RISING STARS
Mathematics

Year **6**

Concept developed by
Caroline Clissold and Cherri Moseley

Year 6 Author Team
Caroline Clissold, Heather Davies, Linda Glithro, Steph King

Homework Sheets written by
Jo Chambers

Practice Book written by
Paul Broadbent

Teacher's Guide

Every effort has been made to trace all copyright holders, but if any have been inadvertently overlooked, the Publishers will be pleased to make the necessary arrangements at the first opportunity.

Although every effort has been made to ensure that website addresses are correct at time of going to press, Rising Stars cannot be held responsible for the content of any website mentioned in this book. It is sometimes possible to find a relocated web page by typing in the address of the home page for a website in the URL window of your browser.

Hachette UK's policy is to use papers that are natural, renewable and recyclable products and made from wood grown in sustainable forests. The logging and manufacturing processes are expected to conform to the environmental regulations of the country of origin.

ISBN: 978-1-78339-533-0

Text, design and layout © Rising Stars UK Ltd 2016

First published in 2016 by
Rising Stars UK Ltd, part of Hodder Education,

An Hachette UK Company

Carmelite House
50 Victoria Embankment
London EC4Y 0DZ

www.risingstars-uk.com

Authors: Jo Chambers, Caroline Clissold, Heather Davies, Linda Glithro, Steph King

Programme consultants: Caroline Clissold, Cherri Moseley, Paul Broadbent

Publishers: Fiona Lazenby and Alexandra Riley

Editorial: Kate Baxter, Jane Carr, Jan Fisher, Lucy Hyde, Lynette James, Jackie Mace, Jane Morgan, Denise Moulton, Christine Vaughan, Sara Wiegand

Answer checking: Deborah Dobson

Project manager: Sue Walton

Text design: Steve Evans and Mark Walker

Illustrations by Steve Evans

Cover design: Steve Evans and Words & Pictures

Printed by Ashford Colour Press Ltd, Gosport, Hants

A CIP record for this book is available from the British Library.

Contents

Introduction

What is *Rising Stars Mathematics*?

Rising Stars Mathematics is a primary mathematics programme developed specifically for the 2014 National Curriculum Programmes of Study. The programme offers a complete solution to primary mathematics, adapting the best teaching and learning approaches from high-performing jurisdictions such as Shanghai and Singapore, but written bespoke to develop mathematics mastery in the context of UK classrooms.

Rising Stars Mathematics has been designed, developed and written by UK mathematics experts and educators to meet the Mathematics Textbook Guidance produced by the National Centre for Excellence in the Teaching of Mathematics (NCETM).

> 'A high-quality mathematics textbook is an educational resource that can be used by pupils in lessons and independently, and that also provides both subject knowledge and pedagogy support to teachers of mathematics. It is a comprehensive learning tool, providing support for the development of both procedural fluency and conceptual understanding in mathematics.'
>
> NCETM, January 2015
> (https://www.ncetm.org.uk/files/21383193NCETM+Textbook+Guidance.pdf)

Following these guidelines, *Rising Stars Mathematics*:

- provides the rigour teachers expect from quality schemes, without the prescription of scripted day-by-day lesson plans
- contains all the resources and CPD support teachers need to design outstanding mathematics lessons
- offers a wealth of opportunities for children to explore, practise, embed and extend learning
- follows the Concrete-Pictorial-Abstract approach to deepen children's understanding of mathematical concepts
- covers all the curriculum content with a wide variety of teaching ideas whilst respecting teachers' professionalism, to enable them to decide how best to teach their classes.

The pedagogy, approach and rationale

Rising Stars Mathematics is designed to develop fluency, build conceptual understanding and embed reasoning through an enquiry-based approach. It provides a 'light touch' comprehensive structure that allows teachers to retain the control, freedom and flexibility to adapt the timing and teaching activities to meet the needs of their own class. This means that they can focus their time and skills on teaching outstanding lessons in their own way. Carefully organised to provide a clear route through the yearly programmes of study, the curriculum concepts are revisited in a spiral way to reinforce and extend understanding and make links between content areas.

The programme has been developed based on the following key pedagogical beliefs:

1. Mathematical understanding is developed through using **concrete, pictorial** and **abstract** representations.

2. High-quality **textbooks used effectively as teaching tools** support teachers in explaining mathematical concepts clearly, encourage investigative thinking, questioning, discussion and application, all while encouraging children to engage with the wonder of mathematics (see page 6).

3. Children will only fully understand topics and **master concepts** through **step-by-step teaching** and **intelligent practice**. This means teaching concepts at a slower pace and dealing with each aspect of that concept in very small steps, in order to give children time to embed understanding. To achieve mastery, therefore, it is important to spend more time on teaching fewer topics in greater depth rather than moving on to a new topic or concept every few days (see page 6).

4. Mathematics is an interconnected subject in which children need to be able to **make connections** across mathematical ideas. This enables them to develop fluency, mathematical reasoning and problem-solving skills (see page 7).

5. Using **precise mathematical vocabulary** from the beginning is vital in ensuring children's understanding. **Rich talk and discussion** between teachers and children, and amongst peers, using mathematical terminology and constant probing questioning is an essential tool in the ongoing assessment of conceptual understanding for all children (see page 7).

Each of these key points of pedagogy is expanded on and explained in the following sections.

1. Concrete-Pictorial-Abstract (CPA) approach

Rising Stars Mathematics is based on the belief that mathematical understanding is developed through using **concrete, pictorial** and **abstract** (or symbolic) representations. Children will travel along this continuum again and again, often revisiting previous stages when a concept is extended.

Children use **concrete** objects to help them make sense of the concept or problem. This could be anything from real or plastic fruit, to straws, counters, cubes or something else meaningful. Whatever the objects are, they can be moved, grouped and rearranged to illustrate the problem. As the child's experience and confidence grows, they may no longer need physical objects to actually move around. Instead, they draw them. These simple **pictures** to represent the problem could be pictures of real objects they have used in the past, objects mentioned in the problem or something else meaningful. As understanding develops, children move on to use some form of **abstract** representation. This could be giving values to rectangular bars (bar model) to identify what is known and what is unknown, using a symbol to stand for a number, or something else.

It is important to realise that these are not stages gone through once, but a continuum. There will be occasions when a particular child will use concrete, pictorial and abstract representations all in one session. A child who uses abstract representations in one area may need concrete representations in another. On a different occasion, a child may need to revisit a concrete representation before moving on to a pictorial or abstract one.

Using the CPA approach encourages children to start by modelling a problem with concrete objects, before moving on to pictorial and abstract representations. It is important to ensure that a variety of manipulatives are available in all classrooms, not just for Key Stage 1 children. This will help children to develop their understanding more quickly and securely.

A variety of representations are used throughout *Rising Stars Mathematics*. These are both the teacher's and children's toolkit for illustrating and understanding a concept or a

Introduction

particular problem. Children will need to explore the various representations for themselves and be allowed the opportunity to choose which representations they use for a particular activity. (See pages 12–14 for examples and explanations of the main concrete resources and pictorial representations used throughout the *Rising Stars Mathematics* programme.)

2. Textbooks as teaching tools

Rising Stars Mathematics follows the Singapore and Shanghai approach to the use of textbooks. In these high-performing jurisdictions the textbook is a starting point for high-quality teaching. Teachers lead the usage of the textbook with the whole class as a starting point for high-quality teaching, rather than giving a textbook to children to work through on their own. This latter misuse of published resources unfortunately became common in England over a number of years and led to textbooks being seen as synonymous with poor-quality lessons. However, when used effectively as a teaching tool, evidence shows that this is not the case. Instead textbooks provide a framework for teachers to both introduce and develop new content, as well as providing a resource for children to refer back to as required.

The *Rising Stars Mathematics* Textbooks are designed specifically to be used as a teaching tool in conjunction with the teaching guidance and ideas provided in the corresponding Teacher's Guide pages. It is not intended that the Textbooks are given to children to work through in isolation. The Teacher's Notes tabs at the bottom of each Textbook page reference the relevant Teacher's Guide pages, so that the resources can be used in tandem.

The 'Let's learn' pages in the Textbooks should be used by the teacher as a starting point to introduce, teach, model and demonstrate new concepts. To support them in doing this, they can use the ideas in the Teacher's Guide or their own activities if preferred.

The 'Let's practise' pages in the Textbooks provide initial practice opportunities. They lead from basic practice and practice in context, to investigative, open-ended practice. These guided practice activities should be introduced by the teacher. The Teacher's Guide provides suggestions on questioning and how to give targeted support to children who may need additional help in order to move on with the group. The 'Let's practise' sections can be used to provide opportunities for independent working as appropriate for different children or as assessment opportunities to identify whether children have mastered the concept. This will then enable teachers to judge how much additional practice each child requires using the *Rising Stars Mathematics* Practice Books (or other practice materials that they choose to use).

3. The mastery approach

A mastery approach underpins the 2014 National Curriculum. This approach advocates spending longer on topics in order to embed understanding and developing rich connections across topics.

NCETM has identified further principles and features that characterise a mastery approach:

- Teachers reinforce an expectation that all pupils are capable of achieving high standards in mathematics.
- The large majority of pupils progress through the curriculum content at the same pace. Differentiation is achieved by emphasising deep knowledge and through individual support and intervention.
- Teaching is underpinned by methodical curriculum design and supported by carefully crafted lessons and resources to foster deep conceptual and procedural knowledge.
- Practice and consolidation play a central role. Carefully designed variation within this builds fluency and understanding of underlying mathematical concepts in tandem.
- Teachers use precise questioning in class to test conceptual and procedural knowledge, and assess pupils regularly to identify those requiring intervention so that all pupils keep up.

NCETM, October 2014
(https://www.ncetm.org.uk/public/files/19990433/Developing_mastery_in mathematics_october_2014.pdf)

In December 2012, The Advisory Committee on Mathematics Education (ACME) published a report called 'Raising the bar: developing able young mathematicians'. The report identified that England needs to increase the number of young mathematicians with a robust grasp of the range of mathematical ways of thinking and working, through experiencing a deep, rich, rigorous and challenging mathematics education. Children should not be accelerated through the school curriculum: 'acceleration encourages only a shallow mastery of the subject, and so promote procedural learning at the expense of deep understanding'. Not allowing children enough time to secure deep understanding can lead to feelings of insecurity and dislike of the subject.

Consequently, there is an expectation in the 2014 National Curriculum that most children should 'move through the programmes of study at broadly the same pace'. Children should not be accelerated into a future year group's work. Instead, it is expected that children who grasp concepts rapidly should be challenged through being offered rich and sophisticated problems before any acceleration through new content. There is also the expectation that those who are not sufficiently fluent with earlier material should consolidate their understanding, including through additional practice, before moving on. The aim is for mastery, which is the approach used by many of the high-performing jurisdictions in the international league tables.

With this in mind, there are some important questions for schools to consider when teaching for mastery, which should be discussed and agreed with the whole staff:

- To support the expectation that all children are capable of achieving high standards, what are the implications for whole-class teaching, class groupings or setting within the school?
- How will differentiation be managed to enable all children to access what is being taught? How and when will intervention be given to ensure misconceptions are dealt with immediately and shared with the whole class, so that no children fall behind?
- How will questioning and scaffolding be varied to provide support as needed? What different problems will be provided so that children who grasp the concept quickly are given complex problems which deepen their knowledge of the same content?
- Is there enough focus on the important ability to recall facts and manipulate them to work out other facts, so that children develop the fluency which comes from deep knowledge and practice?
- How will enough time be allowed for different types of intelligent practice (basic practice, variations such as practice within different contexts, extended practice which goes deeper and deeper), so that longer can be spent on key concepts? Will more than one mathematics session per day be required?
- How will practice and consolidation be provided within different contexts, e.g. time, money or length, to ensure connections are made across different areas of mathematics?
- How will teaching focus on the development of deep structural knowledge and the ability to make connections?
- Is the use of precise mathematical vocabulary consistent across the school? Is correct vocabulary introduced from the beginning of teaching? Are all teaching staff comfortable with mathematical terminology?

Practice and variation

Intelligent practice underpins the mastery approach. 'Intelligent practice' is a term used to describe practice that develops procedural fluency while at the same time exposing mathematical structures, patterns and relationships in order to deepen conceptual understanding.

Intelligent practice is clearly structured and incorporates carefully-designed variations. These variations may be conceptual or procedural:

- Procedural variation can be introduced by extending a problem (e.g. varying the number, the unknown or the context), varying the processes of solving a problem or varying the application of a method (e.g. applying the same method to a group of similar problems).
- Conceptual variation can be introduced by varying the representation of a problem.

The practice in *Rising Stars Mathematics* is based on the principles of intelligent practice.

- The 'Let's practise' pages in the Textbook are clearly structured. Steps 1 and 2 comprise bare (or, decontextualised) practice and include procedural variations. Step 3 provides practice within a variety of contexts (including time, money and statistics) and Step 4 offers open-ended, investigative practice. By working their way through the practice, children will build procedural fluency across a range of question types and in a range of contexts, while also developing their understanding of the concepts covered in the 'Let's learn' pages.
- The corresponding 'Let's practise' pages in the Teacher's Guide extend the opportunities for conceptual variation by suggesting a range of physical and pictorial representations that teachers may want to use to support children's practice.
- The Practice Book offers further carefully-crafted practice exercises. These exercises have been planned to include structured variation of a number or unknown (procedural variation), a range of representations (e.g. a question on length may use a variety of visuals such as ribbons, snakes and pencils) and open questions (e.g. 'What do you notice?') that encourage children to reason and spot patterns.

Teachers can use the carefully-designed questions and exercises as a starting point to introduce intelligent practice into their teaching. However, they retain the freedom to develop their own questions and activities, incorporating variation that best suits the needs of their children.

4. Making connections

The 2014 National Curriculum states that:

> 'Mathematics is an interconnected subject in which pupils need to be able to move fluently between representations of mathematical ideas. The programmes of study are, by necessity, organised into apparently distinct domains, but pupils should make rich connections across mathematical ideas to develop fluency, mathematical reasoning and competence in solving increasingly sophisticated problems. They should also apply their mathematical knowledge to science and other subjects.'
>
> *National Curriculum in England*, Department for Education, 2013

In *Rising Stars Mathematics* there are a wide variety of opportunities to develop mathematics in other areas of the curriculum and in real life, e.g. the opening pages of each unit in the Textbook contain interesting photos and visuals to encourage children to identify instances of mathematics in the world around them, in order to make connections between what they are learning and how it might apply in real life. The programme is designed to provide opportunities to link together different areas of mathematics together, e.g. when children practise a concept, such as addition, they will have the opportunity to do this through an area of measure, e.g. length, mass, temperature or time. This has the benefit of allowing more time to be spent on the big ideas of mathematics within its everyday applications.

The units in *Rising Stars Mathematics* are structured to focus on one of four key mathematical themes: Number Sense, Additive Reasoning, Multiplicative Reasoning or Geometric Reasoning (see page 9). These cover concepts from the related Programmes of Study areas, incorporating Measurement and Statistics where appropriate. This ensures that the end-of-year statements for these areas are covered through a multitude of practice opportunities across the units.

5. Mathematical vocabulary

The 2014 National Curriculum states that:

> 'The National Curriculum for mathematics reflects the importance of spoken language in pupils' development across the whole curriculum – cognitively, socially and linguistically. The quality and variety of language that pupils hear and speak are key factors in developing their mathematical vocabulary and presenting a mathematical justification, argument or proof. They must be assisted in making their thinking clear to themselves as well as others, and teachers should ensure that pupils build secure foundations by using discussion to probe and remedy their misconceptions.'
>
> *National Curriculum in England*, Department for Education, 2013

Using correct mathematical language is crucial for thinking, learning and communicating mathematically. Children may build knowledge through remembering information that they hear, but it is only when they put these ideas into their own words that it becomes clear whether concepts have been learnt effectively. It is in listening to children talking about mathematics that teachers can best assess what they are actually learning and understanding, which in turn enables them to identify and address any misconceptions that might be developing.

Children should be encouraged to explain what they are doing and why they are doing it, through probing questioning from the teacher if necessary. Offering opportunities to use mathematical language frequently, e.g. by participating in paired activities, group discussions and games, will ensure that rich talk develops in the classroom. Spoken language in mathematics can be thought of as a rehearsal for recording, as well as an outcome in its own right. It allows children to extend and develop their reasoning skills as they explain and justify their thinking. It provides the opportunity to review existing knowledge, to explore new ideas and to extend their understanding.

The productive use of spoken language in mathematics allows children to evaluate their learning, support others' suggestions, challenge ideas, reason or justify and ask questions. Therefore, it is important to encourage children not just to learn and remember the correct vocabulary, but also to use these words regularly to communicate mathematically. Using mathematical vocabulary can help all children to make links across areas of mathematics, across the curriculum as a whole and also within real life situations. It can enable them to build confidence, communicate and problem-solve, so should be an integral part of every mathematics lesson.

Teachers need to plan the introduction of new words into lessons and provide opportunities for children to rehearse and use them on a regular basis. It is also essential that other adults working with children use mathematical vocabulary accurately and consistently. The 'Mathematical vocabulary' sections in the *Rising Stars Mathematics* Teacher's Guide identify key words that should be covered when teaching each concept. The glossary in the Textbook provides explanations for children and the glossary at the back of this Teacher's Guide offers detailed definitions on a wide variety of key mathematical terms.

Introduction

Getting started with *Rising Stars Mathematics*

The components

Rising Stars Mathematics includes a wealth of resources for children and teachers. The pupil materials include full-colour Textbooks, single-colour write-in Practice Books and Homework Sheets (found at the back of the Teacher's Guides). The teacher materials comprise the Teacher's Guide and a variety of additional CPD, teaching resources, and digital teaching and learning resources be found on the My Rising Stars website. The contents for each of these components is summarised below.

Textbook

- Opportunities for children to develop problem-solving and reasoning skills.
- 14 units covering all the concepts to be learnt in Year 6.
- Glossary.

Practice Books

- 14 units providing further independent practice of all the concepts to be learnt in Year 6.
- Answers can be found on the My Rising Stars website.

Homework Sheets

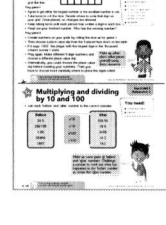

- 84 expansion activities to enable children to explore mathematics further outside the classroom.
- Ideal for engaging parents/carers in children's learning.

Teacher's Guide

- CPD guidance on the pedagogy, approach and how to use the *Rising Stars Mathematics* resources.
- Scope and sequence chart and curriculum mapping grids to aid planning.
- Non-prescriptive teaching guidance for all 14 units in the Textbook.
- Photocopiable Homework Sheets and answers.
- Glossary.
- Bibliography for further reading.

Website and digital resources

- **CPD resources** including:
  1. Short, sharp **CPD videos** providing bite-sized insights into key areas of importance when teaching mathematics, as well as background subject knowledge videos for every theme.
  2. Ready-made **INSET Training PowerPoint presentation** to offer a time-saving way to introduce the principles and resources of *Rising Stars Mathematics* to staff.

- **Planning resources** including:
  1. **Scope and sequence charts** and **curriculum mapping grid** for each year group.
  2. The Rising Stars *Primary Maths Planning Framework* and **posters** for long-term planning support.
  3. Editable **medium-term planning grids** including references to other useful resources.
  4. Mathematical vocabulary **glossaries**.
  5. **Bibliography** of research papers and recommended further reading, including guidance documents from NCETM.

- **Teaching resources** including:
  1. **Teacher Toolkit** containing useful digital tools, which can be used to model concepts on the interactive whiteboard. Tools include:
     - Counters
     - Numerals & Symbols
     - 100 Squares
     - Place Value & Abacus
     - Number Line
     - Clock & Timer
     - Calendar & Timezone
     - Money
     - Calculator
     - Dice, Coin & Number
     - 2D Shapes
     - Tangrams
     - 3D Shapes
     - Fraction Wall
     - Graphs & Charts
     - Geometry Instruments
  2. **eTextbook** – a digital version of the Textbook that can be displayed in the classroom on the interactive whiteboard or shared with parents/carers, so that children can access it from home. The eTextbook is enhanced with fun animations to help explain concepts.
  3. **Animations** from the eTextbook (available separately) are organised by unit, so they can be accessed quickly to play on the interactive whiteboard when required.
  4. PDFs of the **Teacher's Guide notes**, organised unit by unit, can be viewed anytime without needing the book to hand.
  5. Editable versions of the **Homework Sheets**.
  6. Printable versions of the colour **gameboards** from the Textbooks.
  7. Editable versions of the **game instructions** from the Teacher's Guide.
  8. **Answers** to the Practice Books and Homework Sheets.

- **Pupil resources** including:
  1. **eTextbook** – see Teaching resources above.
  2. **Animations** – see Teaching resources above.
  3. **Printable gameboards** and **instruction sheets** organised unit by unit.
  5. Editable versions of the **Homework Sheets** organised unit by unit.
  6. **Answers** to the Practice Books and Homework Sheets.

Themes

Rising Stars Mathematics is built around four themes: Number Sense, Additive Reasoning, Multiplicative Reasoning and Geometric Reasoning. Each covers the concepts from the related Programme of Study areas. This approach ensures that clear connections are made between areas of mathematics.

1. **Number Sense** is about understanding our number system, with a focus on how our numbers work and fit together, and applying this understanding in different contexts. Units on Additive Reasoning and Multiplicative Reasoning are usually preceded by a unit on Number Sense, which explores the understanding needed for the subsequent unit.

2. **Additive Reasoning** is about understanding addition and subtraction together and the relationship between them, and using this understanding to solve problems.

3. **Multiplicative Reasoning** is about understanding multiplication and division together and the relationship between them, and using this understanding to solve problems.

4. **Geometric Reasoning** is about understanding the properties of shapes and the relationships between them, using this understanding to solve problems related to measure and movement within space.

Measures and statistics are included throughout as contexts for all four themes. These contexts are examples and teachers may wish to select different contexts to support each concept. **Algebra** (a new domain in Year 6) appears in all themes as part of generalisation of mathematical understanding.

The unit structure

Each year level of *Rising Stars Mathematics* contains 14 units. These units all follow the same structure as explained below. The Textbook and Teacher's Guide work alongside each other. Each double-page spread in the Teacher's Guide contains a reproduction of the corresponding Textbook page for ease of reference. The Textbook has teaching notes tabs at the bottom of each page to enable teachers to quickly find the corresponding Teacher's Guide page.

Textbook and Teacher's Guide: unit opener pages

In the Textbook, each unit begins with engaging photos of mathematics in real life. These unit opener pages give children the opportunity to discuss what they see and explore what could be going on, looking for mathematics in the world around them. 'I wonder…' questions encourage thinking around the topic. This sets the scene for exploring the underlying concepts in more depth throughout the unit. Such discussions give the teacher the opportunity to check current understanding before moving on to the concept explanation, modelling, exemplification, practice and application.

The corresponding Teacher's Guide pages highlight the main mathematical focus of the unit, expected prior learning and key new learning to be covered throughout the unit. It also provides: support for making connections across areas of mathematics or between concepts; a 'Talk about' section that focuses on the use of precise mathematical vocabulary; a variety of activities and questions about the visuals in the Textbook to engage and explore with children; a list of questions for teachers to think about regarding organisation and planning. Finally, there is brief guidance to support teachers in checking understanding as the unit progresses.

Textbook and Teacher's Guide: concept pages

Each has two pages: 'Let's learn' and 'Let's practise'. The 'Let's learn' page begins with a discussion between the year group character guides, illustrating a possible misconception. The key information about the new concept to be learnt is explained, supported by relevant pictorial representations.

The 'Let's practise' section develops children's reasoning incrementally through guided practice. In *Rising Stars Mathematics*, the first steps provide bare, decontextualised practice. The third step gives practice in a context (e.g. an area of measurement or statistics), while the fourth step is a more open-ended, investigative practice of the concept.

The corresponding Teachers' Guide pages for these sections provide: a list of key mathematical vocabulary, representations and resources; useful background knowledge; activities for warming up, modelling and teaching, digging deeper through practice and follow-up activity ideas. There is also a section on ensuring progress, with ideas for supporting and broadening understanding. These are ideas which can be adapted to the needs of the class – there is no specific script. There are also notes on how to identify when the key concepts have been mastered and answers to the 'Let's practise' activities in the Textbook.

Textbook and Teacher's Guide: gameboard pages

Each unit contains fun activities to encourage children to apply their knowledge and skills, whilst consolidating conceptual understanding. The attractive colour gameboards for these are contained in the Textbooks. Two versions of games that can be played using each gameboard are provided and children are also encouraged to invent their own game using the gameboard. The invented games are often a useful means of assessing understanding.

The corresponding Teachers' Guide pages provide further detail about playing each of the games, including the mathematics focus, resources needed, instructions for how to play and support for making the game activities easier or harder. A photocopiable sheet of 'How to play' instructions is also provided, should teachers wish to send the games home as an out-of-class activity. Printable versions of the gameboards are available to download from the website.

Textbook and Teacher's Guide: 'And finally …' review pages

The final part of each unit is a review section, which provides a variety of assessment tasks. The Textbook pages include three assessment tasks, followed by a colourful 'Did you know?' fun facts section to complete the unit. (For further information about assessment see page 11.)

The corresponding Teachers' Guide review pages provide further detail of any resources needed, instructions for how to run the tasks and guidance on what to look for in children's responses, in order to evidence mastery. There is also some background knowledge about the 'Did you know?' facts and a summary list of all the concepts children are expected to have mastered by the end of the unit.

Introduction

Practice Books

The Practice Books provide further opportunities for children to consolidate understanding and explore, explain and reason through different types of practice activities. These activities include conceptual and procedural variations, in order to develop fluency and conceptual understanding. There is practice for every concept in the Textbook. The write-in format ensures that children always have a record of their work that they can refer back to, so that they can learn from their mistakes and see the progress they are making.

The relevant Practice Book pages for each concept in the Textbook are referenced at the top of the corresponding Teacher's Guide page for each new concept.

Homework Sheets

The photocopiable Homework Sheets can be found at the back of the Teacher's Guide. Editable versions are also available on the My Rising Stars website. They provide expansion activities for children to continue to explore mathematics outside the classroom. Two activities are provided for each of the concept pages in a unit.

The relevant Homework Sheets for each concept in the Textbook are referenced at the top of the corresponding Teacher's Guide page for each new concept.

Teaching a unit

Teachers are advised to begin by looking at the Teacher's Guide to familiarise themselves with the content to be covered within a particular unit and reviewing the related CPD videos on the website if necessary.

1. Develop subject knowledge

- Watch the short online CPD videos to develop background subject knowledge before planning lessons.
- Refresh knowledge by reviewing the INSET training presentations as necessary.

2. Design lessons

- Plan and design lessons using the suggested activities in the Teacher's Guide.
- Choose how much time to spend on each activity to fit the needs of each class.
- Gather all the concrete resources and visual representations needed.
- Review the recommended Teacher Toolkit tools and any relevant concept animations on the My Rising Stars website.

3. Explore new concepts

- Introduce the unit using the Textbooks as a teaching tool. Remember to check the teaching notes tab at the bottom of each page and the corresponding Teacher's Guide pages before the lesson.
- Play any relevant animations (from the eTextbook or direct from the website) to the class and discuss them together.
- Explore, model and teach new concepts to children using a variety of representations and practical resources, following the 'Let's learn' page.
- Use tools from the Teacher Toolkit to model concepts on the interactive whiteboard where appropriate.
- Embed conceptual understanding and dig deeper into concepts through intelligent practice, using the 'Let's practise' page.

4. Embed and expand understanding

- Consolidate understanding using the fun games to provide extra practice and aid mastery. Print extra copies of the game boards and instructions from the website as necessary.
- Set expansion or out-of-class activities using the Homework Sheets or Practice Books. Answers can be found on the website.
- Encourage parents/carers to engage with children's learning by sharing the eTextbook to view the pages and animations at home.
- Provide further independent practice using the Practice Books to deepen understanding of the concepts taught using the Textbooks.

5. Assess progress and mastery

- Review the content covered throughout the unit using the assessment tasks to ensure children have mastered the concepts.
- Finish the unit by finding out some fun mathematical facts in the 'Did you know?' section.
- Use *Rising Stars Assessment Half-Termly Progress Tests* to measure progress independently, if desired.

Timing

As a guide, the expectation is that each unit will take two to three weeks to teach. The length of time spent on each unit will vary depending on the topic, the number of new concepts covered within it and how quickly children master the concepts. If teachers are confident that children have mastered a concept, then it is perfectly acceptable to move on more quickly, just as it is important to allow children to spend longer on a topic if necessary to ensure that they have fully mastered it before moving on. It is better to spend more time on fewer topics to ensure that they are fully understood and children have embedded what they have learnt, so that they can remember and apply it later on.

Mixed-age classes

For schools with mixed-age classes, the *Rising Stars Mathematics* resources can be used to teach the same topic to the whole class, as long as this is done age-appropriately. The pitch should be year group based, regardless of the perceived ability of children within those year groups. It is important that however the classroom is managed, each year group sticks to what is expected for that year in order to meet the National Curriculum Programme of Study requirements. Children should therefore all be using the Textbooks and Practice Books appropriate for their year group. As teachers in this kind of setting will know all too well, this is like teaching two or more classes. This brings huge challenges in planning and organisation, especially in small schools where there are three to four year groups per class.

However, because the units in *Rising Stars Mathematics* all have a main focus on one of four themes (Number Sense, Additive Reasoning, Multiplicative Reasoning or Geometric Reasoning), similar topics are generally covered in the same unit in each year group. Therefore corresponding units from Year 1 and Year 2, Year 3 and Year 4, Year 5 and Year 6 will work together neatly as they focus on the same themes, e.g. Unit 1 in all year groups across the *Rising Stars Mathematics* resources is focused on Number Sense, so teachers are able to focus on similar topics at a different level within mixed-age classes.

On the website, there are Medium-term Planning Grid templates which break down the units into half-termly plans. These may be useful for teachers of mixed-age classes to compare the different year groups.

Assessment

Assessment opportunities

Each unit in *Rising Stars Mathematics* provides the opportunity for teachers to check existing understanding through the opener pages. Discussions around what children can see, how they interpret what they see and their response to the 'I wonder…' questions will reveal children's current level of understanding.

Likewise, the cartoon at the beginning of each concept, provides an opportunity to check understanding through class discussion of the misconception or error. Throughout each unit, there are continual opportunities for assessment. Teachers will probe conceptual and procedural understanding through questioning and observation as they model and teach. The way children respond to the modelling and teaching provides the teacher with valuable information on what to spend a little more time and what to move through quickly, as well as information on individual needs.

The Textbook activities provide further assessment opportunities, particularly the non-routine, open-ended types of activities offered in Step 4.

The final review activities are particularly useful assessment tasks, since they are designed to give children the opportunity to demonstrate what they know and the concepts they have mastered. In this way assessment is ongoing throughout the unit, with a summative assessment at the end of each unit.

End points to be tested in Key Stage 2 national tests

Some elements of the National Curriculum cannot be assessed in statutory tests although they will need to be assessed by teachers as part of their statutory assessment of the whole National Curriculum. Over time, all the end point requirements that can be tested in the 2014 National Curriculum will be tested at the end of Key Stage 2. It is therefore important to make a note of these, particularly for teachers in Years 5 and 6, and to make sure children are up to speed with these requirements, e.g. Roman numerals need to be taught from Years 3 to 5. There is no mention of them in Year 6. However, they could be tested in the end of Year 6 tests. *Rising Stars Mathematics* suggests times when these can be rehearsed and reinforced during the warm-up activities, practice or follow-up tasks.

Measuring progress

In a new world of assessment free from levels, it is now up to teachers to decide how best to assess the progress their children are making against the new Programmes of Study. For schools who wish to do this using regular half-termly or end-of-term tests using an independent resource outside of the *Rising Stars Mathematics* teaching materials, the *Rising Stars Assessment Half-termly Progress Tests* are an ideal resource to measure progress and inform future learning. They are organised to assess the content in the same order that it is covered in the scope and sequence of the Rising Stars Mathematics units, so that teachers can be sure that children are not being tested on content that they have yet to be taught. For more information, please visit www.risingstars-uk.com.

Ensuring progress for all children

If we consider any particular concept area as a pool, some children will paddle, others will swim with armbands and others will swim freely. They are all in the same pool, but accessing it at different levels and in different ways. This is a good metaphor for how differentiation should be managed when following a mastery approach. It will ensure that the broad majority of children all move on together into a new pool, as required by the National Curriculum.

Rising Stars Mathematics assumes that all children within the class will be taught the same content and given the same opportunities to understand the concepts. The 'Let's learn: Modelling and teaching' and 'Let's practise: Digging deeper' sections both include suggestions for a variety of representations, models and images that can be used to explain the concepts. The expectation is not that all children should be able to use all representations or methods, but rather that different representations will trigger understanding for different children. By using a wide variety of representations like this and multiple ways to explain concepts, teachers give each individual child the best possible chance of finding something that works for them. Some children may fully grasp the concept being introduced using the first or second representation, however that does not mean the rest of the lesson is irrelevant for them. Seeing the concept represented in different ways will give them the opportunity to deepen their understanding and make connections between the different methods.

Rising Stars Mathematics recognises that in every class it is likely that there will be some children who will need more support than others to achieve understanding of concepts. The Teacher's Guide includes a section on 'Supporting understanding' for children who need a little more reinforcement. The same section also offers ideas for 'Broadening understanding', for those children who have a good understanding of the concept.

In order to give all children the best possible chance to make progress in mathematics, the *Rising Stars Mathematics* approach to differentiation is that it should be managed through support and intervention, not through changing the content. Difficulties and misconceptions should be addressed as they occur and children should be challenged through more demanding problems, rather than being accelerated to future curriculum content.

Some schools are organising mathematics so that there are two shorter sessions each day. The first session is used for teaching the concept, the second is for practice. Using *Rising Stars Mathematics* for this approach, teachers would focus on the 'Let's learn' part of the unit in the first session and on the 'Let's practise' section in the second session. During the second session, the teacher could work with children who have struggled to understand as a guided group, whilst others work through the three or four steps in the Textbook more independently. A further 15-minute intervention session may be offered later the same day. Intervention must be carried out immediately to ensure that the majority of children move through the materials at the same pace. Some schools may wish to pre-teach a small group of children. This 10-minute session could be used to revise what children already know about today's concept and its vocabulary, before the concept is extended in the main session.

Children with significant special needs may require an individual programme of work. Although these children are unlikely to master concepts as deeply as others, they should still aim for mastery at a level appropriate for the individual.

Fast finishers can be challenged to deepen their understanding by generalising. Depending on the concept, they might be asked if what they have just explored will always, sometimes or never be true. They might be asked to give an example of the concept in money or measures. Alternatively, some of the other strategies to embed problem solving could be used. *Rising Stars Mathematics* provides some suggestions for broadening understanding in every unit.

Resources and representations

Representations are hugely important in helping children to develop a conceptual understanding of what they are learning. *Rising Stars Mathematics* aims to encourage all teachers to make use of these with all children from Year 1 through to Year 6. In the past, manipulatives and visual representations have often only been used in Key Stage 2 for children struggling to grasp certain concepts, but they are necessary for all. There are two main types of representations: visual (pictorial) and manipulative (concrete apparatus).

The key manipulatives included in this programme are:

- Straws (Years 1-3)
- Base 10 apparatus
- Place-value counters
- Place-value cards
- Number rods
- Double-sided counters
- Bead strings
- Plates
- Digit cards
- Coins
- Counting sticks
- Interlocking cubes
- Coloured counters
- 2-D shapes
- 3-D shapes
- Clock faces
- 1–6 dice
- 1–10 dice
- Percentage cards
- Modelling clay
- Number cards
- Tangrams

See below for further details.

The key visual representations included in this programme are:

- Number tracks
- Ten frames
- 100 squares
- Number lines
- The bar model
- Place-value grids
- Gattegno charts

See below for further details.

Concrete manipulatives

Straws

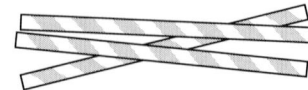

Straws are a great resource to enable children to see the cardinality of numbers. They could make bundles of ten and compare tens and ones. They could put ten bundles together to make 100 and compare these. Straws are particularly useful for younger children, when they still need to see and touch quantities.

Base 10 apparatus

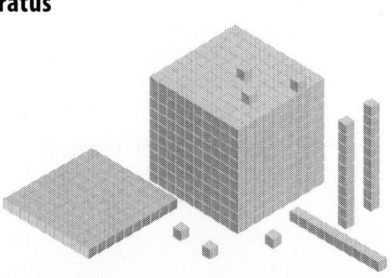

These are representations of numbers. In the first instance, the small cubes represent ones, the rods tens, the flats hundreds and the large cubes thousands. Children find these helpful because the size of the individual pieces helps to denote their value. Later, when children encounter decimals, the flats represent ones, the rods tenths and the small cubes hundredths. If children are familiar with using different manipulatives to represent numbers, it will be easy for them to make this transfer.

Place-value counters

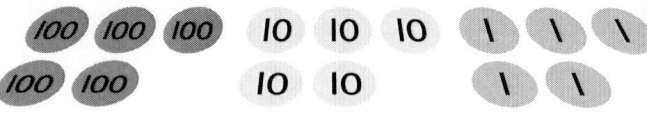

These also represent numbers. You can see clearly what each colour represents through the values written on each (often greens are hundreds, yellows are tens, and reds are ones). They are more abstract than Base 10 apparatus because the counters are all the same size and are therefore not proportional to their value. It is recommended that these are used in late Key Stage 1 and in Key Stage 2, when children are working with larger numbers. When children have used these, you may find that they can use any coloured counters and assign their own values to them.

Number rods

Coloured number rods are excellent for helping children to become flexible in their thinking about numbers. The rods represent any number that you would want them to represent. Assign a value to one and children can work out the values of the other rods. The rods are fractions of other rods, e.g. some are halves, quarters and eighths of others. This is a great resource to use when dealing with multiplication, division and fractions.

Coloured rods can also be used as bars to support thinking when using the bar model. Using a rod to represent a bar allows bars to be changed or manipulated to illustrate the problem under consideration. See the section on the bar model for further information on this.

Double-sided counters

These are great for helping children to develop reasoning and fluency. You could give children three counters each and ask them to show you 2, then 3, then 12. Children need to consider how they could represent 12 using three counters. The only rule is that one colour needs to represent the same number. So, two yellow sides could be 5 each and a red side could be 2. Or one yellow side could be 8 and one red side 4. There are numerous ways to represent 12 or other numbers using these counters.

Bead strings

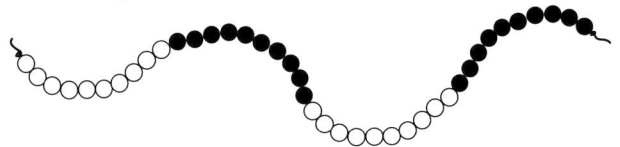

Bead strings are helpful for early calculation. When children are familiar with them and know that each string of colour is 10, they can add, subtract, multiply and divide using them and develop the ability to do this without counting one at a time, e.g. for 10 + 6, they add 6 onto 10, without the need to count ten beads, six beads and then count them all. These can be used to represent other numbers, e.g. the whole string could represent 1, each coloured section would then be one tenth and one bead would be one hundredth. This flexibility makes the bead string a very useful manipulative for fractions, decimals and percentages.

Plates

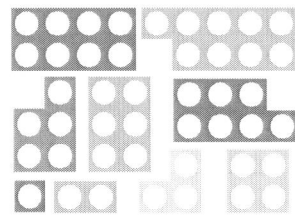

Plates like these are another manipulative which help children to move on from counting everything, e.g. if they add 5 and 9, they put the plates together. They match the result with 10 and 4 to give the answer 14. Paper 10 frames can be cut and used to represent a number in exactly the same way.

Visual representations

The bar model

The bar model is a very effective visual representation. It helps children to make sense of problems. Take missing number statements such as 35 – □ = 16. We know that 35 is the larger number, so it will be the larger bar. A smaller bar of 16 can be drawn below it. Drawing a bar from the end of the 16 bar to fill the space to the end of the 35 bar represents the missing number. We can then work out the missing number by counting back from 35 to 16 or counting on from 16 to 35.

35	
16	?

This can support children as they work out families of addition and subtraction facts.

$a = b + c$
$a = c + b$
$a - b = c$
$a - c = b$

a	
b	c

Addition and subtraction calculations can be represented using this model, e.g.

1) Samir scored 145 points on a computer game, Alex scored 76 more points. How many points did Alex score?

145	76
?	

(Alex scored 221 points.)

2) Jenny had a collection of shells. She gave her friend 123 of them. She was left with 146. How many shells did she have before giving some to her friend?

123	146
?	

(Jenny had 269 shells.)

3) Ben went for a run. He ran 12.5 km to the shop and 6.75 km back. Then he stopped to talk to a friend. How much further did he need to run to get home?

12.5 km	
?	6.75 km

(Ben has to run another 5.75 km.)

4) Ella has some cherries. She eats two. Then she eats half of what is left. She now has six. How many did she have to begin with?

?		
6	6	2

(Ella started off with 14 cherries.)

This model can be used very effectively for representing multiplication, division and fractions, as well as ratio and proportion problems. It is often helpful to use double-sided counters or coloured rods to set out the problems first and then move on to drawing them as bars, e.g.

1) There are 27 red flowers in the garden. There are three times as many red flowers as there are white flowers. How many white flowers are there?

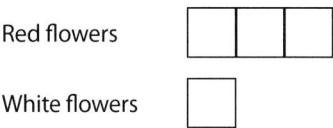

If there are 27 red flowers, each part is worth 9. So there are 9 white flowers.

2) Sam had five times as many marbles as Tom. If Sam gives 26 marbles to Tom, the two friends will have exactly the same amount. How many marbles do they have altogether?

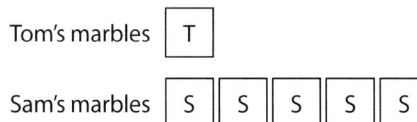

Sam gives 26 marbles to Tom.

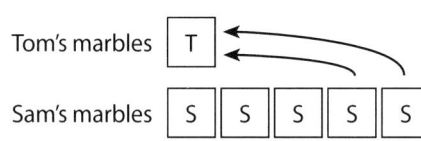

So, the model will look like this:

T	S	S
S	S	S

We now know that each part is worth 13. So they have 78 marbles altogether.

3) David spent $\frac{2}{5}$ of his money on a book. The book cost £10. How much money did he start off with?

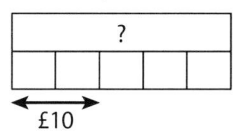

We know $\frac{2}{5}$ is equal to £10. Each part must be £5. So he started off with £25.

Introduction

4) In Class 4, 80% of children like crisps. 75% of children who like crisps also like chocolate. What percentage of Class 4 like both crisps and chocolate?

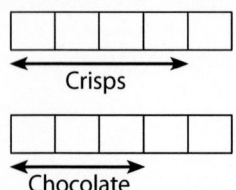

Each part in the model is worth 20%. So 60% of Class 4 like both crisps and chocolate.

5) A computer game was reduced in a sale by 20% and it now costs £48. What was the original price?

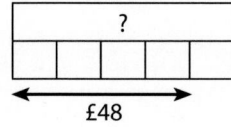

We know from this model that each part is worth £12. So, £12 is equivalent to the discount. Therefore the original cost was £60.

6) A gardener plants tulip bulbs in a flower bed. She plants 3 red bulbs for every 4 white bulbs. She plants 60 red bulbs. How many white bulbs does she plant?

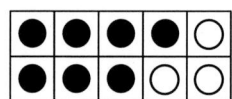

If she plants 60 red tulips, each part is worth 20. Therefore she must have planted 80 white bulbs.

Ten frames

There are different types of ten frames. This is one example.

It draws out the odd and even properties of number. They are helpful for finding number bonds to 10, as well as for addition and subtraction.

These can also be used to represent fractions and decimals, e.g. if the whole frame is worth 1, what are the black counters worth? (0.7, $\frac{7}{10}$.)

Place-value grids

1000	100	10	1	.	10th	100th	1000th
				.			

Place-value grids are very useful for helping children to gain an understanding of the four main aspects of place value.

Gattegno charts

0.001	0.002	0.003	0.004	0.005	0.006	0.007	0.008	0.009
0.01	0.02	0.03	0.04	0.05	0.06	0.07	0.08	0.09
0.1	0.2	0.3	0.4	0.5	0.6	0.7	0.8	0.9
1	2	3	4	5	6	7	8	9
10	20	30	40	50	60	70	80	90
100	200	300	400	500	600	700	800	900
1000	2000	3000	4000	5000	6000	7000	8000	9000
10000	20000	30000	40000	50000	60000	70000	80000	90000

Gattegno charts are another useful resource that will help to secure children's conceptual understanding of place value.

Delivering the aims of the National Curriculum

Developing fluency

The first aim of the 2014 National Curriculum states that teachers must ensure that children: 'become fluent in the fundamentals of mathematics, including through varied and frequent practice with increasingly complex problems over time, so that pupils develop conceptual understanding and the ability to recall and apply knowledge rapidly and accurately'. Fluency includes:

- knowing number bonds for all numbers to 10, then 20 and 100
- knowing multiplication facts up to 12×12.
- using these facts flexibly to create other facts, e.g. if you know that $6 \times 7 = 42$, you can work out that $6 \times 70 = 420$, $6 \times 35 = 21$ and so on.
- knowing efficient mental calculation strategies and written procedures for the four operations and using them efficiently.
- knowing when to use these methods appropriately. Children need to develop conceptual understanding, so that they know the facts and the procedures and how and why they work.

Developing reasoning skills

The second aim of the 2014 National Curriculum states that we should ensure that children: 'reason mathematically by following a line of enquiry, conjecturing relationships and generalisations, and developing an argument, justification or proof using mathematical language'.

Reasoning is about:

- making and testing predictions, conjectures or hypotheses
- searching for patterns and relationships
- making and investigating general statements by finding examples that satisfy them
- explaining and justifying solutions, results, conjectures, conclusions, generalisations and so on:
  - by testing
  - by reasoned argument
- disproving by finding counter-examples.

Many of the activities in *Rising Stars Mathematics* encourage reasoning. You can also provide extra activities to encourage reasoning. Only children can actually do the reasoning, but teachers can help them acquire and refine the necessary skills to do this. Teachers can also model reasoning by 'thinking out loud'.

The problem-solving strategies outlined in this introduction are useful ones to look at for developing reasoning. See also the introduction to the Textbooks, where there are some useful reminder prompts to help children think critically about reasoning and solving problems.

Strategies to embed problem solving

There are many strategies that will embed problem solving, which is the third aim of the 2014 National Curriculum. We need to ensure that children: 'can solve problems by applying their mathematics to a variety of routine and non-routine problems with increasing sophistication, including breaking down problems into a series of simpler steps and persevering in seeking solutions'.

Here are a few strategies that you might like to use, particularly when you work on activities that seek to deepen children's understanding of what you are teaching. Further guidance, detailed examples and activities using these strategies can be found in the Rising Stars *Problem Solving and Reasoning* programme developed by Tim Handley.

Always, sometimes, never

'Always, sometimes, never' is when you give children a statement and then ask whether it is always, sometimes or never true. This encourages the development of the skills of proof, generalisation and algebraic thinking. These are part of reasoning, which is the second aim of the National Curriculum. This strategy also encourages children to make connections between different areas of mathematics.

Another, another, another

'Another, another, another' is a strategy which involves giving children a statement and asking them to give you an example that matches it, and then another and another, e.g. say that $\frac{1}{2}$ and $\frac{2}{4}$ are equivalent fractions, then ask for another pair of equivalent fractions…and another…and another.

This strategy encourages children to give specific examples which meet a given general statement. It provides a good opportunity to assess children's conceptual understanding of an area of mathematics.

Convince me

'Convince me' activities are a useful way to encourage children to explore the structure of a mathematical concept. The teacher makes a statement to children and asks them to decide whether it is accurate or not, and then explain why. Their explanations to convince you allow them to develop their skills of reasoning in the context of mathematical proof, generalisation and algebraic thinking, which is the second aim of the National Curriculum.

Hard and easy

'Hard and easy' is an example of a strategy that encourages children to think closely about the structure of mathematics. It enables you to assess children's conceptual understanding of their mathematics. Ask them to give you an example of a 'hard' and 'easy' answer to a question and explain why one is 'hard' and the other is 'easy'. The choices children make when responding to this often provide valuable information about what they find difficult.

If this is the answer, what's the question?

'If this is the answer, what's the question?' activities encourage children to think creatively and explore the structure of mathematics. The strategy also allows children to develop their skills of generalisation. Give children an answer such as 25% and ask them to come up with as many questions as possible that could have that answer, e.g. 'What is $\frac{1}{4}$ of 100%?' or 'A jumper costs £15 in a sale and the original price was £20. What is the percentage discount?'

Mathematics stories

Giving children a number, geometric concept or measure and asking them to write its 'story', is a strategy that encourages children to explore everything they know about a mathematical concept. It is therefore particularly effective at developing children's subject knowledge, whilst also encouraging them to reason. Through telling a 'story', children are also likely to form and use their own generalisations and patterns, which can be a great starting point for further discussion.

Odd one out

'Odd one out' is a strategy which encourages conjecturing, making generalisations and reasoning about items in a set. All you need to do is give children a set of three or more numbers, shapes or statements and ask them to identify which is the odd one out and why. There will often be several potential responses involving each of the numbers, shapes or statements.

Peculiar, obvious, general

'Peculiar, obvious, general' is a strategy that encourages children to think about the structure of mathematics and to reason about it. Through focusing on what makes a peculiar, obvious or general example of a given statement, children have to think carefully about the statement given, the criteria needed to meet the statement, and what examples they could give.

Silly answers

'Silly answers' encourages children to make generalisations. In giving you a 'silly' answer to a question and explaining why it is such, they will have to reason about possible 'correct' answers. This will require them to consider the properties relating to the topic in the question, therefore deepening their conceptual understanding.

What do you notice?

The 'what do you notice?' strategy encourages children to look deeply at the structure of mathematics. By asking them 'What do you notice?' about a number, set of numbers, shape or mathematical statement, they will need to make their own generalisations and test them against specific examples.

What else do we know?

'What else do we know?' is a strategy that encourages children to see the links that exist in all areas of mathematics. It encourages them to reason and combine other known facts with a given statement, e.g. give children a statement such as 'If we know $8 \times 9 = 72$, what else do we know?' They could then create new statements by doubling, halving and multiplying or dividing by 10, such as $8 \times 90 = 720$, $8 \times 45 = 360$ and $4 \times 45 = 180$.

What's the same? What's different?

'What's the same? What's different?' is a strategy that encourages children to compare and contrast. Children will need to spot patterns and similarities, as well as making generalisations and connections between different aspects of mathematics.

Zooming in

'Zooming in' is a strategy that encourages children to reason about mathematical properties, e.g. give a criterion such as an odd number. Ask children to give an example that fits the criteria. Then 'zoom in' to give another criterion, e.g. an odd number which is also a multiple of 7. This strategy also encourages children to re-evaluate their decisions and helps them to try to make more reasoned choices for their initial 'answers'.

Effective questioning

Questioning is an important strategy which can help embed problem solving and reasoning into day-to-day mathematics teaching. It also allows you to assess children's conceptual understanding. Here are some examples of question structures and routines:

Can you give me an example of …?

- a prime number which is not odd
- an irregular quadrilateral
- a percentage fraction and decimal equivalence

What is the quickest or easiest way to …?

- find out if a number is prime
- find the area of a rectangle
- find out how many chairs will fit into our school hall

What are 7, 11 and 13 examples of …?

What about 36?

What about 72 cm²?

How can we be sure that …?

- all multiples of 6 are multiples of 3
- the area of a triangle $= \frac{1}{2}$ base $\times$ height
- $\frac{6}{8}$ is equal to $\frac{12}{16}$

What's the link between …?

- 12, 24 and 36
- $\frac{6}{8}$, 0.75 and 75%
- a rectangle and a square

Introduction

Developing mental and written calculation skills

Mental calculation strategies

Throughout the 2014 National Curriculum Programme of Study for Mathematics, children are expected to use mental calculation strategies as appropriate. Very often, after written methods have been introduced, children tend to use these as their default methods for answering calculations, whether they are appropriate or not. It is therefore important to provide opportunities where children are given calculations and have to decide which methods would be the most efficient to solve them. This encourages them to continue using mental arithmetic as much as possible.

If schools still have copies of the 1999 National Numeracy Strategy Framework, teachers may find the section on mental calculation strategies for addition, subtraction, multiplication and division a useful reference tool for identifying key mental calculation strategies to teach and practise regularly. The 1999 QCA booklet, Teaching mental calculation strategies: guidance for teachers at key stages 1 and 2, is another useful resource.

Key mental calculation strategies include:

- Partition and recombine: $36 + 24 = 30 + 20 + 6 + 4 = 50 + 10 = 60$
- Sequencing: $135 + 78 = 135 + 70 + 8 = 205 + 8 = 213$
- Doubles and near doubles: $154 + 153 = $ double $154 - 1 = 307$
- Using number pairs to 10 and 100: $462 + 138 = 460 + 130 + 10 = 400 + 100 + 100 = 600$
- Adding near multiples of 10 and adjusting:
  $1458 + 2998 = 1458 + 3000 - 2 = 4456$
- Using known number facts: if we know that
  $12 \times 7 = 84$ then $12 \times 14 = 168$, $1.2 \times 7 = 8.4$, $2.4 \times 7 = 16.8$
- Bridging though tens, hundreds, tenths:
  $36 + 8 = 36 + 4 + 4 = 40 + 4 = 44$
- Using relationships between operations: if $256 + 135 = 391$, then $135 + 256$ must also be 391, $391 - 256$ must be 135 and $391 - 135$ must be 256
- Counting on: $365 - 178$, $178 + 22 = 200$, $200 + 165 = 365$, so $365 - 178 = 22 + 165 = 187$
- ×4 by doubling and doubling again: 280×4, double $280 = 560$, double $560 = 1120$
- ×8 by doubling, doubling and doubling again: 56×8, double $56 = 112$, double $112 = 224$, double $224 = 448$
- ×5 by ×10 and halving: $364 \times 10 = 3640$, half $3640 = 1820 = 364 \times 5$
- ×9 by ×10 then subtracting: ×1
  $17 \times 9 = (17 \times 10) - (17 \times 1) = 170 - 17 = 153$
- ×20 by ×10 and doubling:
  $470 \times 20 = 470 \times 10 \times 2 = 4700 \times 2 = 9400$
- ×25 by ×100 then halving and halving again:
  37×25, $37 \times 100 = 3700$, half $3700 = 1850$, half $1850 = 925 = 37 \times 25$.

Rising Stars Mathematics encourages teachers to rehearse mental calculation strategies regularly with children during the 'Warming up' sections.

Mental strategies are often used in conjunction with written strategies, so the two do, in fact, go hand in hand. Children will use mental strategies to estimate the solution to a number statement. They will also use, e.g. their mental calculation skills in each column of a written calculation and when using an algorithm.

Approach to written algorithms

In the 2014 National Curriculum Programme of Study for Mathematics, formal written algorithms are introduced during Key Stage 2. It is not necessary to introduce any algorithms into Key Stage 1, these children should be focusing on mental calculation strategies. However, recording addition and subtraction in columns can be introduced if teachers wish to support understanding of place value and prepare for formal written methods later on.

When written algorithms are introduced, children need to develop a conceptual understanding of these and not just learn a method using a rote learning process. It is therefore very important that they use manipulatives, such as those outlined in the Resources and Representations section (see pages 12–14), when they learn a new method or use a method that they have previously learnt but are beginning to apply to larger numbers or decimals.

In Key Stage 2, Base 10 apparatus and place-value counters are very important for developing this conceptual understanding. It is useful for the teacher to model the procedure using this apparatus (which could be on the interactive whiteboard) and children follow their lead. The teacher should then model the written method and ask children to identify what is the same and what is different about the two methods. Some suggestions for how to model this for each operation are given below.

It is often a good idea, when beginning a series of lessons on one of the four operations, to write a selection of calculations on the whiteboard. Children can then discuss with a partner which methods would be the best to use. This highlights the fact that mental calculation strategies are often the most efficient methods to use.

Mental calculation uses the multiplicative property of place value and written methods use the positional property, e.g. if using the strategy of sequencing, one number needs to be partitioned, $246 + 132 = 246 + 100 + 30 + 2$. If subtracting 4567 and 1281, children will refer to the digits positioned in their columns. This is one reason that children need to have a deep conceptual knowledge of place value.

Addition

45 + 77

Encourage children to group the ones. They will have 12, 10 of which need to be changed to one ten. They then add the tens to give 12. 10 of these need changing to one hundred. Model the written method as children progress through each stage with the Base 10 apparatus.

$$\begin{array}{r} 4\ 5 \\ +\ 7\ 7 \\ \hline 1\ 2\ 2 \\ \scriptstyle 1\ \ 1 \end{array}$$

How are these models different?
How are they the same?

Using the correct vocabulary is also important. With addition, the vocabulary is:

augend + addend = sum

Subtraction

182 – 147

In this example, children set out 182. When they need to subtract 7 from 2, they can see that there are not enough ones. They therefore need to exchange a ten for 10 ones. They can then take away the other numbers. Again, teachers should model the written method as children progress through the stages of the calculation using the Base 10 apparatus.

Using the correct vocabulary is also important. With subtraction, the correct vocabulary is:

minuend – subtrahend = difference

Multiplication

Arrays are a key visual representation for multiplication. They highlight the links with repeated addition and division. In this example, 38×3, 38 is made three times using manipulatives and then grouped. The model below shows how the physical array links to the grid method and then to the written method:

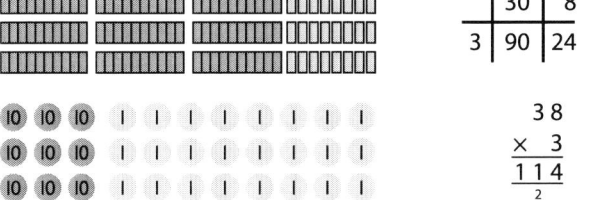

	30	8
3	90	24

$$\begin{array}{r} 38 \\ \times\ 3 \\ \hline 114 \\ {\scriptstyle 2} \end{array}$$

What's different about all these models?
What's the same?

The correct vocabulary for multiplication is:

multiplicand $\times$ multiplier = product

Division

Division is basically grouping, i.e. how many groups of the divisor can be made out of the dividend? When children set out the number (the dividend) using manipulatives, they can clearly see how many groups of the divisor (the number they are dividing by) they can make out of the numbers of each particular value.

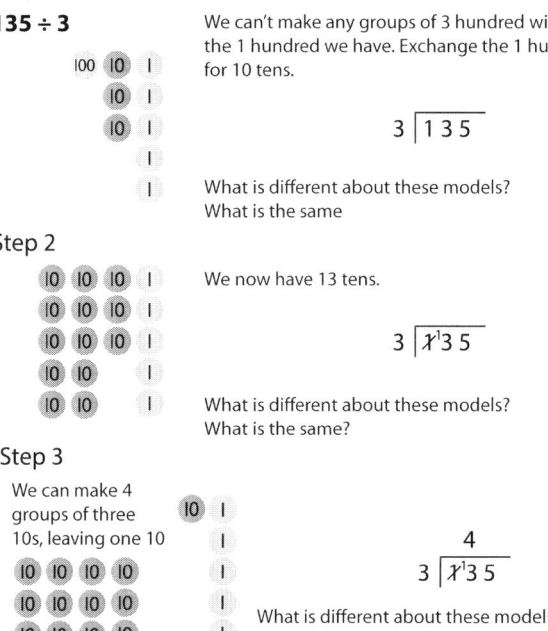

Step 1

135 ÷ 3

We can't make any groups of 3 hundred with the 1 hundred we have. Exchange the 1 hundred for 10 tens.

$3\,|\,1\,3\,5$

What is different about these models?
What is the same

Step 2

We now have 13 tens.

$3\,|\,\cancel{1}^{1}3\,5$

What is different about these models?
What is the same?

Step 3

We can make 4 groups of three 10s, leaving one 10

$\dfrac{4}{3\,|\,\cancel{1}^{1}3\,5}$

What is different about these models?
What is the same?

Step 4

We need to exchange the one 10 for ten 1s

$\dfrac{4}{3\,|\,\cancel{1}^{1}3^{1}5}$

What is different about these models?
What is the same

Step 5

We can make 5 groups of three 1s, giving an answer of 45

$\dfrac{45}{3\,|\,\cancel{1}^{1}3^{1}5}$

What is different about these models?
What is the same

The correct vocabulary for division is:

dividend ÷ divisor = quotient

Use of calculators

The 2014 National Curriculum states that: 'Calculators should not be used as a substitute for good written and mental arithmetic. They should therefore only be introduced near the end of Key Stage 2 to support pupils' conceptual understanding and exploration of more complex number problems, if written and mental arithmetic are secure. In both primary and secondary schools, teachers should use their judgement about when ICT tools should be used'.

It is extremely important that children do not learn to rely on calculators instead of being able to use mental and written calculation methods securely. The calculations given to children as practice should be carefully chosen, so that they are able to perform them using appropriate mental or written methods. However, when working on a real life problem with a large amount of data, teachers may wish to allow children to perform calculations on a calculator, so that they focus more deeply on the problem-solving task at hand.

Calculators are also a very effective way to rehearse recognising numbers for Key Stage 1 and understanding place value in both Key Stage 1 and Key Stage 2, e.g. to rehearse place value, give children the following instructions. They must work out what operation to use at each stage:

- key in 3
- put 5 in front of the 3 (they must add 50)
- put a 2 in front of the 5 (they must add 200)
- change the 5 to a 2 (they must subtract 30)

and so on.

Mathematics outside the classroom

Homework

Rising Stars Mathematics provides a range of homework options:

1. The Textbook can be sent home for children to complete a particular step in the 'Let's practise' section. Within the Textbook, children will have access to the concept explanation, modelling, exemplification, practice and application that they have already explored in the 'Let's learn' section. This enables them to pick up where they left off in class. For schools that do not wish to send Textbooks home, eTextbook versions on the website can be shared with parents/carers, so that the content can be accessed online from home.

2. All the gameboards and game instructions can be downloaded and printed from the website and sent home for children to play with parents/carers/siblings/friends. Children can also be asked to design their own game using the game boards in the Textbook.

Introduction

3. There is a bank of Homework activities at the back of this Teacher's Guide, which can be used as expansion activities outside the classroom. There are two activities for each concept spread in the Textbook. These are also available as editable files on the website, enabling teachers to choose both the homework and its frequency.

4. The Practice Books provide a wide range of additional questions to consolidate and reinforce understanding of concepts taught using the Textbook in class. These extra practice activities can be set as homework or used as further practice within the classroom. Either way, they provide a good record for the child of their understanding and progress and will help teachers identify any misconceptions or gaps in understanding.

Engaging parents/carers

In order to engage parents/carers in their children's learning, it is important to share and explain the way in which mathematics is being taught in school and the key features and benefits of the *Rising Stars Mathematics* approach. An example of a letter to parents/carers is set out below:

Dear Parent/Carer,

As you know, mathematics is an integral part of your child's learning. We are using the innovative *Rising Stars Mathematics* programme to ensure mathematics is accessible for all children and that they achieve personal success in the subject.

Throughout the programme, there is a focus on the development of deep subject knowledge and the ability to make connections. The approach places importance on different types of practice, as well as the ability to recall facts and manipulate them to work out other facts.

The questioning in *Rising Stars Mathematics* is tailored to your child's needs, with a variety of different problems to solve. Any misconceptions are dealt with immediately. Children who grasp mathematical concepts quickly will be given complex problems which deepen their knowledge of the same content, rather than being accelerated into content from the next year level.

There is a focus on practice and spending longer on key concepts to embed understanding. This includes different types of practice, each of which requires a deeper level of understanding:

1. Basic practice, i.e. without any contexts

2. Variations or intelligent practice, this shows children patterns or helps them to make connections

3. Practice and consolidation within different contexts, e.g. time, money or length

4. Open-ended, investigative practice. This goes deeper and deeper, requiring greater reasoning.

Precise mathematical vocabulary will be taught from the start and used consistently throughout the school, including these terms:

Augend + addend = sum/total

Minuend − subtrahend = difference

Multiplicand × multiplier = product

Dividend ÷ divisor = quotient.

We are very excited to be using this unique programme and appreciate your continued support.

Yours faithfully,

The style of the *Rising Stars Mathematics* resources is clear and engaging, which will help to capture the interest of parents/carers. In the Textbook, explanations are supported by clear pictorial representations and followed by guided, step-by-step practice. This will enable parents/carers to quickly familiarise themselves with both what is being taught and how it is being approached. This is especially important if children are asked to complete activities from the Textbook as homework. Since the concepts are set out clearly in the 'Let's learn' section, children will be able to show and explain what they have been learning. Parents/carers will feel able to help without confusing their child by introducing different method, particularly if they were taught mathematics in a different way themselves.

For schools that do not wish to send Textbooks home, online versions can be shared as eTextbooks and accessed online by parents/carers or children at home. These provide an enhanced version of the print Textbooks, with a number of pop-up animations throughout that help to explain key concepts. Parents/carers may wish to watch these with their child, to enable them to participate in their learning.

It may also be useful to share the school's Calculation Policy or the pages from this Teacher's Guide introduction on the *Rising Stars Mathematics* approach to mental arithmetic and written algorithms (see pages 16–17). This could help parents/carers understand how their child will be tackling calculations during practice or homework activities and explain how best they can support this

Planning grids

Year 6 scope and sequence

The following grid shows the concepts and objectives that are covered within each *Rising Stars Mathematics* Year 6 unit and provides page references to each of the various components.

Unit	Concept	Objectives	Textbook	Teacher's Guide	Practice Book	Homework Sheets
1	1a Place value	• Identify the value of each digit in numbers given to two decimal places, and multiply and divide numbers by 10 and 100 giving answers up to two decimal places. • Solve problems that involve number and place value. • Use, read, write and convert between standard units, converting measurements of mass from a smaller unit of measure to a larger unit, and vice versa, using decimal notation up to two decimal places.	12–13	26–7	4–7	198
	1b Comparing, ordering and rounding numbers	• Read, write, order and compare whole numbers to at least 5 000 000. • Round any whole number to a required degree of accuracy. • Solve problems that involve number and place value. • Use, read, write and convert between standard units, converting measurements of mass from a smaller unit of measure to a larger unit, and vice versa, using decimal notation up to two decimal places.	14–15	28–9	8–10	199
	1c Comparing, ordering and simplifying fractions	• Compare and order fractions. • Use common factors to simplify fractions; use common multiples to express fractions in the same denomination. • Solve number and practical problems that involve fractions.	16–17	30–1	11–14	200
	1d Equivalences	• Recall and use equivalences between simple fractions, decimals and percentages, including in different contexts.	18–19	32–3	15–17	201
2	2a Calculating mentally with 3- and 4-digit numbers	• Perform mental calculations, including with mixed operations and large numbers. • Solve addition and subtraction multi-step problems in contexts, deciding which operations and methods to use and why. • Solve problems involving addition, subtraction; use estimation to check answers to calculations and determine, in the context of a problem, an appropriate degree of accuracy. • Interpret line graphs and use these to solve problems.	26–7	40–1	18–24	202
	2b Using the order of operations	• Use knowledge of the order of operations to carry out calculations involving the four operations. • Perform mental calculations, including with mixed operations and large numbers. • Solve problems involving the calculation and conversion of units of measure, using decimal notation to three decimal places where appropriate.	28–9	42–3	25–7	203
	2c Using formulae	• Use simple formulae. • Find pairs of numbers that satisfy an equation with two unknowns.	30–1	44–5	28–30	204
3	3a Using long multiplication	• Multiply multi-digit numbers up to four digits by a 2-digit whole number using the formal method of long multiplication. • Solve problems involving multiplication.	38–9	52–3	31–4	205
	3b Calculating mentally with large numbers	• Perform mental calculations with large numbers. • Give reasons for choosing a particular method.	40–1	54–5	35–8	206
	3c Multiply and divide up to 2 decimal places	• Multiply single-digit numbers with up to two decimal places by whole numbers. • Use written division methods in cases where the answer has up to two decimal places. • Calculate and interpret the mean as an average.	42–3	56–7	39–41	207
	3d Solving problems with ratio and proportion	• Solve problems involving the relative sizes of two quantities, where missing values can be found by using integer multiplication and division facts. • Solve problems involving unequal sharing and grouping using knowledge of fractions and multiples.	44–5	58–9	42–4	208
4	4a Areas and properties of 2-D shapes	• Draw 2-D shapes, using given dimensions and angles. • Recognise that shapes with the same areas can have different perimeters and vice versa. • Calculate the area of parallelograms and triangles. • Recognise when it is possible to use the formulae for area. • Express missing number problems algebraically.	52–3	66–7	45–9	209
	4b Finding angles	• Draw 2-D shapes, using given dimensions and angles. • Compare and classify geometric shapes based on their properties and sizes and find unknown angles. • Recognise angles where they meet at a point, are on a straight line, or are vertically opposite, and find missing angles. • Express missing number problems algebraically and find pairs of numbers that satisfy an equation with two unknowns.	54–5	68–9	50–3	210
	4c Describing 3-D shapes and making nets	• Recognise, describe and build simple 3-D shapes, including making nets. • Recognise when it is possible to use formulae for finding the volume of shapes.	56–7	70–1	54–7	211
5	5a Negative numbers in real life	• Use negative numbers in context, and calculate intervals across zero. • Solve problems that involve number and place value. • Interpret and construct line graphs and use these to solve problems.	64–5	78–9	58–60	212
	5b Decimals in context	• Identify the value of each digit in numbers given to three decimal places, and multiply and divide numbers by 1000 giving answers up to three decimal places. • Solve number and practical problems that involve all of the above.	66–7	80–1	61–3	213

Introduction

Unit	Concept	Objectives	Textbook	Teacher's Guide	Practice Book	Homework Sheets
6	6a Calculating mentally to solve problems	• Perform mental calculations, including with mixed operations and large numbers. • Solve problems involving addition and subtraction; use estimation to check answers to calculations and determine, in the context of a problem, an appropriate degree of accuracy. • Use negative numbers in context and calculate intervals across zero.	74–5	88–9	64–7	214
	6b Solving multi-step problems	• Solve addition and subtraction multi-step problems in context deciding which operations and methods to use and why. • Solve problems involving addition and subtraction; use estimation to check answers to calculations and determine, in the context of a problem, an appropriate degree of accuracy.	76–7	90–1	68–71	215
	6c Rounding to solve problems	• Solve problems which require answers to be rounded to specified degrees of accuracy. • Solve problems involving the calculation and conversion of units of measure, using decimal notation to three decimal places where appropriate.	78–9	92–3	72–4	216
	6d Describing number sequences	• Use simple formulae; generate and describe linear number sequences. • Express missing number problems algebraically.	80–1	94–5	75–9	217
7	7a Fraction equivalences	• Use common multiples to express fractions in the same denominator. • Compare and order fractions, including fractions greater than one. • Add and subtract fractions with different denominators and mixed numbers, using the concept of equivalent fractions.	88–9	102–3	80–4	218
	7b Fraction, decimal and percentage equivalences	• Recall and use equivalences between simple fractions, decimals and percentages, including in different contexts. • Associate a fraction with division and calculate decimal fraction equivalents (e.g. 0.25) for a simple fraction (e.g. $\frac{1}{4}$).	90–1	104–5	85–7	219
	7c Formulae	• Use simple formulae. • Recognise when it is possible to use formulae for area and volume of shapes. • Calculate the area of parallelograms and triangles.	92–3	106–7	88–93	220
	7d Missing number statements	• Express missing number problems algebraically.	94–5	108–9	94–6	221
8	8a Identifying common factors, multiples and prime numbers	• Identify common factors, common multiples and prime numbers. • Solve problems involving addition, subtraction, multiplication and division.	102–3	116–17	97–9	222
	8b Multiplying and dividing decimal numbers	• Multiply and divide numbers by 10, 100 and 1000, giving answers up to three decimal places. • Multiply and divide numbers, giving answers up to three decimal places.	104–5	118–19	100–3	223
	8c Solving problems with percentages	• Calculating percentages of amounts. • Calculating what percentage one amount is of another.	106–7	120–1	104–7	224
	8d Solving equations	• Find pairs of numbers that satisfy an equation with two unknowns. • Enumerate possibilities of combinations of two variables.	108–9	122–3	108–9	225
9	9a Circles and scaling	• Illustrate and name parts of circles, including radius, diameter and circumference and know that the diameter is twice the radius.	116–17	130–1	110–12	226
	9b Finding missing values	• Compare and classify geometric shapes based on their properties and sizes and find unknown angles in any triangles, quadrilaterals and regular polygons. • Calculate, estimate and compare volume of cubes and cuboids, using standard units, including cubic centimetres (cm³) and cubic metres (m³), and extending to other units.	118–19	132–3	113–17	227
	9c Translation over four quadrants	• Describe positions on the full coordinate grid (all four quadrants) and draw and translate simple shapes.	120–1	134–5	118–21	228
10	10a Unknowns and variables	• Find pairs of numbers that satisfy an equation with two unknowns. • Enumerate possibilities of combinations of two variables. • Interpret and construct pie charts and use these to solve problems.	128–9	142–3	122–3	229
	10b Linear number sequences	• Generate and describe linear number sequences. • Interpret and construct line graphs and use these to solve problems.	130–1	144–5	124–6	230
11	11a Solving multi-step problems	• Solve addition and subtraction multi-step problems in contexts, deciding which operations and methods to use and why. • Perform mental calculations, including with mixed operations and large numbers. • Use estimation to check answers to calculations and determine, in the context of a problem, an appropriate degree of accuracy.	138–9	152–3	127–8	231
	11b Solving problems involving fractions	• Add and subtract fractions with different denominators and mixed numbers, using the concept of equivalent fractions. • Interpret and construct pie charts and use these to solve problems. • Calculate and interpret the mean as an average.	140–1	154–5	129–32	232
	11c Finding possible solutions for equations	• Use simple formulae. • Express missing number problems algebraically. • Find pairs of numbers that satisfy an equation with two unknowns. • Enumerate possibilities of two variables. • Interpret and construct line graphs and use these to solve problems.	142–3	156–7	133–5	233

Unit	Concept	Objectives	Textbook	Teacher's Guide	Practice Book	Homework Sheets
12	12a Equivalences	• Associate a fraction with division and calculate decimal fraction equivalents (for example, 0.375) for a simple fraction ($\frac{3}{8}$). • Recall and use equivalences between simple fractions, decimals and percentages, including in different contexts. • Interpret and construct pie charts and use these to solve problems.	150–1	164–5	136–41	234
	12b Formulae and sequences	• Use simple formulae. • Generate and describe linear number sequences.	152–3	166–7	142–6	235
	12c Unknowns	• Express missing number problems algebraically. • Find pairs of numbers that satisfy an equation with two unknowns.	154–5	168–9	147–9	236
13	13a Using long division	• Divide numbers up to four digits by a 2-digit number using the formal written method of long division. • Interpret remainders as whole number remainders, fractions or by rounding, as appropriate for the context.	162–3	176–7	150–2	237
	13b Choosing operations to solve problems	• Solve problems involving addition, subtraction, multiplication and division.	164–5	178–9	153–4	238
	13c Multiplying and dividing fractions	• Multiply simple pairs of proper fractions, writing the answer in its simplest form. • Divide proper fractions by whole numbers.	166–7	180–1	155–7	239
14	14a Making and measuring 3-D shapes	• Recognise, describe and build simple 3-D shapes, including making nets. • Calculate, estimate and compare volumes of cubes and cuboids using standard units, including cubic centimetres (cm^3) and cubic metres (m^3) and extending to other units, e.g. mm^3 and km^3.	174–5	188–9	158–62	240
	14b Drawing shapes and finding angles	• Draw 2-D shapes using given dimensions and angles, including using compasses to construct triangles. • Find unknown angles in triangles, quadrilaterals and regular polygons.	176–7	190–1	163–6	241
	14c Reflections and equations	• Describe positions on the full coordinate grid (all four quadrants) and draw and reflect simple shapes. • Use simple formulae and find pairs of numbers that satisfy an equation with two unknowns.	178–9	192–3	167–72	242

Introduction

Curriculum mapping grid

The following grid shows what children should be taught during Year 6, as laid out in the 2014 National Curriculum Programme of Study for Mathematics and how these are covered within the *Rising Stars Mathematics* Year 6 units.

Domain	Sub-domain	Statement	Unit 1	Unit 2	Unit 3	Unit 4	Unit 5	Unit 6	Unit 7	Unit 8	Unit 9	Unit 10	Unit 11	Unit 12	Unit 13	Unit 14
NUMBER	Number and place value	read, write, order and compare numbers up to 10 000 000 and determine the value of each digit	b													
		round any whole number to a required degree of accuracy	b													
		use negative numbers in context, and calculate intervals across zero					a	a								
		solve number and practical problems that involve all of the above	a, b					b								
		read Roman numerals to 1000 (M) and recognise years written in Roman numerals														
	Addition and subtraction, multiplication and division	multiply multi-digit numbers up to four digits by a 2-digit whole number using the formal written method of long multiplication			a, c											
		divide numbers up to four digits by a 2-digit whole number using the formal written method of long division, and interpret remainders as whole number remainders, fractions, or by rounding, as appropriate for the context			c										a	
		divide numbers up to four digits by a 2-digit number using the formal written method of short division where appropriate, interpreting remainders according to the context														
		perform mental calculations, including with mixed operations and large numbers		a, b	b			a					a			
		identify common factors, common multiples and prime numbers									a					
		use their knowledge of the order of operations to carry out calculations involving the four operations		b												
		solve addition and subtraction multi-step problems in contexts, deciding which operations and methods to use and why		a	b			b					a			
		solve problems involving addition, subtraction, multiplication and division		a	a			a, b	a						b	
		use estimation to check answers to calculations and determine, in the context of a problem, an appropriate degree of accuracy		a				a, b					a			
	Fractions (including decimals and percentages)	use common factors to simplify fractions; use common multiples to express fractions in the same denomination	c							a						
		compare and order fractions, including fractions > one	c							a						
		add and subtract fractions with different denominators and mixed numbers, using the concept of equivalent fractions								a			b			
		multiply simple pairs of proper fractions, writing the answer in its simplest form [e.g. $\frac{1}{4} \times \frac{1}{2} = \frac{3}{4}$]												c		
		divide proper fractions by whole numbers [e.g. $\frac{1}{3} \div 2 = \frac{1}{6}$]												c		
		associate a fraction with division and calculate decimal fraction equivalents [e.g. 0.375] for a simple fraction [e.g. $\frac{3}{8}$]								b				a		
		identify the value of each digit in numbers given to three decimal places and multiply and divide numbers by ten, 100 and 1000 giving answers up to three decimal places	a				b			b						
		multiply single-digit numbers with up to two decimal places by whole numbers								b						
		use written division methods in cases where the answer has up to two decimal places								b						
		solve problems which require answers to be rounded to specified degrees of accuracy	c					c								
		recall and use equivalences between simple fractions, decimals and percentages, including in different contexts	d							b					a	

Domain	Sub-domain	Statement	Unit 1	Unit 2	Unit 3	Unit 4	Unit 5	Unit 6	Unit 7	Unit 8	Unit 9	Unit 10	Unit 11	Unit 12	Unit 13	Unit 14
RATIO AND PROPORTION	Ratio and proportio	solve problems involving the relative sizes of two quantities where missing values can be found by using integer multiplication and division facts			d											
		solve problems involving the calculation of percentages [e.g. of measures, and such as 15% of 360] and the use of percentages for comparison									c					
		solve problems involving similar shapes where the scale factor is known or can be found														
		solve problems involving unequal sharing and grouping using knowledge of fractions and multiples			d											
ALGEBRA	Algebra	use simple formulae		c				d	c				c	b		c
		generate and describe linear number sequences						d				b		b		
		express missing number problems algebraically				a, b		d	d				c	c		
		find pairs of numbers that satisfy an equation with two unknowns		c		b					d	a	c	c		c
		enumerate possibilities of combinations of two variables									d	a	c			
MEASUREMENT	Measurement	solve problems involving the calculation and conversion of units of measure, using decimal notation up to three decimal places where appropriate		b				c								
		use, read, write and convert between standard units, converting measurements of length, mass, volume and time from a smaller unit of measure to a larger unit, and vice versa, using decimal notation to up to three decimal places	a, b													
		convert between miles and kilometres														
		recognise that shapes with the same areas can have different perimeters and vice versa				a										
		recognise when it is possible to use formulae for area and volume of shapes				a, c			c							
		calculate the area of parallelograms and triangles				a			c							
		calculate, estimate and compare volume of cubes and cuboids using standard units, including cubic centimetres (cm³) and cubic metres (m³), and extending to other units [e.g. mm³ and km³]									b					a
GEOMETRY	Properties of shapes	draw 2-D shapes using given dimensions and angles				a, b										b
		recognise, describe and build simple 3-D shapes, including making nets				c										a
		compare and classify geometric shapes based on their properties and sizes and find unknown angles in any triangles, quadrilaterals, and regular polygons				b					b					b
		illustrate and name parts of circles, including radius, diameter and circumference and know that the diameter is twice the radius									a					
		recognise angles where they meet at a point, are on a straight line, or are vertically opposite, and find missing angles				b										
	Position and direction	describe positions on the full coordinate grid (all four quadrants)									c					c
		draw and translate simple shapes on the coordinate plane, and reflect them in the axes									c					
STATISTICS	Statistics	interpret and construct pie charts and line graphs and use these to solve problems		a			a					a, b	b, c	a		
		calculate and interpret the mean as an average			c								b			

Mathematical focus

★ **Number: number and place value, fractions**

★ **Measurement: length, mass, capacity**

Prior learning

Children should already be able to:

- read, write, order and compare numbers to at least 1 000 000 and determine the value of each digit

- count forwards and backwards in steps of powers of 10 for any given number up to 1 000 000

- round any number up to 1 000 000 to the nearest 10, 100, 1000, 10 000 and 100 000

- solve number and practical problems that involve all of the above

- compare and order fractions whose denominators are all multiples of the same number.

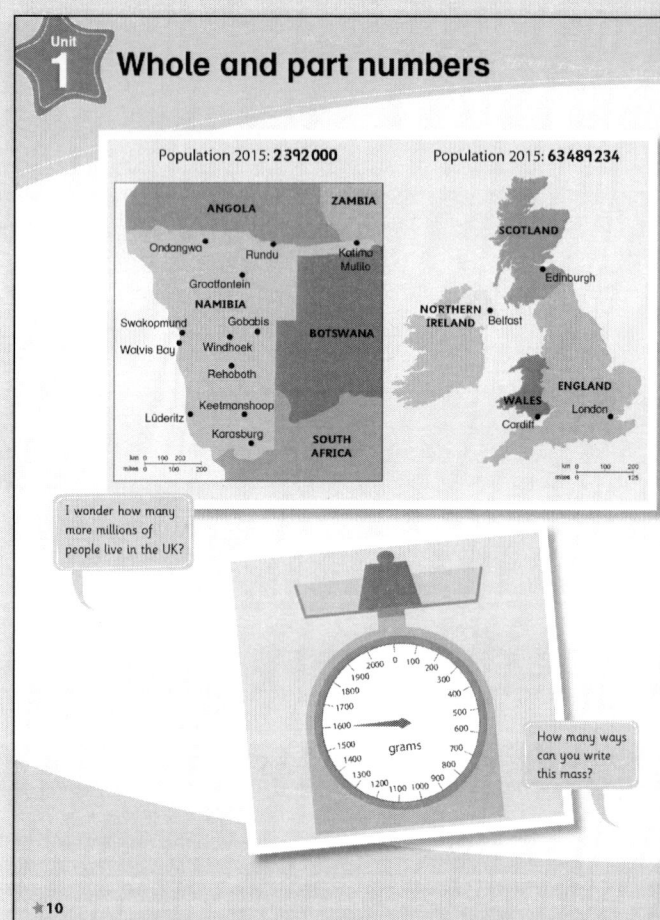

Unit 1

Whole and part numbers

Population 2015: **2 392 000**

Population 2015: **63 489 234**

I wonder how many more millions of people live in the UK?

How many ways can you write this mass?

★ 10

Key new learning

- Identify the value of each digit in numbers given to two decimal places, and multiply and divide numbers by 10 and 100 giving answers up to two decimal places.

- Solve problems that involve number and place value.

- Read, write, order and compare whole numbers up to 5 000 000.

- Round any whole number to a required degree of accuracy.

- Use common factors to simplify fractions; use common multiples to express fractions in the same denomination.

- Solve number and practical problems that involve fractions.

- Compare and order fractions.

- Recall and use equivalences between simple fractions, decimals and percentages, including in different contexts.

Making connections

- Linking work on fractions to measures and statistics gives children an opportunity to practise the main concept whilst making connections to other areas of mathematics.

- To reinforce number sense, provide children with food packages that display information in fractions and percentages on pie charts.

Talk about

Use careful questioning to encourage discussion of the vocabulary of place value. Ask children to tell you what each term refers to. Expect them to be able to tell you that positional is the position where the digit is placed, multiplicative is when the digit is multiplied by the position it is in, and additive is when all the numbers are added to make the whole number. Base 10 indicates that our number system increases and decreases by powers of 10.

Engaging and exploring

Invite children to look at each picture and discuss the accompanying question in pairs.

Establish if children know where Namibia is and find out how familiar they are with the UK. Ask them to read the population numbers. Discuss how it is possible to work out how many more millions of people there are in the UK. Ascertain that we need to compare the digits that represent millions, and agree that there are 61 more millions of people in the UK. You could also spend some time looking at both maps to establish that Namibia is much larger than the UK. Are children surprised that the UK has a larger population than Namibia? You could draw in concepts that children are learning about in geography, such as settlements, to highlight this real-life application of mathematics. Challenge children to use the scales on each map to find the distances from one place to another in both kilometres and miles.

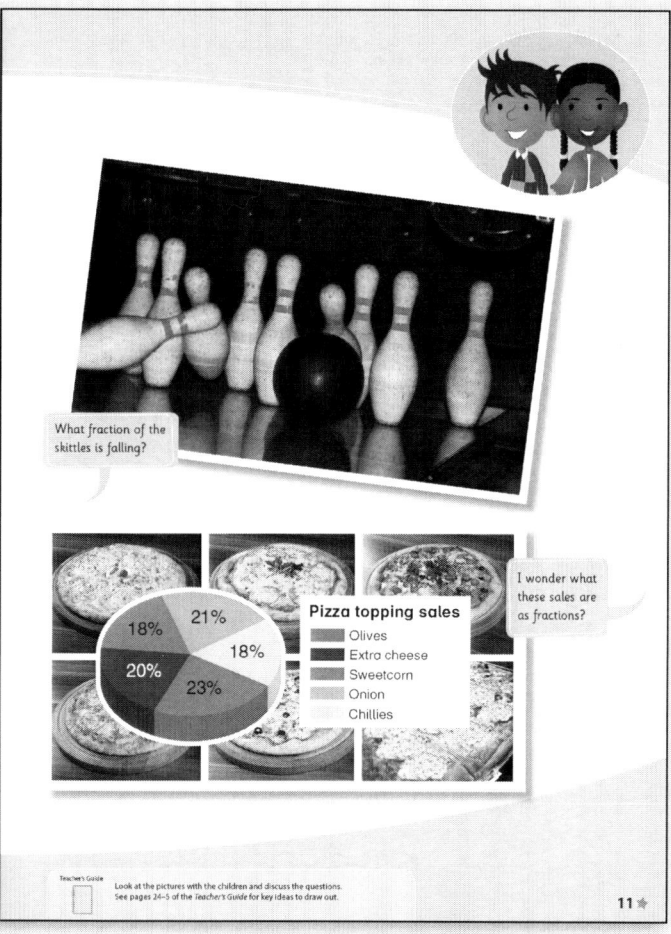

What fraction of the skittles is falling?

Pizza topping sales

18% 21%
20% 18%
23%

■ Olives
■ Extra cheese
■ Sweetcorn
□ Onion
□ Chillies

I wonder what these sales are as fractions?

Teacher's Guide — Look at the pictures with the children and discuss the questions.
See pages 24–5 of the *Teacher's Guide* for key ideas to draw out.

11

Focus on the picture of the weighing scales. Ask children what mass is shown. Invite them to tell you the answer in as many ways as they can (1600 g, 1.6 kg, 1 kg 600 g). Call out other masses and ask children to write these down in all the possible ways. You could also ask them to tell you what the mass would be if you added more grams or took some away. Focus on the decimal aspects of the amounts each time, asking children to tell you how many grams they represent.

Ask children if they know how the game 10-pin bowling gets its name. Then explore the question: 'What fraction of the skittles is falling?' Use resources such as counters to represent the picture. Focus on the part–whole relationship by asking: *If the whole is all the skittles, what part are the falling ones?* Establish that the whole is 10 and the falling skittles are three of those 10. Explain that this can be represented as a fraction. Draw the line of the fraction first to show you are breaking something up, then write a denominator of 10, then the numerator of three. It is also a good idea when introducing fractions to circle each number to make the link to division. This will enable children to see the division symbol, ÷. You could also ask children to turn the fraction into a decimal fraction. Agree that $\frac{3}{10}$ is 0.3 as a decimal. Ask children to use counters to represent a different number of falling skittles, challenging a partner to write the number of falling skittles as a fraction and decimal fraction.

Moving on to the final image, remind children that a percentage is a fraction where the whole is 100. Ask them where they see percentages in real life and agree that they can be useful for comparison. Invite children to tell you how the information about pizza topping sales is presented (a pie chart). Ask them to convert the percentages they see to fractions, first out of 100 and then reduced to their lowest terms. Then ask them to convert the percentages to decimals. Extend by asking children to create their own pie chart to show that, out of a class of 28, half the class has cats, one quarter has dogs, one eighth has hamsters and the rest has none. On completion, they can label each section with the appropriate percentages.

Checking understanding

You will know children have mastered the concepts in this unit when they can:

- represent and explain the multiplicative nature of the number system, understanding how to multiply and divide by 10 and 100

- make appropriate decisions about when to use their understanding of counting, place value and rounding for solving problems

- convert between simple fractions, decimals and percentages, and use equivalences in different contexts.

Things to think about

- How will you organise mixed attainment groupings?

- How will you use Base 10 apparatus, place-value counters or regular counters to help children understand the place value of decimal numbers?

- How will you encourage children to explain the relationship between fractions, decimals and percentages?

- How will you ensure children experience practical opportunities to measure length, mass and capacity?

- Identify the value of each digit in numbers given to two decimal places, and multiply and divide numbers by 10 and 100 giving answers up to two decimal places.
- Solve problems that involve number and place value.
- Use, read, write and convert between standard units, converting measurements of mass from a smaller unit of measure to a larger unit, and vice versa, using decimal notation up to two decimal places.

 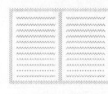 

Homework 1 and 2   Practice Book pp 4–7   Place Value & Abacus

Representations and resources

100 squares, sets of digit cards, place-value grids, money (coins and notes).

Mathematical vocabulary

Millions, hundred thousands, ten thousands, thousands, hundreds, tens, ones, round, place value, positional, multiplicative, additive, Base 10

Warming up

Ask children to add and subtract different numbers using the mental calculation strategy of rounding and adjusting, e.g. to add 19, add 20 and subtract one; to subtract 18, subtract 20 and add two. Give children a 100 square and ask them to put a finger on 5. Call out directions for them to follow, e.g. add 11, add 29, subtract 19. After five or six instructions stop to check what number everyone is on.

Background knowledge

Children need to understand the positional, multiplicative, additive and Base 10 aspects of place value. The positional aspect of place value is about where each digit in a number is positioned. This is important for written methods. The multiplicative aspect gives the digit its true value, e.g. if 3 is positioned in the thousands position, it is multiplied by 1000 to give 3000. This is important for mental calculation. The additive aspect is when the numbers are added together to give the whole number. Base 10 tells us that our number system goes up and down in multiples of 10. This is important for multiplying and dividing by powers of 10.

Let's learn: Modelling and teaching

Place value

- Give children a set of digit cards and a laminated place-value grid. Ask them to make 3 456 187 in the grid. Together, describe the place value of the digits using the correct language, e.g. the 4 is placed in the hundred thousands position.

- Ask children to make up a 6-digit number using digit cards. Ask questions such as who has an odd digit in the thousands position, an even digit in the tens position, the closest number to 5000?

- Ask children to describe the position of each digit in the second row of the grid in the Textbook. Then children make up a 3-digit number with two decimal places. Ask them what measurements their numbers could be. Invite children to record their number in pounds and pence,

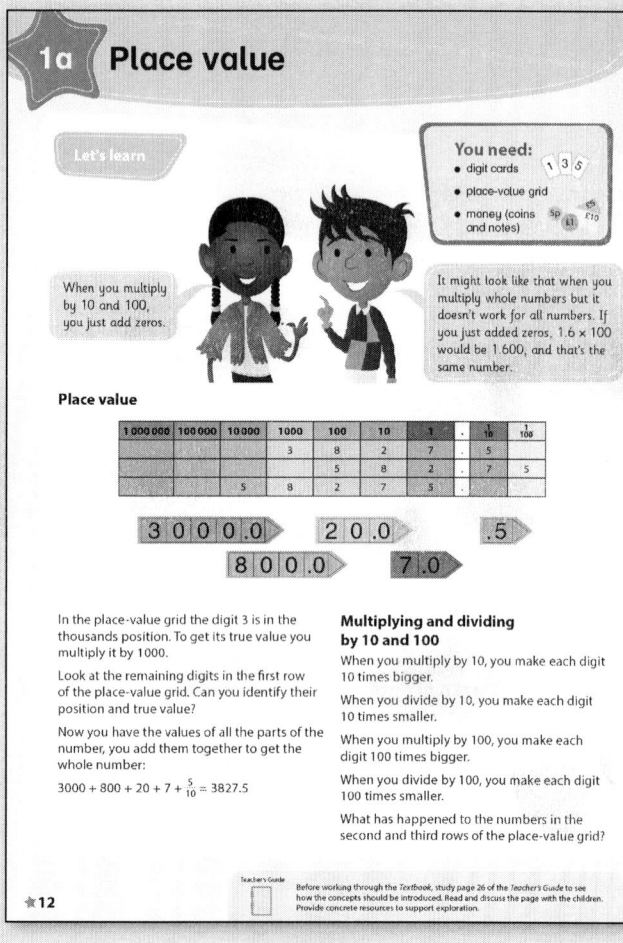

- e.g. £125.79 and 12579p. Next they record it in metres and centimetres.

Multiplying and dividing by 10 and 100

- Ask children what is wrong with Eva's thinking about adding zeros to numbers when multiplying by powers of 10. Ensure they understand that when multiplying by 10 or 100 each digit of a number gets 10 or 100 times bigger.

- Ask them to make up a 4-digit whole number using digit cards and some extra zeros. They place it in their place-value grid. Ask them to multiply the number by 10 and then 100 and to explain what is happening. What do they notice about multiplying by 100? Agree that it is the same as multiplying by 10 and then 10 again. Repeat for dividing by 10 and 100.

Let's practise: Digging deeper

Step 1

This question reviews children's understanding of place value. Encourage them first to establish the position of the 6 and 5, and then the true value of each digit.

Step 2

Before children begin the task, recap the Base 10 aspect of place value. Ask children to describe what happens when numbers are multiplied and divided by 10.

Step 3

Before children begin the task, recap the coins used in our monetary system. Discuss equivalences between them in terms of, e.g. ten 10p coins are equivalent to £1, ten 20p coins are equivalent to £2. Discuss the relationship between different coins, e.g. 1p is $\frac{1}{100}$ of a pound, 20p is $\frac{1}{5}$ of a pound. The task asks children to make amounts of money using the fewest coins. Ensure that you have sufficient notes and coins for them to use. They multiply and then divide the amounts by 10 and 100 and make the new amounts, again using the fewest coins.

Step 4

Children need to work out four possible numbers that Luke could have made and explain what he could have done to the numbers to give the result. Encourage children to work systematically without a calculator. If they need prompting, remind them that to find out the possible starting numbers they will need to do the opposite of what Luke did, e.g. they begin with 23.48 and divide by 10 to find the number Luke multiplied by 10. When they have finished, ask them to make up their own similar problems to give to a partner to solve.

Let's practise

1 **Work out.**

Write the position and value of the 6 in these numbers:

a   12 469   c   452 456

b   262 985   d   3 245 652

Write the position and value of the 5 in these numbers:

e   172 156   g   127 501

f   512 386   h   2 815 210

2 **Calculate.**

Multiply these by 10.

a   12   c   10.2

b   7.5   d   15.8

Divide these by 10.

e   14   g   8

f   21   h   5

3 **Apply.**

Make these amounts using the fewest coins.

a   3p   c   21p

b   15p   d   49p

Make these amounts using the fewest notes and coins.

e   £2   g   £11

f   £4   h   £13

Multiply the amounts by 10 and 100. Show each new amount using the fewest coins.

Divide the amounts by 10 and 100. Show each new amount using the fewest coins.

4 **Think.**

On a calculator Luke keyed in a number. He multiplied or divided it by 10 or 100. The result was 23.48. What number could he have started with and what might he have done to the number?

Find another 3 possibilities.

Teacher's Guide See page 27 of the *Teacher's Guide* for ideas of how to guide practice. Work through each step together as a class to develop children's conceptual understanding.

13

Follow-up ideas

- Children could make up some number problems that involve multiplying and dividing measures by 10 and 100. They give them to a partner to solve.

- Children could measure different items around the classroom in centimetres and millimetres and order these. They could then work out what the lengths would be if they were 10 and 100 times longer or shorter. They could records their results in a table.

- You could write a distance or length on the board, e.g. 2450 km or 250 m. Ask children to multiply and then divide these by 10 and 100. They should then explain the place value of the different digits in the new amounts.

Ensuring progress

Supporting understanding

It is vital that by Year 6 all children have a conceptual understanding of place value. If there are children in your class who don't, it would be wise to find additional time to ensure this understanding is developed. Provide them with place-value grids and digit cards when they answer the questions; the use of visual representations should help.

Broadening understanding

Provide opportunities for children to explain the different elements of place value to a child who hasn't mastered them yet. This will help you to assess their true understanding.

 Concept mastered

Using place-value grids, children can explain and demonstrate the positional, multiplicative, additive and Base 10 aspects of place value.

Answers

Step 1

a   6 tens, 60

b   6 ten thousands, 60 000

c   6 ones, 6

d   6 hundreds, 600

e   5 tens, 50

f   5 hundred thousands, 500 000

g   5 hundreds, 500

h   5 thousands, 5000

Step 2

a   120   e   1.4

b   75   f   2.1

c   102   g   0.8

d   158   h   0.5

Step 3

a   1p, 2p; 30p, £3

b   10p, 5p; £1.50, £15.00

c   20p, 1p; £2.10, £21.00

d   20p, 20p, 5p, 2p, 2p; £4.90, £49.00

e   £2; 20p, 2p

f   £2, £2; 40p, 4p

g   £10, £2, £1; £1.10, 11p

h   £10, £2, £1; £1.30, 13p Check children have correctly listed the fewest coins.

Step 4

0.2348 × 100, 2.348 × 10, 2348 ÷ 100, 234.8 ÷ 10

- Read, write, order and compare whole numbers to at least 5 000 000.
- Round any whole number to a required degree of accuracy.
- Solve problems that involve number and place value.
- Use, read, write and convert between standard units, converting measurements of mass from a smaller unit of measure to a larger unit, and vice versa, using decimal notation up to two decimal places.

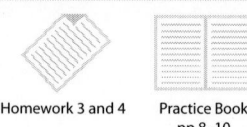

Homework 3 and 4   Practice Book pp 8–10

Representations and resources

Sets of digit cards, place-value grids, money (coins and notes).

Mathematical vocabulary

Order, compare, ascending, descending, round, place value

Warming up

Rehearse the mental calculation strategy of adding by near doubling. Pick pairs of numbers for children to total by doubling one number and then adjusting. Use numbers similar to these: 25 + 26, 75 + 76 and then multiples of 10, such as 150 + 160, 1500 + 1600.

Background knowledge

Comparing, ordering and rounding numbers relies on a conceptual understanding of place value. Some numbers may begin with the same digits, so children need to be able to identify the position of the digits they can use to order the numbers.

Rounding is a useful skill. We use it to carry out some mental calculation strategies, e.g. addition and subtraction of near multiples of 10 and 100. It is also useful for estimating answers to calculations and checking.

Let's learn: Modelling and teaching
Ordering and comparing numbers

- Ask children to read the numbers in the place-value grid in the Textbook to a partner. Discuss how these could be ordered. Ask: *Do the first four digits help?* Establish that they do not and to order the numbers children need to look at the digits in the hundreds position. Agree that none of the other digits matters.

- Ask children to write the same numbers in numerals and words. Encourage them to compare the numbers in different ways to ascertain how they are the same and how they are different.

- Give children digit cards and a place-value grid. Ask them to make up a 6-digit number with decimals. They compare their number with a partner's to identify similarities and differences. They could repeat this a few times.

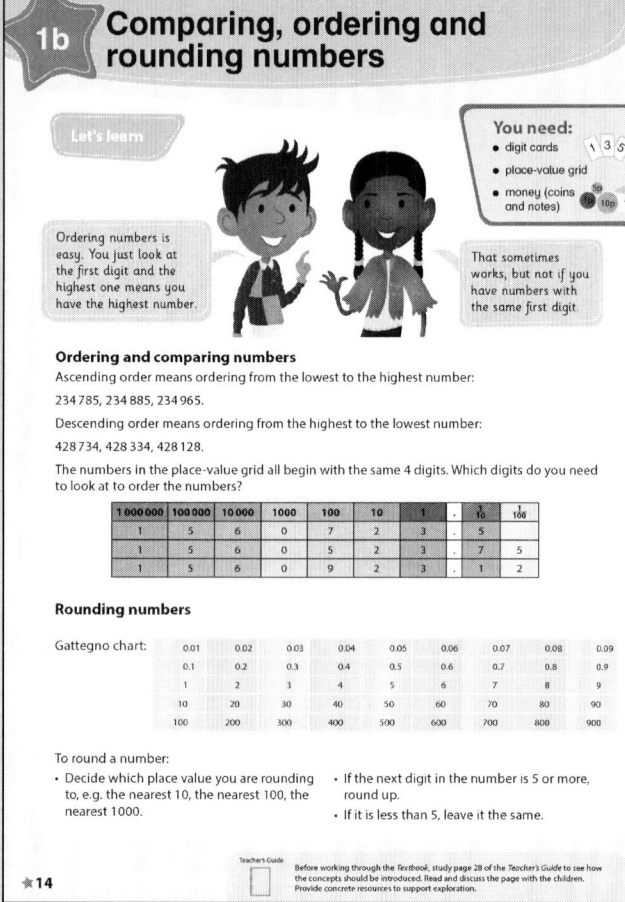

Rounding numbers

- Recap rounding using the steps in the Textbook.

- Ask children to look at the Gattegno chart (named after its developer) and cover the part that has numbers that would be rounded up. Repeat for numbers that would be rounded down.

- Discuss when rounding is useful in real life, e.g. estimating the answer to a calculation.

- Give children amounts of money to add together by taking some from one amount and using it to make the other amount a multiple of 10, e.g. £299 and £159. They could think of this as £300 and £158. The total will be the same.

Let's practise: Digging deeper

Step 1

Children need to order the first two sets of numbers in ascending order and the next two sets in descending order. See if they can remember what ascending order and descending order mean. The numbers in each part a–d all have the same first digit and some of the following digits are also the same. Children need to use their reasoning skills so that they can order the numbers successfully.

Step 2

This task rehearses rounding and reinforces place value. The visual representation of the Gattegno chart helps develop children's understanding of these areas of maths. Before the task, explore the chart by asking children what is happening along each row and then down each column. For the task, children make up a 3-digit number with two decimal places. They then round the number to the nearest tenth, whole number, ten and hundred.

Step 3

Give pairs of children a selection of notes and coins. Ask them to make different amounts of money using the fewest number of notes and coins, e.g. £13.25. Take feedback, finding out if all children were able to do this. If any found this difficult, support them during parts a–f. Parts g and h involve addition to solve word problems. Children should use the mental calculation strategy discussed, e.g. £115 + £249 could be rearranged to make £114 + £250. On completion, ask the class whether they can think of other ways to add the amounts. Which do they think are the most efficient?

Step 4

Children make two numbers using the Gattegno chart and compare them, finding as many similarities and differences as they can. Encourage them to consider the properties of place value and number, such as odd and even numbers of the whole number, as well as the positional aspect of place value.

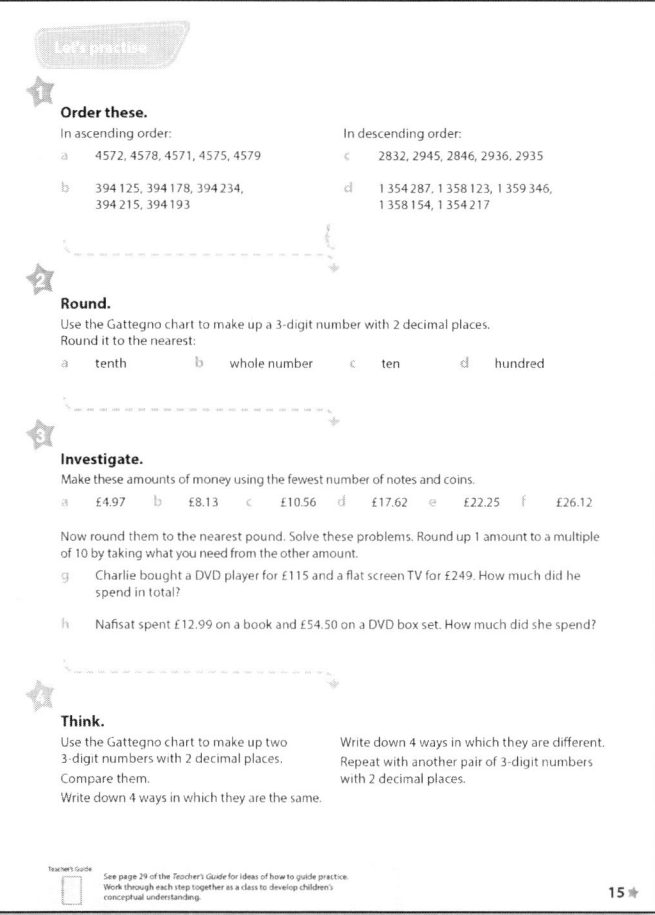

Ensuring progress

Supporting understanding

For children who struggle to understand rounding, ask them to draw number lines that go from, e.g. 100 to 200. They mark on 150 and write some numbers that would be rounded up (anything over 150) and then some that would be rounded down (anything below 150). They could extend this to number lines that go from 1000 to 2000 or from 30 000 to 40 000.

Broadening understanding

Provide opportunities for children to explain clearly and concisely the method for ordering and rounding numbers to a child who has difficulty grasping these concepts. Encourage them to make up problems within measures contexts for others to solve.

 Concept mastered

Children can explain and demonstrate that 234 145 is lower than 234 148, find similarities and differences between two numbers, and explain and demonstrate how to round a number.

Follow-up ideas

- Ask children to measure the lengths of different items found in the classroom. They round these to the nearest centimetre and then write them in ascending and descending order.

- Children could measure the mass, in grams and kilograms, of different items in the classroom on a set of kitchen scales. They then write these in ascending and descending order. They could also round them to the nearest 100 g. They could do a similar activity for capacity and/or liquid volume.

- Children could take two measurements they recorded during the above two activities and write what is the same and what is different about them.

Answers

Step 1

a 4571, 4572, 4575, 4578, 4579

b 394 125, 394 178, 394 193, 394 215, 394 234

c 2945, 2936, 2935, 2846, 2832

d 1 359 346, 1 358 154, 1 358 123, 1 354 287, 1 354 217

Step 2

Answers will vary.

Step 3

a £2 + £2 + 50p + 20p + 20p + 5p + 2p; £5

b £5 + £2 + £1 + 10p + 2p + 1p; £8

c £10 + 50p + 5p + 1p; £11

d £10 + £5 + £2 + 50p + 10p + 2p; £18

e £20 + £2 + 20p + 5p; £22

f £20 + £5 + £1 + 10p + 2p; £26

g £114 + £250 = £364

h £13 + £54.49 = £67.49

Step 4

Answers will vary.

- **Compare and order fractions.**
- **Use common factors to simplify fractions; use common multiples to express fractions in the same denomination.**
- **Solve number and practical problems that involve fractions.**

Homework 5 and 6   Practice Book pp 11–14   Fraction Wall

Mathematical vocabulary

Order, compare, denominator, numerator, simplify, factors, multiples, common factor, equivalent, lowest terms, simplest form, unit fraction, non-unit fraction

Representations and resources

Strips of paper 21 cm × 2 cm (4 per child), strips of paper 10 cm long (8 per child).

Warming up

Rehearse the mental calculation strategy of sequencing for addition and subtraction (keeping the first number whole and partitioning the second),
e.g. $147 + 123 = 147 + 100 + 20 + 3 = 270$;
$4732 - 2346 = 4732 - 2000 - 300 - 40 - 6 = 2386$.
Use numbers similar to these: $147 + 123$, $5365 + 1239$, $348 - 125$, $5218 - 1724$. Write them horizontally on the board as you also say them aloud.

Background knowledge

Be aware of the misconceptions that children might have when it comes to fractions, e.g. children may treat denominators and numerators as individual numbers, and they will think that the largest denominator will lead them to the largest fraction. This may indicate that they don't fully understand the part–whole relationship of fractions. The denominator is the number of parts we divide the whole number into and the numerator is the part we are considering. It is helpful to write the vinculum first to show something is being broken into parts, the denominator next to show the whole and then the numerator last to show the part needed.

Let's learn: Modelling and teaching

Comparing and ordering fractions

- Discuss Eva and Ali's comments. Can children see where Eva has got her thinking wrong? Ask them to look at the fraction strips in the Textbook and use them to order $\frac{1}{2}$, $\frac{3}{4}$, $\frac{1}{8}$, $\frac{7}{16}$, $\frac{3}{5}$ and $\frac{1}{10}$ from smallest to largest fraction.

- Focus on Ali's comment about breaking the bars of chocolate. Ask children to suggest other examples he could have given. Lead them into thinking of money. How much would $\frac{1}{5}$ of a pound be worth? What about $\frac{1}{10}$? What other fractions of a pound can children make?

- Call out pairs of non-unit fractions, e.g. $\frac{3}{10}$ and $\frac{2}{5}$. Ask children to compare them by working out which is the largest.

- Give each child four strips of paper. They keep one whole and divide a second into thirds as accurately as they can. They label each part of one with the fraction $\frac{1}{3}$.

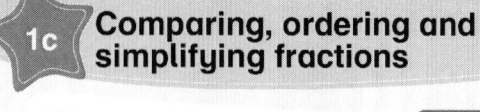

1c Comparing, ordering and simplifying fractions

Let's learn

You need:
- strips of paper

$\frac{1}{10}$ is obviously bigger than $\frac{1}{5}$ because 10 is bigger than 5.

$\frac{1}{5}$ is bigger. Imagine 2 bars of chocolate the same size. If you break 1 into tenths, that will be 10 pieces. If you break the other into fifths that will be 5 pieces. The fifths are bigger than the tenths!

Comparing and ordering fractions
Sometimes you need to compare and order fractions according to their size. For unit fractions, the smaller the denominator, the larger the fraction.

Look at the fraction strips. Can you see that $\frac{1}{2}$ is bigger than $\frac{1}{4}$ and $\frac{1}{8}$?

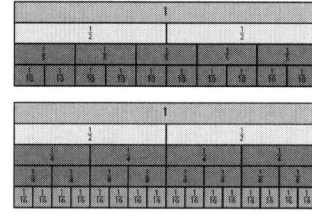

Simplifying fractions
You can simplify fractions to make calculations easier.
Find a common factor of the numerator and denominator and divide it into them.

Look at $\frac{75}{100}$. A common factor of 75 and 100 is 25. So $\frac{75}{100}$ is equivalent to $\frac{3}{4}$. It is much easier to find $\frac{3}{4}$ of a number than $\frac{75}{100}$!

Teacher's Guide Before working through the Textbook, study page 30 of the Teacher's Guide to see how the concepts should be introduced. Read and discuss the page with the children. Provide concrete resources to support exploration.

★16

- Children repeat to divide the remaining strips into sixths and ninths. Ask them to use the strips to order the unit fractions and compare non-unit fractions.

Simplifying fractions

- Ask children to use the strips in their Textbooks and the strips they have made to identify and make lists of equivalent fractions. Ask them to look for all the equivalences that they can.

- Once they have listed the equivalences, ask them to explore each set. Ask: *What do you notice?* Discuss how what they have found out can help them find other equivalent fractions.

- Write $\frac{15}{20}$ on the board. Ask children to discuss with a partner how they could simplify this fraction.

Let's practise: Digging deeper

Step 1

For parts a–d children need to order the fractions from smallest to largest. Encourage them to do this without using fraction strips. They should have understood by now that, for unit fractions, the larger the denominator the smaller the fraction. For parts e–h they write two statements, one using < and the other >.

Step 2

Before children begin the task, recap how to simplify fractions. Write a few examples similar to those in the task on the board. Discuss how these can be simplified. During the discussion, ask questions such as *Is it easier to divide by the highest common factor or several smaller factors?*

Step 3

Provide each child with eight 10 cm strips of paper. They then find the different fractions listed. Observe whether they decide to fold the strips or divide by the denominator and measure. Once they have completed this part of the task, they imagine that the whole strip represents 1 kg and then £5 and work out the different values of the fractions. Encourage them to apply the same reasoning that they used in the first part of the task.

Step 4

Children need to use their reasoning skills to find the possibilities for the original fractions that Dan could have simplified. Before they begin the task, discuss what it is asking them to do and methods by which they could find solutions. You could encourage them to list multiples of 40 and make connections to multiples of the denominators 5 and 8 to find equivalent unit fractions and then adjust, e.g. if the denominator was 40, $\frac{1}{5}$ is equivalent to $\frac{8}{40}$; therefore $\frac{2}{5}$ would be $\frac{16}{40}$.

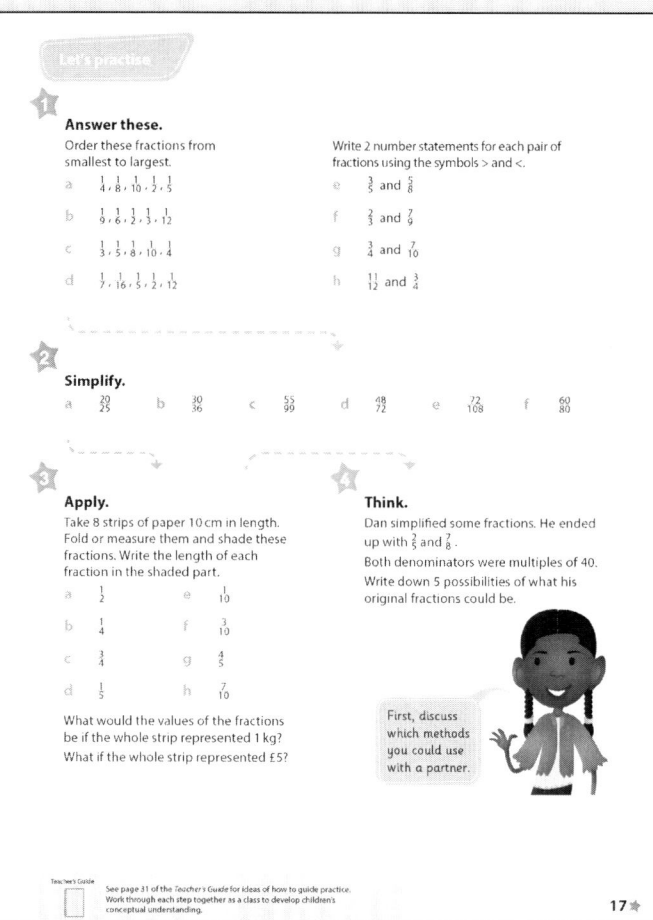

Ensuring progress

Supporting understanding

If some children need support to complete steps 1 and 2, let them use the fraction strips they made and those in the Textbook. You may need to work with these children to reinforce the concept. Encourage them to keep simplifying until the lowest terms are achieved.

Broadening understanding

Extend the tasks, e.g. once children have answered step 3, ask them to find all the fractions, plus thirds, sixths and ninths, of 1.8 kg. Ask them to explain their strategy to a partner.

✓ Concept mastered

Children can explain and demonstrate how to compare, order and simplify fractions.

Follow-up ideas

- Give children different lengths of paper to measure, then ask them to find the lengths of the fractions considered in this concept spread.

- Give pairs of children 24 pieces of small card. They make pairs of cards. On the first card is a fraction with a 2-digit numerator and a 2-digit denominator. On the other card is the fraction in its simplest form. Children shuffle the cards and lay them face down on the table. They pick pairs. If the cards are a match they keep them; if not they replace them. The winner is the child with the most pairs.

Answers

Step 1

a $\frac{1}{10}, \frac{1}{8}, \frac{1}{5}, \frac{1}{4}, \frac{1}{2}$

b $\frac{1}{12}, \frac{1}{9}, \frac{1}{6}, \frac{1}{3}, \frac{1}{2}$

c $\frac{1}{10}, \frac{1}{8}, \frac{1}{5}, \frac{1}{4}, \frac{1}{3}$

d $\frac{1}{16}, \frac{1}{12}, \frac{1}{7}, \frac{1}{5}, \frac{1}{2}$

e $\frac{3}{5} < \frac{5}{8}, \frac{5}{8} > \frac{3}{5}$

f $\frac{2}{3} < \frac{7}{9}, \frac{7}{9} > \frac{2}{3}$

g $\frac{3}{4} > \frac{7}{10}, \frac{7}{10} < \frac{3}{4}$

h $\frac{11}{12} > \frac{3}{4}, \frac{3}{4} < \frac{11}{12}$

Step 2

a $\frac{4}{5}$ d $\frac{2}{3}$

b $\frac{5}{6}$ e $\frac{2}{3}$

c $\frac{5}{9}$ f $\frac{3}{4}$

Step 3

a   5 cm   a   500 g   a   £2.50

b   2.5 cm   b   250 g   b   £1.25

c   7.5 cm   c   750 g   c   £3.75

d   2 cm   d   200 g   d   £1

e   1 cm   e   100 g   e   50p

f   3 cm   f   300 g   f   £1.50

g   8 cm   g   800 g   g   £4

h   7 cm   h   700 g   h   £3.50

Step 4

Many possibilities. Accept multiples of 10, e.g. $\frac{160}{400}$ and $\frac{360}{400}$, $\frac{1600}{4000}$ and $\frac{3500}{4000}$. Accept a combination such as, $\frac{16}{40}$ and $\frac{70}{80}$, $\frac{32}{80}$ and $\frac{350}{400}$.

- Recall and use equivalences between simple fractions, decimals and percentages, including in different contexts.

Homework 7 and 8

Practice Book pp 15–17

Tangrams

Mathematical vocabulary

Order, compare, fractions, decimals, percentages, denominator, numerator, simplify, factors, multiples

Representations and resources

Strips of paper 21 cm × 4 cm, tangrams, counters, 10 × 10 square grids, containers and measuring jugs, calculators (optional).

Warming up

Rehearse the mental calculation strategy of counting on for subtraction. Pick pairs of numbers and ask children to find the difference between them. Use numbers similar to these: 56 and 84, 175 and 250, 2398 and 4126. Write these horizontally on the board as you say them aloud. Allow children to make jottings if they need to.

Background knowledge

Equivalent fractions of shapes do not need to look the same. Fractions need to have the same area and therefore won't necessarily be the same shape.

Some children don't make the connection that decimals and percentages are also fractions. They see them as separate ideas that they need to learn about. It is important to teach fractions, decimals and percentages together when each new aspect is introduced into the curriculum and not as isolated topics.

During this concept children will explore equivalences in two ways - first through parts of shapes and then between fractions, decimals and percentages.

Let's learn: Modelling and teaching
Comparing fractions within shapes

- Discuss the comments of Eva and Ali. Give each child a rectangular strip of paper, a ruler and scissors. Ask them to draw diagonal lines from one corner to the other. Challenge them to prove the parts are quarters. To make the quarters identical they will need to make eighths. $\frac{2}{8}$ is equivalent to $\frac{1}{4}$, therefore the four triangles are quarters.

- Ask children to look at the tangram in the textbook and figure out what fraction of the whole square each shape is. Give them each a tangram. Ask them to cut it out and explore the different equivalences, e.g. the medium triangle, square and parallelogram are all the same fraction.

Equivalences between fractions, decimals and percentages

- Discuss the part–whole relationship of fractions as you did in the unit opener. Demonstrate this using five red counters and three yellow. The whole is the counters. They have been divided into eight. Five parts are red counters and three parts are yellow counters. Link this to percentages. As a percentage is out of 100, the whole is 100 and the part is the percentage given. Link this to

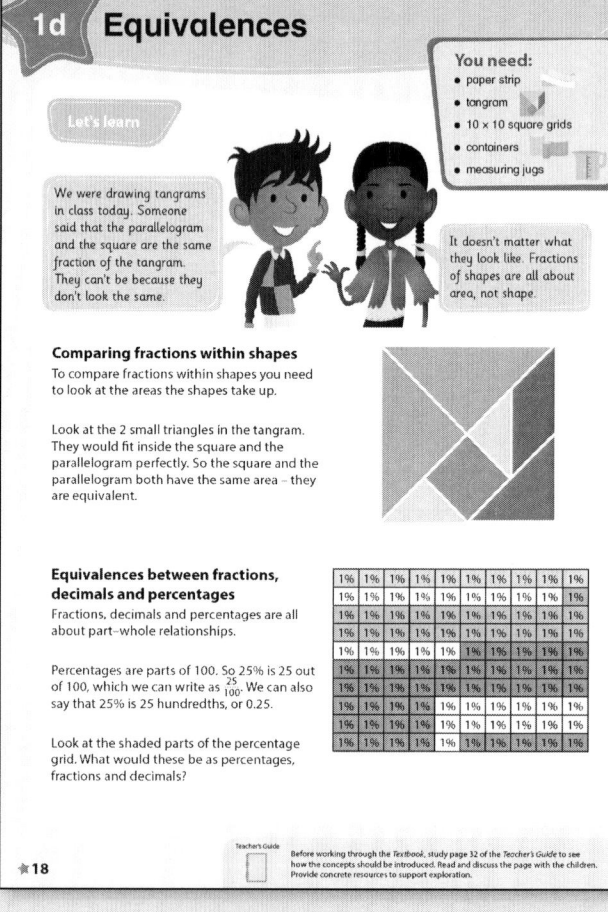

decimals. A percentage is out of 100, which connects to the decimal value of hundredths. Ensure that children make these connections.

- Ask children to identify the percentages shaded in the grid in the Textbook. As they do, they write them as fractions and decimals.

- Give children two 10 × 10 square grids. Ask them to keep the first grid whole and to cut horizontally along the rows of the second grid to create 10 strips. Ask them to use whole strips and part strips to create their own percentages. They list these and write them as fractions and decimals.

- Ask questions, such as, *If the whole grid represents £2, what do your percentages represent?* Change the values of the grid according to the confidence of your children.

Let's practise: Digging deeper

Step 1

The first part of this task focuses on equivalence; the second asks children to simplify fractions. Recap how to make equivalent fractions and how to simplify to the lowest terms. If children have difficulty, let them work with the visuals in the Textbook to model simplification. Children need to be encouraged to simplify fractions whenever they can, so that this becomes second nature.

Step 2

Recap converting between fractions, decimals and percentages before asking children to complete parts a–h. You could add extra questions here or, if children are confident, ask them to make up more percentages and decimals to convert to fractions.

Step 3

Give children water, containers and measuring jugs. They measure 1.2 l in a measuring jug, then work out the percentages of the volume listed. Ensure that they use the correct units when writing down their answers. Children then measure out the new volumes into different containers. Encourage them to be as accurate as possible.

Step 4

Read the introduction to the task together and ask children to prove that the example in the Textbook is correct. Agree that $\frac{1}{3}$ is equivalent to $\frac{2}{6}$, and $\frac{2}{6} + \frac{1}{6} = \frac{3}{6}$, which is $\frac{1}{2}$. Ask children, in pairs, to find the unit fractions to make the other fractions listed. If children struggle, discuss the relationship between the denominators in the example given ($\frac{1}{2} = \frac{1}{2+1} + \frac{1}{2(2+1)}$). Ensure children check the additions they write. Ask *What do you notice about the common denominator you need to use?* (It is the same as the larger denominator, e.g. $\frac{1}{4} + \frac{1}{12} = \frac{3}{12} + \frac{1}{12} = \frac{4}{12} = \frac{1}{3}$.) Challenge children to describe the pattern in the fractions, either algebraically ($\frac{1}{n} = \frac{1}{n+1} + \frac{1}{n(n+1)}$) or in words as appropriate, and continue it to make $\frac{1}{6}$, $\frac{1}{7}$ and so on. You could allow them to check the additions using a calculator as the numbers get larger.

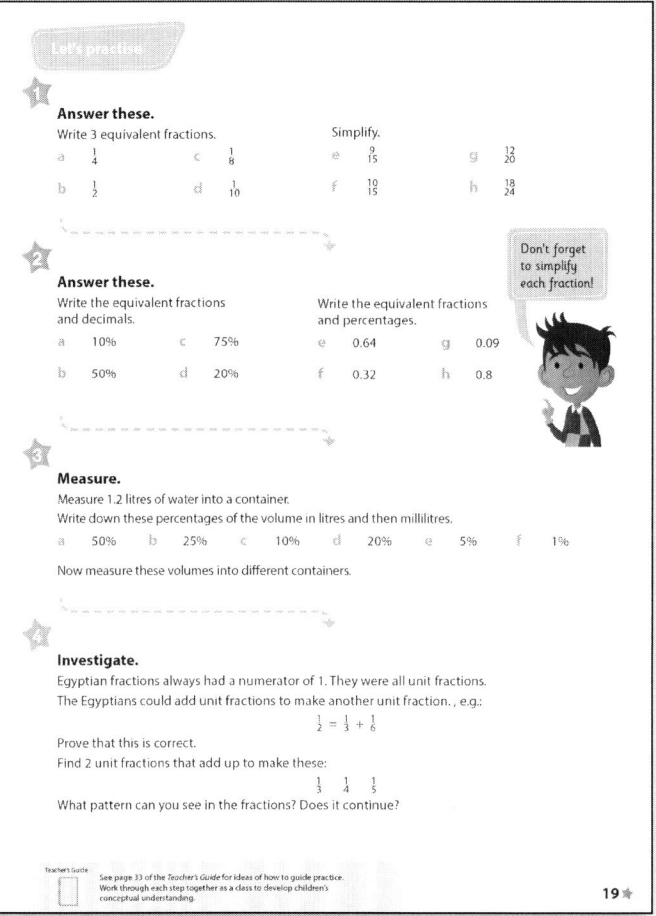

Follow-up ideas

- Children could make their own tangram which is different from the one in their Textbooks and that has more shapes. They then explore the fractions that are equivalent and work out what fraction of the whole each piece is.

- Give children pie charts with total values and percentage labels. There are plenty of examples on the I nternet. Ask them to convert the percentages to fractions and decimals, and then to work out the value of each part in numbers.

- Children could make posters about fractions, decimals and percentages, writing what each one is and how they connect. Encourage them to show examples.

Ensuring progress

Supporting understanding

In order to develop a conceptual understanding of the connections between fractions, decimals and percentages, children need to understand the part–whole relationship these share. They also need an understanding of hundredths. If any struggle, arrange a few intervention sessions in which you teach them the content of the lesson again, using familiar visual representations such as place-value grids and the grid they have been using during this concept spread.

Broadening understanding

Develop a deeper understanding by asking children to repeat step 3 for 1.5 l and 750 ml.

✓ Concept mastered

Children can explain and demonstrate how to find equivalences between fractions of shapes and numbers, and also between fractions, decimals and percentages.

Answers

Step 1

a–d Answers will vary. Ensure that the fractions are multiples of the numerator and denominator.

e $\frac{3}{5}$

f $\frac{2}{5}$

g $\frac{3}{5}$

h $\frac{3}{4}$

Step 2

a $10\% = \frac{1}{10} = 0.1$

b $50\% = \frac{1}{2} = 0.5$

c $75\% = \frac{3}{4} = 0.75$

d $20\% = \frac{2}{10} = \frac{1}{5} = 0.2$

e $0.64 = \frac{64}{100} = \frac{32}{50} = \frac{16}{25} = 64\%$

f $0.32 = \frac{32}{100} = \frac{16}{50} = \frac{8}{25} = 32\%$

g $0.09 = \frac{9}{100} = 9\%$

h $0.8 = \frac{80}{100} = \frac{8}{10} = \frac{4}{5} = 80\%$

Step 3

a 0.6 l, 600 ml

b 0.3 l, 300 ml

c 0.12 l, 120 ml

d 0.24 l, 240 ml

e 0.06 l, 60 ml

f 0.012 l, 12 ml

Step 4

$\frac{1}{3} = \frac{1}{4} + \frac{1}{12}$

$\frac{1}{4} = \frac{1}{6} + \frac{1}{12}$ or $\frac{1}{5}$ or $\frac{1}{20}$

$\frac{1}{5} = \frac{1}{6} + \frac{1}{30}$

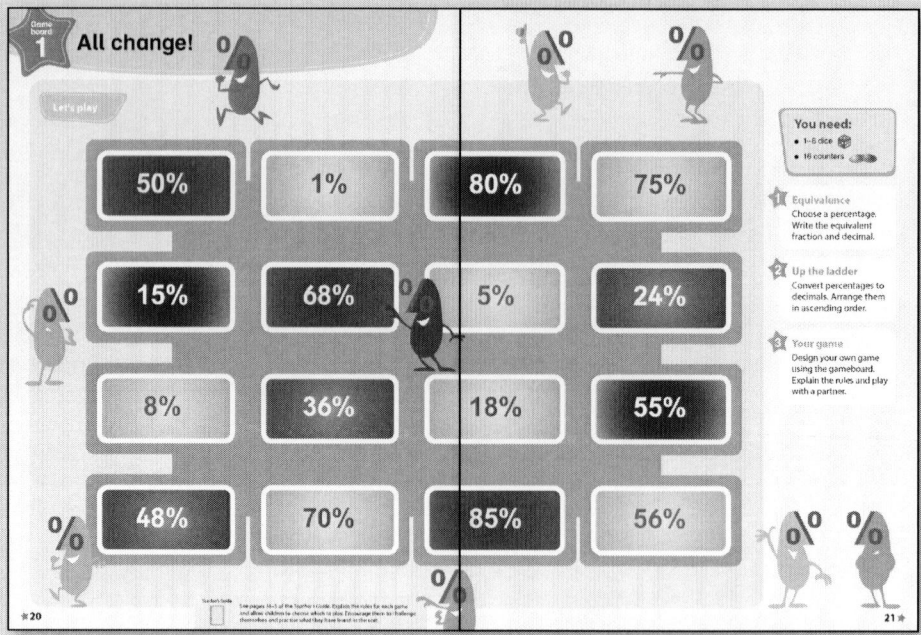

Game 1: Equivalence

This game gives children practice in converting percentages to fractions and decimals. They can choose which percentage to convert, so can start with the easier ones, but the game ends only when all the percentages have been converted.

Maths focus

• Find equivalences between percentages, decimals and fractions

Resources

1–6 dice (1), 16 counters.

How to play

This game is best played in pairs, but small groups could also work. Children take it in turns to throw the dice. If they throw an odd number they miss a turn. If they throw an even number they pick a percentage from the grid. As they do, they cover it with a counter. Percentages can only be used once. They write the percentage on paper and then write the equivalent fraction (in its lowest form) and the equivalent decimal. Play continues until all the percentages have been covered. The winner is the player with the most equivalent statements.

Making it easier

Children could write either the equivalent decimal or fraction (not necessarily simplified).

Making it harder

When children change the percentages to fractions, ask them to write all the equivalences when they simplify, e.g. $\frac{70}{100}, \frac{35}{50}, \frac{7}{10}$.

Game 2: Up the ladder

This game requires children to convert percentages to decimals and place them in ascending order. They will need to think about the size of the chosen percentage and the remaining percentages in order to fill their ladder.

Maths focus

• Convert percentages to decimals; order decimals

Resources

16 counters.

How to play

This game is best played in pairs, but small groups could also work. Children draw a ladder with 10 rungs. They then take it in turns to pick a percentage from the grid and cover it with a counter. Percentages can only be used once. They change their percentage to a decimal and write it on a rung of their ladder. The idea is that the decimals go in ascending order. Children keep doing this until their ladder is full. The player who completes their ladder first is the winner. Children need to consider carefully which percentages to pick and where to place them in order to complete the ladder.

Making it easier

Children could add the percentage to the ladder without making the equivalent decimal.

Making it harder

Turn this into a game of strategy, challenging children to try to stop the other players from completing their ladders. When children have completed their ladders, they could round each decimal to the nearest tenth and whole number.

Game 3: Your game

Children should invent their own game, designing rules that use the concepts covered in the unit.

Challenge children to make their game easier or harder.

All change!

Choose a game to play.

Game 1: Equivalence

You need:
- 1–6 dice
- 16 counters

How to play
- Take it in turns to throw the dice.
- If you throw an even number:
  - pick a percentage from the grid
  - cover that percentage with a counter (percentages cannot be used twice)
  - write down the percentage and the equivalent fraction and equivalent decimal (remember to simplify the fraction to its lowest terms).
- If you throw an odd number, miss a turn.
- Keep doing this until all the percentages have been used.
- The winner is the player with the most equivalent statements.

Game 2: Up the ladder

You need:
- 16 counters

How to play
- Draw a ladder with 10 rungs.
- Take it in turns to pick a percentage from the grid.
- Cover that percentage with a counter (percentages cannot be used twice).
- Change your percentage to a decimal and write it on a rung of your ladder.
- Keep going until you have filled your ladder.
- The numbers must be in ascending order.
- The first player to fill their ladder is the winner.

Game 3: Your game

- Make up your own game using the gameboard.
- Your game could include arranging the percentages in descending order.
- Perhaps it could involve the players scoring points.
- What are the rules of your game? Explain them to someone.

Please help your child by reading the instructions and playing the game together.

And finally …

Assessment task 1

Running the task

Before children begin the task ask them to tell you the word used to describe numbers that are ordered from the smallest to the largest (ascending). Repeat for numbers written in order from the largest to the smallest (descending). Ask them to choose their own numbers and to write these in ascending and then descending order. Invite children in groups to discuss the problem and explain to each other why Eva is wrong. Circulate among the groups to listen to the discussions. Encourage children to identify the value of the first digit of each number and to write it down. Once children have established that 96 257 is the largest number, ask them to identify what mistake Eva made. They should notice that Eva ordered the numbers according to the number of digits.

Evidencing mastery

If children are able to notice Eva's mistake quickly and explain what the order should be and what she in fact did, you can be assured that they have mastered ordering numbers. For children who cannot understand why Eva is incorrect, provide targeted questions on this area of mathematics during warm-ups in the next unit. Give opportunities for children who do understand to explain their reasoning to these children.

Assessment task 2

Running the task

Ask children what happens when a number is multiplied by 10 and 100. Expect them to be able to tell you that the digits move one or two places to the left and all digits are 10 or 100 times bigger than they were. Repeat this for dividing by 10 and 100. Expect them to say that the digits move one or two places to the right and all digits are 10 or 100 times smaller than they were. Call out some numbers for children to practise multiplying and dividing by 10 and 100. Next, recap rounding to hundredths, tenths and whole numbers. Ask them to round the numbers they multiplied and divided to the nearest whole number. The task asks children to use five given digits to make a 3-digit number with two decimal places. They multiply and divide their number by 10 and 100. Then they round each answer and repeat all the steps with another 3-digit number with two decimal places.

Evidencing mastery

If children are able to multiply and divide numbers by 10 and 100 and explain the effect, they are evidencing mastery of this area of maths. If they can round any number to the nearest whole number, they have mastered this aspect of rounding. If children haven't mastered this it may be because they simply add zeros when multiplying. This needs addressing immediately, so work with them as a focus group for short periods of time outside the maths lesson.

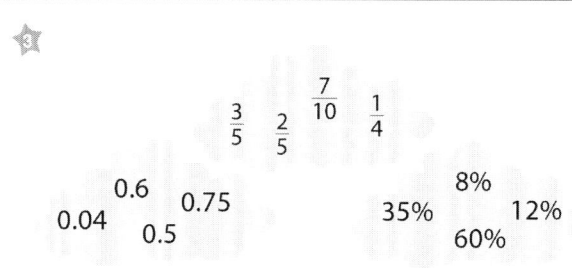

$$\frac{3}{5} \quad \frac{2}{5} \quad \frac{7}{10} \quad \frac{1}{4}$$

0.6   0.75   8%
0.04   35%   12%
     0.5   60%

Pick 2 numbers from each of the clouds.
Write each number in 3 different ways, so that they are equivalent.
Each statement must include a fraction, a percentage and a decimal.

Order the fractions from largest to smallest. Explain how you did this.

Did you know?

We often use percentages to report survey results, because they are easy to compare.

Logitech, the computer accessory and remote controls manufacturer, found out that about 50% of lost remote controls were stuck between the cushions on a sofa, 4% were found in the fridge or freezer, and 2% turned up somewhere outdoors or in the car!

23

Concepts mastered

✓ Children can explain and demonstrate using place-value grids the positional, multiplicative, additive and Base 10 aspects of place value.

✓ Children can explain and demonstrate that 234 145 is lower than 234 148, find similarities and differences between two numbers, and explain and demonstrate how to round a number.

✓ Children can explain and demonstrate how to compare, order and simplify fractions.

✓ Children can explain and demonstrate how to find equivalences between fractions of shapes and numbers and also between fractions, decimals and percentages.

Assessment task 3
Running the task

Before children begin the task spend a few minutes rehearsing converting between fractions, decimals and percentages. Call out a mixture of these for children to convert. They could write these down on paper or whiteboards. Then ask them to explain to a partner how they made their conversions. Write $0.2 = \frac{2}{100}$ on the board and ask children if you are correct. Agree you are wrong and ask someone to explain why. Expect them to be able to tell you that 0.2 is equivalent to two tenths not hundredths. The task asks children to choose six numbers from the clouds and write number statements showing two equivalent values. When appropriate, encourage children to simplify any fractions to their lowest terms. Encourage them to be careful when they convert single-digit percentages and tenths. When they have done this, they order the fractions from the largest to the smallest. Children who complete the task early could repeat it using the remaining numbers.

Evidencing mastery

All children should be able to make up some equivalences. Those who show mastery will be able to find all equivalences and simplify the fractions to their lowest terms without any assistance.

Some children may convert, e.g. 8% to 0.8. If this is the case, provide an opportunity for them to explore this using the percentage grid on page 18 of the Textbook, with a child who shows mastery.

Did you know?

Ask children if they have ever lost the remote control and where they found it. Do their answers fit in with any of the statistics? What percentage of the class has lost the remote control?

You could also discuss whether it is easier to compare the percentages 2%, 4% and 50% than the equivalent decimals (0.02, 0.04, 0.5) or equivalent fractions ($\frac{1}{50}, \frac{1}{25}, \frac{1}{2}$).

Calculations and algebra

Mathematical focus

★ **Number: addition, subtraction, multiplication and division**

★ **Algebra: simple formulae, equations with unknowns**

★ **Measurement: capacity, length, mass, area**

★ **Statistics: interpret and construct, interpret and calculate**

Prior learning

Children should already be able to:

- add and subtract mentally with increasingly large numbers
- use rounding to check answers to calculations and determine, in the context of a problem, levels of accuracy
- solve problems involving numbers up to three decimal places
- convert between different units of metric measure, e.g. kilometres and metre; centimetre and metre; centimetre and millimetre; gram and kilogram; litre and millilitre).

Key new learning

- Perform mental calculations, including with mixed operations and large numbers.
- Solve addition and subtraction multi-step problems in contexts, deciding which operations and methods to use and why.
- Solve problems involving addition, subtraction; use estimation to check answers to calculations and determine, in the context of a problem, an appropriate degree of accuracy.
- Use knowledge of the order of operations to carry out calculations involving the four operations.
- Use simple formulae.
- Find pairs of numbers that satisfy an equation with two unknowns.
- Interpret line graphs and use these to solve problems.

Making connections

- Solving problems involving the calculation and conversion of units of measure, using decimal notation to three decimal places where appropriate, will help children to solve real-life problems and across the curriculum, e.g. in art and design, science and geography.
- The ability to convert measurements of length, mass and time from smaller to larger units and vice versa is a vital tool in other subjects such as science and geography
- Interpreting and constructing pie charts and line graphs and using them to solve problems is a cross-curricular skill.

Calculations and algebra

Premier League						
	Season tickets		Match-day tickets			
Club	Cheapest	Most exp	Cheapest	Most exp	Cheapest day out	Programme
Arsenal	£1014.00	£2013.00	£27.00	£97.00	£36.30	£3.50
Aston Villa	£335.00	£615.00	£22.00	£45.00	£30.40	£3.00
Burnley	£329.00	£685.00	£35.00	£42.00	£42.30	£3.00
Chelsea	£750.00	£1250.00	£50.00	£87.00	£57.50	£3.00
Crystal Palace	£420.00	£720.00	£30.00	£40.00	£39.70	£3.50
Everton	£444.00	£719.00	£33.00	£47.00	£41.50	£3.00
Hull	£501.00	£574.00	£16.00	£50.00	£24.00	£3.00
Leicester	£365.00	£730.00	£19.00	£50.00	£27.50	£3.00
Liverpool	£710.00	£869.00	£37.00	£59.00	£45.80	£3.00
Man City	£299.00	£860.00	£37.00	£58.00	£45.80	£3.50
Man United	£532.00	£950.00	£36.00	£58.00	£45.50	£3.00
Newcastle	£525.00	£710.00	£15.00	£52.00	£23.30	£3.00
QPR	£499.00	£949.00	£25.00	£70.00	£33.40	£4.00
Southampton	£541.00	£853.00	£32.00	£52.00	£42.50	£3.50
Stoke	£344.00	£609.00	£25.00	£50.00	£33.60	£3.00
Sunderland	£400.00	£525.00	£25.00	£40.00	£33.20	£3.00
Swansea	£429.00	£499.00	£35.00	£45.00	£43.50	£3.50
Tottenham	£765.00	£1895.00	£32.00	£81.00	£41.00	£3.00
West Brom	£349.00	£449.00	£25.00	£39.00	£33.00	£3.50
West Ham	£620.00	£940.00	£20.00	£75.00	£29.00	£3.50

> Is the difference between the cheapest and most expensive season tickets always greater for London clubs than for the rest of the country?

★24

Talk about

It is important to use precise mathematical vocabulary from the beginning so that children have the tools to construct mathematical sentences to explain their thinking and convince others. Language stems, such as, 'My estimate is … because … ' encourage children to reason and consider estimates carefully.

Engaging and exploring

Focus on each photograph in turn, asking children to discuss ideas with a partner.

Looking at the football ticket prices, you could discuss strategies that can be used to find the difference. Ask children to work in pairs to model these on a number line. Then read through the question in the Textbook. Encourage children to reason and estimate before calculating. Look at a map of England to confirm the location of clubs before making generalisations relating to the question. To link with other areas of mathematics, children could look at distances between clubs and at train timetables. Encourage children to order a set of season ticket prices, perhaps calculating the mean and rounding values appropriately for the context of money. Children could also look up and compare capacities of stadiums and relate them to ticket prices and predict possible maximum and minimum takings, perhaps based on

the cheapest day-out costs.

Return to the table after completing 2c – Using formulae and look at constructing a pie chart to compare the number of clubs with programme prices of £3.00, £3.50 and £4.00.

Use a class calculator to consider the results of $3 + 4 \times 5$. Show children arithmetic calculators (calculation carried out in order of input) and algebraic calculators (carried out following rules of order of operations). Ask them to experiment to find other sets of calculations that result in different answers. Ask children to sort those calculations that do and do not result in two different answers. Challenge them to generalise about those that do, i.e. the order of the calculations $10 + 7 - 9$ or $10 \times 7 \div 9$ does not matter because within each calculation, the operations have equal priority, e.g. addition and subtraction are of equal priority. However, $10 + 7 \times 9$ or $10 - 7 \div 9$ does, as both calculations involve operations that have different levels of priority, i.e. multiplication and division have higher priority than addition and subtraction. Tell children that they will be looking closely at the importance of doing calculations in a particular order.

Ask children to make up possible prices for each piece of fruit that add to £2.00, assuming each type of fruit costs the same, e.g. bananas 40p, apples 25p and orange 30p. Ask children to suggest different ways of expressing the problem in words and symbols, e.g. three bananas + two apples + one orange equals two pounds or two pounds subtract three bananas subtract two apples equals one orange. Ask children: *Could we use letters to express the problem? Would this be helpful? Does it change the problem?* Take feedback from the class. Suggest that the price of one apple is a multiple of five pence and the price of the orange is a multiple of six pence. Ask children to investigate and present possibilities. Give the price of two of the fruits and children use the formulae created to calculate the cost of the remaining piece. Use the inverse to check solutions.

Return to the photograph after completing 2c – Using formulae to look at expressing the problem as $3b + 2a + O = $ £2.00. Consider the use of brackets in the equation, e.g. £2.00 $- (2a + O) = 3b$.

I wonder why I get 2 different answers?

$3+4\times5$ 23.

35.

I spent £2 on fruit altogether. I wonder how much 1 banana costs?

Teacher's Guide
Look at the pictures with the children and discuss the questions.
See pages 38–9 of the *Teacher's Guide* for key ideas to draw out.

25

Checking understanding

You will know children have mastered these concepts when they can solve addition and subtraction problems in different contexts, appropriately choosing and using number facts, understanding place value and mental and written methods. They can explain their decision, making and justify their solutions and levels of accuracy.

Things to think about

- How will you raise the profile of mental calculation?
- How will you organise groupings for discussions and activities?
- How will you support and develop mathematical language?
- What opportunities will you provide for children to carry out practical tasks that develop their fluency when working with measures and statistics?

- How will you provide opportunities to develop problem-solving strategies outlined in the introduction?
- Which problem-solving strategies are most appropriate in this unit, for your Year 6 children, e.g.
  - ▶ Convince me
  - ▶ What's the same? What's different?

Calculating mentally with 3- and 4-digit numbers

- Perform mental calculations, including with mixed operations and large numbers.
- Solve addition and subtraction multi-step problems in contexts, deciding which operations and methods to use and why.
- Solve problems involving addition, subtraction; use estimation to check answers to calculations and determine, in the context of a problem, an appropriate degree of accuracy.
- Interpret line graphs and use these to solve problems.

Homework 9 and 10   Practice Book pp 18–24

Representations and resources

Tape measures, number lines, place-value counters, Base 10 apparatus

Mathematical vocabulary

Operations, rounding, inverse, accuracy, estimation

Warming up

Ask children to use a method of their choice to solve the division $35 \div 8$. Discuss the methods that have been used, including seeing the calculation as $32 \div 8 + 3 \div 8 = 4\frac{3}{8}$.

Share a range of word problems that suit this calculation, e.g. *a box of eight pens cost £35. Approximately how much does one pen cost? 35 litres of water is divided equally between eight containers. How many litres are in one container? Janet bakes 35 cookies. She places them in tins in groups of eight. How many full tins are there?*

Children should reason about the degree of accuracy required each time and decide when the answer needs to be rounded up or down.

Background knowledge

Children must continue to use and refine mental methods even when they have mastered a range of written methods. Sequencing and representing calculations using number lines continue to be important methods. Rounding helps children to make useful estimates. Support children to make decisions about the most appropriate methods, e.g. subtraction calculations where numbers are close to a boundary can be best answered using a 'counting up' strategy to find the difference.

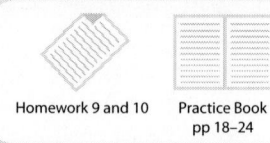

2a Calculating mentally with 3- and 4-digit numbers

Let's learn

You need:
- number lines
- tape measures

I used rounding to help me make an estimate. My estimate for 1612 + 562 is 3000.

I don't think that is a very helpful estimate. You must think carefully about the rounding you use.

Solving problems mentally

Would you use addition or subtraction to solve these problems?

Can you solve all of these problems only using mental methods?

How much rainwater was collected between 2 hours and 2½ hours?

A further 562.5 ml is collected between 4 hours and 5 hours. How much rainwater is there in the container now?

250 ml of water was collected after 1 hour. How much more water was collected after 2 hours?

Making estimates

It is important to make an estimate before you calculate so that you have an idea of the size of the answer. This helps to avoid place-value errors, but the estimate has to be useful.

A useful estimate for the calculation 2344 + 1955 is 4000 or even 4300.
How have the numbers been rounded each time?
Now complete the calculation using the sequencing method and the rounding and adjusting method. How close is the estimate?

$$2344 + 1955 = 2344 + 1000 + 900 + 55$$
$$= 3344 + 900 + 55$$
$$= 4244 + 55$$

$$2344 + 1955 = 2344 + 2000 - 45$$

Teacher's Guide Before working through the *Textbook*, study page 40 of the *Teacher's Guide* to see how the concepts should be introduced. Read and discuss the page with the children. Provide concrete resources to support exploration.

⭐ 26

Let's learn: Modelling and teaching

Solving problems mentally

- Ask children to interpret the line graph in the Textbook. Can they tell you what the scale is on the axes? Can they add any missing values to the scales?

- Encourage children to explain how they know how much water was in the container at different times, e.g. 'I know that there was 250 ml of water in the container after one hour because it is halfway between 0 and 500 ml.'

- Consider the problems posed and challenge different groups of children to focus on each one. They should then convince the rest of the class which operation to use. Encourage them to use a suitable representation, such as a number line, to support them. Explore other questions of your own.

- Children complete the calculations using a range of mental methods. Discuss method choices and model as necessary.

Making estimates

- Revisit the purpose of making estimates and what makes a useful estimate. Refer back to Eva and Ali's discussion, reasoning about the estimate that was made and why Ali thought it was unhelpful. Discuss a better estimate for this calculation, asking children to explain why.

- Discuss the estimates for the given calculation, 2344 + 1955. Ask: *What estimates would be unhelpful and why?*

- Consider how the order of calculation may help when faced with more than one operation

Let's practise: Digging deeper

Step 1

Children should consider different mental strategies, choosing which to use each time for the addition and subtraction calculations. Three of the questions include more than one operation, so encourage children to look carefully before calculating. As children complete the calculations, ask: *Why have you chosen this method?* This exercise includes spotting number bonds.

Step 2

Children choose numbers from the grid to generate their own calculations. Before calculating, they should make a helpful estimate each time. Children should draw a table like the one in the Textbook and then decide which of the three mental methods to use. Ask children to evaluate how accurate their estimates were. If there are any errors, challenge them to find the mistake using a different mental calculation strategy.

Step 3

This is a practical task that requires children to measure lengths to the nearest millimetres, drawing on knowledge of conversion between metres, centimetres and millimetres. Children find the difference between lengths and calculate a perimeter. They should apply mental calculation strategies where possible but also explain when a written method would be more appropriate.

Step 4

This open-ended task allows for children to find their own solutions as long as they meet the criteria given about the costs of the airline tickets. They should be encouraged to record ideas clearly and consider systematic approaches to the problem. The problem should encourage children to use rounding to add or subtract £199 each time, depending on the method used.

Solutions could be displayed in a table.

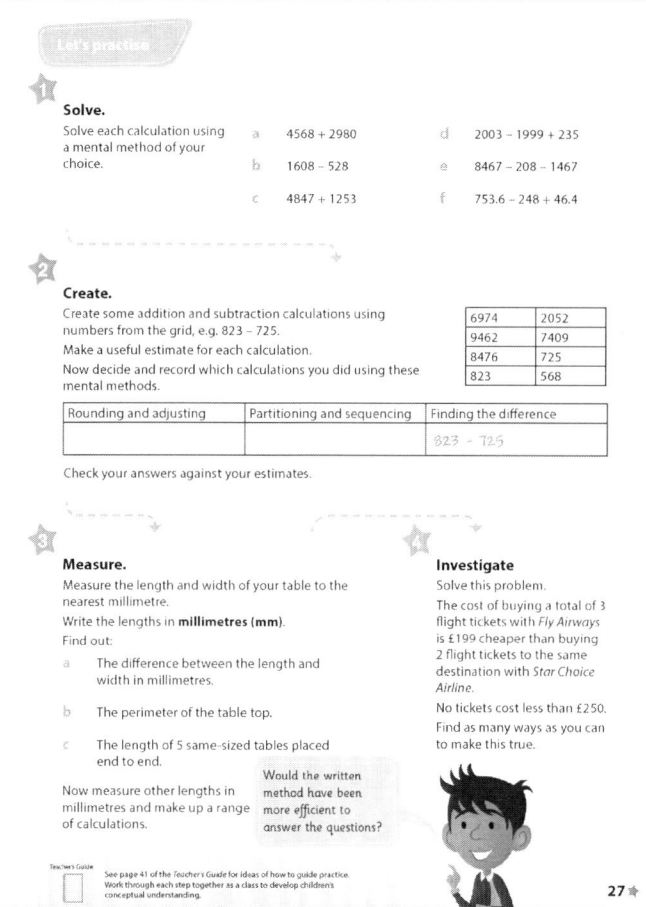

Ensuring progress
Supporting understanding

Place-value counters or Base 10 apparatus clearly represent adding or subtracting a near multiple of 10, 100 or 1000.

e.g. 243 + 99

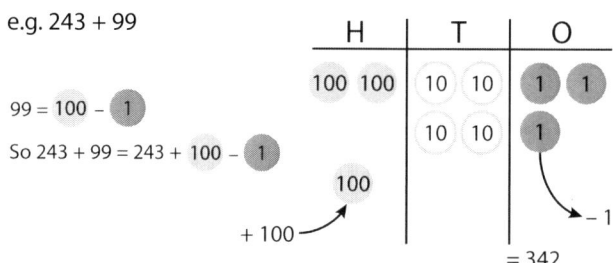

$99 = 100 - 1$

So $243 + 99 = 243 + 100 - 1$

$+ 100$

$= 342$

Broadening understanding

Encourage children to further explore calculations that involve a mix of operations, extending to decimal numbers that are close to a whole number or where number bonds can be used to aid mental calculations.

Concept mastered

Children can draw on a range of mental methods and explain their choices relating these to the numbers involved. They make sensible estimates and return to these to check the accuracy of their solutions.

Follow-up ideas

- Write a 3- or 4-digit number in the middle of a large sheet of paper. Children create as many addition and subtraction calculations (or ones involving a mix of operations) as they can that result in this number.

- Explore kitchen brochures or Internet sites to find measurements for cupboard units, etc. in millimetres. Children plan layouts for different dimensions of kitchens using estimates and mental methods to reason and calculate.

- Use digital kitchen weighing scales to first estimate and then weigh a set of four of five objects. Children reason about two objects with a total mass of approximately 3 kg. The total mass can be calculated using an appropriate method and then checked on the scales.

Answers

Step 1

a	7548	d	239
b	1080	e	6792
c	6100	f	552

Step 2

Children's own calculations and workings.

Step 3

Children's own measuring and workings.

Step 4

Children's own investigations.

Examples of solutions are:

Fly Airways	Star Choice Airline
£250	£275.50
£251	£277
£999	£1399

- Use knowledge of the order of operations to carry out calculations involving the four operations.
- Perform mental calculations, including with mixed operations and large numbers.
- Solve problems involving the calculation and conversion of units of measure, using decimal notation to three decimal places where appropriate.

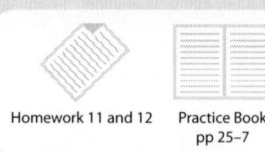

Homework 11 and 12   Practice Book pp 25–7

Representations and resources

Straws or lolly sticks, rulers, number lines.

Mathematical vocabulary

Order, commutative, operation, addition, subtraction, brackets, BIDMAS (or BODMAS), orders and indices, equivalent, conversion

Warming up

4.5	120	1.25	275	?

Children randomly pick one of the numbers and write it using a measurement, e.g. 4.5 kg, 4.5 cm or 4.5 litres. The question mark can be a value of their choice. They convert their chosen measurement using knowledge of place value to find equivalents, e.g. 4.5 cm = 0.045 m = 45 mm.

How many different equivalent measurements can children make using different units each time?

Background knowledge

Children in Year 6 are required to use their knowledge of the order of operations to carry out calculations involving the four operations, i.e. BIDMAS. This stands for 'Brackets, Indices, Division, Multiplication, Addition and Subtraction. Any part of the calculation that is in brackets must be carried out first, followed by indices, e.g. 5^2, followed by division and multiplication (with equal priority) and finally addition and subtraction (with equal but lowest priority). In the example $120 - 15 \times 5$, it is necessary to evaluate 15×5 before subtracting from 120.

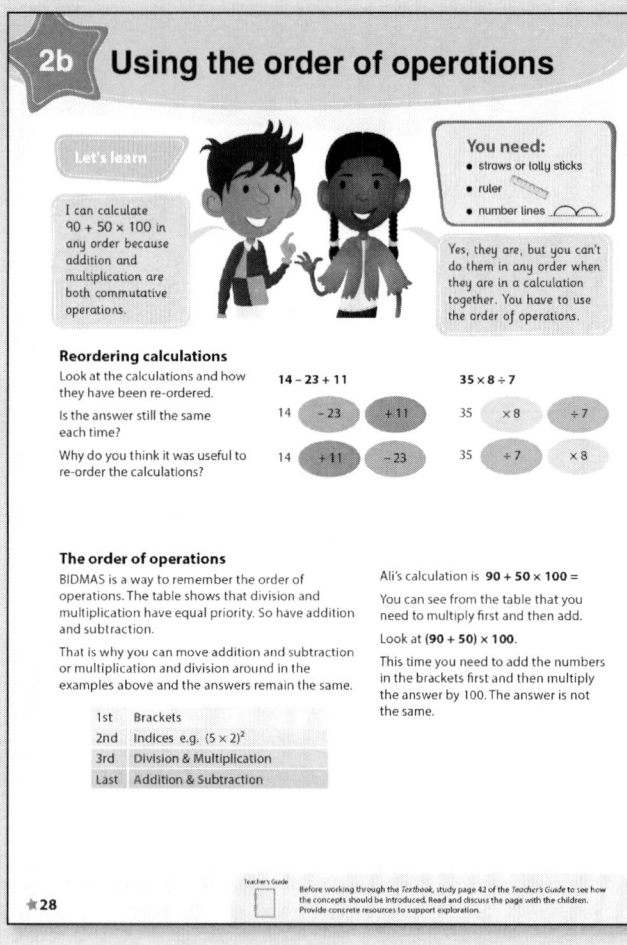

Let's learn: Modelling and teaching

Reordering calculations

- Look at the calculations in the Textbook. Ask: *Why are the answers the same?* Refer back to Ali's comments about the commutative law.

- Using a number line, show the result of doing subtraction first and then second. Highlight the need to count back into negative numbers for 14 – 23 + 11 but not for 14 + 11 – 23. Use this to show that it can be useful to reorder calculations. Link this to related facts.

- Consider calculations where it would not be useful to reorder, e.g. 2400 ÷ 6 × 5 or 793 – 193 + 25 and those where it would e.g. 1520 + 699 – 320. Ask: *Why can calculations like these can be carried out in any order, but Ali's calculation cannot?* You may want to refer to inverse operations.

The order of operations

- Discuss Ali and Eva's problem and refer back to the pictures of the calculators from the unit opener. Have a go at the calculation as 90 + 50 × 100 and then as 50 × 100 + 90 or even 90 × 100 + 50. What do children notice about the answers?

- Practise the rules of BIDMAS. Show a range of calculations and ask: *Does the calculation need reordering? Why?* Reinforce the concept by exploring the calculations on a number line.

- Ask children to decide upon the order in which the calculation 50 × 100 + 90 should be carried out. Ask children what is the same and what is different about the original calculation and the calculation (90 + 50) × 100. Establish that the brackets have priority and the addition must be done first. The answer is different this time.

Let's practise: Digging deeper

Step 1

Children work through calculations that involve mixed operations. In some examples, the calculation can be reordered as the priority of the operations is equal. Look for children who apply knowledge of related facts, e.g. number bonds.

Step 2

These calculations encourage children to think carefully about units of measurement before they calculate. Two of the calculations are set in more of a problem-solving context where children need to elicit the calculation from the information given and then decide upon the order of the operations.

Step 3

This practical activity uses straws or lolly sticks of the same length. Children should measure the length of the straws or lolly sticks, and then make shapes and calculate the perimeters. They compare the perimeters of the shapes, find the difference and record the calculations, e.g. an equilateral triangle and a pentagon with 20 cm straws could be recorded as $(20 \text{ cm} \times 5) - (20 \text{ cm} \times 3)$ or even $20 \text{ cm} \times (5 - 3)$. Observe whether children are using a range of mental calculation strategies. Children could go on to explore a range of irregular shapes, comparing them in the same way.

Step 4

Children must generate calculations using the numbers in the grid to find as many ways as possible to achieve an answer of 250. They should use more than one operation each time and consider the order of operations, including brackets and indices. After finding one solution, ask them to consider what can be changed to help find other solutions.

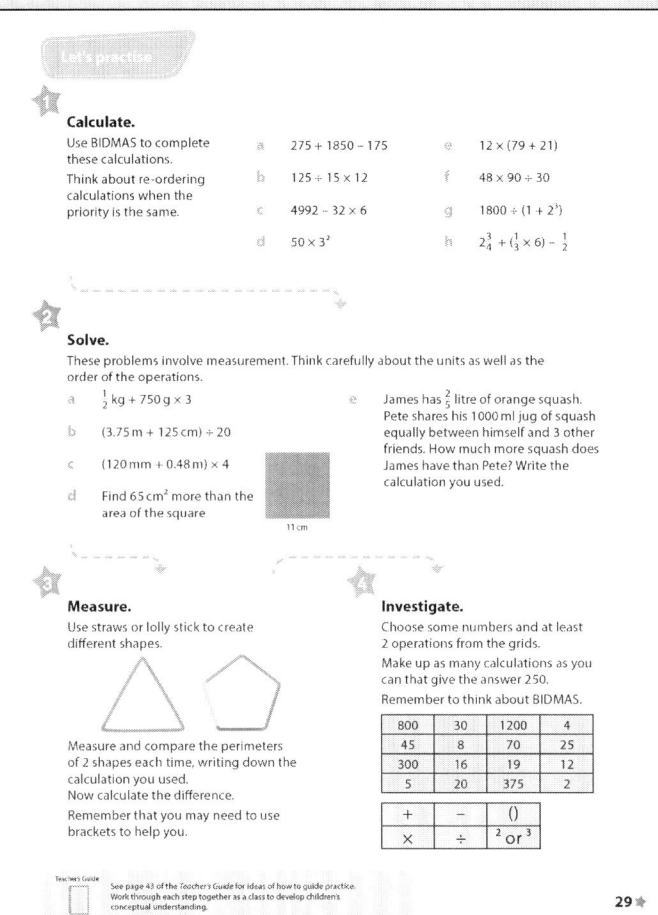

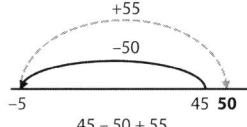
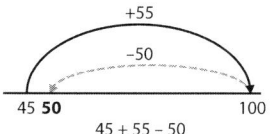

Ensuring progress

Supporting understanding

Number lines are a good way to help children visualise calculations involving addition and subtraction. A calculation, such as $45 - 50 + 55$, can be modelled in two ways, but both result in the same answer.

Broadening understanding

Extend the practical activity by including some shorter straws of equal length, e.g. 15 cm so that perimeters have to be calculated in more than one step. You could also look at combining shapes and subtracting a length that is no longer included in the compound shape.

Rectangle $(15 \times 2) + (20 \times 2)$

Triangle $20 + 15 \times 2$

Compound shape $20 + 15 \times 4$

✓ Concept mastered

Children can use their knowledge of the order of operations to carry out calculations involving the four operations. They can also rearrange calculations involving operations of equal priority to draw on related facts.

Follow-up ideas

- Use 'Countdown-style' activities to increase fluency of mental calculation but also encourage children to consider the order of operations. Challenge them to remember to use brackets to ensure that a lower priority operation is carried out first, if required.

- Further explore different calculators looking at calculations that give rise to different answers.

Answers

Step 1

a	1950	e	1200
b	100	f	144
c	4800	g	200
d	450	h	$4\frac{1}{4}$

Step 2

- a   2750 g or 2.75 kg
- b   25 cm or 0.25 m
- c   240 cm
- d   186 cm²
- e   150 ml, i.e. $400 \text{ ml} - 1000 \div 4$

Step 3

Children's own investigations.

Step 4

Children's own calculations, but could include:

2×5^3

$16 \times 20 - 70$

$25 \times (12 - 2)$

$25 \times (20 \div 2)$

- **Use simple formulae.**
- **Find pairs of numbers that satisfy an equation with two unknowns.**

Homework 13 and 14   Practice Book pp 28–30

Mathematical vocabulary

Algebra, expression, algebraic equation, formula, formulae, unknowns, variables, equivalence, commutative law, distributive, inverse

Representations and resources

Number rods, number shapes, cubes, pie charts.

Warming up

Use the 'zooming in' strategy to reason about decimal numbers and make links to fractions. Give a criterion such as a number between 5 and 6 and then 'zoom in' using the following criteria: a number that rounds to 5 when rounded to the nearest whole number; a number to two decimal places; a number that can be represented as a mixed number; a number where the fraction can also be shown with denominator 4. This will zoom in to the number 5.25. Repeat with other numbers.

Background knowledge

Children have been building up the foundations of algebra since the Foundation Stage. They will have experienced statements with empty boxes in different positions and found possible ways to satisfy a given set of parameters, e.g. finding pairs of numbers that total one whole, finding all possible pairs of multiples of 50 that add to 1000; suggesting possible values for the other two angles in a triangle when the third has a value of 35° and so on.

Draw on these experiences as you extend their learning to include using letters to represent unknown values.

Let's learn: Modelling and teaching

Understanding algebra

- Use number rods to create the representation shown in the Textbook. Children can use the values of the number rods to suggest values of a, b and c or suggest their own values, including fractions and decimals, e.g. $a = 1$, $b = \frac{2}{3}$ or $\frac{6}{9}$ and $c = \frac{1}{3}$ or $\frac{3}{9}$.

- Discuss the algebraic statements given and consider what is the same and what is different about these sets of facts. Link to related facts and confirm statements are true by substituting some of the numbers suggested previously.

- Give other values for rods, e.g. rod $a = 90$ or 45. Encourage children to reason about possible values of b and c. Ask: *What are the possible values of b and c when rod a has the value 90?* Encourage children to model their solutions using a combination of number rods and the bar model.

Using algebra with four operations

- Ask children to give the differences between the second representation in the Textbook and the first, e.g. more than

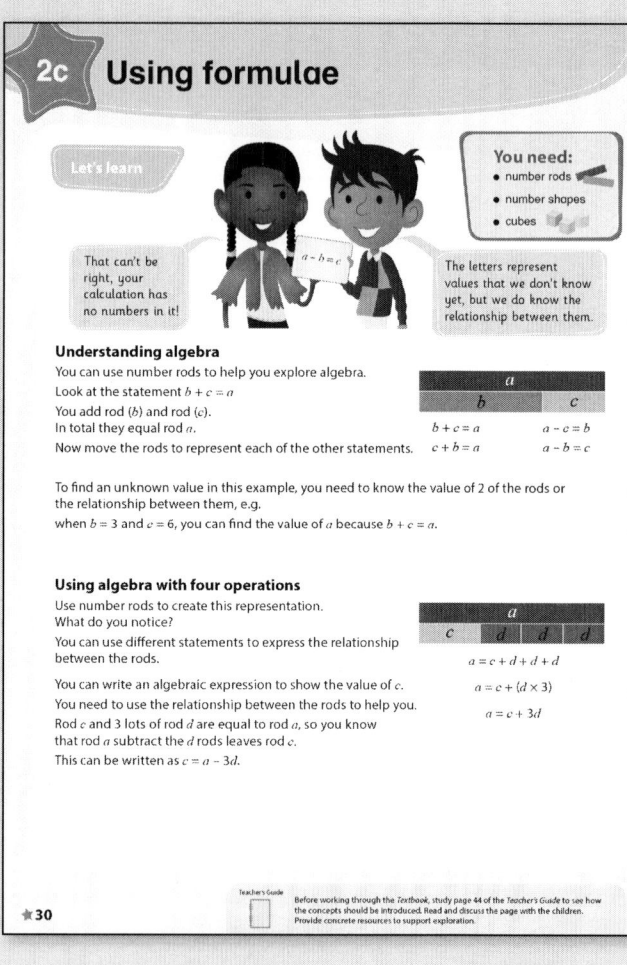

one rod of the same value is shown, c is the same rod as before, there is no value b, there is now a new value d.

- Ask different groups of children to explore each of the algebraic expressions using number rods. You could ask one group to apply additive reasoning to make sense of the first expression, whilst others apply multiplicative reasoning. Ask: *What are the possible values of c and d when rod a still has the value 90?*

- Model how to use number rods to express the equations in terms of rod c. Discuss how the values of the variables change this time when the value of a remains as 90, as in the previous example. Ask children how they might model the equation using the car model.

Let's practise: Digging deeper

Step 1

Children are given four different representations to recreate with number rods. Following the modelling in Let's learn, they should physically move the rods to help them find different ways to express the relationships algebraically. They should be encouraged to apply multiplicative reasoning as well as additive reasoning.

Step 2

Algebraic expressions are represented using number shapes. Two images match representations shown in Step 1. Children interpret the equation using manipulatives, as necessary, to confirm solutions. Encourage them to explain and convince others of their choices.

Step 3

Ask children to reflect on the models shown in the Let's Learn page of the Textbook. They should use number rods and the bar model to help them determine an algebraic expression. Encourage them to also use these to make sense of the problem where $c = 60$ cm. Encourage children to reason about other lengths when c is given a different value, e.g. 0.8 m.

Step 4

Children use the two representations to find the missing values a and c when b has the value 40. They should draw on the relationship between the number rods shown to help find the values. Children then suggest their own values for b.

Ensuring progress

Supporting understanding

Use the colours of the number rods rather than using letters initially. In this way, the first representation in the Textbook could be interpreted using the expressions:

light green + dark green = blue, or blue – dark green = light green, and so on. This can be further developed as $lg + dg = b$ as children move from words to letters to represent values.

Broadening understanding

Encourage children to link algebraic expressions to finding missing values related to measurement. These can be given as word problems or as statements, e.g. Eva pours 1200 ml of squash into five glasses. (Three glasses are the same size and the remaining two glasses are the same size as each other, but different to the first three.) She always puts an equal amount of squash into glasses of the same size. How much squash could there be in each glass?

The algebraic expression $3a + 2b = 1200$ ml would work here so one set of possible values is $a = 300$ ml and $b = 150$ ml.

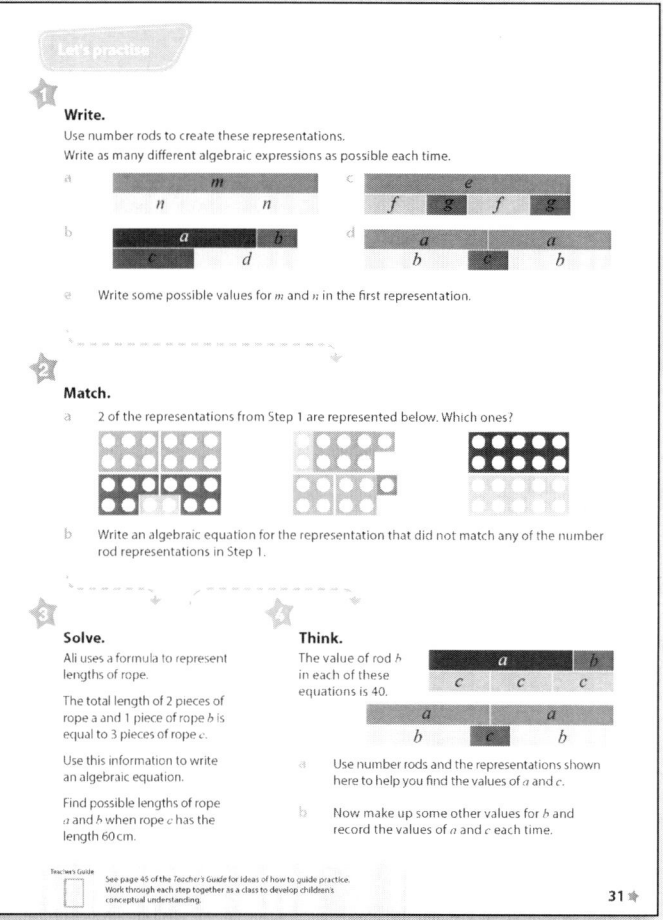

Let's practise

1. **Write.**
   Use number rods to create these representations.
   Write as many different algebraic expressions as possible each time.

   e Write some possible values for m and n in the first representation.

2. **Match.**
   a 2 of the representations from Step 1 are represented below. Which ones?

   b Write an algebraic equation for the representation that did not match any of the number rod representations in Step 1.

3. **Solve.**
   Ali uses a formula to represent lengths of rope.

   The total length of 2 pieces of rope a and 1 piece of rope b is equal to 3 pieces of rope c.

   Use this information to write an algebraic equation.

   Find possible lengths of rope a and b when rope c has the length 60 cm.

   Think.
   The value of rod b in each of these equations is 40.

   a Use number rods and the representations shown here to help you find the values of a and c.

   b Now make up some other values for b and record the values of a and c each time.

   Teacher's Guide
   See page 45 of the *Teacher's Guide* for ideas of how to guide practice. Work through each step together as a class to develop children's conceptual understanding.

   31

Follow-up ideas

- Return to the fruit picture in the unit opener and look at how algebra can be used to solve the problem.

- Use a pie chart as a representation to explore algebra further, e.g. with the value of c given as 72° calculate the size of angle b when $a + d = 2c$ or $a + d = b$.

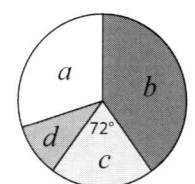

- Continue to develop opportunities to work with pie charts by giving contexts and sample sizes for one or two of the unknowns or for the whole. Children could also create pie charts to fit a given equation, e.g. $4a = b + c$ where $c = 45°$. What are the possible values of a and b?

Concept mastered

Children can use manipulatives to confidently explain relationships between the variables given or represented. They can draw on these experiences to enumerate one or two unknowns when the value of a third variable is given, and they can find pairs of numbers that satisfy an equation with two unknowns.

Answers

Step 1

a $n + n = m$, $2n = m$,
$n = m - n$, $n = m \div 2$,
$n = \frac{m}{2}$

b $a + b = c + d$,
$a = (c + d) - b$, etc.

c $e = f + g + f + g$, $e = 2f + 2g$,
$2g = e - 2f$, $f = (e - 2g) \div 2$,
$g = e - \frac{2f}{2}$

d $a + a = b + b + c$,
$2a = 2b + c$, $c = 2a - 2b$,
$a = (2b + c) \div 2$, etc.

e Children's own answers,
e.g. $m = 100$ and $n = 50$,
$m = 1$ and $n = \frac{1}{2}$, etc.

Step 2

a Image 1 matches Image d
Image 3 matches Image c

b Any letters can be used as long as they match the representation,
e.g. $a + b = 2c + d$

Step 3

a $2a + b = 3c$ or any other equivalent equation.
$2a + b = 180$ cm so a could be 50 cm and b 80 cm i.e. any values that fit the relationships between a and b and total 180 cm.

Step 4

a Image 1, $a = 140$ and $c = 60$
Image 2, $a = 48$ and $c = 16$

b Children's own investigation using the relationship between the rods, e.g. in image 1, b is always $\frac{2}{3}$ of c.

Dicey operations!

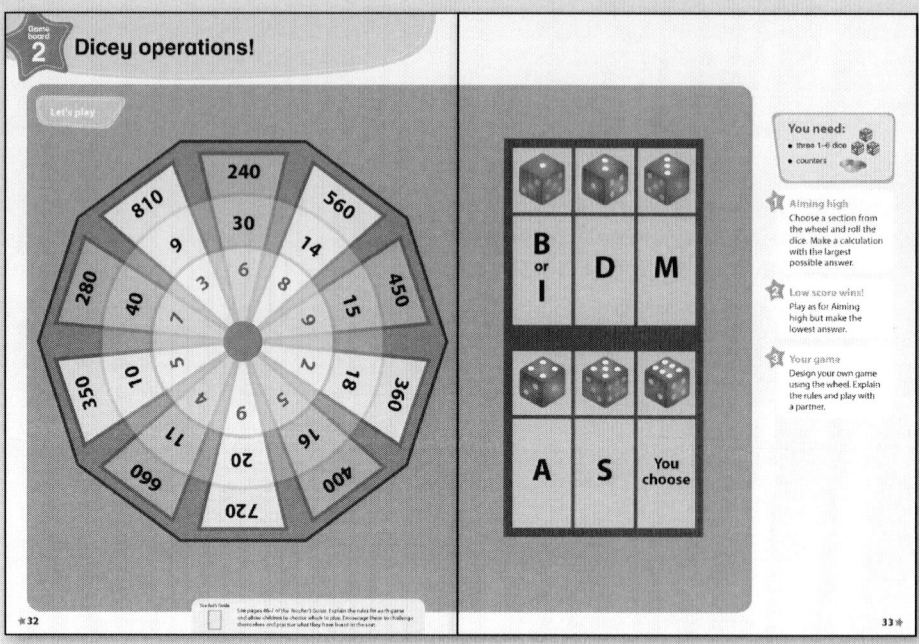

Game 1: Aiming high

The aim of the game is to finish with the highest possible answer, but children have to think carefully about the order in which the operations are used.

Maths focus

- Using the order of operations

Resources

1–6 dice (3), set of small counters for each player (1 colour per player).

How to play

Children take turns to choose a section from the wheel and then roll three dice to make operations.

Using the numbers in the chosen section of the wheel and the rolled operations, children should make the largest possible answer. They must follow the rules of the game so that:

- they use at least two of the operations each time
- only the red numbers can be squared or cubed to draw on known facts
- rolling three ones results in only squaring or cubing the red number; no other calculations can be made in this case.

Each player can use a section from the wheel only once and places a counter on it to show it has been used. The winner is the player with the highest single answer after both players have used all ten sections.

Making it easier

Children could use calculators to make larger calculations easier to work out so that they can still reason about the order of the operations.

Making it harder

Square numbers could also be made from the middle numbers in each section, e.g. 30^2, 14^2, 15^2.

Children could also choose the section of the wheel after they have rolled the dice to add a strategic challenge.

Game 2: Low score wins!

The aim of this game is to finish with the lowest possible answer. Again, the roll of the dice will determine which operations to use, but now children must consider the order of the operations to make the lowest possible answer each time.

Maths focus

- Using the order of operations

Resources

1–6 dice (3), set of small counters for each player (1 colour per player).

How to play

Children play the game in the same way as for Aiming high, but this time they try to achieve the lowest answer possible, e.g. they roll a 1, 3 and a 4 and make
$400 + 5^3 \times 16 = 2400$ or $(16 + 400) \times 5 = 2080$

Making it easier

The game can be played with a partner or in teams so that the order of operations can be discussed.

Making it harder

Children could also choose the section of the wheel after they have rolled the dice to add a strategic challenge, i.e. they do not want to use smaller numbers for addition or subtraction and so be forced to use larger ones for multiplication and so on.

Game 3: Your game

Children should invent their own game, designing rules that use the concepts covered in the unit. Challenge children to make their game easier or harder.

Dicey operations!

Choose a game to play.

Game 1: Aiming high

You need:

- 1–6 dice (3)
- counters (1 colour per player)

How to play

- Take turns to choose a section from the wheel and then roll the 3 dice to determine which operations to use.
- You must use at least 2 operations each time.
- Only the red numbers can be used for squares and cubes.
- If you roll 3 ones, you can only square or cube the red number.
- Each player can use a section from the wheel only once. Place a counter on it to show it has been used.
- The winner is the player with the highest answer after both players have used all 10 sections.

Game 2: Low score wins!

You need:

- 1-6 dice (3)
- counters (1 colour per player)

How to play

- Take turns to choose a section from the wheel and then roll the 3 dice to determine which operations to use.
- You must use at least 2 operations each time.
- Only the red numbers can be used for squares and cubes.
- If you roll 3 ones, you can only square or cube the red number.
- Each player can use a section from the wheel only once. Place a counter on it to show it has been used.
- The winner is the player with the lowest answer after both players have used all ten sections.

Game 3: Your game

- Make up your own game using the gameboard.
- Perhaps you could double your score if you use all 3 dice?
- You could change the rules so the winner is the first to reach 500 000, or start on 500 000 and the winner is the first to reach a 2-digit number by subtracting scores.
- What are the rules for your game? Explain them to someone.

Please help your child by reading the instructions and playing the game together.

Assessment task 1

Resources

Place-value counters or Base 10 apparatus.

Running the task

You may wish to discuss any strategies children have used recently to solve calculations mentally and discuss why mental methods had been used, e.g. think about rounding or looking for numbers that are close together or close to boundaries when subtracting. Look for those who make estimates first before calculating and then adopt appropriate mental strategies for the numbers involved, e.g. finding the difference, rounding and adjusting, and so on, rather than opting for a written method.

Children should discuss any patterns they have noticed so far and how these have helped them with further calculations or to check answers. They should prove, using place-value counters, that the sums of all the addition calculations are the same and why this is the case, recognising that as the first addend increases by two each time, the second decreases by the same amount. They should adopt a similar approach to explain patterns found in the subtraction calculations, also thinking carefully about place value as for the calculations 3502 – 1199 and 3512 – 2199.

You could also ask children to write another set of addition calculations where the sum is the same each time but the pattern used is different, i.e. not increasing and decreasing by two.

Evidencing mastery

Children show mastery through making connections between the sets of calculations and realising that each one does not need to be recalculated, i.e. they use what they already know. Further evidence of mastery is apparent when children confidently prove and explain their thinking using manipulatives and demonstrate how a pattern is developed.

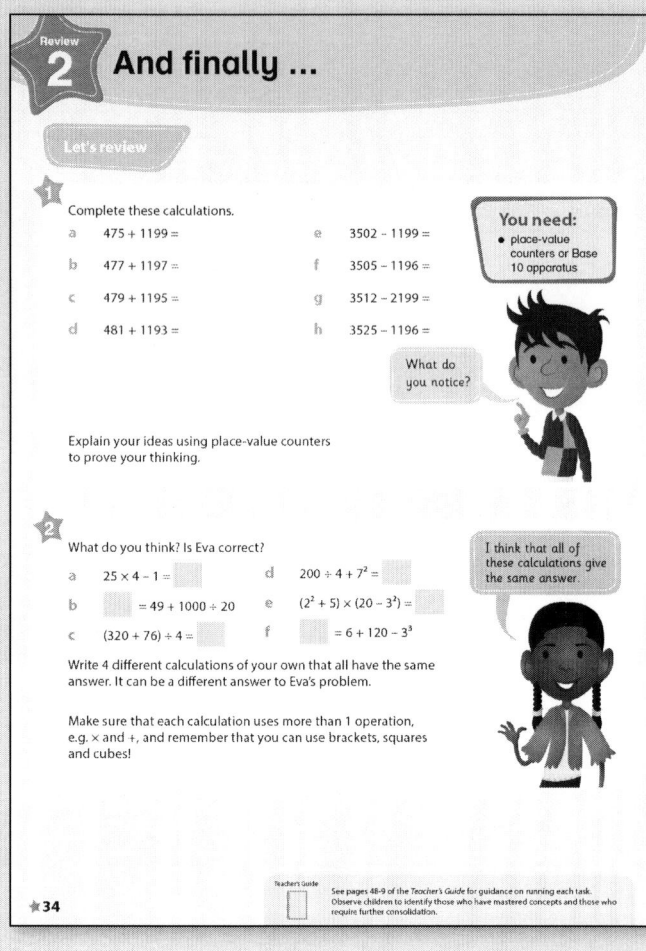

Assessment task 2

Running the task

This task requires children to apply their knowledge of the order of operations to decide whether or not Eva is correct (she is and all the calculations have the same answer (99)). Some children may find it helpful to revisit the mnemonic BIDMAS before they begin, but the majority should be able to confidently draw on this. You could practise applying BIDMAS to some simple calculations and discussing the order each time.

Children can work in pairs or in a group so they can discuss their thinking with others. Perhaps each child or partnership can solve one of the calculations and share their findings with the rest of the group by proving the answer they have obtained.

They are then required to make up a set of four different calculations that all have the same answer but use a range of operations in each one. The use of squares and cubes should be encouraged along with brackets. Children can check each other's calculations and decide if they agree with the order in which the operations have been written.

Discuss a possible word problem that would also use one of the calculations in order to solve it, encouraging children to think about which step of the calculation needs to come first and how this relates to BIDMAS, e.g. $(320 + 76) \div 4 = \boxed{}$ as 'Four friends run a car wash. They take £320 in the morning and £76 in the afternoon. All money is shared equally between them. How much does each friend get?'

Evidencing mastery

Children who fluently draw on the order of operations, and recognise when an error has been made, show evidence of mastery. They should be able to explain why brackets have been used and how the answer to the calculation may differ if the brackets were removed. Children's ability to use brackets should then be applied when making up their own set of calculations and when creating a word problem that would require the steps to be taken in a particular order.

a   Write an algebraic expression to match the representation shown here.

b   Now find the mass of objects a, b and c using the information below:

$$a + c = 420\,g$$
$$c - a = 60\,g$$

Did you know?

Algebra was first developed in ancient Egypt and Babylon where people learned to solve many different equations.

The word *algebra* is Latin but comes from the Arabic word *al-jabr*. It was first used in the title of a book, *Hidab al-jabr wal-muqubala*, written in Iraq, in about 825 AD by the Arab mathematician Mohammad ibn-Musa al-Khwarizmi.

35

Concepts mastered

✓ Children can draw on a range of mental methods and explain their choices relating these to the numbers involved. They make sensible estimates and return to these to check the accuracy of their solutions.

✓ Children can use their knowledge of the order of operations to carry out calculations involving the four operations. They also rearrange calculations involving operations of equal priority to draw on related facts.

✓ Children can use manipulatives to confidently explain relationships between the variables given or represented. They can draw on these experiences to enumerate one or two unknowns when the value of a third variable is given, and they can find pairs of numbers that satisfy an equation with two unknowns.

Assessment task 3

Running the task

Allow children time to discuss what they notice about the image of the weighing scales. Look for those who recognise and can explain that the mass on both sides is equal but is made up of different objects. They should use the information to express the relationship algebraically, i.e. $2a + c = 3b$.

You could ask them to explain what they know about the value of b, i.e. it is a third of the total value of $2a + c$.

The task develops as children must find a pair of masses (a and c) that suit the two given criteria.

They should be encouraged to think about possible values from the information given before calculating. Identifying the mass of objects a and c (180 g and 240 g) will then determine the mass of object b as 200 g.

Evidencing mastery

Children who make links to previous work in this unit using multiple representations show evidence of mastery. They should be able to explain the relationship between the three objects and make a conjecture about the possible value of each before calculating, e.g. object c must be heavier than a, but neither can be a multiple of 100 g as a difference of 60 g is then not possible, or they have to be close to half of 420 g because the difference between them is only 60 g.

Did you know?

Children are given a brief history about the origin of the concept 'algebra' and of the word itself. The development of algebra began in ancient Egypt and Babylon where people learned to solve many different equations, e.g. linear equations and quadratic equations. Children may be interested to find out more about the ancient city of Babylon and its archaeological remains which can still be seen in modern-day Iraq.

You may wish to explore other Latin words that are connected to mathematics, e.g. multiplication from *multiplicare*, division (divide) from *dividere*, subtraction from *subtrahere* and addition from *addere*.

Tell children that the title of the book, *Hidab al-jabr wal-muqubala*, has been translated to mean 'The Book of Completion and Cancellation' or 'The Book of Restoration and Balancing.'

Encourage children to further explore the connection between the words 'cancellation' and 'balancing' as used in the alternative titles of the book, and how this relates to examples of algebra, e.g. $3 + a = a + b$ means that we know immediately that b must equal 3 as the 'a' on each side can be cancelled.

Larger numbers

Mathematical focus

★ **Number: addition, subtraction, multiplication and division, fractions (including decimals and percentages)**

★ **Ratio and proportion**

★ **Measurement: length, mass, capacity, time, money**

★ **Statistics: interpret and calculate, interpret and construct**

Prior learning

Children should already be able to:

- multiply numbers up to four digits by a single- or 2-digit number using a formal written method
- multiply and divide whole numbers, and those involving decimals, by 10, 100 and 1000
- multiply and divide numbers mentally drawing upon known facts
- convert between different units of metric measure and know the relationship between metric units
- recall multiplication and division facts up to 12 × 12
- work with money in £ and p and as decimals of a pound.

Key new learning

- Multiply multi-digit numbers up to four digits by a 2-digit whole number using the formal written method of long multiplication.
- Solve problems involving multiplication.
- Perform mental calculations with large numbers.
- Give reasons for choosing a particular method.
- Multiply single-digit numbers with up to two decimal places by whole numbers.
- Use written division methods in cases where the answer has up to two decimal places.
- Calculate and interpret the mean as an average.
- Solve problems involving the relative sizes of two quantities, where missing values can be found by using integer multiplication and division facts.
- Solve problems involving unequal sharing and grouping using knowledge of fractions and decimals.

Making connections

- Children can apply understanding to real-life contexts, including solving problems involving capacity, time and conversion of metric units of length and mass.
- Children can solve problems involving proportional relationships in science and geography.

Unit 3 Larger numbers

How can I work out the cost of 8 of these if they cost £2.36 each?

DAFFODILS £2.36 per bunch

I wonder how many slabs will be needed?

★36

Talk about

The vocabulary of multiplication and division should be familiar to children from previous years. It may be necessary to explain it for some and a labelled diagram works well here. It makes it easier to refer precisely to the structure of a calculation, e.g. multiplicand × multiplier = product, dividend ÷ divisor = quotient.

Engaging and exploring

Explain that there are many instances where multiplication and division are required in real life and the context gives a check on whether an answer is sensible. Look at the photo of the daffodils. Ask children where they might have seen a number of identical plants? In a restaurant? Beside the road or in parks in a town? Ask if they have been to a garden centre to buy plants. Can they recall any prices? You could ask children to carry out research on the website of some stores to see what prices are charged for the plants. Read the question in the Textbook together and ask children to discuss with their partner how they would approach calculating the answer. Ask for feedback and model children's strategies on the board. Ask: *Which strategy do you think is the most efficient?*

Look at the photo of the patio. Suggest that the paving slabs measure 300 m by 200 mm and 25 cm by 25 cm. The area of ground measures 8.4 m by 5 m. Ask children to give an estimate of how big the paving slabs are by drawing them in the air. How good are they at estimating 30 cm? Ask children to check their estimate using a ruler. Ask: *How big might the piece of ground for the patio be?* Can they compare it to something in the classroom or playground? *Can you estimate how many slabs of each size would be used?* They could discuss how they would solve the problem for each size of paving slab. Would it make sense to use both types of slab? Dealing with a mixture of measures is where many children lose track of their calculation and cannot see that their answer is not sensible. Therefore it may be helpful to ask children to model the area of ground and paving slabs using tiles or paper.

Ask children to imagine that their parents are taking them on a driving holiday in the UK. Ask them to suggest what costs there may be. Draw out the idea that the petrol will be one cost. Ask if they have stopped at a petrol station recently. Can they remember how much it cost to fill up the car? Can they remember how much petrol costs per litre? Ask questions such as: *While on holiday, you find a petrol station which charges 128 pence per litre. How much will 24 litres cost? If the car does an average of 13 miles per litre, how far will the car travel for that amount of petrol?* Children should to discuss approaches to the calculations. At the end of the unit, refer back to their suggestions to see if they have changed their minds.

Look at the photo of the cupcakes and discuss home baking or children's experience of baking in school. 150 g flour, 100 g butter, 75 g sugar, 1 egg is a recipe that makes 10 cupcakes; the available ingredients are 500 g bag of flour, 500 g bag of sugar, 500 g pack of butter and a box of 6 eggs. You could ask if there are any ingredients missing in the list (some milk might be helpful). You could talk about the problem of running out of ingredients, and consider the real life implications. *Do you make fewer cakes? Do you go out to the shop to get more?* You could relate this context to lessons which involve cooking and so bring some mathematics into other subjects. Children could discuss the problem in pairs or groups. Encourage them to break it down into smaller steps and to use coloured counters to model the problem. When they decide, no, there is not enough to make 50 cupcakes. Ask: *How many can you make?* Some children may notice that dividing up an egg is tricky and ways around that can be discussed. Interpreting answers in context brings out any lack of understanding of the purpose of the calculation and the size of numbers and measures.

The last question is more open. Work with children to agree the assumptions before challenging them to attempt a calculation. You could ask them to discuss in pairs or groups: *How large are the cups? How much cordial is needed for each drink? How many people are you catering for?* This is another opportunity to discuss the size of measures, in this case for capacity. Reinforce understanding by asking children to model the problem using bottles, plastic cups and coloured water.

How much will the petrol cost?

I wonder if I have enough to make 50 cupcakes?

I wonder if there would be enough cordial to make drinks for everybody if we need 1 part of cordial to 4 parts of water?

1 litre

Teacher's Guide Look at the pictures with the children and discuss the questions. See pages 50–1 of the *Teacher's Guide* for key ideas to draw out.

37

Things to think about

- How aware are children that these are calculations someone may wish to do?

- How far do you want to go into calculation strategies at this stage?

- Will you come back to these scenarios as you work through the sections of the unit?

- Do you want to use paired work to discuss other situations where similar mathematics might be used?

- Do you want them to seek out examples for homework?

- Do you want to create a display on the working wall of real-life calculations?

Checking understanding

You will know children have mastered these concepts when they can solve problems involving multiplication and division in different contexts, appropriately choosing and using number facts, understanding of place value and mental and written methods. They can explain their decision making and justify their solutions.

Using long multiplication

- Multiply multi-digit numbers up to four digits by a 2-digit whole number using the formal method of long multiplication.
- Solve problems involving multiplication.

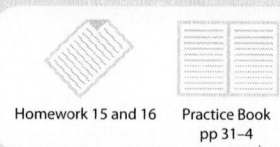

Homework 15 and 16   Practice Book pp 31–4

Mathematical vocabulary

Multiplier, multiplicand, product, digit, tens, ones, solve, commutative

Representations and resources

Arrays, place-value counters, calculators, whiteboards, markers.

Warming up

Practise times table facts. Use the context of length for this, e.g. *I have 8 sticks of length 7 cm. They are placed end to end. How long is the line of sticks?* This can be done using time, e.g. *How many seconds in 8 minutes? How many minutes in 7 hours?*

Background knowledge

The National Curriculum for England expects children to use the formal method of long multiplication. It is the end point of a journey of increasing efficiency in calculation. It arises from the array representation via the grid method. It requires less recording, hence the greater efficiency of the method. The journey through the representations in the unit should enable children to reconstruct the method, rather than merely recall it. It is better to start with the ones digit of the multiplier, then move to the tens – it makes the 'zero' seem more natural as you gradually move to the left and gives a lower threshold to the algorithm. Mathematically, the order of multiplication makes no difference because the operation of multiplication is commutative.

Using the vocabulary of multiplicand × multiplier = product precisely will enable children to explain their understanding more clearly because they can name the different parts of the multiplication. It also supports more precise thinking about mathematics. Using precise language about multiplication prevents misconceptions when learning about division.

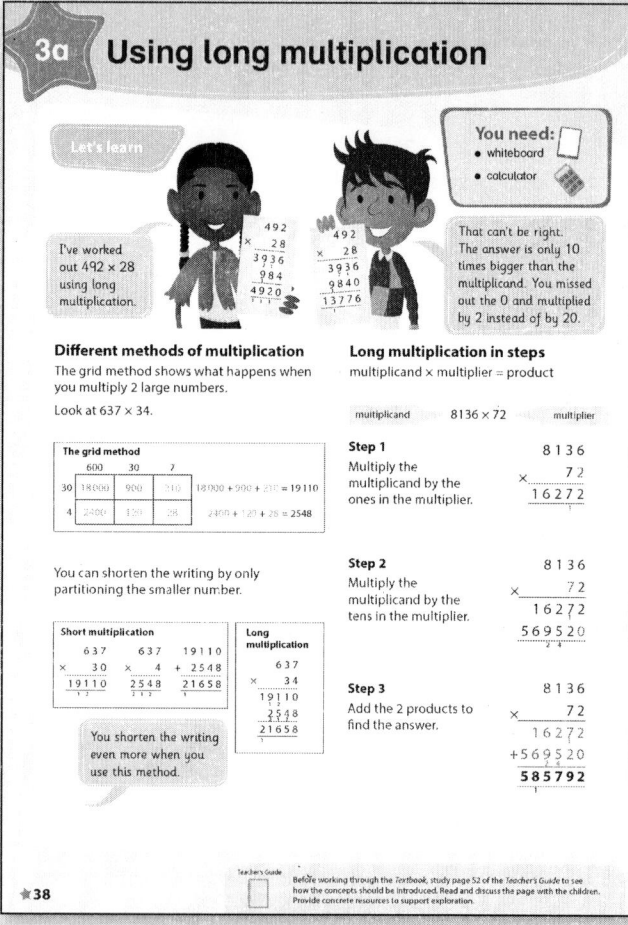

★38

Let's learn: Modelling and teaching

Different methods of multiplication

- The three methods to do the same calculation show increasing efficiency.
- Ask children what is the same in each version. These include: the same number facts are being used such as 7 × 3 = 21 and 6 × 4 = 24; the same products are being calculated such as 19 110; the same addition is done in the final step to get 21 658. Allow children time to notice this, discussing it between themselves.

Long multiplication in steps

- Separating the steps ensures that the working is not overwhelming. As you explain each step to children, ask them to follow the method on the Textbook page.
- The first step is to multiply the multiplicand by the ones digit of the multiplier. The calculation required is 8136 × 2.

Start with the ones digit of the multiplicand, 6 × 2 = 12. Next multiply the tens digit (3) by two to give six tens. Add one ten carried over from the ones column to give seven tens. Next multiply the hundreds digit (1) by two to give two hundreds. This is recorded on the answer line as 2 in the hundreds column. Finally, multiply eight by two to give 16. This is actually multiplying eight thousand by two to make 16 000. This is recorded by placing the 6, representing six thousand, in the thousands column and the 1 in the ten thousands column.

- The second step is to multiply the multiplicand by 70. Recording a zero in the ones column allows you to proceed as above, multiplying by seven.
- The third step is to add the two products to get the final answer.

Let's practise: Digging deeper

Step 1

Children can choose to go straight to the formal method or do the grid or short multiplication method as a stepping stone. They should check their answer using a calculator.

Step 2

These questions encourage children to think about where the different numbers in the long multiplication method come from. Prompt children by asking *Where does that number come from? What do you know about that number?* Encourage children to refer back to the Let's learn page in order to find a sensible strategy.

Step 3

Encourage children to draw a bar diagram to confirm that multiplication is required to solve the problems. Ask: *What do you think is the most efficient way to do this problem?* Compare the methods that the class used and agree which are the most efficient.

Step 4

Ask children which method they might use to solve part a. Look for them to say long multiplication. Ask: *Where does the ones digit of the answer come from? Does this always happen? Why? Is it a useful way to check your answer?* In part b, ask children what is the same and what is different with a 3-digit multiplier. Do the patterns seen in part a happen in this case?

Ensuring progress

Supporting understanding

Children can use whiteboards to draft their workings before recording them in hard copy, allowing them to correct any errors without leaving a trace.

Children who still need support can use place-value counters. Model the process of using the place-value counters to represent the size of the digits using an example such as 46×32.

This emphasises the place value of the digits, and how to multiply powers of ten. You could try asking *Why does $10 \times 10 = 100$?* Ask : *For $6 \times 3 = 18$, where can you see 18 in the grid?*

Broadening understanding

Some children can extend the method to use larger numbers still. Challenge them to write out a long multiplication calculation and remove as many digits as possible, whilst still being able to work back and fill them in from the information that is still there.

✓ **Concept mastered**

Children can calculate using the formal method of long multiplication, explaining why it works and why they chose to use this method.

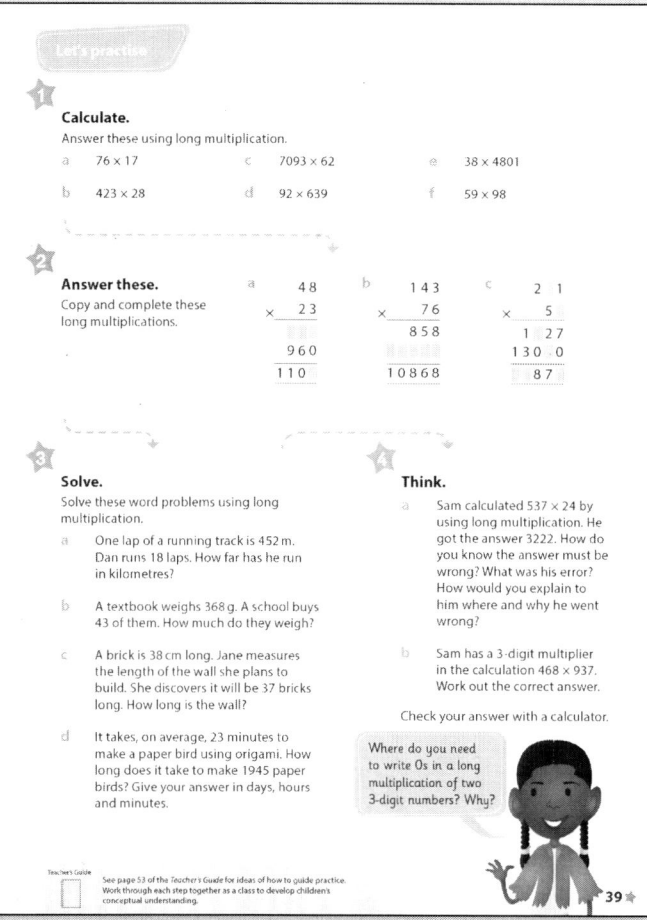

Follow-up ideas

- Ask children to write out a long multiplication calculation and give the workings only to a friend. They should challenge their partner to work out the numbers that were multiplied.

- Have a class debate, e.g. 'This house believes that long multiplication is outdated and should not be taught in schools'.

Answers

Step 1

a	1292	d	58788
b	11844	e	182438
c	439766	f	5782

Step 2

a
```
      4 8
    × 2 3
    1 4 4
    9 6 0
    1 1 0 4
```

b
```
      1 4 3
    ×   7 6
      8 5 8
  1 0 0 1 0
  1 0 8 6 8
```

c
```
      2 6 1
    ×   5 7
    1 8 2 7
  1 3 0 5 0
  1 4 8 7 7
```

Step 3

a	8.136 km
b	15824 g or 15.824 kg
c	1406 cm or 14.06 m
d	44735 minutes = 31 days, 1 hour, 35 minutes.

Step 4

a Either because $4 \times 7 = 28$ so it should end in an 8. Or because $500 \times 20 = 10000$ and so the answer is too small. He forgot to fill in the zero.

b 438516

- Perform mental calculations with large numbers.
- Give reasons for choosing a particular method.

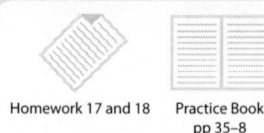

Homework 17 and 18   Practice Book pp 35–8

Mathematical vocabulary

Operator, divisor, dividend, factorising, commutative, associative, multiplier, multiplicand, product, digit, tens, ones, solve, commutative

Representations and resources

Whiteboards, markers, calculators, interlocking cubes, place-value counters.

Warming up

Practise multiplying and dividing by 10, 100 and 1000 with whole numbers, e.g. *Work out 37 × 100. What do you multiply 7 by to get 7000? How many times larger is 2300 than 23?*

Practising multiplying 10, 100 and 1000 by each other, e.g. *Work out 100 × 1000. What do you multiply 10 by to get 1000?*

Background knowledge

It is useful to be able to do arithmetic mentally but multiplying and dividing large numbers mentally is not easy. The use of jottings to support informal methods is completely acceptable and is to be encouraged. Those who can move onto purely mental methods will do so because they can do it more quickly. The mathematical ideas involved are factorising numbers so that 600 may be rewritten as 6 × 100; the commutative law so that 100 × 8 may be rewritten as 8 × 100; the associative law so that 6 × 8 × 100 × 10 may be rewritten as (6 × 8) × (100 × 10). These ideas apply when dividing mentally but, because division is not commutative, more consideration needs to be given to what is equivalent. Calculating 4500 ÷ 30 uses factorising to rewrite it as 45 × 100 ÷ (3 × 10). This can be rewritten as 45 × 100 ÷ 3 ÷ 10. Division and multiplication may be done in any order so rewrite as 45 ÷ 3 × 100 ÷ 10. You can then calculate to get 15 × 10. The answer is 150. These ideas are important for algebraic work later.

Let's learn: Modelling and teaching

Strategies for mental calculations

- Model 400 × 30 using place value counters set out in an array. Ask questions, e.g. *What part shows 4 × 3?*

- Ask children to use the array to suggest mental calculation strategies for solving 400 × 30. Ask: *Which strategies do you find hard? Which are the most efficient? Why?*

- Rewrite the calculation as 4 × 100 and 3 × 10. Ask children what this is called (factorising). Ask: *Why do we write 400 in that way and not 16 × 25?* Continue to model the calculation as shown in the Textbook.

- Ask children to make 5600 using place-value counters and to suggest how they might divide 5600 by 80. Draw out the idea that you could divide by 8 and then by 10. Ask how the counters could be divided into 8 equal groups.

- Elicit the idea that the thousands can be changed to hundreds, giving 56 hundreds and 7 hundreds in each group. Ask: *What do we need to do next?* The 7 hundreds need to be divided into ten equal groups, giving 7 tens or 70 in each group. Ask children to explain what is the same and what is different about this method compared to the method in the Textbook

Deciding on a method

- The numbers in the calculation suggest the method. There is no right answer to 'which method should I use?'.

- Give children calculations such as 615 × 26. Ask them to devise and then share their strategies. Discuss which strategies are the most efficient.

Let's practise: Digging deeper

Step 1

These could all be done mentally. Children may prefer to view the divisions as the inverse of multiplication, e.g. 'What do I multiply 50 by to get 200?' Encourage children who immediately use a written method, to attempt a mental calculation strategy. Use questions such as: *How would you factorise these numbers? How could you rearrange the calculation? What facts do you know about these numbers?'*

Step 2

There is no right method for any question. The questions offer a variety of numbers that suggest different strategies. Part a is most likely separated to $6 \times 9 = 54$ then $\times 1000$. Part b could be done by jottings, using the 17 times table and noticing that 34 and 85 are both there. Part c is most likely $2 \times 251 = 502$ and then multiplying by 10. For Part d could be 'What do I multiply by 25 to get 2000 then 1 more for 2025?'

For part e children use jottings, multiplying by 25 and subtracting 7820, rather than by a formal written method. Part f could be done by halving then dividing by 10. Ask children to verbally justify which strategy they chose and why. Their justifications should refer to using known facts and efficient methods.

Step 3

Children could draw bar models to help them decide what calculation is required and then write down the calculation. Ask: *What is the most efficient way to work this out? Is there a mental method that would solve it quickly?*

Step 4

Encourage children to draw a square of 1 cm in area and one of 1 mm inside it. These will be very small but it is important that children develop an understanding of the measures at the outset. Look for children to scale up the squares and then count. For square metres, prompt children by asking: *Could you draw this one? Could you use what you have done so far to help you?*

Small interlocking cubes can be used to model part b. Draw on the questions asked during part a to support children as required.

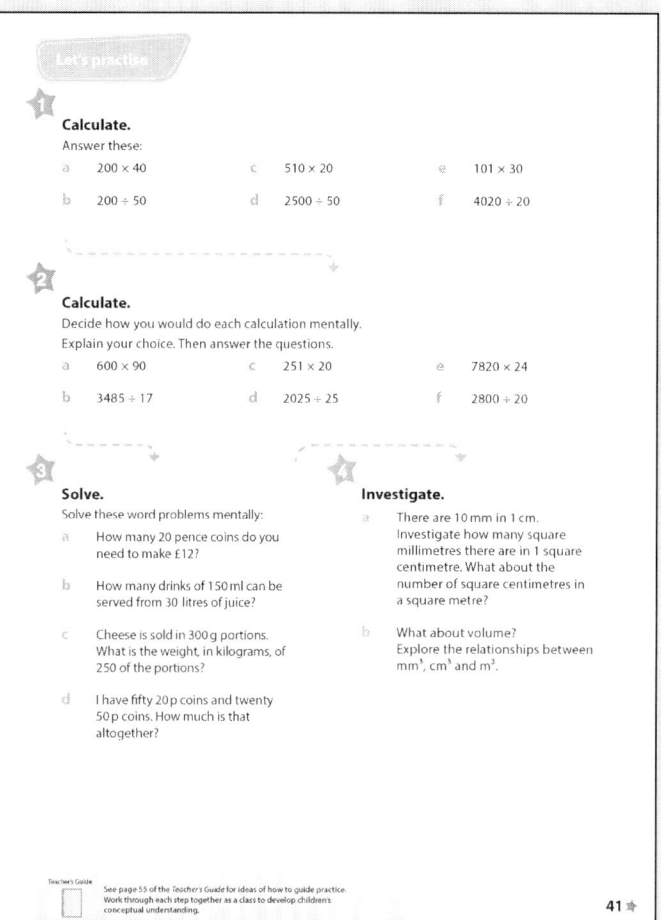

Ensuring progress

Supporting understanding

Encourage children to work collaboratively, modelling the calculations using place-value counters before deciding on an appropriate calculation strategy.

Broadening understanding

Children can explore using mental methods for even larger numbers. They can generate the numbers randomly and try to find a mental method to calculate the answer. This will encourage them to look very carefully at the properties of the numbers they are working with.

> ✓ **Concept mastered**
>
> Children can solve problems involving multiplication and division in different contexts, appropriately choosing and using number facts, understanding of place value and mental and written methods. They can explain their decision making and justify their solutions.

Follow-up ideas

- Set children problems with or without the ability to make jottings, e.g. Use the numbers 2, 3, 6, 7, 25 and 50 up to once each, and addition, subtraction, multiplication or division to make 473.

- Play a game by giving a starting number to the class. Then give a series of calculations for children to do mentally, without any check on progress. After a suitable time, stop and ask the class what number they have got to. The numbers can be large or small and any operations may be used.

Answers

Step 1

a	80 000	d	50	
b	4	e	3030	
c	10 200	f	201	

e   187 680 – written

f   140 – mental or jottings

Step 2

a   54 000 – could be mental or jottings

b   205 – most likely written but could be done mentally too

c   5020 – jottings likely

d   81 – written or jottings likely but could be done mentally

Step 3

a	60	c	75 kg
b	200	d	£20

Step 4

a $100 \text{ mm}^2 = 1 \text{ cm}^2$, $10 000 \text{ cm}^2 = 1 \text{ m}^2$

b $1000 \text{ mm}^3 = 1 \text{ cm}^3$, $1 000 000 \text{ cm}^3 = 1 \text{ m}^3$, $1 000 000 000 \text{ mm}^3 = 1 \text{ m}^3$

Star **3c**

Multiply and divide up to 2 decimal places

- **Multiply single-digit numbers with up to two decimal places by whole numbers.**
- **Use written division methods in cases where the answer has up to two decimal places.**
- **Calculate and interpret the mean as an average.**

 Homework 19 and 20

 Practice Book pp 39–41

 Multiplying by decimals

Representations and resources

Dice, Gattegno chart, Base 10 apparatus, place-value counters, calculators, whiteboards, tape measures

Mathematical vocabulary

Average, mean, product, quotient, multiplicand, multiplier, dividend, divisor

Warming up

Practise times table facts in a variety of forms including division, e.g. *Which numbers divide 30? What do you multiply 8 by to get 56?*

Practise multiplying and dividing whole numbers and decimals up to two decimal places by 10, 100 and 1000, e.g. $100 \times 3.4 = ?$, $560 \div ? = 0.56$

Background knowledge

Multiplying and dividing decimals is best done by reasoning from known facts, usually involving whole numbers. It builds on, and embeds, understanding of place value and multiplication and division by powers of ten.

This reinforces the idea of mathematics as an interconnected subject that makes sense. A product with a whole number as the multiplier and a decimal number as the multiplicand can be rewritten in the same way:

$$1.2 \times 6 = 12 \div 10 \times 6$$
$$= 12 \times 6 \div 10$$
$$= 7.2$$

Let's learn: Modelling and teaching

Multiplying with decimals

- Model 7×3 using place-value counters set out in an array. Next, set out 7×0.3 as in the Textbook. Ask: *What is different about this array?* Explain that each item in the array is worth 0.1. Ask children to work out 21×0.1.

- Now ask them to represent 0.7×3 using counters and work it out. Continue with further variations of 7×3, e.g. 0.07×3. Record their solutions on the board.

Dividing with decimals

- Show children the calculation $0.24 \div 6$ in the Textbook. Discuss why the 0.01 counters are arranged like this and why they shared into 6 groups. Identify how much is in each group.

- Ask children to consider variations such as $2.4 \div 4$. They should model them using the place-value counters and justify their answers. Provide prompts such as: *How do you know that is the correct answer? Explain it in another way.*

Calculating the mean

- Discuss the bars representing the mean. Encourage

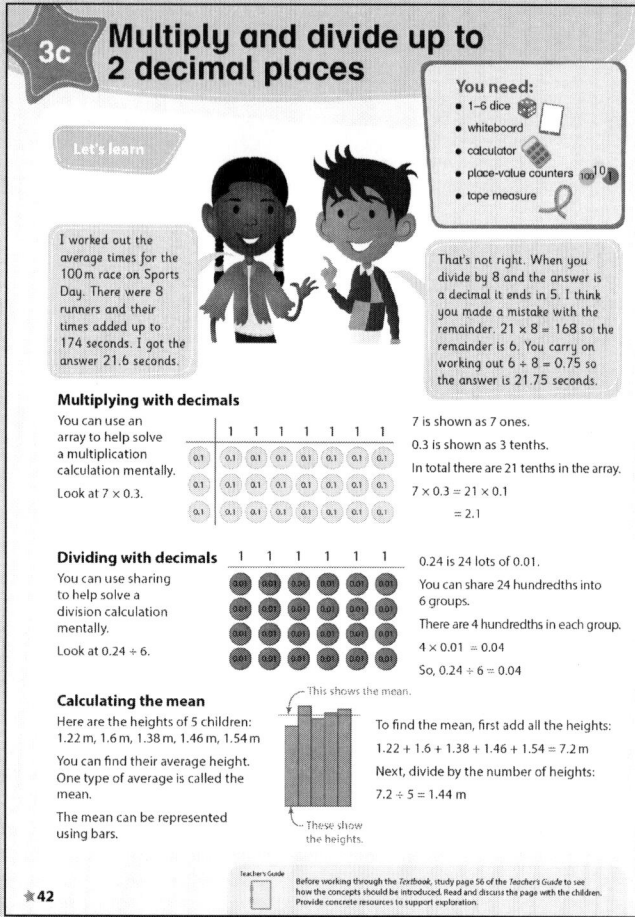

children to identify what the red line represents in relation to the bars and to explain what they notice about the sections above and below the lines.

- Explain that an average is a typical value that represents the whole set of data. The mean is one way of working out an average.

- Using the example in the Textbook, demonstrate that the mean is the total of the bars (or data items) divided by the number of bars (or data items). Show children how this looks as a written calculation.

- Measure the height of five children. Ask children to find the mean height, using bars and written recordings.

- Reflect on the misconception cartoon. Can children explain what Eva did wrong?

Let's practise: Digging deeper

Step 1

Children can represent the multiplications using place-value counters arranged in an array. For the divisions, they can represent the dividend using place-value counters. Ask them what they will do with the remainders.

Step 2

The questions exploit the inverse relationship between multiplication and division. They also emphasise the equivalence interpretation of the equals sign. Ask children to recall the multiplication fact that is related to the numbers in the question. Encourage them to use place-value counters to model the calculation. Part c has more than one possible solution and you may wish to challenge some learners to search for some of these and then express them using a generalisation.

Step 3

Children work in pairs to agree the wording for their survey and an appropriate format to record results. You could carry out the measuring as a class by asking children to measure their partner. Ask children to record the data and find the mean. Compare answers as a class. Ask children to suggest subjects for their second survey. Discuss why subjects such as favourite colour would not be appropriate. Drawing out the idea that data must be numerical and adding frequencies does not give the mean.

Step 4

Children write the numbers on blank pieces of paper and manipulate them in order to select the arrangement that will produce the largest product and quotient. Encourage them to work methodically, thinking about the one or tens spaces first.

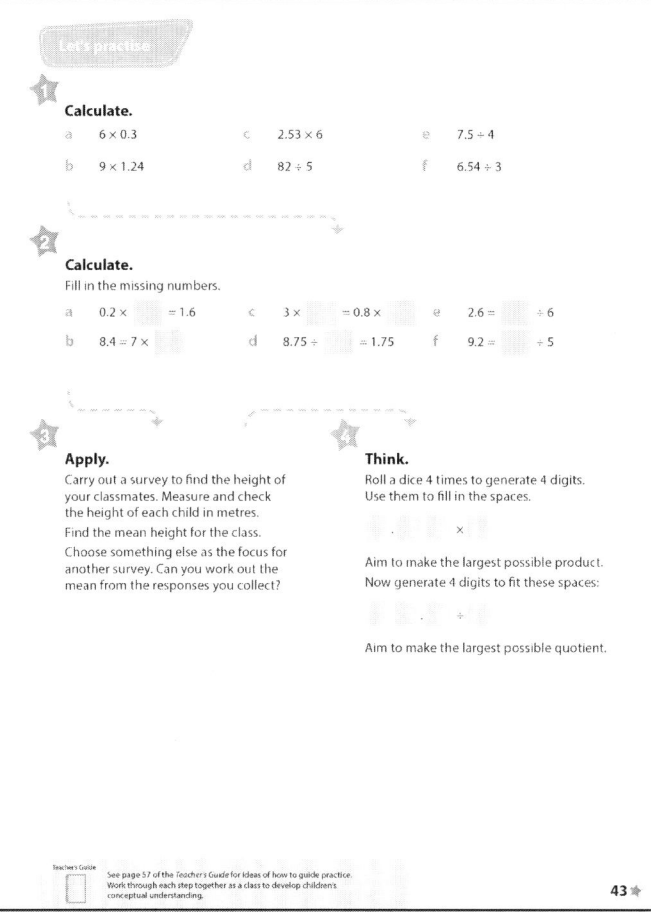

Follow-up ideas

- One child divides two whole numbers under 50 on a calculator and challenges someone else to work out what the two numbers are.

- Discuss where people may use averages. Think about jobs or headlines in newspapers to get ideas. Choose those where the average works out to be a decimal number and write about them in your exercise book.

Ensuring progress

Supporting understanding

Spend more time on deducing number facts from known multiplication and division facts. Make sure that children are confident with doing this with whole numbers and multiples of ten and a hundred. Use Gattegno charts and Base 10 apparatus to show the relative size of the numbers. Ask: *How many times larger is 600 than 6? How many times smaller is 0.6 than 6?* Use place-value counters to model the numbers in the multiplicand and dividend before calculating with them. Start by multiplying by small single digits to develop the concept.

Broadening understanding

Encourage children to explore multiplying and dividing with numbers that have more than two decimal places. This will begin to prepare them for multiplying and dividing decimals by each other at Key Stage 3.

✓ ## Concept mastered

Children can multiply and divide decimals up to two decimal places by whole numbers to solve problems. They can explain why the method they are using works. They can calculate the mean of a set of numbers.

Answers

Step 1

a	1.8	d	16.4
b	11.16	e	1.875
c	15.18	f	2.18

Step 2

a   8

b   1.2

c   1.6 and 6 but there are other possibilities

d   5

e   15.6

f   46

Step 3

Answers will depend on the class.

Step 4

Largest possible product is $6.66 \times 6 = 39.96$

Largest quotient is $\frac{66.6}{1} - 66.6$

- **Solve problems involving the relative sizes of two quantities, where missing values can be found by using integer multiplication and division facts.**
- **Solve problems involving unequal sharing and grouping using knowledge of fractions and multiples.**

Homework 21 and 22   Practice Book pp 42–4

Representations and resources

Number rods, multiplication square.

Mathematical vocabulary

Scale factor, scaling, maps, unit fractions

Warming up

Practise working out mentally using known facts, e.g. What is 400 × 8? (Work this out from 40 × 8) What is 60 × 3? (Work this out from 6 × 3). Move on to simple decimals that link to multiplication table facts, e.g. What is 9 × 0.4? (Work this out from 9 × 4) What is 1.2 × 3? (Work this out 12 × 3).

Background knowledge

There are two models for multiplication. The first one that children meet is repeated addition. The other involves the relative size of the two quantities, e.g. 'is five times as long as' involves mapping a number to that which is five times the size, e.g. 8 maps to 40. It is this model that we consider in this unit. The relation is referred to as scaling. It relates to the scale on a map or drawing, and to the scale factor of an enlargement. It is like magnification. Number rods demonstrate the idea extremely well.

Division as sharing or grouping is first explored with equal parts. Here, we consider unequal parts but only as, e.g. of $\frac{3}{4}$ and $\frac{1}{4}$. The next step after this, at Key Stage 3, is sharing in a given ratio. Finding $\frac{3}{4}$ of 28 builds on knowledge of unit fractions and multiplying fractions by whole numbers from previous years.

Let's learn: Modelling and teaching

Multiplication as a relation

- Ask children to hold up two rods where one is two times as long as the other. Repeat with other examples. Ask for examples of pairs of rods (or trains of rods) where one is three times as long as the other. Each time, ask children to give the scale factor and explain what the scale factor does to the size of the smaller rod to get the size of the larger rod.

- Compare children's rods to the representation in the Textbook. Explore how the number rods could be drawn as a bar model. It is important to say 'three times as long as' not 'three times longer'.

- Ask children to record their work by drawing bar models. Discuss how they know that the pair demonstrates the relation. Challenge them to find pairs for 'is half as

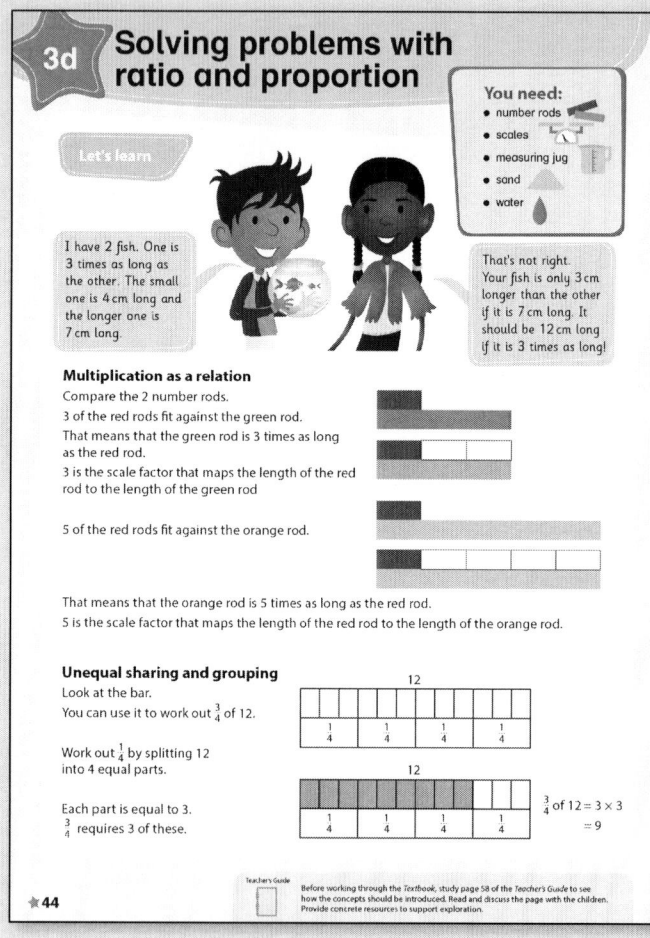

long as', and 'is four times as long as'. Discuss the inverse relation between 'is twice as long as' and 'is half as long as'.

Unequal sharing and grouping

- Ask children how they would work out $\frac{3}{4}$ of 12. They may suggest the bar model. If not, ask: *How does the diagram in the Textbook help show you to work out $\frac{3}{4}$ of 12?*

- Draw out the idea that 12 is divided into 4 equal parts. Ask children to explain why each part is equal to 3 and how many threes make 12. Explore the role of the numerator by asking: *Why do we need 3 of the quarters? How do we know it has to be 3 of them?* Invite them to work out $\frac{3}{4}$ of 20 using a bar model to support them. Then $\frac{2}{5}$ of 20.

Let's practise: Digging deeper

Step 1

Number facts can be used to answer these questions, however some children may benefit from modelling them using number rods. Remind children of the definition of a scale factor. Emphasise the idea by asking questions such as, *What is the scale factor to get from 4 to 100?*

Step 2

Encourage children to use multiplication facts by asking: *What numbers do you know here? Which is the larger number? What is the scale factor?* They should support their understanding of the relationship between the numbers by drawing a bar diagram for each question. Part f has two possible answers.

Step 3

Recipes are a context that is meaningful for children. Start by asking children what the recipe would be if all the amounts were doubled. Using this conceptual understanding they can answer parts a–c. The three answers are the same, which should prompt children to check their working carefully and hence deepen their understanding. Ask different groups to measure out the amounts for each version of the recipe.

Step 4

This question may be solved algebraically by using a letter or symbol to represent the total or the mean of the numbers, writing and then solving the equation. Trial and improvement is another strategy. Knowledge of factors will help this process as the numbers are all whole numbers. Support children by asking: *If you know that the mean is one fifth of the total, what do you know about the number of items of data? What do the fractions add up to? What does that tell you about 4?* Ask children to justify their answer.

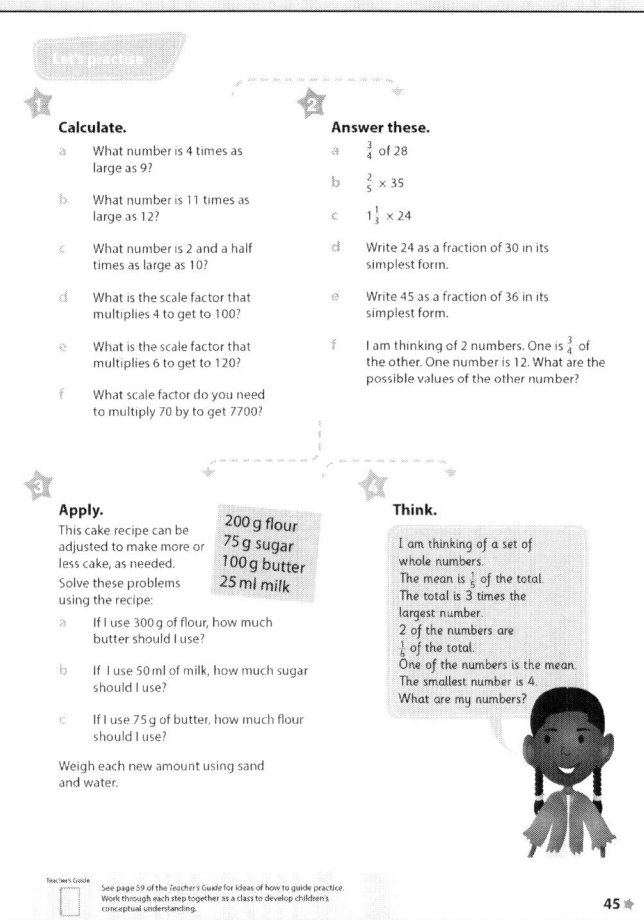

Ensuring progress

Supporting understanding

The number rods can continue to be used to identify the scale factor between pairs of numbers. Using the white as '1' enables them to represent numbers. Moving the smaller rods to match the larger rod models the process done mentally to calculate scale factors. Having worked out an answer using the rods, children record what they have done by translating the rods, to a bar model. A multiplication square can be made available to support less secure knowledge of number facts.

Broadening understanding

Challenge children to make up some problems of their own like Step 4.

✓ ## Concept mastered

Children can solve problems involving scaling and problems involving unequal sharing.

Follow-up ideas

- Children can do some practical measuring and calculate scale factors, e.g. *how many pencils will fit along the length of a desk? How many paces is the width of the playground?*

- Children can gather some data, such as what pets they prefer, or who has blue eyes, brown eyes, green eyes or black eyes and present it in a pie chart.

Answers

Step 1

a	36	d	25
b	132	e	20
c	25	f	110

Step 2

a	21	d	$\frac{4}{5}$
b	14	e	$1\frac{1}{4}$
c	32	f	9, 16

Step 3

a	150 g	c	150 g
b	150 g		

Step 4

a   4, 5, 5, 6, 10

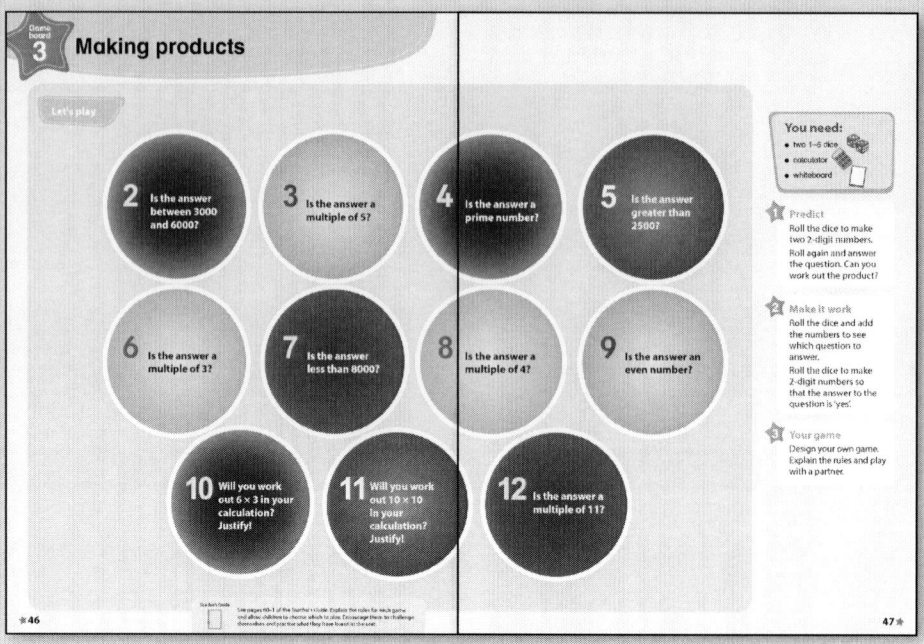

Game 1: Predict

Maths focus

- Multiplying and dividing numbers with more than one digit
- Estimating to check answers
- Reasoning

Resources

1–6 dice (2), calculator, whiteboards, markers.

How to play

Children roll the dice twice each to get four numbers to make two 2-digit numbers. Children then roll the dice again to get two numbers which they add together. Children find the question on the gameboard that matches this tota. They calculate the produce of their 2-digit numbers and answer the question, recording answers on the this whiteboard. Another player uses the calculator to check both answers. Players score a point for each correct answer.

Some tips:

3   At least one of the numbers must be a multiple of five for this as five is prime. Ask: *How do you know if a number is a multiple of 5?*

4   No, it won't be. It is a product. Ask: *What do you know about prime numbers?*

8   At least one of the numbers must be a multiple of four for this or both must be even.

10 For long multiplication you need a six in one number and a three in the other for a 'yes' answer.

11 Unlikely for long multiplication, you need a one as the tens digit in both numbers. A mental method may use it.

Making it easier

Using three numbers to make a 2-digit × single-digit calculation. Allow children to choose which of the 11 questions they answer.

Making it harder

Using five numbers to make a 3-digit × 2-digit calculation.

Game 2: Make it work

Maths focus

- Multiplying and dividing numbers with more than one digit
- Estimating to check answers
- Reasoning

Resources

1–6 dice (2), calculator, whiteboards.

How to play

Roll the dice once each and add the numbers. Children find the question on the gameboard that matches the total.

Roll the dice twice each to get four numbers.

Arrange them in the boxes to work out the product ▢▢ × ▢▢ in order to make the answer to the question 'yes'. Work out the product using long multiplication or a mental method. Another player checks using a calculator. Score a point for getting a 'yes' answer to the question and a point for a correct calculation.

Prompts for this game are similar to the prompts for Game 1.

Making it easier

Using three numbers to make a 2-digit × single-digit calculation.

Making it harder

Place the four numbers to work out the quotient ▢▢▢ ÷ ▢.

Game 3: Your challenge

Children should invent their own game designing rules that use the concepts covered in the unit. Challenge children to make their game easier or harder. They could change the challenges on the boxes. They could use numbers with more, or fewer, digits.

Unit 3: Making products

Choose a game to play.

Game 1: Predict

You need:
- two 1–6 dice
- calculator
- whiteboard

How to play
- Roll the dice twice each.
- Make two 2-digit numbers with the numbers you roll.
- Then roll the dice once each. Add the numbers you get. Match this total to the question on the gameboard.
- Answer the question for your numbers and work out the product.
- Score a point for correctly answering the question. Score a point for correctly calculating the product.
- The winner is the player with the most points at the end of the game.

Game 2: Make it work

You need:
- two 1–6 dice
- calculator
- whiteboard

How to play
- Roll the dice once each and add the numbers you get. Match this total to the question on the gameboard.
- Roll the dice twice each. Make two 2-digit numbers with the digits you get.
- Arrange the digits so that the answer to your question on the board is 'yes'.
- Work out the product.
- Score a point for getting a 'yes' answer. Score a point for correctly calculating the product.
- The winner is the player with the most points at the end of the game.

Game 3: Your challenge

- Design your own game. Explain the rules and play with a partner.
- How will you make your game easier or harder?

Please help your child by reading the instructions and playing the game together.

Unit 3 — And finally …

Assessment task 1

Running the task

The task is to identify the error and then write an explanation. Explain that children are taking on the role of the teacher. Discuss what children find helpful when a teacher marks their work. Elicit that feedback should be clear and help learning by explaining why the answer is incorrect. Write $42 \times 12 = 404$ on the board. Identifying the error together and discuss how the child may have got this answer. When completing the task, children could copy the wrong version of the calculation and use callouts to point to the place where the error occurred, before explaining and correcting it.

In part a the numbers carried over from each calculation have been ignored; in part b the error is in dealing with the powers of ten; in part c the remainder has not been dealt with appropriately (it has been placed after the decimal point); and in part d the price for five pencils has been multiplied by eight but the price for one pencil (unit price) should have been worked out before multiplying it by eight.

Evidencing mastery

Correctly identifying the error is evidence of mastery. Careful and clear explanations that address the misconceptions show that the concept has been properly understood, e.g. in part a children may use the language of carrying over ten tens into the hundreds column of the answer to give 946 as the first part of the product; in part b their explanation may refer to place value; in part c they could note the different ways of dealing with remainders following division and how this applies to decimals; in part d, they may refer to the need to consider the structure of the question, without relying on cue words.

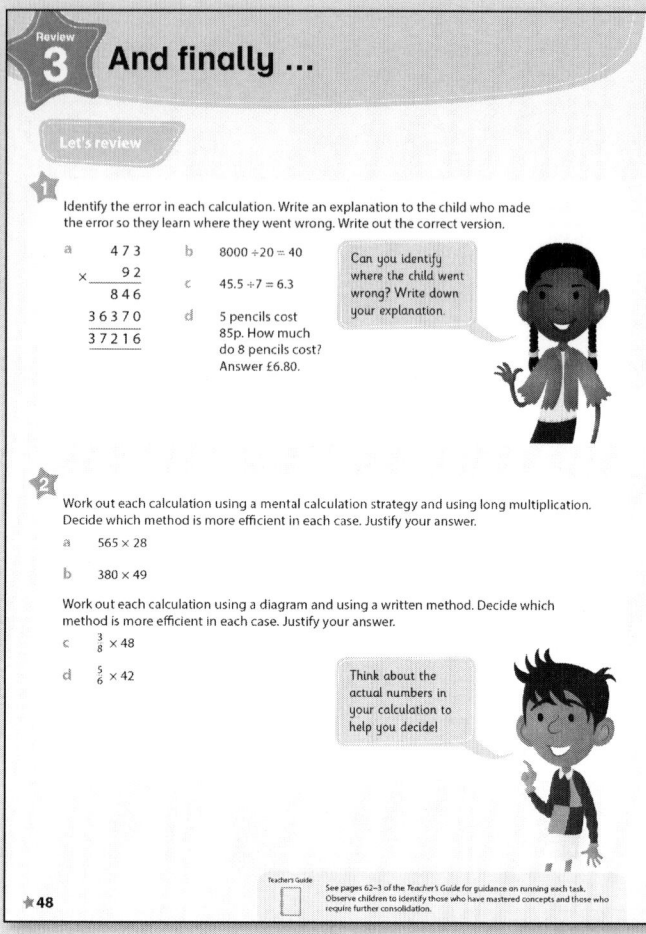

Assessment task 2

Running the task

Explain that there are often several ways of doing a calculation but that some are more efficient than others. Efficient methods are quicker and more reliable; they give the correct answer in a short time. Encourage children to show their method for both written and mental approaches. Emphasise it is important that you can follow what they have done. If necessary, model 23×15 as an example. Write down the long multiplication calculation and a suggested mental calculation strategy, e.g. $23 \times 10 = 230$, $23 \times 5 = 115$, $230 + 115 = 345$. Ask children to identify which is the more efficient method and why. Before completing the second part of the task, ensure that children remember how to use the bar model to represent calculations involving multiplication of fractions and whole numbers.

Evidencing mastery

Clearly set-out calculations, with appropriate digits carried across, indicates mastery of mental calculation strategies and long multiplication. To demonstrate mastery of choosing and using an appropriate method, children should justify their preferred method, referring to both accuracy and speed for justification of their preferred method.

Children showing mastery of unequal sharing draw appropriate diagrams showing the calculation for the fractions alongside the calculation itself. They should be able to explain that the diagram shows the structure of the calculation and aids understanding but calculating with just the numbers is much more efficient.

Assessment task 3

Running the task

Writing questions is a good way to deepen understanding of a concept. If necessary, model this in advance of setting this task. Discuss possible contexts for the word problems, including mathematical and real-world contexts. Prompt children to consider: all of the information is included in the question; if it is clear what the question is asking; if everyone would know the context; if you need to know the context in order to do the question?

Part a is likely to have 847 as some measure or quantity that is repeated 78 times, e.g. *I buy 78 sofas at £847 each, what is the total cost?* £66 066.

Part b could be an estimate for another calculation, e.g. *I need to work out an estimate for 589 × 83. What calculation should I do?* 48 000.

Part c could be the last step of a calculation of the mean of some lengths or weights, or an amount that is to be shared equally amongst eight people. 3.575.

Part d may be around the number of children in Year 6 or Key Stage 2, depending on the size of the school. Perhaps $\frac{3}{7}$ are boys, how many boys is that? 27.

A common error is to pre-empt the answer and that becomes one of the numbers in the question so the inverse operation is required.

Evidencing mastery

There are several aspects that could suggest mastery. The problem must require that calculation and not some alternative version, e.g. if a multiplication problem is required it is not appropriate to write a word problem that involves a division calculation. Getting the multiplicand and multiplier the right way round indicates mastery. This may happen by chance so always ask children to explain their problem to you using precise vocabulary. Lastly, the size of numbers should ideally be appropriate for the context.

Concepts mastered

- ✓ Children can calculate using the formal method of long multiplication, explaining why it works and why they chose to use this method.

- ✓ Children can solve problems involving multiplication and division in different contexts, appropriately choosing and using number facts, understanding of place value and mental and written methods. They can explain their decision making and justify their solutions.

- ✓ Children can multiply and divide decimals up to two decimal places by whole numbers to solve problems. They can explain why the method they are using works. They can calculate the mean of a set of numbers.

- ✓ Children can solve problems involving scaling and problems involving unequal sharing.

Did you know?

Some methods for multiplying large numbers have been around for 4000 years and look much more complicated than long multiplication. This method is basically the same as long multiplication but the digits are arranged slightly differently. The lattice method is criticised for not supporting understanding, it is an algorithm for multiplying large numbers and so you 'turn the handle' to use it.

Leonardo of Pisa, also known as Fibonacci, also brought the idea of numerals within a place-value system to Europe, which eventually ousted Roman numerals and allowed the development of a flourishing bureaucracy and an increasingly technological society.

Mathematical focus

★ **Geometry: properties of shape**

★ **Measurement: length, area**

★ **Algebra: simple formulae, number problems**

Prior learning

Children should already be able to:

- use the properties of rectangles to deduce related facts and find missing lengths and angles

- distinguish between regular and irregular polygons, through reasoning about equal sides and angles

- measure and calculate the perimeter and area of composite rectilinear shapes using appropriate units

- estimate volume (e.g. using 1 cm³ blocks) and capacity (e.g. using water).

Key new learning

- Draw 2-D shapes, using given dimensions and angles.

- Recognise that shapes with the same areas can have different perimeters and vice versa.

- Calculate the area of parallelograms and triangles.

- Recognise when it is possible to use the formulae for area.

- Express missing number problems algebraically.

- Compare and classify geometric shapes based on their properties and sizes and find unknown angles in any triangle, quadrilateral or regular polygon.

- Recognise angles where they meet at a point, are on a straight line, or are vertically opposite, and find missing angles.

- Find pairs of numbers that satisfy an equation with two unknowns.

- Recognise, describe and build simple 3-D shapes, including making nets.

- Recognise when it is possible to use the formulae for finding the volume of shapes.

Making connections

- Working out the possible dimensions of shapes with the same area involves solving the equation $A = xy$ for whole number values.

- Children will use simple CAD software in ICT to draw 3-D models, e.g. playground or bedroom designs.

- Cardboard boxes and containers of all types can be opened to examine nets.

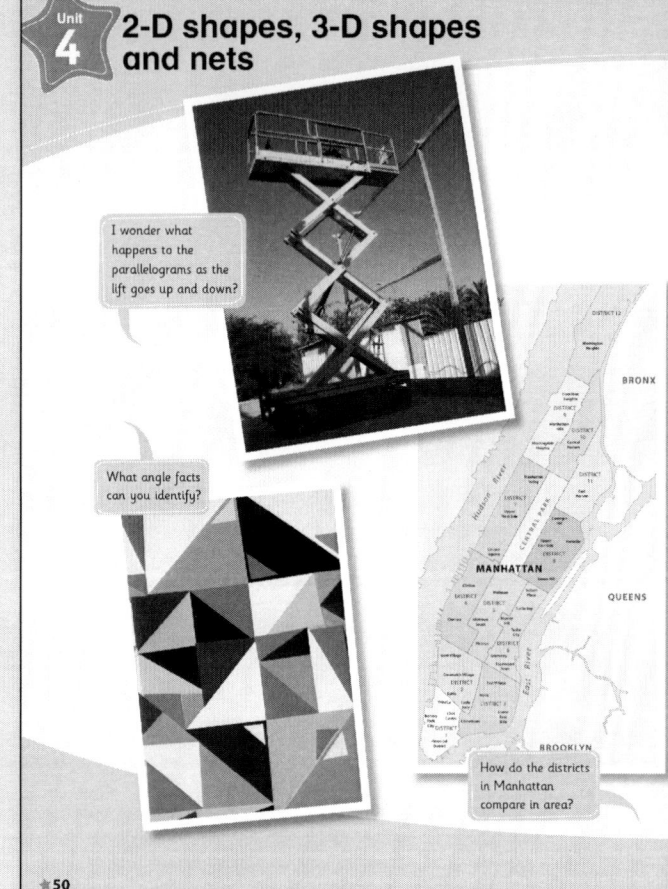

Unit 4

2-D shapes, 3-D shapes and nets

I wonder what happens to the parallelograms as the lift goes up and down?

What angle facts can you identify?

How do the districts in Manhattan compare in area?

★50

Talk about

The word 'net' has many meanings in everyday English, including the goal in football or a shortened form of Internet. In geometry, a net is a 2-D shape composed of polygons which, by folding, can form a 3-D shape or polyhedron. A solid may have a number of different nets. A perpendicular line is one that is at right angles to another line. The correct way to describe lines that cross one another is to say that they intersect. The point where they cross is the intersection. Vertically opposite angles describe the pair of equal angles between two intersecting straight lines. There are two pairs of such lines.

Engaging and exploring

Let children study the pictures and discuss the questions with a partner. Listen to their comments to assess their understanding of how they relate to the unit and the mathematics that they identify in each picture. Focus on each picture in turn.

The first picture shows a scissor lift. You could ask children to identify the parallelograms and think about how they change shape to make the lift go up and down. Elicit the idea that when the lift is closed the angles in the parallelogram are small acute angles and large obtuse ones, so that the height is minimised. As the lift is cranked up, the acute angles become larger and the obtuse ones become smaller. This change causes the overall height to increase. You might like to ask children where else they may see parallelograms in everyday life, e.g. floor tiles or the cross-section of a school rubber. You could use the opportunity

I wonder how the perimeter of this rolling bridge changes?

Which shapes' nets are used for fast food containers?

Teacher's Guide
Look at the pictures with the children and discuss the questions. See pages 64–5 of the *Teacher's Guide* for key ideas to draw out.

51

to revise quadrilaterals.

In the abstract picture of triangles, children look for angles. They should be able to find angles that meet at a point, are on a straight line or are vertically opposite (new in this unit). They will be able to identify different types of angles and triangles. Ask children to create their own triangle artworks and discuss with a partner the angles that they can see. Use this opportunity to reinforce the learning of angle facts, that angles meeting at a point total 360°, a straight line angle is 180° and the angles of a triangle total 180°.

The next picture shows the districts of Manhattan in New York. Explain that Manhattan is a borough of New York City that is very popular with tourists. Have any children been to Manhattan? Explain that Manhattan is divided into districts. Ask children which districts they think have similar-sized areas. How do they know? How could they check? You might like to ask them why only some of the lines on the map are straight. Revisit how to measure the perimeter of a shape and how to calculate area. Ask children what units area and perimeter are measured in and to explain why. Quiz them whether they think a map of their own nearest town or city would have areas with straight lines. Can they explain their answers?

The fourth photo shows a rolling bridge, designed by Thomas Heatherwick. Give children time to look at the pictures and think about how the mechanism works. Ask them to think about the change in perimeter as the bridge folds and unfolds. To simulate and measure this they could join six equilateral triangular prisms from magnetic 3-D shape construction kits, measure the perimeter, then roll up the model and re-measure the new reduced perimeter. You could ask children if the movement reminds them of any creature. Heatherwick was inspired by animatronic dinosaurs made for Jurassic Park. The Rolling Bridge is part of the redevelopment area of Paddington Basin in London. When open, it is quite unremarkable but watching it curl up is very impressive. You can watch it opening and closing on YouTube. Ask children to think about the change in perimeter as the bridge folds and unfolds.

The final photo shows the net of a fast food container. You might like to ask children to tell you about other fast food containers and make a collection. They may bring in pizza boxes and you could ask them to open them out carefully to see how they are constructed. They could also investigate individual lunch boxes that fold to include a handle. Children could draw their own nets to make containers based on these observations.

Things to think about

- How will you organise your class to give opportunity for paired talk?

- How will you plan focus group work?

- How will you make effective use of manipulatives to support understanding, e.g. 2-D and 3-D shapes, cubes, 3-D shape construction kits? If children have not had sufficient experience of handing manipulatives, their spatial awareness and understanding may be less developed.

- How will you check conceptual understanding of area, angle problems, volume and nets?

- How will you promote and develop reasoning through questioning and problem-solving activities?

Checking understanding

By the end of this unit, children are able to calculate the area of parallelograms and triangles, understanding and using the appropriate formulae. They are able to understand that the perimeter of shapes with the same area may differ and vice versa. They know and use these angle facts:

- angles on a straight line total 180°

- vertically opposite angles are equal

- angles that meet at a point total 360°.

They are able to find missing angles using these facts, expressing missing number problems algebraically. They can recognise, describe and build simple 3-D shapes, including making nets.

- Draw 2-D shapes, using given dimensions and angles.
- Recognise that shapes with the same areas can have different perimeters and vice versa.
- Calculate the area of parallelograms and triangles.
- Recognise when it is possible to use the formulae for area.
- Express missing number problems algebraically.

Homework 23 and 24   Practice Book pp 45–9   2D Shapes

Representations and resources

Two dice (1–6), 2-D shapes, cm-squared paper, protractor, ruler, tape measure.

Mathematical vocabulary

Perimeter, area, parallelogram, base, perpendicular

Warming up

Revise finding the area of rectangles. Roll two 1–6 dice to determine the lengths of the sides (if both values are equal, then the shape is a square). You could tell children to draw the shape on squared paper and calculate the area using a mental calculation strategy of their choice. Check that they remember that area is measured in square units, e.g. cm².

Background knowledge

In Year 5, children learnt to measure and calculate the perimeter of rectilinear shapes. They learnt how to find the area of rectilinear shapes by counting squares and know that area is measured in square units, e.g. cm² or m². This is because two measurements are required (this is why we use the term two-dimensional, or 2-D).

The area of a rectangle, A, is equal to the length (l) times the width (w). Expressed as a formula, this is $A = l \times w$ or $A = lw$.

This formula can be used to calculate area. If the area and the length of one side are known, then the length of the missing side can be expressed algebraically in order to find the missing value.

Let's learn: Modelling and teaching

Finding the area of a triangle

- Ask children to recall the formula for the area of a rectangle, $A = lw$, where l = length and w = width.

- Give children two 2-D right-angled triangles to put together. Elicit that they have made a rectangle with one side equal to the base of the triangle and the other equal to its height. Establish that the area of the triangle is therefore $\frac{1}{2}(bh)$ where b = base and h = height. Repeat to encourage children to find this is true for any pair of right-angled triangles.

- Ask children to put together two identical isosceles or scalene triangles. Ask what shape they have made (a parallelogram).

- Look at the diagrams in the Textbook and let children experiment folding and cutting a parallelogram, or drawing their own diagrams on squared paper. Establish that the area of any triangle can be expressed using the same formula, $A = \frac{1}{2}(bh)$.

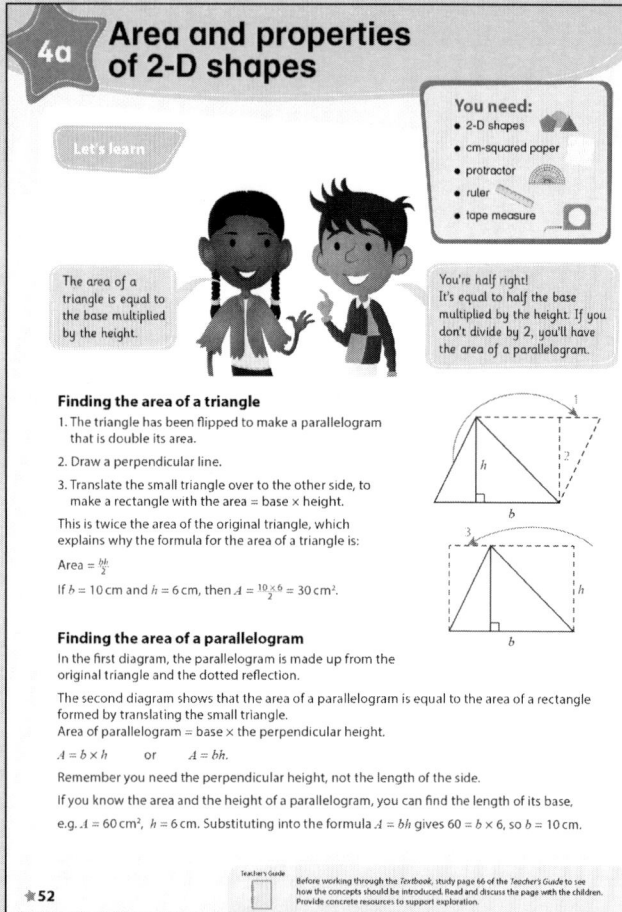

Finding the area of a parallelogram

- As a class, describe the properties of a parallelogram. Ask children to draw a parallelogram on card, fold in a right-angled triangle and then carefully cut it off. Highlight that the triangle fits on the other side of the parallelogram, making it into a rectangle with one side equal to the base of the parallelogram and the other equal to its perpendicular height.

- Explain that this happens with every parallelogram. Discuss how you could use this information to deduce the formula for finding the area of a parallelogram. Compare their ideas to the formula in the Textbook: $A = b \times h$ or $A = bh$, where A = area of a parallelogram, b = base and h = height.

- Prove this by working through a set of examples.

Let's practise: Digging deeper

Step 1

Ask children to tell you what measurements they need to calculate the area of a triangle. The questions have been structured to reinforce the learning objective that shapes with the same areas can have different perimeters, and vice versa.

Step 2

Before they begin, ask children to tell you the possible lengths of the base and perpendicular height for parallelograms with an area of 12 cm². Establish that the solutions are the factor pairs of 12 : 1 and 12, 2 and 6, and 3 and 4. This will prepare them for part c. Children draw and label diagrams for their chosen dimensions. Encourage them to draw these with attention to relative lengths, so that a line they label as 4 cm is approximately half the length of one that they label as 8 cm.

Step 3

This multi-step activity requires children to measure the school hall, round the measurements, calculate the perimeter for the skirting board and the area for the flooring. You may need to explain to children that the skirting board is the trim where the walls meet the floor. Children then need to calculate the cost of replacing the skirting board and the flooring for each alternative material. Children may find it helpful to draw a sketch to aid their calculations. Encourage children to find all four possible permutations for the total cost.

Step 4

Ask children to discuss strategies for tackling the problem. Encourage children to work systematically by increasing the base incrementally, (base 1 cm, 2 cm, 3 cm, etc.). Ask questions such as: *What do you notice?* to encourage children to spot the pattern of square numbers. Finally, discuss children's predictions for part c. Ask them to prove that their prediction is correct. They should spot that since the area for a triangle is $\frac{bh}{2}$, if $h = 2b$ then the area can be simplified to b^2.

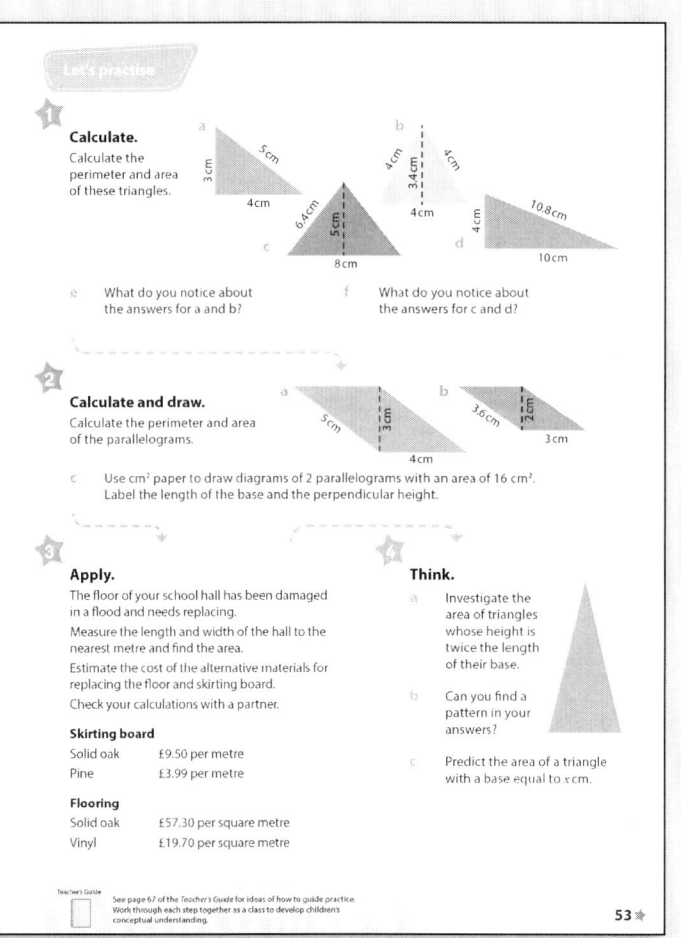

Ensuring progress

Supporting understanding

It is important that all children understand the formulae and are not put off by the use of algebra. You may like to work with some children in a guided group to help them become familiar with using the appropriate formulae. Some children need considerable practice to fully understand the concept of area.

Broadening understanding

Provide opportunities for children to make up missing length and area problems within the theme of the spread. This will enable you to determine their true understanding. Children may enjoy trying the investigations 'Formulae' and 'Chickens' from the Rising Stars *Problem Solving and Reasoning Year 6 book*.

> ✓ **Concept mastered**
>
> Children can find the area of triangles and parallelograms and understand the formulae for calculating areas. They are able to express a missing value algebraically and use the correct formula to find the value. They can draw 2-D shapes with given dimensions and angles. They understand that shapes with the same areas can have different perimeters and vice versa.

Follow-up ideas

- Challenge children to draw large chalk triangles or parallelograms, with given dimensions, as accurately as possible on the playground. You could let them suggest the equipment that they need.

- Use software to draw shapes and calculate their areas and perimeters.

- Measure perimeters and areas of places within the school and its grounds.

Answers

Step 1

a	$A = 6\,cm^2$	$P = 12\,cm$
b	$A = 6.8\,cm^2$	$P = 12\,cm$
c	$A = 20\,cm^2$	$P = 20.8\,cm$
d	$A = 20\,cm^2$	$P = 24.8\,cm$
e	The perimeters are both 12 cm.
f	The areas are both 20 cm

Step 2

a	$A = 12\,cm^2$	$P = 18\,cm$
b	$A = 6\,cm^2$	$P = 13.2\,cm$

c   Possible parallelograms have base = 4 cm and perpendicular height = 4 cm or base = 8 cm and perpendicular height = 2 cm

Step 3

Individual answers.

Step 4

a

Base	1	2	3	4	5	b
Height	2	4	6	8	10	$2b$
Area	1	4	9	16	25	b^2

b   The answers are square numbers

c $x^2\,cm^2$.

- Draw 2-D shapes, using given dimensions and angles.
- Compare and classify geometric shapes based on their properties and sizes and find unknown angles.
- Recognise angles where they meet at a point, are on a straight line, or are vertically opposite, and find missing angles.
- Express missing number problems algebraically and find pairs of numbers that satisfy an equation with two unknowns.

Homework 25 and 26   Practice Book pp 50–3   Geometry Instruments

Representations and resources

2-D shapes, protractor, 1 cm-wide card strips, hole punch, paper fasteners, cm-squared paper.

Mathematical vocabulary

Vertically opposite angles, intersect, perpendicular

Warming up

Divide the class into two teams. Each team rolls two dice and makes a proper fraction, e.g. 3 and 2 gives $\frac{2}{3}$. Change the fractions to a common denominator and compare the fractions. The bigger fraction scores the team one point. Repeat.

Background knowledge

Children should have mastered the following angle facts:

angles on a straight line total 180°;

angles in any triangle total 180°;

angles around a point total 360°.

Vertically opposite angles formed by the intersection of two straight lines are equal. The four angles total 360° because they are angles around a point.

Let's learn: Modelling and teaching

Vertically opposite angles

- Give children two thin card strips fastened in the centre with a paper fastener. Ask them to tell you what happens to the opposite angles as they move the strips to increase and decrease the angle size. Elicit that the opposite angles change size but still look equal. Let them use a protractor to check that the opposite angles are actually equal.

- Look at the diagram in the Textbook. Draw other examples with one known angle and ask children to calculate the missing values using their angle facts.

Equations with two unknowns

- Give children a semicircle of paper. Ask them to fold it along the radius, cut along the fold and measure the angle of one piece. Ask: *Can you predict the angle of the second piece?* Explain that the two angle values are linked – they add up to 180°. They can deduce the size of the angle by subtracting the angle they measured from 180°. Measure

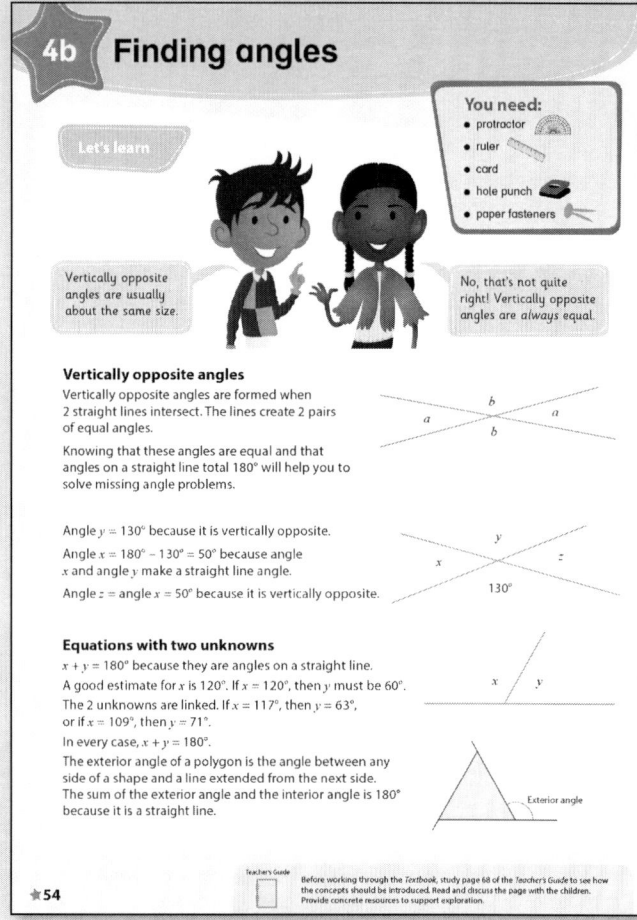

the second angle to check. Repeat the exercise, cutting in a different position.

- Look at the diagram in the Textbook. Ask: *How many whole number solutions are possible if there are no limits on the value of x and y?* Theoretical solutions for x range from 1° up to 179°, with the corresponding values for y going from 179° down to 1°. Introducing this type of equation, where the meaning of the equation is visually evident, is a good way of helping to build algebraic understanding.

- Challenge children to explain how they could find the exterior angle of a polygon using these facts.

Let's practise: Digging deeper

Step 1

The equation $x + y = 180°$ is the equation for two unknown angles on a straight line. Vertically opposite angles are equal. In part a, children are told that x is a multiple of 5 and given a range of possible values. Ask children how they will use this information to find pairs of numbers that will satisfy the equation. Collect their ideas before they complete the question. Part b is similar, but has different conditions.

Step 2

Children have learnt a number of symbols used in geometry diagrams. To find the missing angles, they must use the information that the symbols provide. Check they know geometry symbols and their angle facts before completing the questions.

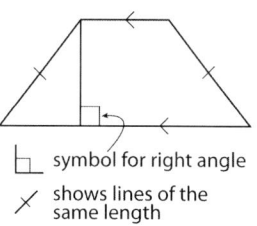

⌐ symbol for right angle

✕ shows lines of the same length

⤚ shows parallel lines

Step 3

Children measure and record the sizes of angles in a parallelogram. Encourage them to record their measurements systematically and to come up with as many general statements as possible. As a class, check the statements by substituting in numbers.

Step 4

Children should sketch regular polygons and extend the lines to form the exterior angles in the same direction around each polygon. They can calculate the size of the interior angles by drawing isosceles triangles from the centre of each polygon. They can deduce the size of the angle in the isosceles triangle and double it to give the interior angle. Next, they find the exterior angle and then calculate the total of the exterior angles. The sum is always 360° because each line changes direction until it gets back to the start.

Ensuring progress

Supporting understanding

Work with children in focus groups to provide further opportunities to manipulate angles using card strips and paper fasteners. Children can estimate and measure angles to reinforce their understanding of angle size, which angles are equal and what angles add up to 180° and 360°.

Broadening understanding

Challenge children to write and draw their own missing angles problems for their peers to solve. Look at world flags that include triangles and quadrilaterals, e.g. Bahamas, Congo, Czech Republic, Guyana, Seychelles, and ask children to calculate the sizes of the angles.

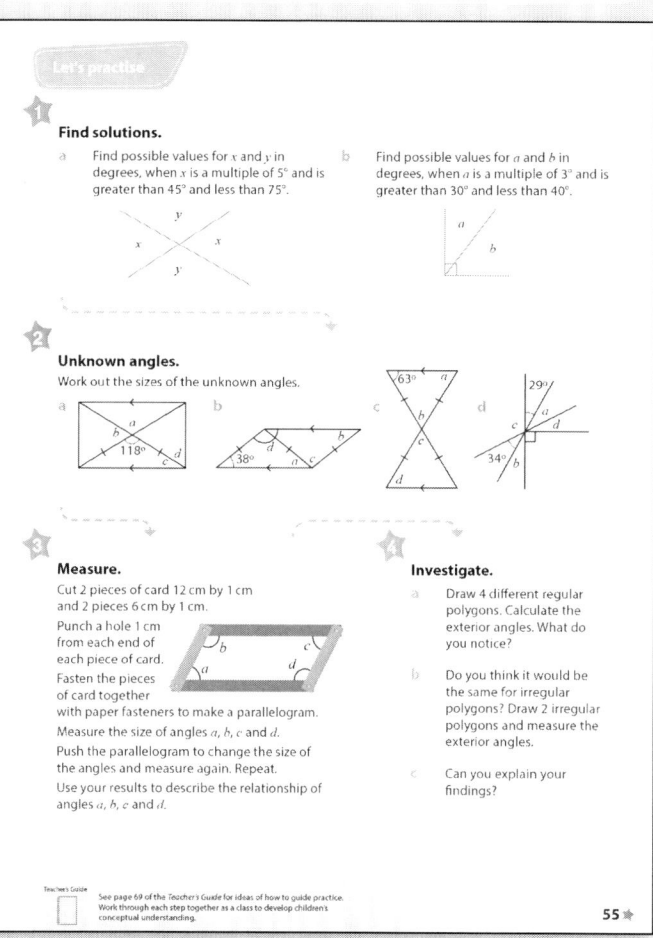

Let's practise

1 Find solutions.

a Find possible values for x and y in degrees, when x is a multiple of 5° and is greater than 45° and less than 75°.

b Find possible values for a and b in degrees, when a is a multiple of 3° and is greater than 30° and less than 40°.

2 Unknown angles.

Work out the sizes of the unknown angles.

3 Measure.

Cut 2 pieces of card 12 cm by 1 cm and 2 pieces 6 cm by 1 cm.

Punch a hole 1 cm from each end of each piece of card.

Fasten the pieces of card together with paper fasteners to make a parallelogram. Measure the size of angles a, b, c and d.

Push the parallelogram to change the size of the angles and measure again. Repeat.

Use your results to describe the relationship of angles a, b, c and d.

4 Investigate.

a Draw 4 different regular polygons. Calculate the exterior angles. What do you notice?

b Do you think it would be the same for irregular polygons? Draw 2 irregular polygons and measure the exterior angles.

c Can you explain your findings?

Teacher's Guide: See page 69 of the Teacher's Guide for ideas of how to guide practice. Work through each step together as a class to develop children's conceptual understanding.

55

Concept mastered ✓

Children can express missing number problems algebraically and find pairs of numbers that satisfy an equation with two unknowns. They recognise angles where they meet at a point, are on a straight line, or are vertically opposite, and use angle facts to find missing angles. They can compare and classify geometric shapes based on their properties and sizes and find unknown angles in triangles, quadrilaterals and regular polygons.

Follow-up ideas

- Children could make up and solve their own question that involves finding pairs of numbers that satisfy an equation with two unknowns.

- You might like to ask children to design a poster to show the angle facts for 180° and 360°.

- Children could create a piece of art that involves aspects of the geometry that they have been studying. You could leave the brief open or give them a list of features to include. The artist Wassily Kandinsky might provide inspiration.

Answers

Step 1

a Possible solutions for x and y are 50°, 130°; 55°, 125°; 60°, 120°; 65°, 115°; 70°, 110°

b Possible solutions for a and b are 33°, 57°; 36°, 54°; 39°, 51°

Step 2

a $a = 118°$ $b = 62°$
$c = 31°$ $d = 59°$

b $a = 38°$ $b = 38°$
$c = 104°$ $d = 142°$

c $a = 63°$ $b = 54°$
$c = 54°$ $d = 63°$

d $a = 34°$ $b = 29°$
$c = 117°$ $d = 27°$

Step 3

General statements are angle a = angle c, angle b = angle d, angle a + angle b = 180° and the total of all four angles = 360°.

Step 4

a In each case the angles add up to 360°.

b The angles add up to 360° (+/− a few degrees drawing and measurement error).

c The exterior angles add up to one complete turn because when you have turned through all the external angles you are facing the way you started - you have turned through 360°.

Describing 3-D shapes and making nets

Homework 27 and 28   Practice Book pp 54–7   3D Shapes

- Recognise, describe and build simple 3-D shapes, including making nets.
- Recognise when it is possible to use formulae for finding the volume of shapes.

Mathematical vocabulary

Net, cuboid, prism, pyramid, volume, formula

Representations and resources

2-D and 3-D shapes (including cubes), 3-D shape construction kits, cm-squared paper, cuboid food boxes

Warming up

Choose a child to pick out two 3-D shapes from a bag of polyhedra. Ask the class to name common properties of the shapes. Repeat with other pairs of shapes. Use the activity to revise shape vocabulary (e.g. face, vertex/vertices, edge, pyramid, prism, cross-section, parallel, perpendicular).

Background knowledge

Children may not have studied 3-D shapes for some time. The warm-up activity should refresh their knowledge.

Volume is defined as the amount of space that a 3-D object occupies. Take care that children do not confuse volume and capacity (capacity is the amount something can hold). Children should have mastered how to find volumes by counting cubes. In Year 5 they began to explore the formula for finding the volume of a cuboid, $V = abc$, where a, b and c are the dimensions of the cuboid. Build on this understanding to explain and apply the formula for volume.

A net is defined as a plane figure composed of polygons which, by folding, can form a polyhedron. A solid shape may have a number of different nets.

Let's learn: Modelling and teaching

Nets of a triangular prism

- Ask children to make a triangular prism using 3-D shape construction kits and unfold it carefully into a 2-D polygon. Ask them to remake the prism and unfold it in a different way to make another net. Ask: *Can you see any similarities in the nets?*

- Ask them to separate the pieces and make a 2-D polygon that will not fold into a triangular prism. They may find that their polygon will not make a prism when it cannot be folded or the faces overlap.

- Look at the images in the Textbook. Ask them to predict which are nets and to explain why the others will not work. Repeat this with other 3-D shapes.

Formula for the volume of a cuboid

- Use cm³ cubes to build a cuboid 4 cm long × 3 cm wide × 2 cm high. As a class, count the cubes in the first 4 cm × 3 cm layer. Remind children that this is an array and equal to 4 × 3. The height of the cuboid is 2 cm so the total volume is (4 × 3 × 2) cm³.

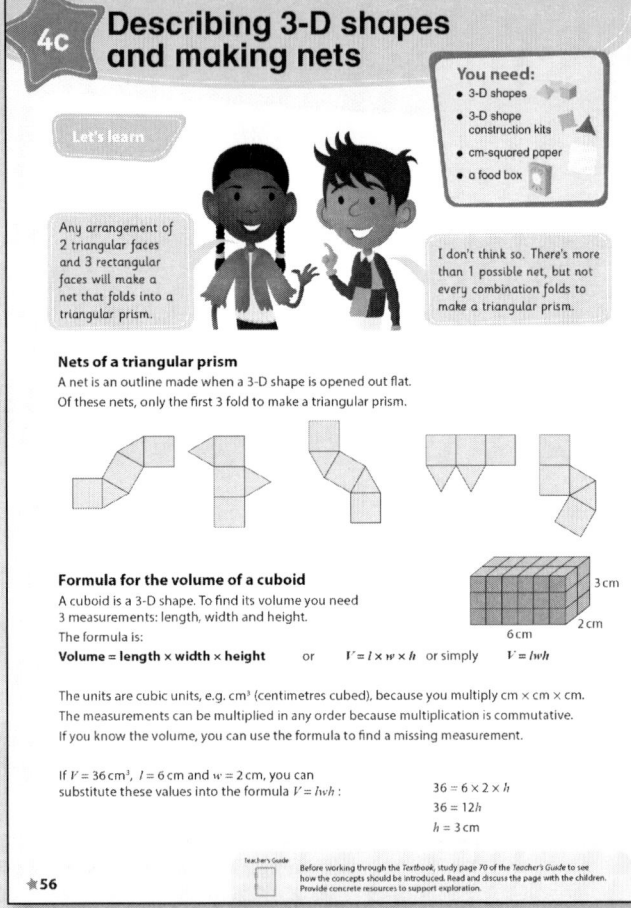

- Repeat with another cuboid. Draw out the idea that volume can be calculated by multiplying the three dimensions together.

- Highlight that volume is measured in cubic units, cm³ and m³.

- Ask children if they can deduce the formula for finding the volume. Compare their ideas to the formula: $V = lwh$. Ask: *Why can the measurements be multiplied in any order?* Explain that if three of the four values are known, they can be substituted into the formula to calculate the missing value.

Let's practise: Digging deeper
Step 1
Ask children to predict which nets will make a 3-D shape. Do all children agree? Ask children to visualise the nets and predict which 3-D shapes they make. They could then check their answers by making making and folding copies of the nets. You could further consolidate understanding by asking children to draw two more nets for each shape – one that will work and one that will not.

Step 2
Children begin by finding volumes from labelled diagrams. Check that they use the correct units in their answers. In the final part children are asked to find two sets of measurements for a given volume. Help any who find this challenging to think of factors and suggest using squared paper to sketch their cuboids.

Step 3
Children investigate the volume of a cuboid food packet and make a net. Discuss tabs or overlaps that are necessary to fasten or glue the shape together, which we do not need to measure. You could ask children to open the box out carefully to look at the actual net and compare the area of this to the net they made. Commercial nets may often be constructed quite differently.

Step 4
Finding and recognising the nets of a cube is a classic investigation. The net of six equal-sized squares is known as a hexomino. There are 35 different hexominoes, with distinct arrangements of the squares that are not rotations or reflections. Of these, only 11 make cubes. Children who find spatial exercises challenging may benefit from using 3-D shape construction kits to try out their ideas. Encourage them to be systematic in their approach and to record the arrangements that are not nets, as well as those that are.

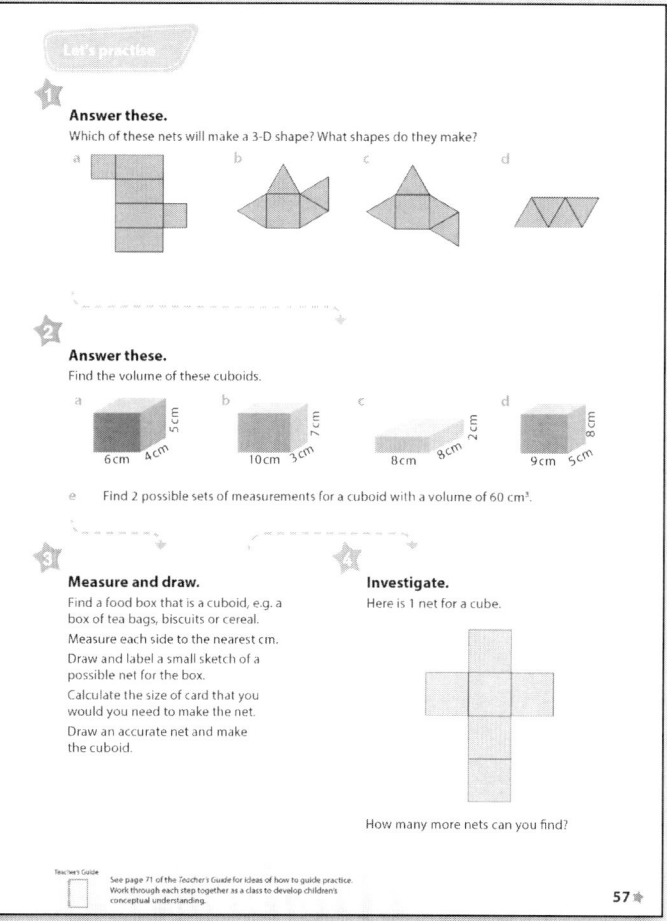

See page 71 of the *Teacher's Guide* for ideas of how to guide practice. Work through each step together as a class to develop children's conceptual understanding.

57

Follow-up ideas
- Collect a few large boxes and carefully take them apart to look at the nets. The boxes often do not exactly match conventional cuboid nets. Discuss possible reasons for this, e.g. to give strength, to provide overlap, to fit together more efficiently and thus to be cheaper to manufacture.

- Make a display of fast food boxes. Perhaps compare different pizza boxes. Again, you could ask children to think about the strength of the packaging and cost.

- Calculate the approximate volume of the classroom in m³.

- Use long bamboo canes and rubber bands to make 3-D structures, such as a tetrahedron or triangular prism.

Ensuring progress
Supporting understanding
Children's ability to visualise folding nets will differ. They can be supported by using 3-D shape construction kits to test the net. Alternatively, you could give them paper with large squares to draw the nets, cut them out and fold them.

Broadening understanding
There are further opportunities for children to explore more complex nets on the Internet.

✓ Concept mastered
Children can recognise, identify and describe 3-D shapes and use the formula for the volume of a cuboid to find its volume in cm³ or m³. They understand, recognise and use nets for 3-D shapes.

Answers
Step 1
a a cuboid

b not a net

c square-based pyramid

d tetrahedron

Step 2
a 120 cm³

b 210 cm³

c 128 cm³

d 360 cm³

e Possible measurements include 6 cm × 5 cm × 2 cm or 10 cm × 3 cm × 2 cm

Step 3
a Individual answers

Step 4
a There are 11 possible nets for a cube.

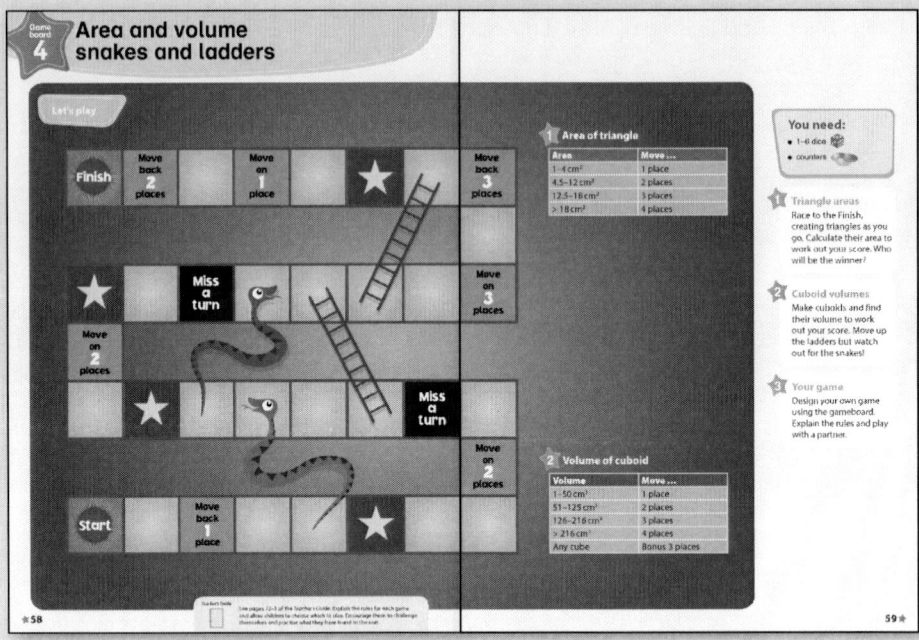

Game 1: Triangle areas

In this game a dice throw determines the base and height of a triangle. The bigger the area of the triangle, the higher the player's score.

Maths focus

- Finding the area of a triangle using the formula, $A = \frac{bh}{2}$, where b = base and h = height

Resources

1 counter per player (1 colour per player),
1–6 dice (2), 1–9 dice (2) for extension.

How to play

Each player places a counter on the Start and take turns to throw the dice. The numbers thrown are the base and height of the triangle in centimetres. Children use them to make a diagram of the triangle and work out its area in centimetres squared. They find their area on the table. They move their counter the number of places indicated and carry out any instructions on the board.

If children are not familiar with snakes and ladders, explain to them that they go up the ladders and down the snakes. The winner is the person who completes the board first.

Making it easier

If children land on a star, they have an extra turn.

Making it harder

Use 1–9 dice instead.

Game 3: Your game

Children should invent their own game designing rules that use the concepts covered in the unit. Challenge children to make their game easier or harder.

Game 2: Cuboid volumes

In this game a dice throw determines the dimensions of a cuboid. The bigger the volume of the cuboid, the higher the player's score. If all three dice are the same, they make a cube and score a bonus!

Maths focus

- Finding the volume of a cuboid using the formula, $V = lwh$, where l = length, w = width and h = height

Resources

1 counter per player (1 colour per player),
1–6 dice (3), 1–9 dice (3) for extension.

How to play

Each player places a counter on the Start and take turns to throw the dice. The numbers thrown are the length, width and height of the cuboid in centimetres. Children use them to sketch the cuboid and work out its volume in centimetres cubed. They find their volume on the table; the bigger the cuboid, the higher the score! If the three dice have the same value, they make a cube which scores an additional bonus of three places, even if it is tiny. They move their counter the number of places indicated and carry out any instructions on the board.

If children are not familiar with snakes and ladders, explain to them that they go up the ladders and down the snakes. The winner is the person who completes the board first.

Making it easier

If children land on a star, they have an extra turn.

Making it harder

Use 1–9 dice instead.

Unit 4 ⟩ Area and volume snakes and ladders

Choose a game to play.

Game 1: Triangle areas

How to play

- Each player places a counter on the Start.
- Take turns to throw the 2 dice. The numbers thrown are the base and height of a triangle in centimetres. Sketch the triangle and work out its area.
- Find your area on the table. Move your counter, following any instructions on the board.
- If you land on a square with the base of a ladder on it, you go up the ladder.
- If you land on a square with the head of a snake on it, you go down the snake.
- The winner is the first to reach the Finish.

You need:

- 1 counter per player (1 colour per player)
- two 1–6 dice
- paper and pencils

Game 2: Cuboid volumes

How to play

- Each player places a counter on the Start.
- Take turns to throw the 3 dice. The numbers thrown are the length, width and height of a cuboid in centimetres. Sketch the cuboid and work out its volume.
- Find your volume on the table and move your counter, following any instructions on the board.
- If the 3 dice values are the same, you make a cube which scores a bonus of 3 places.
- If you land on a square with the base of a ladder on it, you go up the ladder.
- If you land on a square with the head of a snake on it, you go down the snake.
- The winner is the first to reach the Finish.

You need:

- 1 counter per player (1 colour per player)
- three 1–6 dice
- paper and pencils

Game 3: Your game

- Design your own game using the gameboard.
- What resources will you need to play your game?
- What are the rules for your game? Explain them to someone.

Please help your child by reading the instructions and playing the game together.

Assessment task 1

Resources

Squared paper, ruler.

Running the task

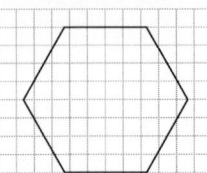 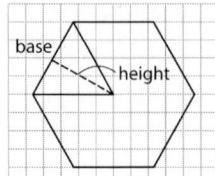

Show children a regular hexagon and ask them what measurements they would need to know to be able to calculate its area. Agree that one way would be to draw the diagonals, so that they can find the area of one of the six identical equilateral triangles that make up the hexagon. They would then need to know the length of the base and the height, as indicated in the second diagram.

Ask children to do the same exercise for the shapes in the Textbook. Drawing the horizontal diagonal on the kite gives two triangles, so the area can be found. Diagram b is a simple parallelogram. Diagram c can be divided into two triangles, but the base and height of the small triangle are not whole numbers of squares so the area cannot easily be accurately measured. The trapezium in d can be divided into a parallelogram and a triangle to calculate the area. Give children thinking time before providing support.

Evidencing mastery

Children who are able to explain the measurements that they need and then calculate the areas quickly and efficiently, clearly demonstrate mastery of the mathematics of this unit.

Here are the measurements required for each polygon.

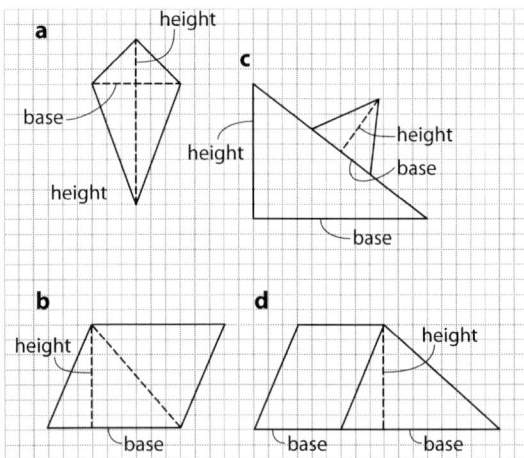

The area answers are: **a** = 33 squares; **b** large triangle area = 54 squares, small triangle cannot be measured accurately; **c** = 63 squares; **d** = 80.5 squares. Note that if cm² paper is used 'squares' become 'cm²'.

Recognising that the diagonals are not whole squares is evidence of a good level of understanding.

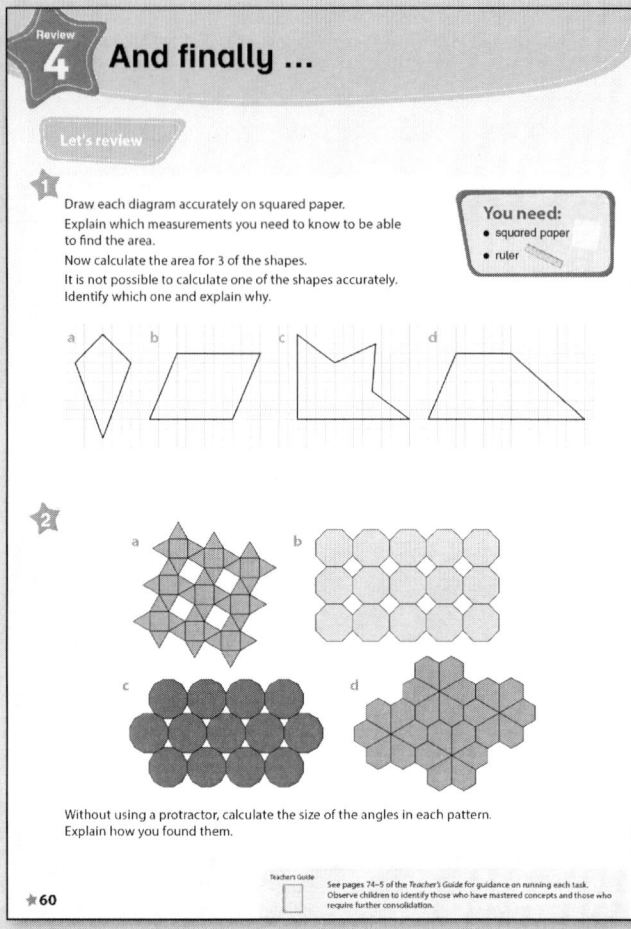

Review

4 And finally ...

Let's review

1. Draw each diagram accurately on squared paper.
Explain which measurements you need to know to be able to find the area.
Now calculate the area for 3 of the shapes.
It is not possible to calculate one of the shapes accurately. Identify which one and explain why.

You need:
- squared paper
- ruler

a   b   c   d

2. Without using a protractor, calculate the size of the angles in each pattern. Explain how you found them.

Teacher's Guide See pages 74–5 of the Teacher's Guide for guidance on running each task. Observe children to identify those who have mastered concepts and those who require further consolidation.

★ 60

Assessment task 2

Running the task

Before children begin the task, you might like to revise the concept of tessellation of single shapes. Give children 2-D kite shapes to tessellate. Ask them to explain how they can tessellate and to describe the angle patterns. Parts, a, b and c are semi-regular tessellations where two regular shapes tessellate. In part d, the shapes that tessellate are irregular pentagons. Listen to what children say to one another as they tackle each question. To carry out the task children need to draw on their knowledge of angle facts, including angles in an equilateral triangle equal 60°, angles in a triangle total 180° and angles around a point total 360°.

Evidencing mastery

If children are able to do this task independently and explain what they are doing using precise vocabulary, they demonstrate a confident grasp of calculating angles and mastery of this aspect of the unit.

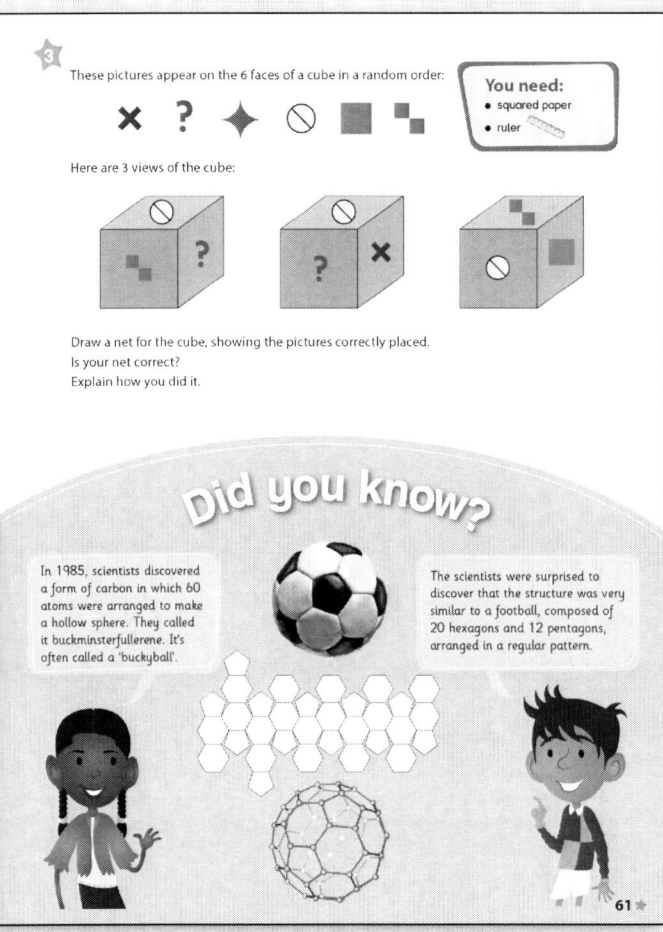

Concepts mastered

✓ Children can find the area of triangles and parallelograms and understand the formulae for calculating areas. They are able to express a missing value algebraically and use the correct formula to find the value. They can draw 2-D shapes with given dimensions and angles. They understand that shapes with the same areas can have different perimeters and vice versa.

✓ Children can find pairs of numbers that satisfy an equation with two unknowns. They recognise angles where they meet at a point, are on a straight line, or are vertically opposite, and use angle facts to find missing angles. They can compare and classify geometric shapes based on their properties and sizes and find unknown angles in triangles, quadrilaterals and regular polygons.

✓ Children can recognise, identify and describe 3-D shapes and use the formula for the volume of a cuboid to find its volume in cm^3 or m^3. They understand, recognise and use nets for 3-D shapes.

Assessment task 3

Resources

Squared paper, ruler.

Running the task

You might like to let children tackle the task in their own way and observe the strategies that they use. Some children may draw a net and try to fill the squares. Others may start with a single square filled and build up the net square-by-square. Some children may make some progress and then cut out a net with one or two empty squares in order to locate the final pictures. Other children may complete the net on paper and then cut out another net to confirm their drawn net. This is sound practice and allows self-correction if they have made an error. Children who are very secure in their spatial awareness may be able to manipulate and visualise the net completely in their head, without cutting or folding the shape at all.

If children need support, you could advise them to begin with two faces that they know are next to each other and build the net up from there.

Evidencing mastery

The problem is quite challenging, but children who have mastered the concept of nets will be able to interpret and complete the task without error. The finished net can be drawn in different ways. Here is one correct version.

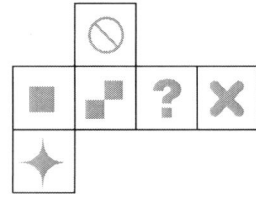

Did you know?

You could tell children about an interesting net with a story. In 1985, scientists discovered a form of carbon in which 60 atoms were arranged to make a hollow sphere. They called it buckminsterfullerene because the shape of it resembled the geodesic domes made by the American architect, Buckminster Fuller. These days, it is sometimes known as a buckyball.

The scientists were surprised to discover that the C_{60} structure was very similar to a football, composed of 20 hexagons and 12 pentagons, arranged in a regular pattern. When a football is blown up, the leather stretches a little and each face expands slightly so that the ball becomes spherical.

Numbers in everyday life

Mathematical focus

★ **Number: number and place value, fractions (including decimals and percentages)**

★ **Measurement: length, mass, volume, capacity, time**

★ **Statistics: interpret and calculate, interpret and construct**

Prior learning

Children should already be able to:

- interpret negative numbers within the context of temperature and count forwards and backwards with positive and negative whole numbers, including through zero

- read, write, order and compare numbers to at least 1 000 000 and determine the value of each digit

- identify the value of each digit in numbers given to two decimal places, and multiply and divide numbers by 100 giving answers up to two decimal places.

Key new learning

- Use negative numbers in a variety of different contexts, and calculate intervals across zero.

- Solve problems that involve number and place value.

- Identify the value of each digit in numbers given to three decimal places, and multiply and divide numbers by 1000 giving answers up to three decimal places.

- Solve number and practical problems that involve all of the above.

- Interpret and construct line graphs and use these to solve problems.

Making connections

- Multiplying and dividing by 100 and 1000 are important skills. They enable children to convert between standard units of measure and link to writing measurements using decimal notation with up to three decimal places. Children should be given opportunities to practically solve problems involving length, mass, capacity and volume, and to record their solutions accurately in different ways, including decimals.

- Measurements with decimal units are often seen in recipes. Cooking is a good way to practise measuring and links well to design technology.

- Working with line graphs and scales such as those found on thermometers can help children understand the meaning of negative numbers. Temperature, depth below sea level, bank balances and the level of floors in buildings are common contexts for negative numbers.

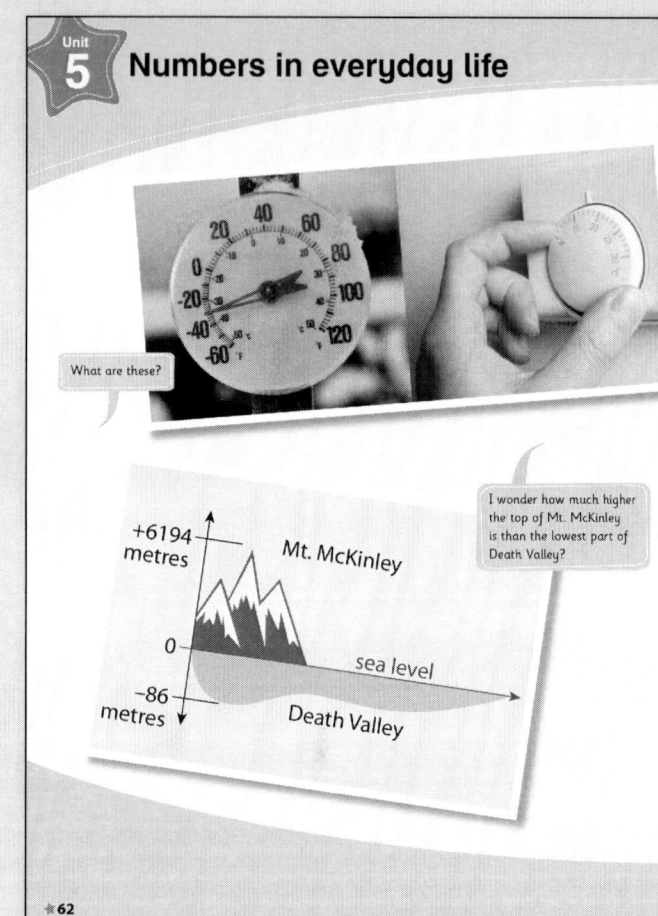

Unit 5 Numbers in everyday life

What are these?

I wonder how much higher the top of Mt. McKinley is than the lowest part of Death Valley?

+6194 metres

Mt. McKinley

0

sea level

−86 metres

Death Valley

★62

Talk about

Build on your discussions at the start of Unit 1– Whole and part numbers by asking children to tell you the properties of place value and to explain the meaning of the words positional, multiplicative, additive and Base 10. Move the conversation on to discuss the fact that −4 is called negative four and not minus four.

Engaging and exploring

Ask children to work in pairs to look at each picture and discuss the accompanying question. Focus on each picture in turn.

For the pictures of the temperature gauges, ask children if they can identify these objects. The first is a thermometer that records the temperature in Fahrenheit. Ask them what they notice about the scale. Agree that its range is from –60° to 120°, the divisions represent 20° and the unit of measure is F. Establish that F is degrees Fahrenheit, a unit that was commonly used in the UK and one that is still used in the US. Ask children to read the temperature on the gauge. It reads –30 °F, which is equivalent to about –34 °C. Ask them where they think this thermometer might be located in the world. Look at the next gauge. Agree that one of these is likely to be in someone's home as it is a central heating thermostat. A person would set this so that a

certain temperature is reached in their home. Ask children to look at the scale and identify the intervals. Write the words 'room temperature' on the board, and invite children to tell you what this term means. Challenge them to guess the temperature of the classroom. Write their suggestions on the board. If possible, check the temperature of the classroom using a thermometer. Agree that in the UK a comfortable room temperature is 20 °C. Ask children to work out the difference between –34 °C and 20 °C. They could draw a number line to help them count on from the lowest to the highest temperature.

Ask children what the chart with Mt. McKinley and Death Valley shows. Agree the height of Mt. McKinley and the lowest point of Death Valley. Ask children to find the difference between these measurements in metres. Ask children what they notice about the measurements below sea level. Agree that they are written in negative numbers.

For the picture of the bank balance, ask children how the information is presented. Establish that it is a line graph. This line graph shows that in February, March, July, August and September there are negative amounts of money. Establish that this is when a person owes the bank money. You could ask children why this might be. If time allows, ask questions about amounts the person had in their account during other months. You could then ask children to write a story based on the whole-class discussions.

Focus on the picture of the stopwatch. Challenge children to tell you the time shown on the stopwatch. Discuss what each digit represents, paying particular attention to the last two digits. Establish that they are hundredths of seconds. Ask children to write what the 30 would look like as a number (0.30). Talk about where time to the hundredth second is used in real life. Examples may include sport, e.g. to record race times in Formula One, swimming and sprinting. Give pairs a stopwatch to experiment with. They could time themselves doing short tasks and then convert any hundredth seconds to a decimal number, as above.

Checking understanding

You will know children have mastered the concepts in this unit when they can represent and explain negative numbers in context and can find differences between them. They will be able to interpret information from a line graph. They will also be able to explain times on a stopwatch and convert simple times to seconds with two decimal places.

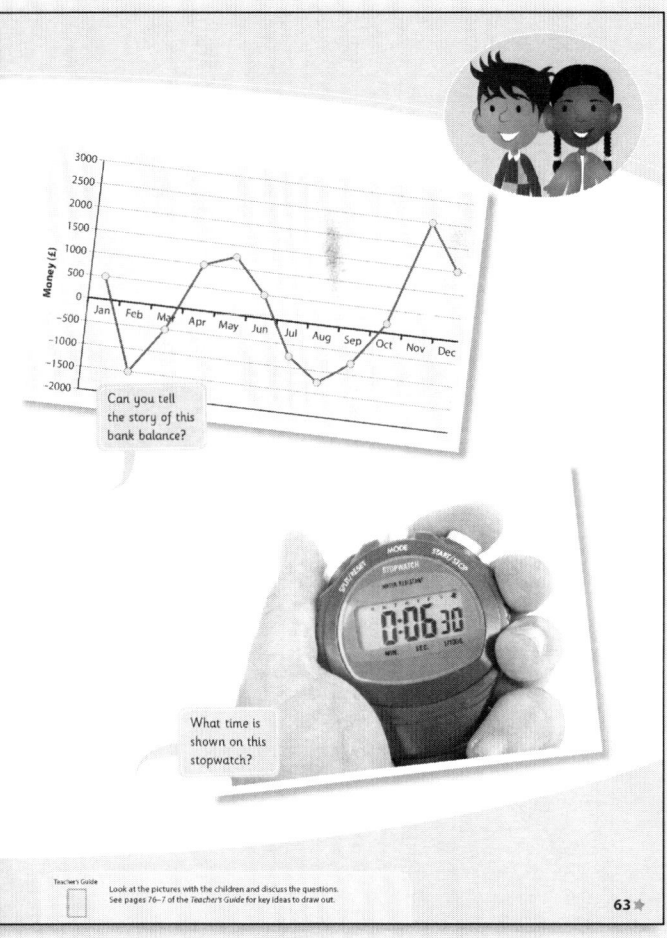

Can you tell the story of this bank balance?

What time is shown on this stopwatch?

Teacher's Guide Look at the pictures with the children and discuss the questions. See pages 76–7 of the *Teacher's Guide* for key ideas to draw out.

63

Things to think about

- How will you make effective use of additional adults in the classroom? One idea might be to use them as the eyes and ears of the classroom when children are measuring masses and volumes, spotting any children who may be struggling to understand a concept.

- How will you organise quick intervention sessions outside the mathematics lesson for those children who need extra support? Good practice in mastery suggests that any children needing extra teaching should be taught by the teacher for around 15 minutes at another time during the day.

Negative numbers in real life

- **Use negative numbers in context, and calculate intervals across zero.**
- **Solve problems that involve number and place value.**
- **Interpret and construct line graphs and use these to solve problems.**

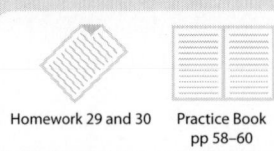

Homework 29 and 30   Practice Book pp 58–60

Mathematical vocabulary

Negative numbers, positive, negative, line graphs, time, continuous data

Representations and resources

Metre ruler, counters in two different colours, temperature and time graphs, bank statements, squared paper, number line, 10 × 10 grid.

Warming up

Show children a metre ruler. Tell them that zero is at one end and one is at the other end. Challenge them to tell you what steps they need to count in to get from zero to one. Agree tenths. Together, count from one end to the other in tenths. Repeat this but at points stop and ask: *How many tenths are there?* Seek answers and invite a child to give the appropriate multiplication statement, e.g. $0.1 \times 7 = 0.7$.

Background knowledge

The middle of our number system is zero and numbers increase infinitely to the right (positive numbers) and decrease infinitely to the left (negative numbers). Ensure that you use the term 'negative' and not 'minus'.

The effect of adding and subtracting negative numbers is opposite to the effect of adding and subtracting positive numbers. When adding positive three, the answer will be higher; when adding negative three, the answer will be lower. When subtracting positive three, the answer will be lower; when subtracting negative three, the answer will be higher.

Let's learn: Modelling and teaching

Calculating with positive and negative numbers

- Together, look at the Textbook page and discuss how to add and subtract negative and positive numbers. Ask children to put a finger on a number on the number line, say four, and add negative five. Discuss the fact that the answer is smaller because you have added a negative number. Repeat for other calculations, such as $-3 + -4$, $-7 + 9$, $-5 - -2$.

- Set up $-4 + 3$ using counters as shown in the Textbook. Discuss why $-4 + 3$ and $3 + -4$ give the same answers. Bring out the idea of commutativity. Ask children to practise adding positive and negative numbers by pairing their own counters. The answer will be the number of counters that remain.

- Move on to calculating positive and negative 2-digit numbers, e.g. $29 + -21$, $-35 + -15$, $10 - -12$. Allow children who need support to draw number lines but encourage all children to write down the number statements correctly.

Negative numbers on graphs

- Discuss when negative numbers are used in real life. Look

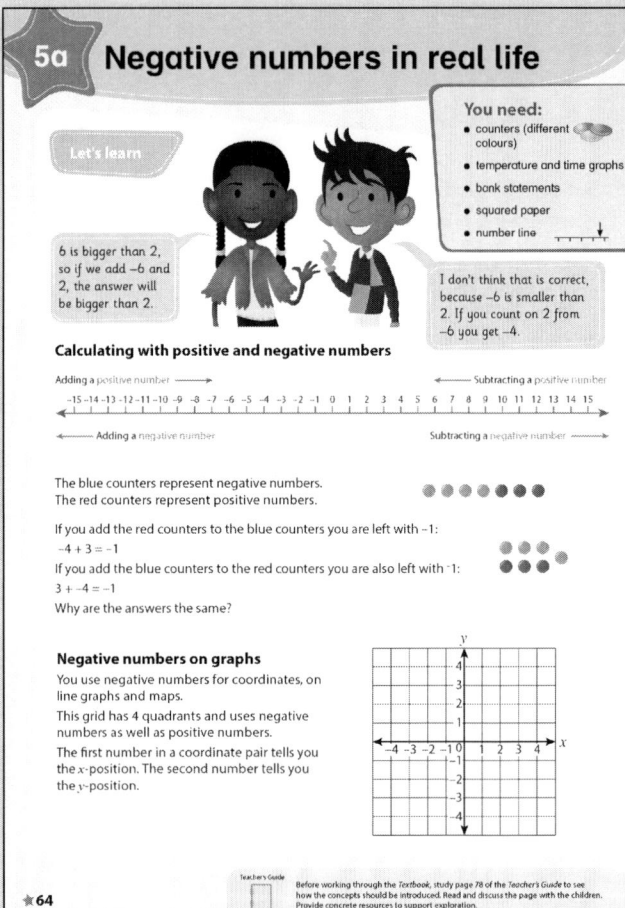

back at the unit opener and ask children if they can think of any other examples (such as lifts that go below the ground floor of buildings). Highlight examples which can be represented on graphs and maps.

- Give them some temperature and time graphs to explore and make statements from. Provide data (including negative numbers) so that they can create their own graphs, e.g. temperatures recorded over a week.

- Give children squared paper. Ask them to make a copy of the four-quadrant grid in the Textbook. Call out two pairs of coordinates for children to plot in each quadrant. They then join the points to make a shape. What shape have they made?

Let's practise: Digging deeper

Step 1

The task requires children to add and subtract positive and negative numbers. If necessary, remind them that when adding positive numbers the result increases and when subtracting it decreases. When dealing with negative numbers the opposite happens. Demonstrate this using a number line, emphasising when you are moving to the right (increasing) and when to the left (decreasing). Some children may be able to answer the questions by mental calculation; others might benefit from using number lines.

Step 2

Recap the procedure of plotting the coordinate on the horizontal axis first and then the one on the vertical axis. Give children squared paper. Ask them to draw their own coordinate grid like the one in the Textbook. They then need to plot the coordinates given with a cross and join the crosses to make a shape. If time allows, encourage them to write coordinates for other shapes to give to a partner to plot and draw.

Step 3

Briefly recap how to draw a line graph. Include labelling the vertical and horizontal axes, deciding what would be sensible multiples for the divisions on the vertical axis and giving the graph a title. Ask children what a line graph shows. Agree that it shows information over a period of time and that this is called continuous data. Lead children to conclude that the data in the line graph is connected to ice turning to boiling water. They work out the difference between the highest and lowest temperatures and make up a story for the graph. They should write this down or tell a partner. They then draw their own line graph and tell its story. Observe how confidently children draw their axes and whether they decide to include negative numbers.

Step 4

Recap adding and subtracting positive and negative numbers. During the task children need to answer the two addition and two subtraction calculations. They write down what they notice for each: the answer to $4 + -2$ is the same as the one for $4 - 2$. They then try to work out a rule. Use careful questioning to support children in explaining what they notice.

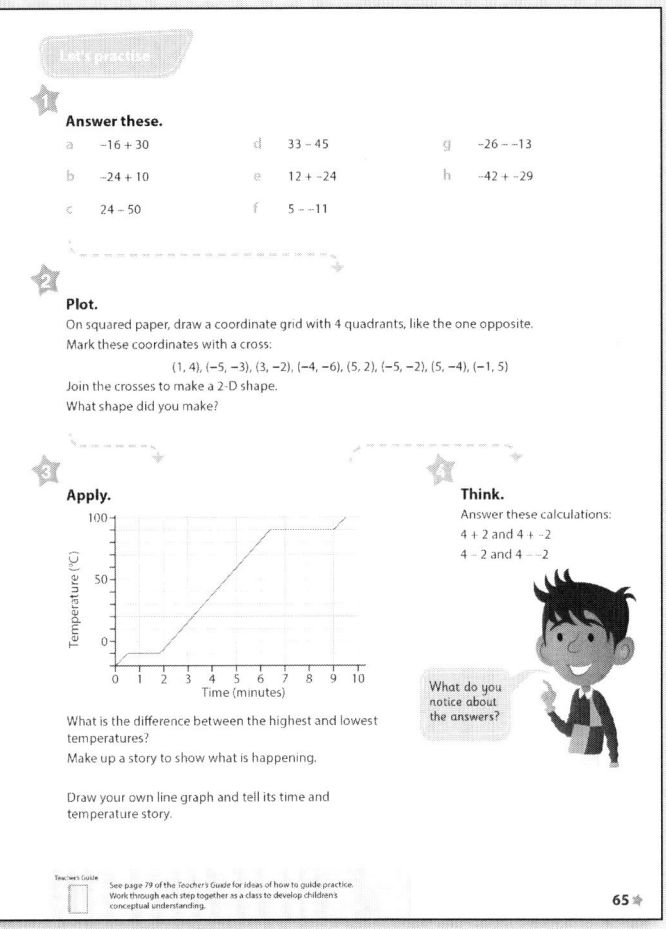

Ensuring progress

Supporting understanding

Adding and subtracting negative numbers can confuse some children. For those who need extra support, use the hot air balloon model to help them. Add hot air (positive number), the balloon goes higher. Add sandbags (negative number), the balloon goes lower. Subtract hot air (positive number), the balloon goes lower. Subtract sandbags (negative number), the balloon goes higher.

Broadening understanding

If children find any of the questions simple, give them higher positive and negative numbers to add and subtract.

> ✓ **Concept mastered**
>
> Children can explain and demonstrate how to add and subtract negative numbers. They can give examples of where negative numbers can be found in real life.

Follow-up ideas

- Children could work in small groups to make a poster about negative numbers in real life. Expect them to use examples worked on in class and any others they can think of. They should include an illustration and a written explanation for each.

- Give 20 small cards to pairs of children. They each write an addition symbol on one card and a subtraction symbol on another and keep these two cards. They then write a negative number on half of the remaining cards, and a positive number on the other half. They place the negative and positive number cards face down on the table in two piles. Children pick one of each and place them face up. They place their operation card between the two numbers and work out the answer.

Answers

Step 1

a	14	b	−14
c	−26	d	−12
e	−12	f	16
g	−13	h	−71

Step 2

Check the crosses are in the correct positions. Shape: (irregular) heptagon.

Step 3

Answers will vary. Difference 120 °C.

Step 4

$4 + 2 = 6$ (sum increases); $4 + -2 = 2$ (sum decreases)

$4 - 2 = 2$ (difference decreases); $4 - -2 = 6$ (difference increases)

- **Identify the value of each digit in numbers given to three decimal places, and multiply and divide numbers by 1000 giving answers up to three decimal places.**
- **Solve number and practical problems that involve all of the above.**

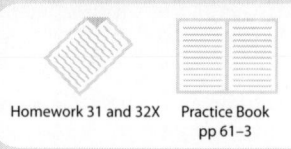

Homework 31 and 32X   Practice Book pp 61–3

Representations and resources

Pendulum (three interlocking cubes on a piece of string), place-value grids, sets of digit cards, stopwatches, jugs and water, weighing scales and sand.

Mathematical vocabulary

Two decimal places, hundredths, three decimal places, thousandths, place value

Warming up

Rehearse multiplication facts. Swing a pendulum from side to side. As it swings, ask children to count in steps of seven from seven to 84 and back again. Call out one of the numbers they said, e.g. 56. Ask them to write down the multiplication and division facts for that number, e.g. $8 \times 7 = 56$, $7 \times 8 = 56$, $56 \div 7 = 8$, $56 \div 8 = 7$. Repeat this for other multiples of seven. Then move on to count in different steps, e.g. eight and nine. Focus on other facts that you might want children to rehearse and recall.

Background knowledge

In Unit 1, children spent time focusing on the place value of digits in numbers to 1 000 000 with up to two decimal places. They also multiplied and divided by 10 and 100. This concept spread extends those themes to numbers with three decimal places and multiplying and dividing by 1000. This is an opportunity to put what children know and what they learn into the contexts of length, time, mass, capacity/volume.

Let's learn: Modelling and teaching

Two decimal places in context

- Give children a laminated place-value grid and a set of digit cards. Ask them to make up 2-digit numbers with two decimal places. Tell them to imagine that these are metres. Challenge them to write the measurements in three ways, e.g. 23.14 m, 23 m 14 cm, 2314 cm. Ask children to explain their method for doing this. Ensure that they talk about place value ($14\,cm = \frac{14}{100}\,m$) and multiplying or dividing by 100.

- Give pairs of children a stopwatch. There should be no times on the display. Ask them to press start. After a few seconds they press stop and then write down the time in seconds to two decimal places (hundredths of a second).

- Ask children to convert 2 minutes 15 seconds to seconds. Agree that because there are 60 seconds in a minute, this would be 135 seconds. Repeat with other examples. Stop watches can record hundredths of a second. 0:02:13.24 is 133.24 seconds This is 2 minutes, 13 seconds and $\frac{24}{100}$ of a second. 2 minutes = 120 seconds, $120 + 13 = 133$ seconds so total = 133.24

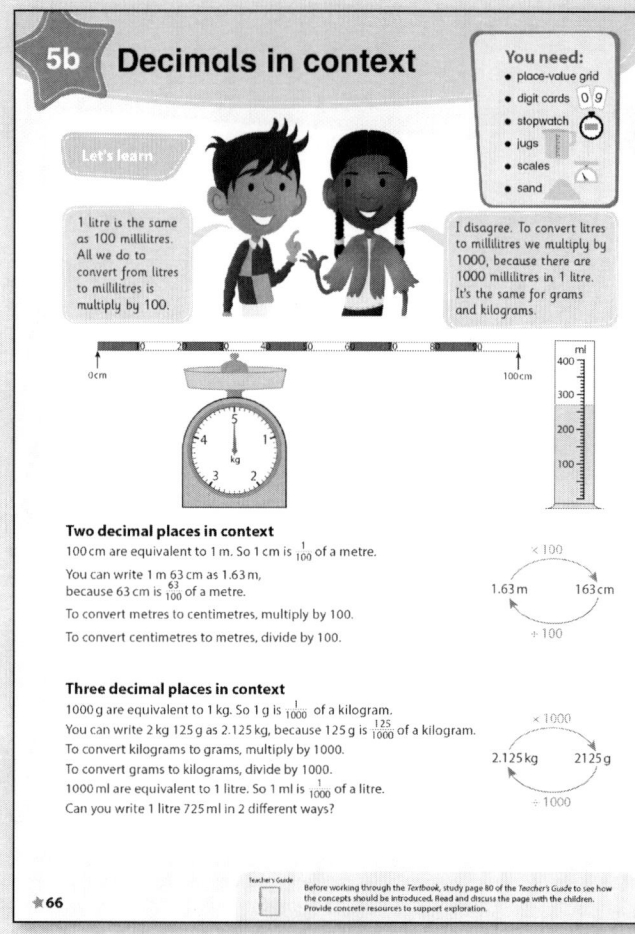

Three decimal places in context

- Give children a place-value grid that has a thousandths column and a set of digit cards. Ask them to make up 2-digit numbers with three decimal places. Explore the place value of each decimal digit. Ask them to imagine that the numbers are a mass. They write the measurements in three ways, e.g. 15.145 kg, 15 kg 145 g, 15 145 g. Establish that you can convert between grams and kilograms by multiplying and dividing by 1000. Repeat for different volumes.

- Give children measuring jugs and water. Ask them to measure volumes that are litres and millilitres and to write the results as litres and millilitres and litres. Repeat this with weighing scales and sand.

Let's practise: Digging deeper

Step 1

The first part of the task asks children to convert from centimetres to metres, covering measurements with two decimal places. The second part requires them to convert from millilitres to litres, covering measurements with three decimal places.

Step 2

The task asks children to convert the stopwatch times to seconds with two decimal places. They need to convert any minutes to seconds and add on the seconds already there, then write the times. Before they begin the task, rehearse converting different numbers of minutes to seconds. Write some times on the board, e.g. 4 minutes 34.45 seconds, and ask children to write them as seconds to two decimal places.

Step 3

Ask children to discuss with a partner the small tasks that they could choose to do. They could do those suggested and think of two more, or they could make up four of their own. Once they have decided they gather any equipment they need to use. They then use a stopwatch to time each other as they carry out the tasks. They record their times in minutes and seconds to two decimal places.

Step 4

This task requires children to make as many different gram masses as they can from six, three, nine and two. It asks them to be systematic. Discuss what systematic means. Agree that it means working in a way that is methodical, organised and efficient. Encourage them to find the masses that begin 63, then 69 and finally 62. They then move on to masses that begin 36, 39 and 32 and so on. You could ask children to find the sum of all the masses and to then suggest a real-life object that may weigh this.

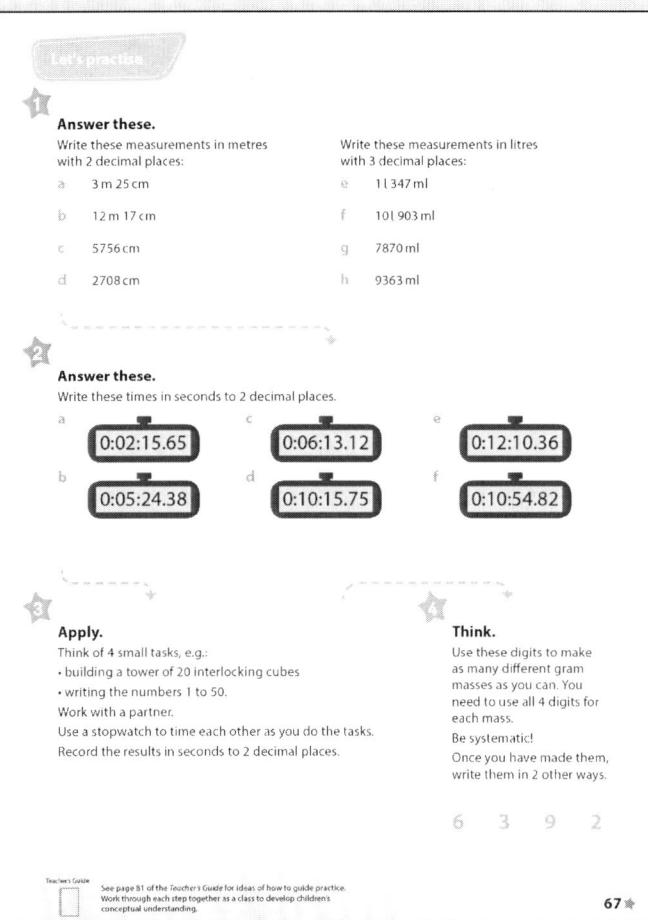

Ensuring progress

Supporting understanding

Ensure less confident children work in a mixed attainment group when measuring. Give them a specific role to play to ensure they take part. You may need to work with them in a focus group to give them further support in deciding how to record measurements such as 2 kg 250 g to two or one decimal place. This will enable them to approach step 2 with confidence.

Broadening understanding

Once children have completed the tasks, ask them to make up stopwatch times that have a digit in each position, including the hour, and to convert these to seconds with two decimal places. They could also make masses with three digits and a zero. Ask them to compare the number of different masses they make with the number made in step 4. Can they explain why there are fewer?

 Concept mastered

Children can explain and demonstrate how to record measurements to two and three decimal places. They are able to tell you what each digit in the decimal positions represents. They can convert between units of length, mass and volume/capacity.

Follow-up ideas

- Provide opportunities for children to practise measuring lengths. They should measure in centimetres and millimetres, then record the lengths in centimetres with one decimal place. Once they have four or five measurements, ask them to compare pairs of measurements to identify what is the same and what is different about them.

- Groups of children could organise an outdoor running competition. They decide the start and finish lines and then time each other, recording the times in seconds to two decimal places.

Answers

Step 1			
a	3.25 m	e	1.347 l
b	12.17 m	f	10.903 l
c	57.56 m	g	7.870 l
d	27.08 m	h	9.363 l

Step 2

a 135.65 seconds

b 324.38 seconds

c 373.12 seconds

d 615.75 seconds

e 730.36 seconds

f 654.82 seconds

Step 3

Answers will vary.

Step 4

6392 g, 6329 g, 6932 g, 6923 g, 6239 g, 6293 g, 3692 g, 3629 g, 3962 g, 3926 g, 3269 g, 3296 g, 9632 g, 9623 g, 9362 g, 9326 g, 9263 g, 9236 g, 2639 g, 2693 g, 2369 g, 2396 g, 2963 g, 2936 g

Children should also write each mass in two other ways, e.g. 6.392 kg and 6 kg 392 g.

Game 1: How low can you go?

Players compete against each other to make the lowest possible number with three decimal places.

Maths focus

- Identify the value of digits in numbers with up to three decimal places; compare and order decimal numbers

Resources

2 decimal point cards, 1 counter per player (1 colour per player), 2 sets of digit cards.

How to play

This game should be played in pairs. Each player takes a decimal point card. They then place their counter on Start. One player shuffles the digit cards together and places them face down on the table. Each player takes four digit cards and uses them, plus their decimal point card, to make a number with three decimal places. The player who makes the lowest number moves their counter one place towards the dartboard. Players return the digit cards to the pack, shuffle them and repeat. The winner is the first player to land on the dartboard.

Making it easier

Children could take three digit cards and make a number with two decimal places.

Making it harder

Children could take five digit cards and make a 2-digit number with three decimal places.

Game 3: Your game

Children should invent their own game, designing rules that use the concepts covered in the unit. Challenge children to make their game easier or harder.

Game 2: Add or subtract?

Children add and subtract negative and positive numbers. They must get the right answer to move across the board.

Maths focus

- Add and subtract positive and negative numbers; calculate intervals across zero

Resources

Number cards from −10 to 10 (omitting 0), 1 counter per player (1 colour per player), 1–6 dice (1).

How to play

This game should be played in pairs. The cards with the numbers from −10 to 10 should be placed face down on the table in two piles, one of negative numbers and the other of positive numbers. Each player places their counter on Start. They then each pick a card, one player picking from the negative pile and the other from the positive pile. They take it in turns to throw the dice. The first player to throw an even number decides how to add or subtract the numbers on the two cards to find the total or difference. Their partner checks the answer. If the first player's answer is correct, they move their counter forward one space towards the dartboard. Play continues until one player reaches the dartboard and wins.

Making it easier

The pair each pick two cards, one from the negative number pile and the other from the positive number pile. Whoever has the closest number to zero moves one space towards the dartboard.

Making it harder

Children aim to achieve the highest possible result for each pair of cards. If their partner can see a way to get a higher result, they explain this and then they move forward instead.

Unit 5

Number darts

Choose a game to play.

Game 1: How low can you go?

You need:
- 2 decimal point cards
- 1 counter per player (1 colour per player)
- 2 sets of digit cards

How to play

- Each take a decimal point card.
- Place your counter on Start.
- Shuffle the digit cards together.
- Each take 4 digit cards. Use them, plus your decimal point card, to make a number with 3 decimal places. Make the lowest number you can.
- Compare your number with your partner's. The player who made the lowest number moves 1 place towards the dartboard.
- Put the digit cards back in the pack and shuffle them.
- Keep going until a player lands on the dartboard and wins.

Game 2: Add or subtract?

You need:
- number cards from −10 to 10 (not 0)
- 1 counter per player (1 colour per player)
- 1–6 dice

How to play

- Place the number cards face down in 2 piles, 1 of negative numbers and 1 of positive numbers.
- Place your counter on Start.
- One player picks a card from the positive pile, the other player from the negative pile. Place the 2 cards face up on the table.
- Take it in turns to throw the dice.
- If you throw an even number, add or subtract the numbers on the cards to work out an answer.
- If your partner agrees it is correct, move your counter forward 1 space.
- Pick 2 cards as before and place them face up on the table.
- Keep playing until a player reaches the dartboard and wins.

Game 3: Your game

- Make up your own game using the gameboard.
- What are the rules for your game? Explain them to a friend.

Please help your child by reading the instructions and playing the game together.

Assessment task 1

Resources

Number line.

Running the task

Before beginning the task, recap the work children have done on negative numbers. Can they remember what happens when a negative number is added to another number? What about when a negative number is subtracted from another number? Agree that adding and subtracting negative numbers is the opposite to adding and subtracting positive numbers. Ask children to describe the contexts they considered for negative numbers. Expect them to talk about temperature, money, below sea level and other examples.

Direct children to the diagram of the cliff and water. Check they understand the information shown.

During the task, listen to groups of children discuss the problem and explain to each other what the actual difference is. Work with any children who find the task difficult by showing them the difference on a number line. This will enable them to visualise the difference between the two numbers. With this help, they should be able to see that the two numbers need adding together. You could start with numbers that have a smaller difference, e.g. −2 and 24, and gradually work up to those in the task. Once children have established that the difference between the two numbers is 118 m, ask them to identify what Anya did to get a difference of 102 m.

Evidencing mastery

If children are able to identify the actual difference and what Anya did wrong quickly and confidently, you can be assured that they have mastered this aspect of negative numbers.

Work with children who have not yet mastered this in an intervention group and determine the difference between negative and positive numbers as described above.

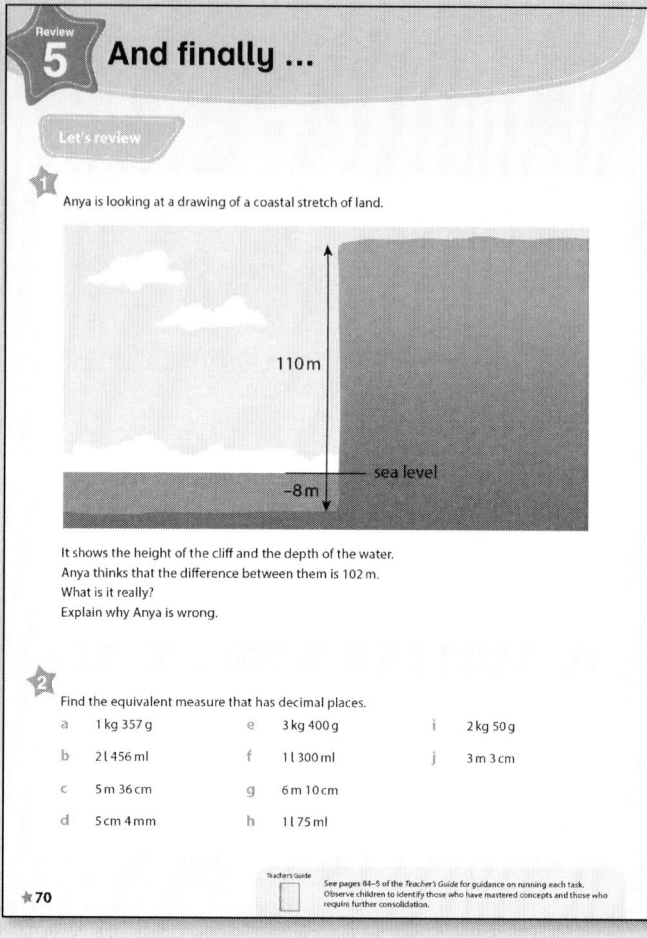

Review 5

And finally …

Let's review

1 Anya is looking at a drawing of a coastal stretch of land.

110 m

sea level

−8 m

It shows the height of the cliff and the depth of the water.
Anya thinks that the difference between them is 102 m.
What is it really?
Explain why Anya is wrong.

2 Find the equivalent measure that has decimal places.

a	1 kg 357 g	e	3 kg 400 g	i	2 kg 50 g
b	2 l 456 ml	f	1 l 300 ml	j	3 m 3 cm
c	5 m 36 cm	g	6 m 10 cm		
d	5 cm 4 mm	h	1 l 75 ml		

Teacher's Guide — See pages 84–5 of the *Teacher's Guide* for guidance on running each task. Observe children to identify those who have mastered concepts and those who require further consolidation.

★ 70

Assessment task 2

Resources

Place-value grids, digit cards.

Running the task

Recap converting between units of measure. Remind children that to convert measurements from the higher unit to the lower unit they would need to multiply by 100 or 1000. Ask children to talk to a partner and come up with examples. Take feedback and invite children to demonstrate an example of what they were talking about on the board. Write some decimal measures on the board, e.g. 2.3 kg. Ask children to write them as mixed units and grams. Repeat for metres and centimetres, kilometres and metres, and litres and millilitres.

Sit with groups of children and observe how they carry out the task. The task asks children to convert the mixed unit measures to the largest unit and show the smaller unit as decimals. Expect most children to be able to, e.g. write 3 kg 400 g

as 3.4 kg. Expect some to be able to identify that in, e.g. 1 l 75 ml there are no hundreds of millilitres and therefore a place holder is needed in the tenths position. The answer will be 1.075 l. You may need to support children in this. If so, work with them to help them understand what happens on these occasions. Give them place-value grids and digit cards so that they can physically make the number. On completion of the task, ask children to change the decimal notation to a fraction in its lowest term.

Evidencing mastery

All children should be able to convert some of the measurements successfully. Children who show mastery will be able to convert all of them and explain why 1.075 l isn't recorded as 1.75 l. Make a note of the names of any children who struggle to complete the task. Work with them in an intervention group at a time outside the mathematics lesson.

Use the digits to make up some volumes in litres that have 1, 2 and 3 decimal places.

Find all the possibilities.
Explain how you know you have found them all.

Write each volume using litres and millilitres.

For example,
28.86 l = 28 l 860 ml

Did you know?

Negative numbers weren't commonly used in Europe until the nineteenth century.

In India negative numbers were used much earlier. The mathematician Brahmagupta wrote the first set of rules in the seventh century. He used the ideas of fortunes and debts for positive and negative.

71

Concepts mastered

✓ Children can explain and demonstrate how to add and subtract negative numbers and also give examples of where negative numbers can be found in real life contexts.

✓ Children can explain and demonstrate how to record measurements to two and three decimal places and tell you what each digit in the decimal positions represents. They can convert between units of length, mass and volume/capacity.

Assessment task 3

Resources
Digit cards, rubber (decimal point).

Running the task
Children use the digits two, five, eight and six to make up as many volumes as they can using decimals. Some of them will be able to write, e.g. 2.586 l, 25.86 l and 258.6 l for each set of six possible combinations for the digits given. Encourage them to be systematic and persevere to find as many decimal numbers as they can. During the task visit groups and ask individuals you particularly want to assess to tell you the place value of the digits in the numbers they have made. Expect them to tell you the positional and multiplicative properties of each. Check they can relate the numbers in the decimal places to millilitres. Some children may benefit from using digit cards and a rubber or something similar as the decimal point. They set their digit cards out, and place the rubber in different positions to make the new numbers.

Evidencing mastery
Most children should be able to make some decimal numbers independently. There are numerous possibilities and time may not allow children to find them all. If children can confidently make as many possibilities as time allows systematically and they can demonstrate understanding of what each digit in the numbers represents and how they have changed from one number to the next, they will have evidenced mastery. Some children may not work systematically. This is an important skill, so work with them in a focused group next time this type of working is needed.

Did you know?

The use of negative numbers wasn't common in Europe until the nineteenth century, when British mathematicians including De Morgan and Peacock used logic to set out the laws of arithmetic. Previously, Western mathematicians considered negative numbers mysterious and nonsensical, although by the seventeenth century a few were more open-minded and decided that negative numbers could be used in calculations, although they still deemed negative solutions false.

In India negative numbers were used much earlier. In the seventh century, the mathematician Brahmagupta wrote the first set of rules using the ideas of fortunes and debts for positive and negative. Brahmagupta was also the first to describe how to calculate using zero.

In China negative numbers were used as early as 200 BCE. The Chinese had a rod system where red rods represented positive numbers and black rods represented negative numbers. Again, this was relating to money. Red meant someone had received some money and black meant that someone had paid out some money. Money appears to be the first reason for introducing positive and negative numbers.

Mathematical focus

★ **Number: addition, subtraction, multiplication and division, fractions (including decimals and percentages)**

★ **Algebra: simple formulae, linear number sequences, number problems**

★ **Measurement: length, time**

★ **Statistics: interpret and calculate, interpret and construct**

Prior learning

Children should already be able to:

- add and subtract numbers mentally with increasingly large numbers

- interpret negative numbers in context

- identify the value of each digit in a number given to two decimal places

- round decimals with two decimal places to the nearest whole number and to one decimal place.

Key new learning

- Perform mental calculations, including with mixed operations and large numbers.

- Solve problems involving addition and subtraction; use estimation to check answers to calculations and determine, in the context of a problem, an appropriate degree of accuracy.

- Use negative numbers in context and calculate intervals across zero.

- Solve addition and subtraction multi-step problems in contexts, deciding which operations and methods to use and why.

- Solve problems which require answers to be rounded to specified degrees of accuracy.

- Solve problems involving the calculation and conversion of units of measure, using decimal notation to three decimal places where appropriate.

- Use simple formula; generate and describe linear number sequences.

- Express missing number problems algebraically.

Making connections

- Children can relate negative numbers to temperature. They can also see how negative numbers are used in banking and business.

- Using pie charts and line graphs to solve problems will be useful across the curriculum, e.g. in geography and science.

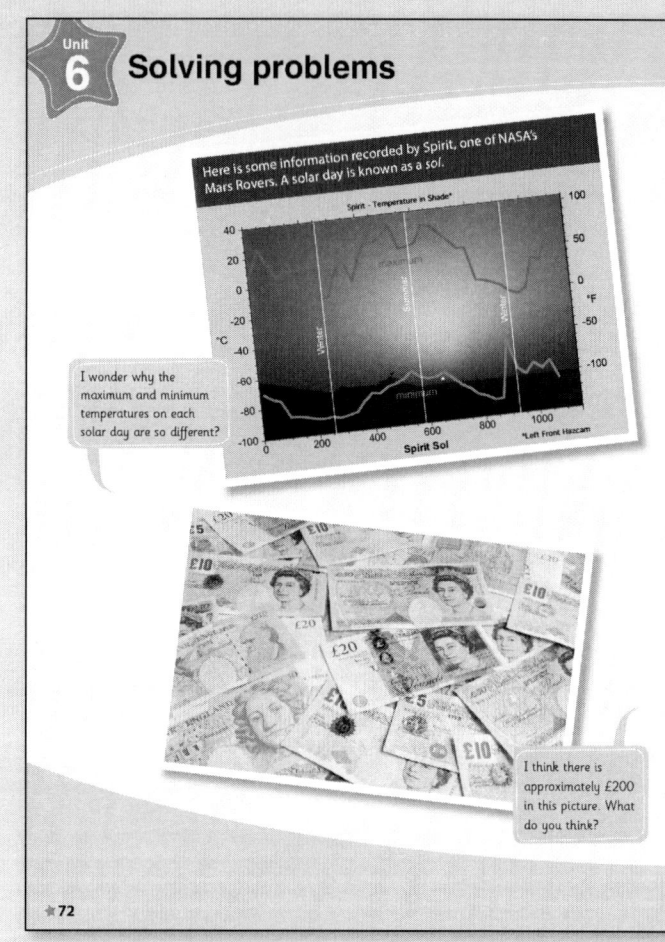

Unit
6 Solving problems

★72

 Talk about

It is important to use precise mathematical vocabulary from the beginning and encourage all adults to use it consistently. Throughout this unit, continue to reinforce the vocabulary that children have built up, such as augend + addend = sum and multiplicand × multiplier = product. Children should be confident to use a range of language, interchanging fluently, e.g. the difference between 7.5 and 9.2 is 1.7, 9.2 is 1.7 more than 7.5, 9.2 subtract 7.5 equals 1.7, the sum of 7.5 and 9.2 is 16.7, etc.

Engaging and exploring

Focus on each picture in turn, asking children to discuss ideas with a partner. Use this as an opportunity to assess children's understanding about negative and positive numbers, estimating, fractions and sequences.

For the picture of the line graph, you could ask children what they know about Mars or any of the other planets in terms of their temperatures. Discuss the 'story' of the line graph so that children understand the terms used, e.g. a sol is a solar day on Mars, and why there are two sets of data. Agree the scale of the graph and identify a range of temperatures. Find the difference between some of the maximum temperatures. Consider the question and discuss possibilities, e.g. day and night temperatures, thinking also about the differences in day and night temperatures on Earth.

Research the places on Earth with extreme temperatures and compare these with the ones on Mars. Is the lowest temperature recorded at the poles lower or higher than on Mars? (−89.2 °C was recorded at the Soviet Vostok Station in Antarctica, on July 21, 1983.) You could find out more about the length of a sol and compare it to a day on Earth. (A sol is 39 minutes 35.24409 seconds longer.) *How can we round this to the nearest hundredth of a second?*

For the picture of the money, you could ask children to quickly find the number of each denomination of the notes. Without calculating the total, discuss the estimate to determine whether children feel it is sensible. Discuss how a quick estimate could be made. *Where would we start?* You could suggest that children spot the largest value notes first. Encourage children to use multiplication to find the value of the money in the photo. Focus on mental strategies for multiplying twenties, e.g. multiplying by 10 and then doubling, and for mentally adding values. Give children plastic money and ask them to make the final amount using the fewest notes possible.

For the photo of the clocks, you could discuss strategies to calculate how long Eva took on her homework, focusing on the way the times are shown on the different clocks. Revisit Roman numerals and the 24-hour clock using real clocks and alongside the images in the Textbook. Ask children what they think Ali means by a 'fraction of the time'. What fractions could he mean? Encourage children to calculate different fractions of 80 minutes, e.g. $\frac{1}{2}, \frac{3}{4}, \frac{3}{8}, \frac{4}{5}, \frac{7}{10}$. Ask what would be a silly fraction to use here, e.g. $\frac{4}{7}$ as Ali would have to record that he had done his homework in 45.714284 seconds! Suggest that Ali started his homework at the same time as Eva. Using their chosen fraction, encourage children to record the time that he finished using 24-hour clock notation.

For the photo of the building bricks, ask children to recreate the pattern using similar manipulatives, discussing how the pattern grows each time. *What is different and what stays the same?* Challenge children to describe or create the next pattern in the sequence, carefully explaining to each other the change that needs to be made. Suggest that the pattern increases by the same number of individual pieces (cubes) each time. Can they prove this to be true? Record the number of cubes each time and use this to predict the number needed for the fifth, sixth and then tenth pattern in the sequence. Encourage children to make up a linear pattern of their own using cubes or building bricks and be ready to explain how it changes each time.

Things to think about

- How will you continue to raise the profile of mental mathematics and challenge inappropriate methods?
- How will you model and encourage the use of precise mathematical vocabulary when explaining thinking and reasoning?
- How will you organise groupings? Could a stronger reader be paired with a less confident reader so that language does not impede accessing problems?
- How will you use manipulatives and visual representations to help all children with their conceptual understanding?
- How will you make effective use of additional adults? Could they support children to rehearse explanations and model their own thinking?

Checking understanding

You will know children have mastered these concepts when they can solve addition and subtraction problems in different contexts, appropriately choosing and using number facts, place value and mental and written methods. They can explain their decision making, justifying their solution and level of accuracy.

6a Calculating mentally to solve problems

- Perform mental calculations, including with mixed operations and large numbers.
- Solve problems involving addition and subtraction; use estimation to check answers to calculations and determine, in the context of a problem, an appropriate degree of accuracy.
- Use negative numbers in context and calculate intervals across zero.

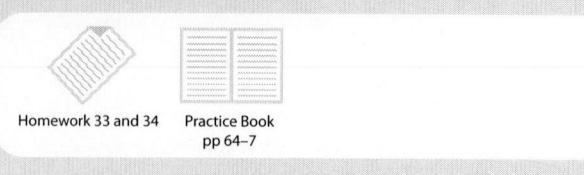

Homework 33 and 34   Practice Book pp 64–7

Representations and resources

Bead strings, + and - number lines, thermometer, line graph from page 72, flip chart.

Mathematical vocabulary

Positive, negative, interval, temperature, Celsius, Fahrenheit, addition, subtraction, difference, difference between, sum

Warming up

Pose the following problem for children to reason about and find a range of possibilities: *Two clocks display times with a difference of 36 minutes. What possible times could the clocks show?* You could use the 'Another, Another, Another' strategy for children to give you a range of possibilities. Extend the problem by suggesting that the 'hours' are not the same on each clock. Discuss which solutions are no longer possible and consider the different ways that the times could be displayed, e.g. analogue, 12-hour digital and 24-hour digital.

Background knowledge

Continue to encourage children to refine mental strategies so that they make appropriate decisions when faced with a calculation. Both time and temperature are valuable contexts to explore the strategy of 'difference' to make sense of intervals, especially those that require children to cross zero or to cross an hour boundary. When partitioning a number across zero, the first step should land on zero. There is an opportunity to explore converting between Fahrenheit and Celsius using the formula $°C = (°F − 32) × \frac{5}{9}$.

Let's learn: Modelling and teaching
Calculating intervals and crossing zero

- Discuss Eva's misconception and why it has arisen. Use the bead string to confirm. Rehearse other differences of 10 that cross zero, drawing on knowledge of number bonds.

- Explain why the calculation 7 – 10 = has been rewritten as 7 – 7 – 3. Use the language of subtrahend and minuend. Ask children to rewrite other difference calculations, e.g. 9 – 10 as 9 – 9 – 1.

- Look at how number bonds of 100 support 53 – 100, using the bead string again to confirm that 53 + 47 sum to 100. Ask children to identify other calculations that number bonds of 100 support, e.g. 65 – 100 or –65 + 100? Model how to draw a number line to show one or more of these calculations. Record the calculation above the number line.

- Explore intervals that cross zero using the bead string representation, e.g. the interval that represents the

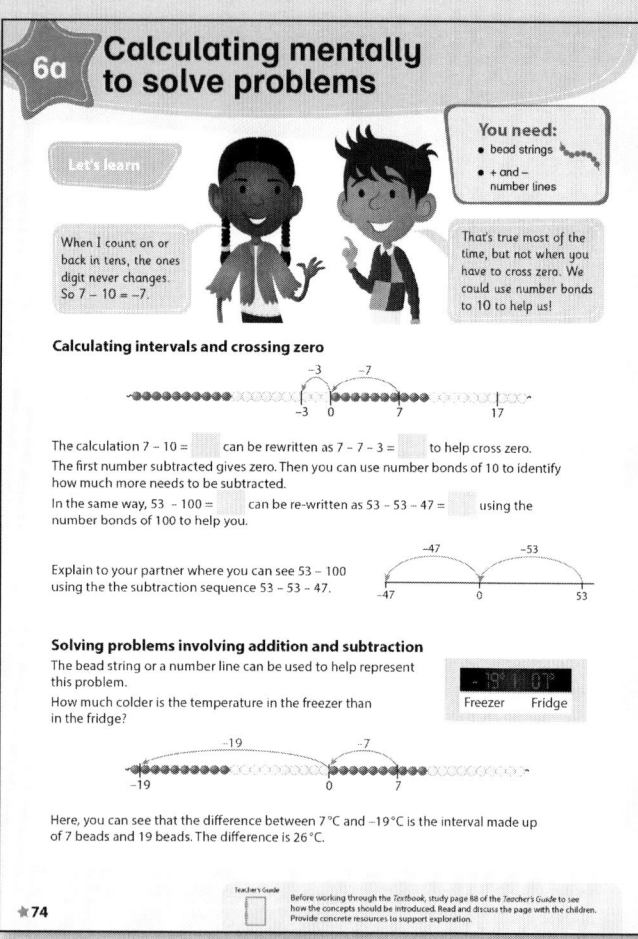

difference between 17 and –12. Then, ask children to draw number lines to show these intervals. Ask them to explain what is the same and what is different about the bead string and number line representations.

Solving problems involving addition and subtraction

- Discuss different real-life examples of positive and negative numbers, including the fridge-freezer display. You could also refer back to the Mars data from page 72.

- Ask children to represent the problem on the bead string or a number line. Discuss strategies to find the difference.

- Encourage them to use a range of language structures to make comparisons, e.g. the temperature in the freezer is 26 °C lower/colder than in the fridge.

Let's practise: Digging deeper

Step 1

Children should draw on patterns and number bonds to 10 to solve the calculations. The questions are written as equations or in words to focus on the use of language to explain or demonstrate an addition or subtraction. Children should continue to use the bead string and number line to model calculations.

Step 2

For this task, children should look for patterns in the numbers and make decisions before calculating. In several questions, only an adjustment in place value is needed rather than having to recalculate. Ensure that children spot this by asking questions such as: *What do you notice? Why is this the case?*

Children should apply mental strategies, such as partitioning and sequencing, and draw on their knowledge of number bonds.

Step 3

The line graph provides a context for comparing positive and negative numbers and calculating intervals. Children first calculate the difference on the 400th solar day. This provides scaffolding so that they can interpret the word 'compare' in part b. They can choose to calculate differences using Celsius or Fahrenheit. Estimates should be encouraged where a value cannot be accurately identified. Children can design their own tables for results and can further develop the activity by making statements about their findings, e.g. the maximum difference in temperature was … ; the minimum temperature was below … for a total of … sols, etc.

Step 4

This logic puzzle is based on the magic square. It requires children to explore differences between positive and negative numbers and find a solution where the centre number is the difference between all adjacent pairs. Some children may benefit from modelling the problem by writing the numbers on squares of paper and experimenting with different positions for each number. However, reinforce that they should not be afraid of writing down their workings and that they may need a few attempts before getting the correct response.

For the second part of the problem, children may well need to refine their solution to meet a second criterion of all corners summing to a single digit. They should consider which pairs of numbers or individual numbers can be moved so that the solution fits both criteria.

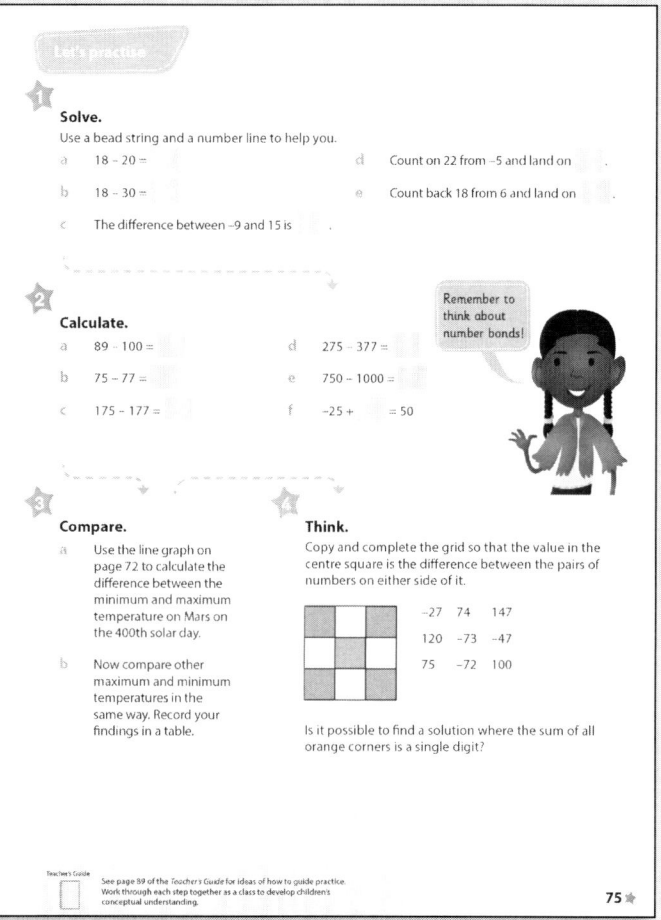

Follow-up ideas

- Use timetables to practise calculating intervals of time, including planning journeys and testing hypotheses, e.g. It is always faster to travel by aeroplane than by train.

- Explore other ways of representing an interval crossing zero using different manipulatives, e.g. number rods.

- Encourage further research of the places on Earth with extreme temperatures and compare these with the ones recorded on Mars (see page 72), or research other data collected by different Rovers on Mars.

Ensuring progress

Supporting understanding

Continue to use the bead string as a visual aid, placing it on flip chart paper and modelling the number line around it. Children should use and explain the pattern of counting back in tens and describe how a ten is formed when it crosses zero, e.g. '3 white beads and 7 red beads, because I need to subtract 7 red beads to get back to zero and I still have 3 white beads to subtract'.

Broadening understanding

Challenge children to make up their own number puzzle as for Step 4, thinking carefully about the number to place in the centre square.

✓ **Concept mastered**

Children can use mental strategies to calculate a difference or an interval between a positive and negative number, and relate this to the context of temperature.

Answers

Step 1

a	−2	d	17
b	−12	e	−12
c	24		

Step 2

a	−11	d	−102
b	−2	e	−250
c	−2	f	75

Step 3

a The maximum temperature is approximately 17 °C and the minimum is −75 °C so the difference is approximately 92 °C.

Step 4

e.g.

−73	120	75
−47	147	100
−72	−27	74

6b Solving multi-step problems

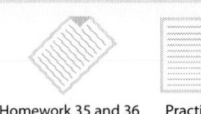

- **Solve addition and subtraction multi-step problems in context deciding which operations and methods to use and why.**
- **Solve problems involving addition and subtraction; use estimation to check answers to calculations and determine, in the context of a problem, an appropriate degree of accuracy.**

Homework 35 and 36   Practice Book pp 68–71

Representations and resources

Coins (£2, £1, 50p, 20p 10p, 5p, 2p, 1p), large squared paper, templates of 6-squared shapes for Step 4, bead strings, number rods and/or number lines.

Mathematical vocabulary

Addition, subtraction, sum, total, difference, reason, pound, pence, estimate, more than

Warming up

Play a conversion game between grams and kilograms. All children start by writing down 2.5 kg. Tell them to add 150 g; they must now record the new mass in grams, i.e. 2650 g. Now tell them to subtract 300 g; they must now record in kg, i.e. 2.35 kg. Then tell them to add 650 g; they now record 3000 g and so on. Shorten the time given as children become more fluent.

Background knowledge

Using money as a practical context provides opportunities to secure fluency when adding and subtracting a multiple number of different coins, and demonstrates the need to apply multiplication for greater efficiency and accuracy. Throughout, encourage children to reason about the language used for addition and subtraction and, therefore, which operations to use and in what order. Draw on BIDMAS (which gives the order of operations). When indices have the same priority, look at ways that number bonds or other known facts can be used to simplify the calculation.

Let's learn: Modelling and teaching

Multi-step money problems

- Ask children to recreate the grid using plastic or real money and to estimate the total value of the grid. Encourage reasoning to help make estimates of how much money is on the grid, e.g. I know there are six £2 coins so there is more than £12 on the grid. Consider different calculation strategies and focus on the relationship between repeated addition and multiplication.

- Explore ways to calculate the total value of the grid. Consider order (e.g. is it better to start with the larger coins?) and strategies to work with a multi-step calculation. Ask: *Can brackets be used to help organise the calculation?* Discuss which were the most efficient strategies.

Choosing operations

- Discuss Ali's statement in the speech bubble, and ask children to suggest examples where this is true. Focus on

Eva's statement and consider examples where subtraction is required. Model examples using a bead string, number rods or a number line, e.g. Ali saves £10 more than Eva. Eva has £12, how much does Ali have? or Ali has £12 how much does Eva have? Consider each problem in the Textbook. What is the same and what is different about the first two problems? i.e. both use 'more than' but one implies addition and the other subtraction.

- Children to work in pairs to find a solution to each of the problems. They can use sketches or jottings to help them. Encourage them to reason about starting points by estimating the values of rows or columns first.

- Again, encourage estimates. Suggest that you will start by considering ways to make 70p.

Let's practise: Digging deeper

Step 1

These questions require children to solve two-step or multi-step calculations using addition and subtraction. Children should also reason about the order in which to calculate as in several questions, reordering will reduce the complexity of the calculations, e.g. part b. Parts c, d and e use the phrase 'more than' so children will need to decide whether to add or subtract.

Step 2

Children must calculate sums of pairs or groups of coins in sections from the original grid. Some might find it helpful to sketch the grids first. Encourage them to use brackets to organise their calculations, and to make use of known totals rather than recalculating. They must then find the differences by looking at subtraction calculations.

Step 3

This provides a practical opportunity to investigate rows and columns, reasoning about the effect of greatest and smallest amounts.

Step 4

Children are required to investigate a hypothesis that involves adding and subtracting amounts formed by two different shapes on the grid. Ensure that children reason about possible combinations rather than calculating randomly. Observe whether children record their findings clearly and systematically. Children can work in groups or an adult can also play the role of a problem solver.

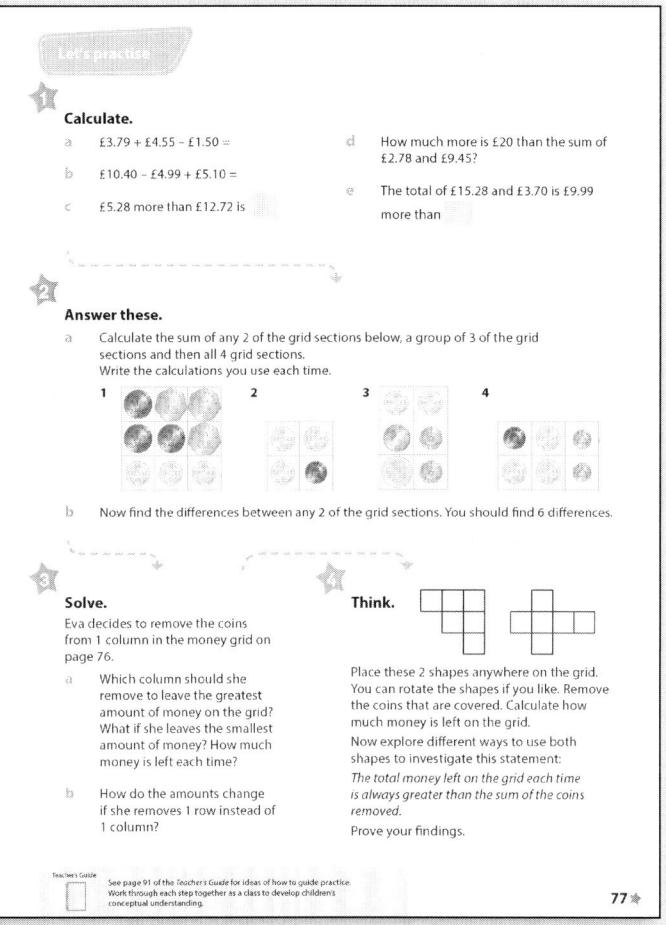

Follow-up ideas

- Children could sort a range of word problems into a Venn diagram using the criteria 'Requires addition', 'Requires subtraction' and, therefore, the overlap requires both. They could create other word problems to add to the diagram.

- Children could continue to explore the order of operations and the use of brackets to organise a more complex calculation. They could look at reordering a calculation requiring addition and subtraction to avoid unnecessary calculations, e.g. $7563 - 9000 + 2300$.

- Children could use catalogues or the Internet to look at purchasing two or more items, working out change from £50 or £100. Extend this to larger numbers by comparing the price of new cars which may have equipment as standard or may require the customer to purchase an optional extra.

Ensuring progress

Supporting understanding

Focus on the language used in different word problems, role-playing each problem and deciding whether it requires addition, subtraction or a combination of both. Give children key words that they have to use to make up problems of their own and model the method to solve it by using manipulatives.

Broadening understanding

Children can create their own money grid, perhaps using a 6 by 6 grid or an 8 by 8 instead. They should consider patterns of coins and the number of each needed to ensure, perhaps, that the total value of the grid is between £15 and £20. They can design grid shapes to use in different investigations, e.g. can they design a grid where the value of the coins left on the grid is always greater than the sum of the coins removed?

 Concept mastered

Children can recognise where addition and/or subtraction are required to solve a problem, explaining why this is the case. They can make appropriate estimates and consider the order of a calculations.

Answers

Step 1

a	£6.84	d	£7.77
b	£10.51	e	£8.99
c	£18.00		

Step 2

a e.g.
$£3.00 + (50p \times 3) + 6p = £4.56$
so $£4.56 + £3.01 = £7.57$ or
spot $£6 + (50p \times 3) + 7p$

b e.g.
$£3.00 + (50p \times 3) + 6p = £4.56$
so $£4.56 - £3.01 = 1.55$
or simply $£1.56 - 1p$ by ignoring the pound coins

Step 3

a Removing column 6 leaves the greatest amount ($£28.62 - £2.00 = £26.62$) on the grid.

Removing column 1 leaves the smallest amount ($£28.62 - £6.80 = £21.82$) on the grid.

b Removing row 2 leaves the greatest amount. It is more than removing column 6 because there are two 2p coins instead of two 5p coins so 6p less is removed. It leaves £26.68 on the grid.

Removing row 7 leaves the same smallest amount as before as all coins are the same as in column 1.

Step 4

Children's own investigation to prove that the statement is not true, e.g. the first shape can be used to cover all the £2 coins (£12 in total) and the second shape can be used to cover four £1 coins and two 50p coins (£5 in total). The total of the grid is £28.62 so the amount left on the grid is $£28.62 - (£12 + £5) = £11.62$. The amount left is less than the amount covered by the shapes.

- Solve problems which require answers to be rounded to specified degrees of accuracy.
- Solve problems involving the calculation and conversion of units of measure, using decimal notation to three decimal places where appropriate.

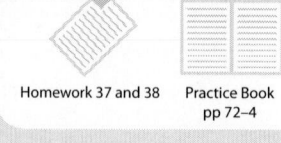

Homework 37 and 38   Practice Book pp 72–4

Representations and resources

Base 10 apparatus, stopwatches.

Mathematical vocabulary

Round, estimate, decimal place, tenth, hundredth, thousandth, sum, difference

Warming up

Provide children with a set of addition/subtraction statements to work out, with at least three numbers in each. Include a range of whole numbers, decimals and fractions (with the same denominators). Challenge children to highlight the two numbers they will use first and explain their decision each time, e.g. 'I noticed the number bond …' or 'I noticed that both have the same decimal value so when I subtract, the result is a whole number'. Children should choose a few examples to write the reordered calculation for.

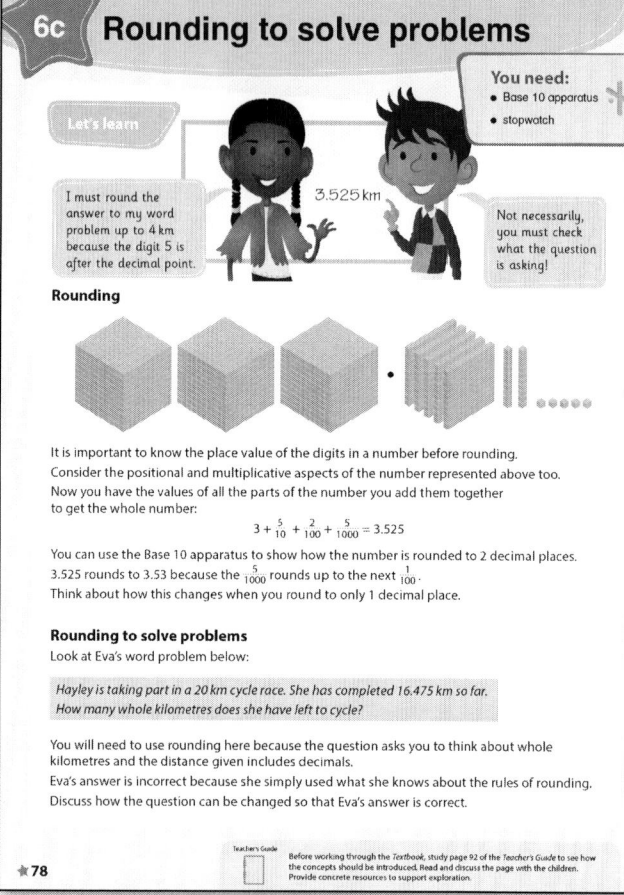

Background knowledge

Children need a secure understanding of place value in order to understand the concept of rounding, particularly when it involves decimals up to three places. Ensure that they experience problems and other tasks that require rounding to a degree of accuracy or to suit the criteria of a problem.

Let's learn: Modelling and teaching

Rounding

- Ask children to use Base 10 apparatus to represent the number 3.525, explaining the positional and multiplicative aspects of the number to their partner, e.g. the 2 is in the hundredths column and its value can be worked out by dividing 2 by one hundred (2 hundredths). Explore how this can be represented as a fraction and decimal using an equivalence wall. Practise representing other decimal numbers in this way and then recombining the parts using addition.

- Focus on rounding 3.525 to 2 decimal places using Base 10 apparatus to model rounding up to 3.53. Explain that 5 thousandths would be rounded up to the nearest 10 thousandths and $\frac{10}{1000}$ is equal to $\frac{1}{100}$. Children should suggest other numbers that round up in this way, e.g. 4.638 rounding to 4.64. Discuss how the number 3.525 should be rounded to 1 decimal place. Again, modelling that this time it rounds down to 3.5 and not up. Children should suggest other numbers that would round up to 3.6.

Rounding to solve problems

- Discuss the word problem, asking children to look carefully at the part of the question that shows that they will need to use rounding.

- Encourage children to make an estimate and consider mental strategies they can use to solve the problem. Does it require addition or subtraction?

- Model the calculation using Base 10 apparatus and the number line, focusing on the positional and multiplicative aspect of the numbers involved, including representing 20 km as 20.000 km.

- Consider changing numbers in the problem that would have required the use of a column method, again encouraging children to use Base 10 apparatus to represent the calculation.

- Refer back to Eva and Ali's discussion about the answer to the problem. Discuss the mistake that Eva has made here, even though she has followed the conventions of rounding. How will the question need to change so that Eva's answer is correct?

Let's practise: Digging deeper
Step 1
Children should describe the positional and multiplicative aspects of the decimal numbers. Children then round the numbers as required. Children should use Base 10 apparatus to represent, describe and reason about rounding numbers up or down.

Step 2
Remind children to think about equivalences that they know and how to work out a decimal equivalence using division, e.g. for $\frac{5}{8}$. Observe whether children decide to use mental or written strategies to find sums and differences of the decimal numbers.

Step 3
Children should use a stopwatch to time the length of different activities to $\frac{1}{100}$ of a second. Activities can be inside or outside the classroom. Encourage children to use number lines to avoid any place-value issues when working with time.

Step 4
Children are required to add pairs of decimal numbers to give a sum that rounds to 13.2 rather than exactly totalling it. Ask questions, e.g. Why does 13.25 not round to 13.2? Encourage them to consider numbers to 3-decimal places. Children should reason about the lowest possible values of a pair of numbers, each written to 2-decimal places. They should identify that 13.15 is the lowest possible sum. The problem can be extended to reason about a pair of highest possible values.

Ensuring progress
Supporting understanding
Children could use Base 10 apparatus to explore the positional and multiplicative aspects of a range of decimal numbers, perhaps starting with those written to one decimal place. They should recombine numbers using addition, carefully explaining the positions of the digits.

Encourage children to explore physically adding and subtracting amounts to the numbers represented, making estimations using rounding.

Broadening understanding
Children could make up their own decimal calculations and set them in a range of word problems. They should be challenged to create problems in different contexts that require rounding up or down to answer the question.

✓ Concept mastered
Children can round a range of decimal numbers to the nearest whole number, tenth or hundredth. They can reason about the need to round values up or down in a range of contexts and problems.

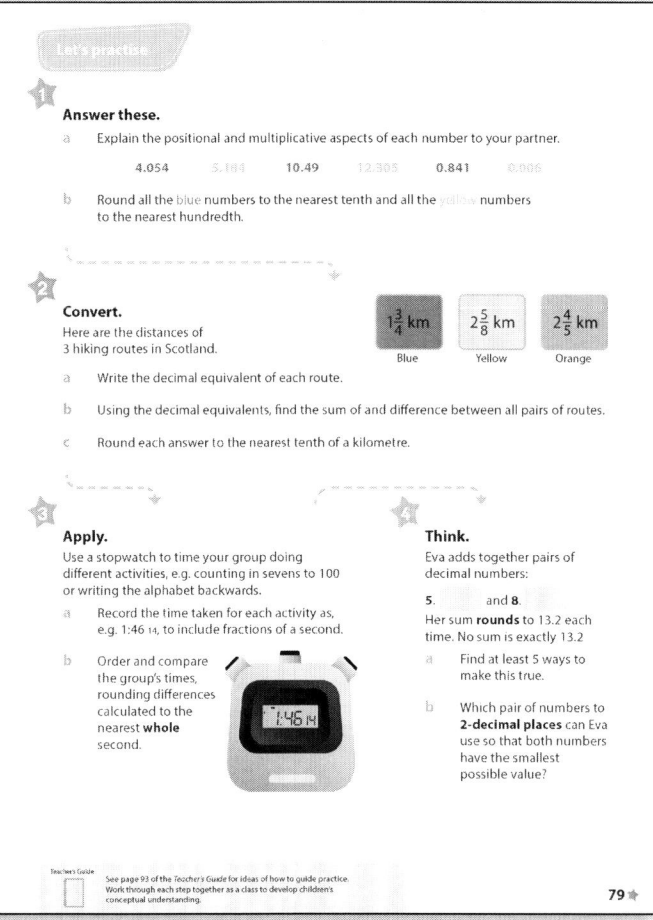

Follow-up ideas
- Children use digital kitchen scales to estimate and then weigh a set of four of five objects. Children can reason about two objects that would weigh approximately 3 kg, using their estimates to help them. The total mass can be calculated using an appropriate method and then checked on the scales. They should show all measurements in grams and kilograms. Similarly, children can calculate what will be left on the scales as they start with three different objects and then take one away each time.
- Using the results of the task above, children could create word problems that require rounding to different degrees of accuracy. Include those that require unconventional rounding.

Answers
Step 1
a Using Base 10 apparatus to help describe numbers, children could say, e.g. the third digit in 4.054 (5) is positioned in the hundredths position; it is divided by 100 to give $\frac{5}{100}$ or 0.05

b Green numbers: 4.1, 10.5, 0.8
Red numbers: 5.18, 12.31, 0.01

Step 2
a 1.75 km, 2.625 km, 2.8 km

b Sum of blue and yellow route is 4.375 km and difference is 0.875 km

Sum of blue and orange route is 4.55 km and difference is 1.05 km

Sum of yellow and orange route is 5.425 km and difference is 0.175 km

c 4.4 km and 0.9 km; 4.6 km and 1.1 km; 5.4 km and 0.2 km

Step 3
a Children's own timings of activities, e.g. 1:46 14, 1:57 87, 1:35 07 and 2:01 23

b Timings written in order and then differences calculated, e.g. 1:57 87 – 1:46 14 = 0:11 73 so 12 when rounded to the nearest whole second.

Step 4
a Children own investigations and recording of at least five possible pairs of numbers, e.g. 8.21 + 5.03 = 13.24 (rounds down to 13.2), 8.17 + 5.01 = 13.18 (rounds up to 13.2), etc.

Encourage children to consider systematic approaches.

b Lowest sum is 13.15 so pairs of numbers where both are at their lowest is 5.07 and 8.08 or 5.08 and 8.07

- **Use simple formula; generate and describe linear number sequences.**
- **Express missing number problems algebraically.**

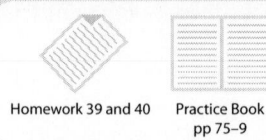

Homework 39 and 40   Practice Book pp 75–9

Mathematical vocabulary

Linear sequence, term, position, algebraic expression, total, sum, pattern, predict

Representations and resources

Counters, cubes or pegs, number rods, counting stick.

Warming up

Use a counting stick to practise counting on and back in steps of different sizes, e.g. fraction steps or steps of 7 or 25. Children should reason about other numbers that will or will not be in the count, explaining their thinking carefully each time using precise mathematical language. They should explain why a count in, say $\frac{3}{8}$, will not land on zero when counting backwards from 10. Children should notice, after counting back several steps, that the count lands on every third whole number, i.e. 7, 4 and 1 but not zero.

Background knowledge

Algebra was introduced formally in Unit 2– Calculations and algebra, focusing on unknown values. Here, the use of algebra extends to describe linear sequences involving pattern and number. To find the rule in a linear sequence, it is useful to draw a table listing the position in the sequence and the value of the term. This makes it easier to find a relationship that is true for each set of values, e.g.

Term	2	3	4
Value	5	6	7

The value is 3 more than the term. The rule is $n + 3$ (where n is the position of the term).

Let's learn: Modelling and teaching

Describing patterns and linear sequences

- Ask children to represent the pattern using counters or cubes, describing carefully how it changes each time. Ask: *What is the same and what is different?* Present an incorrect fourth term for children to discuss. They should explain why it does not fit the pattern.

- Invite children to represent the fourth term and prove their thinking. Reason about the number of red and blue counters each time, looking carefully at the relationship between the coloured counters. Ask how we know that a term with 132 blue and 131 red counters will never be in this particular sequence.

Using simple formulae

- Before looking at the completed table in the Textbook, assign different groups the task of finding the number of red or blue counters, and another the task of finding the total each time. Collect feedback on any patterns they notice. Explain that a table is an efficient way to record information and helps to spot relationships between the numbers.

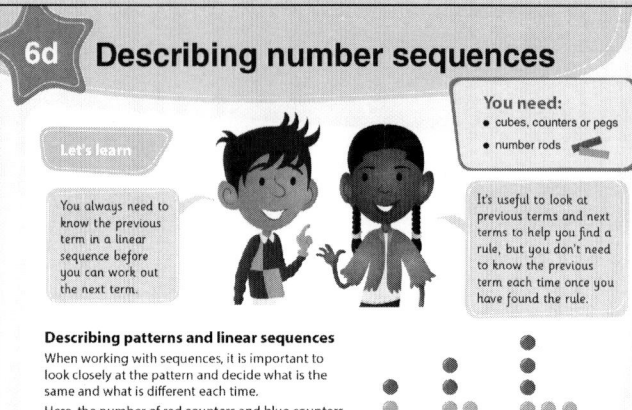

- Consider the way that the rule for the number of red counters is described in the Textbook, and why the number of blue counters is described in a different way even though both sets of counters increase by one each time.

- Discuss the use of n to represent the position of the term and why this may be a useful approach. Agree that we want to be able to find the total of any term, even when we do not know the value of the previous terms.

- Establish that the algebraic rule for the number of red counters is $n + 1$, and is simply n for the blue counters. Ask children how this helps us to make sense of the different ways that the total number of counters is expressed in the Textbook. Agree that if red is $n + 1$ and blue is n, we can see two lots of n plus one, which is $(2 \times n) + 1$ or simply $2n + 1$.

Let's practise: Digging deeper

Step 1

Allow children to use counters to continue the pattern up to at least the seventh term, so that they are secure with using and checking that the formula does still work before considering higher terms. Ask them to think about the number of blue counters each time.

Step 2

Some of the terms from Step 1 are repeated here so that children can use what they know to check their workings. Again, they go on to identify the total numbers in higher terms and use, e.g. the inverse to find the term with the given total of 101. Encourage children to record their results in a table to help them spot patterns.

Step 3

Children should generate their own linear sequence using

the given rule $3n + 2$ and represent it using counters or cubes. They could extend the activity by including a different number of coloured counters each time that also follow a term-to-term rule. Children are required to use a table to record totals each time and predict future terms in the sequence.

Step 4

This task introduces a different representation where each part of the pattern within a term has a value. Here, different coloured number rods determine the values. Encourage children to use a table to list the position of the terms and the value each time. This will help them to determine the rule.

Let's practise

⭐1 Calculate.
Use the formula $n + 1$. Calculate the total number of red counters each time as the pattern on page 80 continues.

a	5th term	c	10th term	e	25th term	g	200th term
b	7th term	d	20th term	f	100th term	h	1000th term

⭐2 Calculate
Use the formula $2n + 1$. Calculate the **total** number of counters each time as the pattern on page 80 continues.

a	7th term	d	24th term
b	10th term	e	75th term
c	16th term	f	Which term in the sequence will have a total of 101 counters?

⭐3 Apply.
Use the algebraic rule: Total = $3n + 2$.
Use counters or cubes to make up a pattern to follow the rule.

a Record the total number in each term in a table.

b Predict the total number of counters in the 100th term, and other terms of your choice.

⭐4 Think.

Use number rods to represent the start of the linear sequence shown here.
The white cube has the value 1, the red bar has the value 2 and so on.

a Investigate to find the total value of each term in the sequence and find a way to describe the rule in words.

b Express the rule algebraically using n and use it to find the value of other terms, e.g. the 50th term.

Teacher's Guide See page 95 of the *Teacher's Guide* for ideas of how to guide practice. Work through each step together as a class to develop children's conceptual understanding.

81

Follow-up ideas

- Return to the shape pattern image from page 73 and use the term-to-term rule to help children identify the algebraic expression $(3n + 4)$ by looking at the patterns generated from the totals 7, 10, 13, etc. in relation to the position in the sequence, n.

- Children write an algebraic expression and challenge another group to generate a linear sequence to represent it.

- Children could relate linear sequences to line graphs, e.g. they could plot values of the position in a sequence (x-axis) and the value of each term (y-axis), so for the red and blue counter sequence used in the Textbook, they would plot (1, 3), (2, 5), (3, 7) and so on. Discuss the line that is created each time.

Ensuring progress

Supporting understanding

Initially focus on describing the sequence using term-to-term rules, e.g. add 2 each time, until children are secure with finding other terms in the sequence using the value of the previous term to help them. Begin to look at some simple sequences that involve only additive reasoning, giving rise to expressions such as $n + 2$ or $n + 3$.

Broadening understanding

Challenge children to assign their own values to the rods used in the linear sequence in Step 4, as long as the relationship between each rod remains in ratio. They can investigate how the algebraic expression will change to suit the new values each time, e.g. assigning white as 10, red as 20, etc. will change the rule to $20n + 30$.

✓ **Concept mastered**

Children can describe the term-to-term rule using words and numbers. They recognise that the position in the sequence is key to finding subsequent terms without having to enumerate the previous term each time. They apply additive and multiplicative reasoning to help identify algebraic expressions and use these to identify future terms.

Answers

Step 1

a	6	e	26
b	8	f	101
c	11	g	201
d	21	h	1001

Step 2

a	15	d	49
b	21	e	151
c	33	f	50th

Step 3

a Children's own patterns following the rule $3n + 2$.

A table of results to show the position in the term and the total counters, e.g.

Term	1	2	3	4	5
Total	5	8	11	14	17

b 100th term is 302, and then children's other examples.

Step 4

a The rule could be described as, e.g. 'The next term is the sum of the previous term + 2' or 'The totals go up in steps of 2' or 'Double the position/term number add 3', etc.

b $2n + 3$ and then 50th term is 103. Children's own list of other terms.

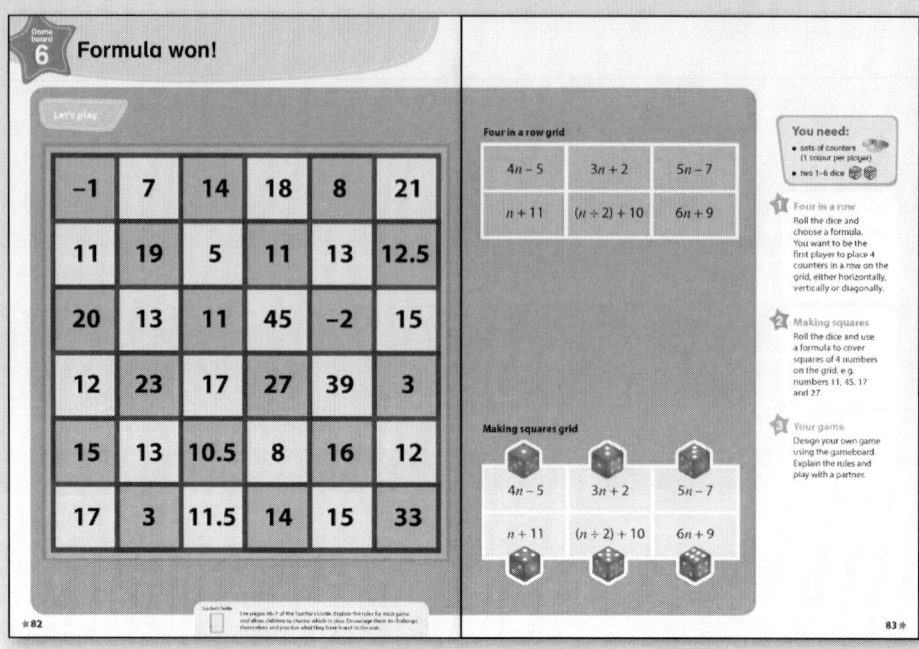

Game 1: Four in a row

Children have to make decisions about which formula to use each time to help them cover four numbers in a row.

Maths focus

- Use simple formula

Resources

Sets of counters (1 colour per player), 1–6 dice (1).

How to play

Children must aim to get four counters in a row, either horizontally, vertically or diagonally. Players take turns to roll one dice. The number rolled represents n for this turn, e.g. roll a 4, so $n = 4$. Children choose a formula from the Four in a row grid that will give them an answer in a useful position on the board. They cover this number with their counter. If the number is no longer available, the counter cannot be placed.

You could point out that it is sometimes a better strategy to block your opponent's moves than to add to your own.

Making it easier

Children could work in teams to discuss the decisions that they need to make.

The game could be played without the dice. Children could think about the number they want to cover and then decide their own value for n and the formula they would like to use.

Making it harder

Children may decide to only allow horizontal and vertical rows as winning counters and not include diagonals. They could pick a formula to use before they roll the dice, which would require them to think ahead and consider different possibilities.

Game 3: Your game

Children should invent their own game, designing rules that use the concepts covered in the unit. Challenge children to make their game easier or harder.

Game 2: Making squares

This game requires children to make two decisions each time: which value to choose for n and which formula to use.

Maths focus

- Use simple formula

Resources

Sets of counters (1 colour per player), 1–6 dice (2).

How to play

Children take turns to roll two dice. Of the numbers rolled, one will represent n and the other will determine the formula to use from the Making squares grid. Children need to look at the formulae in the Making squares grid which are labelled 1–6, according to the roll of the dice, e.g. a player rolls a 3 and a 5. They can choose to use 5 as n and formula 3 ($5n - 7$) or choose 3 for n and formula 5 (($n \div 2$) + 10). They work out the answer using their numbers and chosen formula and cover the answer on the board with their counter. If the number is no longer available, they cannot place their counter.

The winner is the player with the most squares of four counters covered after all or most of the numbers have been used.

Making it easier

Children could work in teams so that they can discuss the decisions that they need to make.

The game could be played with only one dice that determines the formula that must be used. Children could make their own decision about the value of n.

Making it harder

Use the same rules as before but, when an answer is no longer available on the board, a player could swap their opponent's counter for one of their own and remove it from the board.

Formula won!

Choose a game to play.

Game 1: Four in a row

You need:
- sets of counters (1 colour per player)
- 1–6 dice

How to play

- Take turns to roll the dice. The number you roll represents n for this turn, e.g. roll a 4, so $n = 4$.
- Choose a formula that will give you an answer on the board that will be a useful position for your counter. If the formula you choose gives an answer that is no longer available on the board, you cannot place a counter this time.
- The winner is the first player to get 4 counters in a row, either horizontally, vertically or diagonally.

Game 2: Making squares

You need:
- sets of counters (1 colour per player)
- two 1–6 dice

How to play

- Try and cover numbers on the board so that you cover 4 numbers in a square, e.g. numbers 13, 11, 23 and 17.
- Take turns to roll 2 dice.

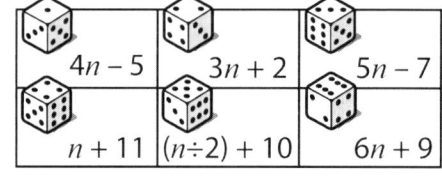

| $4n - 5$ | $3n + 2$ | $5n - 7$ |
| $n + 11$ | $(n÷2) + 10$ | $6n + 9$ |

- Choose one of the numbers rolled to represent n. The other number tells you which of the 6 formulae from the Making squares grid you must use, e.g. roll a 3 and a 5, choose 5 for n and formula 3 or choose 3 for n and formula 5.
- Use your numbers to work out the answer and place your counter over that number.
- You cannot place a counter if the answer you get is not available on the board.
- The winner is the player with the most squares of 4 counters covered.

Game 3: Your game

- Make up your own game using the gameboard
- You could use a 1–8 or 1–9 dice for 'Four in a row'.
- You could decide on your own formulae to use. You will need to check all the possible answers.
- Change the shape of numbers to cover so that there are more possibilities, e.g. make L shapes with 4 counters. What are the rules for your game? Explain them to someone.

Please help your child by reading the instructions and playing the game together.

Assessment task 1

Running the task

Children can work though these tasks on their own or in pairs so they can discuss their thinking. You may wish to discuss other sequences that children have worked with recently, including those with fractions.

The sequences focus on different aspects of learning including place value, negative numbers and fractions. All sequences include positive and negative numbers. Children are required to count across zero or calculate intervals that cross zero. Children should relate sequences to finding the difference between terms to help them find the rule. All sequences have directly adjacent terms so that the rule can be found using only a one-step calculation.

Look for children who make use of mental strategies, e.g. adding or subtracting 1000 and multiples of 100, to find the missing values in each sequence. No calculations require a formal written method. One of the sequences includes fractions, which gives children an opportunity to demonstrate fluency in this aspect of learning and convert between proper and improper fractions. Look for children who make use of equivalence when calculating and when simplifying fractions.

Evidencing mastery

Children showing mastery can apply additive reasoning to identify the step sizes each time, recognising that they have to find the difference between a pair of terms. They draw on mental strategies, fluently counting and calculating. They draw on place value and other aspects of additive reasoning to help them calculate. Children confidently partition numbers to cross zero, and use this to help calculate intervals. They add and subtract fractions fluently, recognising the need to use knowledge of equivalence to convert to fractions with the same denominators.

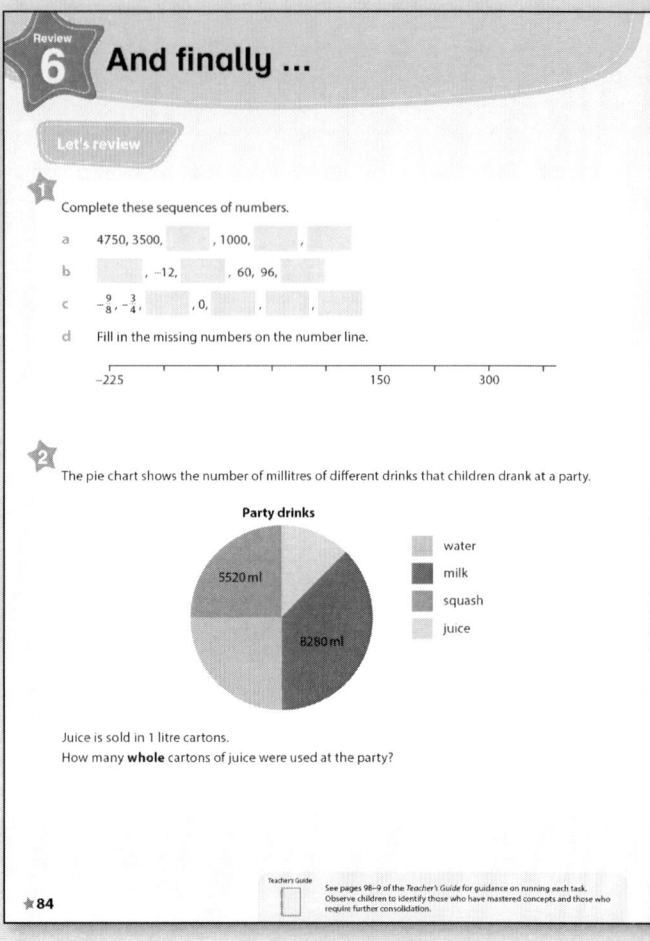

Assessment task 2

Running the task

Encourage children to discuss the pie chart and what it represents. They could think about other pie charts they have used and the type of information they have represented. Children should focus on the relationship between the sectors, recognising those that are equal and the relative size of each. Ask children to label any fractions of the circle that they recognise and those that they will need to check. Also ask them to discuss what they notice about the pie chart and whether or not they do need to identify the actual fractions or angles to answer the question.

Look for those who recognise that the sum of the milk and squash is one half of the pie chart and, therefore, the sum of the juice and water is equivalent to this. You may find it useful to cut up a copy of the pie chart or use fractional representations to prove that this is true.

Look for children who apply mental strategies of doubling 5520 ml to find the amount of juice represented by half the pie chart or those who halve 5520 ml because they recognise that

the fraction of juice is half of $\frac{1}{4}$ or $\frac{1}{8}$ of the total.

Remind children to look carefully again at the question should they give 2760 ml as the answer, and look for those who recognise that they will need to convert millilitres to litres and round in the given context. You may also wish to think about how the question would need to change so that children would need to round the answer up to three cartons rather than down to two cartons.

Evidencing mastery

Children who can explain why the problem involves steps of both addition and subtraction show clear evidence of mastery. Some children will go further and apply multiplicative reasoning, recognising that the number of litres of juice can be calculated by finding $\frac{1}{2}$ of 5520 ml that represents the squash or $\frac{1}{3}$ of 8280 ml that represents the water. Being able to apply knowledge of conversion and explain why 2.76 litres (2760 ml) must be rounded down for the context of the question is clear evidence of mastery.

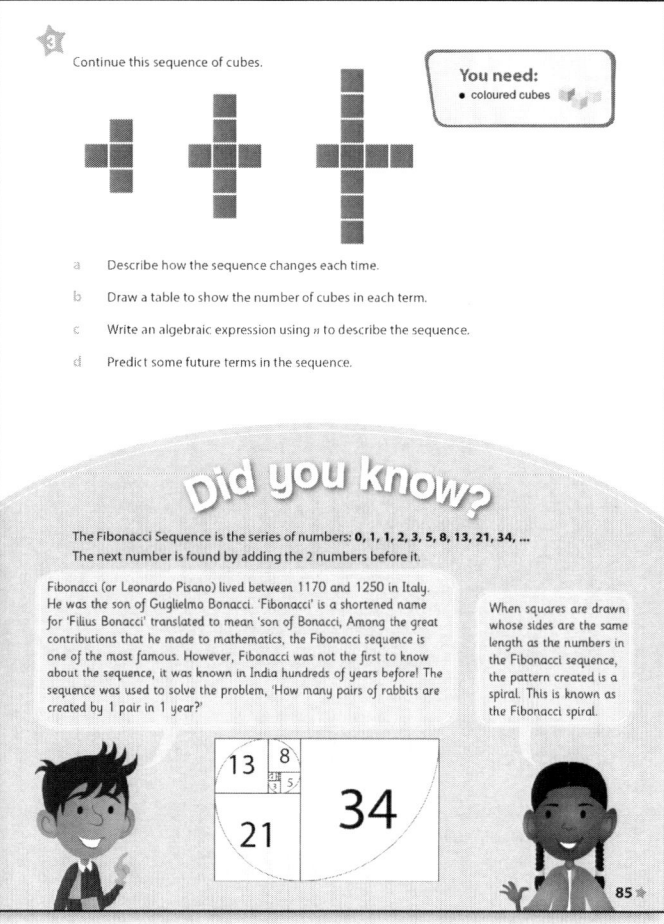

Assessment task 3

Resources

Coloured cubes.

Running the task

Children can work though the task on their own or in pairs. They should discuss how the pattern changes each time as the pattern continues. Cubes should be made available so that the pattern can be made or represented using drawings, providing a stimulus for discussion and reasoning.

Children create their own table to record results and use these to begin to look for patterns. The task requires them to express the sequence algebraically using n and continue to identify future terms.

Evidencing mastery

Children can explain how the pattern changes each time and recognise that the sequence can be expressed algebraically as $3n + 1$. Choosing headings for their own tables and organising results in the clearest way to help identify patterns is further evidence of mastery. Some children may go on to look at the patterns for the number of blue and pink cubes, relating these expressions to the total number of cubes.

Being able to fluently apply the algebraic rule to find future terms in the sequence is clear evidence of mastery.

Did you know?

Children are introduced to the Fibonacci sequence of numbers **0, 1, 1, 2, 3, 5, 8, 13, 21, 34**. The next number is found by adding the two numbers before it.

You may find it interesting to look at the 'Rabbit' problem on the Internet so that children can see how the sequence of numbers is generated.

The illustration of the Fibonacci spiral can promote interesting discussions as children predict where subsequent squares should be drawn to continue the pattern and make the spiral for themselves. You can find out more about this on the Internet.

There are lots of connections between the Fibonacci sequence, the golden ratio and nature.

It is said that the Fibonacci sequence is nature's numbering sequence as they appear in arrangements of leaves, petals and even the scales of a pineapple!

Concepts mastered

- ✓ Children can use mental strategies to calculate a difference or an interval between a positive and negative number, and relate this to the context of temperature.

- ✓ Children can recognise where addition and/or subtraction are required to solve problems, explaining why this is the case. They make appropriate estimates and consider the order of calculations.

- ✓ Children can round a range of decimal numbers to the nearest whole number, tenth or hundredth. They reason about the need to round values up or down in a range of contexts and problems.

- ✓ Children can describe the term-to-term rule using words and numbers. They recognise that the position in the sequence is key to finding subsequent terms without having to enumerate the previous term each time. They apply additive and multiplicative reasoning to help identify algebraic expressions and use these to identify future terms.

Let's explore fractions and algebra!

Mathematical focus

★ **Number: fractions (including decimals and percentages)**

★ **Algebra: simple formulae, number problems**

★ **Measurement: length, volume, area**

Prior learning

Children should already be able to:

- use common factors and multiples to express fractions in the same denominator
- compare and order fractions
- recall and use equivalences between simple fractions, decimals and percentages, including in different contexts
- associate a fraction with division and calculate decimal fraction equivalents
- use formula for area and perimeter of rectangles, including squares.

Key new learning

- Use common multiples to express fractions in the same denominator.
- Compare and order fractions, including fractions greater than one.
- Add and subtract fractions with different denominators and mixed numbers, using the concept of equivalent fractions.
- Recall and use equivalences between simple fractions, decimals and percentages, including in different contexts.
- Associate a fraction with division and calculate decimal fraction equivalents (e.g. 0.25) for a simple fraction (e.g. $\frac{1}{4}$).
- Use simple formulae.
- Recognise when it is possible to use formulae for area and volume of shapes.
- Calculate the area of parallelograms and triangles.
- Express missing number problems algebraically.

Making connections

- Children will make connections between fractions, decimals and percentages through using, reading, writing and converting between standard units of measure, such as litres and millilitres.
- Measurement also includes finding perimeters, areas and volumes. Children will have opportunities to calculate the areas of different shapes including parallelograms and triangles. They will also explore when it is possible to use formulae for areas of shapes.

Unit 7
Let's explore fractions and algebra!

What fractions can you see in this picture?

How could you show this information on a pie chart?

★86

Talk about

At the beginning of this unit, recap the vocabulary involved in fractions: vinculum, denominator and numerator.

It would also be worth briefly recapping the vocabulary of tenths, hundredths and thousandths and the terms positional, multiplicative and additive in relation to place value.

Engaging and exploring

First look at the photos of the egg boxes. Remind children of the whole/part nature of fractions, by asking them what the whole is for the larger egg box. Agree 12. Next ask what the parts are (eggs and empty) and then ask them to write what these would be as fractions. Remind them to write the vinculum first to show that the whole has been broken, then the denominator and finally the numerator. Repeat this for the other egg box.

Ask children for a simplified equivalent fraction for $\frac{3}{6}$. Agree $\frac{1}{2}$. Establish that each part can be divided by the common factor of three. Ask them to list other equivalent fractions for $\frac{3}{6}$ by focusing on finding common multiples of each part.

Ask children to tell you how many eggs there are altogether as a fraction. Agree $\frac{10}{18}$ and $\frac{8}{18}$. They simplify these by finding common factors. Establish that all parts can be divided by

two to give $\frac{5}{9}$ and $\frac{4}{9}$. If added there will be the whole.

Finally, ask them to compare and order the fractions that they have made, then rehearse adding and subtracting fractions with the same denominators and those that are multiples of the same number, e.g. $\frac{1}{3} + \frac{1}{6}$.

Ask children to explore the fractions they can see in the picture of the fruits, e.g. each section is one quarter, the types of fruit $\frac{5}{20}$. Again explore equivalence, beginning with these two fractions. Ask questions, e.g. if one of the parts was taken away, what would the fractions be this time. You could, again, explore addition and subtraction using the picture, e.g. $\frac{1}{4} + \frac{1}{4} + \frac{1}{4} + \frac{1}{4} = 1$, $\frac{3}{4} + \frac{1}{4} = 1$, $1 - \frac{3}{4} = \frac{1}{4}$.

This is a good opportunity to rehearse finding equivalent decimals, e.g. $\frac{1}{4} = 0.25$, $\frac{3}{4} = 0.75$, and talk about percentages. Agree that each section is 25%, because that is equivalent to $\frac{1}{4}$ and 0.25. You could ask children to draw a pie chart to represent the picture and label each section with the appropriate percentage. They could go on to draw other pie charts of different fractions of small items, e.g. toys or coloured counters.

Ask children if they know where the road sign pictured might be. Establish that it is in part of Australia. Alice Springs is in the north of the country. Ask children what units the distances might be in. Agree kilometres.

Remind children that there are 1000 metres in one kilometre. Ask them to write the distance to Glendambo in mixed units and to explain why 113.5 is an equivalent representation.

If appropriate, inform children that there are 0.62 miles in a kilometre and ask them to convert the kilometres to miles using whatever method they prefer, e.g. $0.62 \times 113 = 70.06$, $0.62 \times 0.5 = 0.31$, $70.06 + 0.31 = 70.37$ miles. Ask children to tell you the place value of the decimal numbers and then to convert these to fractions. Repeat this for other distances.

Find out how many children in your class play football. How many have been to some form of league match? You could display this information in a two-criteria Carroll diagram showing 'play football/not play football' and 'been to football match/not been to football match'. Analyse the results using structured questions, e.g. *How many in the class have done both? How many in the class have done neither?*

Ask children to identify the lengths of the various parts of the pitch, then convert the decimals to fractions. Talk about how they could find the perimeter of the pitch. Agree they could add all four sides together. Ask them if they remember the formula for this. Establish that it is $2l + 2w$ or $2(l + w)$. Repeat for the area of the pitch, agreeing that the formula is $l \times w$.

A87 STUART HWY
Glendambo 113.5
Coober Pedy 366
Cadney Park 517
Marla 597
Alice Springs 1050
MAJOR REST AREA
LAKE HART 40

How else could you represent 113.5?

Radius 1 rm
120 m
I wonder how far it is around the outside of the pitch?
7.32 m
11 m
Radius 9.15 m
16.5 m
90 m

Look at the pictures with the children and discuss the questions. See pages 100–1 of the *Teacher's Guide* for key ideas to draw out.

87 ★

Things to think about

- How will you use practical equipment and/or visual representations to help children develop a conceptual understanding of simplifying fractions and finding equivalences?

- How will you develop ways to incorporate the concepts covered in this unit within the context of measurement?

- How will you encourage children to verbalise their reasoning as they discuss the various elements that involve converting between units of measure and the various forms of fraction?

Checking understanding

Children can identify, simplify and find equivalent fractions. They can represent fractions as decimals and percentages. They can convert metres to kilometres and vice versa. They can convert distances from kilometres to miles. They can find perimeters and areas of shapes.

Fraction equivalences

- Use common multiples to express fractions in the same denominator.
- Compare and order fractions, including fractions greater than one.
- Add and subtract fractions with different denominators and mixed numbers, using the concept of equivalent fractions.

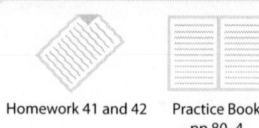

Homework 41 and 42   Practice Book pp 80–4

Representations and resources

Strips of paper about 2 cm in width, money (coins and £5 notes), measuring jugs, water (or rice or sand).

Mathematical vocabulary

Multiple, factor, denominator, numerator, vinculum, equivalent, common denominator

Warming up

Draw a clock face on the board with numbers from one to 12. Decide which multiplication table you wish children to practise, e.g. nine. Write this in the middle of the clock. Point to each hour number in turn. As you do, children call out the answer when that number is multiplied by nine. Move round from one to 12 and then point at numbers at random. Keep going back to any that children struggle to recall instantly. You could then replace the numbers one to 12 with nine to 108. Repeat but ask children what you need to divide the number you are pointing at by to get nine.

Background knowledge

In earlier years children will have begun to develop a conceptual understanding of what a fraction is, the relationship between the denominator and numerator and the idea of equivalence. Both finding equivalent fractions and simplifying fractions require a knowledge of multiples and factors. Once children have a depth of understanding in these aspects, they will be able to use this to add and subtract fractions with different denominators.

Let's learn: Modelling and teaching

Comparing and ordering fractions

- Write some unit fractions on the board and ask children to make a list of fractions that are equivalent. Agree that to do this they find common multiples of both the numerator and denominator. Repeat for non-unit fractions, e.g. $\frac{32}{48}$. This time they find common factors, e.g. $\frac{16}{24}$, $\frac{8}{12}$. Ask children to compare and order some of the fractions, using the equivalent fractions they have found.

- Write pairs of fractions that are greater than one (improper fractions) on the board. Ask children to compare them. Agree that they could start by turning them into mixed numbers, e.g. $\frac{13}{8}$ ($1\frac{5}{8}$) is clearly smaller than $\frac{25}{12}$ ($2\frac{1}{12}$); but for $\frac{7}{4}$ ($1\frac{3}{4}$) and $\frac{9}{5}$ ($1\frac{4}{5}$) it is necessary to find the common denominator. Give children examples to work through.

- Ask children to compare centimetre and metre lengths in the same way, e.g. $2\frac{3}{4}$ cm and $2\frac{4}{5}$ cm.

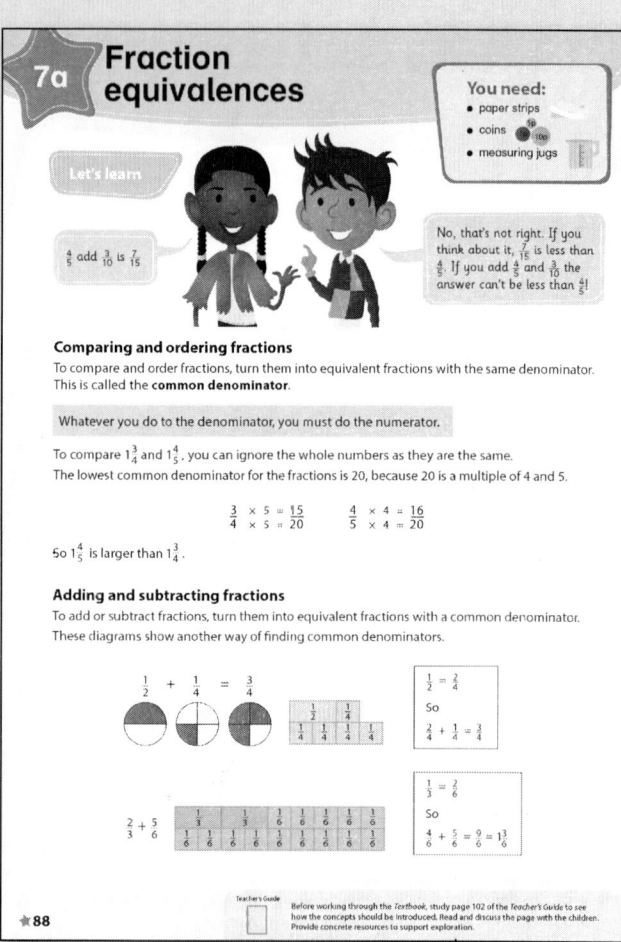

Adding and subtracting fractions

- Discuss the the misconception cartoon. Write some incorrect examples on the board in which the denominators are all multiples of the same number. Establish that they need to ensure the fractions are equivalent, so they need to find common denominators.

- Ask children to describe to a partner what the models in the Textbook show. Agree that they show addition of fractions within the same family (where denominators are common multiples). Ask children to use strips of paper to make halves, quarters and eighths. They then practise adding and subtracting pairs of these fractions, such as one quarter and three eighths. Change any improper fraction results to mixed numbers.

Let's practise: Digging deeper

Step 1

Before the task ask children what they need to do to compare fractions with different denominators. Expect them to tell you that they would find common denominators, which is a common multiple and that they need to multiply the numerator by the same number that they multiplied the denominator by. The task asks children to work out either the smallest or the largest fraction, including some pairs of fractions greater than one. Some of the fractions in the first part of the task are in the same family, so are relatively simple to convert. Once they have completed the task ask children to make some up for a partner to compare.

Step 2

Ask children why they can't simply add or subtract denominators and numerators when they add or subtract fractions. Expect them to be able to explain that the fractions need to be in the same unit to do this, so equivalent fractions need to be found. Write up some examples on the board for them to practise before beginning the task.

Step 3

This task is a practical application of the mathematics they have been learning. For the first part, they need to work out the fractions of each amount of money and then find the total and make it using the fewest coins. The second part asks them to subtract volumes of litres and then round the difference between them and measure it with water into containers. Before they begin, discuss the equipment with children and ask: *What will your strategy be to answer these questions?* Observe to what extent children plan to use the equipment.

Step 4

Children need to use their knowledge of converting fractions and apply this to the problem. Ask them to try to solve it without any prompts. They could discuss approaches with a partner. Some children may decide to compare two jugs at a time. They might convert two of the volumes to equivalent fractions and need prompting to convert the third. Some might decide to work out how many millilitres the fractions represent. Others may try to judge by eye, in which case you will need to intervene. Encourage them to use one method and then to check using an alternative one.

Ensuring progress

Supporting understanding

Keep the denominators in 'families' so that children are converting one fraction to another, e.g. halves and quarters, thirds and sixths. Let them use fraction strips so that they have a visual representation when they do this.

Broadening understanding

Give children more complex pairs to compare, add and subtract, e.g. eighths and tenths, fifths and twelfths.

✓ Concept mastered

Children can explain and demonstrate how to convert fractions to a common denominator and to use this understanding to compare, add and subtract fractions.

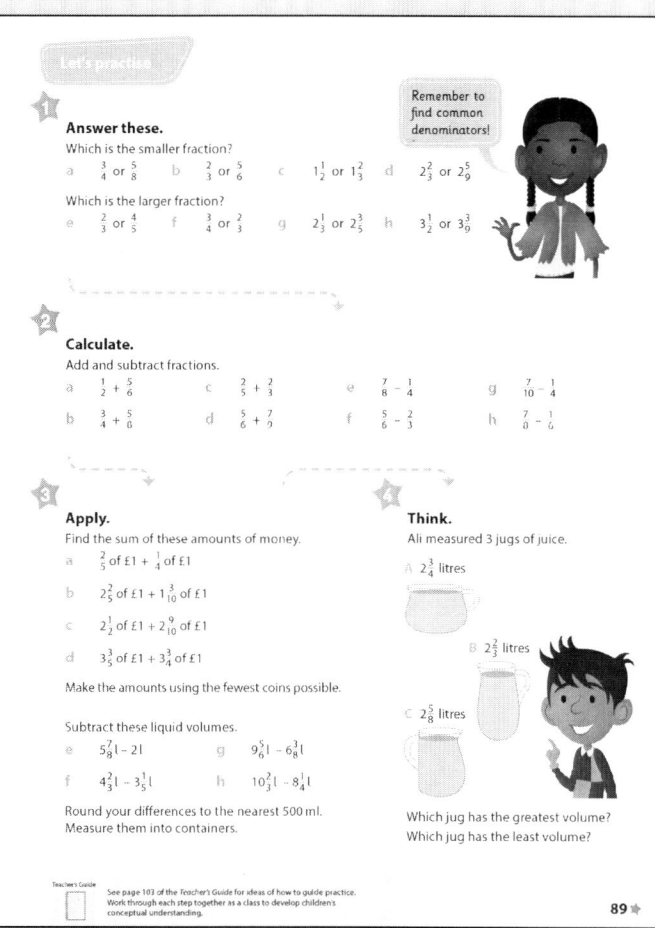

Follow-up ideas

- Ask children, in pairs, to make an instruction poster to demonstrate, with words and diagrams, how to find common denominators to compare, add and subtract fractions.

- Give 16 small cards to pairs of children. On them, they write different fractions with a variety of denominators. They then make a pile of the cards and each pick one from the top. They compare the cards – the player with the highest fraction keeps theirs; the other player replaces theirs in the pile. They continue until all but one of the cards is used. The winner is the player with the most cards.

- Children could use the cards again. This time they each take two and find the total of their fractions. They keep doing this until all the cards have been used. They then find the total of their cards. The winner is the player with the highest total.

Answers

Step 1

a $\frac{5}{8}$

b $\frac{2}{3}$

c $1\frac{1}{2}$

d $2\frac{5}{9}$

e $\frac{4}{5}$

f $\frac{3}{4}$

g $2\frac{3}{5}$

h $3\frac{1}{2}$

Step 2

a $\frac{8}{6}$ or $1\frac{2}{6}$ or $1\frac{1}{3}$

b $\frac{11}{18}$ or $1\frac{3}{8}$

c $\frac{16}{15}$ or $1\frac{1}{15}$

d $\frac{29}{18}$ or $1\frac{11}{18}$

e $\frac{5}{8}$

f $\frac{1}{6}$

g $\frac{9}{20}$

h $\frac{17}{24}$

Step 3

a 65p, 50p + 10p + 5p

b £3.70, £2 + £1 + 50p + 20p

c £5.40, £5 + 20p + 20p

d £7.35, £5 + £2 + 20p + 10p + 5p

e $3\frac{7}{8}$ l

f $1\frac{7}{15}$ l

g $3\frac{11}{24}$

h $2\frac{5}{12}$

Step 4

Jug A has greatest volume. Jug C least volume.

Fraction, decimal and percentage equivalences

- Recall and use equivalences between simple fractions, decimals and percentages, including in different contexts.
- Associate a fraction with division and calculate decimal fraction equivalents (e.g. 0.25) for a simple fraction (e.g. $\frac{1}{4}$).

 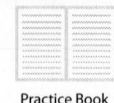 

Homework 43 and 44   Practice Book pp 85–7   Fraction Wall

Representations and resources

Strips of paper about 2 cm in width, calculators, money (coins and notes), counters.

Mathematical vocabulary

Fraction, decimal, percentage, equivalent, division

Warming up

Rehearse finding fractions of numbers. Call out fractions and whole numbers, e.g. one twelfth of 72, three fifths of 25, three eighths of 16. Children write the answers on their whiteboards. Allow them to make jottings should they need to. Ask children what it is helpful to know in order to be able to do this efficiently. Establish that knowing multiplication facts and corresponding divisions is very helpful because finding fractions is all about multiplication and division. You may wish to begin by asking children to find unit fractions first and then move on to non-unit fractions.

Background knowledge

Fractions encompass decimals, percentages, ratio and proportion as well as the part-whole and division relationships that children began studying Year 1. Decimals occur when the denominator is divided into the numerator. It is worth giving children the opportunity to use calculators to explore what decimals they can make from different fractions, e.g. $\frac{1}{3}$ and $\frac{1}{9}$. This will enable them to explore recurring fractions. Percentages are fractions that are always out of 100.

Let's learn: Modelling and teaching

Fractions and division

- Discuss the comments in the misconception cartoon. Ask: *Why does Ali think that $\frac{1}{4}$, 0.4 and 4% are equivalent?* Look at Eva's explanation.

- Ask how children could work out what half is as a decimal and then one quarter. Agree they divide the whole by two to give 0.5 and by four to give 0.25.

- Give each child a calculator, call out different fractions and ask them to divide the denominator into the numerator to find the decimal. Do this for one third. What do they notice? Establish that this is a recurring decimal which will go on forever. Ask children what they should do to make this a decimal they could work with more easily. Agree that they could round to the nearest tenth or hundredth. Repeat with different sixths and ninths.

Finding equivalences mentally

- Write some unit fractions on the board and ask children to write down the equivalent decimals and then percentages.

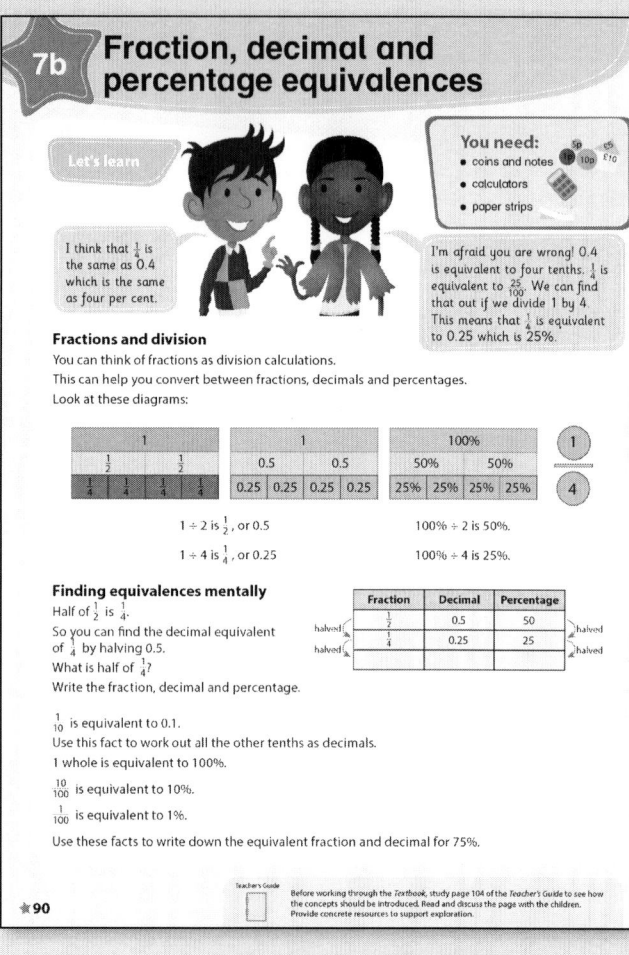

Ask children to sketch a diagram to show the equivalence, as shown in the Textbook. Repeat with percentages and then decimals.

- Give children strips of paper. Ask them to make up fraction strips for a whole and then by halving make halves, quarters and eighths. They label each section with the appropriate fraction, decimal and percentage. When they find the equivalent percentage for one eighth point out that a percentage is out of 100. One eighth as a decimal is 0.125. How do they think they can represent this as a percentage? Establish that it is $12\frac{1}{2}$%. Repeat for fifths and tenths.

- For each of the above, tell children that the whole is a measure, e.g. 12 kg, 8 m, 15 l. Ask them to work out what each fraction, decimal and percentage will be.

Let's practise: Digging deeper

Step 1

Before the task, ask children to tell you the names of the different parts of a fraction and explain the purpose of each. Include vinculum, numerator and denominator. Next ask them to describe how they could change a fraction into a percentage. Agree that they have to find what to multiply the denominator by to make it into 100 and then multiply the numerator by the same amount. Percentages are hundredths so it is then simple to make the decimal equivalent. Let any children who need support use their fraction strips if they are helpful.

Step 2

Before the task, discuss possible strategies for finding the fractions, decimals and percentages of 12, e.g. 25% is equivalent to one quarter, so they could find one quarter of 12 by halving and halving again. Some of the fractions and

decimals are mixed numbers, so children will need to think in more depth. Allow them to attempt these questions independently at first, then if necessary give the clue that the one is equivalent to 12; they then need to work out the other part and add it.

Step 3

This first part of this task asks children to find the percentages given for £36. Ask: *Will you find ten per cent or one per cent first? Which do you think is simplest? Why?* Once they have found the percentages they make the new amounts using the fewest number of notes and coins possible. Then they total all the amounts and show this using the fewest notes and coins. Observe how confidently children apply their understanding of addition and money, after they have been working closely on fractions, decimals and percentages. They should be starting to move fluently across these different areas of mathematics.

Step 4

Rehearse the task first. Write an amount on the board, e.g. £180. Ask children to tell you what ten per cent is and model how to write this: 10% = £18. Expect them to record their answers in this way, so that others know what percentages they found. Encourage them to find interesting percentages such as $17\frac{1}{2}$%. You could challenge them to find all the whole number percentages by using what they have already found to make others.

Ensuring progress

Supporting understanding

In Step 1, you could ask children to focus on changing the unit fractions. In Step 2, support them as they answer the parts involving whole numbers. You could give them counters to represent the fractions, decimals and percentages, e.g. one counter represents 20%, they set out five to represent the whole which is 12. They should be able to see clearly that 12 needs to be divided into five equal parts to give 20%.

Broadening understanding

After completing each step, ask children to make up examples of their own for a partner to answer. In Step 4, ask children to think of some word problems that involve £180 and the different percentages that they have made up.

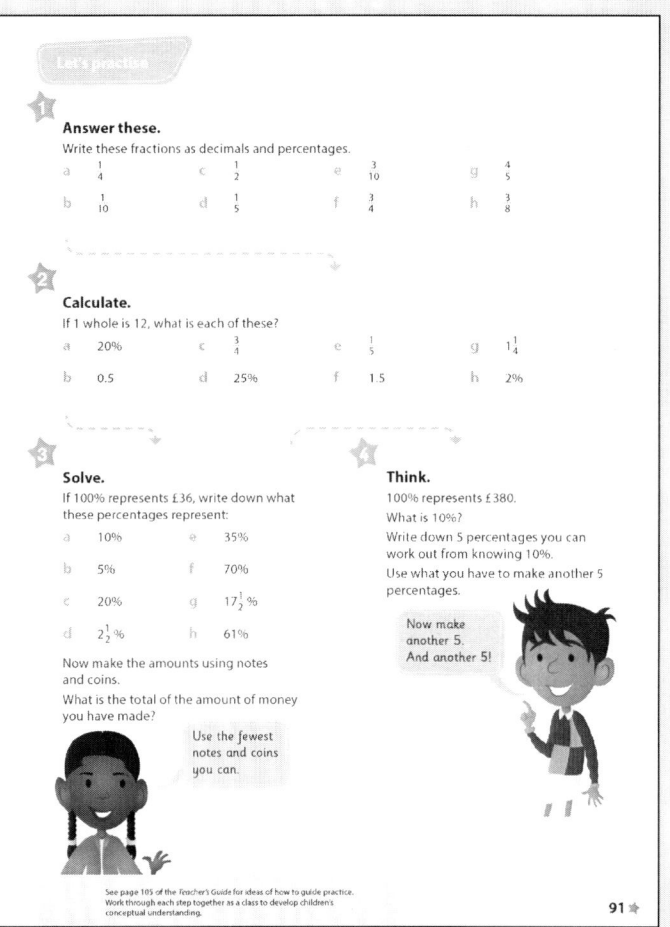

Concept mastered

Children can explain and demonstrate how to convert from fractions to decimals and percentages and vice versa.

Follow-up ideas

- Ask children to work in pairs to make a leaflet which shows how to convert fractions, decimals and percentages. They could share this with any children who haven't mastered this to see if it helps their understanding.

- Give 36 small cards to pairs of children. They share these equally into three piles. On one card from each pile they write a fraction and the equivalent decimal and percentage. When they have done this, they play a 'Happy Families' type game where they have to collect trios of equivalences.

- Give children a shopping catalogue. Ask them to select different items. They then pretend there is a ten per cent sale and work out new prices. They will need to be careful that the new prices are whole numbers of pence. If they are not, they will need to find prices that can be reduced to whole pence.

Answers

Step 1

a	0.25, 25%	**e**	0.3, 30%
b	0.1, 10%	**f**	0.75, 75%
c	0.5, 50%	**g**	0.8, 80%
d	0.2, 20%	**h**	0.375, 37.5%

Step 2

a	2.4	**f**	18
b	6	**g**	15
c	9	**h**	0.24
d	3		
e	2.4		

Step 3

a	£3.60, £2 + £1 + 50p + 10p
b	£1.80, £1 + 50p + 20p + 10p
c	£7.20, £5 + £2 + 20p
d	£0.90, 50p + 20p + 20p
e	£12.60, £10 + £2 + 50p + 10p
f	£25.20, £20 + £5 + 20p
g	£6.30, £5 + £1 + 20p + 10p
h	£21.96, £20 + £1 + 50p + 20p + 20p + 5p + 1p
	Total: £79.56, £50 + £20 + £5 + £2 + £2 + 50p + 5p + 1p

Formulae

- **Use simple formulae.**
- **Recognise when it is possible to use formulae for area and volume of shapes.**
- **Calculate the area of parallelograms and triangles.**

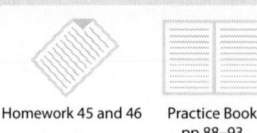

Homework 45 and 46   Practice Book pp 88–93

Mathematical vocabulary

Formula, equation, perimeter, area, square, rectangle, triangle, parallelogram

Representations and resources

Pendulum (three interlocking cubes), centimetre-squared paper, rulers, scissors.

Warming up

Rehearse number pairs to ten, then 20 and 100. Swing the pendulum from side to side. As it swings one way, call out a number to ten. As it swings the other way children call out the number that goes with it to make ten. Repeat this for number pairs to 20 and then 100. Begin with multiples of ten, then five and finally any number, such as 27, 38 or 63.

Background knowledge

Algebra is the part of mathematics in which letters and symbols are used to represent numbers and quantities in formula and equations. This concept focuses on developing formulae for finding areas of parallelograms and triangles. This builds on children's experience of looking at formulae for perimeter and area of squares and rectangles.

Let's learn: Modelling and teaching

Formulae for perimeter

- Discuss the misconception cartoon. Do children remember the formulae for the perimeter of a rectangle? If so, ask them to explain them to a partner. Ask: *Why is using a formula quicker than adding or counting squares? Can you think of an example where you would have to use a formula rather than count?* Use the example in the Textbook to explore how using a formulae is more efficient.

- Give each child a piece of centimetre-squared paper and a ruler. Ask them to draw different-sized rectangles, including squares, and find their perimeters using the formulae.

- Ask children to find all the possible rectangles for a given perimeter, e.g. ten centimetres. They then write the calculations they would use, based on both formulae.

- Challenge children to work out formulae for finding the perimeters of other regular shapes.

Formulae for area

- Spend some time exploring the formula for the area of a rectangle. Do children come up with the formula in the Textbook? Establish that area is measured in two dimensions, so the unit is cm². The superscript two indicates the two dimensions.

- Give each child a piece of centimetre-squared paper and a ruler. Ask them to draw different-sized rectangles and find

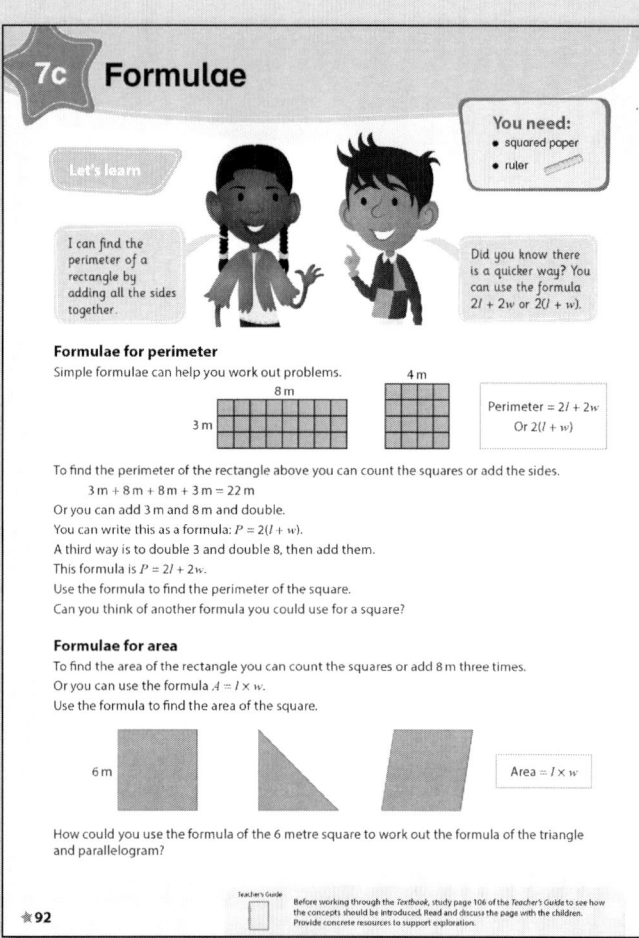

their areas using the formula.

- Ask children to draw a right-angled triangle and discuss with a partner how to use the formula for the area of a rectangle to find the area of their triangle. Establish that a triangle is half a rectangle. Ask them to complete the rectangle around their triangle, work out its area and halve it. Can they think of a formula? Agree that they could use $A = \frac{1}{2}(l \times w)$.

- Repeat for a parallelogram. Establish that they could cut this out and make it into a rectangle by cutting a triangle from one side and adding it to the other diagonal side. Agree that the formula is the same as for a rectangle. The only difference is that they need to measure the vertical height of the parallelogram. Ask children to draw parallelograms and find their areas.

Let's practise: Digging deeper
Step 1
Children draw squares and use the formula to find their areas. They are given the length of one side, so must be familiar with the fact that all sides on a square are equal. You could link this to square numbers. If they have a square with sides of 10 cm and they are using the formula $A = l \times w$, then A could also be l^2 which here would be 10 cm². Call out some whole number lengths for children to square to find the shape's area. The last three lengths are millimetre lengths. Encourage children to multiply using the grid method or long multiplication.

Step 2
In this task children draw rectangles to given dimensions and then use the formulae to find out perimeters and areas. Encourage them to use mental calculation strategies with jottings. For the area part of parts f and g allow them to use long multiplication or the grid method.

Step 3
This task asks children to work out the area of a patio. Before they begin, spend some time recapping area. Draw and label rectangles on the board and ask children how to use $l \times w$ to find the areas. Remind them of the notation used, e.g. m², cm². Then ask them to tell you how they can use their knowledge of finding areas of rectangles and apply this to finding areas of parallelograms and triangles. Work through a few examples with children telling them what to do. Children then design a patio using two parallelograms and two triangles. Encourage them to take care with their measuring to ensure their shapes are accurately drawn. Discuss that they need to measure in centimetres and then scale their measurements up to metres. Ask them what scale factor they are using to do this (100). Once they have made their design they work out its area. As an extra part to the task, you could ask them to find its perimeter.

Step 4
Children are given the perimeter of a rectangle and need to work out and draw the possible whole number rectangles Eva might have drawn. Ask them to write down the lengths first in a systematic way, e.g. width 1 cm and length 11 cm, width 2 cm and length 10 cm. Encourage them to look for a pattern. Once they have drawn them they then work out their areas. If any finish quickly, ask them to work out some possibilities involving decimal lengths.

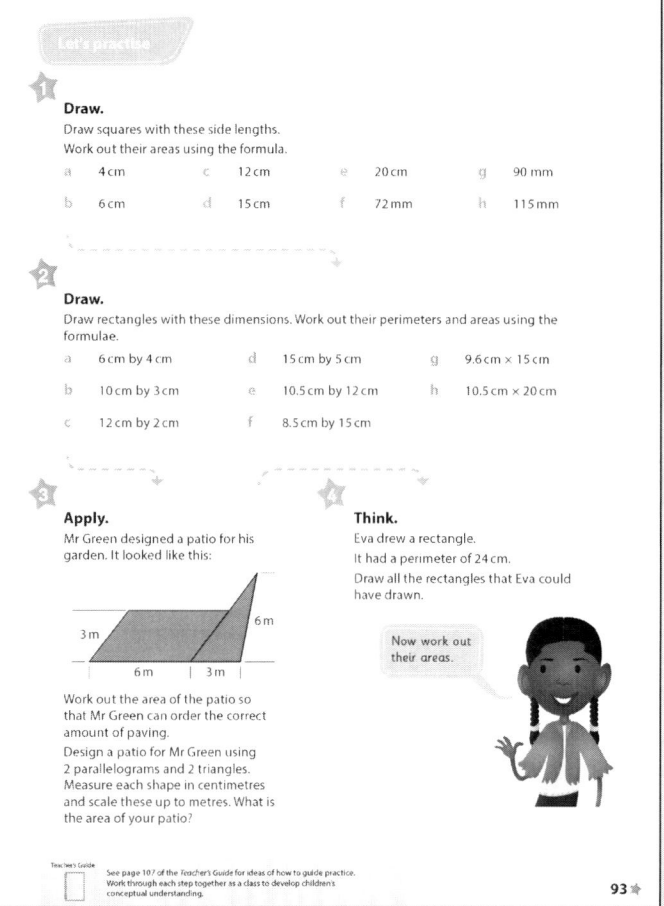

Ensuring progress
Supporting understanding
Begin by finding perimeters and areas of rectangles, including squares. When children are secure move on to triangles. It is important that they draw triangles on squared paper and make the associated rectangle, so they can visualise that a triangle is half the rectangle.

Broadening understanding
You could ask children to explore how to find perimeters and areas of other quadrilaterals, e.g. two types of trapezium. Ask them to work out how they can rearrange this trapezium to make a rectangle and then work out the formula.

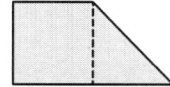

For this type of trapezium they find the area of the rectangle and then add the area of the extra triangle.

Follow-up ideas
- Children could make up information posters giving instructions on how to find the perimeters and areas of rectangles, including squares, triangles, parallelograms and other quadrilaterals.

- Ask children to explore the formula for finding perimeters of other regular shapes. You could then ask them to draw round these shapes and see if they can work out how to find their areas.

- Ask children to draw a shape with straight sides and challenge a partner to find the perimeter in the quickest way they can. They then ask their partner to find its area by cutting the shape into different rectangles, and possibly triangles, and finding and combining the areas of those.

Concept mastered
Children can explain and demonstrate how to use simple formulae to find perimeters and areas of rectangles, triangles and parallelograms.

Answers

Step 1

a	16 cm²	e	400 cm²	
b	36 cm²	f	5184 mm²	
c	144 cm²	g	8100 mm²	
d	225 cm²	h	13225 mm²	

e $P = 45$ cm, $A = 126$ cm²
f $P = 47$ cm, $A = 127.5$ cm²
g $P = 49.2$ cm, $A = 144$ cm²
h $P = 61$ cm, $A = 210$ cm²

Step 2

a $P = 20$ cm, $A = 24$ cm²
b $P = 26$ cm, $A = 30$ cm²
c $P = 28$ cm, $A = 24$ cm²
d $P = 40$ cm, $A = 75$ cm²

Step 4

1 cm × 11 cm (area 11 cm²),
2 cm × 10 cm (area 20 cm²),
3 cm × 9 cm (area 27 cm²),
4 cm × 8 cm (area 32 cm²),
5 cm × 7 cm (area 35 cm²),
6 cm × 6 cm, (area 36 cm²).

- **Express missing number problems algebraically.**

Homework 47 and 48   Practice Book pp 94–6

Mathematical vocabulary

Equation, unknown, balancing, bar model

Warming up

Give each child a clock face and ask them to find different analogue times and show you. State whether they are a.m. or p.m. times and ask them to write down the equivalent 24-hour digital time. Set problems, e.g. *My watch says five minutes to 12. It is 17 minutes slow. Show me what time it should say.*

Representations and resources

Clocks with moveable hands, centimetre-squared paper, rulers, scissors, pan balances, cubes.

Background knowledge

All the way through primary school children have been given missing number statements to solve. These are the first steps in algebra. If children are not already familiar with the term 'algebra', introduce it now. Algebra is about finding unknowns. In earlier years these unknowns were indicated by shapes. In Year 6 children are introduced to letters. This spread looks at using the bar model and also the idea of balancing to find unknowns. The latter is a method they will use in secondary school.

Let's learn: Modelling and teaching

Find missing numbers using the bar model

- Look at the cartoon in the Textbook. Ask children to discuss what Eva might have done. Then look at the Ali's response. Does this match their thinking?

- Look at the example of the bar model in the Textbook. Ask: *Why might you use this model?* Establish that it can help them to visualise a missing number problem. Discuss each step in the Textbook.

- Write some missing number statements on the board, e.g. $n + 34 = 53$, $m - 15 = 31$. Ask children to draw bar models for each:

n	34
53	

m	
15	31

- Establish that they can find n by counting on from 34 to 53; they can find m by adding 15 and 31. Repeat this for examples such as $25 + n = 42$, $35 - n = 17$, then move on to 3- and 4-digit numbers.

- Write up some statements such as $34 + 15 = ? + 17$. Ask children to solve these using the bar model.

Find missing numbers using balancing

- Ask children to look at the balances in the Textbook. Establish that they show balancing as a way of isolating the unknown. Recap the importance of the equals symbol

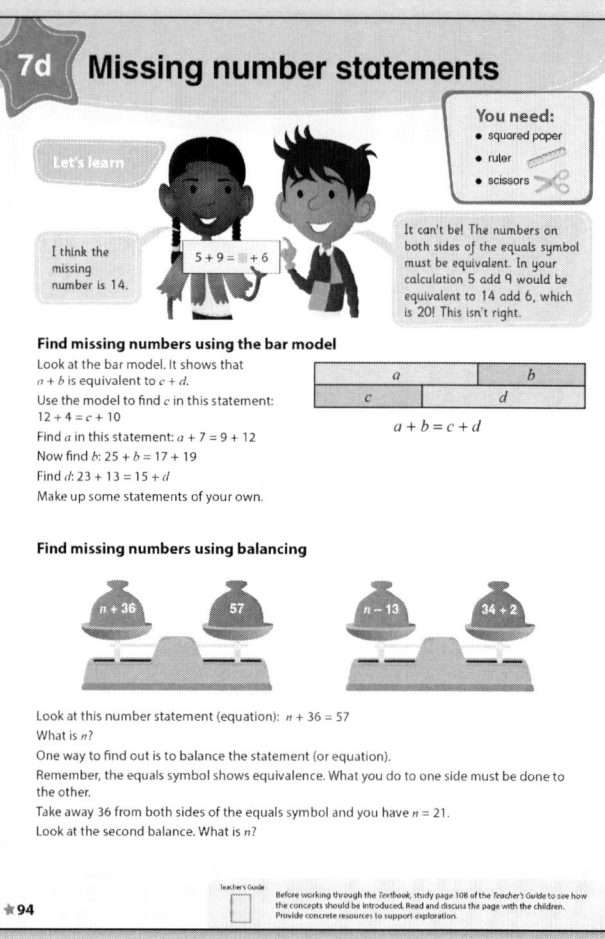

as a sign of equivalence, therefore, what is done on one side must be done to the other. Work through the first example in the Textbook, agreeing that children need to take 36 from both sides to leave $n = 21$. Then give a few more examples, e.g. $n + 15 = 24$ (take 15 from both sides to leave $n = 9$).

- Look at the second example in the Textbook. Establish that you need to add 13 to both sides to cancel out the −13. So n equals $34 + 2 + 13$. Remind children of the inverse nature of addition and subtraction. Give similar examples for them to work through. Include some examples involving multiples of n and some with negative answers.

Let's practise: Digging deeper

Step 1

Children need to work out the unknown numbers. They do this by drawing the bar model, writing the known numbers in two sections of the model. They then count on or add to find the unknown and write this in the third section. Rehearse a few of these before they begin the task. You could do this using procedural fluency, such as $12 + m = 26$, $12 + m = 27$, $m + 16 = 28$. Some of the number statements in the task involve two parts for each bar. Ensure that you have covered this in your teaching.

Step 2

The task asks children to use balancing to find the unknown number in each number statement. Before the task recap this method. Remind them that for questions like $p - 46 = 27$, 46 has to be added to each side to give $p = 27 + 46$ and for $138 - n = 87$, n has to be added to both sides to give $138 = 87 + n$. You may wish to write examples of the questions, particularly those that involve several balancing steps and different multiples of n, before they carry out the task and discuss these. Observe the supports that children use to help them complete this task, e.g. strips of paper, pictures, words or simply numbers. This will help you to assess the depth of their understanding.

Step 3

This task asks children to measure and cut strips of paper of four different lengths. They then use these to make bar models to show missing number statements, e.g. they lay the 6 cm strip above the 23 mm strip, work out the missing value and then draw a strip of this size. Encourage them to find as many different possibilities as they can and to make strips of these lengths. Observe how children check their answers.

Step 4

This is a well-known investigation that involves children in algebraic reasoning. Encourage children to find all the possible answers and to talk to a partner or write down what they notice about their results and how they can be sure that they have all possibilities. They need to work systematically.

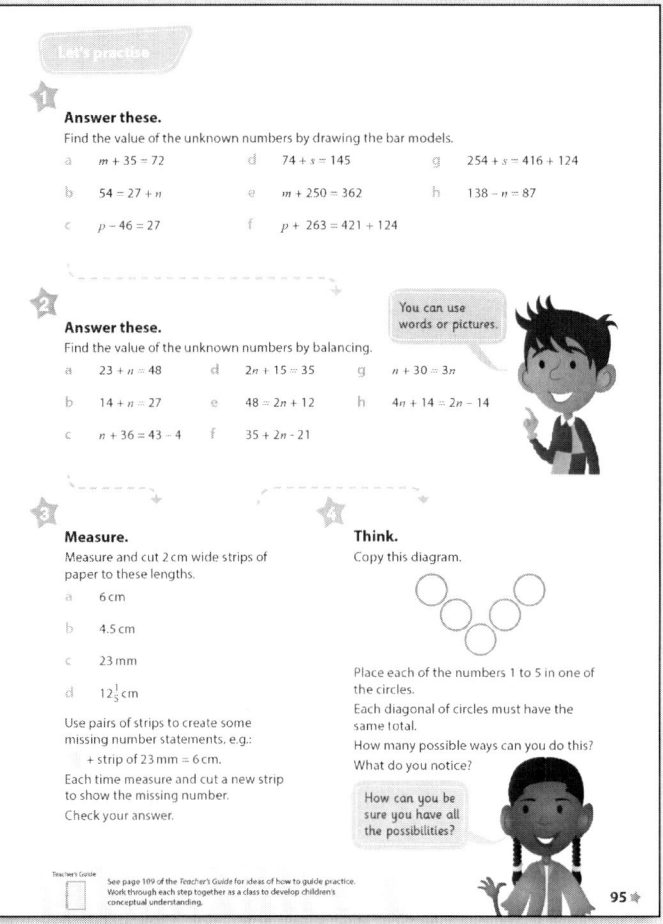

Follow-up ideas

- Ask children to make up missing number statements for a partner to solve using the bar model. They could then make some up for their partner to solve using balancing.

- Children could make up their own missing number statements and solve these using the bar model and also balancing method and consider the pros and cons of both methods with a partner.

- Children can make up word problems within the context of measures and ask the class to solve them using both the bar model and balancing method.

Ensuring progress

Supporting understanding

For children that need support on balancing equations you could work with them using pan balances and cubes. Place, e.g. 10 cubes in one pan and 6 in the other. The unknown is the amount that needs to be added to the pan with 6 to make them balance.

Broadening understanding

If children work quickly through Step 4, you could extend what they do by asking questions such as: *What happens if you use the numbers from 37 to 41? From 103 to 107? What if you use five consecutive odd numbers? What do you notice about a similar pattern with the same rules that has arms of length four using any seven consecutive numbers that you want?*

> ✓ **Concept mastered**
>
> Children can use a bar model and balancing to find unknown numbers.

Answers

	Step 1				Step 2			
a	$m = 37$	**e**	$m = 112$		**a**	$n = 25$	**e**	$n = 18$
b	$n = 27$	**f**	$p = 282$		**b**	$n = 13$	**f**	$n = 28$
c	$p = 73$	**g**	$s = 286$		**c**	$n = 3$	**g**	$n = 15$
d	$s = 71$	**h**	$n = 51$		**d**	$n = 10$	**h**	$n = -14$

Step 4

There are three distinct possibilities. The number that appears in both diagonals must be odd.

```
  2       4        1       4        1        3
   5    3        5    2        4    2
    1             3                5
```

There are 8 different arrangements for each of these 3 possibilities; e.g. in the first, the 2 and 5 must be in one diagonal and 3 and 4 in the other, but they could be swapped over and their order doesn't matter.

Unknown numbers

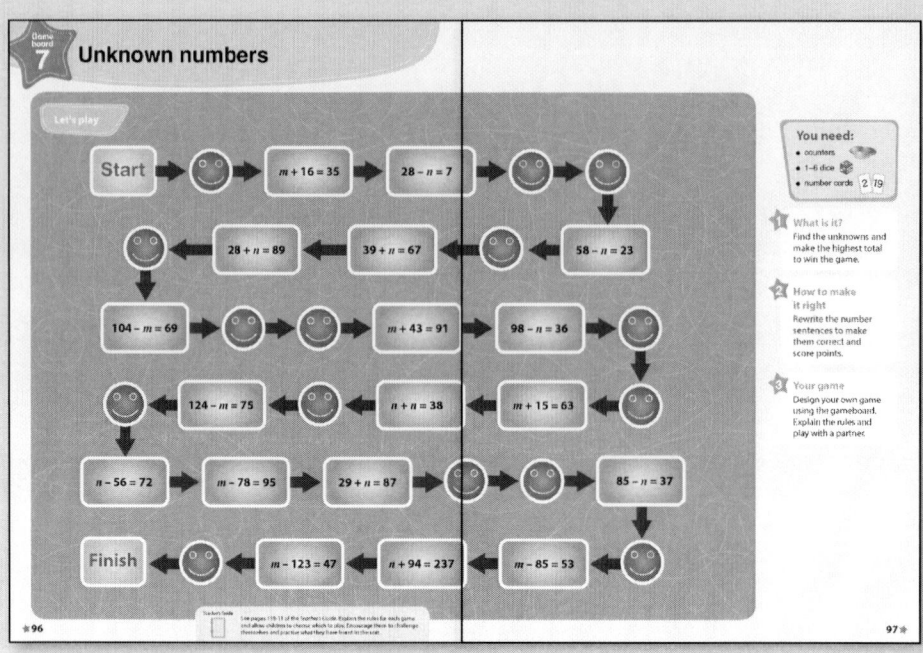

Game 1: What is it?

In this game children have to find the unknown numbers as they make their way around the board. They total their unknowns at the end – who will get the highest total?

Maths focus

- Find unknown numbers

Resources

1 counter per player (1 colour per player), 1–6 dice (1).

How to play

This game should be played in pairs. Each player puts their counter on Start on the gameboard. They throw the dice and move that number of spaces around the board. If they land on a smiley face, they stay there until their next throw. If they land on a number statement, they work out the unknown number and write this down. They can use either the bar model or balancing to do this. Play continues this way until both players land on Finish. They then work out the total of all the unknowns that they found. The winner is the player with the highest total. They could play this three times, the winner being the player with the highest final total.

Making it easier

When children land on a statement, they should draw the bar model to work out the unknown number. To save some time, you could have premade bar models for them to populate with the numbers.

Making it harder

When children land on a statement, they should use balancing to work out the unknown number. Encourage them to explain to their partner what they are doing.

Game 3: Your game

Children should invent their own game designing rules that use the concepts covered in the unit. Challenge children to make the game easier or harder.

Game 2: How to make it right

In this game, children rewrite the number statements – they must get them right in order to score points.

Maths focus

- Recreate number statements to make them correct

Resources

1 counter per player (1 colour per player), 1–6 dice (1), number cards from 10 to 50.

How to play

This game should be played in pairs. First children shuffle the number cards and put them in a pile face down on the table. Each player puts their counter on Start on the gameboard. They throw the dice and move that number of spaces around the board. If they land on a smiley face, they stay there until their next throw.

If they land on a statement, they pick a number card. This replaces the unknown in the number statement. They then rewrite the number statement so that it is correct, e.g. if they land on $m + 16 = 35$ and pick the number card 23, the number statement becomes $23 + 16 = 35 + 4$. If their partner agrees that the new statement is correct they score five points.

They keep playing until a player reaches Finish. They then add up the total points scored. The winner is the player with the highest score.

Making it easier

Children could use digit cards from one to nine to substitute for the unknowns.

Making it harder

Children could use number cards from 50 to 99 to substitute for the unknowns.

Unknown numbers

Choose a game to play.

Game 1: What is it?

You need:
- 1 counter per player (1 colour per player)
- 1–6 dice

How to play

- Place your counters on Start. Take it in turns the throw the dice and move around the board.
- If you land on a smiley face, stay there until your next throw.
- If you land on a number statement, work out the unknown number and write it down.
- Keep playing until you both land on Finish.
- Work out the total of all the unknowns you found. The winner is the player with the highest total.

Game 2: How to make it right

You need:
- 1 counter per player (1 colour per player)
- 1–6 dice
- number cards from 10–50

How to play

- Shuffle the number cards and put them in a pile face down. Place your counters on Start.
- Take it in turns the throw the dice and move around the board.
- If you land on a smiley face, stay there until your next throw.
- If you land on a number statement take a number card from the pile:
  - use this number to replace the unknown in the number statement
  - rewrite the number statement so it is correct.

  If you land on $m + 16 = 35$ and pick the number card 23, the number statement becomes $23 + 16 = 35$.

  You need to add 4 to the right-hand side to make it correct: $23 + 16 = 35 + 4$.
  Ask your partner to check your statement, if they agree, you score 5 points.
- Keep playing until one of you lands on Finish.
- Add up your scores to find the total. The winner is the player with the highest score.

Game 3: Your game

- Make up your own game using the gameboard.
- What are the rules for your game? Explain them to someone.

Assessment task 1

Before children begin this task recap finding equivalent fractions. Ensure that children can explain how to do this and they know that in order to compare, add and subtract fractions finding equivalent fractions is important. Expect them to be able to tell you that equivalent fractions have the same denominator and to find this they need to find a common multiple.

They also need to explain that because a fraction has a numerator and a denominator which are linked to each other, anything done to the denominator must also be done to the numerator, e.g. to change four fifths to tenths, the denominator must be doubled and therefore so must be the numerator.

During the first part of the task children need to find equivalent fractions to find the largest; two pairs need changing to mixed numbers first. In the second part of the task some children may be able to visualise the equivalence of some of the fractions in the questions through their work using fraction strips. If this is the case, ask them to explain how they have worked out their answers. Others will convert each pair of fractions to make two equivalent fractions with the same denominator. Ensure that they show you what they have done with a brief written explanation.

The third part of the task asks children to convert between fractions, decimals and percentages. You may need to work with some of the class to recap this before they begin.

Evidencing mastery

If children can add and subtract fractions by finding equivalent fractions and can convert between fractions, decimals and percentages with clear explanations of what they have done, they have mastered this area of mathematics.

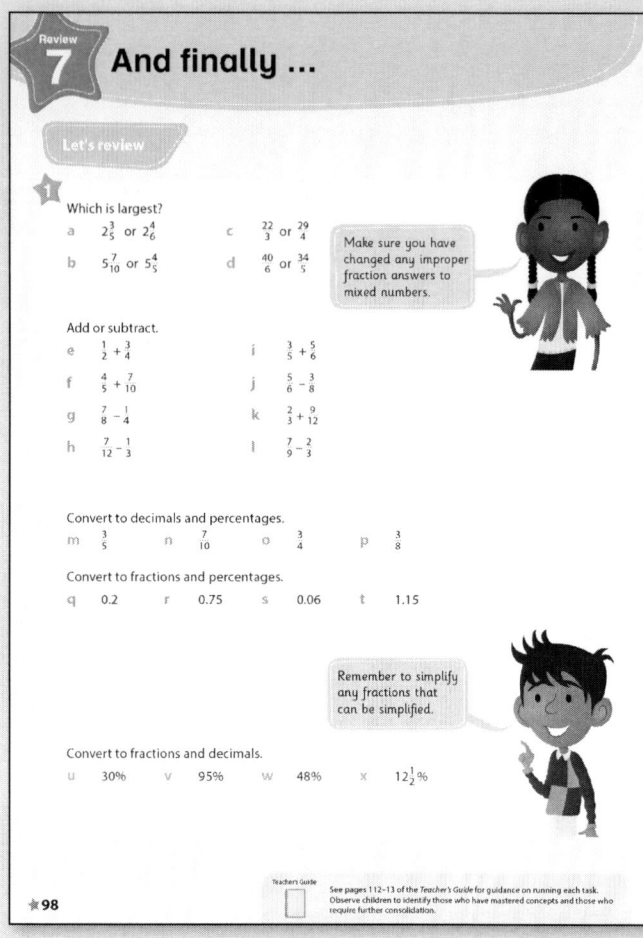

Assessment task 2

Running the task

Before children begin the task, recap the bar model for finding unknowns. Encourage them to practise a few examples, such as $m + 45 = 72$, $3n = 24 + 12$, $24 + t = 12 + 40$. Once you have done this, discuss the balancing method. Write examples on the board for them to answer. Discuss why these methods are helpful in developing their algebraic reasoning. You could focus on the fact that the bar model is helpful visually in allowing children to understand what they need to do and that balancing isolates the unknown.

The task asks children to find the unknown numbers. They can choose which method they use. You could encourage less confident children to sketch and use the bar model. You could encourage children who have grasped the concept well to use the balancing method.

Evidencing mastery

If children can find unknown numbers using either method confidently and efficiently they are evidencing mastery of this element of algebra at this level.

Concepts mastered

✓ Children can explain and demonstrate how to convert fractions to a common denominator and to use this understanding to compare, add and subtract fractions.

✓ Children can explain and demonstrate how to convert from fractions to decimals and percentages and vice versa.

✓ Children can explain and demonstrate how to use simple formulae to find perimeters and areas of rectangles, triangles and parallelograms.

✓ Children can use a bar model and balancing to find unknown numbers.

Assessment task 3

Resources

Centimetre-squared paper, rulers.

Running the task

Before children begin the task recap finding the perimeters and areas of rectangles. Encourage them to tell you the formulae for both. Write some dimensions on the board and ask them to use the formulae to find their perimeters and areas. You could ask them to draw the rectangles accurately on paper first.

After they have done this, ask them how they can use this method to find areas of triangles and parallelograms. You could ask them to look at the appropriate pages in the Textbook as a reminder. Agree that to find the area of a triangle they could halve the area of a rectangle that can be made using two identical triangles. Remind them of the formula they discussed: $\frac{1}{2}$ length × width. For parallelograms, they explored how to make one into a rectangle and used the formula height × width.

The task asks children to draw triangles and parallelograms on squared paper and find their perimeters and areas. Encourage them to make simple statements about what they notice, e.g. the longer the sides of the triangle the longer the perimeter. This part of the task is to help develop their reasoning skills.

Evidencing mastery

If children can confidently explain and demonstrate how the formulae for the perimeter and area of rectangles, including squares, triangles and parallelograms work, they will have evidenced mastery.

Did you know?

Algebra has been around for centuries. Research has shown that mankind is essentially a 'symbolic species'. We have the need to make ideas visible in the mind, in other words we need to visualise things in order to make sense of them.

In early civilisations people used to visualise things that they were not sure of or problems that they wanted to solve. Egyptian hieroglyphics, as shown in the Textbook, are an early example of how people represented number using visual symbols. Gradually over time these visualisations became actual representations and abbreviations.

Finally, in the 17th century they became algebraic symbols close to what we use today in school.

Mathematical focus

★ **Number: addition, subtraction, multiplication and division, fractions (including decimals and percentages)**

★ **Ratio and proportion**

★ **Algebra: simple formulae, number problems**

★ **Measurement: mass, capacity, volume, money, length, distance, time**

★ **Statistics: interpret and construct, interpret and calculate**

Prior learning

Children should already be able to:

- find factor pairs of a number identifying multiples of numbers and prime numbers

- multiply and divide whole numbers by 10, 100 and 1000, using short multiplication with whole numbers and use short division with whole numbers

- interpret a percentage as the number of parts per hundred using tenths and hundredths and recalling number facts.

Key new learning

- Identify common factors, common multiples and prime numbers.

- Solve problems involving addition, subtraction, multiplication and division.

- Multiply and divide numbers by 10, 100 and 1000, giving answers up to three decimal places.

- Multiply and divide numbers, giving answers up to three decimal places.

- Calculating percentages of amounts.

- Calculating what percentage one amount is of another.

- Find pairs of numbers that satisfy an equation with two unknowns.

- Enumerate possibilities of combinations of two variables.

Making connections

- Money is one of the most widely recognised uses of percentages. It is a familiar use of decimal notation and can be used to underpin understanding of decimal notation.

- Common factors are used for simplifying fractions and, eventually, for factorising in algebra. Common multiples are used when adding and subtracting fractions to obtain a common denominator.

Unit 8 — Using what you know

I wonder what the sale price is if it cost £50 to start with?

20% off

I wonder how I can get the right amount of electricity to go around this circuit?

★ 100

Talk about

The techniques in this unit involve building on prior learning, by applying it in different situations or extending it a little. It is important to present it in this way, as it reinforces what has been learnt. For each concept, use phrases such as 'we already know this, so we can now ...'. Encourage children to verbalise their prior learning as they are introduced to new concepts, through rich mathematical talk with adults and peers.

Engaging and exploring

Percentages are used to communicate reductions in a sale, as in the first photo. Children will be familiar with this. Ask: *Have you seen percentages when you are shopping?* After collecting some examples, ask: *What do you think 20% off means?* It is worth prompting recall of the idea that percentage means number of parts per hundred. Ask children how they would deduce the reduction on an item that cost £50, as in the photograph. A common misconception is that the percentage amount is the same as the monetary amount. Ensure that children understand that this is not the case by presenting further examples, e.g. *What if the item cost £10? What about if it cost £20?* Extend the discussion to collect instances of other uses of percentages they may have come across.

A common complaint from children is that algebra is of no use in real life, perhaps because they have not used it in their daily lives or they may find it difficult. The most likely situation that they will come across it is when using spreadsheets in the workplace. The cells may contain formulae used to calculate costs or wages, for example. A grasp of algebra is essential when using speadsheets.

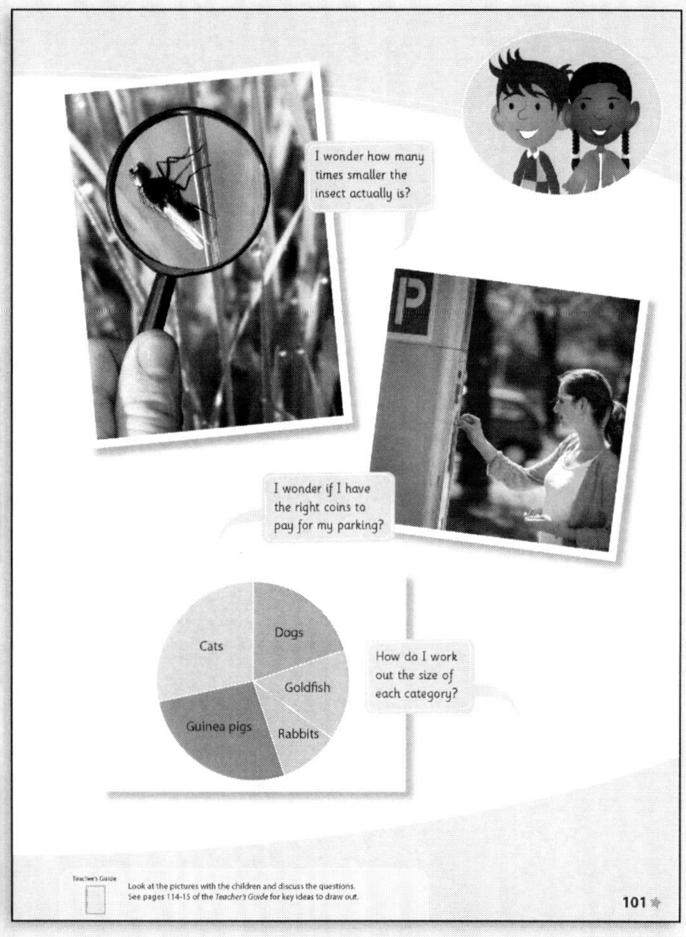

The second picture shows an electrician. Tell children that $V = RI$ means voltage = resistance × current. Discuss what this might mean using their knowledge of circuits from their science lessons. They have not met resistance but they should recognise voltage (batteries) and current (potential for electric shocks). Discuss how the electrician could use this formula in order to get the right amount of electricity flowing around the circuit. Draw out the idea that numbers can be substituted into the formula.

Ask children what insect is shown in the photograph. And to estimate how long it is. Ask children to suggest mathematical questions to ask about the image, e.g. How long is the insect in centimetres? What is the scale factor for the magnifying glass? Challenge children with your own questions, e.g. An ant is 2 mm long. How long will it look in the magnifying glass? Ask children if they have used a telescope or binoculars to look at far away objects. Encourage them to estimate how much larger things looked.

Many children will have come across Pay and Display parking machines. They may recall the search for the right coins in order to pay for the time needed. Ask: *What amounts of money it is sensible to charge via a machine? Is there a limit to the amount you could charge? What would that limit be?* Challenge children with problems such as: Parking costs £1.70 per hour and I have 3 £1 coins, two 50p coins, 7 20p coins coins. How many hours can I buy? Can I pay for it exactly?

Pie charts are used to show information in many different contexts. Discuss what children can say about the pets from the pie chart. Encourage them to say what they can and cannot tell from the pie chart. They may suggest that they can say which pet is most popular, which is least popular, what proportion are guinea pigs. This is also a good opportunity to link to angles.

I wonder how many times smaller the insect actually is?

I wonder if I have the right coins to pay for my parking?

How do I work out the size of each category?

Cats · Dogs · Goldfish · Guinea pigs · Rabbits

Teacher's Guide   Look at the pictures with the children and discuss the questions.
See pages 114-15 of the *Teacher's Guide* for key ideas to draw out.

101

Checking understanding

You will know that children have mastered these concepts when they can explain how to find common factors and multiples; multiply and divide confidently using numbers up to three decimal places in the multiplicand, product, dividend and quotient; identify data which can best be represented in a pie chart and explain how to construct that pie chart; work out percentages of quantities in order to solve problems; find all the possibilities of a combination of two variables.

Things to think about

- How will you ensure that children are aware that these are calculations someone may do in real life?

- How will you use realistic contexts and numbers?

- How will you encourage children to use their reasoning skills to work out what to do?

- How will you develop independence in your learners?

- How will you ensure that importance is placed on a systematic approach?

- How will you come back to these scenarios as you work through the sections of the unit?

- How will you use group work to discuss other situations where similar mathematics might be used?

- How will you ask children to seek out examples for homework?

- How will you create a display on the working wall of real-life calculations?

8a Identifying common factors, multiples and prime numbers

- Identify common factors, common multiples and prime numbers.
- Solve problems involving addition, subtraction, multiplication and division.

Homework 49 and 50

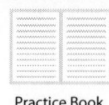
Practice Book pp 97–9

100 Squares

Multiplying by decimals

Mathematical vocabulary

Factor, proper factor, multiple, common factor, common multiple, prime, product

Representations and resources

Arrays, number lines, whiteboards and pens, adhesive notes, calculator, multiplication table squares, counters.

Warming up

Practise identifying factors of a number by saying a number and asking children to write all its factors on whiteboards. You could also practise in context, saying *I have 30 children in my class and I want them to work in groups, all of the same size. How many can I have in each group? How many groups could I have?* This reinforces the idea of factor pairs.

Practise counting in multiples of numbers from 2 to 12, e.g. 7, 14, 21, 28 and so on.

Background knowledge

Factors are the building blocks of numbers. The first step is the connection between even numbers and multiples of two, implying that two is a factor of the number. This links with the multiplication table for two, as well as doubling and halving. Further multiplication tables, and the associated division facts, continue to link factors and multiples of numbers to give children an enhanced understanding and recall of these number facts.

Prime numbers are numbers with exactly two factors, themselves and one. This means that one is not prime, but two is prime. All other even numbers have two as a factor, so cannot be prime.

Let's learn: Modelling and teaching

Finding factors

- Challenge children to find as many different mental methods as they can for working out 48×13. Tell them that they can use jottings to help. Ask them to identify advantages and disadvantages for each.

- Explain that the first strategy is to identify prime factors. Demonstrate this using the example in the Textbook. Ask children to suggest the benefits of this strategy.

- The second strategy involves doubling. Highlight that this can be done entirely mentally. Ask children: *Work out $3 \times 13 = 39$ mentally. Double it $(2 \times 3 \times 13) = 78$, double again $(2 \times 2 \times 3 \times 13) = 156$ and so on, until reaching 624.* Look at the example in the Textbook: 48×13. 48 has 2^4 as a factor; doubling can be done four times.

- It is important to stress that there is no 'correct' method.

Common factors and multiples

- In mathematics, common means 'belonging to each one'.

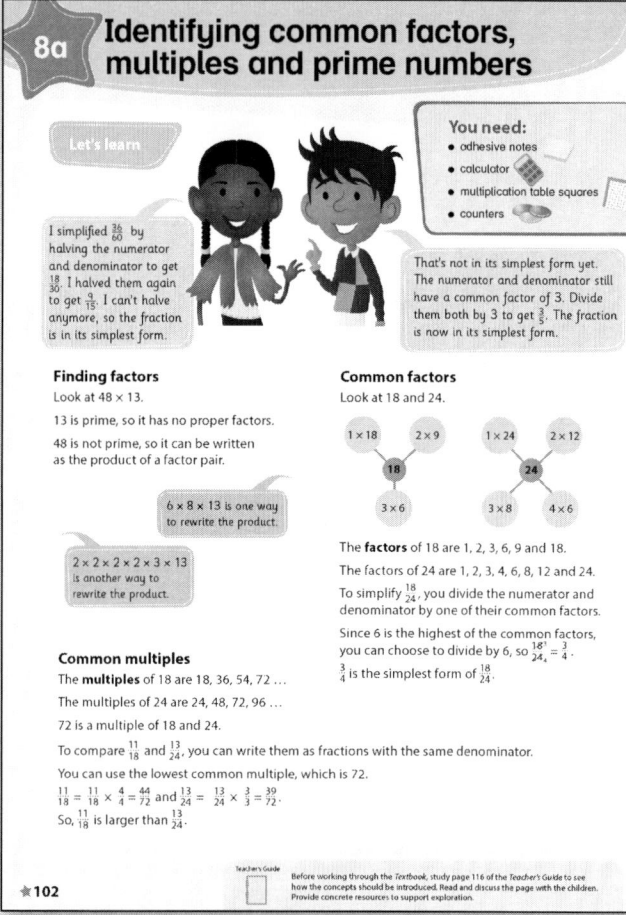

e.g. six is a common factor of 12 and 30, which means six is a factor of both 12 and 30.

- Ask children how they could find common factors quickly. Look together at the diagram in the Textbook showing the factor pairs for 18 and 24. Explain that the diagram is easy to draw because of the patterns involved. Ask children to identify the links that they see between the factor pairs. Discuss whether they need all of the information from the diagrams to simplify fractions.

- Use this opportunity to revisit equivalent fractions using fraction bars.

- Ask children to generate a set of factors and multiples, and to identify those common to both lists. Discuss what they notice. Explore how they could identify a common multiple most efficiently.

Let's practise: Digging deeper

Step 1

Children apply their knowledge of factors, exploiting their properties to find efficient methods. Challenge children to find shortcuts. *Do you need to write down every factor? Can you eliminate some immediately? What pattern can you see in the common multiples? Why do you think that happens?*

Step 2

The first question has one prime number, so it is clear that 42 requires factorising. Ask: *What is special about 31?* Exploring the options for part b will yield 23 × 5 × 2 × 7 and the opportunity to multiply by ten once 7 × 23 has been calculated. Simplifying part c requires noticing the single common factor of seven, whereas part d has many common factors and finding the largest is a challenge you could offer children. Part e requires the use of equivalent fractions. This is increased to three fractions in part f. Noticing that $\frac{3}{7}$ must be smallest, since it is less than half, makes this less labour-intensive. You could also ask: *How do we know that $\frac{3}{7}$ must be first?* to encourage thinking about efficient methods.

Step 3

There is more than one answer to the first three questions. Children can generalise to describe the whole collection of correct answers. Encourage children to use jottings and diagrams to model the problems, particularly as they become more complex.

Step 4

It is possible to answer part a quickly, if you deduce that six must be a factor of both numbers. There are several answers to this question. By creating their own problems, children will consolidate their understanding of the mathematical concept. Prompt children by asking: *Can you give me a hard problem? What would an easy problem look like? Why is that?*

The search for the number with the most factors could be approached systematically if you consider the prime factors. It is also possible to rule out prime numbers and prime multiples of prime numbers quite quickly, which demonstrates a deep understanding of the ideas in this section.

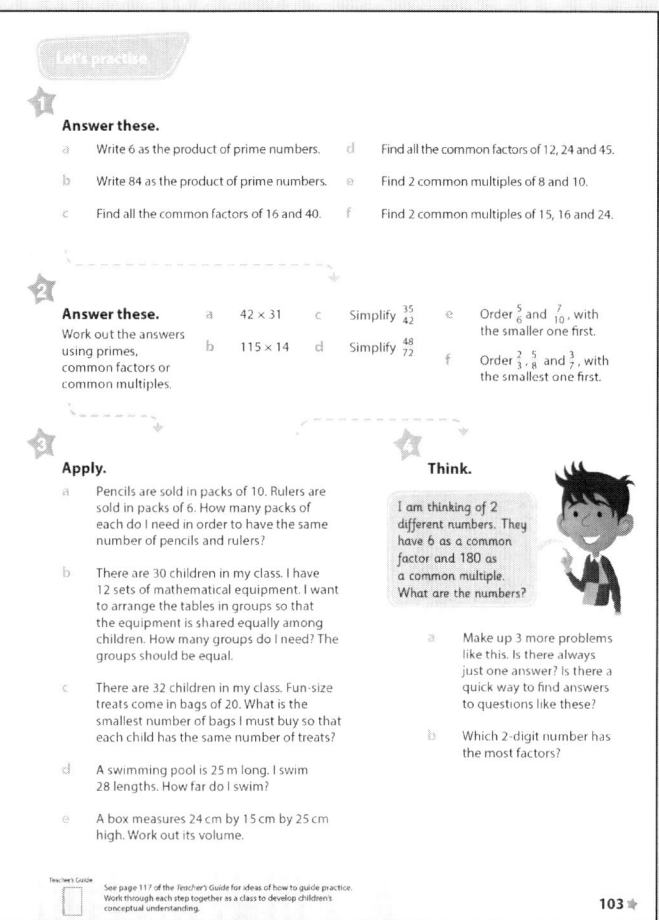

Follow-up ideas

- Make up more questions like Step 4 to try on other children.

- Discuss other times when knowing about primes, common factors or common multiples can be helpful.

- Make up other number puzzles for a 'Puzzle of the week' series.

Ensuring progress

Supporting understanding

Children can arrange numbers as arrays to identify factors, or have a copy of the multiplication table square.

Broadening understanding

Ask children to work in pairs to explain why the strategies using prime numbers work and to identify more situations, both mathematical and contextual, where the ideas of common factors and multiples may be used.

 Concept mastered

Children can identify common factors and common multiples. They can decide whether a number is prime, in order to choose a strategy for calculating with it.

Answers

Step 1

a 2 × 3

b 2 × 2 × 3 × 7

c 1, 2, 4, 8

d 1, 3

e 40, 80, any multiple of 40

f 240, 480, any multiple of 240

Step 2

a 1302   d $\frac{2}{3}$

b 1610   e $\frac{7}{10}, \frac{5}{6}$

c $\frac{5}{6}$ f $\frac{3}{7}, \frac{5}{8}, \frac{2}{3}$

Step 3

a Five packs of rulers and three packs of pencils, or multiples of this

b Six groups, three groups or two groups

c Eight bags

d 700 m

e 9000 cm³

Step 4

a 6 and 30 and there are several others

b 60, 72, 84, 90 and 96 all have ten proper factors (not including 1 or themselves)

Multiplying and dividing decimal numbers

- Multiply and divide numbers by 10, 100 and 1000, giving answers up to three decimal places.
- Multiply and divide numbers, giving answers up to three decimal places.

Homework 51 and 52   Practice Book pp 100–3

Mathematical vocabulary

Decimal, divisor, dividend, quotient, average, metric

Representations and resources

Whiteboards and pens, calculators, Gattegno charts, place-value counters, place-value charts, coins.

Warming up

Practise multiplying and dividing whole numbers by 10, 100 and 1000, e.g. *Work out 56 × 100, 304 × 10, 6700 ÷ 100. What do I need to divide 5000 by to get 50?* Practise in context by converting between metric units. How many centimetres are in 12 metres? *How many litres is 23 000 millilitres? How many kilograms is 1500 grams?*

Background knowledge

Children met multiplication and division of decimals up to two decimal places by whole numbers in Unit 3–Larger numbers. When multiplying or dividing decimals by a single-digit whole number, it is possible to use short multiplication and division. These do not extend easily when multiplying or dividing decimals by two or more digit numbers, or by decimals. The most effective approach is to multiply or divide using the whole numbers that are formed by the digits, and then decide where to replace the decimal point. Estimating by rounding the numbers to get a sensible size for the answer is one way. Reasoning about how many times larger or small the answer may be is another way.

Let's learn: Modelling and teaching

Multiplying and dividing by 10, 100 and 1000

- Ask children what they notice in the Gattegno chart in the Textbook. Ask: *What do you do to the numbers in each line to get the numbers in the line below? What is happening mathematically?*

- Ask children how they can find the answer to 0.027 multiplied by 1000. Guide them to understand that 0.027 can be partitioned into 0.02 and 0.007. Ask children to 'take their fingers for a walk' along the chart as they multiply each by 1000. Ask children to explain the same calculation using place-value counters. Carry out a variety of calculations such as 0.4 ÷ 100, 1.03 × 10, 218 ÷ 100, 2.18 ÷ 100 using the Gattegno chart and place-value counters. Ask children to explain what is happening each time.

Multiplying and dividing decimals with answers up to three decimal places

- Ask children to explain what they think is happening in

the multiplication calculation in the Textbook. Ask: *Why is there an eight written at this (right-hand) end? Why do you think we multiply the one by the eight?* Ask children to interpret the steps in the calculation using the Gattegno chart. Continue until children can follow the method with understanding.

- Ask children to explain what is happening in the division calculation in the Textbook. If necessary, prompt them by asking questions such as: *Why is there a zero above the three? Why is there a small three by the nine?* Continue until children can follow the method with understanding.

Let's practise: Digging deeper

Step 1

The first two questions are bare practice of multiplying and dividing decimals by 100, which children will have met when converting metric units. The next two involve 1000 and contain zeros as place-holders or as part of the number. Parts e and f progress to multiplication and division involving three decimal places and single-digit whole numbers. Children can use short multiplication and division to work these out. Part g uses a 2-digit divisor, but within multiplication table knowledge. Part h involves a whole number dividend, but the quotient has three decimal places.

Step 2

Missing number questions reinforce the inverse relationship between multiplication and division. Having one number on the right-hand side of the equals sign reinforces the role of equals as an equivalence relation. Ensure that children understand this by asking questions such as *What do you notice?* Part c has an operator missing, so children have to decide between multiplication and division.

Step 3

Encourage children to look carefully at the description in the question and the labels on the axes. Ask: *Why is there a gap at the start? How do you think the data was obtained?* Prompt children to indicate how tall the plant was at different times by holding their hand at that height above the floor or desk. Ask: *Does your answer make sense?* to draw out the different units used.

Step 4

Trial and improvement is one strategy to solve this problem. If children decide to use this strategy, ensure that they work carefully and logically. Provide support by asking them to think about how many combinations there might be and whether they have tried them all. Remind children to think carefully about whether a mental strategy or short division is the most efficient method. Ask: *Was there a remainder when you did that division? Could you see a pattern in the answers?* You may wish to prompt some children to move beyond three decimal places in order to see a pattern.

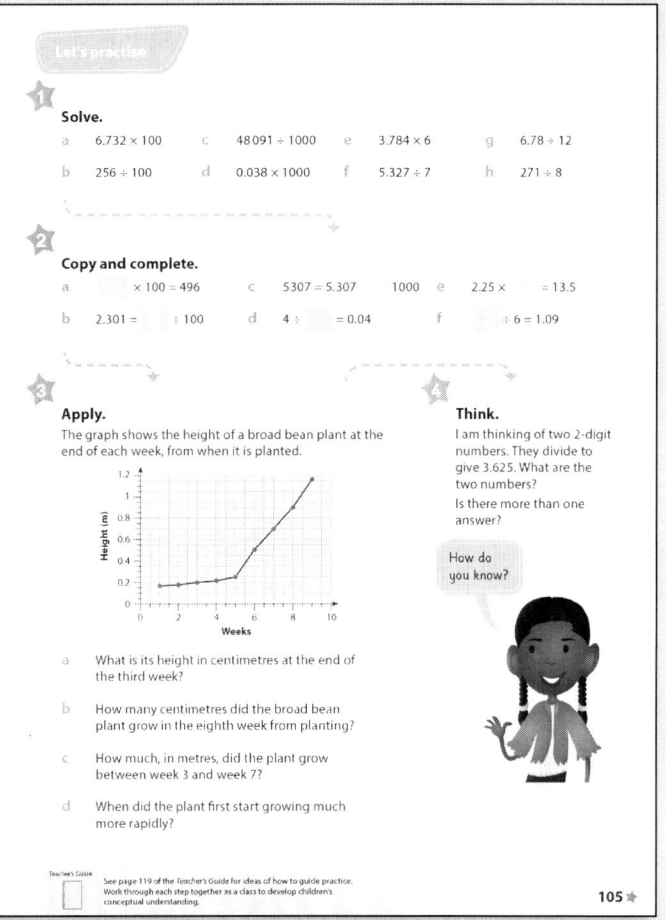

Ensuring progress

Supporting understanding

Place-value charts can be used to support multiplying and dividing by 10, 100 and 1000. Place-value counters that extend into decimals, $\frac{1}{10}$ and $\frac{1}{100}$, can support short division with decimals. You might like to show children how it works with money if they still need support. Drawing a bar diagram or other diagram of the context could also help. It requires selecting information from the question and is useful for visual learners.

Broadening understanding

Ask children to explain how they solved a problem, so that someone else could understand. This is more effective if there are still children who are struggling. You could ask children to write their own version of the questions, as this makes them think more deeply. Step 4 can be extended to different quotients or numbers of digits.

✓ **Concept mastered**

Children can multiply and divide whole numbers and decimal numbers by 1000. They can solve multiplication and division problems involving decimal numbers.

Follow-up ideas

- Grow some pea plants and measure them weekly, drawing a line graph of the results. Children can then write 'pea plant' quizzes for each other to answer.

- Children can explore the words used for 1000 times bigger than a kilogram or kilometre, then 1000 times bigger than that and so on. They can consider where they might use these measures.

- Children can make up 'What am I?' questions about decimal numbers, e.g. *I have a six as my tenths digit. The digits that form me are three, five and six. To make me whole, you must multiply by 1000. Round me to the nearest whole number and you get four. What am I?*

Answers

Step 1				Step 3	
a	673.2	e	22.704	a	20 cm
b	2.56	f	0.761	b	46 cm
c	48.091	g	0.565	c	0.5 m
d	38	h	33.875	d	After 5 weeks

Step 2				Step 4	
a	4.96	d	100	The answer must be in the ratio 29:8, so there are two possible answers: 58 and 16, 87 and 24.	
b	230.1	e	6		
c	×	f	6.54		

- **Calculating percentages of amounts.**
- **Calculating what percentage one amount is of another.**

Homework 53 and 54

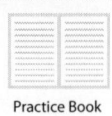
Practice Book pp 104–7

100 Squares

Mathematical vocabulary

Percentage, equivalent, ratio, deduce, reasoning

Representations and resources

Percentage bar, 100 squares, whiteboards and pens.

Warming up

Practise converting between fractions and decimals. Ask questions such as: *What is 0.25 as a fraction? What is $\frac{2}{5}$ as a decimal? What is $\frac{1}{10}$ as a decimal?*

Practise multiplication table facts as quotients. *What is 84 ÷ 12? What is 96 ÷ 8?*

Background knowledge

Percentages, together with fractions and decimals, are a way of describing part of a whole. Many children find percentages more accessible than decimals, perhaps because they are expressed as whole numbers, but find calculating with percentages difficult. Percentages are just a fraction, hundredths, in disguise. Always return to the language such as 'out of 100', 'number of parts per 100', 'hundredths' and drawing the image on a 100 square to reinforce the idea.

The most efficient way of working out a given percentage of an amount is to write it as a decimal and multiply the amount by the decimal. Children lose touch with their understanding if this is introduced too soon and need to instead use increasingly efficient methods of reasoning towards their answers. Identifying 10% and 1% as particularly useful quantities is the first step towards greater efficiency. Some will find the idea of a 'shortcut' appealing and finding 1% as a routine strategy is the most efficient at this stage. Using the percentage bar is an extension of earlier work using bar models and, like the earlier applications, is a clear way of showing the equivalences and the chains of reasoning.

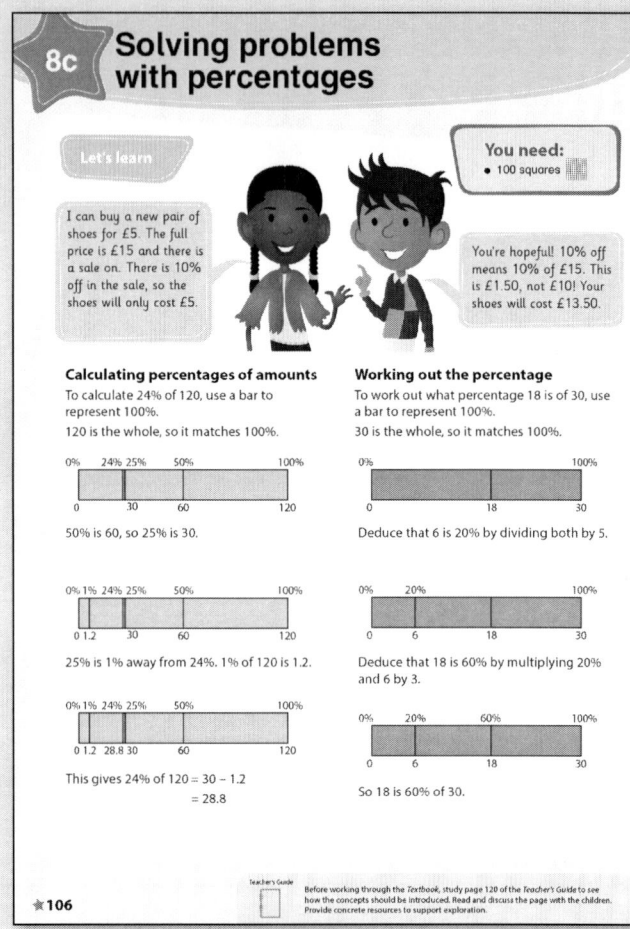

Let's learn: Modelling and teaching

Calculating percentages of amounts

- Draw the percentage bar in the Textbook with 100% at one end. You could ask children to say what number in the question matches it. Then place 24% on the bar, roughly in the right place. The bars do not need to be to scale. Ask children what they can deduce from what is there. 50% and 25% are likely to be the first suggestions, but any could be added. Ask children to work in pairs to see what else they can find out. Some may reach 24% themselves. It is worth taking time to allow children to think this through independently.

- Collect feedback on the strategies that children used and discuss the advantages and disadvantages of each. Choose one or two strategies to model using a different calculation, e.g. A survey was carried out to find the favourite colours of children in a primary school. 120 children were surveyed and 24% gave red as their favourite colour, 32% blue, 20% green and the rest yellow. How many liked each colour?

Working out the percentage

- Draw the bar in the Textbook with no markings. You might like to ask: *Where shall I put 100%?* If children are unsure, you could say *I am going to put it at the end here – why do you think I am doing that?* The next number to add is 30. Ask: *What number shall I put to match 100%?* Both are the full amount or whole. Now place 18 and explain that you are looking for the percentage that matches 18.

- You could invite children to discuss their method with a partner. Reflect on which solutions are more efficient.

Let's practise: Digging deeper
Step 1

The questions can be completed by deducing from the definition of percentage as number of parts per hundred. 10% is ten parts per hundred and 5% is five parts per hundred. Encourage children to draw a percentage bar as in 'Let's learn'. You might say: *Remember a percentage is the number of parts per hundred, what do you think 12% means?* Children should be flexible in their approach to doing calculations. They should look at the numbers involved to choose an appropriate and efficient strategy. The percentage bar encourages this approach.

Step 2

The missing number structure prompts children to approach calculations in a different way. They should still be reasoning from the definition of percentage, e.g. *20% of something is 17, so 40% is 34 and 60% is 51,* or they may get straight to 100% is

five times 17, which is 85. Encourage children to look at the numbers involved to decide an appropriate strategy.

Step 3

Pie charts are a way of using proportions of a circle, or full turn, to represent the proportions of a set of data. 360 degrees is the whole and compares with 100% as the whole in the first two parts. You could ask: *What is the whole amount?* to match with 100%. This supports children through questions on percentages.

Step 4

Children are challenged to decide the truth of an assertion about which discount comes first. Children often find it confusing to combine discounts represented by percentages. Ask children to explain their approach to a a partner. This will prepare them for later work on percentages in Key Stage 3.

Ensuring progress
Supporting understanding

100 squares are a useful image or piece of equipment. Children could shade in squares to represent the percentage. This helps them to understand what it means. The percentage bar is more helpful in terms of carrying out the calculation.

Broadening understanding

Children can make up their own questions with more difficult numbers and work out how to use percentage bars to solve them. Often the transition to awkward numbers, that don't have many factors or common factors with the other numbers in the question, tests understanding. Writing their own questions of this kind allows children to explore how to answer them more readily.

 Concept mastered

Children can calculate percentages of amounts and work out what percentage one amount is of another.

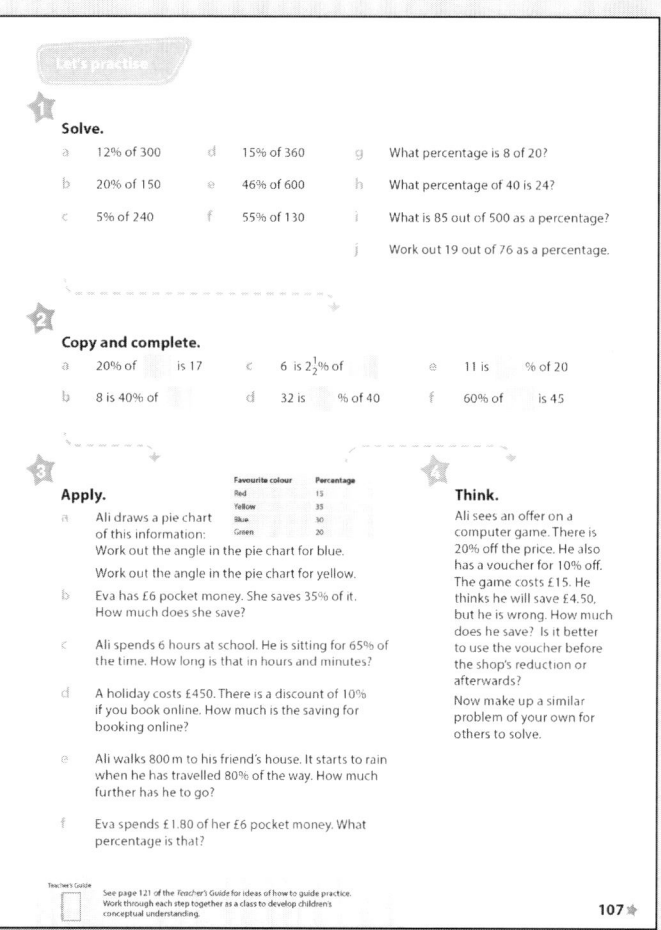

Let's practise

1 Solve.
a 12% of 300
b 20% of 150
c 5% of 240
d 15% of 360
e 46% of 600
f 55% of 130
g What percentage is 8 of 20?
h What percentage of 40 is 24?
i What is 85 out of 500 as a percentage?
j Work out 19 out of 76 as a percentage.

2 Copy and complete.
a 20% of ▢ is 17
b 8 is 40% of ▢
c 6 is 2½% of ▢
d 32 is ▢% of 40
e 11 is ▢% of 20
f 60% of ▢ is 45

3 Apply.

Favourite colour	Percentage
Red	15
Yellow	35
Blue	30
Green	20

a Ali draws a pie chart of this information:
Work out the angle in the pie chart for blue.
Work out the angle in the pie chart for yellow.
b Eva has £6 pocket money. She saves 35% of it. How much does she save?
c Ali spends 6 hours at school. He is sitting for 65% of the time. How long is that in hours and minutes?
d A holiday costs £450. There is a discount of 10% if you book online. How much is the saving for booking online?
e Ali walks 800 m to his friend's house. It starts to rain when he has travelled 80% of the way. How much further has he to go?
f Eva spends £1.80 of her £6 pocket money. What percentage is that?

Think.
Ali sees an offer on a computer game. There is 20% off the price. He also has a voucher for 10% off. The game costs £15. He thinks he will save £4.50, but he is wrong. How much does he save? Is it better to use the voucher before the shop's reduction or afterwards?
Now make up a similar problem of your own for others to solve.

See page 121 of the *Teacher's Guide* for ideas of how to guide practice. Work through each step together as a class to develop children's conceptual understanding.

107

Follow-up ideas

- Make up more puzzle questions like Step 4, involving finding percentage discounts of amounts.
- Make a poster of examples of percentages used in everyday life.
- Use the Internet to research where the idea of percentages came from.

Answers

Step 1
a	36	f	71.5
b	30	g	40%
c	12	h	60%
d	54	i	17%
e	276	j	25%

Step 2
a 20% of 85 is 17
b 8 is 40% of 20
c 6 is 2½% of 240
d 32 is 80% of 40
e 11 is 55% of 20
f 60% of 75 is 45

Step 3
a 108°, 126°
b £2.10
c 3 hours 54 minutes
d £45
e 160 m
f 30%

Step 4
£4.20 and it doesn't matter which way round the discounts are calculated

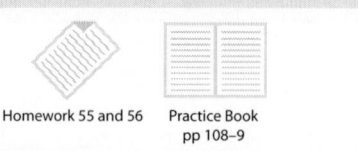

- **Find pairs of numbers that satisfy an equation with two unknowns.**
- **Enumerate possibilities of combinations of two variables.**

Homework 55 and 56   Practice Book pp 108–9

Mathematical vocabulary

Positive, sum, product, commutative, associative, algebraic, variable, equation.

Representations and resources

Number rods, digit cards, counters.

Warming up

Practise number bonds to different sums. *What do I add to 12 to get 21? What do I subtract from 21 to get four?*

Practise multiplication table facts. *What are the common factors of 12 and 20? What are the common multiples of three and five?*

Background knowledge

Children have met algebra previously, e.g. they have completed missing number questions and learned about the rules and properties of arithmetic, such as being commutative or associative. In this concept, using letters to replace numbers exploits the idea of a variable. The letter can take any number of values until constraints are added. The letter stands for an unknown quantity.

When listing all of the possible values for a pair of variables sometimes one and two is considered to be the same as two and one, and other times it is different. It depends whether the order matters. It is usually necessary to think carefully to decide whether both count.

Let's learn: Modelling and teaching

Satisfying equations

- Pose the question $a + b = 6$. Ask: *What could a and b stand for?* Draw the bar model and invite suggestions. Number rods could be available for support. Mark children's responses on the diagram. Compare the bar model that you have drawn together to the image in the Textbook.

- Challenge children to solve $a + b = 8$ for positive whole numbers and show their results in the same way. Continue to use number rods and draw the bar model to make the structure clear.

- Challenge children to make up other examples of equations with two variables and list the solutions, as well as showing them on a diagram.

What are the possibilities?

- Read Ali's equation and ask children to suggest solutions. When you have most of them, ask: *How can we be sure we haven't missed any? What is helpful about these ideas?*

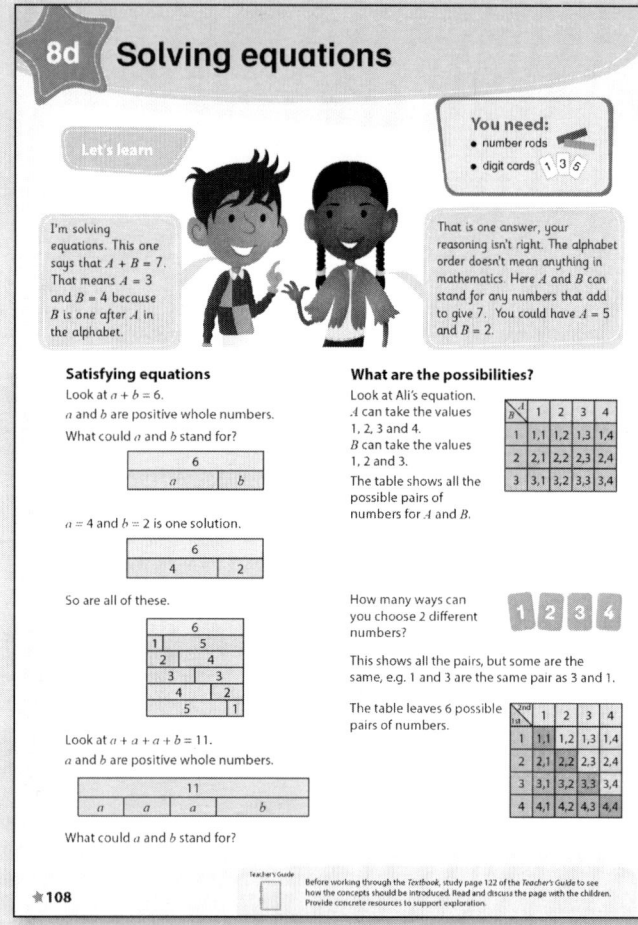

Draw out the idea of being systematic. Show children the table in the Textbook as one way of working systematically. Invite feedback on the format. Pose the next question in the Textbook.

- Ask: *What is different about this question?* Give children digit cards so that they can role play choosing two numbers. Show the full table in the Textbook and on a copy of the table circle the pairs that children have identified. Ask: *Why can't we have this one?* for one that isn't circled. It may be that you can and that one has been missed, or children reason that it is a repeat or double.

Let's practise: Digging deeper

Step 1

Prompt children by asking *what does p + q = 3 mean?* Encourage them to make sense of the question using a bar model. Sometimes the order matters and children should be prompted for all of the possibilities when this happens. A systematic approach is helpful, so you could ask: *How can you check/be sure that you have all of the possible outcomes?* Reviewing a range of responses to the questions can reinforce the idea that a systematic search is useful.

Step 2

Children should represent each question using a bar model. Part a does not specify that the numbers are positive or that they are whole numbers. Prompt children by asking *Are there any other sorts of number we could use?* There are infinitely many pairs.

Step 3

It will be obvious that some routes will not give the shortest route; others may be trickier to spot. Ask children to explain why this is the case, supporting their explanation with a bar model. Prompts such as *Can you swap the 14.5 km for a shorter route?* will support children in developing their strategy.

Step 4

Children can start with a conjecture or by generating some 'data', by finding examples of amounts that can be made. At some point they will see the need to be systematic, if only to check their conjectures. It is much more powerful if this need arises from children as they work on the task. You could have a class discussion about 'what helped' when working on the task.

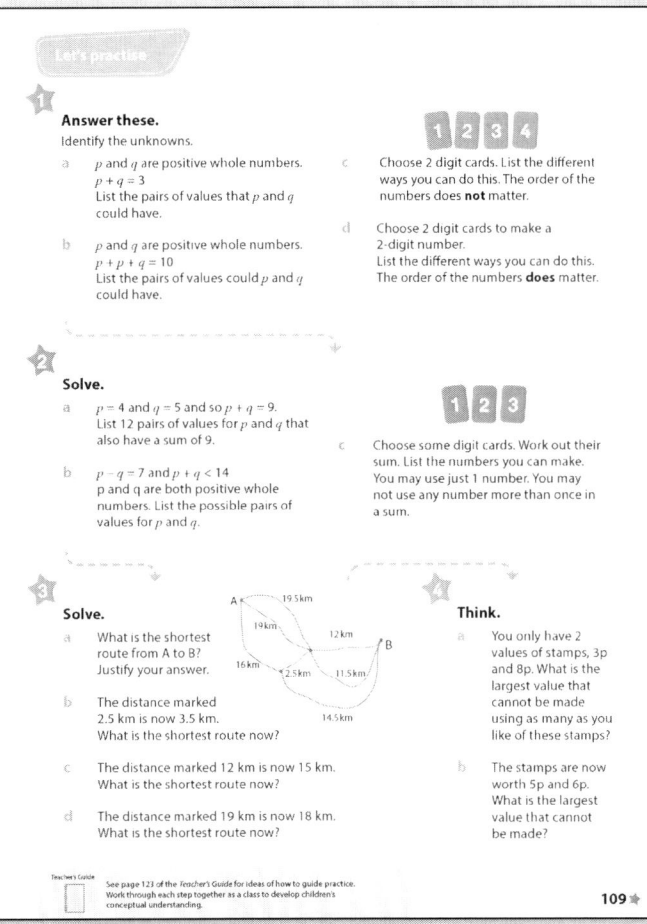

Follow-up ideas

- Step 2 links with binary or Base 2 arithmetic. Searching for the most efficient set of numbers for making others by adding, yields powers of 2 as the most efficient set. Plenty of mathematical thinking and conjecturing can go on during the search.

- Make up some more questions like those in Step 4, or continue the investigation for different values of stamps.

Ensuring progress

Supporting understanding

Children can use counters in some of the questions. They partition them in ways that match the equation. Allow plenty of time for children to make sense of the question and explore ways to answer it. There is no set way, although certain strategies are more helpful than others. Children should be allowed to make those decisions themselves.

Broadening understanding

You might like to ask: *What if the numbers are negative? What if the numbers are not whole numbers?* to encourage children to think more broadly about possibilities. You could ask children to describe all of the possible answers if there are an infinite number. Ask them to justify why there are not an infinite number in the other cases.

 Concept mastered

Children can identify the possible values of the variables for a statement such as $a + a + b = 40$. Children can enumerate all of the possible outcomes when two dice are rolled.

Answers

Step 1

a $p=1$ and $q=2$; $p=2$ and $q=1$

b $p=1$ and $q=8$; $p=2$ and $q=6$; $p=3$ and $q=4$; $p=4$ and $q=2$

c 1 and 2; 1 and 3; 1 and 4; 2 and 3; 2 and 4; 3 and 4

d 12; 13; 14; 21; 23; 24; 31; 32; 34; 41; 42; 43

c 1, 2, 3, 4, 5 and 6 can be made

Step 2

a $p=1$ and $q=8$; $p=2$ and $q=7$; $p=3$ and $q=6$; $p=5$ and $q=4$; $p=6$ and $q=3$; $p=7$ and $q=2$; $p=8$ and $q=1$; $p=9$ and $q=0$; $p=10$ and $q=-1$ and so on

b $p=10$ and $q=3$; $p=9$ and $q=2$; $p=8$ and $q=1$

Step 3

a 30 km

b 30.5 km

c 30 km

d 29.5 km

Step 4

a 13p is the largest amount that cannot be made with the stamps

b 19p

Challenging numbers

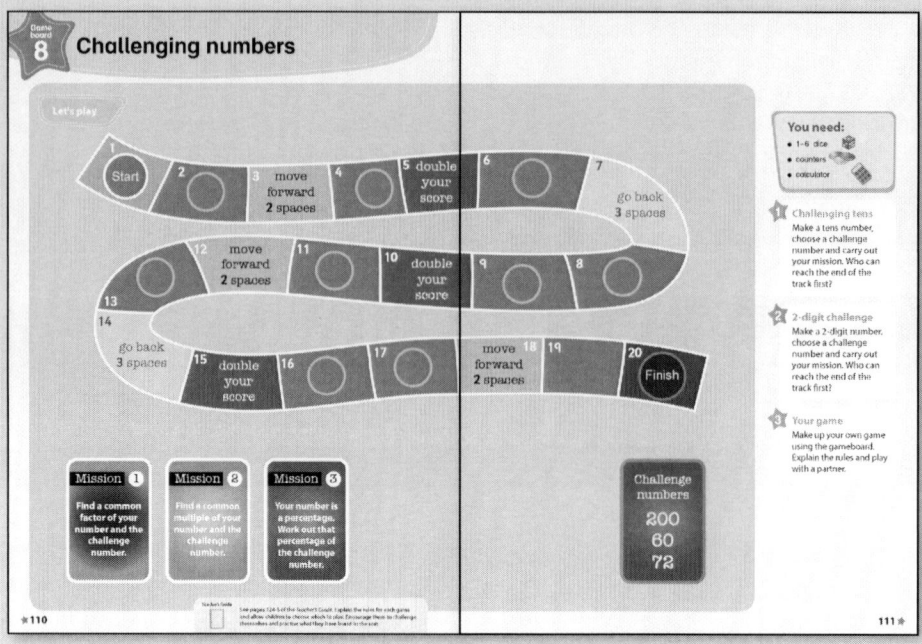

Game 1: Challenging tens

This is a race game. Some positions on the board can speed up progress and two move players back. The number of places moved is given by the challenge number.

Maths focus

* Finding common factors and multiples
* Calculating percentages
* Multiplying and dividing decimals with two decimal places by single-digit numbers

Resources

1–6 dice (1), 1 counter per player (1 colour per player), calculator.

How to play

The ones digit is zero in this game, so children first roll the dice for the tens digit. They roll the dice again to select a mission, choose a challenge number and carry out the calculation. They check their answer on a calculator. If they are correct, they can move 1 place for using challenge number 200, 2 places for using 60 and 3 places for using 72. The first player to the end of the track wins. Checks for the missions:

Mission 1

Divide the challenge number and the player's number by the answer to get a whole number. They are not allowed to answer one.

Mission 2

Divide the answer by the challenge number and then by the player's number. Answers must be whole numbers.

Mission 3

Divide the player's number by 100, then multiply by the challenge number.

Making it easier

Choose challenge number 100 to score 1 point.

Making it harder

Choose challenge number 93 to score 4 points.

Game 2: 2-digit challenge

This is also a race game. Some of the positions on the board can speed up progress along the track and there are two that move players back. The number of places moved is given by the challenge number.

Maths focus

* Finding common factors and multiples
* Calculating percentages
* Multiplying and dividing decimals with two decimal places by single-digit numbers

Resources

1–6 dice (1), 1 counter per player (1 colour per player), calculator.

How to play

This is similar to Game 1, but this time children roll the dice to get both of the digits for the 2-digit number. As with Game 1 children should be encouraged to check their mission is correct.

Making it easier

Choose challenge number 100 to score 1 point.

Making it harder

Choose challenge number 783 to score 4 points.

Game 3: Your game

Children should invent their own game, designing rules that use the concepts covered in the unit. Challenge children to make their game easier or harder.

Unit 8 Challenging numbers

Choose a game to play.

Game 1: Challenging tens

You need:
- 1–6 dice
- 1 counter per player (1 colour per player)
- calculator

How to play
- Roll the dice to get the tens digit of your 2-digit number.
- The ones digit is zero.
- Roll the dice again to get your mission.
- Choose your challenge number and carry out your mission.
- Check the answer using the calculator.
- Challenge number 200 scores 1 point, 60 scores 2 points and 72 scores 3 points.
- Your score tells you how many places to move along the track.
- Race to the end of the track.
- The winner is the first player to reach the end of the track.

Game 2: 2-digit challenge

You need:
- 1–6 dice
- 1 counter per player (1 colour per player)
- calculator

How to play
- Roll the dice to get the digits for your 2-digit number.
- The first roll gives the tens digit, the second roll gives the ones digit.
- Roll the dice again to get your mission.
- Choose your challenge number and carry out your mission.
- Check the answer using the calculator.
- Challenge number 200 scores 1 point, 60 scores 2 points and 72 scores 3 points.
- Your score tells you how many places to move along the track.
- Race to the end of the track. The winner is the player to get there first!

Game 3: Your game

- Make up your own game using the gameboard.
- How will you make your game easier or harder?
- What are the rules for your game? Explain them to someone.

Please help your child by reading the instructions and playing the game together.

Assessment task 1

Running the task

Children should be familiar with this kind of task. If not, discuss approaches with the class. Ask: *If you were marking someone's maths homework, what would you do first?* Prompt that working the answers out themselves might be helpful. It would also be helpful to think about the kind of errors people make. They may have made them themselves when they first learnt about the topic.

Each of the questions has an error that is caused by a classic misconception. Part a involves noticing that the percentage being found needs to be smaller than the number that represents 100%. Part b has an error when carrying digits across the decimal point. Children who are competent when carrying digits with whole numbers can make this error when there is a decimal point. Part c has an error with the zero in the number. Children often make mistakes when zero is involved. Part d contains the misconception that there is only one possible solution. In part e, only one pair of numbers has been considered. In part f the child has not replaced the letter with the number, but instead has kept them in the expression. Part g has included one as a prime number.

Evidencing mastery

Identifying the error in each case, explaining why it is wrong and what is needed to correctly answer the question suggest mastery. Being able to deconstruct their own understanding in order to give feedback that will move the learner on also suggests mastery.

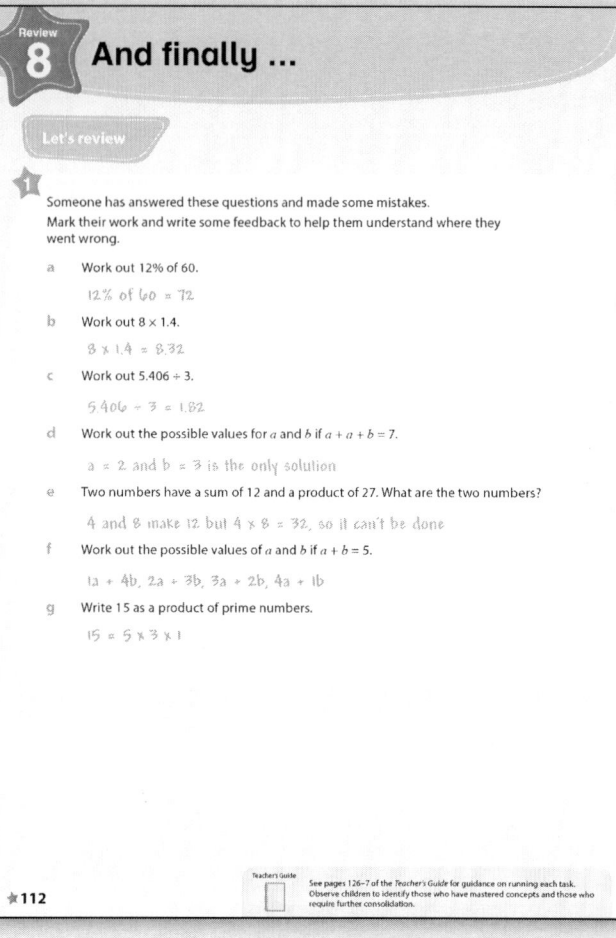

Assessment task 2

Running the task

Goldbach's conjecture states that 'every even number greater than two may be written as the sum of two prime numbers'. It has been proven up to 4×10^{18}, which is four followed by 18 zeros, but has yet to be proven for all even numbers.

To start the task use 28, or invite the class to choose a number, and try to find a way of expressing it as the sum of prime numbers. If you choose 28, that could be 23 + 5, or 17 + 11, 12 could be 5 + 7. Challenge children to use as few prime numbers as possible. When there is plenty of data available to the class, check for correct addition and use of primes. Children should write an account of what they have found out. They should include:

- What number they started with and why they chose it.

- How they decided on the best answer for that number.

- How they continued and why.

- What they noticed.

- Any conjectures they had and how they tested them, including their outcome.

Evidencing mastery

Children show mastery here by describing their thinking, so look for the following: understanding of what prime numbers are; noticing patterns emerging; descriptions and explanations of patterns leading to a conjecture; noticing that even numbers can be made with two primes; noticing that odd numbers after five can be made with three numbers; attempting to explain results.

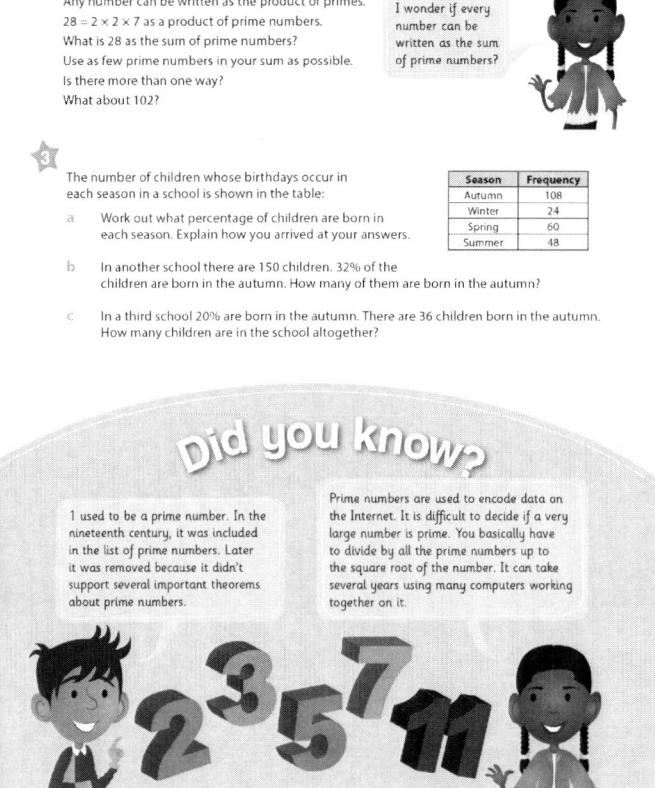

Did you know?

Concepts mastered

✓ Children can identify common factors and common multiples. They can decide whether a number is prime, in order to choose a strategy for calculating with it.

✓ Children can multiply and divide whole numbers and decimal numbers by 1000. They can solve multiplication and division problems involving decimal numbers.

✓ Children can calculate percentages of amounts and work out what percentage one amount is of another.

✓ Children can identify the possible values of the variables for a statement such as $a + a + b = 40$. They can enumerate all of the possible outcomes when two dice are rolled.

Assessment task 3

Running the task

As a class, look at the frequency table. Ask children what information they can deduce from it. Draw out that the frequency is the number of children born in each season. Then, ask children what further information they might need to work out the percentages of children born in each season. Revisit using bar models. Encourage children to draw their own bar models to help them make sense of this problem. If some children are still unsure of where to start, ask: *Which season looks the easiest to work out? What percentage is that?* Encourage children to work independently from this starting point.

Make sure children realise that the second question involves a different school. Ask: *How many children are in the second school? How many are born in the autumn?* Again, encourage them to use a bar model to help them work out their answers.

Children may find it trickier to interpret the final question. Read it together as a class, and discuss what information you know and what information you must find out. Look for children to suggest drawing a bar model to support their thinking. They will need to think carefully about what 100% is for this problem.

Evidencing mastery

Children showing mastery will draw diagrams that show an appropriate approach to finding a solution and an appreciation of the structure of the problem. They will also select the right quantity to be 100% and correctly choosing the operations in order to solve the problem.

Did you know?

You could tell children that for many years prime numbers were considered to have special powers and special significance. More recently, eminent mathematicians spent their careers exploring conjectures about prime numbers. Up until very recently, the study of primes was considered an indulgence as they could not possibly have any use in the real world. The interest of mathematicians in prime numbers was evidence of how irrelevant mathematics was to real life. The rise of the Internet has changed this completely. We can only send information securely because of public key cryptography, which encodes information securely.

Shapes and coordinates

Mathematical focus

★ **Measurement: length, area, volume**

★ **Algebra: simple formulae**

★ **Geometry: properties of shapes, position and direction**

Prior learning

Children should already be able to:

- draw 2-D shapes using given dimensions and angles

- recognise, describe and build simple 3-D shapes, including making nets

- compare and classify geometric shapes based on their properties and sizes, and find unknown angles in any triangles, quadrilaterals and regular polygons

- recognise angles where they meet at a point, are on a straight line or are vertically opposite and find missing angles

- recognise when it is possible to use the formula for area and volume of shapes

- identify, describe and present the position of a shape following a reflection or translation within the first quadrant

- use simple formulae and express missing numbers algebraically.

Unit 9 Shapes and coordinates

Can you describe the circles in this old watch mechanism?

How do the sizes compare?

★114

Key new learning

- Illustrate and name parts of circles, including radius, diameter and circumference and know that the diameter is twice the radius.

- Compare and classify geometric shapes based on their properties and sizes and find unknown angles in any triangles, quadrilaterals and regular polygons.

- Calculate, estimate and compare volume of cubes and cuboids, using standard units, including cubic centimetres (cm³) and cubic metres (m³), and extending to other units.

- Describe positions on the full coordinate grid (all four quadrants) and draw and translate simple shapes.

Making connections

- Children meet circle designs in art and see them in many aspects of everyday life, from soft furnishings to patterns on crockery.

- The concept of scale is seen in computing, geography and art and design lessons. Toys are often scale versions of real objects and maps use many different scales.

- Encourage children to use coordinates in maps and atlases.

 Talk about

Some children may have met the vocabulary of circles in everyday life but this unit introduces the terminology to everyone. Most of the words have Latin derivations. Circle comes from the Latin word 'circus' meaning ring. Radius not only meant 'ray' but also the spoke of a chariot wheel. The plural can be either radii (from the Latin plural) or the conventional English plural, radiuses. Circumference comes from the Latin 'circumferentia' meaning 'carrying around'. Diameter has Greek roots; 'dia' is across and 'metron' is measure.

Encourage children to talk and reason about the mathematics they are learning as this helps to consolidate their knowledge and understanding.

Engaging and exploring

Ask children to look at and discuss each picture with a partner before you talk about them together. Then focus on each picture in turn.

The picture of the watch mechanism may not be something that all children are familiar with as the wearing of a wristwatch becomes increasingly less common. Ask those who know what it is to explain that it is the inside of the back of a watch. Explain that the tiny cogwheels are powered either by a tightly curled spring in an old-fashioned watch or by a battery in a modern one. The cogs are carefully controlled so that the hands of the watch on the unseen side keep the correct time.

Ask children what shape they can predominantly see and establish that it is a circle. Ask them to think about why the circle is such a useful shape. Establish that, like time, it is continuous and so the watch operates without stopping.

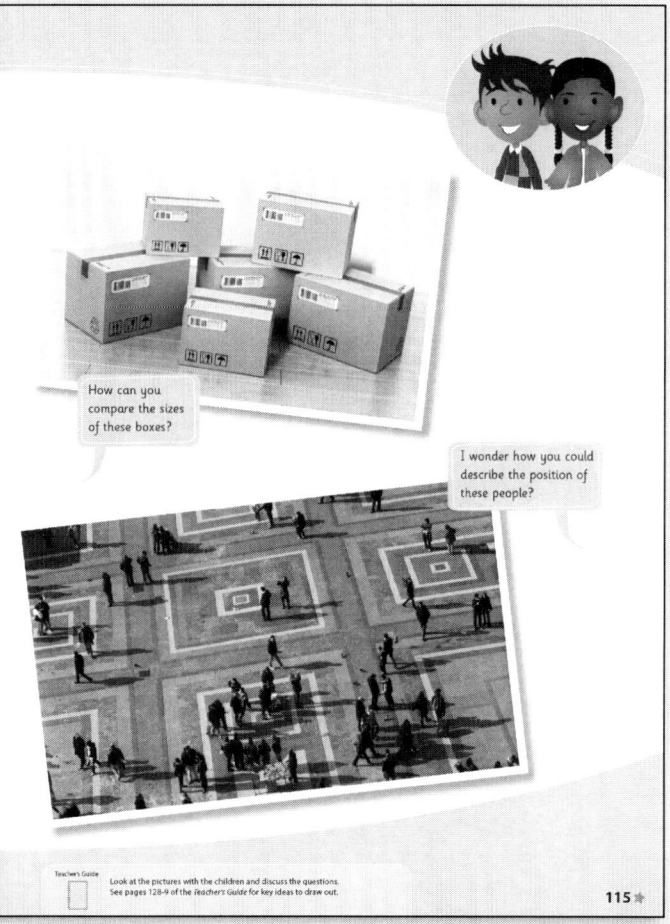

How can you compare the sizes of these boxes?

I wonder how you could describe the position of these people?

Teacher's Guide Look at the pictures with the children and discuss the questions. See pages 128-9 of the *Teacher's Guide* for key ideas to draw out.

115

Ask children to think about whether any other shapes could be used in the watch mechanism. Discuss with children the preciseness and beauty of the instrument. This is a good opportunity to revisit telling the time using an analogue clock.

Children may be more familiar with the Russian nesting doll and some may even have a set at home. In this photo the dolls have been arranged in order of decreasing size. Each doll fits inside the next and in this set there are nine dolls. Traditionally there are never fewer than five (the number is usually odd) but craftsmen have produced sets with several dozen dolls. The innermost doll, the baby, is made from a single piece of wood and does not open. Ask children to think about the relative sizes of the dolls. Reinforce comparative language, such as tallest, shortest, smaller and larger.

Show children a collection of real cardboard boxes and ask for ideas on how you could compare them. Encourage children to think about absolute and relative comparisons. Then look at the photo of the boxes. Guide children to suggest measuring the size of each box, finding the length, width and height. They may remember the formula for volume, $V = lwh$ where l is the length, w the width and h is the height. Ask them if they can tell you the units that volume is measured in and why. Establish that it is measured in cubic units, e.g. cm^3 or m^3 and that it is cubic units because you are multiplying cm × cm × cm. Focus on a particular box and ask children how big they think it is and what could be inside. Use their ideas to estimate measurements and calculate the volume.

The aerial view is of the city square in Milan, Italy. Discuss what time of day children think it is, what the weather is like, where it might be and what the people are doing. There are no correct answers (except that it is definitely sunny because there are strong shadows, nor is it close to midday because the shadows are too long). The question asks how you could describe the position of these people; this may lead children to suggest the use of a coordinate grid. They are familiar with coordinates in the first quadrant and you could revise the way of writing coordinates as a pair of number in brackets with the horizontal x coordinate first followed by the y coordinate (x, y).

Checking understanding

You will know children have mastered the concepts in this unit when they can describe circles using appropriate mathematical vocabulary and understand the term 'scale factor' and use it to solve problems. They can use the formula for calculating the volume of cuboids, estimate and compare volumes using standard units and explain why volume is measured in cubic units. They can also plot coordinates for 2-D shapes on the full coordinate grid (four quadrants) and translate them in the x- and y-axes.

Things to think about

- How will you organise the use of a teaching assistant to ensure their most effective use? You may decide to use them to keep an overview of the class while you work with a particular group of children. This can be followed by short intervention sessions with any children who are identified as requiring additional support.

- How will you check children's conceptual understanding of areas such as scale factor, volume and using four quadrants?

- In what ways can you use higher order questioning to promote and develop reasoning?

- How can you introduce problem-solving activities? Suitable techniques include 'Convince me', 'What do you notice?', 'Silly answers' and 'What's the same, what's different?'. Consider providing 'panic envelopes' to facilitate self-differentiation. Inside the envelope are hints to help children progress, such as additional information, key questions or specific examples. Children decide if and when to use them.

- **Illustrate and name parts of circles, including radius, diameter and circumference and know that the diameter is twice the radius.**

Homework 57 and 58   Practice Book pp 110–12   Geometry Instruments   Drawing circles

Mathematical vocabulary

Radius, diameter, circumference, arc, similar, scale factor

Representations and resources

Three 1–9 dice, cardboard triangles, compasses, rulers, chalk, string, metre sticks, protractors.

Warming up

Use three 1–9 dice to practise mental multiplication of three numbers. Remind children that multiplication is commutative – they can multiply the numbers in any order as this may make the calculation easier, e.g. for $2 \times 9 \times 5$, multiplying 10×9 is easier than 18×5. Ask children how they would choose to multiply $8 \times 9 \times 5$. Ask children to give you some other similar examples.

Background knowledge

Remember a circle is not a polygon because it does not have straight edges. As the number of sides on a polygon increases towards infinity the polygon becomes closer and closer to the shape of a circle.

Children will need to use angle facts learnt in earlier units. These are: the angles in an equilateral triangle are 60°; angles in a triangle total 180°; angles around a point total 360° and angles on a straight line total 180°.

Let's learn: Modelling and teaching

Enlarging with scale factors

- Give children cardboard triangles that have the same measurements as the triangles in the Textbook. Ask: *What is the same and what is different about them?* Elicit that they only differ in the size of the lengths. The triangles are similar. The ratio of their corresponding sides is called the scale factor.

- Model how to find the scale factor by locating the same side on each shape and identifying the ratio of one length to the other.

- Discuss what it means to enlarge a shape by a scale factor. Ask children to draw a 4 cm × 3 cm rectangle. Ask them what the measurements will be if it is enlarged by a scale factor of 2. Ask them to draw the new rectangle. Discuss how many times the original fits in the new rectangle. Children should cut them out to confirm. Repeat with other scale factors.

- Explain that if the scale factor is less than one, the shape will decrease in size.

- Read the misconception cartoon. Explain that in algebraic terms when lengths are multiplied by a scale factor of x the areas increase by $x \times x$.

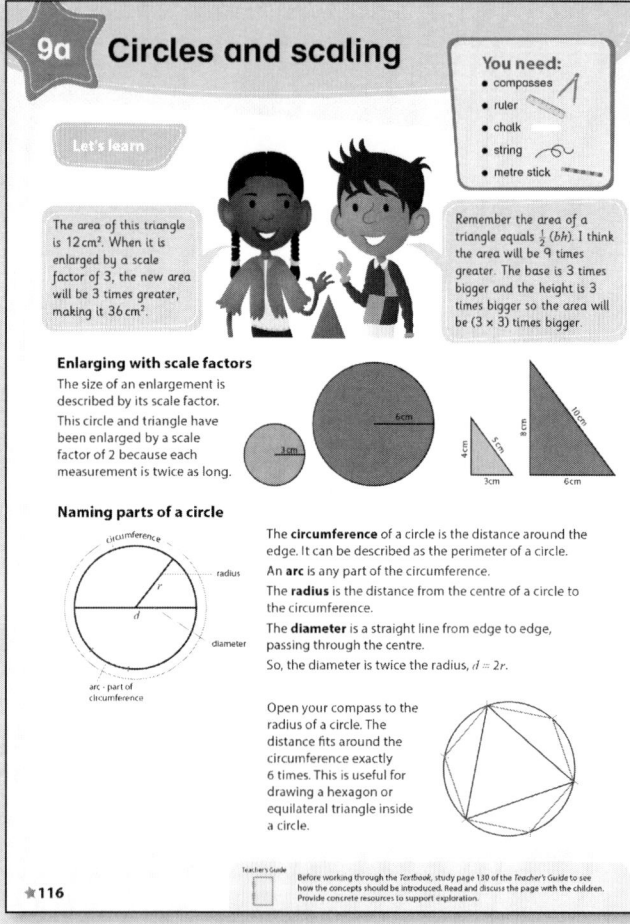

• Naming parts of a circle

- Using the Textbook, ensure that all children are secure with the vocabulary for parts of a circle.

- Ask children to: use compasses to draw a circle with a radius of 5 cm; draw a line through the centre from one side of the circle to the other; and measure this line. Highlight that it is twice the radius. Draw and measure more lines through the centre to check this relationship is true for all lines through the centre. Ask: *Do you think this is true for circles of all sizes? How might you express this rule?* Guide children to understand that $d = 2r$.

- The second diagram in the Textbook shows how the radius fits around the circumference exactly six times. This is the basis for many circle patterns.

Let's practise: Digging deeper
Step 1

In this step children are practising using the rule $d = 2r$ and substituting into the formula. Remind them to pay attention to the units being used. Ask children to estimate the size of the radius with their hands to practise visualising lengths.

Step 2

Children use the rule $d = 2r$ to find the radius and then draw the circles. Remind them to measure the radius accurately on the ruler and draw the circle with a compass without changing the size or allowing the point to slip. Using compasses is a skill that improves with practice. Ensure that children are routinely checking their work.

Step 3

It is unusual for children to work on a large scale. Check that the groups work on a design and size that will challenge them. You may need to show them how to use string to draw a circle. The centre needs to be kept fixed so children will probably need to hold the string and draw one half of the circle and then move to the other side to draw the other half.

Step 4

If necessary, remind children about angle facts. One method of working out the internal angle of the hexagon is to imagine the diagonal lines drawn in; this would give six equilateral triangles and then you can see that the internal angle equals $2 \times 60°$. Once the 120° angle is known the small acute angles can be calculated as $\frac{(180° - 120°)}{2} = 30°$ because the triangle is isosceles.

Ensuring progress
Supporting understanding

Some children find it difficult to understand that using a scale factor does not change the size of the angles. You could suggest that they use a protractor to measure the angles in the original and the enlargement to see for themselves that the angle sizes are unchanged. Using a compass requires physical dexterity, which may be challenging for some children. Ensure that children are supported with short additional sessions.

Broadening understanding

Those children who show good understanding could be given problems with a scale factor 'enlargement' of less than one. Ask them to explain to you why the new shape is smaller than the original. Encourage children to make up problems for their peers to solve which will deepen their understanding. Step 3 can be extended with more complex examples. Children could make their own designs or research them on the Internet.

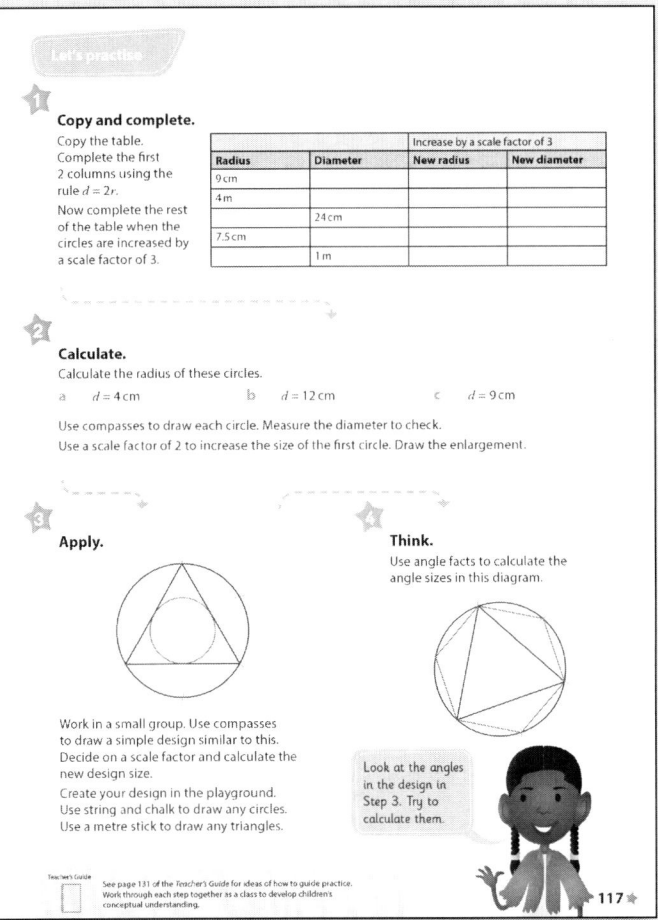

Concept mastered

Children can use the names for parts of a circle and understand and use the simple formula, $d = 2r$ to find the radius from the diameter and vice versa. They understand what a scale factor is and know that using a scale factor does not change the angles of a shape, simply its size. The original and enlarged shapes are similar.

Follow-up ideas

- Children could use the Internet to research circle designs and then use compasses to create their own circle designs. It is possible to draw a huge variety of designs, from simple flower-like pictures, to complex Islamic patterns.

- Explain to children that someone using a scale drawing created every product that we see in everyday life. This includes the work of all kinds of engineers, civil, mechanical, plumbing, industrial and structural, also architects, planners, surveyors and interior designers. Encourage children to research these careers and what the work involves.

- Ask children to look at maps and atlases and check the scales that are used on them.

Answers

Step 1

Radius	Diameter	New radius	New diameter
9 cm	18 cm	27 cm	54 cm
4 m	8 m	12 m	24 m
12 cm	24 cm	36 cm	72 cm
7.5 cm	15 cm	22.5 cm	45 cm
0.5 m or 50 cm	1 m	1.5 m	3 m

Step 2

a   radius 2 cm (4 cm when increased by a scale factor of 2)

b   radius 6 cm

c   radius 4.5 cm

Step 4

Equilateral triangle angles are 60°; obtuse angle is 120° and small angles are 30°.

- Compare and classify geometric shapes based on their properties and sizes and find unknown angles in any triangles, quadrilaterals and regular polygons.
- Calculate, estimate and compare volume of cubes and cuboids, using standard units, including cubic centimetres (cm³) and cubic metres (m³), and extending to other units.

Homework 59 and 60   Practice Book pp 113–17

Representations and resources

Geostrips, paper fasteners, board protractor, metre sticks, long tape measures.

Mathematical vocabulary

Volume, cube, cuboid, isosceles, equilateral

Warming up

Give each child a pair of geostrips fastened with a paper fastener to use as an angle measure. Ask them to show you different sizes of angles. Revise the names of angles – acute, obtuse and reflex and their sizes. You could also show children angles of different sizes on the board and ask them to name the type of angle and estimate its size. Individual children can then check the size of the angle using a large protractor. With practice, children should be able to estimate acute and obtuse angles to within 5° to 10°.

Background knowledge

Volume is the amount of space something takes up. It is measured in cubic units, e.g. cm³ or m². Children learnt to use a formula for this in Unit 4: $V = lwh$, where V = volume, l = length, w = width and h = height. Capacity is the amount a hollow 3-D container can hold and is measured in millilitres or litres. If a one litre cuboid has 500 ml of water in it, the volume of water is 500 ml but the capacity of the cuboid is one litre. In this concept you will extend children's understanding of volume through solving word problems and tackling multi-step and more open-ended tasks.

It is important that children have a secure understanding of angle facts before you attempt to solve angle problems with them.

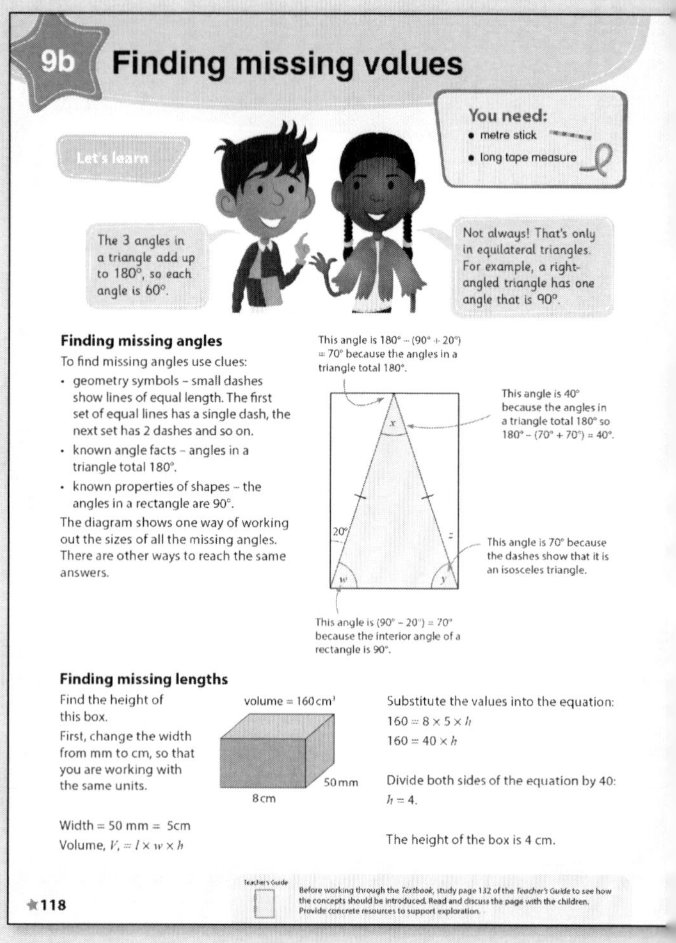

9b Finding missing values

Let's learn

You need:
- metre stick
- long tape measure

The 3 angles in a triangle add up to 180°, so each angle is 60°.

Not always! That's only in equilateral triangles. For example, a right-angled triangle has one angle that is 90°.

Finding missing angles
To find missing angles use clues:
- geometry symbols – small dashes show lines of equal length. The first set of equal lines has a single dash, the next set has 2 dashes and so on.
- known angle facts – angles in a triangle total 180°.
- known properties of shapes – the angles in a rectangle are 90°.

The diagram shows one way of working out the sizes of all the missing angles. There are other ways to reach the same answers.

This angle is 180° – (90° + 20°) = 70° because the angles in a triangle total 180°.

This angle is 40° because the angles in a triangle total 180° so 180° – (70° + 70°) = 40°.

This angle is 70° because the dashes show that it is an isosceles triangle.

This angle is (90° – 20°) = 70° because the interior angle of a rectangle is 90°.

Finding missing lengths
Find the height of this box.
First, change the width from mm to cm, so that you are working with the same units.

volume = 160 cm³

8 cm   50 mm

Width = 50 mm = 5 cm
Volume, V, = $l \times w \times h$

Substitute the values into the equation:
$160 = 8 \times 5 \times h$
$160 = 40 \times h$

Divide both sides of the equation by 40:
$h = 4$.

The height of the box is 4 cm.

Before working through the *Textbook*, study page 132 of the *Teacher's Guide* to see how the concepts should be introduced. Read and discuss the page with the children. Provide concrete resources to support exploration.

★118

Let's learn: Modelling and teaching

Finding missing angles

- Look at the triangle diagram in the Textbook. Challenge children to explain each of the symbols that they see.

- Give children examples of triangles and quadrilaterals. Ask them to measure the sides and add the correct dashes. Ask how would they mark a parallelogram or a kite.

- Ask children to recall the key angle facts: angles in a triangle total 180°, angles in a quadrilateral total 360°, angles on a straight line total 180°, angles around a point total 360°. Challenge them to prove these facts.

- Draw a right-angled triangle, isosceles triangle, scalene triangle and quadrilateral on the board. Ask children to state the facts that they know about each, e.g. each angle

in an equilateral triangle measures 60°, isosceles triangles have two equal angles, angles in a square and rectangle are all right angles, the opposite angles in a rhombus and a parallelogram are equal.

- Once children are secure with angle facts, they can approach missing angle problems and systematically tease out the sizes of the missing angles.

Finding missing lengths

- Ask children to sketch a cuboid of length 90 mm and height 2 cm. Give the volume as 108 cm³. Ask children how they could calculate the width. As a starting point, suggest that you must first ensure that the units match. Collect children's strategies on the board and discuss their efficiency.

Let's practise: Digging deeper

Step 1

The written information and the diagram together provide the necessary information to find the missing angles. In this problem the right angles are not marked because the introduction explains they are rectangles and one property of rectangles is that each angle is equal to 90°. Encourage children to verbalise their reasoning to each other, e.g. *I know the triangle is equilateral because the dash symbol tells me the lengths are all the same, that means the angles equal 60°.*

Step 2

In this step children calculate missing measurements by substituting into the formula, $V = lwh$. Each part has a little more challenge. Part a has a diagram to support children while parts b and c do not. Encourage children to use sketches and jottings as a support. In part c children

need to change the height from mm to cm so that the measurements match.

Step 3

Each of these word problems involves more than one part. Encourage children to articulate their thinking through the whole problem before they begin, e.g. *First I need to find the volume of the whole cake. I do this by using* $V = lwh$ *and I know all the measurements. Next I need to divide the answer by 20 because Ali is sharing the cake into 20 pieces. The answer is a volume so I need to include the units for volume in my answer, that's cm³.* They may wish to use sketches to support their workings.

Step 4

To solve the problem children need to take stock of what they can deduce immediately from the diagram. They can identify the right angles and the fact that angle d is equal to angle i because the triangle is isosceles. They know which pairs of angles total 90°. If they knew angle d, they could work out angles e and f. They would then need to know one more angle before they can deduce the rest. Provide hints if necessary, e.g. *Suppose angle d was 80°, which angles could you deduce?* There are several ways to approach the problem and sharing their reasoning will strengthen understanding.

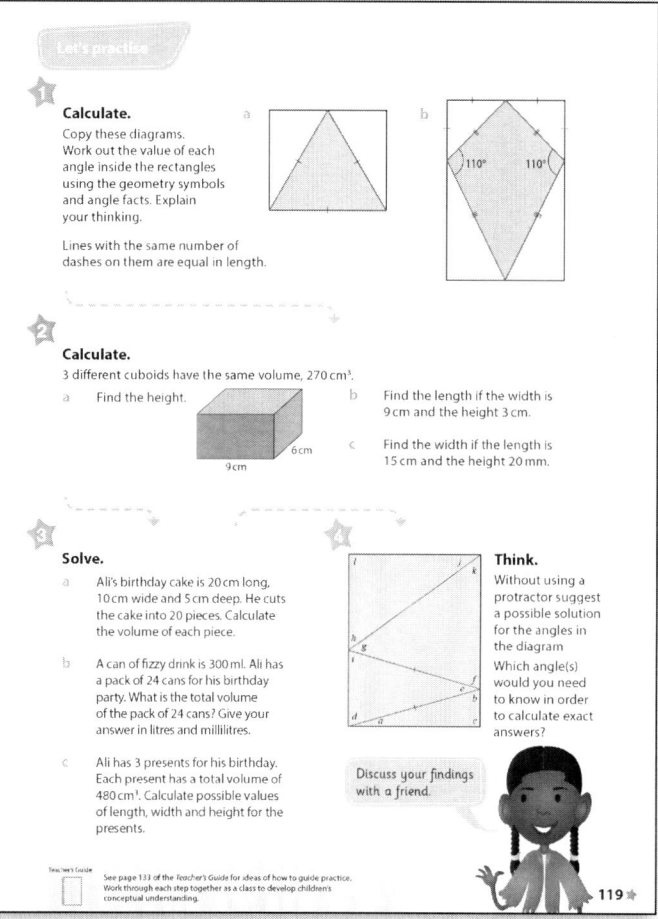

Ensuring progress

Supporting understanding

Look out for children who have gaps in their understanding and provide support sessions to reinforce learning using familiar concrete resources and diagrams. Use questioning to consolidate understanding, e.g. *What examples of angles totaling 180° or 360° can you give? What examples of equal angles can you give? Why is volume measured in cubic units?*

Broadening understanding

Asking children to design their own missing angle problems will also deepen their understanding.

> ✓ **Concept mastered**
>
> Children can find unknown angles in triangles and quadrilaterals. They can estimate, calculate and compare volumes of cubes and cuboids using standard units.

Follow-up ideas

- Ask children to work out the capacity of a swimming pool, preferably one that they use, and the actual volume of water there is in the pool. Encourage them to make drawings, showing the dimensions, including the height of the pool and the depth of the water. Remind them that one litre of water is 1000 cm³ (which is a 10 cm × 10 cm × 10 cm cube). Help them to work out how many litres there are in 1 m³.

- Agree that at a cinema, popcorn is usually available in a variety of container sizes. Ask children to bring in empty popcorn containers and investigate their relative volumes. Ask them to find out which ones are the best value for money.

Answers

Step 1

a Equilateral triangle 60°, 60°, 60°; right-angled triangle 90°, 60°, 30°

b Small right-angled isosceles triangle 45°, 45°, 90°; kite 90°, 110°, 110°, 50°; large right-angled triangle 65°, 90°, 25°

Step 2

a 5 cm   c   9 cm

b 10 cm

Step 3

a Volume = 20 × 10 × 5 cm³
= 1000 cm³ Volume of each piece = $\frac{1}{1000}$ = 50 cm³

b Volume = 300 × 24 = 7200 ml³ = 7 litres 200 ml

c Possible shapes include 6 cm × 8 cm × 10 cm, 5 cm × 8 cm × 12 cm, 5 cm × 6 cm × 16 cm, 2 cm × 10 cm × 24 cm

Step 4

Pupil's own answers with:

$c = l = 90°$

$b = d = f = i = 90 - a°$

$e = 2a$ and $k = h$

Assuming $c = 90$ then need to have values for ONE of a, b, d, e, or i plus ONE of g, h, k or l.

* **Describe positions on the full coordinate grid (all four quadrants) and draw and translate simple shapes.**

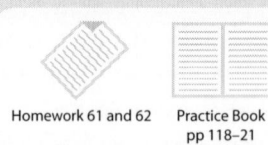

Homework 61 and 62   Practice Book pp 118–21

Mathematical vocabulary

Origin, x-coordinate, y-coordinate, plot, intersection, quadrant, reflection, translation, congruent

Representations and resources

Number lines, squared paper, 1–6 dice, blank dice marked with + and –, transparent rulers.

Warming up

Play a warm-up activity involving addition and subtraction of numbers across zero to revisit negative numbers. Use a number line from –20 to + 20. Split the class into two teams. Each team starts the game with 100 points. Use one 1–6 dice and a blank dice with three faces marked + and three marked –. Start with a counter at zero. The first team rolls the dice to give, e.g. three and – so the counter is moved to –3. Now the other team's turn gives, e.g. four and – so the counter is moved to –7. If moving the counter would result in the counter going off the number line in either direction, that team loses ten points and the counter is put back to zero. The winning team is the one with the larger score when time is up. Remind children that –3 is called 'negative three', not 'minus three'.

Background knowledge

Zero is the middle point of our number system and numbers go to infinity in both directions, positive numbers to the right and negative numbers to the left. Remember, adding a negative number makes a number smaller (moves it left) and subtracting a negative number makes it larger (moves it to the right). Children are familiar with using coordinates in the first quadrant; using four quadrants is a natural extension. Translating a shape means moving it left or right and up or down. Translated shapes do not change their size or shape. Apart from their position, they are exactly the same; the correct way to express this mathematically is to say that they are congruent.

Let's learn: Modelling and teaching

Using four quadrants

* Ask children to draw a horizontal number line from –5 to +5. Ask how they can show that the line continues in both directions. Remind them that this is the x-axis. Agree how a y-axis could be drawn and ask them add it to their diagram. Compare their axes to those in the Textbook. Highlight the equal scaling and explain that the quadrants are numbered in an anti-clockwise direction.

* Practise plotting the position of coordinate pairs in all four quadrants.

* A coordinate pair (–2, –3) is read as 'negative two, negative three'. Tell children that it is good practice to plot their points using a small cross at the intersection.

Translating using a full coordinate grid

* Draw a square in the third quadrant. Make a matching

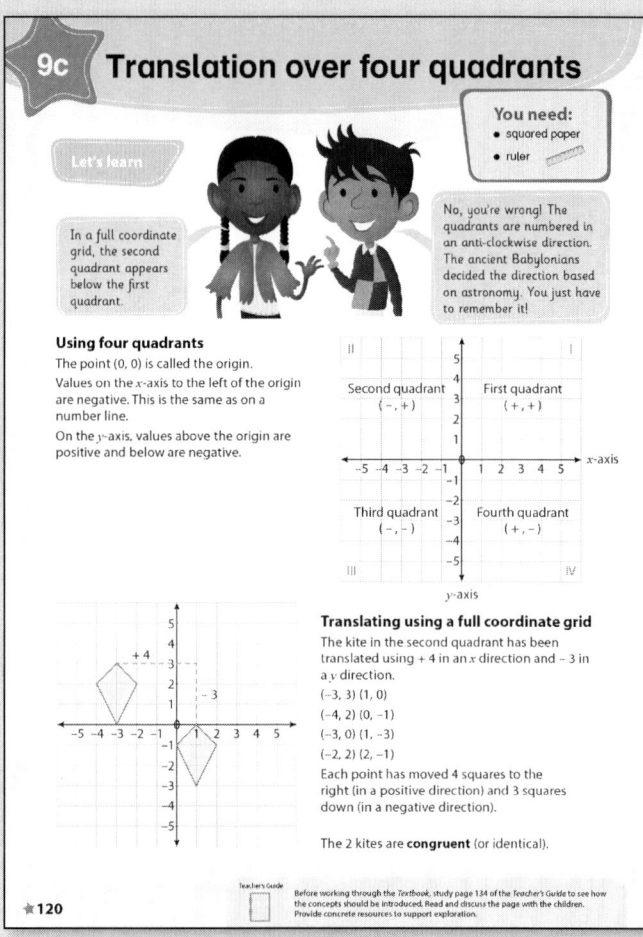

paper square. Place the paper square in a new position and ask children to tell you the coordinates. Elicit that the new value of the x- and y-coordinates have increased by the same number. The relationship between each coordinate pair has not changed. Confirm with more translations.

* Look at the co-ordinates of the kites in the Textbook. Together, count the number of squares and the direction the shape has moved horizontally to find the change in x. Then do the same for the number of squares and the direction the shape has moved vertically to find the change in y. Agree that the kite has been translated + 4 in the x direction and – 3 in the y direction.

* Remind children when a shape is translated it does not change its shape or size. The shapes are congruent.

Let's practise: Digging deeper

Step 1

Ask children how to work out the translation. They should explain that they need to look at the original and translated shapes and focus on the same point in both shapes. You could remind them that moves to the right are positive while moves to the left are negative.

You could suggest to children that they count the squares for a second point in both shapes to check that they have counted correctly.

Step 2

In this step, children look for coordinates to make different quadrilaterals. Encourage them to look carefully at the numbers in the answers to see how the coordinate numbers are related. Challenge children who complete this task quickly to plot coordinates for additional shapes, e.g. a hexagon.

Step 3

Suggest to children that they make the origin about the centre of the robot's body and ask them to explain why this is a good idea. They should explain that it ensures that the coordinates cover all four quadrants. If children choose to draw a symmetrical robot, there will be a pattern in the coordinate pairs for each side. Ask them to point this out to you.

Step 4

This question uses coordinates to construct a code. Check that children use all four quadrants when they plot their additional letters. Ask them if they can think of ways to make the code more difficult to decipher. One possibility is to introduce a translation that has to be applied to every letter. Once they have written their own message they can ask a friend to decipher it.

Ensuring progress

Supporting understanding

One simple error that may still occur is children writing the coordinates in the wrong order, i.e. the y coordinate before the x. Remind them of the mnemonic: *Along the corridor and up the stairs*. It is also important to check that children use a sharp pencil and a transparent ruler to help with the presentation of their work.

Broadening understanding

Provide opportunities for children to explain the full coordinate grid and how to plot and read coordinates. Step 3, where children design their own robot, has potential for extension. Children could design more complex animals or vehicles for their peers to draw.

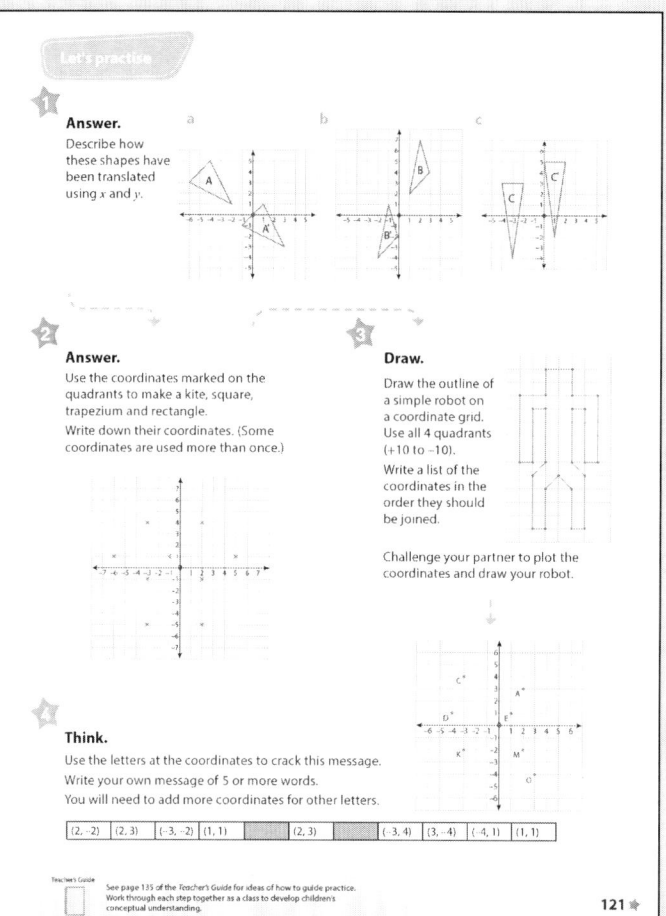

✓ Concept mastered

Children can describe and plot positions accurately in all four quadrants and draw and translate simple shapes on the coordinate plane.

Answers

Step 1

a + 5 in x direction,
   – 4 in y direction

b – 3 in x direction,
   – 6 in y direction

c + 4 in x direction,
   + 2 in y direction

Step 2

Square: (2, 4), (2, –1), (–3, –1), (–3, 4)

Rectangle: (2, 4), (2, –5), (–3, –5), (–3, 4)

Parallelogram: (2, 4), (–1, 1),
(–6, 1), (–3, 4) or (–1, 1), (–6, 1),
(–3, –1), (2, –1)

Kite: (2, 4), (5, 1), (2, –5), (–1, 1)

Irregular quadrilateral – answers will vary.

Step 4

Message: MAKE A CODE.

Follow-up ideas

- Challenge children to find out about lines of latitude and longitude. These lines use a similar four-quadrant system to determine the position of every place in the world. Parallel lines of latitude circle the Earth in an east-west direction. They are numbered from the equator which is 0°, going north to the North Pole at 90°N and south to the South Pole at 90°S. Lines of longitude run from the top of the Earth to the bottom meeting at the north and south poles. They are called meridians. The Prime Meridian (0°) runs through

Greenwich, London. The Earth is then divided into 180° east and 180° west.

- Coordinates are often referred to as Cartesian coordinates. Ask children to conduct research on the Internet to find out why. They are named after the 17th century French mathematician and philosopher, René Descartes, also known as Cartesius, who first used them. He is best known for saying, *'Cognito, ergo sum'*, which means 'I think, therefore I am'.

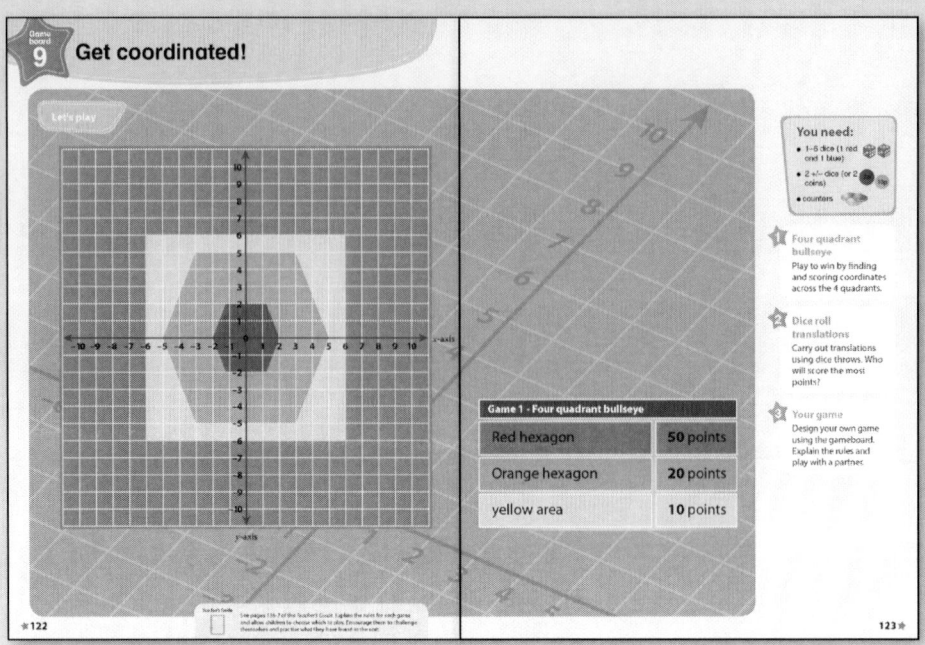

Game 1: Four quadrant bullseye

In this game children use dice to find coordinates in the four quadrants and use the gameboard to score.

Maths focus

- Describe positions on the full coordinate grid (all four quadrants)

Resources

1–6 dice (one red and one blue), two blank dice with three faces marked – and three faces marked +.

How to play

In pairs, children take turns to roll the dice to determine coordinates on the grid. The red dice and one +/– dice determines the x-coordinate; the blue dice and the second +/– dice identifies the y-coordinate, e.g. red 4 and +, blue 5 and – gives (4, –5). Children find the point on the coordinate grid and score according to the points table.

Red hexagon	50 points
Orange hexagon	20 points
Yellow area	10 points

A coordinate that falls on a boundary of the red and orange hexagons scores the higher value for red. Similarly, score the orange value for a coordinate on the orange/yellow boundary. Children play for a specified time and the child with the higher score is the winner.

If children are playing at home and do not have blank dice, they can use coins – heads is positive and tails is negative.

Making it easier

Discuss the board with children before they begin to play and revise plotting coordinates in the four quadrants.

Making it harder

Extend the board by using 1–9 dice, changing the scoring system to introduce a fourth scoring level.

Game 2: Dice roll translations

In this game children locate coordinates and translate them to new positions.

Maths focus

- Describe positions on the full coordinate grid (all four quadrants) and carry out translations

Resources

1–6 dice (one red and one blue), two blank dice with three faces marked – and three faces marked +, 2 small counters (1 colour per player).

How to play

Players can choose to start anywhere on the grid and place their counter on the coordinate of their choice. Both players roll the dice to determine their translation. The red dice and one +/– dice determine the x-direction translation and the blue dice and the second +/– dice identify the y-direction translation. Children move the counters and the player closer to the origin scores ten points. For subsequent turns, children start from where their translation has taken them. If a translation takes a player off the board, the other player scores ten points and the first player starts the next round from the origin.

The winner is the first player to reach 100 points.

Making it easier

Each time start from the origin.

Making it harder

Instead of translating one set of coordinates, translate a small triangle.

Game 3: Your game

Children should invent their own game designing rules that use the concepts covered in the unit. They can either use the gameboard or a blank coordinate grid.

Get coordinated!

Choose a game to play.

Game 1: Four quadrant bullseye

You need:
- 1–6 dice (2)
- 2 +/– dice (or 2 coins: use heads for + and tails for –)

How to play
- Play with a partner. Decide how long to play for.
- Take turns to roll the dice to determine coordinates. The red dice and one +/– dice give the x-coordinate and the blue dice and second +/– dice give the y-coordinate, e.g. red 4 and +, blue 5 and – gives $(4, -5)$.
- Find the point on the coordinate grid.
- Look at the table to find your score. A coordinate that falls on a boundary scores the higher value.
- The winner is the player with the higher score.

Red hexagon	50 points
Orange hexagon	20 points
Yellow area	10 points

Game 2: Dice roll translations

You need:
- 1–6 dice (2)
- 2 small counters (1 colour per player)
- 2 +/– dice (or 2 coins: use heads for + and tails for –)

How to play
- Play with a partner. Both place your counter on any coordinate.
- Both players roll the dice as in Game 1 to determine a translation, e.g. red 3 and +, and blue 2 and – gives a translation of + 3 in the x direction and – 2 in the y direction.
- Each move your counter to your new position.
- The player whose counter is nearer the origin scores 10 points.
- For subsequent turns, start from where you are.
- If a translation takes your counter off the board, your opponent scores 10 points and you start the next round from the origin.
- The winner is the first player to score 100.

Game 3: Your game

- Make up your own game using the bullseye.
- What are rules for your game? Can you explain them to someone?
- How do you win?

Please help your child by reading the instructions and playing the game together.

Assessment task 1

Resources

Compasses, protractors, rulers.

Running the task

Read the task through with children to check that they understand it. You could provide them with a pro-forma of a nine-dot plus central dot geoboard to record their work. However the geoboards are easy to draw free-hand fairly accurately. Ask children if they can think of the best way to do this and listen to their suggestions. One way is to draw a freehand circle, mark the centre and then divide it into thirds. Put points at each of the thirds to give three of the circumference points. Now space two more points evenly within each third and you have the required nine points fairly-evenly spaced.

If children need help getting started, look again at the angle facts and suggest that they begin by focusing on the fact that a complete turn is 360°. Ask them which other facts they think will be useful. The most helpful one is the fact that angles in a triangle total 180°. As there are an odd number of points, none of the lines joining them is a diagonal.

This is a rich task where all children can achieve to their own level. Think carefully about the pairing of children if you are using this for assessment.

Evidencing mastery

Look for children who use the fact that a complete turn is 360° and therefore the angle between two dots is 360° ÷ 9 = 40°. They are able to extrapolate this idea and explain that the angle between two dots is 80°, three dots 120° and four dots 160°. Children can go on to join the dots to make isosceles triangles and use the fact that angles in a triangle total 180° to calculate angles of 70°, 50°, 30° and 10°.

Look for children who, once they have found a few angles, take a systematic approach and list all the multiples of 10° angles, 10°, 20°, 30°, etc. and mark them off their list as they find them.

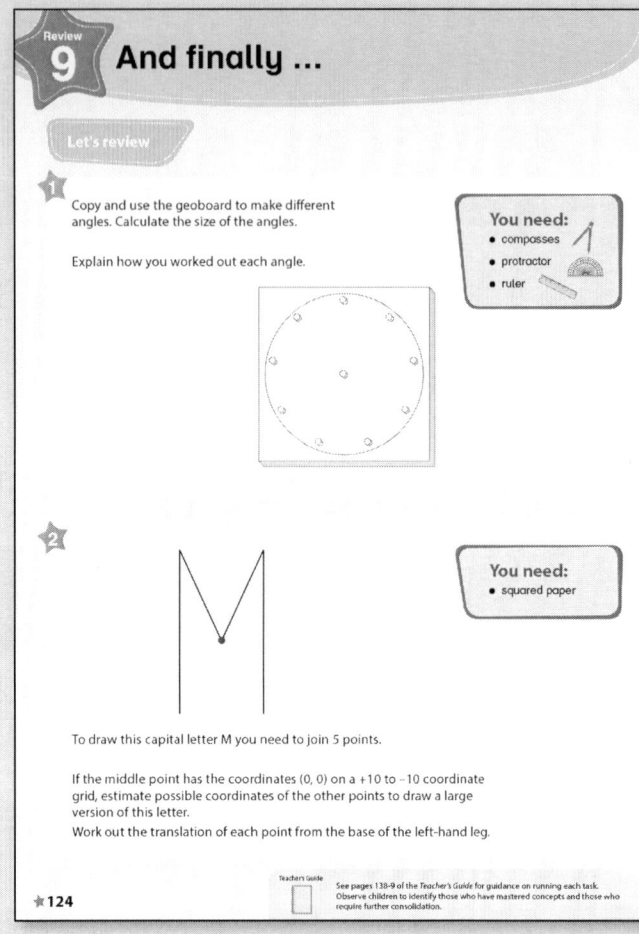

Assessment task 2

Resources

Squared paper or printed grid.

Running the task

Encourage children to discuss the task with each other. They need to decide what size they will make their letter. Encourage them to make it fairly large so that it covers a reasonable amount of the grid. Since the centre of the M is at the origin, the other four coordinates are in each of the four quadrants. As the letter is symmetrical, the coordinates will be related; if one coordinate is (x, y) another will be $(-x, y)$.

Children are asked to describe the translation from the bottom left coordinate. Two of the four coordinate pairs will have one value unchanged because the points have the same x or y value. Discuss what would be the coordinates of the largest and smallest 'M' that they could make.

Evidencing mastery

There are two parts to the task and children evidencing mastery will achieve them both. The first part is to enlarge the letter to fit appropriately on the grid and plot the five coordinate pairs correctly, so that the letter is symmetrical with 'legs' parallel to one another and the same length. Completing this shows that children have mastered using coordinates in all four quadrants.

The second part of the task is to calculate the translation required for each point using x and y. Completing this shows that they have mastered translation across all four quadrants.

Eva and Ali answered a question about scale factors. They have made some mistakes.

Work out the correct answers, then explain their errors.

a   A right-angled triangle has sides 1.5 cm, 2.0 cm and 2.5 cm. An enlarged
    right-angled triangle has sides 6 cm, 7.5 cm and 4.5 cm. What is the scale factor?

    The scale factor is 4.

b   A rectangle 3 cm × 1 cm is enlarged by a scale factor of 4. How many times
    greater is the area of the new rectangle?

    The area is 4 times greater.

c   Enlarge a circle with a radius 3 cm by a scale factor of 4.
    What is the diameter of the new circle?

    The diameter is 12 cm.

Did you know?

Crop circles are large, intricate circular patterns created by flattening crops. They often appear overnight. At first people believed that aliens created them!

They're probably man-made by pranksters. In 1991, 2 men admitted that they were responsible for many crop circles in England. They even made one in front of journalists, using a plank of wood to flatten the crops and a rope as a pair of compasses. The circles are still a bit mysterious though.

125

Concepts mastered

- ✓ Children can use the names for parts of a circle and understand and use the simple formula, $d = 2r$ to find the radius from the diameter and vice versa. They understand what a scale factor is and know that using a scale factor does not change the angles of a shape, simply its size. The original and enlarged shapes are similar.

- ✓ Children can find unknown angles in triangles and quadrilaterals. They can estimate, calculate and compare volumes of cubes and cuboids using standard units.

- ✓ Children can describe and plot positions accurately in all four quadrants and draw and translate simple shapes on the coordinate plane.

Assessment task 3

Running the task

Children can carry out the task on their own but working in pairs will give more opportunity for discussion and reasoning. If children are working in pairs, listen carefully to each individual in order to assess mastery.

Ask children to explain the terms 'scale factor' and 'enlargement'. Then, draw a 4 cm square on the board and ask children what the side of each length would be if the square was enlarged by a scale factor of three. Repeat for a triangle or other polygon, using different measurements and scale factors each time.

In the first part of the task children must work out the correct answers. Ensure that they record their work using jottings or sketches. Part c will be more challenging as children must use the relationship $d = 2r$. Encourage children to recall this rule by thinking about the different parts of a circle and the relationships between them.

The second part of the task provides further challenge because children need to identify and explain the errors. You might wish children to give their explanations verbally (to you or a partner) or write them down. Ensure that children use precise mathematical vocabulary in their explanations.

Evidencing mastery

Children showing mastery in the first part of the task will arrive at the correct solutions to the questions. They will look for corresponding lengths and may check the relationship of the other lengths to be certain they are correct. In part c children will demonstrate mastery by using the relationship $d = 2r$. Children will show mastery in the second part of the task by identifying the error, e.g. in part c that Ali and Eva have correctly multiplied the radius by the scale factor but the question asks for the new diameter, using precise mathematical vocabulary.

Did you know?

Crop circles are beautiful examples of circle patterns that can be reproduced using compasses and a ruler – they are just much bigger, sometimes as much as several hundred metres across! They usually appear overnight in fields of wheat or barley. They are generally constructed by anchoring one end of a rope and using a board on the other end to make circles so that the crop is not cut but laid flat in swirling patterns.

Theories about what make crop circles include whirlwinds, earth energies, aliens and pranksters. In 1991 two hoaxers, Doug Bower and Dave Chorley, admitted that they had been responsible for many of the crop circles in Wiltshire. These days most people believe that crop circles are man-made. Some farmers allow the public on to their land to visit the circles.

Encourage children to research the subject on the Internet. They could try to construct some of the designs.

Mathematical focus

★ **Algebra: number sequences, equations with two unknowns, linear number sequences**

★ **Measurement: length, mass, distance, time**

★ **Statistics: interpret and construct, interpret and calculate**

Prior learning

Children should already be able to:

- use formulae for finding the area and perimeter of rectangles, including squares, and triangles
- multiply and divide using mental calculation strategies.

Key new learning

- Find pairs of numbers that satisfy an equation with two unknowns.
- Enumerate possibilities of combinations of two variables.
- Generate and describe linear number sequences.
- Interpret and construct pie charts and use these to solve problems.
- Interpret and construct line graphs and use these to solve problems.

Making connections

- Children will use algebra to find the area and perimeter of different shapes, including triangles.
- They will also use, read, write and convert between standard units, with opportunities to convert measurements of mass from a smaller unit of measure to a larger unit, and vice versa. They will reinforce using decimal notation to up to three decimal places.
- This unit provides plenty of opportunities to solve problems that include interpreting and constructing pie charts and line graphs. These representations of information are commonly found in real life, e.g. on food packaging, pie charts are used to show the nutritional values of food.

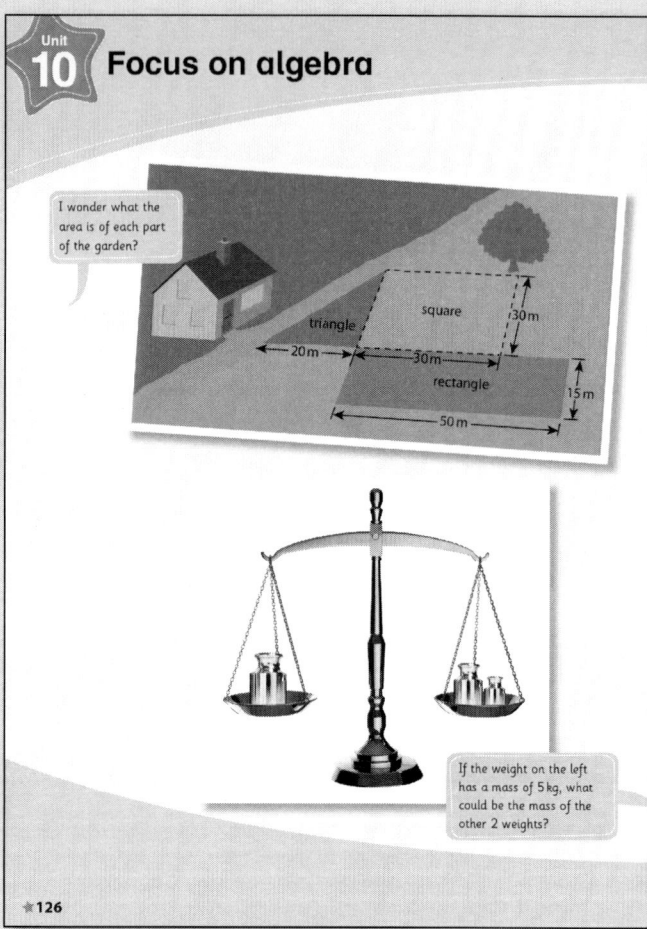

 Talk about

Discuss with children the fact that they have been working algebraically all the way through primary school. Write examples of missing number statements on the board. Explain that anything where children have to find unknowns is algebra. Agree that an unknown number is also called a variable, which is often represented by a symbol or letter. The number that is not a variable is known as the constant. Give examples, such as $y - 7 = 5$, where y is the variable and seven and five are the constants. Discuss what a linear number sequence is. Ensure that children know these are number patterns that increase or decrease by the same amount each time. The amount that the sequence increases or decreases by is called the common difference.

Engaging and exploring

Invite children to look at each picture and discuss the accompanying question with a partner. Then focus on each picture in turn as a class.

Look at the picture of the house and garden. Ask children if they can remember the formula for the area of a rectangle. Write it on the board: $A = l \times w$. Challenge children to find the area of the rectangular patch of grass. Repeat for the square and triangular areas. Agree that because a triangle is half a rectangle, we can find the area of the appropriate rectangle and halve it, so producing the formula $A = \frac{1}{2}(l \times w)$. You could extend this question by asking children to find the total area of grass, or by repeating the above activity, this time focusing on perimeter. You could also give children squared paper and ask them to draw a plan of another garden, using squares, rectangles and triangles. Swapping their drawing with a partner, they work out the areas and perimeters shown.

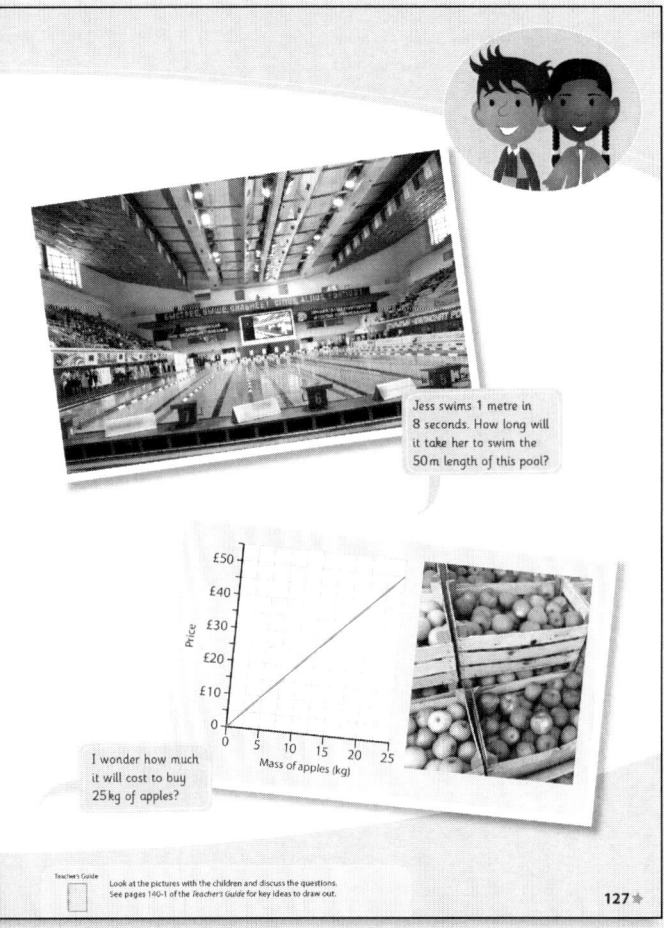

Jess swims 1 metre in 8 seconds. How long will it take her to swim the 50 m length of this pool?

I wonder how much it will cost to buy 25 kg of apples?

Teacher's Guide Look at the pictures with the children and discuss the questions. See pages 140-1 of the Teacher's Guide for key ideas to draw out.

127

Things to think about

- How will you use manipulatives for modelling sequences?

- How will you pair children with a sound understanding of number skills with those whose strengths lie in visualising and spatial skills?

- How will you involve problem-solving strategies, such as 'another and another and another', 'odd one out' and 'zooming in'?

Next look at the picture of the scales. Recap the meaning of the equals symbol. Emphasise that it is a sign of equivalence and not an indicator of an answer. Remind children that what is on one side must be the same as what is on the other. Write some incorrect number statements on the board, e.g. 25 + 16 = 50. Ask children to correct them. Children either add a number to the left side or subtract from the right to make the number statement equivalent.

Ask children to find different possibilities for the two unknown weights if the one on the left pan weighs 5 kg. Remind them that the two unknown weights are different sizes so they will not be the same mass. You could ask children to draw bar models to show their answers. An example is given below:

5 kg	
1.5 kg	3.5 kg

Compare children's answers. Are they all the same?

Repeat, giving a different mass for the weight on the left pan. Encourage children to use decimals and fractions as part of the masses. You could also ask children to solve problems, such as: *Gerri weighed a banana on a balance scale. To make the pans balance she had to put eight 10 g and five 5 g weights on one side and the banana on the other. How much did the banana weigh?*

Turn to the picture of the swimming pool. Find out which children in your class can swim. Have any of them swum in an Olympic-sized pool like the one shown? Tell them that an Olympic-sized pool is 50 metres in length. Can they visualise 50 m? Ask children to explain how they would work out how long it will take Jess to swim 50 m. Agree that if it takes eight seconds to swim one metre, they multiply eight by 50 to get the equivalent time. Discuss ways to multiply by 50 mentally, e.g. multiply by 100 and halve, multiply by five and then 10. Ask further questions using different times and distances.

Finally, look at the graph and the picture of the apples. Ask children what information the graph shows (how much different masses of apples cost). Invite them to discuss the graph with a partner and make statements from it, e.g. it costs £50 to buy 25 kg of apples and 10 kg of apples will cost £20.

Ask children to explain the relationship between the horizontal and vertical axes on the graph. Explain that it is a little like ratio in that for every £10 there are 5 kg of apples. Ask them to scale the amounts up and model this using the bar model or similar drawings. An example is given below:

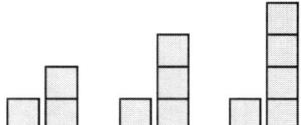

Ask: *If the single square represents 5 kg, what do the others represent? If the single square represents £10, what do the others represent?*

Checking understanding

You will know children have mastered the concepts in this unit when they can represent missing number statements algebraically and explain how to find unknowns. They understand the term 'variable' and can read graphs and identify linear relationships.

- **Find pairs of numbers that satisfy an equation with two unknowns.**
- **Enumerate possibilities of combinations of two variables.**
- **Interpret and construct pie charts and use these to solve problems.**

Homework 63 and 64   Practice Book pp 122–3   Currency

Representations and resources

Number rods, squared paper, rulers, A4 paper, scissors.

Mathematical vocabulary

Algebra, unknowns, equation, variable, formula

Warming up

Write '100% represents £250' on the board. Invite children to write down as many other percentages and equivalent amounts based on this statement as they can. Encourage them to start with 10% and to use this to create other percentages. After one minute take feedback and write some of their ideas on the board. Then give them two minutes to make up more. Less confident children can get ideas from those written on the board and then double, halve or multiply these by 10 to find other percentages.

Background knowledge

Algebra includes finding unknowns. It is also concerned with variables. A variable is a quantity, the value or size of which can vary, e.g. the number of people in a town is variable but the number of letters that make up the word 'town' is not. Variable are likely to be a new concept for children. A common misconception can arise if we are not clear about variables, e.g. suppose you can exchange one euro for 70p. We often think of this relationship as €1 = 70p, so €2 = 140p, and so on; here we are using scaling and the values are fixed, so they are not variables. However, to create a formula, we need to write the relationship using variables. The formula $p = 70e$ tells us that the value of p will be 70 times any value of e, e.g. if $e = 15$, we know that we will get $70 \times 15 = 1050$p or £10.50.

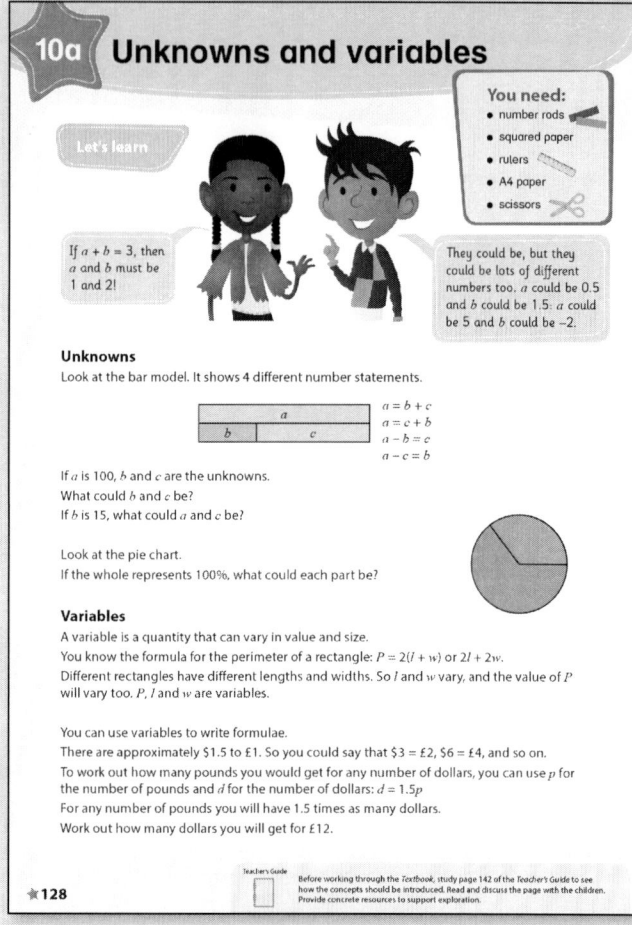

Let's learn: Modelling and teaching

Unknowns

- Give children number rods. Ask them to use three rods to replicate the bar model shown in the Textbook. Review the four possible number statements shown. Tell children that a represents 100. Invite them to find and record possible values for b and c, focusing on the addition statements first.

- Tell children that the shortest piece (b) represents 15. Ask them to find and record possible values for a and c.

- Discuss Ali and Eva's conversation. Ask children to come up with 10 different values for $a + b = 3$. Encourage them to use fractions, decimals and negative numbers.

- Discuss the pie chart in the Textbook. The small part is somewhere between 25% and 50%. Ask questions such as: *If the whole represents 50 people (or 2 kg, 3 m, 10 l) what could each part represent?*

Variables

- Ask children to tell you the formula for the perimeter of a rectangle: $P = 2(l + w)$ or $2l + 2w$. Tell them that the letters are known as variables, because they do not have a fixed value; the value can vary. Explain to children that they can substitute the letters for values, e.g. $P = 2(12 + 8)$. Explain that this is not variable anymore. It can only be used to find the perimeter of one particular rectangle. Give a value for P, l or w. Ask children to work out possible values for the others.

- Work through the currency conversion example in the Textbook. Emphasise that the formula allows us to find the number of dollars equivalent to any number of pounds. Check children understand how to use the formula to find either dollars or pounds.

Let's practise: Digging deeper

Step 1

The task asks children to find five possible values for the unknowns. Encourage them to be creative and think of possibilities that include fractions, decimals and negative numbers, e.g. $-10 + 58 = 48$, $15.3 + 32.7 = 48$. If necessary, model an example, such as $a + 2b = 16$, with children before they tackle parts f to h. In this case, a could be two and b could be seven, or a could be three and b could be 6.5. You could challenge some children to find more than five pairs of possible values.

Step 2

Children need to convert amounts of money from euros to pounds, and vice versa. Some children may need support around the concept of variables and how the formula for converting pounds to euros or euros to pounds works. You could encourage them to draw bar models to help them visualise this.

Step 3

Children apply their knowledge of variables to solve problems in a measures context. For parts a to d they could simply draw any rectangle with the required length or width and then measure or count squares to find the other dimension and perimeter. For parts e and f they will need to think about what lengths and widths will give the required perimeter before or while they draw. Make sure they write the formula for each rectangle they draw (e.g. for $l = 10\,\text{cm}$, one possibility is $26 = 2(10 + 3)$ or $26 = 2 \times 10 + 2 \times 3$). Encourage them to find a variety of possibilities for each rectangle.

Step 4

Children each need an A4 piece of paper and scissors. They fold the paper in half widthways and then cut. They keep one half as it is and fold the other in half and cut. They do this twice more until they have five pieces of paper. They take the smallest piece and label the width a and the length b. They put the largest and smallest pieces alongside each other as shown in the diagram. Can they explain why the perimeter is $10a + 4b$? If not, encourage them to place the smallest piece on the largest piece to see how many times it fits. Support children by asking questions such as: *How many times does the smallest piece fit along the length of the longest? What does this tell you about the length of the longest side? How can you use this to find the length of the two parallel sides of the rectangle?* Ask similar questions about the width. Then ask children how this will help them to prove that the perimeter of the large rectangle is $10a + 4b$. They then make more shapes using the pieces and find their perimeters. It may help them to label the length and width of each piece, e.g. $2a$ and b for the second smallest rectangle.

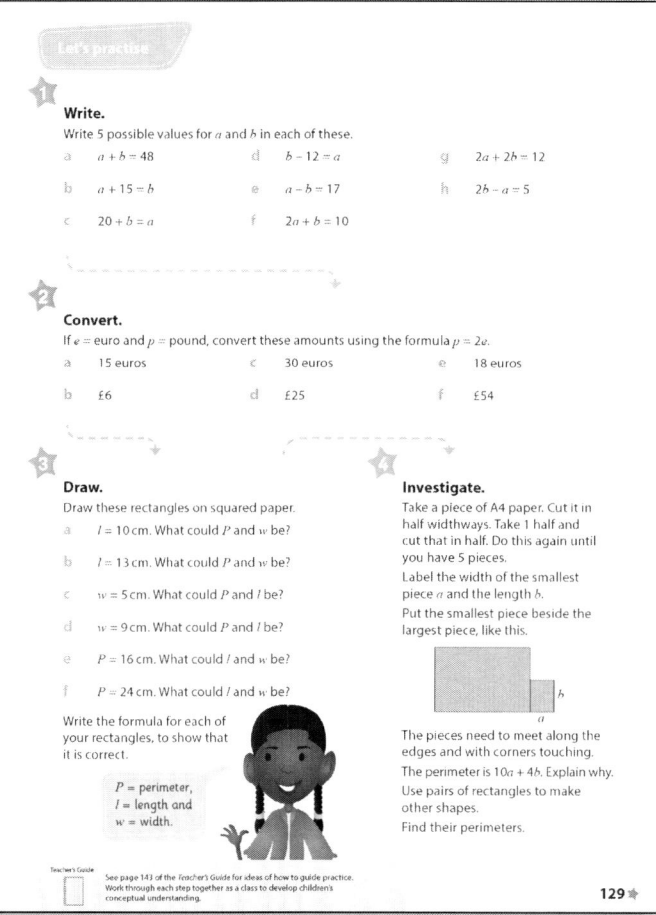

Ensuring progress

Supporting understanding

Initially focus on the concept of finding unknowns that satisfy a number statement. Give children plenty of examples so that they understand that when finding pairs of unknowns there is not necessarily one correct answer.

Broadening understanding

Give children opportunities to create pie charts similar to the one in the Textbook but divided into more sections, so that they can demonstrate how unknowns can be represented, e.g. 100% is equivalent to 32 children, 50 people, 1 kg.

 Concept mastered

Children can explain and demonstrate how to find unknowns. They can explain what is meant by a variable and how variables can be used to solve problems.

Follow-up ideas

- Ask children to draw pie charts. They devise their own criteria, e.g. the whole is £100 and the pie is divided into 50%, 30% and 20%. They work out the value for each part.

- Children could explore currency conversions between currencies of countries of their choice. They could use the Internet to find these and round them to the nearest tenth or hundredth.

- Ask children to make up their own missing number problems, e.g. $12 - a = b$. Encourage them to be creative with their solutions and to draw on their learning of other concepts, including negative numbers: $12 - -15 = 27$.

Answers

Step 1

Answers will vary. Check that children's pairs of values satisfy the statements.

Step 2

a	£30	d	12.5 euros
b	3 euros	e	£36
c	£60	f	27 euros

Step 3

Answers will vary.

Step 4

Answers will vary.

Linear number sequences

- **Generate and describe linear number sequences.**
- **Interpret and construct line graphs and use these to solve problems.**

Homework 65 and 66   Practice Book pp 124–6

Mathematical vocabulary

Linear number sequence, term, nth term, pattern, relationship, variable

Representations and resources

Squared paper, rulers, kitchen scales, apples, interlocking cubes.

Warming up

Write a multiplication fact on the board, e.g. $8 \times 7 = 56$. Ask children to make up as many facts as they can from this by doubling, halving, multiplying and dividing by 10. After two minutes, take feedback. Collect as many different facts as you can and write them on the board. Give children another two minutes to make up some more.

Background knowledge

A linear number sequence is a number pattern that increases or decreases by the same amount each time, e.g. 16, 14, 12, 10. The amount by which it increases or decreases is called the common difference. In the sequence given above, the common difference is two. In this concept spread we explore the idea of the nth term and how to view linear number relationships on a graph. The latter links well to coordinates and so builds on something that children already understand.

Let's learn: Modelling and teaching

Number sequences

- Together look at the cartoon and the number line in the Textbook. Discuss the explanation. Point out that any number multiplied by five will appear in the sequence. Ensure children understand that the nth term represents any number in the sequence.

- On the board, copy the number line shown in the Textbook, but draw curved arrows to show jumps from seven to 12 to 17 to 22. Explain that this sequence still goes up in fives, but now two has been added onto the answer. The nth term is $5n + 2$. Challenge children to tell you the 20th and 100th terms in this sequence. Repeat with other sequences, e.g. 13, 23, 33. Also focus on sequences that decrease, e.g. 20, 18, 16.

- Ask children to study the pattern of squares in the Textbook. How many squares are added each time? Ask them to draw the next pattern in the sequence, and to then find the formula for the nth term ($5n + 3$). Invite them to use the formula to work out the 12th, 15th and 20th terms. Give them similar problems to solve.

Linear relationships

- Explore the graph in the Textbook together. Ask children to describe the information it shows (time taken to travel different distances). Explain that graphs like this always

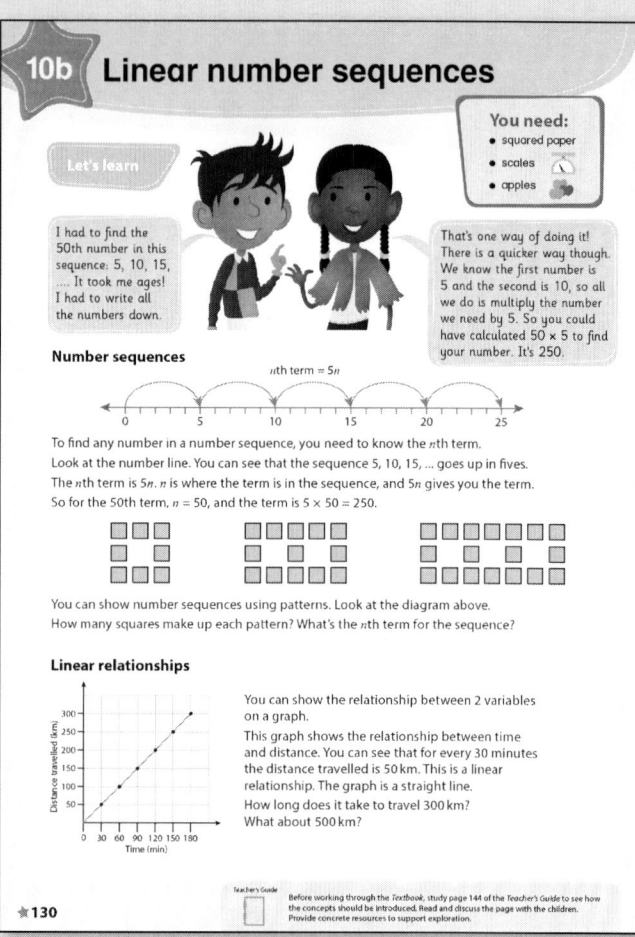

produce a straight line. Ask children to write the sequence for distance (50, 100, 150, 200, 250, 300) and to work out the nth term for distance, using t to represent time (nth term = $50t$). Establish that when $t = 1$, $50t$ tells you the distance travelled in 30 minutes. When $t = 2$, $50t$ tells you the distance travelled in 60 minutes, and so on. Repeat for time (nth term = $30t$).

- Ask questions such as: *What distance will have been travelled in three hours? How long will it take to travel 450 km?*

- Make up and display some data similar to that shown in the graph. Ask children to construct a line graph on squared paper to show the data. Then, ask them to make statements about the data that the graph shows using words and formulae.

Let's practise: Digging deeper

Step 1

Encourage children to look at the difference between the given terms before they attempt to find the next five terms of each sequence. They may wish to sketch a number line to help them with the first questions. They should recognise sequences d and h as the square and cube numbers respectively. If they struggle to write a formula for the nth term for these, encourage them to think about how they would write, e.g. one squared, two squared and three squared. They should then realise that the nth term can be written as n^2.

Step 2

As in step 1, encourage children first to look at the difference between the terms. They can then compare the terms of the sequence to the multiples of that number. Check children understand how to find and use the formulae for the nth term.

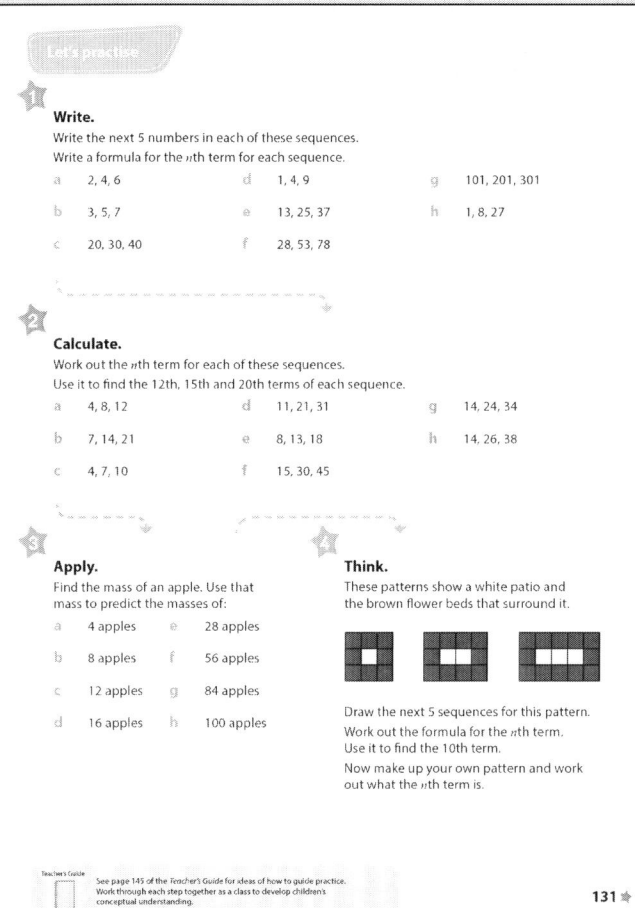

If necessary, work in a focus group with any children who are not confident at finding the formulae. However, expect all children to use the formulae to find the different terms independently.

Step 3

In groups, children weigh an apple or similar fruit to the nearest gram. They then use that mass to work out the masses of different numbers of apples by scaling up. They should look closely at the numbers, because many of the answers can be found by adding results they have already worked out, e.g. 100 = 84 + 16 apples. Discuss the fact that the actual masses of 100 apples will probably be different, because the masses of the individual apples will vary. Children could plot their results on a graph.

Step 4

Children need to draw the next five sequences for the pattern. They then work out what the formula is and find the 10th term. Encourage them to draw the 10th term to check their solution. Some children may need to draw the whole sequence on squared paper to find the 10th term. If they do, work with them as a group. Work through each of the first three terms slowly. Ask children what they notice is happening each time. Find the formula together.

Ensuring progress

Supporting understanding

If children lack the confidence to work independently, work with them in focus groups. Give them some number sequences and discuss how to find the nth term. Resources such as interlocking cubes can be used to show children how the sequences are built up.

Broadening understanding

Ask children to make up their own graphs and make statements about them. They could also make up number patterns and explore how to find the nth term.

 Concept mastered

Children can explain and demonstrate how to find the nth term in a sequence and explain linear relationships.

Follow-up ideas

- Ask children to find and copy existing linear graphs from the Internet. They then make up statements from these.

- Give children coloured counters or cubes. Ask them to make up repeating patterns. Once they have made one, ask them to find the rule which will tell them the nth term.

- Children could work with a partner. One of them starts a number sequence and the other child continues it. They then both work out the rule and the formula for the nth term.

- Explore line graphs in a four quadrant coordinate grid. Ask children to draw a grid on squared paper. They then draw a straight line and write the coordinates that the line passes through. You could also give them coordinates to plot. Ensure that these produce a straight line.

Answers

Step 1

a 8, 10, 12, 14, 16; $2n$

b 9, 11, 13, 15, 17; $2n + 1$

c 50, 60, 70, 80, 90; $10n + 10$

d 16, 25, 36, 49, 64; n^2

e 49, 61, 73, 85, 97; $12n + 1$

f 103, 128, 153, 178, 203; $25n + 3$

g 401, 501, 601, 701, 801; $100n + 1$

h 64, 125, 216, 343, 512; n^3

Step 2

a $4n$; 48, 60, 80

b $7n$; 84, 105, 140

c $3n + 1$; 37, 46, 61

d $10n + 1$; 121, 151, 201

e $5n + 3$; 63, 78, 103

f $15n$; 180, 225, 300

g $10n + 4$; 124, 154, 204

h $12n + 2$; 146, 182, 242

Step 3

Answers will vary, depending on the mass of the apple.

Step 4

Possible formula: $(2f + 6) + 1t$. 10th term is 26 flower bed squares, 10 tiles.

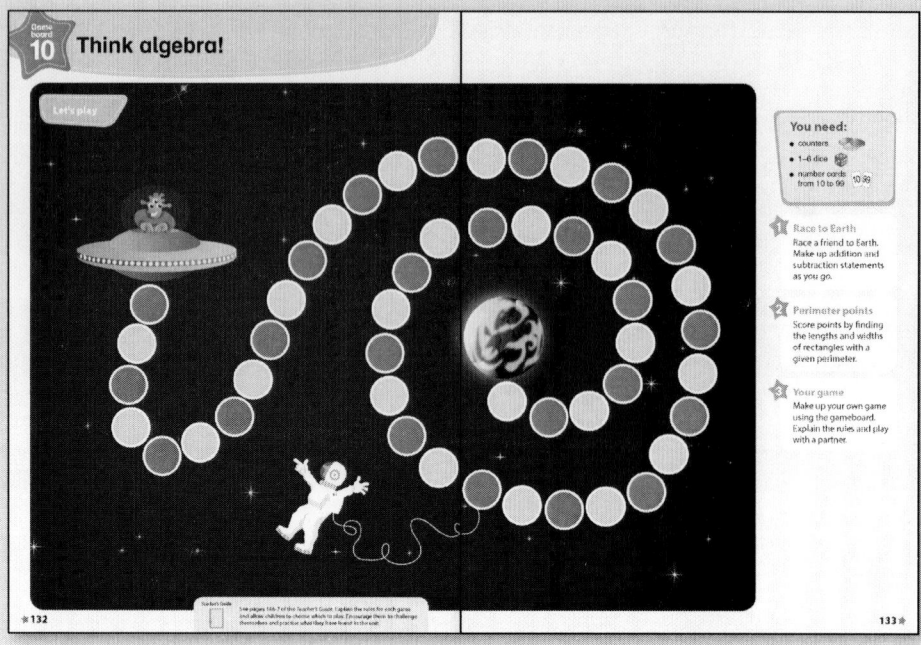

Game 1: Race to Earth

This is a simple race game. Children make up addition and subtraction statements as they move around the board.

Maths focus

- Find pairs of numbers that satisfy an equation with two unknowns

Resources

1 counter per player (1 colour per player), 1–6 dice (1), number cards from 10 to 99.

How to play

Children shuffle the number cards and put them in a pile, face down on the table. They each place their counter on the spaceship. They take it in turns to throw the dice and move their counter that number of places around the board towards Earth. If they land on a blue circle, they stay there until their next throw. If they land on a yellow circle, they pick a number card. They make one addition and one subtraction statement with the number on the card as the answer. Their partner checks their statements – if either is incorrect, the player misses their next turn. The winner is the first player to reach Earth.

Making it easier

Children could make only addition, or only subtraction, statements.

Making it harder

Challenge children to make two addition statements and two subtraction statements each time they pick a card. You could also set some rules, e.g. that at least one of their statements must include a negative number.

Game 3: Your game

Children should invent their own game, designing rules that use the concepts covered in the unit. Challenge children to make their game easier or harder.

Game 2: Perimeter points

Children must write down possible whole number lengths and widths of a rectangle with a given perimeter. The more they find, the more points they score.

Maths focus

- Find pairs of numbers that satisfy an equation with two unknowns

- Enumerate possibilities of combinations of two variables

Resources

1 counter per player (1 colour per player), 1–6 dice (1), cards showing the even numbers from 10 to 98, stopwatches (optional).

How to play

Children shuffle the number cards and put them in a pile, face down on the table. They each place their counter on the spaceship. They take it in turns to throw the dice and move their counter that number of places around the board. If they land on a yellow circle, they stay there until their next throw. If they land on a blue circle, they pick a number card: this is the perimeter of a rectangle. They must find as many whole number lengths and widths for the rectangle as they can. They score a point for each correct pair of dimensions. The number of possibilities ranges from two (for perimeter 10) to 24 (for perimeter 96 or 98) so you might want to set a time limit. The game ends when each player has reached Earth. The winner is the player with the highest total score.

Making it easier

Children could find one pair of dimensions for each number card. They don't score points and, as in Game 1, the winner is the first player to reach Earth.

Making it harder

Use all the cards (10 to 98) and tell children that now the number card they pick represents the area of a rectangle or the area of a triangle.

Choose a game to play.

Game 1: Race to Earth

How to play

- Shuffle the number cards and put them in a pile, face down on the table. Each place your counter on the spaceship.
- Take turns to throw the dice. Move your counter that number of places towards Earth.
- If you land on a blue circle, stay there until your next throw.
- If you land on a yellow circle:
  - pick a number card
  - make one addition statement and one subtraction statement with the number on the card as the answer
  - ask your partner to check your statements. If either is incorrect, miss your next turn.
- The winner is the first player to reach Earth.

You need:

- 1 counter per player (1 colour per player)
- 1–6 dice
- number cards from 10 to 99

Game 2: Perimeter points

How to play

- Shuffle the number cards and put them in a pile, face down on the table. Each place your counter on the spaceship.
- Take turns to throw the dice. Move your counter that number of places towards Earth.
- If you land on a yellow circle, stay there until your next throw.
- If you land on a blue circle:
  - pick a number card; this is the perimeter of a rectangle
  - find as many whole number lengths and widths for the rectangle as you can
  - score a point for each correct pair of dimensions.
- Continue playing until all players reach Earth. The winner is the player with the highest total score.

You need:

- 1 counter per player (1 colour per player)
- 1–6 dice
- even number cards from 10 to 98

Game 3: Your game

- Make up your own game using the gameboard.
- What are the rules for your game? Explain them to someone.

Please help your child by reading the instructions and playing the game together.

Assessment task 1

Resources

Number rods.

Running the task

Before children begin the task, recap scaling by writing on the board, '1 is equivalent to £12.50'. Ask children to find two, four, eight and 16 of the amount and then to add or subtract to find other values. As they begin the task, listen to pairs of children discuss the problem and explain to each other how they can work out the value of the money in dollars. Children need to multiply each number of pounds by 1.5 to get the equivalent number of dollars. Encourage them to use a mental calculation strategy for multiplying, e.g. multiply by one, halve this and add the two amounts together. Encourage children to show how they work out their answers by drawing scaling up models or the bar model. You could give provide them with number rods to explore this if you have them available. Once they have completed this task, you could ask them to change dollars to pounds by scaling down.

Evidencing mastery

If children are able to convert the pounds to dollars using the formula then they are evidencing mastery. If any children have not mastered this, work with them in an intervention group, clearly modelling what they need to do using the bar model or manipulatives. It may be that you need to spend longer on this so that most of your class achieve mastery.

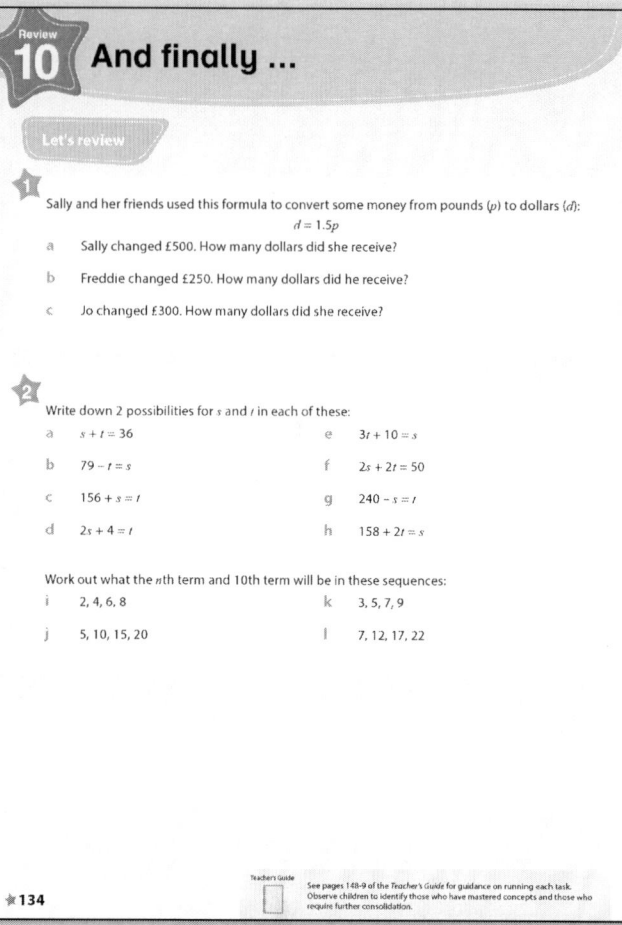

Assessment task 2

Running the task

Before children begin the task, recap similar missing number statements using letters as shown. The second part of the task asks children to find the nth term of a sequence. Before they do this, recap linear number sequences. Write this example on the board: 10, 20, 30. Ask them what the next three or four numbers will be and how they know. Then ask them how they would find the nth term and how this could be expressed algebraically. Repeat this for other sequences to ensure that children understand what to do. In the first part of the task, children need to find possible values of s and t. There are many options; encourage children to find at least two. Notice how children solve part d, for example. If necessary, model an example. For part d, you could say: $10 + 4 = 14$, so $t = 14$ and $2s = 10$. What do I need to do to find s? (halve 10). The second part of the task asks children to find the nth term of a sequence. Before they do this, recap the work they have previously done on this.

Evidencing mastery

If children can confidently and correctly find options for s and t then they are evidencing mastery of this element of algebra at this level.

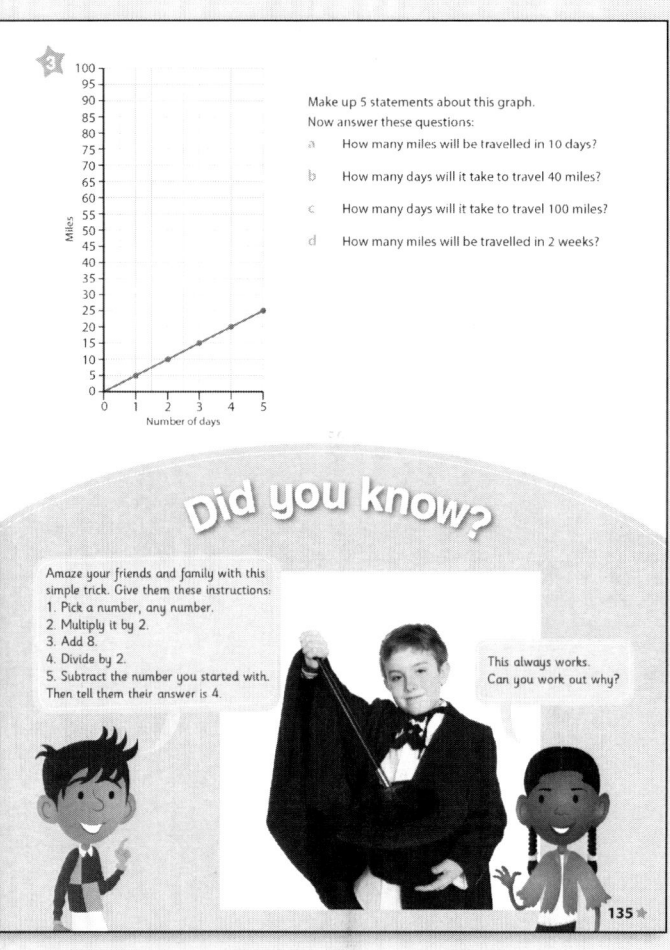

Assessment task 3

Running the task

Children need to explore the graph and make five statements about the information it shows, e.g. the graph shows that 10 miles are travelled in two days. Encourage them to work out facts that are not given on the graph, e.g. you can see from the graph that in three days 15 miles are travelled, so you can work out that in six days 30 miles are travelled. Children answer the four questions. Encourage them to work out the answers using mental calculation strategies and to show their workings as jottings.

Strategies could include doubling and using multiplication facts. Ask them to tell you the relationship between the horizontal and vertical axes, e.g. for every unit on the horizontal axis there are five units on the vertical axis.

Evidencing mastery

If children can confidently explain and demonstrate what the graph shows and the relationship between the two axes, they will have evidenced mastery.

Did you know?

Discuss with children why the 'trick' described in the Textbook works. Establish that the answer will always be the number added in the third step divided by two. Since the number added in the third step was eight, the answer will always be four. The 'trick' can be expressed algebraically as follows:

1 x **2** $2x$ **3** $2x + 8$ **4** $\frac{2x + 8}{2} = x + 4$ **5** $x + 4 - x = 4$

Children could try adding other numbers in the third step instead, e.g. if they add 10, the answer will always be five. What happens if you add an odd number in the third step (it still works, but the answer will always be something and a half)? The 'trick' can be further adapted by multiplying and dividing by a number other than two.

Concepts mastered

- ✓ Children can explain and demonstrate how to find unknowns. They can explain what is meant by a variable and how variables can be used to solve problems.

- ✓ Children can explain and demonstrate how to find the nth term in a sequence and explain linear relationships.

Solving more problems

Mathematical focus

- ★ **Number: addition, subtraction, multiplication and division, fractions**
- ★ **Algebra: simple formulae, missing number problems, equations with two unknowns**
- ★ **Measurement: length, mass, capacity**
- ★ **Statistics: interpret and construct, interpret and calculate**

Prior learning

Children should already be able to:

- add and subtract mentally and using formal written methods
- add and subtract, with increasingly large numbers, mentally and using formal written methods using the concept of equivalent fractions.

Key new learning

- Solve addition and subtraction multi-step problems in contexts, deciding which operations and methods to use and why.
- Perform mental calculations, including with mixed operations and large numbers.
- Use estimation to check answers to calculations and determine, in the context of a problem, an appropriate degree of accuracy.
- Add and subtract fractions with different denominators and mixed numbers, using the concept of equivalent fractions.
- Calculate and interpret the mean as an average.
- Interpret and construct pie charts and use these to solve problems.
- Use simple formulae.
- Express missing number problems algebraically.
- Find pairs of numbers that satisfy an equation with two unknowns.
- Enumerate possibilities of two variables.

Making connections

- Multi-step problems use children's knowledge of the order of operations and demonstrate real-life applications of what they have learnt. Problems involving measure often involve conversion between units and the use of decimal notation with up to three decimal places. This could be linked with their science investigations.
- Understanding the relationship between variables and enumerating possible values, leads into later work on graphs and equations.

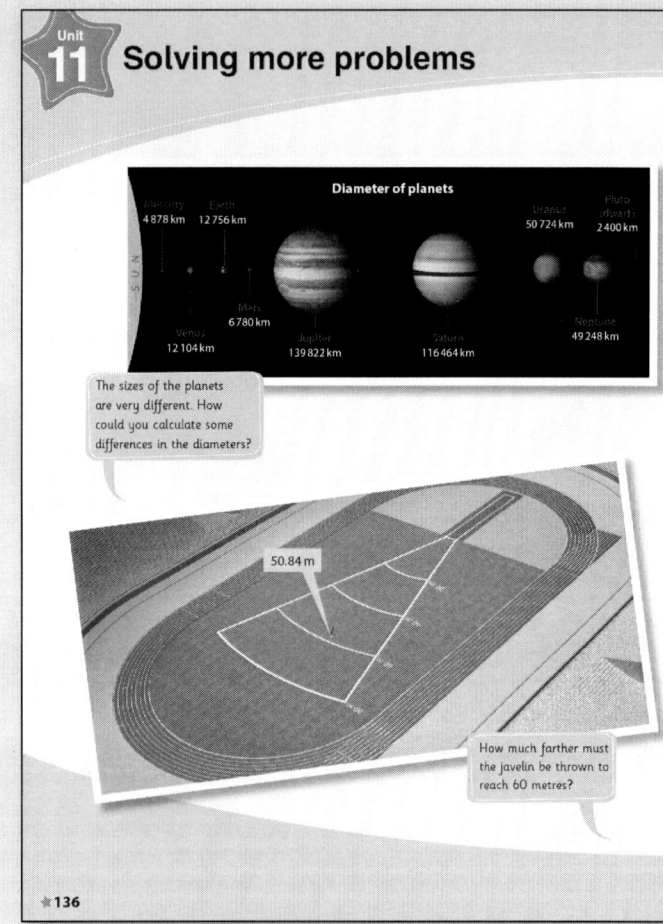

Unit 11 Solving more problems

Diameter of planets

Mercury 4878 km
Earth 12756 km
Uranus 50724 km
Pluto (dwarf) 2400 km
Mars 6780 km
Venus 12104 km
Jupiter 139822 km
Saturn 116464 km
Neptune 49248 km

The sizes of the planets are very different. How could you calculate some differences in the diameters?

50.84 m

How much farther must the javelin be thrown to reach 60 metres?

★136

Talk about

It is important to encourage children to answer in full sentences and refine their choice of technical terms. Consider the mathematical language used in word problems and how this helps us to decide what we may need to do, e.g. sum, difference, etc. Mathematical discussion helps children to reason about the mathematics they are doing, explaining their ideas and justifying their choices. Encourage children to use phrases to help them understand vocabulary, e.g. equivalence: has the same value but may not look the same; variable: its value 'varies'.

Engaging and exploring

Look at the picture of the planets and ask children to order the planets from largest diameter to smallest diameter. Establish that Pluto (a dwarf planet) has the smallest diameter and Jupiter has the largest. Challenge children to calculate the difference between these and to explain the method they have used. Model the calculation using the formal written method, asking children to talk through each step. Suggest that the difference between some of the diameters can be calculated using a mental method. Children should identify possible pairs, e.g. Pluto and Mars, Earth and Venus, Uranus and Neptune, explaining their choices (e.g. close proximity on a number line, multiples of 10 and 100) and methods used. Children can also make up some word problems using the information given and discuss the operations needed to solve them, e.g. *Approximately how many times larger is the diameter of Neptune than Mercury? Two planets have a difference in*

diameter of 23 358 km. Which planets are they?

For the picture of the javelin throw, ask children to tell you what they notice about the measurements they can see, e.g. agree that they are marked every 20 metres. They should recognise that 50 m would be the halfway point, so 50.84 m is more than halfway. This should help them estimate that a throw of 60 m is less than 10 m longer than the throw shown here. Ask children to the question, using the bar model to represent the problem. Focus on the use of number bonds to count up to the next whole number, etc. Consider some other measurements to 2 decimal places that would be closer to 40 m, or the same distance past 40 m as 50.84 m is to 60 m, i.e. 9.16 m so 49.16 m. Challenge children to calculate how much longer the throw would need to be to reach 60 m each time. Consider place value and mental methods of counting up to find the difference to support calculations.

Using the picture of the hats, ask children to explore different fractions of the group that suit criteria of their choice. They should practise using full sentences to explain their thinking, e.g. 'I know that $\frac{1}{3}$ of the hats are dark blue because 4 out of 12 or $\frac{4}{12}$ are dark blue.' Discuss what we need to know to prove or disprove the statement, i.e. the number or the fraction that each represent. Consider strategies to solve the problem. We could represent both the number of hats with ribbons or silver badges as fractions and then find the difference. Focus on the use of equivalent fractions using 12 as the denominator. A more efficient way would be to simply recognise that there are five more with ribbons than silver badges, so the difference is $\frac{5}{12}$. Look at different ways and representations to compare $\frac{5}{12}$ and the fraction $\frac{1}{3}$ to show that $\frac{1}{3}$ is equivalent to $\frac{4}{12}$ which is $\frac{1}{12}$ smaller than $\frac{5}{12}$. You could use paper strips, cubes, fraction bars or something else. You could also explore any two characteristics that do have a difference of $\frac{1}{3}$. What would we need to look for? i.e. a difference of four hats.

Discuss the egg box problem and encourage children to represent it using number rods or the bar model. What would each bar or rod need to represent? i.e. sixes and two remaining. Use the representations to explore different numbers of possible eggs that have been arranged in this way, e.g.

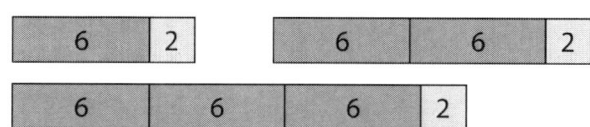

Ask children to suggest and explain 'silly' numbers of eggs that could not have been the number arranged in this way.

Discuss how an algebraic formula can be used to calculate all possible numbers of eggs.

What would the symbol 'n' (or other) need to represent? What changes and what stays the same each time? Agree that the number of eggs in a box (6) and the two left over remain the same, whilst the number of egg boxes changes. The formula $6n + 2$ can be used, where n represents the number of boxes.

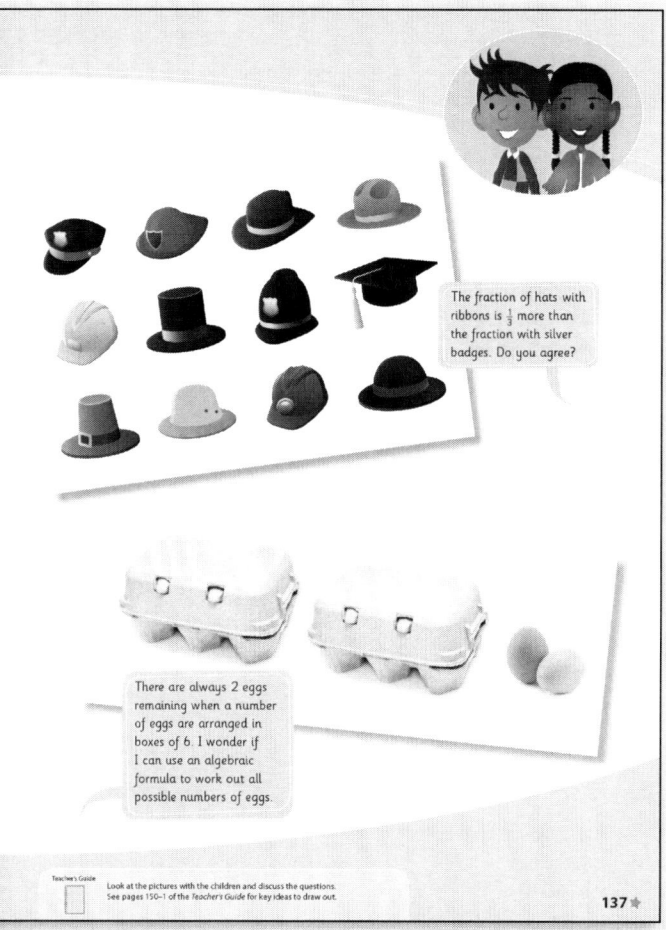

The fraction of hats with ribbons is $\frac{1}{3}$ more than the fraction with silver badges. Do you agree?

There are always 2 eggs remaining when a number of eggs are arranged in boxes of 6. I wonder if I can use an algebraic formula to work out all possible numbers of eggs.

Look at the pictures with the children and discuss the questions. See pages 150–1 of the *Teacher's Guide* for key ideas to draw out.

137

Things to think about

- Continue to raise the profile of mental mathematics and challenge inappropriate methods.

- Model and encourage the use of precise mathematical vocabulary when explaining thinking and reasoning.

- How will you organise groupings? Could a stronger reader be paired with a less confident reader so that language does not impede accessing problems?

- Which manipulatives and visual representations will help all children with their conceptual understanding?

- How could you best use additional adults? Could they support children to rehearse explanations and model their own thinking?

Checking understanding

You will know pupils have mastered these concepts when they can solve calculation problems in different contexts, appropriately choosing and using operations, number facts, understanding of place value and mental and written methods. They can explain their decision making and justify their solutions and level of accuracy.

- **Solve addition and subtraction multi-step problems in contexts, deciding which operations and methods to use and why.**
- **Perform mental calculations, including with mixed operations and large numbers.**
- **Use estimation to check answers to calculations and determine, in the context of a problem, an appropriate degree of accuracy.**

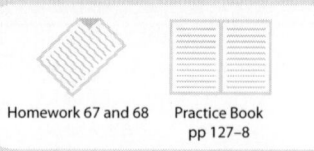

Homework 67 and 68   Practice Book pp 127–8

Representations and resources
Pencils and paper, number rods, word problems (multi-step).

Mathematical vocabulary
Addition, subtraction, multiplication, division, additive reasoning, multiplicative reasoning, half, double

Warming up
Practise making decisions about the order of operations. Present children with six or seven calculations that include addition and subtraction or multiplication and division. They should rewrite them in the order that they would best be solved, recognising that addition and subtraction have equal priority and multiplication and division have equal priority. They should find the answers each time. Ensure that all can be solved using mental strategies, drawing on halving and doubling for multiplication and division e.g. $120 \times 6 \div 2$.

Background knowledge
The bar model helps children to represent problems. Emphasise the relationship between the bars and values that are known to be equivalent. Encourage children to describe the relationship between the bars, the unknown and the values that are known to be equivalent. They should be encouraged to use multiplicative reasoning as well as additive reasoning to improve efficiency and develop their fluency.

Let's learn: Modelling and teaching
Representing problems
- Discuss Eva and Ali's thinking and some two-step problems that children have done recently where they had to add or subtract first before multiplying or dividing. Explain that brackets can be used to show that this step has to be done first.
- Look at the bar model in the Textbook and discuss the relationship between different parts of the bars. Children should notice that two sections are an equal value of 740. Reinforce the idea by modelling the problem using number rods.
- Explore the problem about the car rally, asking children to match parts of the bar model with different parts of the problem.

Solving problems
- Ask children to discuss the different ways that the problem can be solved and the operations they will need to use. Explain that this is a multi-step problem and is likely to involve more than one operation.
- Ask different groups to consider one of the statements and

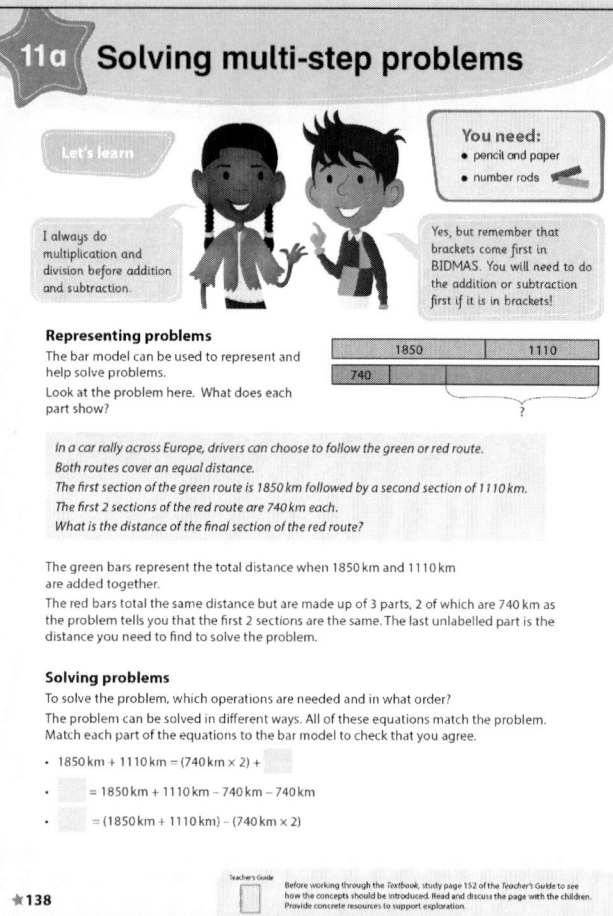

report back to others on its validity. They should prove that the statements are true by using number rods and the bar model in the Textbook.

- Focus on the position of the equals sign and the concept of balancing equations. Discuss the application of multiplicative reasoning for two sections of 740 rather than applying additive reasoning by subtracting 740 twice.

- Ask children whether they will use mental or written methods to solve the problem or a combination of both. Ask: *Which might be the most efficient?* Think about adding and subtracting multiples of ten, hundreds and thousands. Doubling should be encouraged when looking at the two sections of 740.

- Encourage estimates and methods of checking, including the use of the inverse.

Let's practise: Digging deeper

Step 1

Children are provided with four different bar models. They should reason about the relationship between the unknown white bar each time and the given values of the other bars.

They should apply additive and multiplicative reasoning to make sense of each representation, making estimates and checking for accuracy. If needed, allow children to use number rods to model part a, before encouraging them to use only the visual representations of the bar model in parts b-d.

Step 2

Children draw on their knowledge of the order of operations to show the calculations they used to find the value of the white bars in Step 1. They are given an example using additive reasoning but are required to use multiplicative reasoning as well. Remind children that brackets will help to

separate the steps needed and show the order.

Step 3

Encourage children to identify the relationship between the different values in the problem, e.g. the total time is 2 hrs 15 minutes so the time spent on the game and the two lessons is equal to this. Discuss what is known about the length of both lessons and how this can be represented as part of the bar model.

Step 4

Children demonstrate their understanding of multi-step problems by creating word problems to match the representations shown in Step 1. They are asked to set the problems in the context of measure. The numbers (which include decimals to 3 places) lend themselves most appropriately to length, mass and capacity.

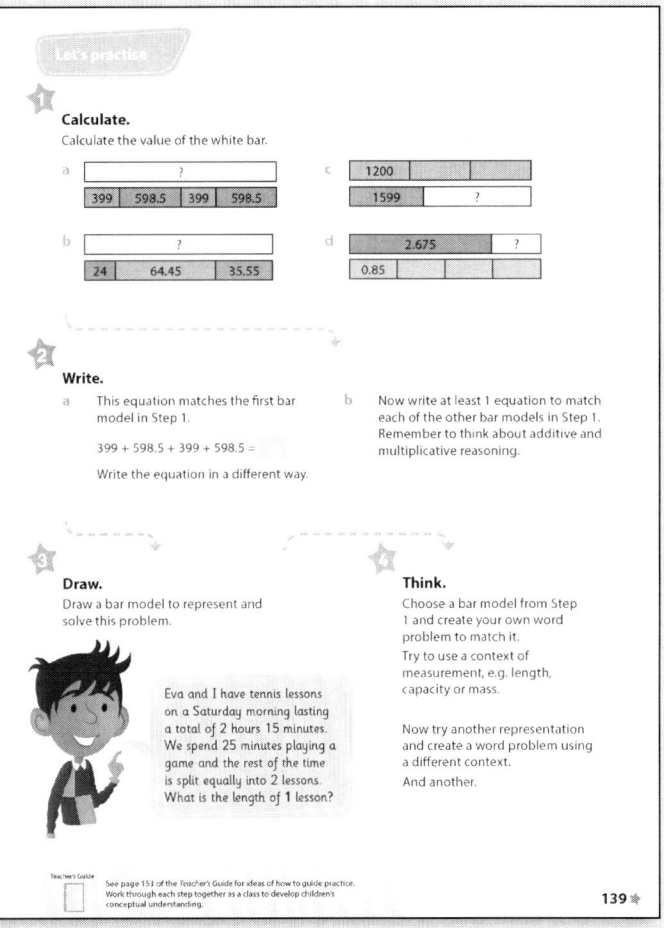

Ensuring progress

Supporting understanding

Working with children in focus groups, look at examples of word problems, perhaps from past papers, and explore ways to represent them using the bar model. Begin with two-step problems and use the dual representations of number rods and the bar model. Ensure that children can identify the operations required, and their order, before moving on to other examples of multi-step problems using just the bar model.

Broadening understanding

Use the representations from Step 1 but remove the values of the bars. Children should reason about other sets of possible values using the relationships to guide them, including the use of decimal numbers. They write problems to match the new values.

✓ Concept mastered

Children can represent problems in a variety of ways and explain which operations are required and the order in which they should be used. They can contextualise a representation, recognising the steps that will need to be taken.

Follow-up ideas

- Use number rods to make up bar models, give the bars values and create word problems. The children should decide which bar represents the answer each time.

- e.g.

0.24	0.24	0.12
?		?

- Children take a problem and draw the matching bar representation along with two other representations that include the same values but do not match the problem. Different groups of children then have to find the correct representation for the problem and decide how the problem would need to change for one of the other representations to be true.

Answers

Step 1

a   1995   c   2001

b   124   d   0.725

d   e.g.
$0.85 \times 4 = 2.675 +$
or
$(0.85 \times 4) - 2.675 =$

Step 2

a   e.g.
$(399 \times 2) + (598.5 \times 2) =$
or even
$- (399 \times 2) = 598.5 \times 2$

b   e.g.
$(64.45 + 35.55 + 24) \div 2 =$
or
$64.45 + 35.55 + 24 = \quad \times 2$
or
$(64.45 + 35.55) + 24 = \quad \times 2$

c   e.g.
$1200 \times 3 = 1599 +$
or
$(1200 \times 3) - 1599 =$

Step 3

2 hours 15 mins		
25 mins	?	?

55 minutes per lesson.

Step 4

Answers will vary.

e.g. for the first bar model:

Pete is measuring the perimeter of a rectangular room. The shorter sides are 399 cm in length and the longer sides are 598.5 cm. What is the perimeter of the room?

- Add and subtract fractions with different denominators and mixed numbers, using the concept of equivalent fractions.
- Interpret and construct pie charts and use these to solve problems.
- Calculate and interpret the mean as an average.

Homework 69 and 70   Practice Book pp 129–32   Fraction Wall

Representations and resources

Fraction bars, multiplication squares, protractors.

Mathematical vocabulary

Fractions, numerator, denominator, common denominator, scaling, equivalent, sum, total, difference, sector, simplify

Warming up

Focus on rounding to degrees of accuracy. Present the children with a range of numbers to several decimal places, e.g. 19.1428 and 25.0365. Children round the numbers to the nearest whole number, tenth, hundredth and thousands, completing as many as they can in the time allowed.

Background knowledge

Children need to practise adding and subtracting fractions with a range of denominators. When denominators are different, children can get into the habit of multiplying the denominators to find a common one, without checking whether they are both already multiples of the same number. A multiplication square is a useful way to explore equivalent fractions, e.g. $\frac{3}{4}$ by looking at the row for 3 and 4. As we move across the columns, we can see how numerator (3) and denominator (4) are scaled by the same factor, giving the string of equivalents $\frac{6}{8}, \frac{9}{12}, \frac{12}{15}$, etc.

Let's learn: Modelling and teaching
Equivalent fractions

- Discuss the title and legend of the pie chart. Ask children to explain what these tell them. Relate the pie chart to the divisions on a clock face to help children make sense of the blue sector. The other sectors can be described by relating them to the blue sector, e.g. the red sector is three times larger than the blue sector, which is $\frac{1}{12} \times 3$. Ask children what they can say about the green sector. Establish that it is $\frac{8}{12}$ and use fraction bars to confirm that $\frac{8}{12} = \frac{2}{3}$.

- Suggest a total number of tickets sold so that children use the fractions to find the number sold each week or suggest the number sold on week 1 or week 3 and children find the total tickets sold.

Adding and subtracting fractions

- Discuss the comments made by Eva and Ali, asking children to give examples of pairs of fractions where it is necessary to multiply the denominators to find a common denominator and where it is not. Use fraction bars to model adding $\frac{1}{4} + \frac{1}{12}$, using fractional language

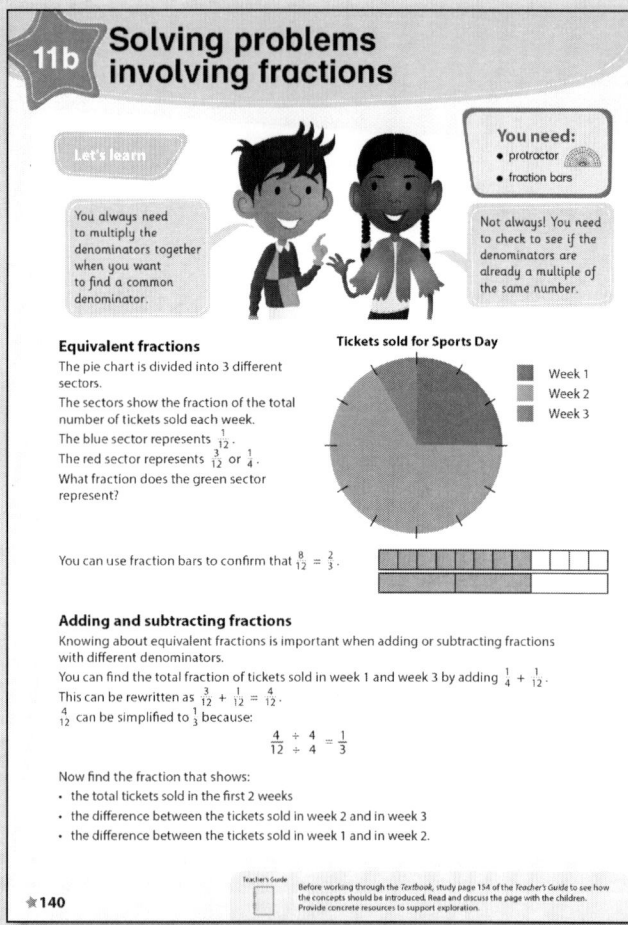

and multiplicative reasoning to scale the numerator and denominator accordingly.

- Encourage children to choose a representation to find the sums and differences set out in the Textbook. Collect feedback on why children used specific representations.

- Return to the suggested totals discussed earlier and check whether the calculations are correct by giving each fraction a value, e.g. *if the suggested total ticket sales are 120, then the blue sector represents 10, the red 30 and the green 80. We calculated $\frac{1}{4}$ (red) + $\frac{1}{12}$ (blue) as $\frac{1}{3}$ so 10 tickets plus 30 tickets should represent $\frac{1}{3}$ of the total sales.*

Let's practise: Digging deeper

Step 1

The flag shows different fractions of the whole. Children must first identify the value of each section and then explore pairs of sums and differences. The flag should be referred to when finding equivalent fractions, as the denominator 24 will help to express fractions using a common denominator.

Step 2

Children practise a set of addition and subtraction calculations. They must determine the common denominator, checking to see if the denominators are already multiples of the same number. Fraction bars will continue to support children to find equivalent fractions.

Step 3

Children must use the clues in this logic problem to determine the fractions, applying knowledge of adding and subtracting fractions along with equivalent fractions. Observe how confidently children make the connection to statistics when drawing their pie charts.

Step 4

This finding-all-possibilities problem is related to statistics as children find sets of fractions that have the mean value of $\frac{1}{2}$. Encourage children to describe how a mean is calculated and discuss how this relates to the problem. Ask them to consider how they can 'undo' the calculation needed to find the mean by applying the inverse. *What do we know now?* (The total of the 3 fractions must be $\frac{1}{2} \times 3$ or $1\frac{1}{2}$.)

Ensuring progress

Supporting understanding

Use the multiplication square to help children find strings of equivalent fractions. They should refer to each column heading in relation to the first so that they recognise that $\frac{1}{4}$ is equivalent to $\frac{3}{12}$ because the numerator is multiplied by three and the denominator is multiplied by three.

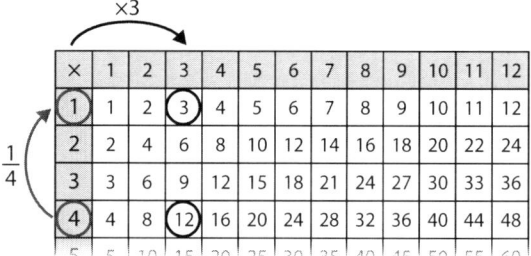

Broadening understanding

Children create their own problems that require them to add and subtract fractions. This could be in the context of a word problem or problems set out in diagrams. Challenge children to think creatively about the diagrams that they could use, drawing on other areas of statistics.

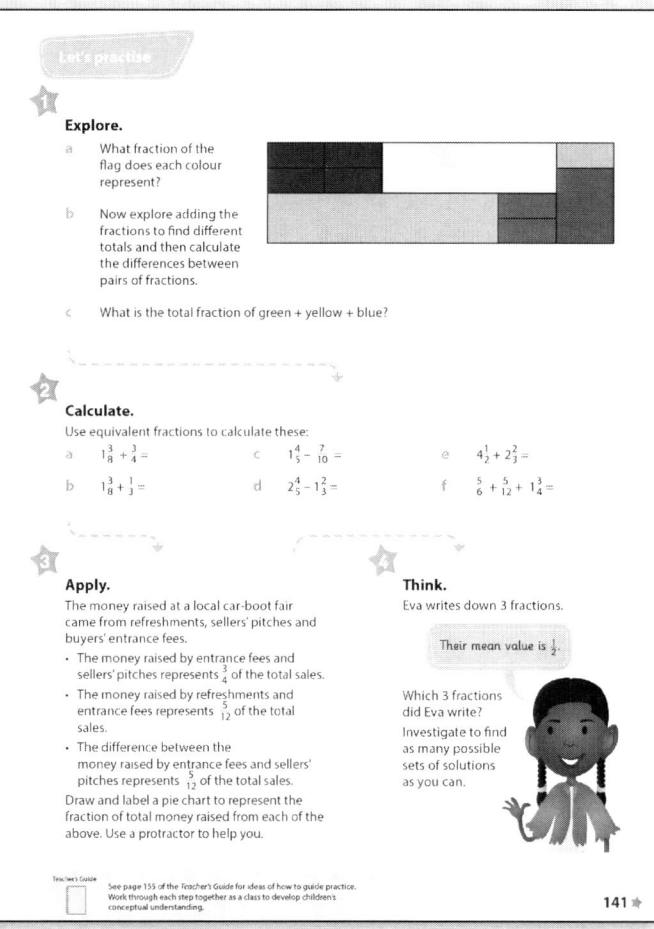

> ## Let's practise
>
> ☆ **Explore.**
>
> a What fraction of the flag does each colour represent?
>
> b Now explore adding the fractions to find different totals and then calculate the differences between pairs of fractions.
>
> c What is the total fraction of green + yellow + blue?
>
> ☆ **Calculate.**
>
> Use equivalent fractions to calculate these:
>
> a $1\frac{3}{8} + \frac{3}{4} =$ c $1\frac{4}{5} - \frac{7}{10} =$ e $4\frac{1}{2} + 2\frac{2}{3} =$
>
> b $1\frac{3}{8} + \frac{1}{3} =$ d $2\frac{4}{5} - 1\frac{3}{3} =$ f $\frac{5}{6} + \frac{5}{12} + 1\frac{3}{4} =$
>
> ☆ **Apply.**
>
> The money raised at a local car-boot fair came from refreshments, sellers' pitches and buyers' entrance fees.
> - The money raised by entrance fees and sellers' pitches represents $\frac{3}{4}$ of the total sales.
> - The money raised by refreshments and entrance fees represents $\frac{5}{12}$ of the total sales.
> - The difference between the money raised by entrance fees and sellers' pitches represents $\frac{5}{12}$ of the total sales.
>
> Draw and label a pie chart to represent the fraction of total money raised from each of the above. Use a protractor to help you.
>
> ☆ **Think.**
>
> Eva writes down 3 fractions.
>
> Their mean value is $\frac{1}{2}$.
>
> Which 3 fractions did Eva write? Investigate to find as many possible sets of solutions as you can.
>
> See page 155 of the *Teacher's Guide* for ideas of how to guide practice. Work through each step together as a class to develop children's conceptual understanding.
>
> 141

> ✓ ## Concept mastered
>
> Children can represent fractions in different ways using knowledge of equivalence and connect them to finding common denominators. They look carefully at the denominators given and check to see whether they are already multiples of the same number.

Follow-up ideas

- Link fractions to area of shapes, including rectilinear and compound shapes. Use squared paper to help determine fractions, writing each in their lowest form. Investigate sums and differences of different areas of the shape, using equivalent fractions as necessary to support calculation, e.g:

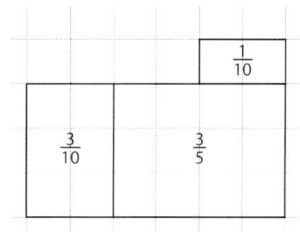

$\frac{3}{5} + \frac{3}{10} = \frac{6}{10} + \frac{3}{10} = \frac{9}{10}$

$\frac{3}{5} - \frac{1}{10} = \frac{6}{10} - \frac{1}{10} = \frac{5}{10} = \frac{1}{2}$

Answers

Step 1

Answers will vary.

e.g. purple + blue is
$\frac{1}{6} + \frac{1}{8} = \frac{4}{24} + \frac{3}{24} = \frac{7}{24}$

purple − blue is
$\frac{1}{6} - \frac{1}{8} = \frac{4}{24} - \frac{3}{24} = \frac{1}{24}$

green + yellow + blue = $\frac{17}{24}$

Step 2

a $2\frac{1}{8}$ d $1\frac{2}{15}$

b $1\frac{17}{24}$ e $7\frac{1}{6}$

c $1\frac{1}{10}$ f 3

Step 3

Refreshments = $\frac{1}{4}$,
entrance fees = $\frac{1}{6}$ and sellers'
pitches = $\frac{7}{12}$.

Pie chart must show the fractions above along with the legend and title.

Step 4

Any three fractions that add up to $\frac{3}{2}$, e.g. $\frac{1}{2}, \frac{1}{2}, \frac{1}{2}$

$\frac{1}{2}, \frac{3}{4}, \frac{1}{4}$

$\frac{3}{4}, \frac{3}{8}, \frac{3}{8}$

$\frac{3}{10}, \frac{7}{10}, \frac{1}{2}$, etc.

- Use simple formulae.
- Express missing number problems algebraically.
- Find pairs of numbers that satisfy an equation with two unknowns.
- Enumerate possibilities of two variables.
- Interpret and construct line graphs and use these to solve problems.

Homework 71 and 72   Practice Book pp 133–5

Representations and resources

1–6 dice, number rods, number shapes, cubes, squared paper, rulers.

Mathematical vocabulary

Algebra, expression, equation, formula, unknown, variable, value

Warming up

Children work in pairs with a 1–6 dice. They roll a starting number, e.g. 4, and then must follow the rule 'double the number and add 12' to create a string of numbers, i.e. in this case 4, 20, 52, 116, 244, etc. They should be challenged to go as far as they can, using mental strategies for doubling. Children may choose to use a decimal number to start with, e.g. 0.4, but still applying the same rule.

Background knowledge

Line graphs are a useful way to show relationships between values. Each point on a line graph has an x value and a y value that can be related to a term and a value in a linear sequence or in other algebraic expressions. We can also represent multiplication tables using line graphs. The x value can represent the term to be multiplied and the y axis can represent the value after the term has been scaled, e.g. (0, 0), (1, 3), (2, 6), (3, 9), etc. would show the multiplication table for 3.

Let's learn: Modelling and teaching

Using simple formulae

- Discuss why the line graph in the Textbook is straight by focusing on the relationship between the x and y values remaining the same.

- Explore some different points on the line, noting the x and y values each time. Record the pattern made by each set of value. Children should notice that they start on different numbers.

- Ask children to suggest how the use of tables, lists and systematic approaches helps to identify patterns, both within and across the variables.

- Discuss the two given algebraic expressions and challenge children to find a way to prove that both are correct.

- Remind children that the line graph shows continuous data so all points along it have values. Consider larger values for x and y beyond the size of the line graph shown as well as values that are between intervals, e.g. when $x = 12.5$

Finding possible solutions

- Discuss missing number problems that children have

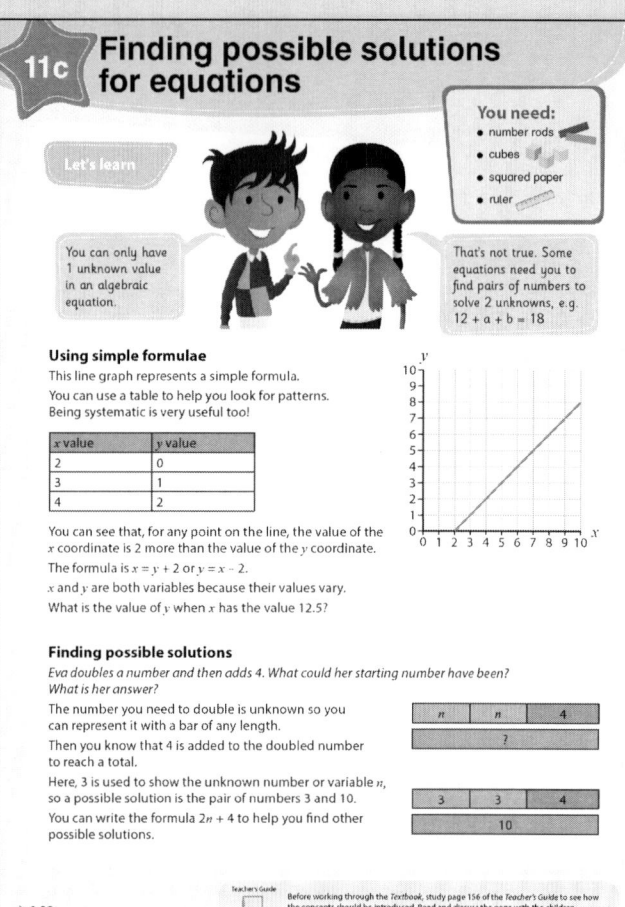

experienced previously.

- Refer to the discussion between Eva and Ali. *Do the algebraic equations shown here have one or more unknowns? Why?* Suggest examples of equations with one unknown, e.g. $25 + a = 100$.

- Encourage children to use number rods to match the representation in the Textbook. Establish that the rod we start with is a variable as its value 'varies'. In this representation, the value is 3, but it can have many other values.

- Challenge children to explain what the second variable is in the problem and why it varies, i.e. the number you end up with will vary depending on the number you start with. Establish that we have found one pair of numbers (3 and 10) to satisfy the equation $2n + 4$.

Let's practise: Digging deeper

Step 1

Children are presented with another formula that has been represented using cubes. They must use the formula to determine the values of n and d in the particular representation and go on to explore other possible values for the variables n and d. Observe how confidently children move to this different representation and encourage them to use cubes to model the problem if necessary.

Step 2

Children use the bar model to help find other pairs of numbers to satisfy the equation $2n + 4 = m$. They are given a set of different values for n, and must use these to find the value of m. They could use number rods as an additional support. Encourage them to record the values systematically in a table.

Step 3

Children draw a line graph to represent the equation $2y + 1 = x$. Observe to ensure they construct their line graphs accurately. They work logically using a table to find possible values to be plotted. Use questioning to draw out the idea that a straight line is formed again because the relationship between x and y remains the same each time.

Step 4

Children investigate a formula for the area of two given shapes. Discuss the first two shapes in the sequence and challenge children to explain how the formula is used to express the areas. They should represent other shapes that suit the formula, using squared paper or cubes. Tables or lists would help children to organise their results.

Ensuring progress

Supporting understanding

Work with children in a focus group. Look at representing the equation $2n + 4 = m$ in different ways, perhaps with number shapes or with cubes. Link this to the idea of a 2-step function machine where n is the input number and m is the output number after n has been doubled and 4 added.

Broadening understanding

Children could be challenged to write equations each time that can be used to check the answers to the problems set out in Steps 1– 4. They should apply knowledge of the inverse and consider the order of operations and the use of brackets.

> ## ✓ Concept mastered
>
> Children can use manipulatives to represent an algebraic equation and find pairs of numbers to suit it. They can explain which parts of an equation are variables and why this is the case.

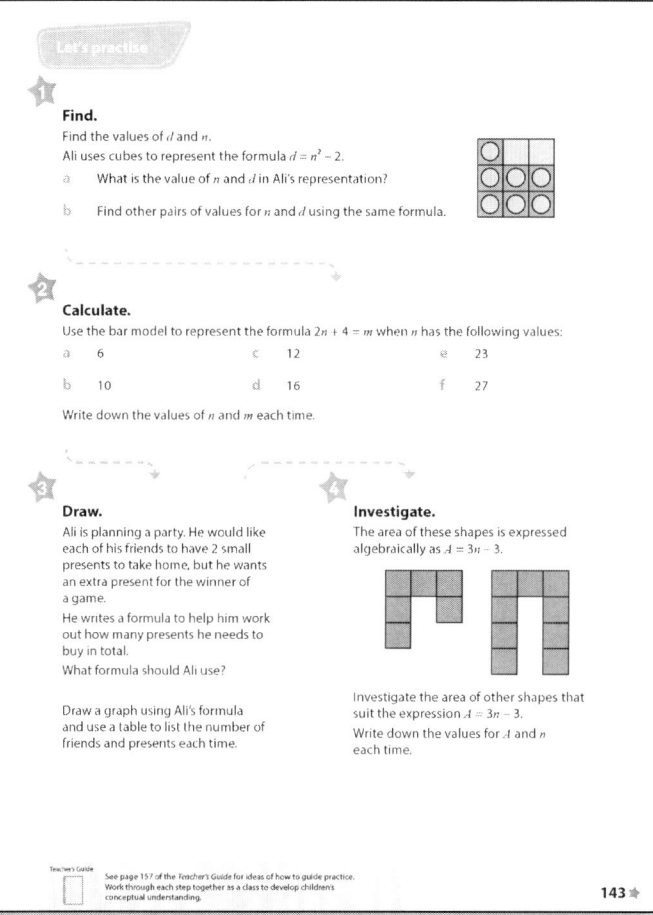

Let's practise

1 Find.

Find the values of d and n.

Ali uses cubes to represent the formula $d = n^2 - 2$.

a   What is the value of n and d in Ali's representation?

b   Find other pairs of values for n and d using the same formula.

2 Calculate.

Use the bar model to represent the formula $2n + 4 = m$ when n has the following values:

a   6   c   12   e   23

b   10   d   16   f   27

Write down the values of n and m each time.

3 Draw.

Ali is planning a party. He would like each of his friends to have 2 small presents to take home, but he wants an extra present for the winner of a game.

He writes a formula to help him work out how many presents he needs to buy in total.

What formula should Ali use?

Draw a graph using Ali's formula and use a table to list the number of friends and presents each time.

4 Investigate.

The area of these shapes is expressed algebraically as $A = 3n - 3$.

Investigate the area of other shapes that suit the expression $A = 3n - 3$.

Write down the values for A and n each time.

Teacher's Guide See page 157 of the Teacher's Guide for ideas of how to guide practice. Work through each step together as a class to develop children's conceptual understanding.

143

Answers

Step 1

a $n = 3$ and $d = 7$

b   Answers will vary.

e.g. $n = 1$ and $d = -1$, $n = 2$ and $d = 1$, $n = 4$ and $d = 14$, $n = 10$ and $d = 98$

b   e.g.

x friends	y presents
1	3
2	5
3	7
10	21
12	25

Step 2

a   6 and 16   d   16 and 36

b   10 and 24   e   23 and 50

c   12 and 28   f   27 and 58

Step 3

a

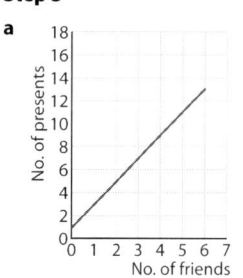

Step 4

Answers will vary.

Possible values for n and A include:

n	3	4	5	15	50	12.5
A	6	9	12	42	147	34.5

Follow-up ideas

- Look at the use of algebra to calculate area and perimeter of shapes. Consider which parts of the formulae are the variables each time and why.

- Use tangrams to explore algebra further, finding relationships between the shapes and how these are put together or cut to make other shapes e.g:

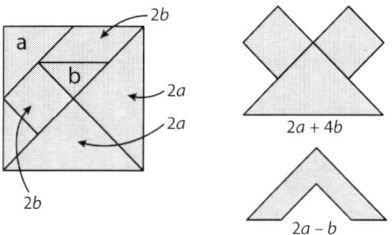

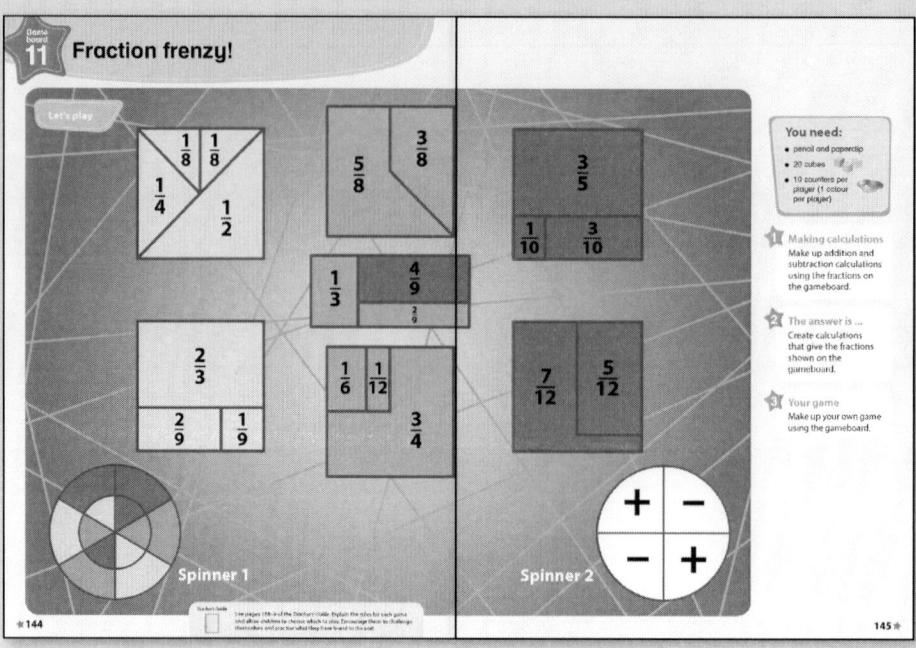

Game 1: Making calculations

Children make up addition and subtraction calculations using the fractions on the gameboard.

The spinners determine the range of fractions and the operation to use. Players can earn bonus points by choosing fractions that give an answer that can be simplified.

Maths focus

- Adding and subtracting fractions

Resources

Pencil and paperclip (for spinners), 20 cubes, 10 counters per player (1 colour per player).

How to play

Players take turns to spin the paperclip, around the pencil, on each spinner. Spinner 1 shows the colours of the pair of fractions that must be chosen, e.g. if the paperclip lands on a section with green and orange then a green fraction and an orange fraction must be picked. Spinner 2 determines whether the fractions should be used for an addition or subtraction calculation. Players make up a calculation using the results on the spinners and then work out the answer; if their partner agrees with their answer, they take a cube. They can take a bonus cube if their answer can be simplified. The winner is the player with the most cubes after all 20 have been taken.

Making it easier

Children work in pairs to help each other with calculations or initially play the game using only spinner 1 and decide if it is an adding game or a subtracting game. They may also like to start by using the top row of shapes on the gameboard only.

Making it harder

Players put a counter on a fraction when they have used it. Each player can only use a fraction once.

There are 20 fractions in total so each player can make 10 pairs. They should think carefully about pairs that may earn them an extra cube because the answer can be simplified.

Game 2: The answer is …

The aim of the game is to create calculations that give the fraction answers shown on the gameboard. Players spin the spinner to find out if they must add or subtract.

Maths focus

- Adding and subtracting fractions

Resources

Pencil and paper clip (for spinner), 10 counters per player (1 colour per player).

How to play

The aim of the game is to be the first to cover 10 fractions with their counters. Players take turns to spin the paperclip, around the pencil, on spinner 2 to find out if they must make up an addition or subtraction calculation. They must think of a pair of fractions that they can use in the calculation to give one of the answers on the gameboard. They cover a correct answer with a counter.

Making it easier

Play with only the three shapes on the top row. These fractions include quarters, halves, eighths, fifths and tenths rather than including sixths, ninths and twelfths, etc.

Making it harder

Players choose an answer to make first before they spin spinner 2. They could also spin spinner 1 to give them the option of the fractions they can pick, e.g. green or orange, green only, etc.

Game 3: Your game

Children should invent their own game designing rules that use the concepts covered in the unit. Challenge children to make their game easier or harder.

Unit 1 Fraction frenzy!

Choose a game to play.

Game 1: Making calculations

You need:
- pencil and paperclip (for spinners)
- 20 cubes

How to play

- Take it in turns to spin the paperclip on each spinner.
- Make up a calculation using the results on the spinners.
  - Spinner 1 shows the colours of the pair of fractions, e.g. if the paperclip lands on a section with green and orange, you need to choose a green fraction and an orange fraction.
  - Spinner 2 tells you to add or subtract them.
- Work out the answer to your calculation and, if your partner agrees with your answer, take a cube. Take a bonus cube if your answer can be simplified.
- The winner is the player with the most cubes after all 20 have been taken.

Game 2: The answer is …

You need:
- pencil and paper clip (for spinners)
- 10 counters per player (1 colour per player)

How to play

- The aim of the game is to cover 10 fractions with your counters.
- Take turns to spin the paperclip on spinner 2 to find out if you must make up an addition or subtraction calculation.
- Think of a pair of fractions that you can use that will give one of the answers on the gameboard.
- Cover the answer with a counter if you are correct.

Game 3: Your game

- Make up your own game using the gameboard.
- You could choose to play with your own colour fractions, e.g. you play with the yellow fractions, your partner with the green, but you can both pick any of the orange ones.
- You may want to choose 3 fractions to add each time when you are playing an adding game.
- Perhaps you could make up your own gameboard with fractions of your choice.
- What are the rules for your game? Explain them to someone.

Please help your child by reading the instructions and playing the game together.

Assessment task 1

Running the task

Children can solve the problem on their own or with a partner. They should discuss a starting point and think about the use of the bar model to help them make sense of the problem.

They should recognise that the problem has several steps and decide what they need to do first.

It would be useful to discuss the operations that they will need to use and what part of the problem suggests these.

They should reason about the price of the two adults by using what they know about the price of one child, i.e. £149 is approximately £150 so the price of three children is approximately £450. The price of two adults must be more than £500. As always, they should consider mental methods first before applying a written method. Look for children who also use a method of checking and refer back to the original question. The problem develops as the children now use the costs for one adult and one child to work out the total cost for a different number of passengers.

Evidencing mastery

Children are showing mastery if they are able to represent and explain stages for the problems using a representation, e.g. the bar model. They reason carefully about the order in which the calculation should be completed, and fluently apply a range of mental strategies for halving and multiplying £149 by rounding to £150 and adjusting. They check their calculations using inverse operations and check that the answer is correct in the context of the problem.

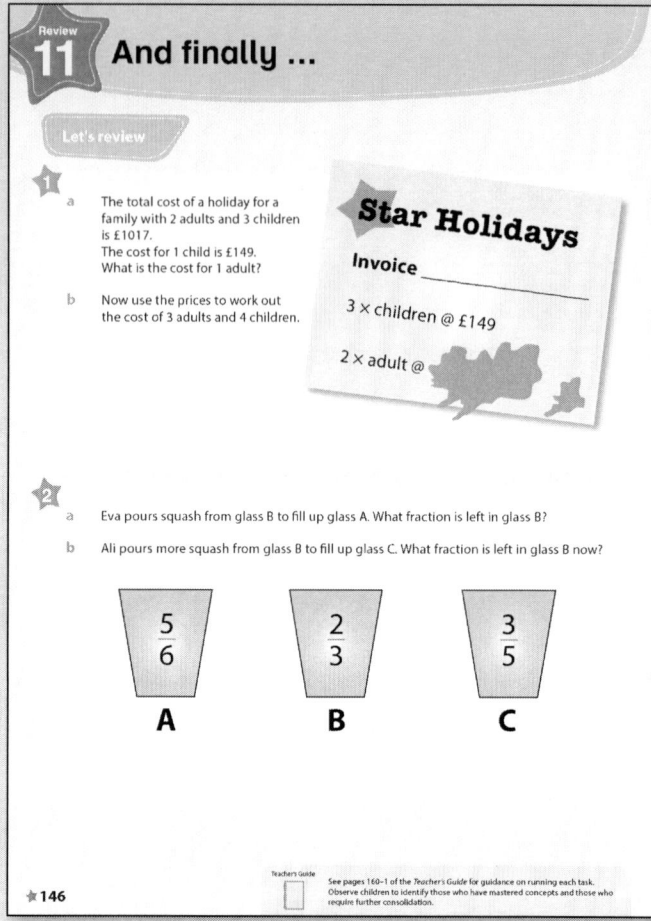

Assessment task 2

Running the task

Discuss the mathematics involved in this problem and what operations children will need to use to help them. Remind children of some of the adding and subtracting that they have been doing with fractions. Discuss pairs of fractions that are easier to add and why, i.e. they have the same denominators or the denominators are all multiples of the same number.

Children may decide to role play the problem and explain what is happening to each glass as the squash is poured from one to another. They should reason about the common denominators that can be used and whether it is best to write

the fraction of squash left in glass B after the first step in its lowest form or to leave it as $\frac{3}{6}$.

Evidencing mastery

Children who recognise and explain that they must first use fraction pairs to one to find out how much squash must be poured from glass B are demonstrating mastery. They fluently apply strategies for subtracting fractions by finding a common denominator. They look carefully for examples where the denominators are both multiples of the same number before simply multiplying the denominators.

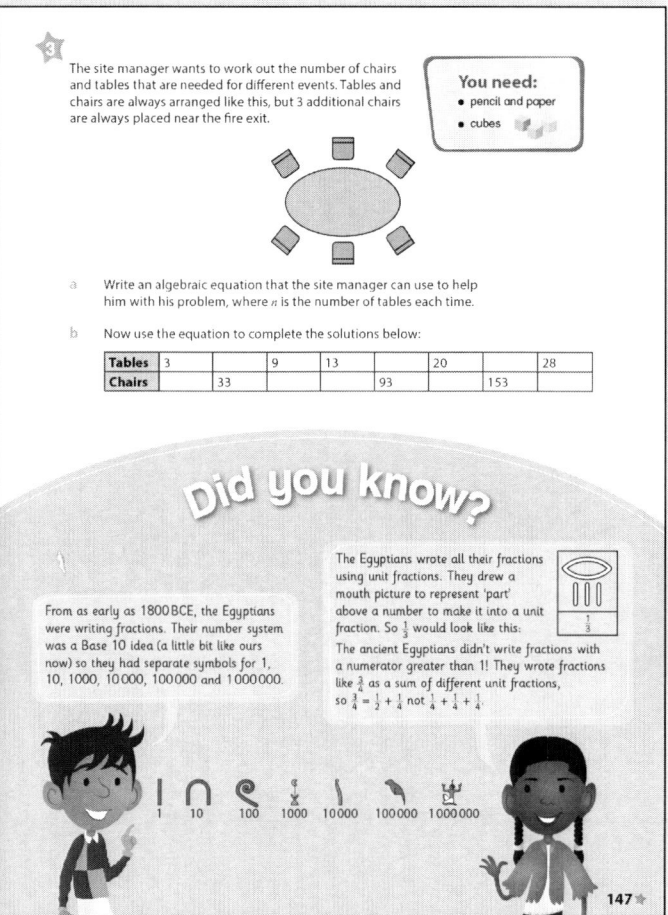

The site manager wants to work out the number of chairs and tables that are needed for different events. Tables and chairs are always arranged like this, but 3 additional chairs are always placed near the fire exit.

You need:
- pencil and paper
- cubes

a Write an algebraic equation that the site manager can use to help him with his problem, where n is the number of tables each time.

b Now use the equation to complete the solutions below:

Tables	3		9	13		20		28
Chairs		33			93		153	

Did you know?

From as early as 1800 BCE, the Egyptians were writing fractions. Their number system was a Base 10 idea (a little bit like ours now) so they had separate symbols for 1, 10, 1000, 10 000, 100 000 and 1 000 000.

The Egyptians wrote all their fractions using unit fractions. They drew a mouth picture to represent 'part' above a number to make it into a unit fraction. So $\frac{1}{3}$ would look like this:

The ancient Egyptians didn't write fractions with a numerator greater than 1! They wrote fractions like $\frac{3}{4}$ as a sum of different unit fractions, so $\frac{3}{4} = \frac{1}{2} + \frac{1}{4}$ not $\frac{1}{4} + \frac{1}{4} + \frac{1}{4}$.

𐌉	∩	૭	𓏤	𓏲	𓆓	𓁨
1	10	100	1000	10 000	100 000	1 000 000

147

Concepts mastered

✓ Children can represent problems in a variety of ways and explain which operations are required and the order in which they should be used. They can contextualise a representation, recognising the steps that will need to be taken.

✓ Children can represent fractions in different ways using knowledge of equivalence and connect them to finding common denominators. They look carefully at the denominators given and check to see whether they are already multiples of the same number.

✓ Children can use manipulatives to represent an algebraic equation and find pairs of numbers to suit it. They can explain which part of the equations are variables and why this is the case.

Assessment task 3

Resources

Cubes.

Running the task

Remind children of some of the work they have been doing with algebraic expressions, including examples with one and two variables. Revisit the meaning of variable and ask children to identify the variables in this problem, i.e. the number of tables and the total number of chairs. They should recognise, e.g. that the number of chairs around the table does not change as it is always six, and so this is not a variable. The three chairs at the fire exit also remain unchanged.

Children may wish to represent the problem using cubes before they begin to find the relationship between the variables and find an algebraic equation to express this.

Children can work in pairs or groups to promote discussion and test possible equations using the cubes to prove or disprove their ideas.

Evidencing mastery

Children identify the variables and explain why they change or 'vary' each time. They recognise that the number of chairs around each table stays the same, as do the three extra chairs by the fire exit. The variables are the number of tables (n) and the total number of chairs needed (let's call this c) for the event. They should find an equation, such as $c = 6n + 3$.

Did you know?

Children are introduced to the idea of Egyptian fractions. The Egyptians wrote all their fractions using unit fractions – these are fractions with 1 as the numerator. They drew a mouth picture to represent 'part' above a number to make it into a unit fraction, as shown in the Textbook.

The Egyptians expressed fractions as the sum of different unit fractions so a fraction such as $\frac{3}{4}$, was written as $\frac{1}{2} + \frac{1}{4}$ and not $\frac{1}{4} + \frac{1}{4} + \frac{1}{4}$.

Children can investigate different ways of expressing non-unit fractions using the Egyptian approach. They may wish to investigate any fractions that can be written in more than one way, e.g. $\frac{3}{5}$ as $\frac{1}{4} + \frac{1}{5} + \frac{1}{10} + \frac{1}{20}$ or as $\frac{1}{2} + \frac{1}{10}$. Egyptian fractions are a great way to link fraction and decimal equivalence and the concept of area.

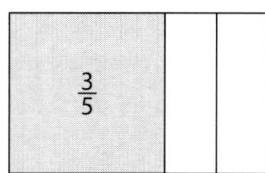
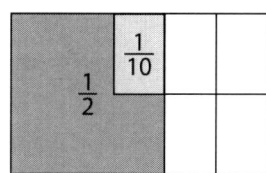

The spread gives children the opportunity to look at the Egyptian number system, also working on the idea of Base 10. They may wish to compare the Egyptian number system to say, the Mayan system.

Fractions, equivalents and algebra

Mathematical focus

★ **Number: fractions (including decimals and percentages)**

★ **Algebra: number sequences, equations with two unknowns, simple formulae**

★ **Measurement: length, money, area**

★ **Statistics: interpret and construct, interpret and calculate**

Prior learning

Children should already be able to:

- find and use simple fraction, decimal and percentage equivalents
- recognise the link between fractions and division
- make and describe number sequences
- solve missing number problems
- solve simple equations with two unknowns
- use formulae for the area and perimeter of rectangles, including squares, and triangles
- multiply and divide using mental calculation strategies.

Key new learning

- Associate a fraction with division and calculate decimal fraction equivalents (for example, 0.375) for a simple fraction ($\frac{3}{8}$).
- Recall and use equivalences between simple fractions, decimals and percentages, including in different contexts.
- Use simple formulae.
- Generate and describe linear number sequences.
- Express missing number problems algebraically.
- Find pairs of numbers that satisfy an equation with two unknowns.
- Interpret and construct pie charts and use these to solve problems.

Making connections

- An understanding of equivalent fractions is important in the context of statistics.
- Children need to be comfortable using formulae as these are widely used across many areas of maths, as well as in other subjects such as science and geography.
- Finding perimeters and areas links to their knowledge of the properties of shape and helps children see visually how the formulae 'work'. Linear number sequences are given a similarly visual element using a 100 square, linking to children's previous experience of counting in multiples and earlier work on patterns.

Unit 12 Fractions, equivalents and algebra

I wonder how tall these trees could be?

What fraction of the coins is made of copper?

★148

Talk about

Remind children that algebra is about finding unknowns. They have experienced this in missing number problems and simple formulae for perimeter and area. Ask them if they can remember what a linear number sequence is and when they first started working on these: counting in steps of equal size, which they have done since Year 1. When working with fractions, ensure that children know and use the terms, vinculum, denominator and numerator.

Engaging and exploring

Look at the picture of the trees. How tall might the tallest tree be? Compare the heights of the trees. Establish that the second tallest tree looks about half the height of the taller one. The smallest looks about half the height of the second tallest tree and about one quarter the height of the tallest. Tell children the height of the tallest tree is 5 m. How can you find the approximate heights of the other trees? Agree that you could divide the height of the tallest tree by two and four. Now tell children the height of the smallest tree is 1.5 m and ask them to find the heights of the other two.

Recap the fact that finding fractions links to division. Ask children to tell you how to find a fraction of an amount (divide by the denominator and multiply by the numerator). Rehearse this by calling out fractions of numbers for children to find, e.g. $\frac{2}{3}$ of 24, $\frac{7}{10}$ of 90, $\frac{5}{6}$ of 126.

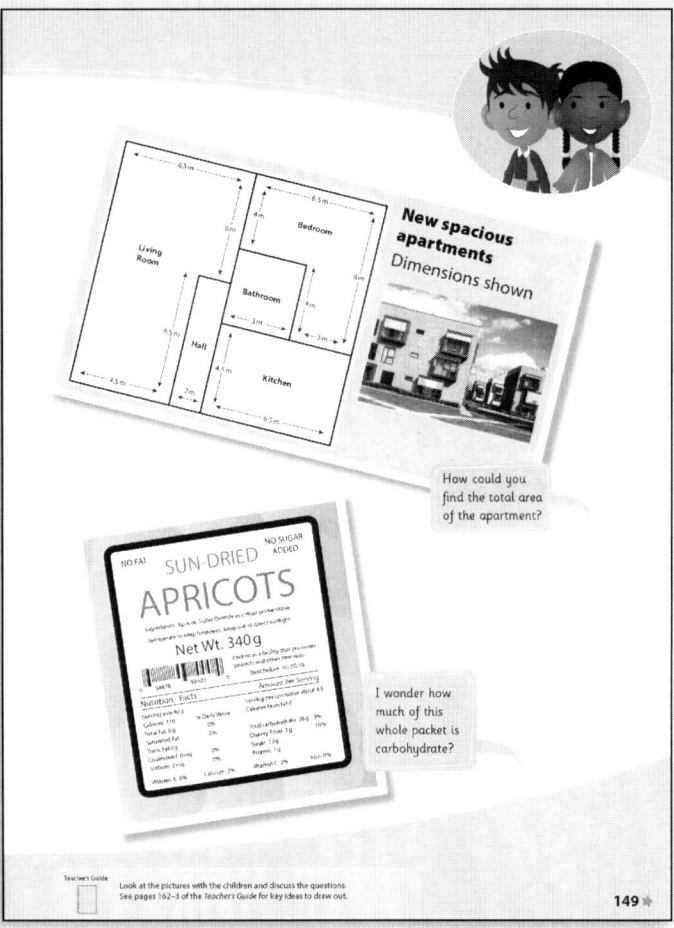

New spacious apartments
Dimensions shown

How could you find the total area of the apartment?

SUN-DRIED APRICOTS

NO FAT   NO SUGAR ADDED

Net Wt. 340 g

Nutrition Facts

I wonder how much of this whole packet is carbohydrate?

Teacher's Guide   Look at the pictures with the children and discuss the questions. See pages 162–3 of the *Teacher's Guide* for key ideas to draw out.   149

Next, recap equivalent fractions, decimals and percentages. Ask children to look at the picture of the trees again and convert the fractions they found earlier to decimals and percentages ($\frac{1}{2}$ = 0.5 = 50%, $\frac{1}{4}$ = 0.25 = 25%).

Ask children to identify the different coins in the pile shown and how many there are of each. You could model this using real coins. Then discuss the whole/part relationship of the coins, e.g. the whole is 20 and the part taken by 50p coins is 4, so $\frac{4}{20}$ of the coins are 50p. Ask children to simplify the fraction ($\frac{1}{5}$). They could do this for all the coins. Next agree that 5 of the 20 coins are copper; the other 15 are not. Ask them to write both amounts as fractions in their lowest terms ($\frac{1}{4}$ copper, $\frac{3}{4}$ not copper).

Look at the plan of the flat. The easiest way to find the total area of the flat is to find its total length and width and multiply. You could also talk about how you can find the area of the different rooms. Agree that for the rectangles you can simply multiply the length by the width. For the compound shapes, encourage children to reason about what they could do. Agree they need to make the shapes into two rectangles, find the areas of these and then total them. Can they identify how to make these shapes into two rectangles? Recap the formula for finding the area of rectangles. Agree that it is $l \times w$. Ask children to use the formula to work out the areas of the different rooms. Next ask them to find the perimeters of the rooms: for some rooms they will need to find the missing lengths first; for the rectangles they can use the formula $P = 2(l + w)$ or $2l + 2w$.

Ask children to design their own flat plan. They need to decide which rooms to include and the sizes of them. They then scale these down from metres to centimetres and draw their plan. They work out the area and perimeter of each room. Those children who recall how to find the area of triangles and parallelograms from Unit 7 could include these shapes (e.g. a triangular ensuite bathroom, or a garden in the shape of a parallelogram).

Ask children to look carefully at the packet of food and make a list of all the different numbers they can see, including masses, dates and percentages. You could discuss what mg stands for (milligram). Remind them that they know that 1000 millilitres equals one litre. Can they use this knowledge to work out what a milligram is worth? Establish that one milligram is one thousandth of a gram, a very tiny amount. Ask children to write the amount they see in grams. Discuss how to work out how much of the whole packet is carbohydrate and work this out together. Then ask children to rewrite the information on the package for a bag twice the size, and then half the size. You could extend the task by giving them other food packaging to explore in the same way.

Things to think about

- How will you organise groupings for discussions and activities?

- How will you provide support for practical activities, such as drawing pie charts?

- What opportunities are there in the classroom to find the areas and perimeters of rectangles?

- Which problem-solving strategies are most appropriate in this unit, for your Year 6 children, e.g.

  ▶ If that's the answer, what's the question?

  ▶ Odd one out

  ▶ What else do we know?

Checking understanding

Children can see the link between division and fractions and use this to calculate decimal fraction equivalents. They can recall equivalences between different fractions, decimals and percentages. They can represent missing number statements and explain how to find unknowns and also explain how different formulae can be used to solve problems.

- Associate a fraction with division and calculate decimal fraction equivalents (for example, 0.375) for a simple fraction ($\frac{3}{8}$).
- Recall and use equivalences between simple fractions, decimals and percentages, including in different contexts.
- Interpret and construct pie charts and use these to solve problems.

 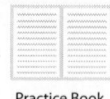 

Homework 73 and 74   Practice Book pp 136–41   Fraction Wall

Representations and resources

Pendulum, individual whiteboards, tracing paper or plain paper, scissors, bags of coloured cubes.

Mathematical vocabulary

Division, multiplication, bar models, vinculum, denominator, numerator, equivalent

Warming up

Rehearse multiplication facts to 12 × 12. Begin by choosing a series of facts that children may not be fluent in recalling, such as the multiplication facts for eight. Swing the pendulum from side to side and, as it swings, children count in steps of eight to 96 and back. Next, call out, e.g. 9 × 8. They find the product and then write down all the other facts they know from this.

Background knowledge

It is important to begin work on fractions by emphasising whole/part relationships. You could do this by using pictures as suggested in Unit 1 – Whole and part numbers. It is also important to use the correct vocabulary: vinculum, denominator and numerator.

Let's learn: Modelling and teaching

Equivalent fractions

- Discuss, with children, the conversation between Eva and Ali. Ask: *Why does Eva think the two fractions are equivalent? What is wrong with her thinking?* Discuss Ali's comment. Ask: *Is he correct?*

- Ask children to explain the bar models in the Textbook. Use them to check that $\frac{2}{5}$ of 40p is 16p. Ask children to tell you what different fifths of 40p would be and to explain how they know, using the words divide, multiply, denominator and numerator. Repeat this for different tenths of 20p.

- Next, you could use the bar models to check that $\frac{2}{5}$ is equivalent to $\frac{4}{10}$. Establish that we can make $\frac{4}{10}$ by multiplying the numerator and denominator of $\frac{2}{5}$ by the same number, (2). Ask children to use this method to find fractions equivalent to fifths (tenths, fifteenths and twentieths). Repeat for fractions equivalent to tenths (twentieths, thirtieths). Expect children to explain how they have found the equivalent fractions.

Types of fractions

- Ask children to convert the fractions in the bar models in their Textbooks to decimals and percentages and explain how they do this.

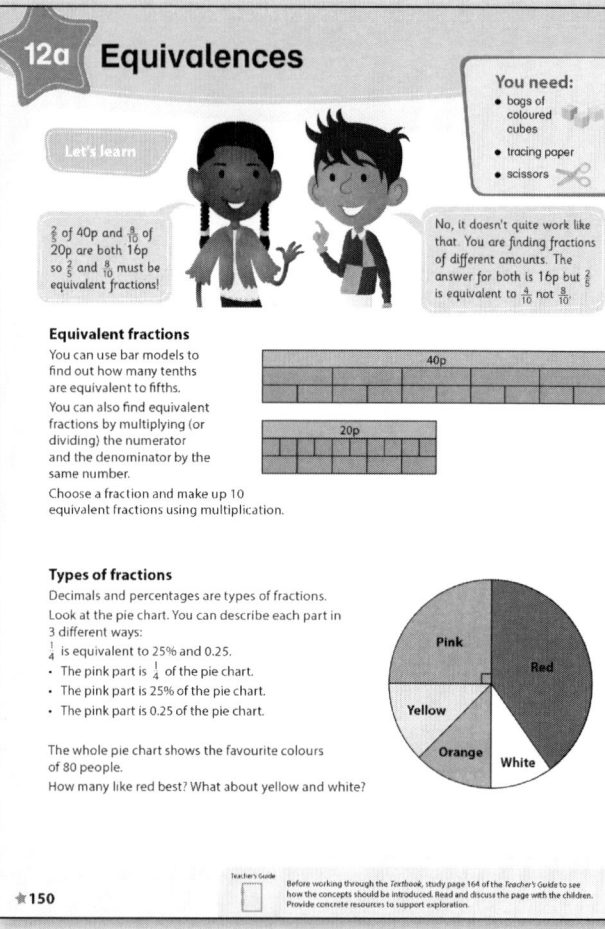

- Children should explain to each other the information shown in the pie chart. Ask them to estimate the percentages represented by each part. Ask them to trace the pie chart, then cut it up and compare the parts. The yellow and orange parts are equal, and together equivalent to the pink part, making each $12\frac{1}{2}$%. The white part fits into the red part four times, so the white part is 10% and the red 40%. Ask children to write the percentages as fractions, in their simplest form, and decimals.

- Tell children that the pie chart shows people's favourite colours. Ask children to work out possibilities for the number of people that could have been surveyed (multiples of 40).

Let's practise: Digging deeper

Step 1

Check children are confident finding multiples before they begin the task, giving them practice if necessary. Parts d and f can be simplified, so children also need to be secure in finding factors. Model the task by writing the fractions $\frac{1}{5}$ and $\frac{12}{18}$ on the whiteboard. Discuss how to find fractions equivalent to $\frac{1}{5}$ (multiplying) first, and then fractions equivalent to $\frac{12}{18}$ (multiplying and dividing). Reinforce the equivalence by sketching a bar model. Remind them that whatever they do to the denominator, they must do to the numerator. Children then complete the task, finding six equivalent fractions for each listed. Allow children to draw models to support them as required.

Step 2

Children convert decimals to fractions and percentages. Prompt them to consider simplifying any fractions that can be simplified.

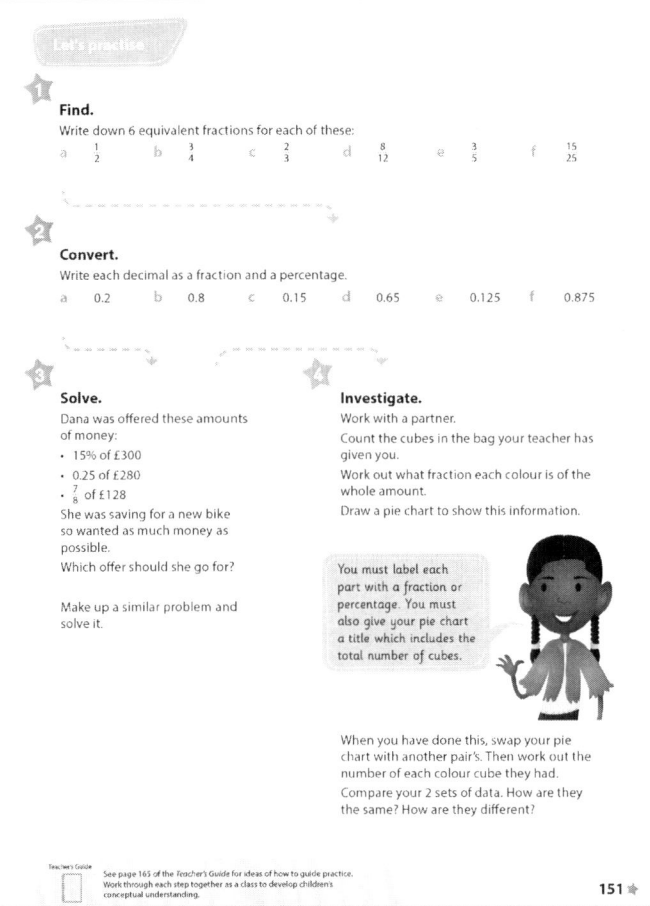

You might wish to go over a few examples with some children before they work independently.

Step 3

Before children do the task, identify any children who need extra input and ask them to practise finding percentages of amounts of money by finding 10% and doubling, halving and so on to make the percentage they need; then ask them to find the decimal and fraction equivalent to the percentages they have made. They can then tackle the task in the Textbook, finding the amounts Dana has been offered and identifying the best offer. You could challenge children to make up their own similar problems to solve.

Step 4

This task asks children to carry out an investigation and display their results in a pie chart. For this to be successful you will need to provide bags of specific numbers of coloured cubes for each pair. Part of the task is to work out another pair's colours and compare the results, so not all bags can be the same. Here are two examples of the bags you could provide:
40 cubes: 5 red, 15 blue, 10 green, 10 black
30 cubes: 10 red, 5 blue, 15 green

The first part of the task asks children to work out the fraction of the whole amount each colour is. Encourage children to write these in the correct sections of their pie chart using either fractions or percentages.

They then swap pie charts with another pair, work out their numbers and then compare both sets of data. Ask what is the same and what is different about their data sets.

Ensuring progress
Supporting understanding

Initially focus on finding equivalent fractions until children have mastered this. Give them unit fractions and ask them to double the numerator and denominator to make other equivalent fractions. Once they are confident, move on to finding decimal and percentage equivalences.

Broadening understanding

Give children opportunities to pick a subject, e.g. favourite sports. They then survey the class to find their favourite sports and create a pie chart to show the information. They could turn the figures collected into fractions so that they can find the parts. Once they have them, they write these as percentages.

Follow-up ideas

- Children print out pie charts from the Internet and make a poster for display, describing what each one shows.

- Children think of a topic and make up their own pie chart, deciding on the percentages for each part. They then make up questions about the pie chart to ask their partner.

- Children could make a snap game, by writing the equivalent fractions that they have looked at in this spread on cards.

- Ask children to make a mind map showing what they have learned about equivalent fractions, decimals and percentages.

 Concept mastered

Children explain and demonstrate how to find fraction equivalents and equivalences between fractions, decimals and percentages.

Answers

Step 1

Answers will vary. Ensure all the fractions are equivalent.

Step 2

a $\frac{1}{5}$, 20%   d $\frac{13}{20}$, 65%

b $\frac{4}{5}$, 80%   e $\frac{1}{8}$, 12½%

c $\frac{3}{20}$, 15%   f $\frac{7}{8}$, 87½%

Step 3

Answers will vary.

Step 4

Dana should opt for $\frac{7}{8}$ of £128

12b Formulae and sequences

- **Use simple formulae.**
- **Generate and describe linear number sequences.**

Homework 75 and 76

Practice Book pp 142–6

100 Squares

Mathematical vocabulary

Algebra, formula, linear number sequences, common difference, nth term, substitute

Representations and resources

Counters, centimetre-squared paper, rulers, individual whiteboards.

Warming up

Write a measure on the whiteboard, e.g. 250 km. Children find as many fractions as they can of this amount and write them on their whiteboards. Give them a minute to make a start and then take feedback, writing some suggestions on the whiteboard. Give them another two minutes to continue. They then share their ideas with a small group of children. The group decides which five are the most interesting and feed this back to you to add to the list you started to create.

Background knowledge

Using formulae to find area and perimeter are real-life applications of algebra. The important formulae for this concept spread are: $A = l \times w$ (for rectangles and parallelograms) and $A = \frac{1}{2}(b \times h)$ (for triangles).

In this concept children will continue to explore linear sequences. A linear number sequence is a pattern that increases and decreases by the same amount. This amount is known as the common difference.

Let's learn: Modelling and teaching

Formulae

- Discuss the cartoon in the Textbook. Do children agree with Eva? Give them centimetre-squared paper and rulers and ask them to draw the rectangles that Eva describes. Then ask them to find any other whole centimetre examples that she did not give. Repeat for a rectangle with an area of 36 cm²; encourage children to be systematic in their working.

- In a similar way, investigate whether all shapes with the same perimeter have the same area. Establish that this is not the case.

- Review the formulae for the area of rectangles, triangles and parallelograms (met in Unit 7 – Let's explore fractions and algebra!). Highlight the fact that the height of a triangle is the vertical height measured from the base to the apex; the height of a parallelogram is the vertical height. Ask children to find the areas of the shapes shown in the Textbook.

Linear number sequences

- Ask children to tell you what they remember about linear number sequences from Unit 10 – Focus on algebra. Look at the 100 square in the Textbook and ask how we can find

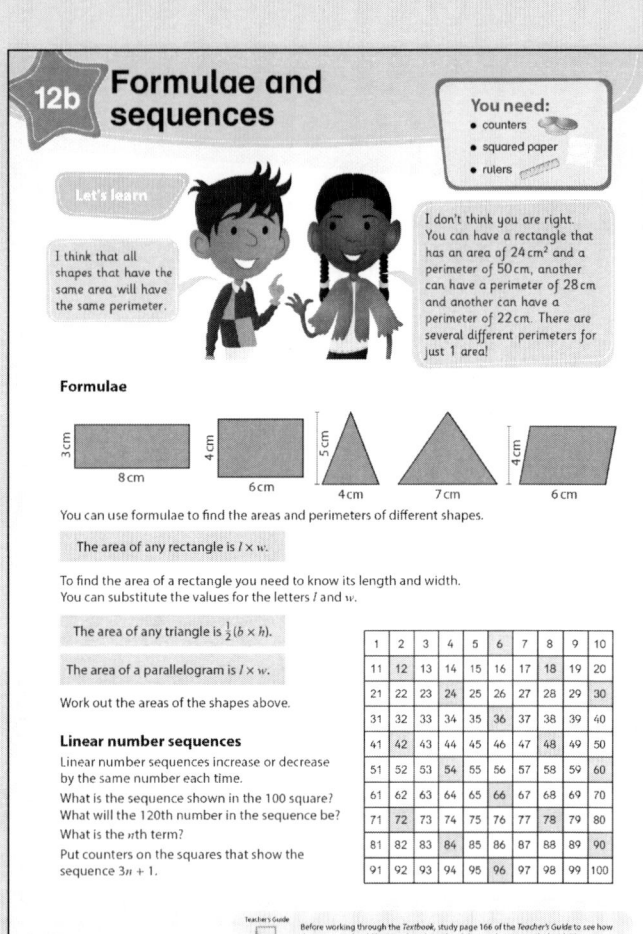

the 120th number in the sequence. Agree it is 120 × 6, which is 720. Review the meaning of 'nth term', agreeing that it represents any term they want to find. Ask children to find the formula for the nth term of the sequence shown ($6n$) and then ask them to find various different terms in the sequence.

- Ask children to put counters on squares in the 100 square to cover the numbers that show the sequence: $3n + 1$. Can they describe the sequence? Establish that each term is a multiple of 3 with 1 added on: 4, 7, 10, 13, and so on.

- Give them other sequences, e.g. $4n – 2$. They could use the 100 square and counters or simply write the sequence. When they are confident, let them make up their own sequences.

166 Rising Stars Mathematics

Let's practise: Digging deeper

Step 1

Children should have had a lot of practice of working out the perimeters and areas of rectangles using the appropriate formulae. If they have not, provide more opportunities before asking them to carry out this task. Expect them to carry out the task independently. Some may benefit from sketching the rectangles on squared paper first.

Step 2

The task asks children to write the first ten numbers in each of the number sequences. Before they begin, ensure children are fully aware what is meant by this. You may need to reinforce what n represents in the formulae. Work through some similar examples first with those children who need extra support.

Step 3

Some children will be able simply to draw the shapes, measure them and find their areas and perimeters. For others, this is an opportunity to explore again the relationship between rectangles and triangles, and rectangles and parallelograms. Encourage these children to draw rectangles around their triangles and establish that the triangle is half of the rectangle; similarly, they should be able to see that a parallelogram can be made into a rectangle. They can then go on to tackle the task. Check all children understand how to find the (vertical) height of the shapes they have drawn. Once they have found the areas, they need to find all the shapes' perimeters by measuring each side accurately.

Step 4

Children need to work out all the possible rectangular enclosures that Farmer Giles can make from 24 m of fencing. This involves working out widths and lengths of the given perimeter. They then need to find the areas of these to see which needs the least grass. Encourage them to draw the possible enclosures on centimetre-squared paper where 1 cm represents 1 m. They should work systematically to find that the enclosure that requires least grass is the narrowest. Ask children to explain their findings to you. You could discuss whether this is a practical shape for an enclosure.

Ensuring progress

Supporting understanding

Initially focus on the concept of using formulae to find areas and perimeters of rectangles. When they have mastered this, children can use what they know to find areas of triangles and parallelograms.

Broadening understanding

If children are confident at finding areas of rectangles, triangles and parallelograms, give them the opportunity to explore how to find the areas of other quadrilaterals such as trapeziums, rhombi and kites.

 Concept mastered

Children can explain and demonstrate how to find areas of shapes using formulae and the nth term in a linear number sequence.

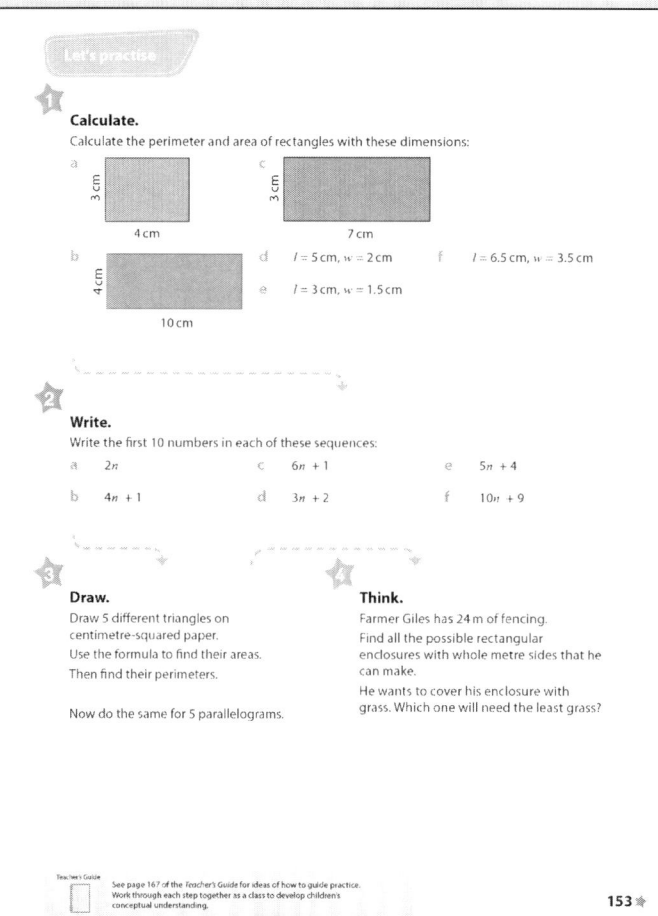

Follow-up ideas

- Children could make information posters, which show their knowledge of using formulae to find areas of rectangles (including squares), triangles and parallelograms.

- Children could make up other linear number sequences, shading appropriate squares on a 100 square, and then ask a partner to identify the pattern and write the formula for the nth term.

- Ask children to make up other number sequences that are not linear, e.g. 2, 5, 11, 23 and to find a rule for their sequence, e.g. $2n + 1$. They work out what is the same and what is different between this and a linear number sequence.

Answers

Step 1

a $a = 12\,cm^2, p = 14\,cm$

b $a = 40\,cm^2, p = 28\,cm$

c $a = 21\,cm^2, p = 20\,cm$

d $a = 10\,cm^2, p = 14\,cm$

e $a = 4.5\,cm^2, p = 9\,cm$

f $a = 22.75\,cm^2, p = 20\,cm$

Step 2

a 2, 4, 6, 8, 10, 12, 14, 16, 18, 20

b 5, 9, 13, 17, 21, 25, 29, 33, 37, 41

c 7, 13, 19, 25, 31, 37, 43, 49, 55, 61

d 5, 8, 11, 14, 17, 20, 23, 26, 29, 32

e 9, 14, 19, 24, 29, 34, 39, 44, 49, 54

f 19, 29, 39, 49, 59, 69, 79, 89, 99, 109

Step 3

Answers will vary.

Step 4

Possible enclosures:
1 m × 11 m (11 m²), (least area)
2 m × 10 m (20 m²),
3 m × 9 m (27 m²),
4 m × 8 m (32 m²),
5 m × 7 m (35 m²),
6 m × 6 m (36 m²).

- **Express missing number problems algebraically.**
- **Find pairs of numbers that satisfy an equation with two unknowns.**

 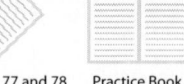

Homework 77 and 78   Practice Book pp 147–9

Mathematical vocabulary

Algebra, inverse operations, bar models, variables, unknown

Representations and resources

Individual whiteboards, number rods, strips of paper, scissors, counters.

Warming up

Write a measure on the whiteboard, e.g. 125 kg. Children find as many percentages as they can of this amount and write them on their whiteboards. Encourage them to find 10% first and then double, halve, add, multiply/divide by ten and so on to generate new facts. Give them three minutes to do this. They then share their ideas with a small group of children. The group decides which five are the most interesting facts. Make a list on the whiteboard.

Background knowledge

This concept spread builds on work on algebra done in Units 7 – Let's explore fractions and algebra! and 10 – Focus on algebra, reinforcing and developing children's understanding of how to find unknowns in equations. They should by now be able to tackle all the ideas presented with some confidence. The bar model is an incredibly helpful visual representation, although be aware that some children may be comfortable with the balancing method introduced in Unit 7.

Let's learn: Modelling and teaching

Two unknowns

- Look at the first bar model in the Textbook. Ask children to write addition and subtraction statements using m, n and p. Those who would benefit from a more concrete approach could use number rods to recreate the bar model.

- Ask children to find possible values for m and n, if $p = 12$. Encourage them to be creative and find at least six options. Repeat in a measures context, e.g. if $m = 12.25$ km, what could n and p be?

- Give children two strips of paper. Ask them to cut one strip into six pieces and make a bar model to show $6 \times 4 = 24$. Repeat with other numerical examples, then move on to statements with two unknowns, such as $n \times m = 86$, $150 \times n = m$. Take feedback to find out if their possibilities work.

- Link to finding areas of triangles. Write the formula on the whiteboard: $A = \frac{1}{2}(b \times h)$. Give a value for one of the letters and ask children to work out what the other two could be. They should use paper strips or sketch a bar model to help them.

Missing number problems

- Look at the cartoon in the Textbook. Work through how to find n using the balancing method. Then look at the

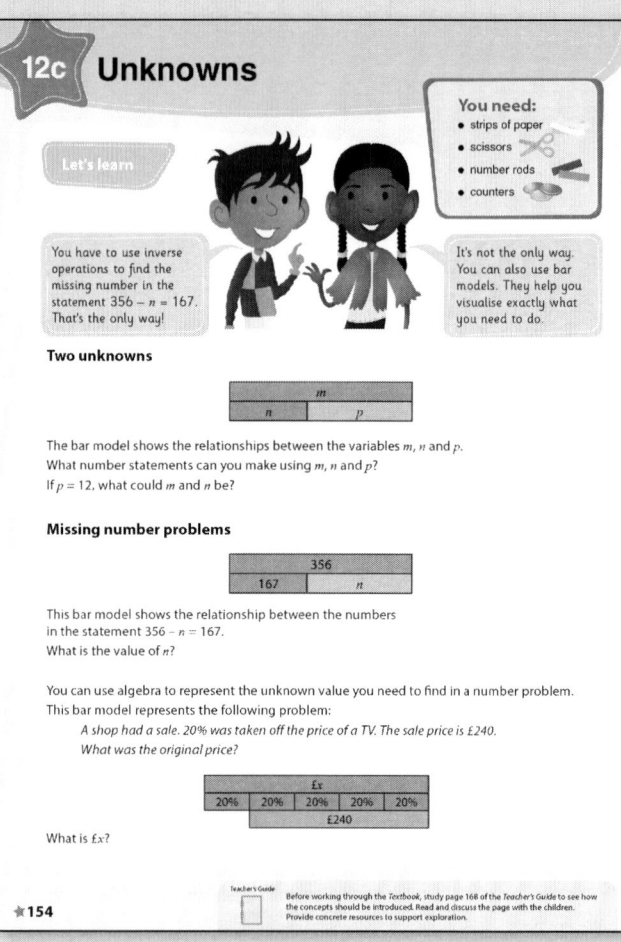

second bar model in the Textbook and discuss ways to find n from that. Which method do children prefer?

- Give children a variety of addition and subtraction calculations to solve, which all involve an unknown number. See Step 1 in Let's practise for similar ideas. Explain that, in a number problem, we can use algebra to represent the unknown value we need to find.

- Read the problem and discuss the bar model in the Textbook. Here £x represents the original price. Solve the problem together, then set similar word problems for children to work on. See Step 2 in Let's practise for similar ideas. Include some involving fractions and ratio, in preparation for Let's practise Step 2.

Let's practise: Digging deeper

Step 1

Before children begin the task, give them the opportunity to answer similar calculations (e.g. $78 - m = 34$) using a bar model. If any children struggle, keep giving them practice until they are confident. For each number statement, they should draw the bar model and label it with the appropriate numbers and letters before using it to find the value of the missing number. Encourage them to find differences by counting on as it can be simpler than subtraction.

Step 2

Building on Step 1, children now must work with number statements involving decimals. They must find the missing numbers in the statements. This is an open-ended task in as much as the two possible missing numbers could vary. Ask children what is the same and what is different about the

number statements, compared with those in Step 1. Then, work through examples together to ensure children are clear about what to do, e.g. $m + n = 12.4$. Ask children to share a variety of possible examples of what m and n could be.

Step 3

This task asks children to solve some more missing number statements, given in the form of word problems. Encourage them to extract the numerical information they need from the question and use it to write the number statement or draw and label the bar model. Some children may need you to work with them on similar examples first, e.g. Cory had eight comics. Adam had five times as many. How many more comics did Adam have? Model how to draw the bars and find the answer.

Adam has $4 \times 8 = 32$ more comics than Cory.

Step 4

Children work through the problem. They could draw a bar model. Some might benefit from using counters, with one counter to represent Abi's sweets and seven to represent Josie's. If Josie gives Abi some sweets and they then have an equal amount, three of Josie's counters need to be placed beside Abi's. The number of sweets is not known so children need to work out six possibilities. Encourage them to share their possibilities with their partner's. Ask: *How many different ones did you find between you? Can you give an easy answer and a hard answer?* Observe their responses carefully. They then make up another similar problem and solve it.

Ensuring progress

Supporting understanding

Initially focus on the concept of finding one missing number. Children who need support must make use of the bar model as this will help develop their conceptual understanding. Once they have mastered this they move on to problems with two unknowns.

Broadening understanding

Children who are confident at finding one and two unknowns may wish to use the balancing method for some questions, but it is worth encouraging them to use the bar model as well because this will help deepen their understanding. They should be given the opportunity to make up problems, similar to those in this spread, for a partner to solve.

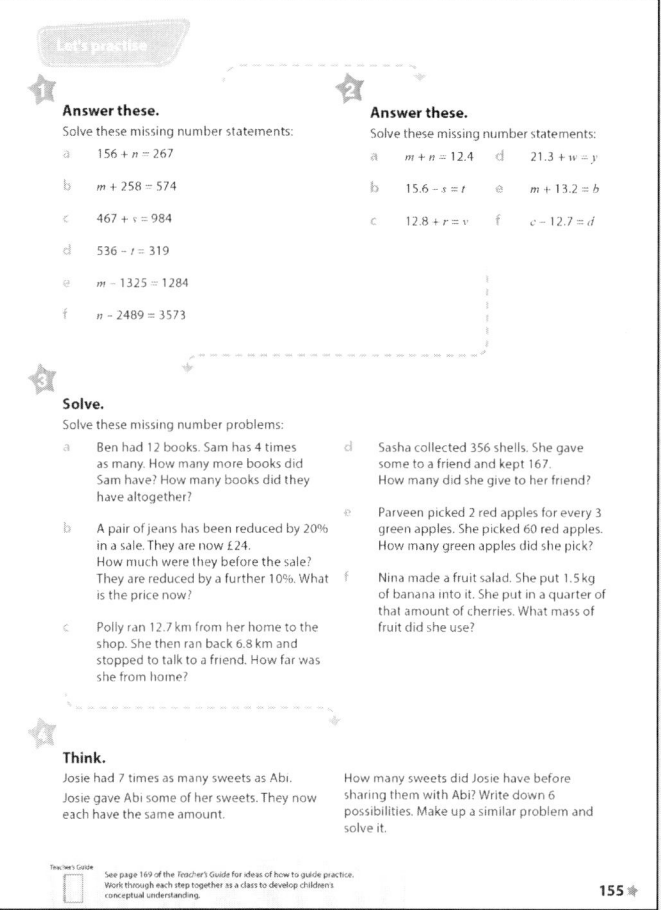

Follow-up ideas

- Children could make information posters to show how to use the bar model to solve missing number addition and subtraction statements.

- Children could make up problems that involve fractions and percentages. They write these on large pieces of paper and then draw diagrams to show how these can be answered using a bar model.

- Children take two different-size strips of paper and measure each of the lengths. They label each with a different letter and give them to a partner with the actual total length of both. Their partner has to estimate what each length must be and write an addition statement with the lengths substituted for the letters. They then measure the strips to see if they are correct.

Concept mastered

Children can explain and demonstrate how to find and solve problems that involve one and two unknowns.

Answers

Step 1

a	$n = 111$	**d**	$t = 217$
b	$m = 316$	**e**	$m = 2609$
c	$s = 517$	**f**	$n = 6062$

Step 2

Answers will vary.

Step 3

a	36, 60	**d**	189
b	£30, £21.60	**e**	90
c	5.9 km	**f**	1.1.875 kg

Step 4

Answers will vary but the number of sweets Josie gives Abi will always be three times Abi's sweets..

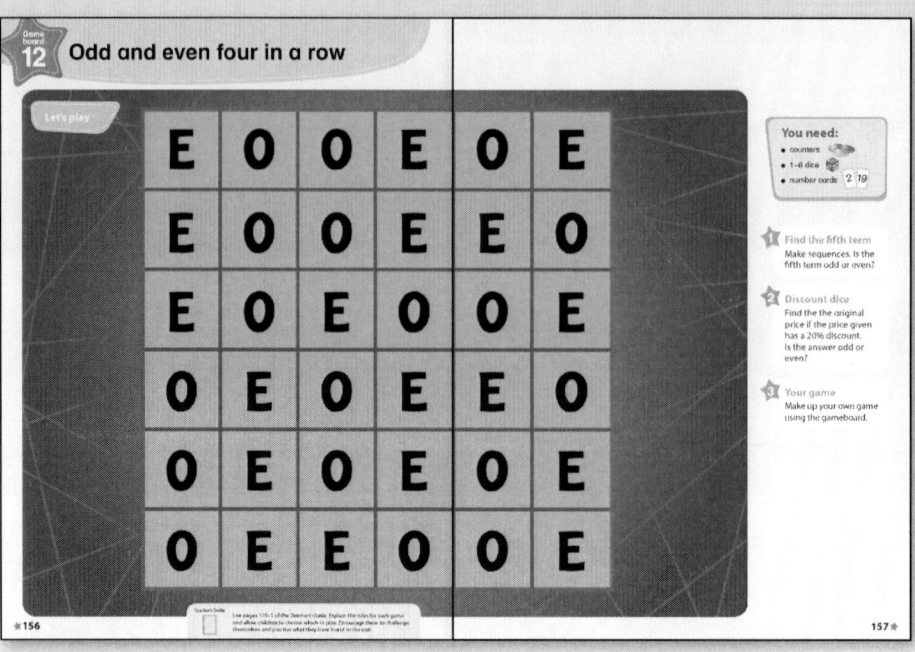

Game 1: Find the fifth term

This game gives children practice in generating linear number sequences, given the formula for the nth term.

Maths focus

- Generate and describe linear number sequences

Resources

36 counters in two different colours (18 of each colour per player), two sets of 1–9 digit cards.

How to play

This game should be played in pairs. Each pair needs 36 counters in two colours (18 of each colour for each player) and two sets of 1–9 digit cards, shuffled and placed face down on the table. Players take it in turns to pick a digit card from each set. They use the card to write down the formula for the nth term of a linear sequence: one card represents the common difference; the other card represents what they add, e.g. if they pick 9 and 4, they could write down nth term = $9n + 4$ or nth term = $4n + 9$. They then work out the fifth term of the sequence. If is even, they place a counter on an E on the gameboard; if it is odd, they place a counter on an O. The winner is the first player to get four counters in a row. This can be horizontal, vertical or diagonal. Encourage them to be strategic and to aim to block their partner as well as to get their own row of four.

Making it easier

Children use one set of digit cards and make their sequence with the number picked as the common difference.

Making it harder

Play as above, but this time one card represents the common difference and the other is subtracted, e.g. if they pick 1 and 5, the formula for the nth term would be $n - 5$ or $5n - 1$, and the sequence would start with −4 or 4 respectively.

Game 2: Discount dice

Children practise finding the original price after a percentage discount, using the bar model to solve the missing number problem.

Maths focus

- Solve missing number problems

Resources

36 counters in two different colours (18 of each colour per player), 1–6 dice (1), number cards 10–99.

How to play

This game should be played in pairs. Each pair needs 36 counters in two colours (18 of each colour for each player) and a set of number cards 10–99, shuffled and placed face down on the table. Players take it in turns to throw the dice. If they throw a 1, 2 or 3 they miss a turn. If they throw a 4, 5 or 6 they pick a number card. This represents the price of something in a sale. The discount is 20%. They must find the original price; encourage them to use a bar model as in 12c– Unknowns. Their partner checks their answer. If they are correct they round their answer to the nearest pound. If the answer is even, they place a counter on an E on the gameboard; if it is odd, they place a counter on an O. The aim is to get four counters in a row.

Making it easier

Children could use even number 2-digit cards to 50.

Making it harder

You could vary the percentage discount, e.g. 25% or 40%.

Your game

Children should invent their own game designing rules that use the concepts covered in the unit.

Challenge children the make the game easier or harder.

Unit 2 Odd and even four in a row PCM 12

Choose a game to play.

Game 1: Find the fifth term

You need:

- 36 counters in 2 different colours (18 of each colour)
- 2 sets of 1–9 digit cards

How to play

- Shuffle each set of digit cards and place them face down on the table in 2 piles.
- Take turns to pick a card from each set.
  Use the cards to write the formula for the nth term of a linear sequence.
  - one card tells you the common difference; the other card tells you what to add.
    e.g. if you pick 9 and 4 you could write: $9n + 4$ or $4n + 9$
- Find the fifth term of the sequence.
  If it is odd, place one of your counters on an O on the gameboard.
  If it is even, place one of your counters on an E on the gameboard.
- The winner is the first player to get four counters in a row, horizontally, vertically or diagonally.

Game 2: Discount dice

You need:

- 36 counters in 2 different colours (18 of each colour)
- 1–6 dice
- number cards 10–99

How to play

- Shuffle the number cards and place them face down on the table.
- Take turns to throw the dice.
- If you throw a 1, 2 or 3, miss a turn. If you throw a 4, 5 or 6, pick a number card.
  The number is the price of something in a sale.
  The discount is 20%. Find the original price.
- Round the number to the nearest pound. If the amount is odd your counter is placed on O, if even it is placed on E.
- The winner is the first player to get four counters in a row.

Game 3: Your game

- Make up your own game using the gameboard.
- What are the rules for your game? Explain them to someone.

Please help your child by reading the instructions and playing the game together.

Assessment task 1

Running the task

This task has four parts to it; all parts assess children's knowledge and understanding of equivalences between fractions and also between fractions, decimals and percentages. Before carrying out this assessment task, work through a few examples with children who may need extra support. Write a few fractions and discuss how to find some other fractions that are equivalent to those you have written. Encourage children to consider multiplying each part of the fraction by the same multiplier. Then discuss the idea of finding decimal and percentage equivalents. Suggest that to turn these into decimals they need to make the fraction into tenths or hundredths. Once they have done this, finding the percentage equivalent is straightforward because percentages are fractions that have a denominator of 100. Once you have done this, ask children to complete the first two parts of the task.

The third part of the task asks children to make lists of their own decimals that haven't been used as yet and convert them to fractions and percentages. The fourth part asks them to do the same for eight percentages. You may need to go through a few examples with children who need support. Observe the complexity of the decimals and percentages that children choose.

For those children who can confidently carry out the task and explain how to convert fractions to decimals and percentages, ask them to apply this knowledge and find different fractions, decimals and percentages of measures, e.g. lengths, masses and volumes.

Evidencing mastery

If children are able to confidently find equivalent fractions and also convert to decimals and percentages they are evidencing mastery. Make a note of any children who have not yet mastered this area and work with them in an intervention group.

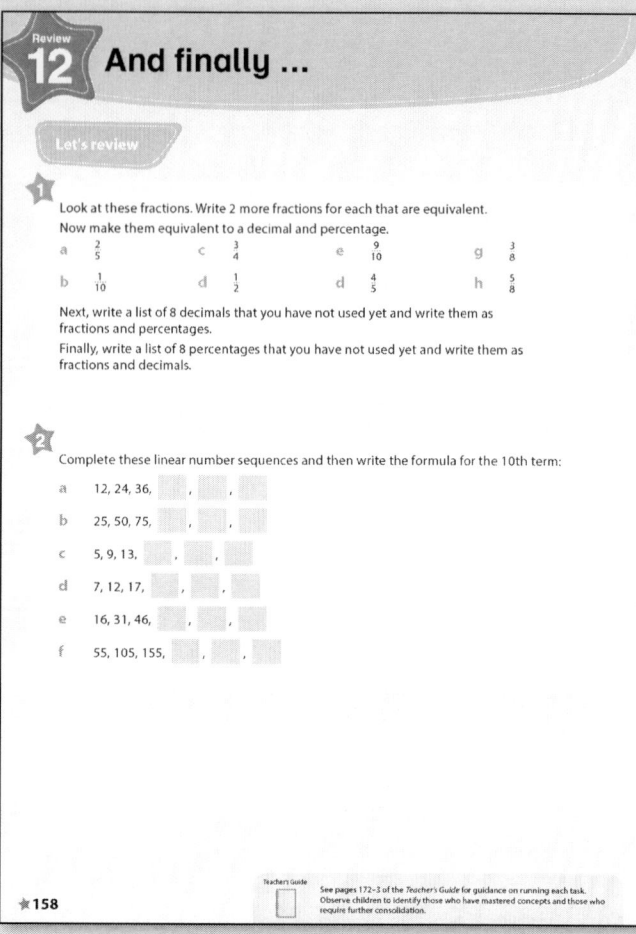

Assessment task 2

Running the task

Before beginning the task recap what is meant by a linear number sequence and the common difference. Work through some simple examples, e.g. 10, 20, 30 ....
Ask children to use a 100 square and counters to continue the pattern. They should then identify the common difference and write the algebraic expression for the nth term. Then give children an example to work through without the 100 square. Repeat this for sequences that expect children to look for the multiple and what they do to it each time, e.g. 3, 5, 7.
Each number in the sequence is a multiple of two with one added. They then identify the algebraic expression for the nth term, $2n + 1$.

Children should work on this task independently. Some children may need to focus on the simple linear sequences as described above, so give them more of these to work through, making them more challenging, e.g. 13, 26, 39 and 75, 150, 225. For those children who can answer these easily, ask them to make up their own more complicated linear number sequences and record the algebraic expression for the nth term.

Evidencing mastery

If children can confidently complete simple linear sequences, and describe and write algebraic expressions for the 10th term they are evidencing mastery.

 ③ Draw each problem using the bar model, then write an algebraic statement for each and solve them:

a   Sam had some marbles. He gave 26 to his friend and was left with 48. How many marbles did he start off with?

b   Adam had 3 times as many football stickers as Tom. Tom had 45. How many did Adam have?

c   Rosie baked 75 muffins. She gave 36 to her friend. How many did she have left?

d   Samira ate 3 times as many cherries as Sally. Samira ate 27 cherries. How many cherries did Sally eat?

What could the values of these letters be? Make up 5 possibilities for each question.

e $n + m = 145$ h $t - w = 2345$

f $1568 - s = t$ i $a + 3568 = b$

g $34510 + k = h$ j $d - z = 32567$

Did you know?

The word 'algebra' came from the Arabic word *al-jabr*.

Algebra was first used in ancient Egypt and Babylon. The Persian mathematician Muhammad ibn Musa Al-Khwarizmi is credited as one of the forefathers of algebra. This Russian stamp commemorates 1200 years since his birth.

159

Concepts mastered

✓ Children explain and demonstrate how to find fraction equivalents and equivalences between fractions, decimals and percentages.

✓ Children can explain and demonstrate how to find areas of shapes using formulae and the nth term in a linear number sequence.

✓ Children can explain and demonstrate how to find and solve problems that involve one and two unknowns.

Assessment task 3

Running the task

This task is twofold. The first part asks children to solve missing number problems in real-life contexts. Children need to draw the bar model to show each problem and then identify the algebraic statement to go with it. They finally need to solve the problem. Work through a few examples together before children work independently on this task, e.g. Luke had 56 stamps, Marie had three times as many. How many stamps did Marie have? Ask children to draw the bar model:

Luke	56		
Maire	56	56	56

Marie had $3 \times 56 = 168$

For the second part of this task children need to work out five possibilities for the letters in each calculation. Encourage them to draw the bar model each time so that they can visualise what each part will look like. Before they tackle the task, rehearse it by writing some examples on the whiteboard and ask children to work through them. This is an open-ended task with no specific answers because there are many possibilities. Ensure that the answers children give work and ask questions such as *Which of your answers is hard and which is easy? Why?*

Evidencing mastery

If children can confidently and correctly explain and demonstrate different possibilities for the letters they are evidencing mastery.

Did you know?

The word algebra came from the Arabic word *al-jabr*, which means 'reunion of broken parts' and was used by Persian mathematician Muhammad ibn Musa Al-Khwarizmi to describe one of the methods he used to solve quadratic equations. Al-Khwarizmi is credited as one of the forefathers of algebra; in Renaissance Europe, he was thought to be its original inventor, but it has since been discovered that his work was based on older Greek or Indian sources.

Algebra did not always appear as it does today. At first, problems and their solutions were written in prose; this was known as 'rhetorical algebra'. In the 3rd century, the Hellenistic mathematician Diophantus was the first to use some symbols and abbreviations in his treatise *Arithmetica*; this marked the invention of 'syncopated algebra'. The third stage, 'symbolic algebra', in which full symbolism is used was largely developed towards the end of the 16th century by mathematicians such as François Viète. He and his successors promoted the formalisation of algebra, creating the symbols and discovering the rules for manipulating symbols that we use today.

Mathematical focus

★ **Number: addition, subtraction, multiplication and division, fractions (including decimals and percentages)**

★ **Measure: distance, length, time, mass, capacity, volume**

★ **Ratio and proportion**

Prior learning

Children should already be able to:

- divide numbers up to four digits by a single-digit number using the formal written method of short division

- write remainders as simple decimals or fractions according to the context

- solve problems involving the four operations

- use common factors to simplify fractions.

Key new learning

- Divide numbers up to four digits by a 2-digit number using the formal written method of long division.

- Interpret remainders as whole number remainders, fractions or by rounding, as appropriate for the context.

- Solve problems involving addition, subtraction, multiplication and division.

- Solve multi-step problems involving multiplication or division.

- Multiply simple pairs of proper fractions, writing the answer in its simplest form.

- Divide proper fractions by whole numbers.

★ 160

Making connections

- The most important link to make in this unit is between the real-world problem and the mathematics that children are using to solve the problem. Dealing with the remainder following the division of two numbers is an example of the interplay between the two.

- Solving word problems relates to many other curriculum areas, as well as the real world. One example is dealing with the remainder in problems involving currency conversion.

- One of the applications of long division is calculating the mean of a set of numbers. These will often be measures and so will involve decimals.

- Multiplying fractions and dividing them by whole numbers can be used when working with pie charts. Reasoning about percentages using fractions is another connection.

 Talk about

The vocabulary of numerator and denominator is fundamental in talking about fractions. Ask children to answer the question: *What does denominator mean? What does numerator mean?* They should refer to the number of equal parts whenever the word denominator is used. Numerator is the number of the equal parts that we are using.

Encourage rich mathematical talk around real-life problems and use this opportunity to reinforce precise use of mathematical vocabulary.

Engaging and exploring

Ask children to look at each picture and the comments or questions that go with it and to discuss with a partner what each might be about.

Look at the first photo together. There are few situations where multiplication of fractions is genuinely required. One example is using a recipe which has cups as the measure.

Tell children that a recipe needs 2 cups flour, 4 tablespoons sugar, 6 tablespoons butter, $1\frac{1}{2}$ cups milk and 2 eggs. You could try measuring it out using cups. Ask children to think about the problems that they might encounter if they wanted to convert the recipe so that it is suitable for a different number of servings. They might suggest making an estimate.

The estimate needs to be based on as accurate a figure as possible as errors soon build up and it can affect the outcome. You could ask children how confident they would feel about converting a recipe for half the number of people. Ask: *What about $\frac{1}{3}$ of the number of people?*

If you have ever organised a trip which requires coaches or minibuses the situation shown in the second photo will be very familiar to you. Ask children whether they have been on trips by coach *Were there many spare seats? How do they think the organiser worked out the number of coaches needed? What calculation might they have done?* What other situations can they think of like this? Packing boxes is one example.

For the calendar photo, you could explain that working out what day of the week an event will take place on can be very helpful, i.e. whether it is on a weekday or at the weekend. Discuss with children what special events are coming up soon. *What day of the week is it on? Do you know the date?* Ask children to identify the dates on a calendar. Working out the total number of days until a specific event involves recalling calendar facts, such as how many days each month has, and adding to find the total. All you need to do is work out the remainder when that total is divided by seven and that tells you how many days to count on. That is much easier than counting through to the date in question.

For the vegetable stand photo, ask children to imagine someone coming back from the shop having bought several items. They might remember the unit cost of several, but not all, of them. Pose a problem such as, I spent £4.50 on 2 kg of onions and 4 kg of carrots. The carrots were 83p per kg. How much were the onions? Discuss strategies to tackle the problem and model children's suggestions on the board or using coins.

School trips are an important part of the curriculum. Prices vary according to the size of the coach and the distance, and also whether the driver can do another trip while waiting for the return journey. Ask children about school trips they have been on and what they cost. Ask them to assume that 26 children are going on the trip and that the cost of the coach is £375. *How can you work out the cost per child?* Encourage children to think about whether to round the answer up or down or give it as a decimal. Develop the discussion by asking questions such as: *What if someone was absent on the day? Should they pay anyway? What if they said they couldn't go in advance? What should happen to manage that?*

I would love a class trip to the seaside! I wonder how much it would cost us each if we hired a coach?

If I bought 2 kg of carrots and 3 swedes for £3.01, how much would that make the swedes each?

Carrots 83p per kg

Teacher's Guide Look at the pictures with the children and discuss the questions. See pages 174–5 of the Teacher's Guide for key ideas to draw out.

161

Checking understanding

You will know children have mastered these concepts when they can divide 4-digit numbers by 2-digit numbers using long division and decide whether to round up or down when the quotient has a remainder, or write it as a decimal or fraction depending on the context. Children can recognise which operation to use when solving a word problem by the relationship between the amounts given in the problem and identify which operations to use when solving problems involving several steps.

They can multiply two simple fractions, giving the product in its simplest form. They can also divide a fraction by a whole number, giving the quotient in its simplest form.

Things to think about

- How will you help all children to relate mathematics to the real world when solving word problems? Some children do this quite naturally, while for others it is more of a challenge. How can you help them to make the connections? How will you organise groupings?

- How can you help children to draw bar models and other diagrams? What problem-solving strategies will you use? How might you use questioning to prompt them?

- How could you use role play to support children in understanding a situation before drawing their diagram or using other concrete materials to solve the problem?

13a Using long division

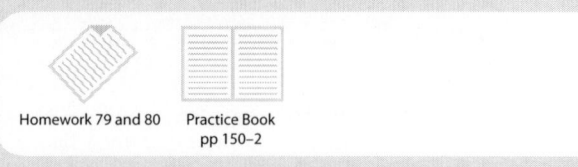

Homework 79 and 80   Practice Book pp 150–2

Representations and resources

Place-value counters, Base 10 apparatus, whiteboards and markers, clocks.

Mathematical vocabulary

Remainder, divisor, decimal, fraction, factor, multiple, quotient, dividend.

Warming up

Practise multiplication table facts in as many different ways as possible, e.g. *Is 45 a multiple of seven? What is 48 divided by six?* Focus on facts in the six, seven and eight multiplication tables.

Background knowledge

Children met short division in Year 5. Use the model of division as grouping to explain the algorithm for short division. Long division is exactly the same process as short division, it just shows more of the steps in the calculation. It can be modelled using place-value counters and Base 10 apparatus.

Dealing with remainders requires some flexibility. Some people will more readily use a fraction and others a decimal. Deciding whether to round will also generate some differences of opinion. The context is important. This is an excellent opportunity for discussing the relationship between the mathematics and the real world. The patterns revealed by remainders link with multiples, a remainder of one following division by eight is because the dividend is one more than a multiple of eight.

Let's learn: Modelling and teaching

Long division

- Explain that long division is just a longer way of setting out short division. Give children the question in the Textbook: 2921 ÷ 23.

- Set up the calculation with place-value counters and work through each step, e.g. for step 1 exchange 2 thousands for 20 hundreds to give 29 hundreds; share those into 23 groups, each with one hundred, leaving a remainder of 600. Continue for the remaining steps. Now write 2921 on the board twice as the starting point for the short and long methods of division. Work through the two methods in parallel, referring back to the place-value counters. Ask children at each step to say what happens next.

- Compare the each step with those shown in the Textbook.

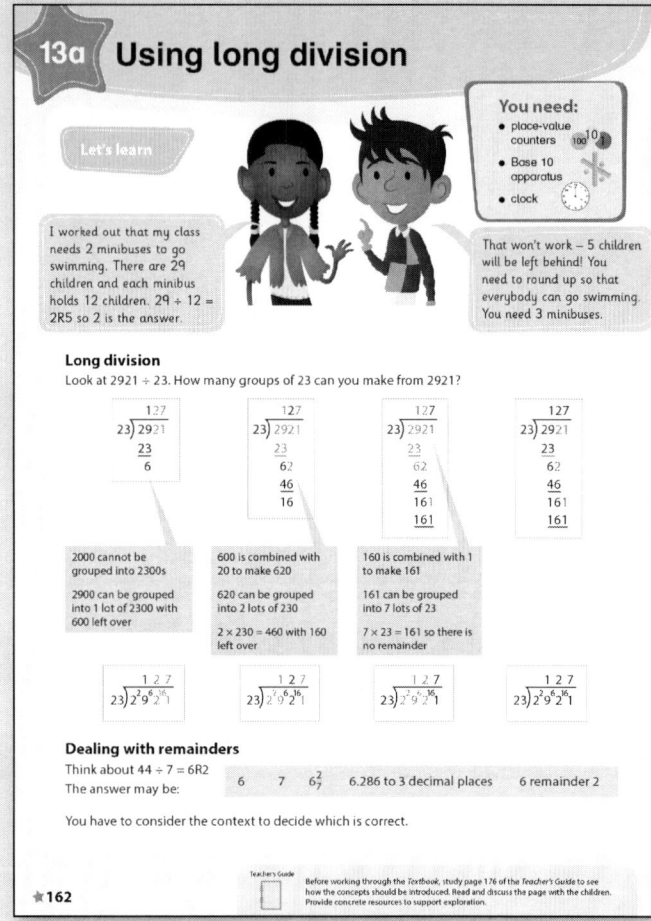

- Ask children to work through several calculations. Give them whiteboards and markers to do the short division method and use this to advise what happens next as you work through using long division with the whole class.

Dealing with remainders

- Explain that there is not always a single answer that may be correct. Sometimes the fraction and decimal versions are interchangeable, sometimes real-life issues will affect it, such as the accuracy required.

- Ask children to write some word problems for each answer in the Textbook. Discuss what other answers may be appropriate.

Let's practise: Digging deeper

Step 1

Children can start using long division but use whiteboards to do the short division version. The first three calculations work exactly, with no remainders and gradually using larger numbers. The next three use smaller numbers but have remainders. The fraction and decimal versions of the remainder become increasingly complex, with recurring decimals. Suggest children round to three decimal places once they reach the fourth digit after the decimal point.

Step 2

Parts d to l prompt children to delve deeper into their understanding of the ways to deal with remainders. Children identify errors and explain why they are incorrect. One way to support this is to ask: *What is the correct answer?* This gives a way into the question as children may be tempted to make the same mistake.

Step 3

Children will need to interpret the questions in context in order to decide how to tackle the remainders and whether to round their answers up or down. Encourage children to share and justify their answers. In part e looking at a clock face may support thinking.

Step 4

Encourage children to search systematically for examples, this will generate , e.g. 5, 9, 13 … linking with work on sequences. *What do you notice about these numbers?* is a useful prompt. Ask: *Why can't you have a remainder of 4?* They can go on to investigate remainders when dividing by other divisors.

Ensuring progress

Supporting understanding

Children can model the calculation using place-value counters and use short division as a way of recording it. Writing out the method for long division in parallel with this helps children become familiar with the sequence of steps as written out in the formal method of long division.

Broadening understanding

Children can write out an example of using long division and annotate each step to explain what is happening and why it is happening at that point in the algorithm.

✓ Concept mastered

Children can divide 4-digit numbers by 2-digit numbers using long division. They can decide to round up or down when the quotient has a remainder, or write it as a decimal or fraction depending on the context.

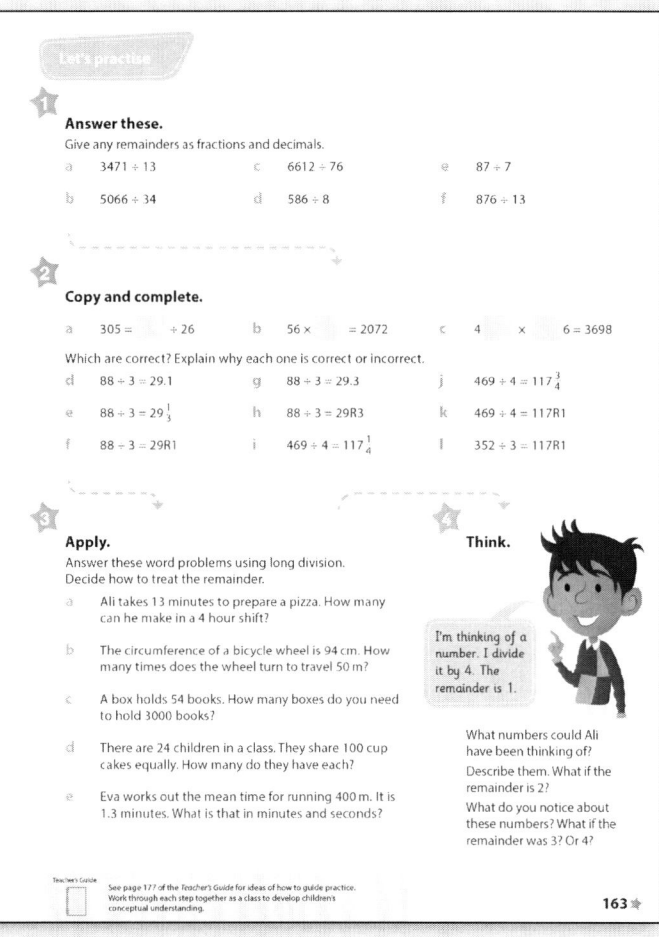

Answers

Step 1

a   267

b   149

c   87

d   73R2, 73.25, $73\frac{1}{4}$

e   12R3, 12.428571 or 12.429 to 3 decimal places, $12\frac{3}{7}$

f   67R5, 67.385 to 3 decimal places, $67\frac{5}{13}$

i   correct, $4 \times 117 = 468$ so the remainder of 1 is $\frac{1}{4}$ since 4 is the divisor

j   incorrect, $4 \times 117 = 468$ so the remainder is 1 and does not give $\frac{3}{4}$

k   correct, $4 \times 117 = 468$ so the remainder is 1

l   correct, $3 \times 117 = 351$ so the remainder is 1

Step 2

a $305 = 7930 \div 26$

b $56 \times 37 = 2072$

c $43 \times 86 = 3698$

d   incorrect, the remainder is 1 so it should be 19.333

e   correct, the remainder of 1 is $\frac{1}{3}$ as 3 is the divisor.

f   correct, $87 = 3 \times 29$ so there is a remainder of 1

g   correct to 1 decimal place

h   incorrect as $3 \times 29 = 87$ so only 1 remaining

Step 3

a   18 pizzas

b   53.2 (or 53 whole) turns

c   56

d $4\frac{1}{6}$ cup cakes

e   1 minute 18 seconds

Step 4

5, 9, 13, are all 1 more than a multiple of 4. 6, 10, 14 … are all 2 more than a multiple of 4 but you can't have a remainder of 4 because you would add 1 to the quotient instead.

Follow-up ideas

- Link the remainder following division by seven with days of the week. It is Monday. What day of the week will it be in 40 days? (40 ÷ 7 has remainder five so count on five days – Saturday.) There are opportunities to do some calendar work here.

- Children can write a selection of word problems to exemplify the different ways of treating the remainder. Rounding up or down, writing it as a fraction or decimal and just identifying it as a remainder.

Choosing operations to solve problems

- **Solve problems involving addition, subtraction, multiplication and division.**

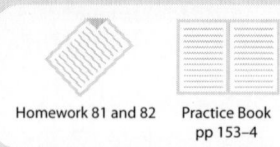

Homework 81 and 82   Practice Book pp 153–4

Mathematical vocabulary

Equivalent, sum, addend, augend, difference, subtrahend, minuend, product, multiplicand, multiplier, quotient, dividend, divisor, operation

Representations and resources

Number rods, whiteboards and markers, coins.

Warming up

Practise multiplication and division facts up to 12 × 12. *What is 56 ÷ 7? What is 11 × 12?*

Background knowledge

Children have applied knowledge of calculation to solve word problems throughout Key Stage 1 and Key Stage 2. To start with they use concrete materials to model the calculation and some may still have recourse to these when they feel challenged. Children now develop the ability to solve problems more efficiently and choose the correct operation.

Relating problems that involve addition to those involving subtraction deepens understanding of the structure of problems. The same can be done with multiplication and division problems.

The words used in a problem can mislead as well as distract children from thinking about the problem itself. Help children to analyse the problem carefully before they attempt to solve it.

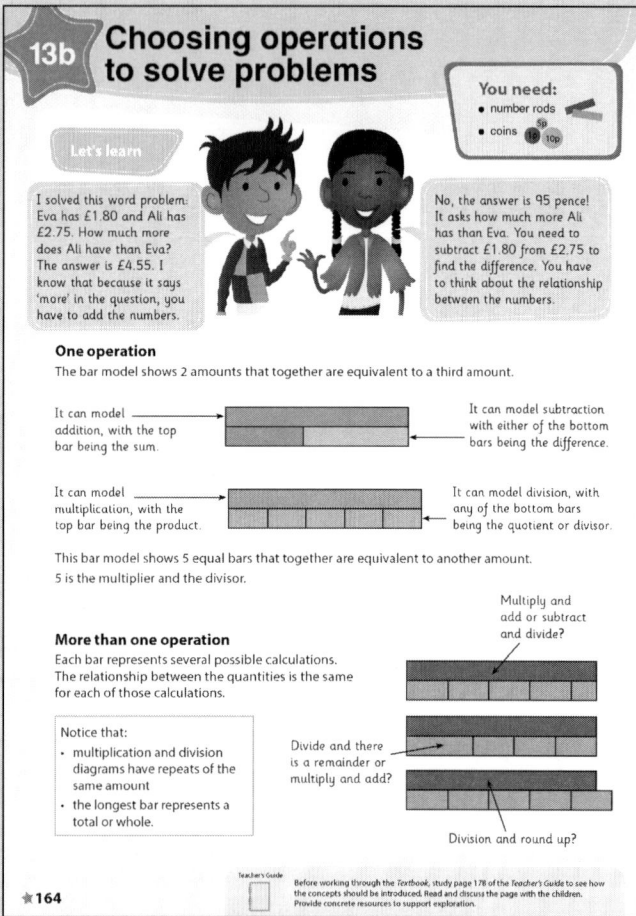

Let's learn: Modelling and teaching

One operation

- Invite children to explain the structure of the first diagram. How does it show addition? How does it show subtraction? Ask children for an example of a word problem that could be modelled by the diagram. Make sure they give both the addition, and both subtraction, versions of the problem. Children can use number rods to model the calculation.

- Next invite children to look at the multiplication bar. Ask: *How does the bar model show multiplication? How does it show division?* Spend time exploring the two division questions to clarify the grouping and sharing models of division. Ask children to write a word problem for each of the interpretations of the diagram. Can they do all three from one situation?

- Ask children to swap one problem with a classmate. They should solve the problems using their bar models alongside an appropriate formal written method.

More than one operation

- There are many different bar models that can be drawn for different multi-step word problems. Those shown in the Textbook are a selection and are open to interpretation in different ways. Explain that some can be more complicated than these. For each one prompt children by asking for some numbers for the bars and then for a word problem for it. They can then attempt to write a version of the word problem for the other interpretations.

- Encourage children to justify their responses. Ask: *Why does it fit the diagram?* and explore other possible diagrams in order to deepen understanding.

Let's practise: Digging deeper

Step 1

The context for these word problems is simple and familiar and the same for each question. Part a has a word clue as it uses the scaling model of multiplication. The other parts avoid giving word clues or use words that might be distractors for children who are dependent on them. Prompt children to draw bar models or use number rods to model the problems. They then identify what is to be found and that dictates the calculation.

Step 2

These questions present a similar context to Step 1 to avoid the context being a distraction. However, they progress from Step 1 by requiring children to find a missing component before they can solve the problem. Money is a known context and so children can refer to their own experience to interpret the questions. These are multi-step problems involving a mixture of operations. Ask: *Can*

you draw a diagram to show this? Can you use number rods to describe this problem?* Probe children's understanding by asking: *How can you tell from your diagram what calculation to do?* Part e is a variation where children meet a different kind of money problem. Challenge them to draw a bar model for it.

Step 3

These word problems provide a variety of contexts, including mass and capacity. Drawing a diagram will help to solve them. Children may start with a 'realistic' model and then you can challenge them to turn that into a bar diagram before solving the problem. The purpose is not to insist on a particular method for solving it but to deepen children's understanding of the structure of the situation. Ask children to identify what in their diagrams tells them what calculations to do. Some children may not recall the number of millilitres in a litre. Prompt them by asking about 'milli' as a prefix for metres.

Step 4

Writing the word problem from the diagram deepens children's awareness and understanding of the structure of different problems. It is an important element in developing mastery of the ideas as they have to think about word problems and their associated calculations in a different way. Writing the different versions of the same problem – where each number takes its turn to be the answer – reinforces the relationships between operations and the idea of inverses. The third diagram can prompt questions on percentages or decimal notation which could be in a measures context.

Ensuring progress

Supporting understanding

Use concrete materials such as coins and number rods to model the question. Allow children plenty of thinking time and space to explore and try out their ideas, even if it means making false starts – these are learning opportunities. Ask them to describe the problem in their own words.

Broadening understanding

Challenge children to write different versions of the same problem with different items being the number to be found.

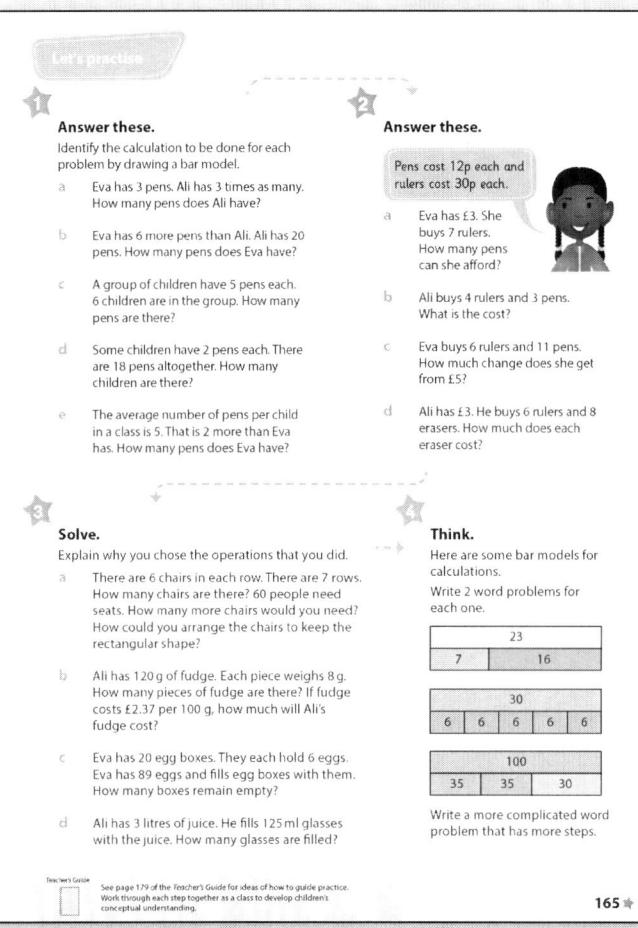

> ✓ **Concept mastered**
>
> Children can recognise which operation to use when solving a word problem by the relationship between the amounts in the problem. They can identify which operations to use when solving problems involving several steps.

Follow-up ideas

- Make posters to summarise what an addition problem is like. Choose a calculation such as 12 + 7, draw the bar model and write some word problems that require that sum (or subtraction or multiplication or division).

- Select a test paper. Classify the questions according to whether they involve addition, subtraction, multiplication or division. Sort them into a two-way table if they involve two different operations.

Answers

Step 1		Step 3	
a	multiplication	**a**	42 chairs – 18 and make 3 more rows.
b	addition	**b**	15 pieces – £2.84 (rounded to nearest penny).
c	multiplication	**c**	5
d	division	**d**	5 boxes
e	subtraction		

Step 2

a	7 pens	**d**	15p
b	£1.56	**e**	24 glasses
c	£1.88		

Step 4

Any question that requires:

$7 + 16 = 23$ or $23 - 7 = 16$

$6 \times 5 = 30$ or $30 \div 5 = 6$

$2 \times 35 + 30 = 100$ or

$100 - 2 \times 35 = 30$

- **Multiply simple pairs of proper fractions, writing the answer in its simplest form.**
- **Divide proper fractions by whole numbers.**

Homework 83 and 84

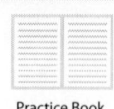
Practice Book pp 155–7

Fraction Wall

Mathematical vocabulary

Equivalent, unit fraction, numerator, denominator, multiplicand, multiplier, product, dividend, divisor, quotient.

Representations and resources

Arrays, counters, whiteboards and markers.

Warming up

Start with quarters. Ask: *Which quarters can you simplify?* (e.g. $\frac{2}{4} = \frac{1}{2}$). Move on to fifths. Which ones can you simplify? (None. Ask children to explain why not.) What about sixths? (Nearly all can be simplified. Ask children to explain why.) Ask which fractions in certain fraction families simplify. Ask: *Is there a way of predicting this?*

Background knowledge

Understanding fractions using diagrams is fundamental to developing understanding of ways of multiplying and dividing fractions. The array model for multiplying generates the equivalent fractions as the two dimensions multiply to give the area. This is the 'common denominator' for the fractions.

It is important to bring out the idea that the array has a total area of one because it is one whole. The sides are therefore both one as well, but you then choose how to divide up each side. You look at the fractions involved and the denominators give the dimensions for the array. This is also a powerful model for multiplying non-unit fractions as the product of the numerators is clearly shown by the number of parts shaded in the array. Dividing a fraction by a whole number is clearly shown to be equivalent to multiplying by its associated unit fraction.

Let's learn: Modelling and teaching

Multiplying fractions

- Look at the array model in the Textbook. Point to the top side and ask: *What is the length of this side?* Children may say four quarters or one whole. Do the same for the other side to establish that the whole 'rectangle' has area one square unit. Remind children of the array model for multiplication and ask: *I am working out one third multiplied by one quarter, how can I use this diagram?* Children identify the top left hand square. Ask: *What fraction of the whole does the square represent?* Use the diagram to calculate other products involving thirds and quarters.

- The bar model in the Textbook shows the same calculation. The multiplicand is shown first, as part of a whole. Ask: *How do you draw the bar for one quarter on the diagram?* Discuss what that is as a fraction of the whole. Ask: *How many of those fit against the whole bar? How do you know?*

- Record the calculation on the board. Ask children to

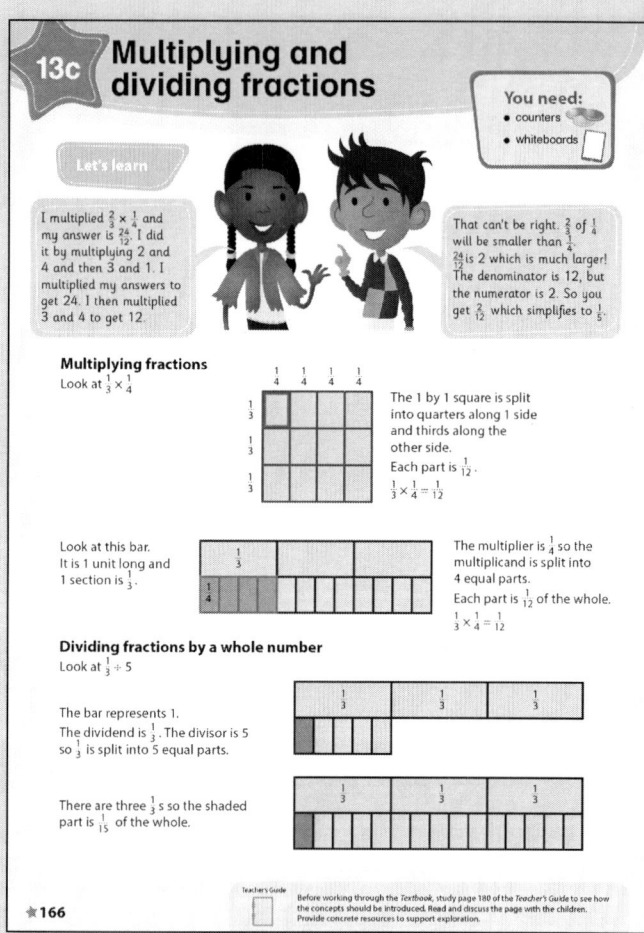

compare the written workings to the array and bar models.

Dividing fractions by a whole number

- First show the dividend as a fraction bar using the Textbook. Ask: *How do we know it is one third?* Prompt for understanding that the thirds are equal. Show the third split into five equal parts. Children can model this using a rectangle of paper to represent the whole, and fold it into the appropriate number of divisions each way to show the fractions when it is opened out. Ask children what fraction of the whole each one is before showing the second diagram. Children should notice that the diagram is exactly the same as the one for multiplying fractions, except with slightly different numbers. Again, record the calculation on the board to discuss as a class.

Let's practise: Digging deeper

Step 1

Parts a-d involve multiplying gradually more difficult fractions. Parts e-h are finding the quotient of a fraction and a whole number with the whole number as divisor. These progress from known facts to less familiar fractions and non-unit fractions that require simplifying. Drawing a diagram such as the bar model and applying knowledge and understanding of multiplication and division to that diagram will support progress through this section.

Step 2

The questions have different parts of the calculation omitted and the quotient on either side of the equals sign to develop understanding of the relationships. Some children see immediately what the missing numbers are from knowledge of number facts. Others may try a number and work out the calculation, noticing where their choice does not work. Trying to draw a diagram forces children to pay attention to what is not known. Some children fill in the gaps by noticing patterns and should be encouraged to explain their thinking using diagrams in order to deepen that understanding of the structure.

Step 3

In parts a-c children first work out what fraction is needed, then use that fraction to calculate the amount. You could prompt, e.g. *What fraction of the recipe do we need? What is the calculation here?* Children should write down the calculation to free space in working memory and to aid recognition of the process needed. Whiteboards can be used for that and to draw a diagram to show the calculation if necessary. The last three questions require children to draw on other skills involving fractions as well as the ones introduced in this unit.

Step 4

It is possible to make all of the numbers from one to ten in this way. The smaller numbers use the new ideas from this unit and larger ones revise previous fraction work. Division by half is accessible to them and readily available if children have mastery of fractions. Ask children to go on to explain why division by a whole number is equivalent to multiplication by a unit fraction.

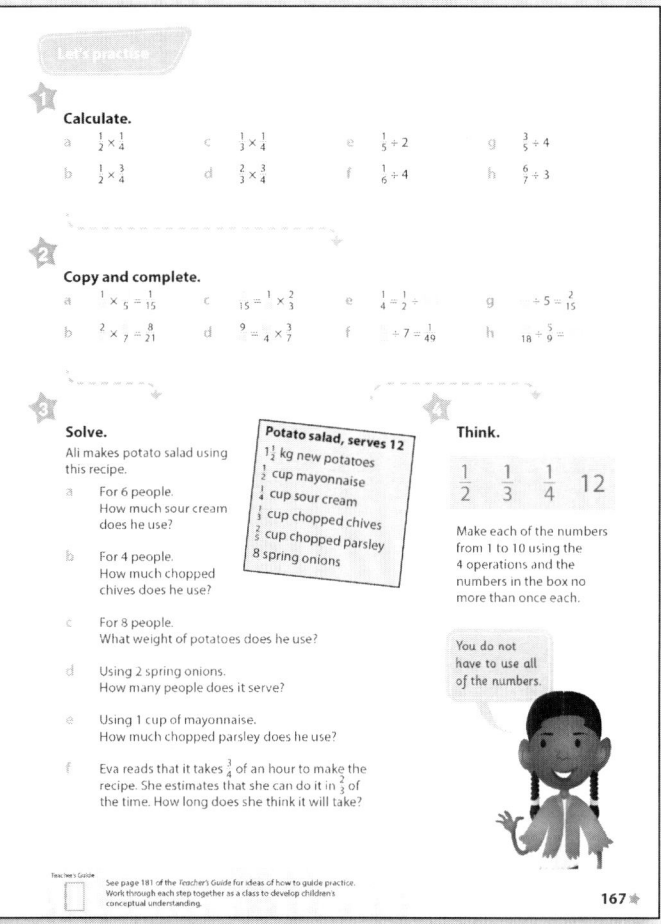

Ensuring progress

Supporting understanding

Use eight counters in a 2 by 4 array, where each counter represents $\frac{1}{8}$ and the length of each side of the array is one. Ask children to identify where $\frac{1}{2}$, $\frac{1}{4}$ and $\frac{1}{8}$ are represented in the array.

Broadening understanding

Children can extend the diagrammatic representations to non-unit fractions and write a poster guide on how to do this.

✓ Concept mastered

Children can multiply two simple fractions, giving the product in its simplest form. They can divide a fraction by a whole number, giving the quotient in its simplest form.

Follow-up ideas

- Children can search for other recipes that use cups to measure quantities of the ingredients. They can adapt them for different numbers of people using their knowledge of multiplying and dividing fractions. Children could make some of the recipes to share with their family and friends.

- Children can extend the first question in Step 4 to make more numbers. They can decide how to change the rules in order to achieve this with as few extra numbers as possible.

Answers

Step 1

a $\frac{1}{8}$

b $\frac{3}{8}$

c $\frac{1}{12}$

d $\frac{1}{2}$

e $\frac{1}{10}$

f $\frac{1}{24}$

g $\frac{3}{20}$

h $\frac{2}{7}$

Step 2

a $\frac{1}{3} \times \frac{1}{5} = \frac{1}{15}$

b $\frac{2}{3} \times \frac{4}{7} = \frac{8}{21}$

c $\frac{2}{15} = \frac{1}{5} \times \frac{2}{3}$

d $\frac{9}{28} = \frac{3}{4} \times \frac{3}{7}$

e $\frac{1}{4} = \frac{1}{2} \div 2$

f $\frac{1}{7} \div 7 = \frac{1}{49}$

g $\frac{2}{3} \div 5 = \frac{2}{15}$

h $\frac{5}{18} = \frac{5}{9} \div 2$

Step 3

a $\frac{1}{8}$ of a cup

b $\frac{1}{5}$ of a cup

c 1 kg

d 3 people

e $\frac{4}{5}$ of a cup

f $\frac{1}{2}$ an hour

Step 4

1 $= \frac{1}{3} \times \frac{1}{4} \times 12$

2 $= \frac{1}{3} \times \frac{1}{2} \times 12$

3 $= \frac{1}{4} \times 12$

4 $= \frac{1}{3} \times 12$

5 $= (\frac{1}{2} \times \frac{1}{3} + \frac{1}{4}) \times 12$

6 $= \frac{1}{2} \times 12$

7 $= (\frac{1}{3} + \frac{1}{4}) \times 12$

8 $= 12 \times \frac{1}{3} \div \frac{1}{2}$

9 $= (\frac{1}{2} + \frac{1}{4}) \times 12$

10 $= (\frac{1}{2} + \frac{1}{3}) \times 12$

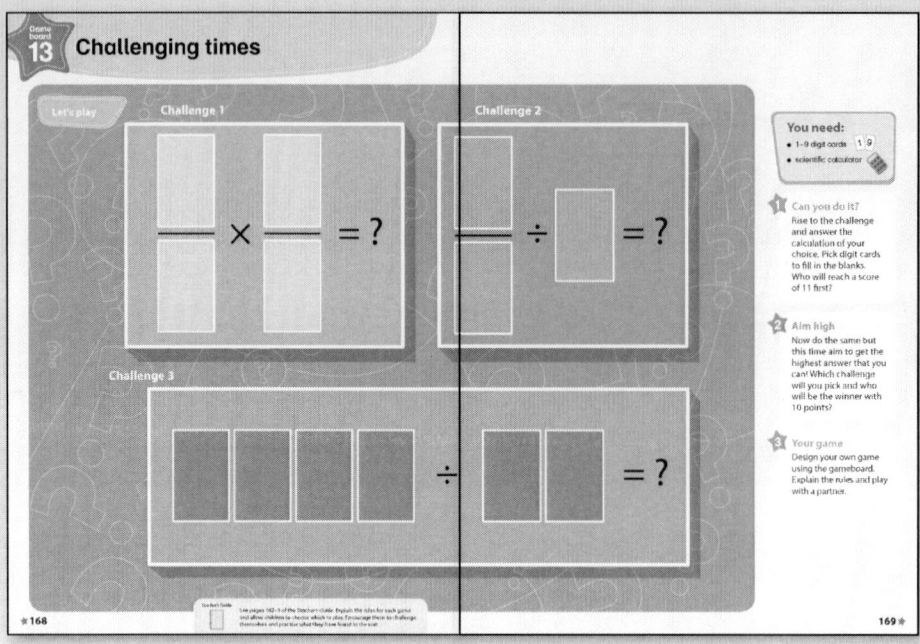

Game 1: Can you do it?

Players compete to build up their score in order to reach 11 first. Success comes from choosing the most difficult challenge they can achieve so rewards risk-taking with self-knowledge.

Maths focus

- Divide 4-digit numbers by 2-digit numbers
- Multiply simple fractions
- Divide fractions by whole numbers

Resources

1–9 digit cards, whiteboards, scientific calculators.

How to play

Play in pairs. Each player chooses one of the challenges. The higher the number of the challenge the more points that are scored. They pick the appropriate number of digit cards: four for Challenge 1, three for Challenge 2 and six for Challenge 3. They arrange them according to the layout for the challenge box. They then work out the answer.

Both players check the answer on a calculator which handles fractions. The points scored are equal to the challenge number. The first player to reach 11 points wins.

Making it easier

The game self-differentiates as players can choose a lesser challenge.

Making it harder

The game self-differentiates as players can choose a greater challenge such as challenge 3.

Game 3: Your game

Children should invent their own game designing rules that use the concepts covered in the unit. Challenge children to make their game easier or harder.

Game 2: Aim high

This game rewards risk-taking and self-knowledge, but with the spoiler that your opponent can stop you scoring by finding a better solution.

Maths focus

- Divide 4-digit numbers by 2-digit numbers
- Multiply simple fractions
- Divide fractions by whole numbers
- Apply understanding of place value

Resources

1–9 digit cards, scientific calculator, counters.

How to play

Play in pairs. Each player chooses one of the challenges. They pick the appropriate number of digit cards: four for Challenge 1, three for Challenge 2 and six for Challenge 3. They arrange them according to the layout for the challenge box. This time, they are aiming to get the highest answer. They work this out and both players check the first player's answer on a calculator. The second player tries to get a higher answer, checking on a calculator. The first player scores 1 if they have the highest answer. The second player scores 2 if they beat them – that means getting a higher answer, not just matching it. That gives the first player an advantage, hence the lesser score.

The first player to reach ten points wins. The game can be easily changed so that the lowest answer wins or there is a different objective, e.g. nearest to one.

Making it easier

The game self-differentiates as players can choose a lesser challenge such as Challenge 1. They can also use concrete materials such as counters in an array model to support the calculation.

Making it harder

Players may insist that fractions are in their simplest form, not requiring further simplification.

Unit 3 Challenging times

Choose a game to play.

Game 1: Can you do it?

You need:
- 1–9 digit cards
- scientific calculator

How to play
- Play in pairs.
- Each choose a challenge.
- Pick a digit card for each empty box.
- Work out the answer.
- Check the answer on a calculator.
- Your points are equal to the challenge number.
- The first player to reach 11 points wins.

Game 2: Aim high

You need:
- 1–9 digit cards
- scientific calculator

How to play
- Play in pairs.
- Each choose a challenge.
- Pick a digit card for each empty box.
- Arrange them to get the **highest** answer.
- Player 1 works out the answer.
- Together check the answer on a calculator.
- Player 2 tries to get a higher answer.
- Player 1 scores 1 point if they have the higher answer.
- Player 2 scores 2 points if they beat them.
- The first player to reach 10 points wins.

Game 3: Your challenge

- Make up your own game using the gameboard.
- What resources will you need to play?
- What are the rules for your game? Explain them to someone.

Please help your child by reading the instructions and playing the game together.

Assessment task 1

Running the task

Children have to match the question to the calculation. You could create the cards for them to actually handle. The same numbers and context are used each time to avoid giving clues that will allow success without understanding of the situation. For the same reason cue words are avoided where possible while still being clear about what is being asked. Prompts should also avoid cue words at all costs. The task is testing whether children recognise the structure of the different situations.

It is vital that children include an explanation for their matching. A diagram, annotated to explain what is happening, is the best way to do this. Encourage children to do this and prompt as necessary: *How can you show that in a diagram? Use a speech bubble to explain what is happening.*

You can infer children's understanding from how they explain it. Correct answers can be arrived at with superficial learning that is based on recall. Children may use a process of elimination to pair the questions and answers, which shows some understanding. Some may work out the answer intuitively and match accordingly. This suggests that that they understand because they know what to do. However, they need to make this explicit via their explanation in order to deepen their understanding and so retain it.

Evidencing mastery

Children demonstrate correct matching. They provide a model and/or explanation of their choice which needs to be convincing. A correct bar diagram with the numbers on the bars would do this. An explanation that identifies which quantity is the whole and how it relates to the other numbers would also indicate mastery.

Assessment task 2

Resources

Calculators.

Running the task

Children should use long or short division to work out the recurring decimal for these divisions. The task uses long (or short) division to investigate another area of mathematics (decimal version of fractions). This allows children to develop their number sense while practising the method of division. They may focus on a particular divisor, e.g. three, and notice that the decimal is either .3333… or .6666 … Dividing by three allows possible remainders of one or two so there could be a 2-digit repeating sequence or two sequences of one digit repeating. Children could use calculators to check their answers. Some answers may go beyond the display as they have so many decimal places but it still serves as a check for the first bit.

Ask: *What do you notice?* This should prompt recording and thinking about what they have found. Then prompt them to try a different divisor. It may or may not repeat – encourage children to record both types as this can also provide insights into the number system. Continuing to investigate the quotients associated with a divisor of seven is another possible path. Division by seven allows possible remainders of one, two, three, four, five and six. This may be one repeating cycle of six digits or three different cycles of two digits, or two different cycles of three digits. Divisors of 9, 11 and 13 are also fruitful.

Evidencing mastery

Correct application of the short or long method of division indicates mastery. Statements that indicate that they have noticed the remainders appearing again and in the same order suggest an element of mastery. Being able to explain this with reference to the idea that any given divisor will have a number of possible remainders equal to one less than itself is evidence of the extra insight required for mastery.

Concepts mastered

- ✓ Children can divide 4-digit numbers by 2-digit numbers using long division. They can decide to round up or down when the quotient has a remainder, or write it as a decimal or fraction depending on the context.

- ✓ Children can recognise which operation to use when solving a word problem by the relationship between the amounts in the problem. They can identify which operations to use when solving problems involving several steps.

- ✓ Children can multiply two simple fractions, giving the product in its simplest form. They can divide a fraction by a whole number, giving the quotient in its simplest form.

Assessment task 3

Resources

1–9 digit cards.

Running the task

Before asking children to work independently on the task, recap the key models - the array and bar models - that could support them to complete the calculations. Children may choose any three digits but one, two and three are good to start with. They test children's competence with dividing fractions by whole numbers without challenging their knowledge of number facts. There are six different ways of placing the digits, which generate three different answers. Both the denominator of the fraction and the divisor divide the numerator so they can be exchanged without affecting the result. Children should notice this as they discover answers being repeated. Prompt them to try to explain it. They may require several more examples of working with the sets of three before they can see why it happens.

Children who manage this confidently can move on to using a set of four digits to fill in $\frac{}{} \times \frac{}{}$.

There are 24 different arrangements for this version and children will need to be systematic to find them all. They generate six different answers. It does not matter which way round the two numerators are, nor does it matter which way round the two denominators are.

Evidencing mastery

If children can correctly find the answers to the fraction calculations they are showing the beginnings of mastery. Explaining why the answers are the same for the pairs of calculations suggests they have mastery of the idea, particularly if their explanation refers to the role of the digits within the calculation. They may be able to draw a convincing diagram to show why it works which again suggests mastery.

Children who move on to investigate and explain the case with four digits and multiplying fractions are showing mastery of that idea as well. Reasoning and problem-solving skills should also be evident in their work. They are evidence of mathematical thinking.

Did you know?

Fractions are a natural next step after whole numbers. Many cultures have developed ways of writing them down. Some have used pictures, others have used symbols inspired by pictures. The way of representing the fractions dictates the ways of manipulating them, e.g. it was not until we had developed a place-value system with zero as a place-holder that we could attempt complex calculations. Multiplication of fractions was unknown as a way of manipulating symbols but people could work out fractions of fractions by actually dividing up the quantities. They worked with the concrete without needing an image.

The realisation that there were numbers that could not be written as fractions was shocking at the time. Now we accept them as part of the rich subject that is mathematics.

Nets, angles and coordinates

Mathematical focus

★ **Geometry: properties of shape, position and direction**

★ **Measurement: length, volume, area**

★ **Algebra: simple formulae, linear number sequences**

Prior learning

Children should already be able to:

- draw 2-D shapes using given dimensions and angles

- recognise, describe and build simple 3-D shapes, including making nets

- compare and classify geometric shapes based on their properties and sizes, and find unknown angles in any triangles, quadrilaterals and regular polygons

- recognise angles where they meet at a point, are on a straight line or are vertically opposite and find missing angles

- identify, describe and present the position of a shape following a translation on the full coordinate grid

- recognise and use simple formulae and express missing numbers algebraically.

Key new learning

- Recognise, describe and build simple 3-D shapes, including making a wider variety of nets.

- Calculate, estimate and compare volumes of cubes and cuboids using standard units, including cubic centimetres (cm³) and cubic metres (m³) and extending to other units, e.g. mm³ and km³.

- Draw 2-D shapes using given dimensions and angles, including using compasses to construct triangles.

- Find unknown angles in triangles, quadrilaterals and regular polygons.

- Describe positions on the full coordinate grid (all four quadrants) and draw and reflect simple shapes.

- Use simple formulae and find pairs of numbers that satisfy an equation with two unknowns.

Making connections

- Children are building relationships between shapes and using this knowledge in mathematics, art and design technology lessons.

- Many computer games involve the use of Cartesian coordinates. Children may meet a third dimension that describes elevation. Computer games may also use scale factors.

Unit 14 Nets, angles and coordinates

What 3-D shapes can you see?

I wonder how these models compare in size to real life?

What angles can you see?

★172

Talk about

Many common shapes words will be firmly established in children's vocabulary but they will need to persevere to remember others. Focus on the derivation of the words so that, e.g. children remember that the word for an eight-sided figure is octagon because of the association of 'oct-' from the eight legs of an octopus. The suffixes, '-gon' and '-hedron' meaning angle and face are used in naming polygons and polyhedra. Children could investigate more definitions for themselves.

When they are solving problems, encourage them to explain their thinking and reasoning using precise vocabulary.

Engaging and exploring

Focus on each picture in turn and use it to assess children's understanding and their recall of facts and vocabulary. There is deliberately limited new learning in this unit so this is an opportunity to focus on any areas where consolidation is required and to reflect on the vast content covered.

The first photo is taken in Staffa, a tiny uninhabited island off the west coast of Scotland. Its Viking name means 'pillar island' because of the dramatic vertical basalt columns. The island has inspired artists (e.g. Turner), writers and poets (e.g. Keats) and composers (e.g. Mendelssohn). The columns are mostly hexagonal prisms, although some columns have between three and eight sides. Elicit from children that the shapes are hexagonal prisms. Ask them to define a prism and name some others using the image for inspiration. Move on to thinking about other 3-D shapes, such as

pyramids which are named in a similar way and where they have seen them in real life. The Giant's Causeway in Northern Ireland has similar geology to Staffa and was formed at the same time.

The photo of the 'tiny' model people is to stimulate a discussion about scale and scale factors. There is actually nothing in the photo that shows the relative size. Ask children what they would need to know to work out the scale factor. To do this they need to think about average heights. Work together to agree the scale factor. Show children other models that you have in the classroom. Ask them to work out the scale factor of these models compared to your height. Ask: *What other models can you think of? What scale factors are they?*

In the football match photo, one player is about to kick the ball in an attempt to score and the question asks about angles. You can see a number of angles in the player on the left, e.g. an acute angle between his left and right legs and between his right arm and body. Discuss the importance of angles and turning in sports generally, including hockey, netball, snooker, gymnastics and diving. You could even show short video clips to support this discussion. Use the context to revise types of angles and to estimate angle sizes. Use the photo or the video clips to generate missing angle problems and use these to revise angle facts.

The striking building with faces that are parallelogram-shaped is the Docklands Building in Hamburg, Germany. Constructed from steel and glass, it tilts over the river more than 40 metres and resembles the prow of a ship. Ask children to identify the shapes of the faces that they can see and use it as a stimulus to revise 2-D shapes and their properties. You can include the concepts of perimeter and area. Ask: *Do you like the building? Explain why or why not.* Ask them what other buildings they know that have interestingly shaped faces. *What buildings would you design?*

The final photo shows reflection. Discuss the words object, image and reflection with children and the mathematics of reflection. Elicit from them that the angles and size of the shape are unchanged but reversed. Ask them to give you examples of reflection in real life, e.g. in water, or in art and design, particularly geometric or stylised graphics such as logos. Think about reflections in two axes, both horizontal and vertical.

What 2-D shapes can you see?

Can you describe the reflections?

Teacher's Guide
Look at the pictures with the children and discuss the questions.
See pages 186–7 of the *Teacher's Guide* for key ideas to draw out.

173

Things to think about

- How will you pair children for most effective learning? Maths partners, friends, mixed-ability, similar-ability? It is important that children become used to working in different types of pairs so that they become adept at explaining their thinking and reasoning in a variety of ways.

- In what ways will you support children with less dexterity in measurement and drawing?

- How will you check conceptual understanding of area, missing angle problems, volume and nets, and translation and reflection across the full coordinate grid?

- How do you plan to introduce problem-solving activities?

Checking understanding

You will know children have mastered the concepts in this unit when they can identify and describe 2-D shapes, use properties and angle facts to solve missing angle problems and calculate perimeter and area. They can calculate the area of parallelograms and triangles. They can also identify and describe 3-D shapes, including nets. Children can use the formula for calculating the volume of cuboids, estimate and compare volumes using a variety of units and explain why volume is measured in cubic units. They are able to plot coordinates for 2-D shapes on the full coordinate grid (four quadrants), translate and reflect them in the x- and y-axes. Children can make appropriate use of algebra within the topic.

Making and measuring 3-D shapes

- Recognise, describe and build simple 3-D shapes, including making nets.
- Calculate, estimate and compare volumes of cubes and cuboids using standard units, including cubic centimetres (cm³) and cubic metres (m³) and extending to other units, e.g. mm³ and km³.

Homework 85 and 86

Practice Book pp 158–62

3D Shapes

Representations and resources

Whiteboards, 3-D shape construction kits, 3-D shapes, compasses, rulers, protractors, thin card, scissors, glue, Base 10 apparatus, Internet access.

Mathematical vocabulary

Net, cube, cubic, cubic units, metres cubed (m³), centimetres cubed (cm³), kilometres cubed (km³), millimetres cubed (mm³), pyramid, apex

Warming up

Explain to children that a mind map is a diagram used to organise information visually. Tell them to write 3-D shapes in the centre of their whiteboard and add words and images to show all that they know about the topic. They may include the names and properties of shapes, measuring volume, units of volume and nets. After a few minutes ask pairs to share with another pair and add to their mind map. An alternative approach is to create a class mind map. Research has shown that the brain works by associating ideas, memories and pieces of information so this is a good way to consolidate children's learning.

Background knowledge

In previous units children have measured volume in cm³ and m³. Here they are extending the range of units. Millimetres cubed (mm³) are used for small volumes. 1 m³ is quite a large unit and can be used for measuring large volumes. Children are unlikely to meet anything measured in km³ in mathematics lessons because it is such an enormous unit. They may meet it in science where it is used to measure the size of planets.

To convert from a larger unit to a smaller one, you multiply. To change from cm³ to mm³, multiply by 1000. To convert from a smaller unit to a larger one, you divide. To change from mm³ to cm³, divide by 1000.

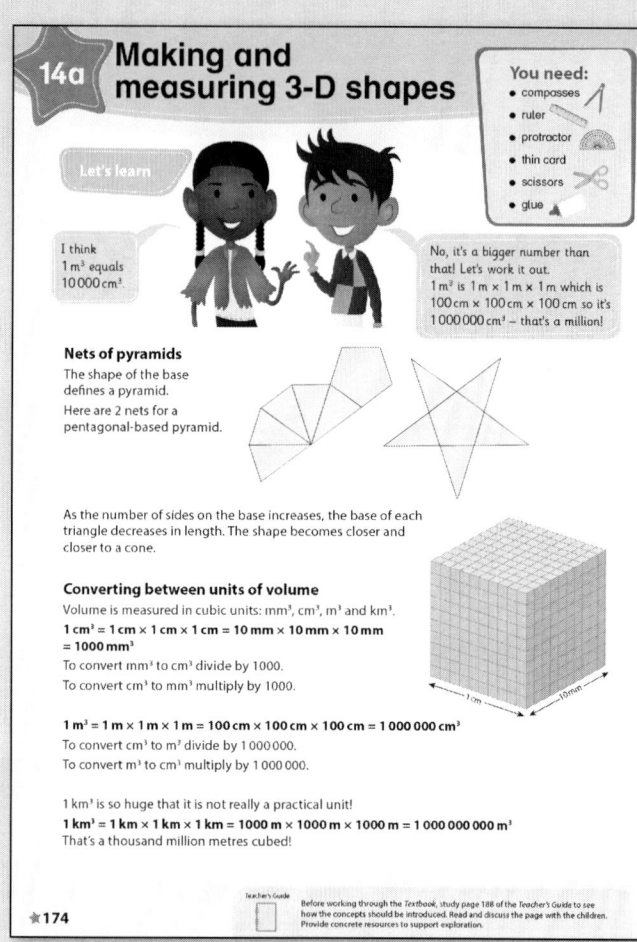

Let's learn: Modelling and teaching

Nets of pyramids

- Ask children to describe the properties of a pyramid.

- Give children 3-D shape construction kits and ask them to make a selection of pyramids, e.g. tetrahedron, square-based pyramid, pentagonal pyramid, hexagonal pyramid. Ask them to open out their models to give the 2-D nets.

- Challenge children to make the two nets for the pentagonal pyramids shown in the Textbook. Ask them what they notice about the number of sides of the base and the name of the pyramid. Use the models to show that as the number of sides on the base of the pyramid increases, the individual triangles become narrower and less distinct, and the net approaches that of a cone.

Converting between units of volume

- Read the misconception cartoon together. Ask children to recall the pattern of cube numbers (1, 8, 27, 64, 125, 216, etc.) to illustrate how cubic measurements increase very rapidly.

- Show children a single unit and a 1000 block of Base 10 apparatus. Ask: *How many times bigger is the block than the cube? How many blocks are needed to make 1m³?* Elicit that 10 blocks × 10 blocks × 10 blocks gives 1000 blocks, i.e. multiply to convert from larger to smaller units..

- Ask: *What do we do when converting a smaller unit to a larger unit?* (We divide.)

- Create a bank of facts children can draw on, e.g. 1 cm³ = 1000 mm³.

Let's practise: Digging deeper

Step 1

In this step children use their knowledge to create the net of a hexagonal pyramid. They will also need to follow a set of instructions carefully. You may need to remind them how to inscribe a regular hexagon in a circle by systematically marking the radius around the circumference. You could ask children to explain how to make the net for other pyramids, e.g. a tetrahedron, a square-based or an octagonal-based pyramid. Support any children who find the practical aspects challenging.

Step 2

Children have learned that 1 cm³ = 1000 mm³. Show them a 1000 block of Base 10 apparatus and ask what the volume is in mm³, cm³ and m³. Use diagrams to establish that the block has a volume of 1 000 000 mm³, 1000 cm³ or 0.001 m³. Discuss which unit they feel most comfortable using. Suggest that they use diagrams when answering the Textbook problems.

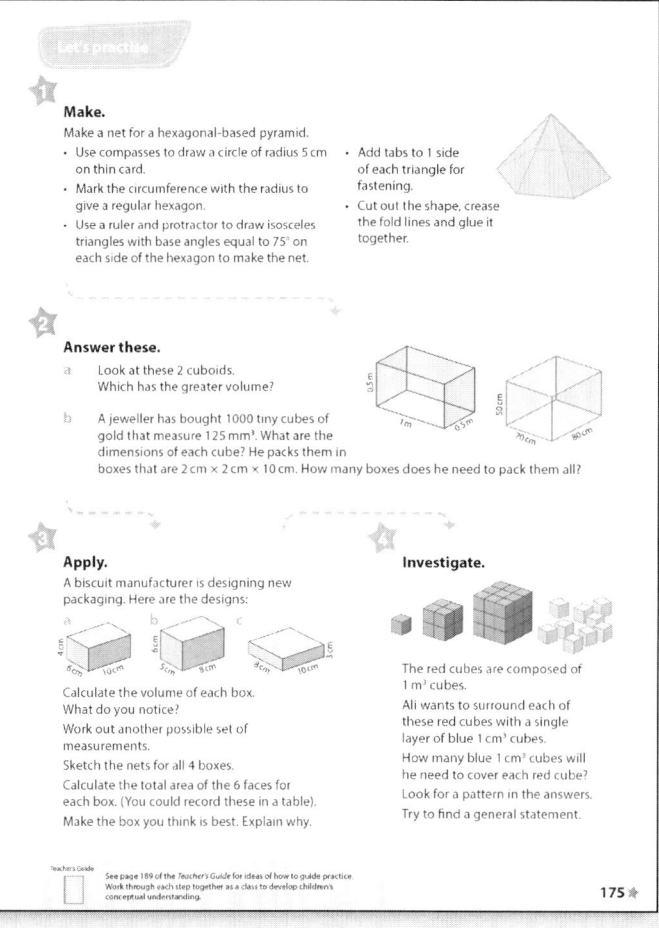

Step 3

The practical element of this task occurs at the end. Children use a number of skills: calculating volumes, areas, finding alternative measurements and comparing sizes. The volume is 240 cm³, which has a large number of factors, so there are a considerable number of alternative measurements. Explain 'surface area'. To find the surface area of the boxes, they have to work out the area of each face and total them. Children make the biscuit box of their choice. Factors to consider are the appearance, practicality of packing the biscuits and the cost. The box closest to a cube (5 cm × 6 cm × 8 cm) has the smallest surface area and is the cheapest to produce.

Step 4

The table shows the thinking needed for this problem.

	1 cm red cube	2 cm red cube	3 cm red cube	x cm red cube
Number of red 1 cm³ cubes	1	8	27	x^3
Size of cube required to cover red cube	3 cm × 3 cm × 3 cm = 27 cm³	4 cm × 4 cm × 4 cm = 64 cm³	5 cm × 5 cm × 5 cm = 125 cm³	$(x + 2)^3$
Number of blue 1 cm³ cubes	27 – 1 = 26	64 – 8 = 56	125 – 27 = 98	$(x + 2)^3 – x^3$

Ensuring progress

Supporting understanding

Asking children to explain the problem to you in their own words is a good way of teasing out any areas where they are unsure. Allow them thinking time and encourage them to use diagrams and jottings to visualise their ideas.

Broadening understanding

Children who find making models from nets easy may enjoy making alternative models. There are many examples of polyhedra nets available on the Internet that could be explored. Really keen children could find out about stellated polyhedra.

✓ **Concept mastered**

Children can recognise, describe and build simple 3-D shapes, including making a variety of nets. They can calculate, estimate and compare volumes of cubes and cuboids using standard units, including cubic centimetres (cm³), cubic metres (m³) and cubic millimetres (mm³).

Follow-up ideas

- Different units have been explored for volume; children have met, but not used, km³. Challenge them to find out when this huge unit is used and to visualise what it would look like.

- Investigate shipping containers. What would you need to pack your household needs? You can get bigger ones but a typical domestic container is 6 m × 2.5 m × 2.5 m. Ask children to work out what this will hold, e.g. how much of the classroom equipment would fit in one container.

- Find a small shed or similar. Ask children to measure the dimensions and draw a diagram of a possible net. They could annotate the diagram with the real measurements, calculate the materials required to construct it or make a scale model of it.

Answers

Step 2

a b (a = 0.25 m³ = 250 000 cm³; b = 0.28 m³ = 280 000 cm³)

b cube = 5 mm × 5 mm × 5 mm; 4 boxes (3 filled with 320 per box, 4th box partly filled with 40 cubes).

Step 3

Volume of each box is = 240 cm³
a = 248 cm²; b = 236 cm²;
c = 268 cm²

Step 4

red cube 1 × 1 × 1 blue cubes 26 (27 – 1)

red cube 2 × 2 × 2 blue cubes 56 (64 – 8)

red cube 3 × 3 × 3 blue cubes 98 (125 – 27)

blue cubes needed for red cube of side $n = (n + 2)^3 – n^3$

- Draw 2-D shapes using given dimensions and angles, including using compasses to construct triangles.
- Find unknown angles in triangles, quadrilaterals and regular polygons.

Homework 87 and 88　　Practice Book pp 163–6　　Geometry Instruments

Mathematical vocabulary

Compasses, arc, intersect (intersection)

Representations and resources

Whiteboards, 2-D shapes, compasses, rulers, pairs of geostrips with split pin, protractors, thin card, scissors, glue.

Warming up

Remind children that a mind map is a diagram used to organise information visually. It is a good way to remember information because it mirrors how the brain itself works. Tell them to write 2-D shapes in the centre of their whiteboard and add words and images to show all that they know about the topic. They may include the names and properties of 2-D shapes, measuring area, units of area, types of angles and angle facts. After a few minutes ask pairs to share with another pair and then add to their mind map. An alternative approach would be to create a class mind map.

Background knowledge

This concept brings together the knowledge and skills in reasoning about 2-D shapes and angles that children have built up during Key Stage 2. They extend their ability to draw shapes accurately by learning to use compasses for constructing triangles.

Remember area is measured in square units and that doubling the dimensions of a rectangle will result in a rectangle with four times the area of the original. This is because area involves two dimensions, doubling both dimensions means doubling twice or multiplying by four.

Let's learn: Modelling and teaching
Constructing triangles using compasses

- Ask children how they would draw an equilateral triangle. They will probably tell you that they need a protractor. Explain that the method shown in the Textbook uses a pair of compasses as a tool to construct triangles accurately. Remind children that every point on the circumference of a circle is equidistant from the centre. See if they can suggest to use this fact to construct an equilateral triangle with sides five centimetres. Help them to follow the instructions in the Textbook. Remind them to place the ruler carefully and tell them not to rub out the construction arcs.

- Ask them to think about how this method can be extended to draw isosceles and scalene triangles where the lengths of the sides are known.

- Ask children to construct an isosceles triangle with base 6 cm and sides 8 cm, and a scalene triangle with sides of 3 cm, 4 cm and 5 cm.

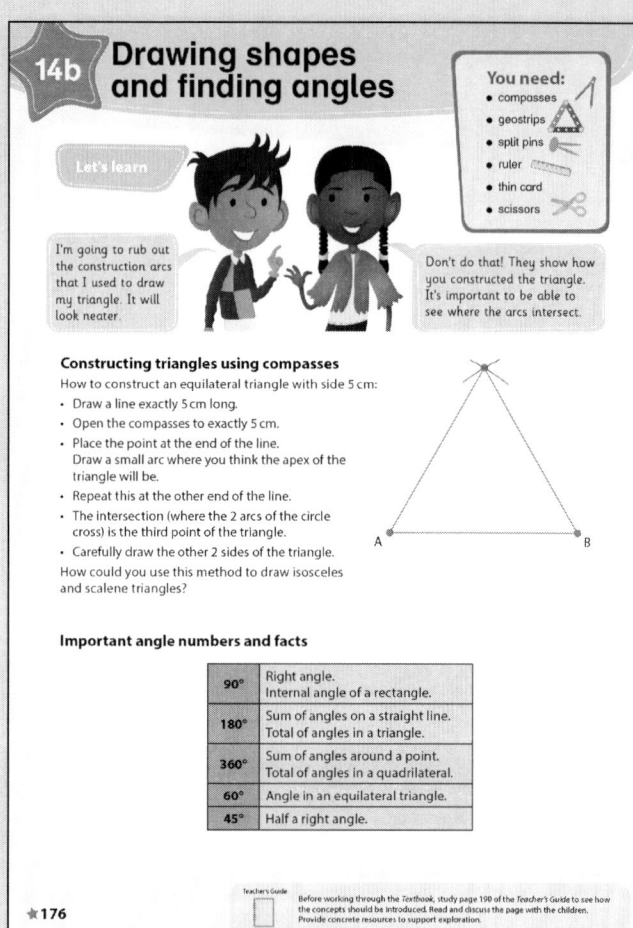

Important angle numbers and facts

- The angle facts in the table in the Textbook have been developed over the course of several years and used in many problems. They are as vital to geometry as multiplication tables are to multiplication and so it is worth spending time to ensure that children understand them fully. Remind them that if they tear the corners off a triangle (or quadrilateral) and put the angles together they will always make 180° (or 360°). Together, explore how you could write these rules using words, letters and symbols.

- Ask children to estimate different size angles using a pair of geostrips joined with a split pin. Write their estimates on the board. Reinforce the dynamic nature of angle as a measure of turn.

Let's practise: Digging deeper

Step 1

Check that children have the correct equipment and correct any errors or bad practice immediately. Ask children to measure the equal angles of their isosceles triangle. If they have constructed the triangle accurately, the angle should be 53°. Allow an error of plus or minus one to two degrees.

Step 2

Using the geometry symbols and angle facts allows children to calculate the angles in the diagrams. The starting point in the first one is the equilateral triangle so children identify the 60° angles. From there they can use the properties of the parallelogram to find those angles and finally the angles in the isosceles triangles.

The second diagram hinges on angles around a point. Encourage children to verbalise their thinking.

Step 3

This practical task gives children the opportunity to practise using compasses for construction of equilateral triangles. Encourage and support them to make their tetrahedrons as accurately as possible, cutting carefully and scoring the fold lines with scissors and a ruler. This is the simplest stellated polyhedron. Children who enjoy the task may also enjoy researching further stellated polyhedra on the Internet.

Step 4

To draw a freehand 5-pointed star without lifting the pencil begin at the bottom left and draw an upside down V; continue up to the left, crossing the V; draw a horizontal line; and joining this to the starting point. In the next part of the task, children solve problems with missing angles. They need to calculate the internal angle of the pentagon. They could draw five isosceles triangles from the centre of the pentagon. The angles at the centre are 360° ÷ 5 = 72° and the other angles are both (180°– 72°) ÷ 2 = 54°. The internal angle is twice this, 108°. Using the facts that angles on a straight line = 180° and angles in a triangle = 180°, the angles in the star point triangles can be calculated as 72°, 72°and 36°. Children go on to explore four-, six- and seven-pointed stars. Ensure that they use mathematical language to describe the shapes in their stars.

Ensuring progress

Supporting understanding

Check the development of children's language of shape. The words are not complicated but there is a large vocabulary to learn and remember. Encourage children to talk about shape, perhaps by introducing a different shape each day to focus on.

Broadening understanding

In Step 4 children may explore more complex stars and use drawing programs to create stars on the computer. Now that children have learnt how to use compasses for construction, they can use this method to draw other nets, e.g. an octahedron or icosahedron.

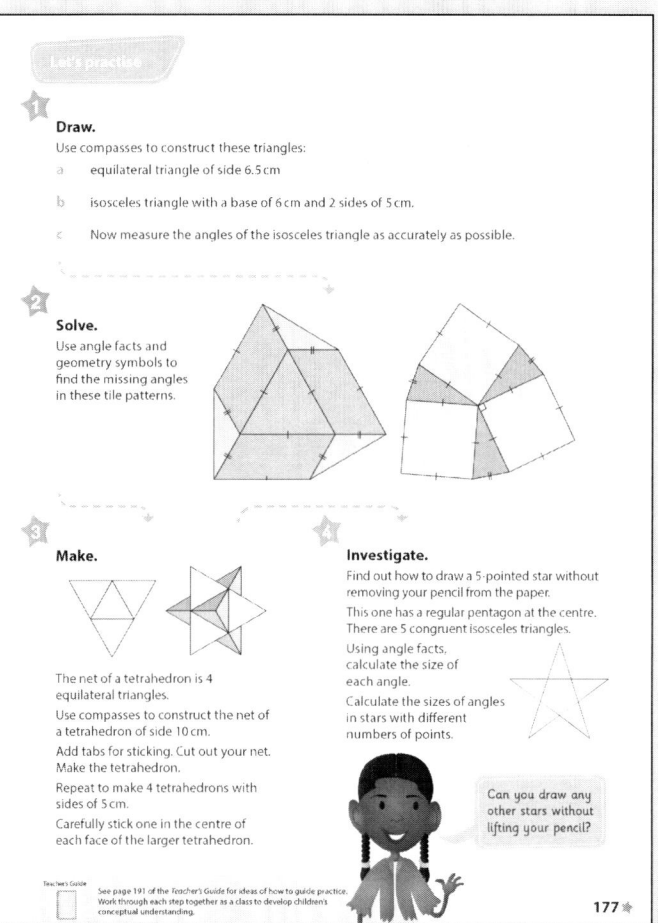

Concept mastered

✓ Children can draw 2-D shapes using given dimensions and angles, including using compasses to construct triangles. They can find unknown angles in triangles, quadrilaterals and regular polygons.

Follow-up ideas

- Develop the mind map produced in the Warming up session into individual or class posters.

- Investigate how the number 360 (degrees in a complete turn) came about. It goes back more than 4000 years to the Sumerians who watched the sun's circular track and noted that it took about 360 days to complete one circuit. They divided the circle into 360° to track its daily movement. In a metric system a complete turn might have been divided into 100 parts. *Would this be better?*

- Challenge children to explore how the work of architects involves careful measurement of angles. Look at architectural drawings for new local buildings or national ones, e.g. The Shard in London.

Answers

Step 1

c   53°, 53, 74° +/– 1° or 2°

Step 2

Angles in equilateral triangle are 60°; angles in parallelograms are 60°and 120°; angles in isosceles triangles are 120° and 30°.

Angles in squares are 90°; angles in isosceles triangles are 30° and 75°.

Step 4

For the 5-pointed star the internal angles of the pentagon are 108° and the angles in the star point triangles are 72°, 72°and 36°.

- **Describe positions on the full coordinate grid (all four quadrants) and draw and reflect simple shapes.**
- **Use simple formulae and find pairs of numbers that satisfy an equation with two unknowns.**

Homework 89 and 90   Practice Book pp 167–72

Representations and resources

Squared paper, rulers, 1–6 dice.

Mathematical vocabulary

Origin, x-coordinate, y-coordinate, plot, quadrant, reflection, translation, intersection.

Warming up

Write the equation $y = 3x + 4$ on the board. Roll a dice to decide the value of x then ask children to work out the value of y. For example, if the dice roll equals two, then $y = 10$. You substitute two for x in the equation so that $y = (3 \times 2) + 4 = 10$. Repeat for more dice rolls and for different equations. This will give children practice in handling equations to support the tasks in the unit.

Background knowledge

An equation with two unknowns such as $y = x + 3$ is known as a linear equation because the solutions can be plotted as coordinate pairs and they lie on the same straight line. To draw a line you must have at least two coordinate pairs.

To find coordinate pairs, choose a value for x and work out the corresponding value of y. Draw a line though the coordinates and extend it in both directions. All the points on the line are solutions for x and y.

Let's learn: Modelling and teaching

Reflection in x- and y-axes

- Ask children to draw the following L-shaped irregular hexagon, A, on a full coordinate grid: (0, 0), (3, 0), (3, 3), (2, 3), (2, 1), (0, 1). Then, ask them to make a paper copy of the shape and reflect it in the x-axis. Ask children to identify and record the new coordinates for A': (0, 0), (3, 0), (3, −3), (2, −3), (2, −1), (0, −1). Ask questions such as: *Have any of the properties of the shape changed? How have the coordinates changed?*

- Now ask children to reflect the original shape in the y-axis. Ask them to analyse the changes. Help them to establish the general rules for reflection in the x-axis – $(x, y) \rightarrow (x, -y)$ – and in the y-axis – $(x, y) \rightarrow (-x, y)$. Elicit that this means that you can work out the coordinate pairs without counting squares.

- Reinforce this by showing the example in the Textbook. Try further examples together.

- Explain the labelling convention: if the original shape is named A, then the shape after reflection (e.g. in the x-axis) is named A' and a second reflection, e.g. in the y-axis, is named A". Ask children to work out the coordinates of shape A": (−3, 2), (−6, 2), (−3, 4).

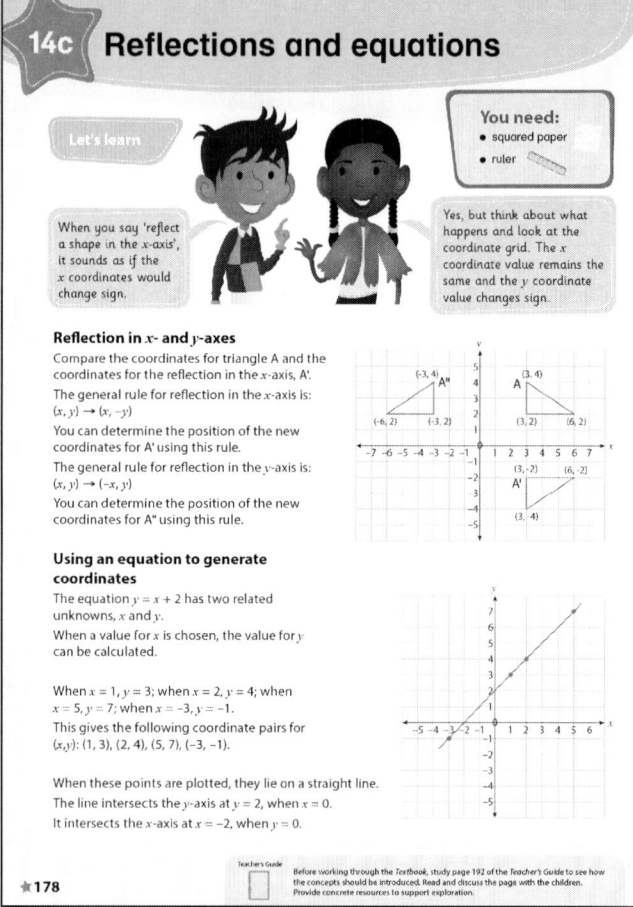

Using an equation to generate coordinates

- Look at the equation $y = x + 2$ in the Textbook. It has two related unknowns, x and y. When a value for x is chosen, the value for y can be calculated. Model how to substitute numbers into the equation to find values. Use the Textbook to show that when the values for the four coordinate pairs in the Textbook are plotted on the coordinate grid, they find that they lie on the same straight line. Reinforce this idea by asking children to plot these points independently. Ask children to calculate further pairs of coordinates and plot them. They will also be on the same straight line. The intersection of the line with the y-axis is at $y = 2$, when $x = 0$ and the intersection with the x-axis is at -2 when $x = -2$ and $y = 0$.

- Ask children to predict where values that satisfy the equation $y = x + 4$ will be found.

Let's practise: Digging deeper

Step 1

This question practises using the general rule to determine the coordinates after reflection in the x-and y-axes as described. Children check their work by plotting the coordinates of the original and the two reflections. Observe how confident children are in drawing and plotting their coordinates. As children become more familiar with the full coordinate grid the structure will become automatic.

Step 2

In this step children use a full coordinate grid to show reflection and translation in the context of a word problem. Encourage children to think about the meaning of the grid. If necessary, discuss the meaning of the x in part f, establishing that the x-coordinate remains unchanged. This is an excellent opportunity to observe whether children are plotting

coordinates consistently accurately. Ask children to discuss part g in pairs before agreeing an answer. Look out for children using the language of coordinates accurately.

Step 3

This step practises generating coordinates from an equation. The partially completed table guides children through the process, providing good preparation for Step 4. You could ask them to add more values and to tell you what they notice about the pattern of the answers (the value of y is always 1 less than the value of x) and how this relates to the equation, $y = x - 1$.

Step 4

This question guides and develops children's understanding of line equations. They work out values for a number of simple equations and plot the coordinate pairs they have generated. All the lines will pass through the origin because in every case when $x = 0$, $y = 0$, generating the coordinate pair (0,0). Gather children's predictions for line $y = 3x$. Ask children to prove their prediction is correct. If it was incorrect, ask: *Explain the reasoning behind your prediction. Can you spot where you went wrong?* Encourage children to explain the pattern by asking: *What do you notice about the length and steepness of the lines?* (The lines become steeper as you move from $y = x$, through $y = 2x$, $y = 3x$, etc.)

Ensuring progress

Supporting understanding

Drawing and labelling x-and y-axes helps to embed this knowledge but for some children this takes valuable learning time. You could provide a pro-forma with or without the numbers. Look out for children who find the abstract nature of algebra and generalisations challenging and give them short sessions of additional support.

Broadening understanding

Step 4 can be extended to more complex equations. Children can predict the pattern of the lines and where the lines will cross the x-and y-axes.

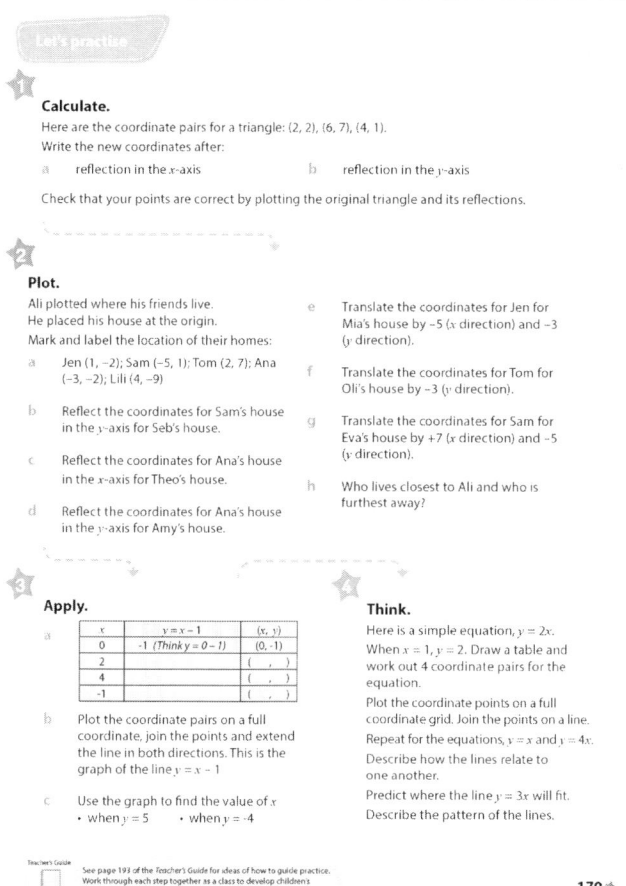

 Concept mastered

Children can describe positions on the full coordinate grid, and draw and reflect simple shapes on the coordinate plane. They understand how the signs of a coordinate pair (x,y) change when reflected in the x- or y-axis. They can use simple equations to generate coordinate pairs and plot them on the full coordinate grid.

Follow-up ideas

- Many computer games use Cartesian coordinates. Ask children to share their experience of games of this type with the class. Some games even use a third dimension. (You may need to check that they are suitable first!)

- Look at the Landranger Ordnance Survey map for the local area and learn how to use six figure grid references to locate important buildings. Children can work out the grid reference for the school and their own home.

- If there are children who are enjoying investigating line equations, you could ask them what to predict might happen when you change the sign and plot the line for $y = -x$. Let them investigate and report their findings.

Answers

Step 1

a $(2, 2) \rightarrow (2, -2)$; $(6, 7) \rightarrow (6, -7)$; $(4, 1) \rightarrow (4, -1)$

b $(2, 2) \rightarrow (-2, 2)$; $(6, 7) \rightarrow (-6, 7)$; $(4, 1) \rightarrow (-4, 1)$

Step 2

b Seb (5, 1)

c Theo (−3, 2)

d Amy (3, −2)

e Mia (−4, −5)

f Oli (2, 2)

g Eva (2, −4)

h Jen is closest and Lili furthest away.

Step 3

a (2, 1); (4, 3); (−1, −2)

c $x = 6$; $x = −3$

Step 4

All lines pass though the origin ($y = 4x$ is the steepest line).

All about nets

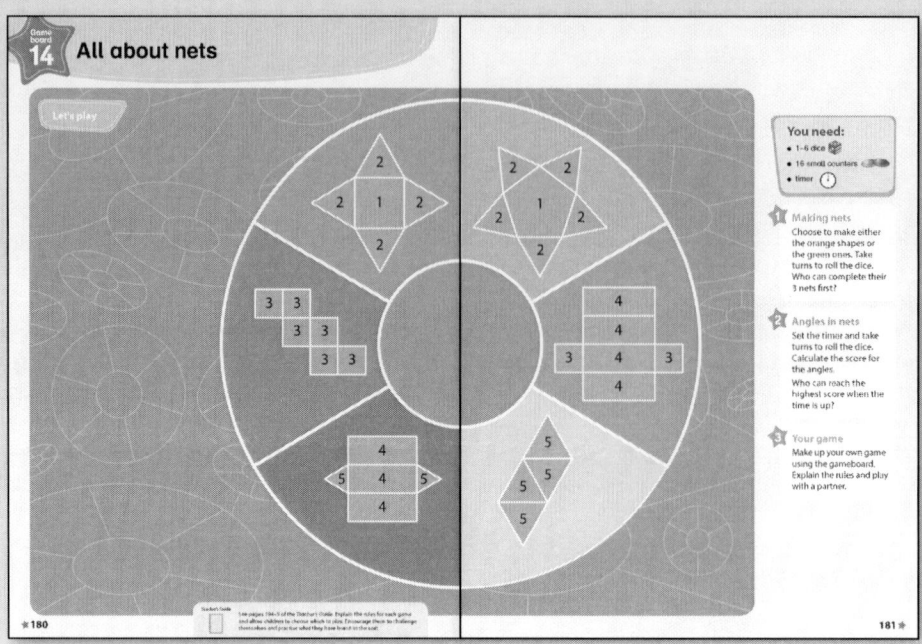

Game 1: Making nets

In this two-player game, children build the nets of common 3-D shapes by taking turns to roll the dice. Once they have 'collected' the faces, the shape is 'folded' by rolling a 6.

Maths focus

- Recognise, describe and build simple 3-D shapes, including making nets

Resources

1–6 dice (1), 16 small counters per player (1 colour per player).

How to play

One player completes the three orange shapes (on the left) and the other completes the three green shapes (on the right). Children take turns to roll the dice and cover one face of one of their chosen shapes, with a counter corresponding to the number rolled. When all the faces have been covered, a 6 must be rolled to 'fold' the net and make the shape. At this point, children stack the counters to show that the shape has been completed. The winner is the first person to complete their three shapes.

Making it easier

A 6 could be used as a 'wild card' and the player may use it to cover any face of their choice.

Making it harder

Instead of covering a face of the correct number with a counter, the player could choose to remove a counter of that number from the other player to slow their opponent's progress.

Game 3: Your game

Children should invent their own game designing rules that use the concepts covered in the unit. You might like to challenge children to make their game easier or harder.

Game 2: Angles in nets

In this more complex game, children analyse the types of angle in the net of the shape that they land on, including angles on a straight line and vertically opposite angles. A table shows how to score and the winner is the person with the highest score after a set time.

Maths focus

- Recognise acute, obtuse and right angles, angles on a straight line and vertically opposite angles

Resources

1–6 dice (1), 1 counter per player (1 colour per player), timer.

How to play

Players take turns to roll the dice and move in a clockwise direction around the board. They score the angles for the net that they land on according to the following table:

Feature	Score
Acute angle	10
Right angle	5
Obtuse angle	20
Angles on a straight line	10
Vertically opposite angles	20

E.g. landing on the triangular prism scores as follows: 6 acute angles scores 60 points, 12 right angles scores 60 points and 4 sets of angles on a straight line scores 40 points, giving a total score of 160 points.

The winner is the person with the higher score when the time is up.

Making it easier

Support children in identifying the vertically opposite angles and the angles on a straight line.

Making it harder

For bonus points, calculate the number of sides of each polygon net, multiply it by 10 and add it to your score.

Choose a game to play.

Game 1: Making nets

You need:
- 1–6 dice
- 16 counters per player (1 colour for each player)

How to play

- Choose either to make the orange shapes or the green ones.
- Take turns to roll the dice.
- Cover with a counter 1 face of a shape containing the number rolled.
- 6 does not score until you have covered all the faces for a net and then you must roll a 6 to 'fold' the net into the 3-D shape.
- The winner is the first person to complete their 3 nets.

Game 2: Angles in nets

You need:
- 1–6 dice
- 1 counter per player (1 colour each)
- timer

How to play

- Set the timer and place your counter on the gameboard on a section of your choice.
- Take turns to roll the dice and move clockwise around the board.
- Calculate the score for the net that you land on using the table (right), e.g. if you land on the triangular prism you will score 160 points: 60 points for 6 acute angles, 60 points for 12 right angles and 40 points for 4 sets of angles on a straight line.
- The winner is the person with the highest score when the time is up.

Feature	Score
Acute angle	10
Right angle	5
Obtuse angle	20
Angles on a straight line	10
Vertically opposite angles	20

Game 3: Your game

- Make up your own game using the gameboard.
- Explain the rules and play with a partner.

And finally ...

Assessment task 1

Resources

Squared paper, plain paper, 3-D shapes, rulers.

Running the task

Children can work through the task individually or in pairs. Working with a partner gives opportunities for discussion about 3-D shapes and reasoning about the types of shapes that fit each statement. Provide 3-D shapes for support so that children can handle them freely. Make plain and squared paper available for drawing the nets.

Evidencing mastery

This task enables children to show understanding of the structure of 3-D shapes as well as knowledge of nets. Eva's nets all have triangles and children who show mastery recognise the general case that all pyramids have triangular faces and therefore have triangles in their nets. Look for children who make this statement and are able to describe pyramids systematically as the number of sides in the base increases, tetrahedron, square-based pyramid, pentagonal-based pyramid, hexagonal-based pyramid, etc. Listen for children who spot that in a triangular prism both ends are triangles and this too fits Eva's statement.

Ali's nets all have rectangular faces. The general statement here is that all prisms have rectangular faces and children showing mastery recognise this. Again, they are able to name the prisms systematically and recognise that a cube with square faces also fits the statement because squares are rectangles. The simplest prism, the triangular prism, is the shape that could appear on both pages. Less secure children may think of shapes one at a time to decide which category they fit.

Children showing mastery confidently sketch the nets, although this ability may be affected by dexterity.

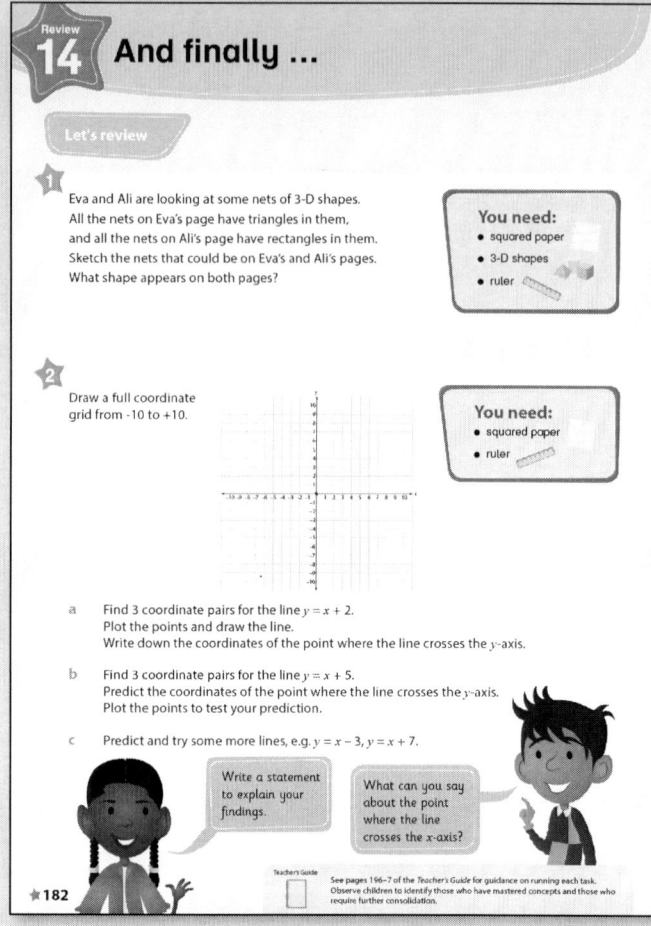

Assessment task 2

Resources

Squared paper, rulers.

Running the task

Prior to the task write a simple line equation on the board, e.g. $y = x + 8$. Work together to find values of y for specific values of x and model systematic recording in a table. Read the task through with children to check that they understand it. If time is limited, you could provide them with a pro-forma of a full coordinate grid.

If children need help getting started, suggest that they find values for y when x equals 1, 3, 5 and -2. Ask children why you should begin with more than two points and why it might be useful to include a negative coordinate. Ask how they will know if the coordinate pairs are correct. Elicit that all the points will fall on the same straight line.

Ensure that all children attempt to formulate a general statement, either verbal or written. They may identify that the

line crosses the y-axis at the number that has been added to x in the equation. If children grasp this quickly, challenge them to express their statement algebraically, e.g. they could state that a line, $y = x + p$, will cross the y-axis at p. Some children may even be able to take this one step further to explain that the line intersects with the x-axis at $-p$. Encourage children to develop their line of thinking as much as possible.

Evidencing mastery

Children showing mastery will carry out the task independently. Look for children who choose a sensible spread of values for x, possibly including a negative value. Listen for children who say that they need three or four coordinate pairs to be certain that they have found the correct line.

Children showing a deeper level of understanding will spot that the lines are all parallel and will be able to formulate a general statement.

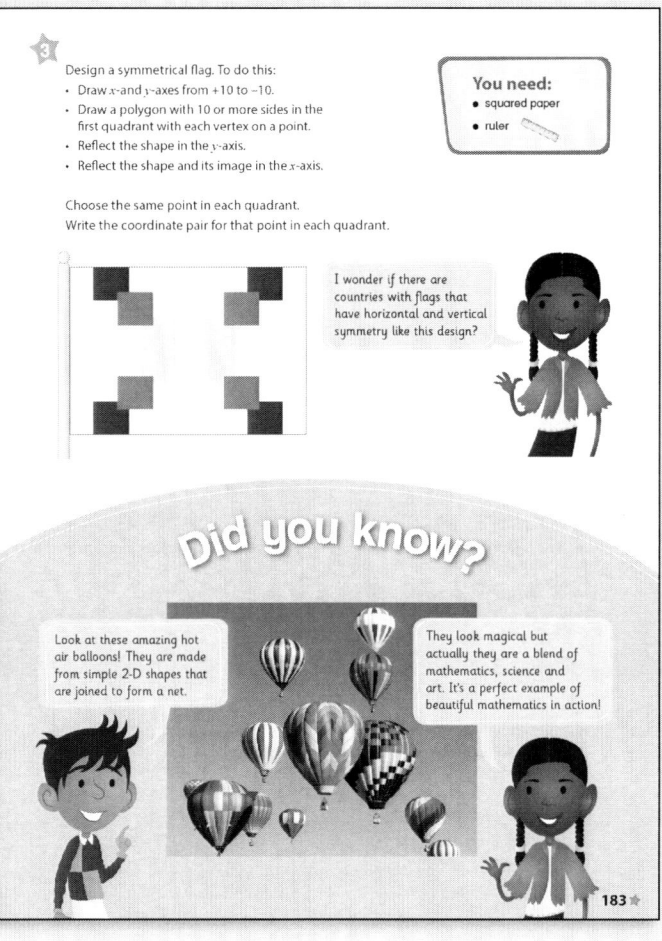

Design a symmetrical flag. To do this:
- Draw *x*-and *y*-axes from +10 to –10.
- Draw a polygon with 10 or more sides in the first quadrant with each vertex on a point.
- Reflect the shape in the *y*-axis.
- Reflect the shape and its image in the *x*-axis.

You need:
- squared paper
- ruler

Choose the same point in each quadrant.
Write the coordinate pair for that point in each quadrant.

I wonder if there are countries with flags that have horizontal and vertical symmetry like this design?

Did you know?

Look at these amazing hot air balloons! They are made from simple 2-D shapes that are joined to form a net.

They look magical but actually they are a blend of mathematics, science and art. It's a perfect example of beautiful mathematics in action!

183

Concepts mastered

✓ Children can recognise, describe and build simple 3-D shapes, including making a variety of nets. They can calculate, estimate and compare volumes of cubes and cuboids using standard units, including cubic centimetres (cm^3), cubic metres (m^3) and cubic millimetres (mm^3).

✓ Children can draw 2-D shapes using given dimensions and angles, including using compasses to construct triangles. They can find unknown angles in triangles, quadrilaterals and regular polygons.

✓ Children can describe positions on the full coordinate grid, and draw and reflect simple shapes on the coordinate plane. They understand how the signs of a coordinate pair (x, y) change when reflected in the *x*- or *y*-axis. They can use simple equations to generate coordinate pairs and plot them on the full coordinate grid.

Assessment task 3

Resources

Squared paper, rulers.

Running the task

Recap the rules of reflection in the *x* and *y* axes. As a class, model the reflection of a triangle in the first quadrant, in the second, third and fourth quandrants. Give children squared paper to carry out the task. Check that children have done this correctly before they proceed. They must first draw and label a full coordinate grid. The polygon should be drawn in the first quadrant with each vertex on an intersection. Ask children to check the number of sides on their polygon to ensure that it has ten or more. They are then asked to reflect the polygon in the *y*-axis and then to reflect both the original and the image in the *x*-axis. This will give a symmetrical 'flag'.

The final task is to choose a particular point on the polygon and write the coordinate pair for that point in each quadrant. Children can colour their 'flag' if they wish.

Evidencing mastery

Children showing mastery will quickly draw a full coordinate grid, labelling and numbering the axes correctly. They will draw a polygon within the first quadrant and reflect it accurately to give a symmetrical design. They will identify the same point in each of the four quadrants and record the coordinate pairs, following the correct order of the quadrants, i.e. (+, +), (–, +) (–, –) and (+, –).

Did you know?

Hot air balloons are complex nets of 2-D shapes that are joined together to make an open 3-D shape, called an envelope. The patterns and designs are colourful and often symmetrical.

Hot air balloons work because hot air rises. As the burner (powered by propane gas) heats the air inside the balloon it becomes lighter than the cooler air on the outside. This causes the balloon to float upwards. If the air is allowed to cool, the balloon begins to come down slowly. Skilled pilots can control the ascent and descent though intermittent use of the burner.

Balloons can fly to amazing heights – the world record is over 21 000 metres. There are some famous balloon festivals around the world; the most famous one in Britain takes place in Bristol during August.

Place value in 6-digit numbers

- Each person draws a grid like this:

You need:

- pencil and paper
- 1–6 dice
- 6 slips of paper with 1, 10, 100, 1000, 10 000, 100 000 written on them
- a partner

Play game 1

- Agree to get either the largest number or the smallest number to win.
- Take turns to roll the dice. Decide where to write that digit on your grid. Once placed, no changes are allowed.
- Keep taking turns until each person has written a digit in each box.
- Read out your finished number. Who has the winning number?

Play game 2

- Create numbers on your grids by rolling the dice as for game 1.
- Then choose a place-value slip from the 6 placed face down on the table.
- If it says '1000', the player with the largest digit in the 'thousand' column scores 1 point.
- Play again. Make different 6-digit numbers and choose a different place-value slip.
- Alternatively, you could choose the place-value slip before creating your numbers. Then you have to choose more carefully where to place the digits rolled.

> Make up other place-value games yourself using these resources.

Please help your child by reading the instructions and doing the activity together.

Multiplying and dividing by 10 and 100

- Join each 'before' and 'after' number to the correct operator.

You need:

- pencil and paper
- partner

Before		After
34.6	×10	569.64
289 700	÷10	18.9
1.89	×100	3460
56 964		14.2
142	÷100	2897

> Make up some pairs of 'before' and 'after' numbers. Challenge a partner to work out what has happened to the 'before' number to create the 'after' number.

Please help your child by reading the instructions and doing the activity together.

1b Comparing and ordering numbers

- Look at the populations of the 8 countries.

Mali	16 259 000
Zambia	15 473 905
Chile	18 006 407
Senegal	13 508 715
Netherlands	16 904 400
Malawi	16 310 431
Ecuador	15 476 000
Kazakhstan	17 476 100

- Which country has the largest population? Which has the smallest?
- Put the countries in order of population size, from smallest to largest.
- Which 2 countries have populations closest to each other by size?

Find out the population of the UK. How does it compare to these country populations?

Please help your child by reading the instructions and doing the activity together.

Rising Stars Mathematics Year 6 © Rising Stars UK Ltd 2016

1b Rounding money amounts

- Look at the final amount of money spent on each shopping receipt. Round each final amount to the nearest pound. Then add them together to find a rounded total of all 3 receipts.
- Next, look back at the original receipts. This time round each final amount to the nearest 10p. Then add them to find the rounded total of all 3 receipts.
- Which rounded total do you think will give an answer closest to the actual total of all 3 receipts? Explain why. Now add the actual numbers using a standard method to see if you were correct.
- Test your theory! Round the individual amounts shown in the grid to the nearest pound and total them. Then round them to the nearest 10p and total them.

	£1243.67 +	£876.32 +	£42.48 =	
Rounded to nearest pound				
Rounded to nearest 10p				

Please help your child by reading the instructions and doing the activity together.

Comparing and ordering fractions

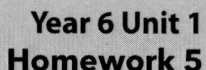

You need:

- pencil and paper
- 1–6 dice
- partner

- Take turns to roll a dice twice to generate a numerator and a denominator, e.g. $\frac{3}{4}$.
- Compare your fraction with your partner's. The person who has made the 'biggest' fraction scores 1 point.
- Continue to play, scoring points and writing down the fractions you make.
- When you have at least 10 different fractions, try to put them in order to find the 'biggest' fraction overall.

> Explain your strategy for creating 'big' fractions. Where should you place the larger rolled digit — on the top (numerator) or on the bottom (denominator)?

Please help your child by reading the instructions and doing the activity together.

Rising Stars Mathematics Year 6 © Rising Stars UK Ltd 201

Simplifying fractions

You need:

- pencil and paper

- Simplify these fractions by looking for a common factor of both the numerator and denominator.

$$\frac{6}{12} \qquad \frac{14}{21} \qquad \frac{35}{40} \qquad \frac{24}{32} \qquad \frac{12}{18}$$

- Now put them in order of size, from smallest to largest.
- Look at these fractions:

$$\frac{4}{7} \qquad \frac{3}{5}$$

Before simplifying they had the same denominator. What could they have been? Is there more than one possibility?

Please help your child by reading the instructions and doing the activity together.

Rising Stars Mathematics Year 6 © Rising Stars UK Ltd 201

Colouring sections of a square

1d

* Draw a square measuring 10 cm by 10 cm.
* Colour $\frac{1}{10}$ of the whole square in green.
* Colour 0.25 of the whole square in red.
* Colour 15% of the whole square in yellow.
* How much of the square has been coloured altogether? Write the amount as a fraction, as a decimal and as a percentage.
* Continue to colour in the square using the 3 colours. Record how much of each colour is used.
* Write a list of each colour and the fraction of the whole square that is now that colour. Add the fractions.

You need:

* pencil
* cm-squared paper
* ruler
* colouring pencils

It is easier to add fractions if they have the same denominator.

Please help your child by reading the instructions and doing the activity together.

Rising Stars Mathematics Year 6 © Rising Stars UK Ltd 2016

Equivalence

1d

* Pick 2 of the digit cards. Use them to make a percentage, e.g. 62. Then write this percentage as a decimal (remember that 62% is 62 hundredths) and as a fraction. If you can, simplify the fraction as well.

You need:

* pencil and paper
* digit cards 1–9 (2 of each)

* Write the numbers in a chart like this:

percentage	decimal	fraction	simplified fraction
62%	0.62	$\frac{62}{100}$	$\frac{31}{50}$

* Do this 8 times.
* Number them in order from 1 to 8, where 1 is the largest amount and 8 is the smallest.
* Is it easier to order the percentages or the simplified fractions? Explain why.

Please help your child by reading the instructions and doing the activity together.

Adding and subtracting with 4-digit numbers

You need:
- pencil and paper

1034 1527 2943 2254

3521 3957

4982 4132 5156 6792

- Which 2 numbers add to make the total nearest to 4000?
- Complete the addition and then subtract the total from 4000 to see how close you were.
- Could you get even closer by adding 2 different numbers?
- Find which pairs of numbers add to create the totals closest to 5000, 6000, 7000, 8000, 9000 and 10 000.

Please help your child by reading the instructions and doing the activity together.

Combining lengths

You need:
- pencil and paper
- tape measure marked in cm and mm
- 6 household objects

- Find 6 objects in your house. Each must have 1 length measuring between 25 cm and 100 cm, e.g. width of a coffee table, length of a table mat, height of a small lamp.
- Record the measurements using decimal notation, e.g. 43.8 cm.
- Which object lengths added together make a total nearest to 1 m?
- Find 2 object lengths which have a difference closest to 20 cm.
- Add all 6 object lengths to find your 'grand total' and convert the answer to millimetres.

Please help your child by reading the instructions and doing the activity together.

2b Order of operations

- Does the order of your calculations matter?
  Will you always get the same answer?
  Try these working from left to right:

You need:
- pencil and paper
- calculator

Start			
2400	× 4	÷ 6	=
2400	÷ 6	× 4	=

Start			
1837	− 500	× 4	=
1837	× 4	− 500	=

- What do you notice?

Some pairs of operations can be done in any order, but some cannot. Investigate to find out which are which.

Please help your child by reading the instructions and doing the activity together.

2b Using all 4 operations in different ways

- Write the digits 1 to 9 in order on a piece of paper. Leave gaps between each digit.

- Now put a + sign between each digit and complete the calculation. What total do you get?

- Write the digits 1 to 9 again. This time put a + sign in the first gap, then a − sign in the next gap and keep alternating + and − signs between each digit. Complete the calculation. What is the final answer?

- Now put a × sign between each digit. What is your answer? You may need to use a calculator!

You need:
- pencil and paper
- calculator

Try using a combination of +, −, × and ÷ signs, one between each digit. How close to 100 can you get? Have a go!

Please help your child by reading the instructions and doing the activity together.

Comparing lengths and writing equations

You need:
- pencil and paper
- scissors

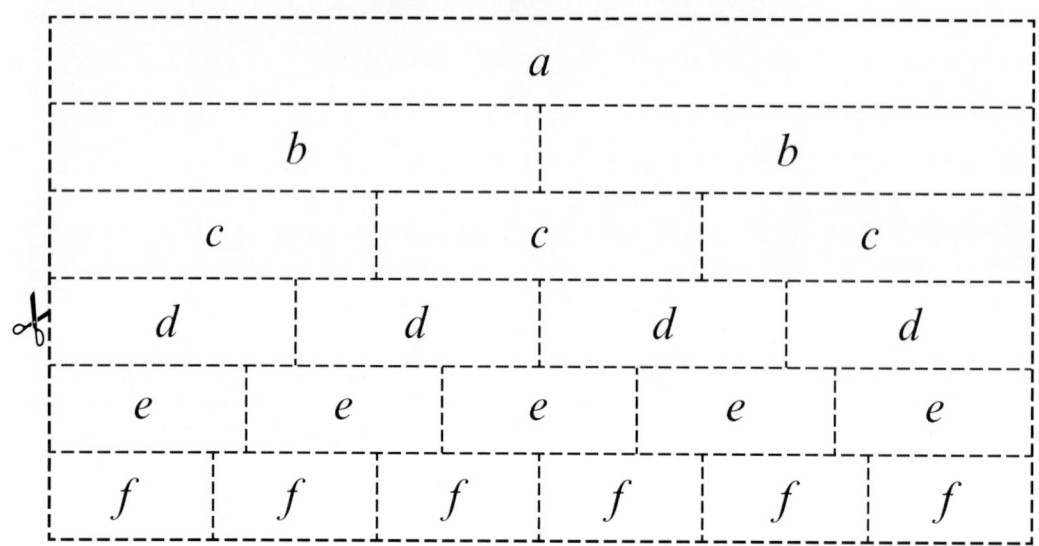

- Cut out these bars and compare them with each other.
- Use them to write some algebraic equations, e.g.

$$d + d + b = a \qquad f + f = c \qquad 3c + 2b = 2a$$

- If the value of c is 12, what are the other values? One value is not a whole number. Which one?

 Please help your child by reading the instructions and doing the activity together.

Rising Stars Mathematics Year 6 © Rising Stars UK Ltd 201

Finding possible answers

You need:
- pencil and paper

The local bus company has 5 buses: A, B, C, D and E. This week the company has been recording the number of passengers travelling at midday on each bus.

Individual bus totals have been lost, but some information remains:

> Bus A + Bus B = 36 passengers
> Bus B + Bus C = 40 passengers
> Bus C + Bus D = 37 passengers
> Bus D + Bus E = 39 passengers

- What could the individual bus totals have been? (There is more than 1 possibility.)
- If the total number of passengers travelling on the buses at midday was 99, which individual totals are the correct ones?

Please help your child by reading the instructions and doing the activity together.

Rising Stars Mathematics Year 6 © Rising Stars UK Ltd 201

3a Multiplication of 3-digit by 2-digit numbers

The number 472 has been multiplied by a 2-digit number. The answer that results is:

▸ an even number

▸ has digits which sum to 15

▸ is larger than 7100.

- Has 472 been multiplied by 15, 24 or 19?

Prove that you have chosen correctly.

Please help your child by reading the instructions and doing the activity together.

Rising Stars Mathematics Year 6 © Rising Stars UK Ltd 2016

3a Cycling times – long multiplication

The average time taken to cycle 10 miles is 24 minutes.

- Joshua cycles at the average speed. How long would it take him to cycle 40 miles at this rate?

- Caitlyn cycles at the average speed for 156 minutes. How far has she travelled?

- If a cyclist completes a 10-mile race at the average speed every day of the year, how much time would he have spent cycling that year? Write your answer in days and hours.

Please help your child by reading the instructions and doing the activity together.

3b Multiplication investigation

You need:

● pencil and paper

- Use the digits 1, 2, 3, 4 and 5 to make multiplications. Each digit can only be used once and the multiplication must be a 3-digit number multiplied by a 2-digit number, e.g. 123 × 45 or 251 × 34.
- Which number arrangement gives the largest product? Which gives the smallest product?
- Explore which 2 arrangements give close totals.

Do you notice any other patterns? Talk about them with a friend or family member.

Please help your child by reading the instructions and doing the activity together.

Rising Stars Mathematics Year 6 © Rising Stars UK Ltd 201

3b Multiplying 3-digit numbers by multiples of 10

You need:

● pencil and paper
● digit cards 1–9
● 1–6 dice
● partner

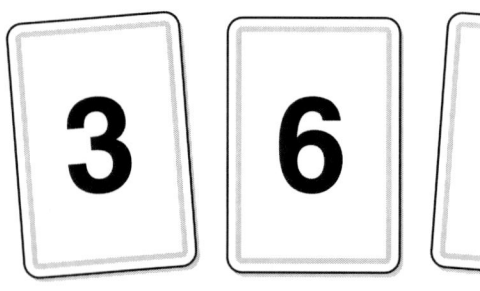

- Each player selects 3 of the digit cards and uses them to create a 3-digit number, e.g. 362.
- Take turns to roll a dice and multiply the number rolled by 10, e.g. if 4 is rolled the number to be used is 40.
- Multiply your 3-digit number by the multiple of 10 you rolled with the dice. Write the product, e.g. 362 × 40 = 14 480.
- The player with the largest product scores 1 point.
- Play the game 5 times. The player with the most points wins.

 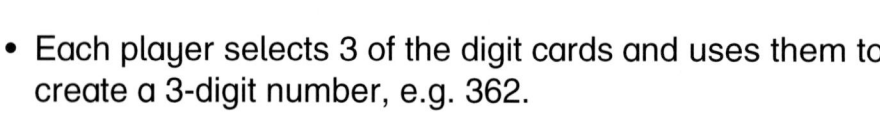 Please help your child by reading the instructions and doing the activity together.

Rising Stars Mathematics Year 6 © Rising Stars UK Ltd 201

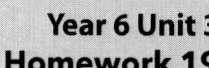

Using place value when multiplying and dividing decimals

You need:
- pencil and paper

These multiplications and divisions are similar to those you know from your multiplication tables. BUT, 1 number is 10 times smaller so your answer will be 10 times smaller, e.g. $6 \times 4 = 24$ ➤ $6 \times 0.4 = 2.4$

- Complete these:

  $8 \times 0.5 =$ $3 \times 0.7 =$ $9 \times 0.6 =$ $5 \times 0.3 =$

  $4.8 \div 6 =$ $1.6 \div 4 =$ $3.5 \div 7 =$ $2.4 \div 8 =$

- Explore what happens when 1 of the multipliers or dividers is 100 times smaller.

- Can your multiplication tables still help?

Try out some multiplications and divisions of your own and use them to explain your discoveries to a grown up.

Please help your child by reading the instructions and doing the activity together.

Rising Stars Mathematics Year 6 © Rising Stars UK Ltd 2016

Finding the mean (average) using division

You need:
- pencil and paper
- catalogue or Internet access

- Charlie bought 8 different CDs. He spent £51.60. What was the mean cost of 1 CD?

- Amanda spent £9.72 on 6 new nail varnishes. Work out the mean cost of 1 nail varnish.

- Look in a catalogue or online at items you might like to buy. Choose a type of product, e.g. stationery sets or model cars or hair accessories.

- Pick 5 different products of that type. Write down their individual prices and add to find the total.

- Now use division to find the mean cost of 1 of those products. You may need to round your answer to the nearest penny.

Please help your child by reading the instructions and doing the activity together.

Mystery numbers

You need:
- pencil and paper

- There are 2 numbers. One number is 4 times bigger than the other. One of the numbers is 20. What could the other number be? Is there more than one possibility?
- There are 2 numbers. One number is 3 times smaller than the other. One of the numbers is 21. What could the other number be? Is there more than one possibility?
- There are 2 numbers. One number is 7 times bigger than the other. Both numbers are less than 50. What could they be? Explain any patterns that you notice.

Remember, patterns always show up better if you work systematically.

Please help your child by reading the instructions and doing the activity together.

Rising Stars Mathematics Year 6 © Rising Stars UK Ltd 201

Using ratio and proportion

You need:
- pencil and paper

Mr Brown bought 100 lengths of copper pipe to sell in his plumbing shop.

He spent exactly £100.

> Long pipes cost £5.00.
> Medium length pipes cost £1.00.
> Short pipes cost 50p.

- How many of each could he have bought for exactly £100?
- Explore different combinations and record your answers.
- Mr Brown bought some of each pipe size. He got the same number of 2 of the pipe sizes. How many of each pipe size did he buy for exactly £100?

Please help your child by reading the instructions and doing the activity together.

Rising Stars Mathematics Year 6 © Rising Stars UK Ltd 201

Garden design

4a

You need:

- pencil
- squared paper
- ruler

- Draw this garden on your squared paper. Your diagram must be drawn to scale. Decide on a suitable scale to use.

> The garden has a length of 15 metres and a width of 12 metres. In the garden you will have some flowerbeds and a paved patio. The patio must have a total area of 100 square metres.

- Investigate different designs for the garden. Mark the measurements on each design you make and check that the area for the patio is the correct size.

> Which design contains a patio with the smallest perimeter?

Please help your child by reading the instructions and doing the activity together.

Rising Stars Mathematics Year 6 © Rising Stars UK Ltd 2016

Triangular areas

4a

You need:

- pencil
- cm-squared paper
- ruler

- Draw 5 rectangles with a length of 8 cm and a height of 4 cm. Mark a point in a different position on the top side of each rectangle and join it to the corners at the bottom to create 5 different triangles, e.g.

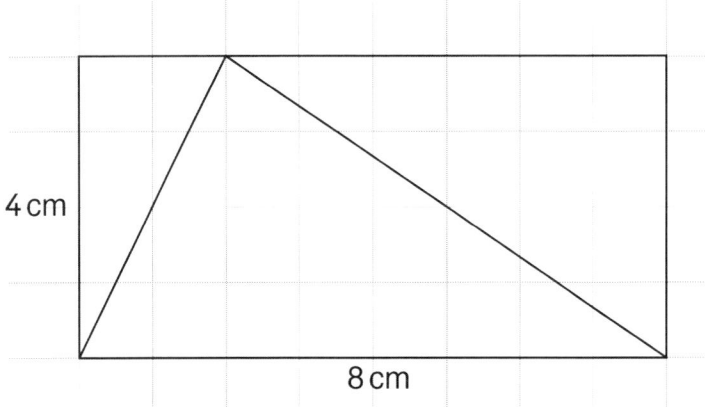

4 cm

8 cm

- Calculate the area of each triangle using the formula $\frac{1}{2}$(base × height).

- Now measure the perimeter of each triangle using your ruler.

- What do you discover? Are all the areas and perimeters the same?

Please help your child by reading the instructions and doing the activity together.

4b Exploring angles

- Angles on a straight line total 180°. Work out the unknown angles in these diagrams.

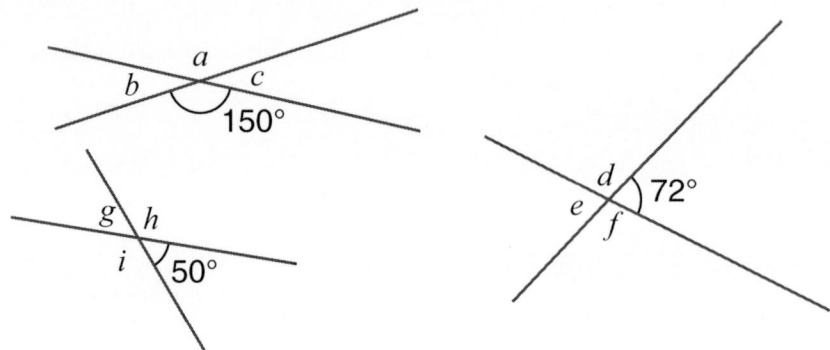

- What do you notice about the opposite angles?
- Draw some other pairs of straight lines which intersect. Look at the angles around the point of intersection to check your theory.
- Use a protractor to measure the angles or use some other method to convince a grown up of your findings.

 Please help your child by reading the instructions and doing the activity together.

Rising Stars Mathematics Year 6 © Rising Stars UK Ltd 201

4b Exterior and interior angles of a triangle

- Draw any triangle. Extend 1 of its sides to create an exterior angle, e.g.

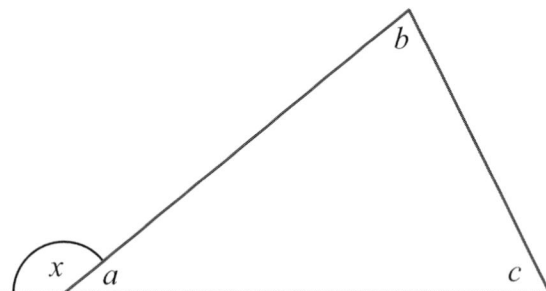

- Measure all 4 angles a, b, c and x.
- Can you see a relationship between any of the angles or pairs of angles?
- Sum angles b and c. Now can you see any relationship?
- Draw other triangles to see whether this happens again.
- Have you found a pattern? Try to write a formula to explain what you have found out.
- Can you explain why this always works?

Please help your child by reading the instructions and doing the activity together.

Rising Stars Mathematics Year 6 © Rising Stars UK Ltd 20

Stacking cubes into a cuboid shape

A packaging firm has 24 equal sized cube-shaped boxes to deliver.

The firm needs to find ways to stack the boxes efficiently on the delivery van.

The best way to do this will be to arrange the boxes into 1 large cuboid shape.

- How many different ways can they do this?
- Draw diagrams and list the dimensions of the different cuboids they could make, e.g.

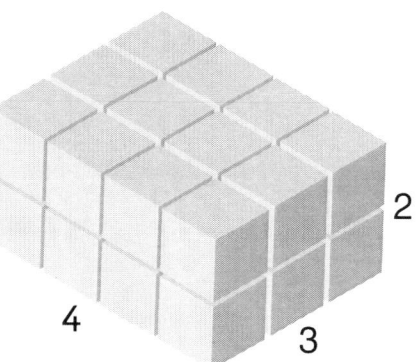

Nets of cuboids

- Choose a box and look for the seams on the edges of the box where the box has been glued together. Slide a ruler down these seams very carefully to open up the box.
- Lay the opened-out flat box on the table. This is the 'net' for the cuboid box. Try folding it back up to create the original box again.
- Repeat this for different-sized cuboid boxes. Does the net always look the same?
- Are the same number and type of 2-D shapes always included in the net, even if they may be joined together in different ways?

Draw diagrams of different nets which all create cuboids when they are folded up to make a 3-D shape.

Exploring coordinates

You need:
- pencil
- squared paper
- ruler

- Draw a *y*-axis on squared paper which goes from −10 to +10. Then draw an *x*-axis which crosses the *y*-axis at 0 and goes from −10 to +10.
- Plot these points on the grid you have drawn:
  (−4, −7) (1, 3) (−3, −5) (−1, −1) (2, 5) (−2, −3) (−5, −9) (0, 1)
- Join the points and explain what you notice.
- Now choose 4 of the points and add 3 to each of the *x*-coordinates. Plot the 4 new points and join them with a line.
- For the other 4 points, subtract 3 from each of the *x*-coordinates. Plot the 4 new points and join them with a line.
- What has happened? Try to explain any patterns you have spotted.
- Predict and then explore what happens when you add or subtract a number from some or all of the *y*-coordinates.

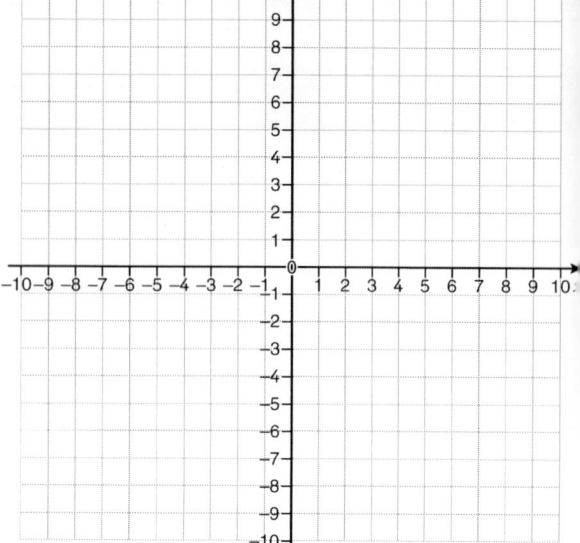

 Please help your child by reading the instructions and doing the activity together.

Rising Stars Mathematics Year 6 © Rising Stars UK Ltd 201

Bank balances and negative numbers

You need:
- pencil and paper
- toy catalogue or Internet access

- Find a toy catalogue or look online at toys and their prices.
- Choose 6 items to buy. Each should cost between £10 and £20.
- Imagine you have £70 of birthday money in your bank account.
- If you buy the 6 chosen items, will you have any money left in your account? Or will you be left with a negative money amount which you owe to the bank?

£70

Please help your child by reading the instructions and doing the activity together.

Rising Stars Mathematics Year 6 © Rising Stars UK Ltd 201

5b Converting measurements

- Each person draws a grid like this. The boxes signify thousands, hundreds, tens and ones in gram measurements.

| | | | | grams |

You need:
- pencil and paper
- 1–6 dice
- partner

- Take turns to roll the dice and decide where to place that digit on your grid. The aim is to make the heaviest gram measurement.

- When both players have rolled the dice 4 times and created a gram measurement, compare the masses and see whose is heaviest. That person scores 1 point.

- Next convert the gram measurement into kilograms and grams and finally into kilograms. Score extra points if you do this correctly, e.g. 4521 g = 4 kg 521 g = 4.521 kg.

Play again!

Please help your child by reading the instructions and doing the activity together.

Rising Stars Mathematics Year 6 © Rising Stars UK Ltd 2016

5b Measuring time

- You need a stopwatch or timer for this task. Ideally it needs to show minutes, seconds and tenths/hundredths of a second, e.g. 1 minute, 24 seconds and 35 hundredths of a second displayed like this:

| 0 | 1 | . | 2 | 4 | . | 3 | 5 |

You need:
- pencil and paper
- stopwatch or timer
- friends and family

Compare results and see who is the fastest! Are there any trends, e.g. are younger people quicker at running?

- Choose some short activities to do and write them down like a mini-Olympics, e.g.
  - ▶ Write your name and address.
  - ▶ Eat an apple.
  - ▶ Go up and down the stairs 5 times.
  - ▶ Run round the garden.

- Complete the tasks yourself and record the time you took to do each.

- Then challenge other family members or friends to do the same task in less time.

Please help your child by reading the instructions and doing the activity together.

Negative numbers, bridging zero

6a

There are 3 versions of this game – easy, medium and hard. Start easy and get harder!

You need:
- pencil and paper
- 1–6 dice
- partner

- **Easy:** each player rolls the dice once, writes down the number and subtracts 10 from it, e.g. 4 − 10 = −6. The first to reach a correct answer scores 1 point. Play again.

- **Medium:** this time roll the dice twice to get a 2-digit number. Write it down and subtract 100 from it, e.g. 52 − 100 = −48.

- **Hard:** roll the dice 3 times to get a 3-digit number. Write it down and subtract 1000 from it, e.g. 341 − 1000 = −659. Keep playing. Do you get quicker with practice?

> Talk about the maths you have used to help you calculate the answers. Do you have any speedy shortcuts to tell each other about?

Please help your child by reading the instructions and doing the activity together.

Rising Stars Mathematics Year 6 © Rising Stars UK Ltd 201

6a

World temperatures

- Look at these December average temperatures from cities around the world.

Toronto, Canada	−14°C
Rio de Janeiro, Brazil	31°C
New York, USA	2°C
Moscow, Russia	−3°C
Helsinki, Finland	−1°C
Madrid, Spain	10°C

You need:
- pencil and paper
- Internet access

- Order the temperatures from hottest to coldest.

- Find the difference between the hottest and the coldest temperatures.

- The December average temperature for London in the UK is 7°C. Calculate the difference between London's temperature and each of the other cities.

- Find and compare the temperatures in each of these cities in July.

- Which country has the greatest temperature range between July and December?

Please help your child by reading the instructions and doing the activity together.

Rising Stars Mathematics Year 6 © Rising Stars UK Ltd 201

Money box totals

You need:
- pencil and paper

- Look at the money boxes.
  Read this information:

  ▶ 8 children have been collecting money for charity. Here are their money boxes.

  ▶ They have collected £84 in total.

  ▶ Each child has collected a different amount (whole pounds only).

  ▶ In this arrangement, every line of 3 money boxes totals £33.

- Can you work out how much money each child has collected?

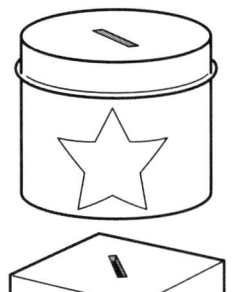
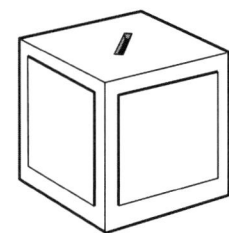

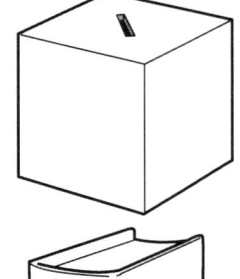
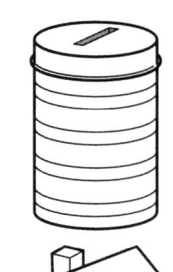

Rising Stars Mathematics Year 6 © Rising Stars UK Ltd 2016

Meal planning

You need:
- pencil and paper
- shopping receipts, or a trip to the shops to look at prices, or Internet access

- Think about the people in your family and what they like to eat.

- You are going to plan a 3-course meal for them and calculate the cost.

- Think of a starter, main course, dessert and drink.

- The main course should include protein (e.g. meat or eggs), vegetables and carbohydrate (e.g. potatoes or pasta).

- Think about the quantity of each item that you will need. Now look through old receipts, or look at prices either online or at a shop, to find out the cost of each item.

- Calculate the cost per person and the cost for your whole family to enjoy your chosen menu.

Fast times

Here are the results of an 800 m world running race. Look how close the results are! They are all under 2 minutes!

You need:
- pencil and paper

- Round each runner's time to the nearest whole second.
- How does this affect the results?
- Instead of having 10 clear places with different times, how many places would there be?
- Round each time to the nearest $\frac{1}{10}$ of a second. Does this provide enough information to place all the runners individually?
- Consider if this is why the results are shown to the nearest $\frac{1}{1000}$ of a second.

1	Adam Kszczot (Pol)	1:45.120
2	Nijel Amos (Bot)	1:45.250
3	Amel Tuka (Bsh)	1:45.450
4	Mohammed Aman (Eth)	1:45.490
5	Nader Belhanbel (Mor)	1:45.940
6	Robert Biwott (Ken)	1:46.170
7	Antoine Gakeme (Bdi)	1:46.820
8	Alfred Kipketer (Ken)	1:46.980
9	Pierre-Ambroise Bosse (Fra)	1:47.010
10	Asbel Kiprop (Ken)	1:47.090

 Please help your child by reading the instructions and doing the activity together.

Rising Stars Mathematics Year 6 © Rising Stars UK Ltd 201

 # Multiplying and rounding decimals

You need:
- pencil and paper
- calculator
- partner

- Each player writes down a 2-place decimal less than 10, e.g. 6.42 and 3.78.
- Together estimate what the product would be if the 2 numbers were multiplied. Write this estimate, e.g. 20.
- Use a calculator to work out the actual product and then round the answer to the nearest whole number, e.g. $6.42 \times 3.78 = 24.2676$, rounded ➡ 24.
- How close was your estimate?

Play several times. Do your estimates get any closer as you play?

⭐ **216** Please help your child by reading the instructions and doing the activity together.

Rising Stars Mathematics Year 6 © Rising Stars UK Ltd 201

Using a formula

Year 6 Unit 6
Homework 39

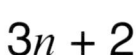

| $3n + 2$ | $4n - 5$ | $n + 12$ |
| $7n - 6$ | $(n \div 2) + 5$ | $6n - 1$ |

You need:
- formula cards, cut out
- 1–6 dice
- partner

- There are 6 rounds to this game. The winner has the largest score at the end of the game.
- Shuffle the formula cards and place them face down on the table.
- Pick a formula card and place it face up for both players to see.
- Each player rolls the dice. The number rolled represents n in the formula.
- Each player calculates their own answer and writes it down.

- Keep turning over the formula cards and rolling the dice until all 6 formula cards have been used and each player has 6 answers recorded. Total the answers to find each player's final score. The highest score wins.
- Does rolling high numbers on the dice guarantee a win?
- Think of other ways you could use the formula cards and dice to create a game.

Please help your child by reading the instructions and doing the activity together.

Describing patterns

Year 6 Unit 6
Homework 40

- Look at this letter T as it grows in size. Count the individual squares.

You need:
- paper and pencil
- ruler

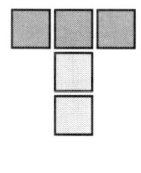 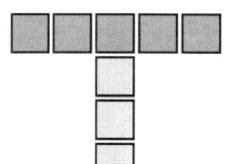 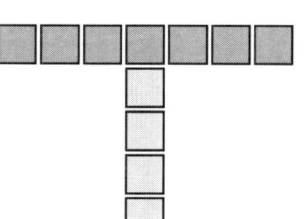

- Describe how the vertical column is increasing in size and how the horizontal row is increasing in size. Is there a pattern?
- Draw the next 3 letter Ts in the sequence. Count the squares to check if your pattern description is correct.
- Now that you have drawn the first 6 letters in the sequence, can you predict the size of the 10th letter?
- Can you predict the size of the 20th letter?
- Can you devise a rule which would help you to predict the number of squares in the 100th letter in the sequence?

Please help your child by reading the instructions and doing the activity together.

Rising Stars Mathematics Year 6 © Rising Stars UK Ltd 2016 **217**

7a Creating and converting fractions

Round 1

- The first player will create quarters and the other will create fifths.
- Each player rolls the dice to generate the numerator for their first fraction.
- Repeat this 3 times so that the first player has 3 fractions each with 4 as the denominator. The other player will have 3 fractions, each with 5 as denominator.
- Each players adds their 3 fractions to find a total.

Round 2

- Play again, but with the first player collecting thirds and the other player collecting sevenths.

Round 3

- Play again, this time deciding for yourself which fractions to collect.
- Investigate how to improve your chances of becoming the winner.
- Now compare your fraction totals to see which player has the largest. You should find a common denominator and convert your fractions to compare them accurately.

You need:

- pencil and paper
- 1–6 dice
- partner

> Remember, a common denominator is a multiple of both the fraction denominators.

Please help your child by reading the instructions and doing the activity together.

Rising Stars Mathematics Year 6 © Rising Stars UK Ltd 201

7a Adding and subtracting fractions

Here are the results of the school shot-put throws.

	Jamie	Anesh	Crystal	Amy
Round 1	$8\frac{2}{3}$ m	$8\frac{5}{9}$ m	$9\frac{1}{3}$ m	$8\frac{4}{6}$ m
Round 2	$9\frac{2}{6}$ m	$9\frac{1}{9}$ m	$9\frac{1}{3}$ m	$8\frac{6}{9}$ m

You need:

- pencil and paper
- ball
- measuring tape

- Convert the fraction lengths so that they have a common denominator. Then compare them to find:
  - ▸ the winner of Round 1 and the winner of Round 2
  - ▸ the difference in individual lengths thrown between Round 1 and Round 2, saying whether their lengths increased or decreased
  - ▸ the total length thrown by each player during both rounds.
- Try throwing a ball in the garden and measuring the length you threw. Does your score increase with practice?

Please help your child by reading the instructions and doing the activity together.

Rising Stars Mathematics Year 6 © Rising Stars UK Ltd 201

Converting fractions, decimals and percentages

You need:
- pencil and paper
- 100 square
- counter (or 5p coin)
- partner

- Takes turns to roll the counter onto the 100 square to select a number.
- Write this as a percentage, e.g. 42%.
- Now convert this percentage into a fraction and a decimal, e.g. $\frac{42}{100}$ and 0.42. Where possible, simplify the fraction, e.g. $\frac{21}{50}$.
- Repeat this 5 times so that each player has 5 sets of equivalents.
- Add these 5 attempts together to see which player has created the largest amount. You can choose whether to add the 5 decimals or the 5 fractions or the 5 percentages but you must be able to compare your result with your partner's result.

Please help your child by reading the instructions and doing the activity together.

Rising Stars Mathematics Year 6 © Rising Stars UK Ltd 2016

Finding fractions, decimals and percentages of amounts

You need:
- pencil and paper

- Choose an even 2-digit number and write it down.
- Find these amounts of your chosen number:

$\frac{3}{4}$ 0.5   20% $1\frac{1}{4}$ 1.5   4% $\frac{1}{5}$ 75%

- Now choose an odd 2-digit number and find the same amounts of it.
- Explain whether it is easier to find these particular amounts of an odd number or of an even number and why this might be.

Choose a 2-digit number that is a multiple of 5 and repeat the experiment. Does being a multiple of 5 help?

Please help your child by reading the instructions and doing the activity together.

7c Making rectangles and using formulae

- Each player chooses 2 number cards, e.g. 4 and 17.
- Each player then draws a rectangle with sides the length of the numbers they have chosen (you do not need to draw these to scale).
- Next each player uses these formulae to find the perimeter and area of their rectangle:

$P = 2l + 2w$

$A = l \times w$

- Score 1 point for the largest perimeter and 1 point for the largest area.
- Do this 5 times so that each player has created 5 rectangles. The winner is the person who scores the most points.

You need:
- 2 sets of 1–20 number cards
- pencil and paper
- partner

Please help your child by reading the instructions and doing the activity together.

Rising Stars Mathematics Year 6 © Rising Stars UK Ltd 201

7c Perimeter and area formulae and patterns

- Remember the formulae for finding the perimeter and area of rectangles:
  Perimeter = 2 length + 2 width
  Area = length × width

You need:
- pencil and paper
- ruler

- Draw a set of 5 rectangles that increase in size. The first rectangle measures 1 cm × 3 cm. The second has double the length and double the width of the first rectangle (i.e. 2 cm × 6 cm). The third is double again and so on. The first 2 are shown here.

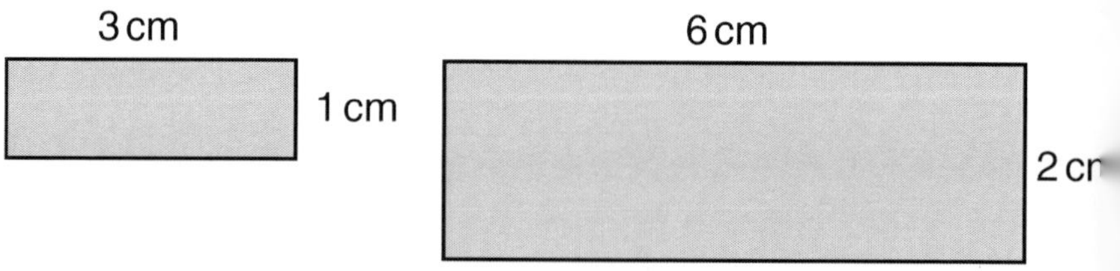

3 cm

1 cm

6 cm

2 cm

- Find and record the perimeter and area of each.
- What patterns can you see? How do the perimeter and area increase each time?
- Can you use your discoveries to predict the area and perimeter of the 8th and 10th rectangle in this series?

Please help your child by reading the instructions and doing the activity together.

Rising Stars Mathematics Year 6 © Rising Stars UK Ltd 201

Algebra puzzle

You need:
- pencil and paper

- What is the value of n in this equation?

  $n + 8 = 17$ A bar model can help:

n	8
17	

- Draw a bar model to help you work out n in this equation.

  $16 + n + n = 28$

- Use the same strategies to solve this puzzle. The numbers show the totals of columns and rows. Find the value of each letter and the remaining totals.

A	C	A	B	
C	B	C	A	25
B	B	B	B	20
A	C	C	A	
			26	

Please help your child by reading the instructions and doing the activity together.

Rising Stars Mathematics Year 6 © Rising Stars UK Ltd 2016

Finding unknown values using balancing

You need:
- pencil and paper

- Work through each of these number balances in order to find the values for a, b, c, d, e and f.

1. $a + 6$ 18
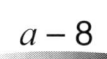

2. $a - 8$ b
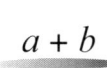

3. $a + b$ c

4. $c + 2$ d

5. $2d + 14$ e

6. $e - c$ $f - 1$

	a	b	c	d	e	f
value						

Please help your child by reading the instructions and doing the activity together.

Prime factors

Here is a set of prime factors.

You need:

- pencil and paper

Investigate which numbers between 1 and 30 cannot be made by multiplying these prime factors.

- Choose 2 or more of these prime factors. Multiply them to see what number you can make, e.g. 2 × 3 = 6 or 3 × 3 × 5 = 45. You can use each number twice because there are 2 of each in the list.
- What is the largest product you can make?
- What is the smallest product?
- Can you create more than 10 different products?

Please help your child by reading the instructions and doing the activity together.

Rising Stars Mathematics Year 6 © Rising Stars UK Ltd 201

Common multiples

- Choose 2 of the digit cards, e.g. 3 and 5.

3 × 5

- Multiply them to find a common multiple, e.g. 3 × 5 = 15.

You need:

- pencil and paper
- digit cards 1–6

- Is that the lowest possible common multiple of your 2 numbers?
- Repeat 4 times with different pairs of numbers.
- Now choose 3 numbers and multiply to find a common multiple. Is that the lowest common multiple?
- Keep finding lowest common multiples of sets of 3 numbers.

Talk about any patterns you notice.

Please help your child by reading the instructions and doing the activity together.

Rising Stars Mathematics Year 6 © Rising Stars UK Ltd 20

Running times

- These runners have all completed a 6-mile cross-country race. Work out each runner's average speed per mile.

Runner 1	43.44 min
Runner 2	42.96 min
Runner 3	43.14 min
Runner 4	42.30 min
Runner 5	43.32 min

- How fast would a runner need to be travelling per mile to achieve a final time of less than 40 minutes?

Please help your child by reading the instructions and doing the activity together.

Rising Stars Mathematics Year 6 © Rising Stars UK Ltd 2016

Multiplying decimals

Here are some decimals:

2.6

3.7

3.4

3.9

4.1

2.9

2 of these decimals have been multiplied.
The answer reached is 9.86.

- Which 2 decimals were multiplied?
- What other products can be made by multiplying 2 of these decimals?

How many products can be made which are smaller than 9.99?

Please help your child by reading the instructions and doing the activity together.

Rising Stars Mathematics Year 6 © Rising Stars UK Ltd 2016 **223**

Calculating percentages

8c

You need:

- pencil and paper
- 1–6 dice

- Roll a dice 3 times to create a 3-digit number. Write your number in the first box: 100% = your number.
- Calculate the other percentages of your number.

100% is	50% is	25% is

10% is	5% is	1% is

- Using the information you have generated, can you easily work out the following percentages of your 3-digit number? Some answers may be decimals.

24% is	17% is	59% is	73% is	46% is

  Please help your child by reading the instructions and doing the activity together.

Rising Stars Mathematics Year 6 © Rising Stars UK Ltd 201

Value Added Tax

8c

You need:

- pencil and paper
- furniture catalogue/ Internet access

- Find a catalogue which sells furniture (or look online), priced between £100 and £900.
- Choose 5 items to buy.
- Customers must pay 20% VAT, which is usually included in the price of the item. Calculate the amount of VAT paid for each of your chosen items and the price of each item before VAT was added.

Item	Catalogue price	20% of catalogue price = VAT	Price before VAT

Please help your child by reading the instructions and doing the activity together.

Rising Stars Mathematics Year 6 © Rising Stars UK Ltd 201

Arrangements of disco lights

You need:
- pencil and paper

- Binoy is arranging disco lights. He has 2 stands and 4 different coloured light bulbs. Each stand holds 1 light bulb.

- How many different ways can he arrange the coloured bulbs in the 2 stands? For this problem an arrangement of blue + green counts as a different arrangement to green + blue as the disco effect would be different.

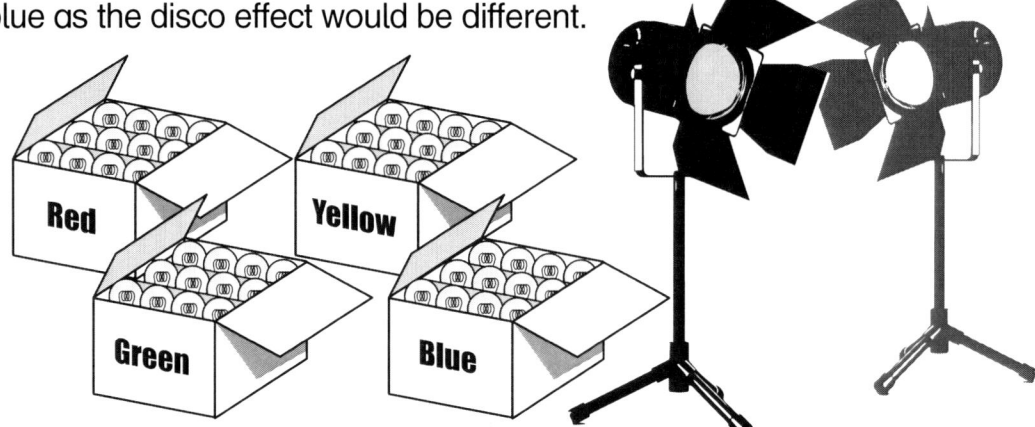

- Explore the possible arrangements if Binoy had 3 stands. Do you think there would be more possible arrangements or fewer?

 Please help your child by reading the instructions and doing the activity together.

Rising Stars Mathematics Year 6 © Rising Stars UK Ltd 2016

Finding unknown values

You need:
- pencil and paper
- partner

- Find all the possible values for A and B if $A + B = 11$. Be systematic and list your answers.

- If the following equation is also true, what must A and B be?

  $A + B + B = 19$

- Decide on values for C and D, but keep them a secret!

- Write out some equations which are true for your chosen values of C and D.

- Challenge a partner to work out the values of C and D.

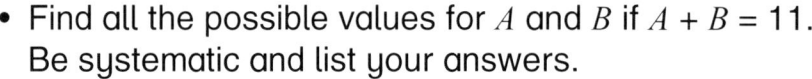 Please help your child by reading the instructions and doing the activity together.

Circles

You need:
- pencil and paper
- compass
- ruler

- Draw a circle on your paper with a radius of 5 cm.
- Then use the compass, set at 5 cm, to make 6 marks around the circumference of the circle.
- Create a geometric design inside your circle – the marks may help you to include either a hexagon or a triangle. Use the compass if you want to insert a smaller circle.
- If your design were to be enlarged by a scale factor of 3, how would the dimensions need to be adjusted?
- Calculate the new dimensions, e.g. radius, marked points on the circumference, length of internal shape's sides. Then draw the scaled up version.
- Compare measurements and angles between the 2 designs. Which measurements change and which stay the same when the design is scaled up? Do all measurements and angles become 3 times larger?

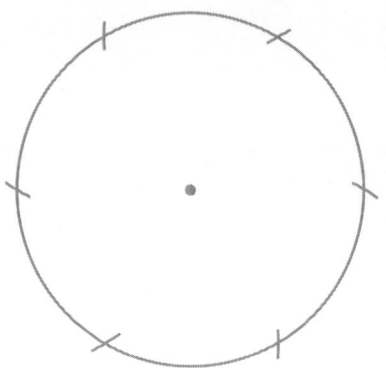

 Please help your child by reading the instructions and doing the activity together.

Rising Stars Mathematics Year 6 © Rising Stars UK Ltd 20

Enlarging triangles

You need:
- pencil and paper
- card
- scissors
- ruler

- Draw a triangle template from card whose sides measure 3 cm, 4 cm and 5 cm.
- Scale the triangle up (i.e. enlarge it) by a factor of 2 and create another card template.
- Finally scale the original triangle up by a factor of 3 and create a third template.
- Use these 3 triangle templates to draw round and create a geometric design on a large sheet of paper.

> Try to include rotation and reflection in your design.

Please help your child by reading the instructions and doing the activity together.

Rising Stars Mathematics Year 6 © Rising Stars UK Ltd 20

Making and measuring angles

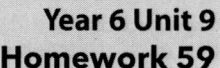

You need:

- pencil and paper
- ruler
- protractor

- Fold a piece of paper in half and then in half again.
- Open it up and draw along the fold lines with a pencil and ruler.
- You have created 4 angles in the centre of the paper where the lines intersect.
- What size are these angles? What do they total when added together?
- Check with a protractor.
- Fold another piece of paper once and then twice, again creating 4 angles. Try to fold the paper so that different sized angles are created.
- Estimate and measure the 4 angles. Add them to find the total. What do you notice?

Is it possible to find a way to fold the paper to create 4 angles which add to make a different total? Explain your reasoning.

Please help your child by reading the instructions and doing the activity together.

Shapes inside shapes

You need:

- pencil
- cm-squared paper
- ruler

- Draw a square with side lengths of 6 cm.
- Mark the midpoints on each side and join them to create a shape inside the square. What is this shape? How does it compare to the large shape it sits inside?
- Use reasoning to calculate or approximate any angles you have created within the large shape.
- Try different starting shapes, each time marking and joining the midpoints to create another shape inside. Make sure to include a triangle, a rhombus, a rectangle and a trapezium among the starting shapes that you investigate.
- Is the inside shape always a small version of the large shape?

Is it always possible to calculate angles without the use of a protractor?

Please help your child by reading the instructions and doing the activity together.

Matching grids

9c

You need:
- pencil
- cm-squared paper
- ruler
- partner

- Draw a 4-quadrant grid with an x-axis from −8 to +8 and a y-axis from −8 to +8, crossing at 0.
- Then draw a small square somewhere on the grid and write its coordinates at each corner.
- Now draw a triangle, star, rectangle and hexagon on the grid, recording the coordinates at each corner of the shapes.
- On another sheet of paper, draw an identical 4-quadrant grid, but do not draw any small shapes on it. Give this empty grid to your partner.
- Choose 1 of your small shapes. Read out its coordinates 1 at a time, asking your partner to plot the points on the grid and then to join them. Repeat with the other shapes.
- Compare grids. Do you have identical shapes drawn in the same places? If not, discuss what might have gone wrong.

Please help your child by reading the instructions and doing the activity together.

Rising Stars Mathematics Year 6 © Rising Stars UK Ltd 201

Translations

9c

You need:
- pencil
- cm-squared paper
- ruler
- colouring pencils
- partner

- Draw a 4-quadrant grid with an x-axis from −8 to +8 and a y-axis from −8 to +8, crossing at 0.
- Then draw a diamond in the top left-hand quadrant of the grid and colour it red. Record the coordinates for its 4 points.
- Now translate the diamond by $(x + 8)$, i.e. each of the x-coordinates has 8 added to it but the y-coordinates remain the same. In which quadrant does the diamond appear now? Colour it green.
- Starting with the red diamond, make up 2 further translations so that the diamond appears in each of the 2 empty quadrants. Colour 1 of the diamonds yellow and the other blue.
- Finally write translations to make the yellow, blue and green diamonds move across the grid and sit on top of the red diamond.
- Explain the changes you needed to make to the x- and the y-coordinates to make this possible.

Please help your child by reading the instructions and doing the activity together.

Rising Stars Mathematics Year 6 © Rising Stars UK Ltd 201

10a Working out unknowns

- Look at this statement: $a + 24 = c$
- If $a = 4$, what must c be?
- Work out all the possible values for a and c where c cannot exceed 35 and a is larger than 0. Work systematically and create a list.
- If c is a prime number, what could a be?
- Is there more than 1 possibility?
- If c is a multiple of 9, what could a be?

You need:
- pencil and paper
- calculator

Please help your child by reading the instructions and doing the activity together.

10a Variables

Here are some rounded exchange rates:
1 UK pound = 1.5 Swiss francs
1 UK pound = 2 Australian dollars

You need:
- pencil and paper
- Internet access or newspaper for exchange rates

- Write these exchange rates algebraically where
  p = UK pound
  f = Swiss franc and
  d = Australian dollar.
- Using these variables, work out:
  ▶ £62 in Swiss francs
  ▶ £128 in Australian dollars
  ▶ 468 Australian dollars in UK pounds
  ▶ 114 Swiss francs in UK pounds
- Can you convert 276 Australian dollars into Swiss francs?

Use the Internet to find out about other exchange rates, e.g. Japanese yen. How many of these would you get for 1 UK pound?

Please help your child by reading the instructions and doing the activity together.

Number sequences

You need:
- pencil and paper

- Here is a number sequence:

5   11   17   23   29 ...

- What is happening to the numbers with each step of the sequence?
- Think about your times tables. Can you see a times table hiding in here? (Tip: the sequence has not started as you might expect. It is like the 6 times table but the first number in the sequence is 5, not 6, i.e. 1 has been subtracted from each of the numbers.)
- We can express this sequence algebraically, where n = number in sequence (e.g. the 3rd number in the sequence has $n = 3$), as $6n - 1$. Can you work out the 10th number in the sequence?

- Now work out the 30th, 75th and 100th numbers in the sequence without writing out the whole sequence!
- Look at this different sequence:

6   10   14   18   22 ...

- Using the same steps as before, identify the sequence step between the numbers.
- Now work out how to express what is happening algebraically.
- Finally, use this to calculate the 10th, 30th, 75th and 100th numbers in the sequence.

Please help your child by reading the instructions and doing the activity together.

Rising Stars Mathematics Year 6 © Rising Stars UK Ltd 201

Handshakes

You need:
- pencil and paper

When 2 people shake hands with each other, there is 1 handshake.

When 3 people each shake hands with each other, they make 3 different handshakes.

- How many different handshakes will there be if 4 people each shake hands with each other?
- What about 5 people and 6 people?
- Can you see a pattern in your results? Have you seen this sequence before?

Explain what is happening algebraically so that you can predict how many handshakes 10 people will make, and 20 people and 100 people!

Please help your child by reading the instructions and doing the activity together.

Rising Stars Mathematics Year 6 © Rising Stars UK Ltd 20

11a Using bar model diagrams

You need:
- pencil and paper

- Read the following information:

> Jessica and Adhnam were collecting donations of money for their school library.
>
> Each child collected for 2 hours.
>
> In the first hour Jessica collected £78.40.
>
> Adhnam collected on average £38 during each $\frac{1}{2}$ hour.
>
> Both children collected the same total figure.

- Use a bar model diagram to help you calculate the amount collected by Jessica in each $\frac{1}{2}$ hour.

 Please help your child by reading the instructions and doing the activity together.

Rising Stars Mathematics Year 6 © Rising Stars UK Ltd 2016

11a 24 hours in 1 day

You need:
- pencil and paper
- ruler

- During a 24-hour period (i.e. 8 a.m. to 8 a.m. the following day), record the following information:

> **Time you spend:**
> Eating
> Watching TV
> Outdoors
> Playing screen games (x-box, DS, Wii, pc games, i-pad, apps, etc.)
> Playing sport
> Sleeping

- Use a bar model to display your results, labelling the top bar '24 hours'.

> How much time was **not** spent on any of the listed activities? How did you use that time?

 Please help your child by reading the instructions and doing the activity together.

Fraction flag

You need:
- pencil and paper
- squared paper
- ruler
- colouring pencils

- Create a colourful design on this flag, but the colours must satisfy these fractions:

$\frac{4}{16}$ blue

$\frac{1}{8}$ red

$\frac{12}{32}$ yellow

$\frac{1}{4}$ green

- Draw a rectangle on your squared paper which encloses 32 squares and measures 8 squares in length and 4 squares in height. Now you can create another flag design, but it must still match the fractions above.

Rising Stars Mathematics Year 6 © Rising Stars UK Ltd 201

Midpoint between 2 fractions

You need:
- pencil
- card
- partner
- scissors

- Write these fractions on pieces of card and then cut them out.

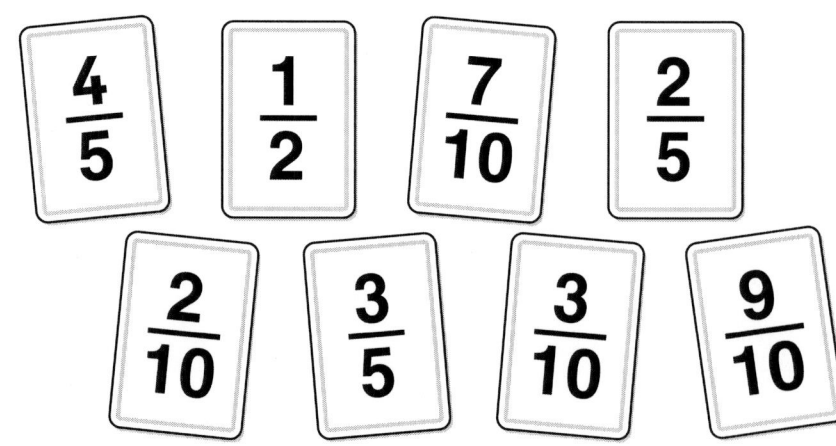

$\frac{4}{5}$ $\frac{1}{2}$ $\frac{7}{10}$ $\frac{2}{5}$

$\frac{2}{10}$ $\frac{3}{5}$ $\frac{3}{10}$ $\frac{9}{10}$

Are there any pairs for which the midpoint cannot be found?

- Shuffle them and place them face down on the table.
- Each player chooses a fraction card and turns it over.
- The challenge is to work out the fraction that is midway between these 2 fractions. (Tip: convert both fractions first so that they have the same denominator.)

Rising Stars Mathematics Year 6 © Rising Stars UK Ltd 20

11c Function machines

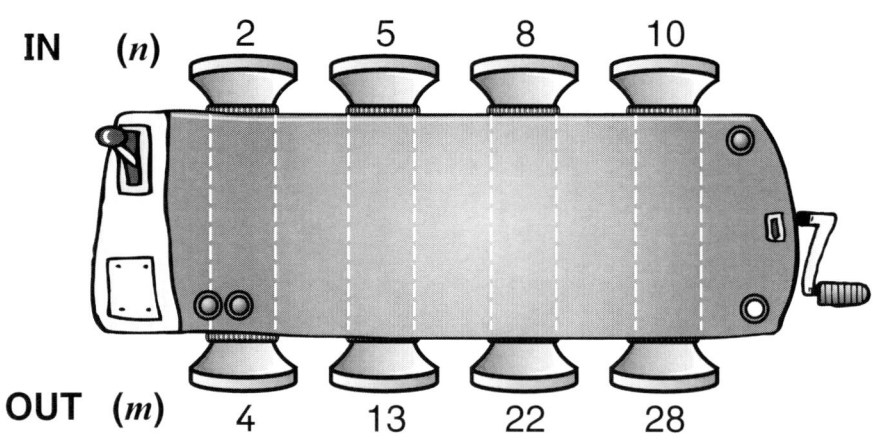

IN (n) 2 5 8 10

OUT (m) 4 13 22 28

- Work out what has happened to the numbers as they pass through the function machine.
- Write it as a formula where the number entering the machine is n and the number coming out of the machine is m. Check that your formula is correct by testing different values of n.

- Draw your own function machine and write a formula to control it.
- Try out the following values for n (i.e. the 'IN' number):
  4, 7, 12, 20, 35.
- Work out what m (i.e. the 'OUT' number) would be in each case.

 Please help your child by reading the instructions and doing the activity together.

Rising Stars Mathematics Year 6 © Rising Stars UK Ltd 2016

11c Formulae for lines on graphs

- Draw 2 quadrants on the squared paper with values of x from −10 to +20 and values of y from 0 to 10.
- Study these formulae:

$y + 3 = x$

$3y + 1 = x$

$y - 2 = x$

$2y - 5 = x$

- Each of these 4 formulae will create a line on the graph.
- Use y values of 1 to 6 in each formula to generate the corresponding x values.
- Plot and join the points that result from each formula.

> Can you come up with 2 further formulae that will create different lines on the graph when values of 1 to 6 are used for y?

 Please help your child by reading the instructions and doing the activity together.

12a Fraction story

You need:

- pencil and paper

- Read the story.
- How many football cards were in the album originally?
- What fraction of the original set of cards did he have left?
- What approximate percentage of the original set of cards did Rohan have left?
- What approximate percentage did he give to Rhys?

Rohan was walking along the road with his friend Rhys, carrying a collector's album of football cards. Unfortunately, the cards began to fall out and blow away in the wind.

- $\frac{1}{3}$ of them blew into the road and out of reach.
- $\frac{1}{6}$ of them got carried along the gutter in a stream of water and disappeared into a drain.
- Rohan and Rhys hurried to pick up the cards that were left, but $\frac{1}{2}$ of those remaining were picked up by some other children who ran off with them.
- Rohan counted those that were left and gave $\frac{1}{3}$ to Rhys for helping him.
- He had 14 football cards left.

 Please help your child by reading the instructions and doing the activity together.

Rising Stars Mathematics Year 6 © Rising Stars UK Ltd 20

12a Fractions and percentages shown on a pie chart

You need:

- pencil and paper
- 1–6 dice
- circle to draw round (e.g. a cup)
- ruler

640 children sat the same English exam and were graded A, B, C, D or E. Here are the results:

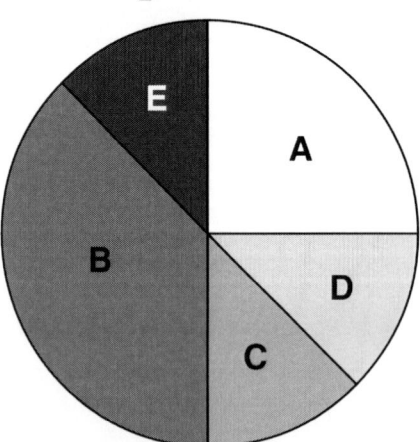

- How many children were given each grade?
- Can you convert these amounts into percentages of the whole?
- Roll a dice 30 times and record which numbers are rolled.
- Draw a pie chart where the whole pie represents the 30 rolls.
- Show the fraction of number 1 rolled, the fraction of number 2 rolled and so on. Then write these as percentages of the whole.

 Please help your child by reading the instructions and doing the activity together.

Rising Stars Mathematics Year 6 © Rising Stars UK Ltd 20

12b Area of the garden

- Imagine that you want to lay down some decking in your garden.
- Go into your garden and measure the section of your choice (it should be a square or rectangular shape). If you don't have a garden, think about your dream garden!
- Round the measurements to the nearest $\frac{1}{2}$ metre. Draw a diagram with the measurements marked on, e.g.:

4.5 m

2.5 m

- You need to buy 2 types of decking.
    - ▸ Type A is laid around the outer edge of your area in a strip that is 50 cm wide.
    - ▸ Type B is laid in the centre of the area.
- Find out the area you need to cover in each type of decking.

 Please help your child by reading the instructions and doing the activity together.

Rising Stars Mathematics Year 6 © Rising Stars UK Ltd 2016

12b Continuing sequences

- Here are some numbers that appear in a sequence:

 16 26 36 46 ...

- We could write this sequence as $10n + 6$.
- Put $n = 1$, $n = 2$, $n = 3$ and $n = 4$ into the equation, in turn, to check that it works.
- Now calculate what numbers in the sequence you would get if $n = 10$, if $n = 50$ and if $n = 85$.
- Here is another sequence of numbers:

 20 23 26 49 ...

- Can you come up with an equation including n to describe this sequence?
- Use your equation to find the numbers in the sequence you would get if $n = 20$, if $n = 32$ and if $n = 45$.

This time think up an equation yourself and then write the first 4 numbers that are made in the sequence. Can anyone in your family work out the equation you started with?

 Please help your child by reading the instructions and doing the activity together.

Calculating unknown values

You need:
- pencil and paper

Kenzie measures the height of 4 sunflowers that she has been growing.

They measure: 1.75 m, 1.23 m, 0.85 m and 2.05 m.

▶ Sunflower A and Sunflower B have a combined height of 2.08 m.

▶ Sunflower B and Sunflower C have a combined height of 2.6 m.

▶ Sunflower C's height is 1.75 m.

▶ The difference in height between Sunflower D and Sunflower B is 1.2 m.

- Use the clues to work out the height of each sunflower and then put them in height order.

- If Sunflower A and Sunflower C each grow a further 0.5 m but Sunflower B and Sunflower D fail to grow any more, what will the new heights be? Will the height order have changed?

Please help your child by reading the instructions and doing the activity together.

Rising Stars Mathematics Year 6 © Rising Stars UK Ltd 201

Making £1.70 in different ways

You need:
- pencil and paper

- If $x + y = £1.70$, work out some possible values of x and y. You must have values for x and y which can be made using £1, 50p and 10p coins only.

- How many different values are there?

Work systematically and look for patterns which will help you.

Please help your child by reading the instructions and doing the activity together.

Rising Stars Mathematics Year 6 © Rising Stars UK Ltd 201

Organising a school trip

13a

You need:

- pencil and paper
- information about your school

- Imagine you are organising a school trip. You need to work out how many children are going and which is the cheapest bus company. You also have to book tickets to the cinema for everyone.

  1 How many are going? Calculate the approximate number of children in your school by multiplying the number of classes by 28 children.

  2 Work out whether to hire bus company A (whose coaches each hold 54 children at a cost of £280 per coach) or bus company B (whose minibuses each hold 18 children at a cost of £100 per minibus). How many of your chosen bus will be required?

  3 Calculate how many rows you must book in the cinema. There are 12 seats per row and you can get a discounted rate of £25 per row.

- How much will the whole trip cost?

- What will you charge each child?

Think how you will deal with remainders at each stage of the problem.

 Please help your child by reading the instructions and doing the activity together.

Investigating remainder patterns

13a

You need:

- pencil and paper

- Work out these 2 puzzles. In each puzzle, 2 children are thinking about numbers and remainders.

- Could they be thinking of the same number? What number could it be?

- Explain your reasoning.

> **Puzzle 1:** Carly is thinking of a number which is 3 more than a multiple of 5.
> Gita is thinking of a number which is 8 more than a multiple of 10.

> **Puzzle 2:** Theo is thinking of a number which is 3 more than a multiple of 6.
> Poppy is thinking of a number which is 2 more than a multiple of 4.

 Please help your child by reading the instructions and doing the activity together.

13b Word problems and bar models

- Work out the missing number in each bar model.
- Then write a word problem that each bar model could represent.

You need:

- pencil and paper

38	
26	?

?			
12	12	12	12

107		
45	?	7

364			
120	120	120	?

Now write your own word problem and matching bar model.

Rising Stars Mathematics Year 6 © Rising Stars UK Ltd 201

13b Holiday club

- Annette is setting up a holiday club. She needs to buy resources for the children to use. Look at the table below to see how many children are coming and what items are needed.

- Browse the Internet or the shops to find good prices for the items. Work out the cost of each.
- If Annette charges £5 per child per day, how much profit would she make?

You need:

- pencil and paper
- Internet access or a trip to the shops

Day	Number of children	Activity	Resources needed
Monday	12	Designing a poster	A pencil, ruler and rubber for each child
Tuesday	15	Decorating biscuits	2 biscuits per child, ready-made icing and sweets for decoration
Wednesday	18	Playing team games	1 football, 1 cricket bat and ball and stumps, 6 cones
Thursday	10	Colouring in	Felt tips to share, colouring book to tear pages from
Friday	14	Swimming	£2 per child for entry to the pool

Rising Stars Mathematics Year 6 © Rising Stars UK Ltd 20

Multiplying fractions

13c

You need:
- pencil and paper
- 2 sets of digit cards 1–9
- partner

- Shuffle the digit cards. Place them face down on the table.
- Each player takes turns to pick 4 cards and to generate 2 fractions, e.g. pick cards 3, 6, 2, 4 and create fractions $\frac{3}{6}$ and $\frac{2}{4}$.
- Each player then multiplies their 2 fractions to find the product, e.g. $\frac{3}{6} \times \frac{2}{4} = \frac{6}{24} = \frac{1}{4}$.
- Compare the products made (it might help to simplify them). The player with the largest product scores 1 point.
- Remember, you can choose how to arrange the 4 numbers chosen into fractions. Think about which fractions multiplied would create the largest product.

Play again.
The winner is the first to score 5 points.

Please help your child by reading the instructions and doing the activity together.

Rising Stars Mathematics Year 6 © Rising Stars UK Ltd 2016

Fraction puzzle

13c

Callum started the week with 60 stickers.

You need:
- pencil and paper

- On Monday he chose $\frac{3}{4}$ of them to keep and shared the rest among his friends.
- He then gave 1 to his younger sister.
- How many did he have left?

- On Tuesday Callum chose $\frac{7}{11}$ of his remaining stickers to keep and shared the rest among his friends.
- He then gave 1 to his younger sister.
- How many did he have left?

- On Thursday Callum chose $\frac{2}{7}$ of his remaining stickers to keep and shared the rest among his friends.
- He then gave 1 to his younger sister.
- How many did he have left?

- On Wednesday Callum chose $\frac{5}{9}$ of his remaining stickers to keep and shared the rest among his friends.
- He then gave 1 to his younger sister.
- How many did he have left?

- On Friday Callum chose $\frac{2}{3}$ of his remaining stickers to keep and shared the rest among his friends.
- He then gave 1 to his younger sister.
- How many stickers did he have left for himself at the end of this week?

Please help your child by reading the instructions and doing the activity together.

Possible nets for a square-based pyramid

- Draw a square with a side length of 5 cm.
- Now draw an isosceles triangle on each of the sides of the square so that the overall shape becomes the net of a square-based pyramid.
- Do the angles of the isosceles triangle need to be a particular size for the pyramid net to work?
- Do the sides of the isosceles triangle need to be a particular length for the net to work?
- If the 4 triangles are equilateral, will the pyramid net still create a square-based pyramid?
- Investigate and explore by making different nets and testing them out.

You need:

- pencil and paper
- ruler
- protractor
- scissors
- sticky tape

Explain what you have discovered to an adult.

Please help your child by reading the instructions and doing the activity together.

Rising Stars Mathematics Year 6 © Rising Stars UK Ltd 20

Making cuboids with a given volume

- How many different cuboids can you make which each have a volume of 36 cm³? If you have 36 bricks, you can build cuboids with them to help you.

- Record the different cuboids by drawing them on squared paper using a ruler.
- Write down the different dimensions.
- Is there a different volume which would generate a greater number of different shaped cuboids than 36 cm³ does?

You need:

- pencil
- squared paper
- ruler
- 36 bricks of the same size (optional)

Please help your child by reading the instructions and doing the activity together.

Rising Stars Mathematics Year 6 © Rising Stars UK Ltd 20

![14b]

Triangle angles

- Each player takes a turn to roll a dice twice to create a 2-digit number. These numbers become 2 angles in a triangle. Draw the triangle. The drawings do not need to be to scale.

- Next calculate what the third angle in the triangle must be, e.g. 46 + 37 + ? = 180. The first player to reach the correct answer wins a point.

You need:

- pencil and paper
- ruler
- 1–6 dice
- partner

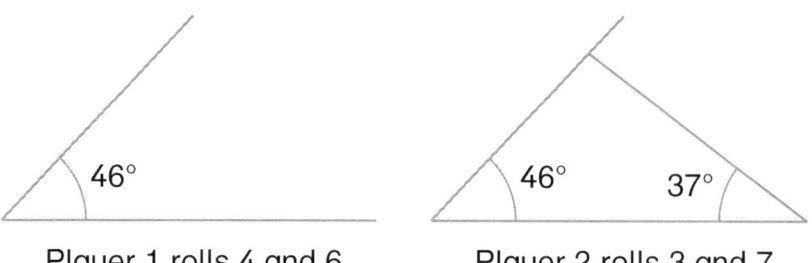

Player 1 rolls 4 and 6   Player 2 rolls 3 and 7

- Play a few times. Talk about the different triangles that have been created. Have any isosceles triangles been drawn? Give reasons for this.

 Please help your child by reading the instructions and doing the activity together.

Rising Stars Mathematics Year 6 © Rising Stars UK Ltd 2016

![14b]

Making 3-D shapes from nets

- These 12 pieces will combine in pairs to make 6 different nets. Each net makes a different 3-D shape. Work out which pieces pair together.

- Then use the diagrams to create your own nets. Can you construct all 6 shapes?

You need:

- pencil and paper
- ruler
- scissors
- sticky tape

Can you draw other nets that make different 3-D shapes?

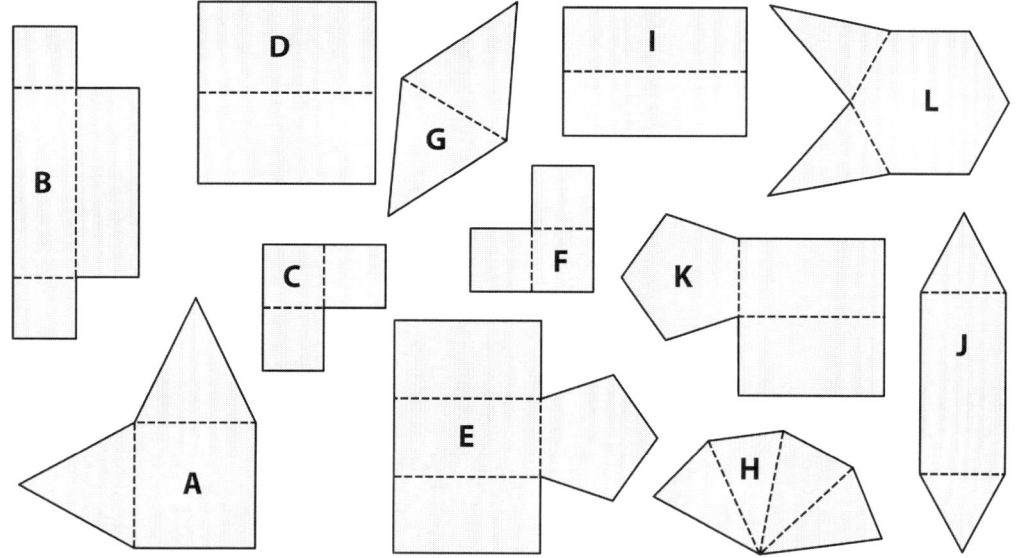

 Please help your child by reading the instructions and doing the activity together.

Castle design

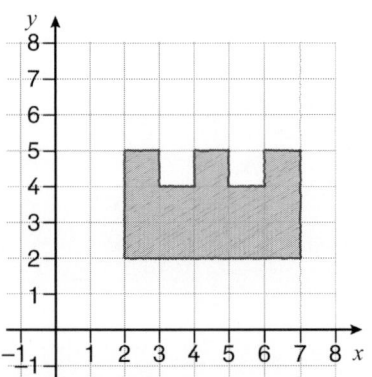

- Draw a 4-quadrant grid with x-axis from −8 to +8 and a y-axis from −8 to +8.

- Draw a castle like this in the first quadrant. Colour it blue. Write each of its coordinates.

You need:

- pencil
- cm-squared paper
- ruler
- blue colouring pencil

- Reflect the castle design across the x-axis and note down the new coordinates. What do you notice?

- Can you predict the new coordinates if you reflect your original blue castle across the y-axis? Try it to find out if you were correct.

- Draw a line on the grid from (−8, 8) to (8, −8) crossing (0, 0).

- Can you reflect your original blue castle across this line? In which quadrant will the new shape appear?

Please help your child by reading the instructions and doing the activity together.

Rising Stars Mathematics Year 6 © Rising Stars UK Ltd 20

Reflecting shapes

- A pentomino is a shape made from 5 small squares joined along their straight sides, e.g.

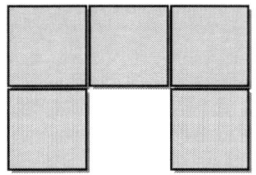

You need:

- pencil
- cm-squared paper
- ruler

You could try this activity using hexominos (made of 6 small squares joined along straight sides).

- Draw several different pentominos on your squared paper.

- If each pentomino is $\frac{1}{2}$ of a shape that has line symmetry, what might the whole shape be? Each of your pentominos should produce 2 or more possible whole shapes. (Tip: it may help to cut out a pentomino and move it into different positions next to your identical drawn pentomino.)

- Which pentomino generated the greatest number of different whole shapes? Why might this be?

Please help your child by reading the instructions and doing the activity together.

Rising Stars Mathematics Year 6 © Rising Stars UK Ltd 20

Homework sheets answers

Homework 2

Multiplying and dividing by 10 and 100

34.6 × 100 = 3460; 289 700 ÷ 100 = 2897;
1.89 × 10 = 18.9; 56 964 ÷ 100 = 569.64;
142 ÷ 10 = 14.2

Homework 3

Comparing and ordering numbers

Chile largest, Senegal smallest.

Senegal, Zambia, Ecuador, Mali, Malawi, Netherlands, Kazakhstan, Chile

Ecuador and Zambia are closest in size.

UK population approximately 64 800 000 in 2016. It has a much bigger population than the other countries.

Homework 4

Rounding money amounts

Rounding to the nearest 10p will give a more accurate rounded total.

	£1243.67 +	£876.32 +	£42.48 =	£2162.47
Rounded to nearest pound	£1244	£876	£42	£2162
Rounded to nearest 10p	£1243.70	£876.30	£42.50	£2162.50

Homework 6

Simplifying fractions

Simplified and in order from smallest to largest:
$\frac{1}{2}, \frac{2}{3}$ and $\frac{2}{3}, \frac{3}{4}, \frac{7}{8}$

There are lots of possibilities with denominators as multiples of 35, e.g. $\frac{20}{35}$ and $\frac{21}{35}$ or $\frac{40}{70}$ and $\frac{42}{70}$.

Homework 7

Colouring sections of a square

If pupils have drawn 10 × 10 as an array of 10 × 10 small squares then colour 10 squares green, 25 red and 15 yellow.

$\frac{1}{2}$ or 50% or 0.5 of the square has been coloured so far. The whole square has been coloured, i.e. 1 in total.

Homework 9

Adding and subtracting with 4-digit numbers

2943 + 1034 = 3977

1527 + 3521 = 5048

5000: 4000 − 3973 = 23

6000: 4982 + 1034 = 6016

7000: 4132 + 2943 = 7075

8000: 5156 + 2943 = 8099

9000: 2254 + 6792 = 9046

10 000: 4982 + 5156 = 10 138

Homework 11

Order of operations

Start			
2400	× 4	÷ 6	= 1600
2400	÷ 6	× 4	= 1600

Start			
1837	− 500	× 4	= 5348
1837	× 4	− 500	= 6848

You can do × and ÷ in a calculation in any order but, if you change the order of − and ×, it will change the answer.

Operations that can be done in any order are ×/÷ and +/−. Operations that cannot be done in any order are ×/−, ×/+, ÷/− and ÷/+.

Homework 12

Using all 4 operations in different ways

45; −3; 362 880

Homework 13

Comparing lengths and writing equations

$a = 36, b = 18, c = 12, d = 9, e = 7.2$ or $7\frac{1}{5}, f = 6$

Homework 14

Finding possible answers

There are numerous possibilities, e.g. A = 30, B = 6, C = 34, D = 3, E = 36; just start with 2 numbers that add to 36 and then carry on through the list of calculations.

Look back at the possibilities you found and choose the solution which totals 99 when each bus is added, e.g. A = 20, B = 16, C = 24, D = 13, E = 26.

Homework 15

Multiplication of 3-digit by 2-digit numbers

472 × 15 = 7080; 472 × 24 = 11 328; 472 × 19 = 8968

So 472 has been multiplied by 24 for the answer to match the 3 criteria given.

Homework 16

Cycling times – long multiplication

Joshua: 4 × 24 = 96 minutes
(1 hour and 36 minutes)

Caitlyn: 156 divided by 24 = 6.5, so she has travelled 6 lots of 10 miles plus 0.5 lots of 10 miles. This makes 65 miles in total.

365 × 24 minutes = 8760 minutes.
That is 146 hours or 6 days and 2 hours.

Homework 17

Multiplication investigation

431 × 52 = 22 412 gives the largest product and 245 × 13 = 3185 gives the smallest product.

Homework 19

Using place value when multiplying and dividing decimals

8 × 0.5 = 4.0　　　　3 × 0.7 = 2.1
9 × 0.6 = 5.4　　　　5 × 0.3 = 1.5

4.8 ÷ 6 = 0.8　　　　1.6 ÷ 4 = 0.4
3.5 ÷ 7 = 0.5　　　　2.4 ÷ 8 = 0.3

If a multiplier or number to be divided is 100 times smaller, then the dividend or product that results will also be 100 times smaller.

Homework 20

Finding the mean (average) using division

£6.45; £1.62

Homework 21

Mystery numbers

Could be 5 or 80.

Could be 7 or 63.

Could be 1 and 7, 2 and 14, 3 and 21, 4 and 28, 5 and 35, 6 and 42, 7 and 49.

Homework 22

Using ratio and proportion

He could buy various combinations for £100.

E.g. 10 long pipes (£50), 10 medium length pipes (£10), 80 small pipes (£40).

Homework 24

Triangular areas

All the areas are 16 cm². Perimeters are different. The largest is 20.9 cm, the smallest is 19.3 cm.

Homework 25

Exploring angles

$a = 150, b = 30, c = 30, d = 108, e = 72, f = 108, g = 50, h = 130, i = 130$

The opposite angles are the same.

Homework 26

Exterior and interior angles of a triangle

$b + c = x$

$x = b + c$

Angles on a straight line equal 180°, so $x + a = 180°$. The internal angles in a triangle equal 180° so $b + c + a = 180°$, meaning that $b + c = x$.

Homework 27  4c

Stacking cubes into a cuboid shape

Possibilities include: $2 \times 4 \times 3$, $1 \times 3 \times 8$, $1 \times 4 \times 6$, $1 \times 2 \times 12$, $2 \times 2 \times 6$, $2 \times 3 \times 4$, $2 \times 6 \times 2$, $3 \times 4 \times 2$, $1 \times 8 \times 3$, etc.

Homework 28 4c

Nets of cuboids

The nets will probably not always look the same as the boxes are all different.

The net should always include 6 rectangles in paired sizes, e.g. the net might have 2 small, 2 medium and 2 large rectangles or 2 large and 4 small rectangles.

Homework 29 5a

Exploring coordinates

The points form a straight line from (–5,–9) to (2,5).

The new line is parallel to the first but is located 3 squares to the right.

The next new line is parallel to the first but is located 3 squares to the left.

Homework 34 6a

World temperatures

Ordered from hottest to coldest: 31°C, 10°C, 2°C, –1°C, –3°C, –14°C

45°C difference between Brazil and Canada.

Difference between the other city temperatures and London UK: Toronto 21°C, Rio 24°C, New York 5°C, Moscow 10°C, Helsinki 8°C, Madrid 3°C

July temperatures: e.g. Toronto 21°C , Rio 21°C, New York 25°C , Moscow 19°C , Helsinki 17°C , Madrid 35°C

Toronto has the greatest difference at 35°C.

Homework 35 6b

Money box totals

£9	£11	£13
£10		£8
£14	£7	£12

Homework 37  6c

Fast times

	Times taken	Rounded to the nearest second (lots of runners have the same result and there are only 3 places)	Rounded to the nearest $\frac{1}{10}$ of a second (runners 3 and 4 have the same time and runners 8, 9 and 10 would have the same time, so you still cannot individually place all the runners)
1	1:45.120	1:45	1:45.1
2	1:45.250	1:45	1:45.3
3	1:45.450	1:45	1:45.5
4	1:45.490	1:45	1:45.5
5	1:45.940	1:46	1:45.9
6	1:46.170	1:46	1:46.2
7	1:46.820	1:47	1:46.8
8	1:46.980	1:47	1:47.0
9	1:47.010	1:47	1:47.0
10	1:47.090	1:47	1:47.1

Homework 40  6d

Describing patterns

The pattern is: vertical 2, 3, 4 increases by 1 each time; horizontal 3, 5, 7 increases by 2 each time; total squares 5 then 8 then 11.

10th letter: vertical = 11, horizontal = 21, total 33

20th letter: vertical = 21, horizontal = 41

If the letter number in the sequence is n, the vertical squares total $n + 1$ and the horizontal squares total $2n + 1$, making the total $(n + 1) + (2n + 1)$ which is $3n + 2$. So, if $n = 100$, the total number of squares would be $(3 \times 100) + 2 = 302$.

Homework 41  7a

Creating and converting fractions

Collecting larger fractions will help improve the chances of winning, i.e. those with smaller denominators.

Homework 42  7a

Adding and subtracting fractions

Round 1: Crystal; Round 2: Jamie and Crystal drew.

	Jamie	Anesh	Crystal	Amy
Round 1	$8\frac{6}{9}$	$8\frac{5}{9}$	$9\frac{3}{9}$	$8\frac{6}{9}$
Round 2	$9\frac{3}{9}$	$9\frac{1}{9}$	$9\frac{3}{9}$	$8\frac{6}{9}$
Difference	$\frac{6}{9}$ m increase	$\frac{5}{9}$ m increase	same	same
Total	18 m	$17\frac{6}{9}$ m, $17\frac{2}{3}$ m	$18\frac{6}{9}$ m, $18\frac{2}{3}$ m	$17\frac{3}{9}$ m, $17\frac{1}{3}$ m

Homework 44  7b

Finding fractions, decimals and percentages of amounts

It is easier to find halves and quarters of even numbers.

It is easier to find fifths of multiples of 5s, but can be harder to find halves and quarters.

Homework 46 7c

Perimeter and area formulae and patterns

Rectangle 1: P = 8 cm, A = 3 cm²
Rectangle 2: P = 16 cm, A = 12 cm²
Rectangle 3: P = 32 cm, A = 48 cm²
Rectangle 4: P = 64 cm, A = 192 cm²
Rectangle 5: P = 128 cm, A = 768 cm²

The perimeter doubles each time and the area quadruples each time.

Rectangle 8: P = 1024 cm, A = 49 152 cm²;
Rectangle 10: P = 4096 cm, A = 786 432 cm²

Homework 47  7d

Algebra puzzle

$n = 9$

$n = 6$

A	C	A	B	27
C	B	C	A	25
B	B	B	B	20
A	C	C	A	28
27	22	25	26	

A = 8, B = 5, C = 6

Homework 48 7d

Finding unknown values using balancing

	a	b	c	d	e	f
value	12	4	16	18	50	35

Homework 49 8a

Prime factors

Largest product 900, smallest 4. There are lots of possible products.

1, 2, 3, 5, 7, 8, 11, 13, 14, 16, 17, 19, 21, 22, 23, 24, 25, 26, 27, 28, 29

Homework 50 8a

Common multiples

Yes.

E.g. $3 \times 2 \times 4 = 24$ but the lowest common multiple of these numbers is 12; $2 \times 5 \times 3 = 30$ which is the lowest common multiple of these numbers.

Homework 51 8b

Running times

Average speeds per mile:

Runner 1   7.24 min

Runner 2   7.16 min

Runner 3   7.19 min

Runner 4   7.05 min

Runner 5   7.22 min

6.66 min per mile would give a time of 39.96 min overall.

Homework 52 8b

Multiplying decimals

3.4 and 2.9

15 products possible in total: 8.84, 13.94, 13.26, 12.58, 9.86, 10.66, 10.14, 9.62, 7.54, 15.99, 15.17, 11.89, 14.43, 11.31, 10.73

4 are smaller than 9.99: 8.84, 9.86, 9.62, 7.54

Homework 55 8d

Arrangements of disco lights

16 different ways: RR, RG, RY, RB, BB, BR, BG, BY, GG, GR, GY, GB, YY, YG, YB, YR

There would be lots more possible arrangement

Homework 56 8d

Finding unknown values

0 + 11, 1 + 10, 2 + 9, 3 + 8, 4 + 7, 5 + 6, 6 + 5, 7 + 4
8 + 3, 9 + 2, 10 + 1, 11 + 0

A = 3 and B = 8

Homework 57 9a

Circles

The angles stay the same but the length of the sides becomes 3 times longer.

Homework 59 9b

Making and measuring angles

If the paper is folded neatly, the angles should be right angles, $4 \times 90° = 360°$.

The angles total 360° again.

No, the 4 angles always total 360° as that creates a full turn about the central point.

Homework 60 9b

Shapes inside shapes

A square; it is smaller and rotated 45°.

No, the inside shape in a triangle is a triangle, but in a rhombus it is a rectangle, in a rectangle it is a rhombus and in a trapezium it is a rhombus.

It is sometimes hard to.

Homework 63 10a

Working out unknowns

$c = 28$

0 and 24, 1 and 25, 2 and 26 …, 10 and 34

26, 27, 29, 31

$a = 5$ or $a = 7$

$a = 3$

Homework 64 10a

Variables

$p = 1.5 f; p = 2 d$

£62 = 93 Swiss francs

£128 = 256 Aust dollars

468 Aust dollars = £234

114 Swiss francs = £76

276 Aust dollars = £138 = 207 Swiss francs

Homework 65  10b

Number sequences

Adding 6

10th number = 59

179, 449, 599

Adding 4

$4n + 2$

42, 122, 302, 402

Homework 65 10b

Handshakes

4 people: 6; 5 people: 10; 6 people: 15

Triangular numbers

E.g. for 4 people: $3 + 2 + 1 = 6$

for 5 people: $4 + 3 + 2 + 1 = 10$

This can be expressed as $n \times (n - 1)$ divided by 2, e.g. where $n = 5$, the handshakes are (5×4) divided by 2 = 20 divided by 2 = 10.
If $n = 10$, handshakes = 45;
where $n = 20$, handshakes = 190;
where $n = 100$, handshakes = 4950.

Homework 67 11a

Using bar model diagrams

Jessica

£78.40	£73.60

Adhnam

£38	£38	£38	£38

Adhnam's total = £38 × 4 = £152. So Jessica's second hour must be £152 – £78.40 = £73.60. Jessica's $\frac{1}{2}$ hour totals were £39.20, £39.20, £36.80, £36.80.

Homework 69 11b

Fraction flag

8 blue, 4 red, 12 yellow, 8 green

Homework 70 11b

Midpoint between 2 fractions

When converted into 20ths all the numerators are even, so midpoints between any 2 can be found.

Homework 71 11c

Function machines

$(n \times 3) - 2 = m$

Homework 73 12a

Fraction story

There were 84 cards to start with. 28 cards blew into the road, 14 went down the drain, 21 cards were taken by other children, he gave Rhys 7 cards or approximately 8%. Rohan had $\frac{14}{84} = \frac{1}{6}$ left or approximately 17%.

[You need to start at the end of the problem and work your way to the beginning using logic and fraction knowledge: 14 cards = $\frac{2}{3}$ of those left, because $\frac{1}{3}$ of 7 cards went to Rhys. He picked up 21, and 21 were taken by the other children; at this point there were 42 cards. $\frac{1}{3} + \frac{1}{6}$ were lost at the start = $\frac{3}{6} = \frac{1}{2}$. If $\frac{1}{2} = 42$, the whole number at the start must have been 84.]

Homework 74 12a

Fractions and percentages shown on a pie chart

160 got A, 240 got B, 80 got C, 80 got D and 80 got E

A 25%, B 37.5%, C 12.5%, D 12.5 % and E 12.5%

Homework 75 12b

Area of the garden

Work out the whole area, e.g. $4.5 \times 2.5 = 11.25$ m² in this example. Then the smaller area inside would be $3.5 \times 1.5 = 5.25$ m² (taking off the 50 cm strip). The smaller area is the Type B decking (5.25 m² here) and the difference between the whole area and the smaller area (11.25 – 5.25 = 6 m² here) is the Type A decking.

Homework 76  12b

Continuing sequences

106, 506, 856

$3n + 17$ so 77, 113, 152

Homework 77 12c

Calculating unknown values

D = 2.05 m, C = 1.75 m, A = 1.23 m, B = 0.85 m

C = 2.25 m, D = 2.05 m, A = 1.73 m, B = 0.85 m

Homework 78 12c

Making £1.70 in different ways

18 different values

Lots of possibilities including:

x	y
£1	70p
£1.10	60p
£1.20	50p
£1.30	40p
£1.40	30p
£1.50	20p
£1.60	10p
£1.70	0p
90p	80p
80p	90p
70p	£1
60p	£1.10
50p	£1.20
40p	£1.30
30p	£1.40
20p	£1.50
10p	£1.60
0p	£1.70

Homework 80 13a

Investigating remainder patterns

Puzzle 1: Adding 3 to multiples of 5 creates numbers with 8 or 3 in the ones column. Adding 8 to multiples of 10 creates numbers with an 8 in the ones column. Every number Gita thinks of is also thought of by Carly.

Puzzle 2: Adding 3 to multiples of 6 always creates odd numbers. Adding 2 to multiples of 4 always creates even numbers. So Theo and Poppy will never think about the same number.

Homework 81 13b

Word problems and bar models

12, 48, 55, 4

Homework 84 13c

Fraction puzzle

Monday: $\frac{3}{4} = 45$, 44 left

Tuesday: $\frac{7}{11} = 28$, 27 left

Wednesday: $\frac{5}{9} = 15$, 14 left

Thursday: $\frac{2}{7} = 4$, 3 left

Friday: $\frac{2}{3} = 2$, 1 left

Homework 86  14a

Making cuboids with a given volume

Answers include: $9 \times 2 \times 2$, $2 \times 6 \times 3$, $4 \times 3 \times 3$, $3 \times 1 \times 12$, $6 \times 6 \times 1$, $2 \times 1 \times 18$, $9 \times 4 \times 1$, $36 \times 1 \times 1$

There are more (13) ways to build a cuboid with 72 blocks because 72 has more factors (12) than 36.

Homework 87  14b

Triangle angles

To draw isosceles triangles would need either both players to roll the same dice numbers or the third angle to be identical to another which has already been drawn. Therefore, the likelihood of drawing scalene triangles is much greater.

Homework 88  14b

Making 3-D shapes from nets

A + G square-based pyramid, B + I cuboid, C + F cube, D + J triangular prism, E + K pentagonal prism, H + L hexagonal-based pyramid

Homework 89  14c

Castle design

The x-coordinates remain the same; the y-coordinates have the same digits but are now negative numbers. The castle is in the 4th quadrant. (Quadrants are numbered 1 to 4 anticlockwise from top right.)

The y-coordinates remain the same; the x-coordinates have the same digits but have now become negative numbers. The castle is in the 2nd quadrant.

It will be in the 3rd quadrant.

Homework 90 14c

Reflecting shapes

Examples

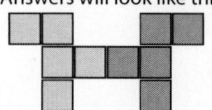

Answers will look like this:

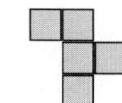

1, 2, 3

2-dimensional (2-D)
Points in 2-dimensional space lie on a flat surface.

3-dimensional (3-D)
Points in 3-dimensional space occupy a space or a volume.

5, 10, 15… minutes past
Ways of counting minutes on an analogue clock. The minute hand takes five minutes to move between each hour mark on the clock face. See also *analogue clock*.

12-hour time
Counting hours of the day in two blocks of twelve. 12.01-12 noon as a.m. and 12.01-12 midnight as p.m. Often told on a 12-hour clock and known as analogue time.

24-hour time
Counting hours of the day from 0-24. Used on digital clocks. 2 p.m. is written as 14:00.

A

a.m.
From Latin ante-meridian, meaning before midday. See also *12-hour time*.

above/below zero
Temperatures are measured relative to 0°C – the freezing point of water, e.g. 4° below zero is –4°C.

acute angle
An angle between 0° and 90°. See also *obtuse, reflex angle*.

add
A mathematical operation to increase one number (the augend) by another to give the sum.

addend
The number being added in an addition calculation. See also *augend*.

addition
A mathematical operation combining two or more numbers to find a total. Augend + addend = sum (or total).

addition fact
An addition statement likely to be frequently used, so worth memorising.

algebra
Generalised calculation using symbols (variables) instead of numbers. It can be used to prove statements and show general relationships.

analogue clock
A dial with hands used to show time. The dial shows 12 hours in a full circle. The minute hand moves one complete turn every hour. Times on these clocks are read, e.g. 20 past five or five to four.

angle
The amount of turn between two straight lines that meet at a point. Usually measured in degrees. Symbol: °. See also *acute, obtuse, reflex angle*.

anticlockwise
A rotation or turn in the opposite direction to the movement of the hands on a clock. See also *clockwise*.

approximate, approximately
A number that is not exact, e.g. 2028 is approximately 2000. Symbol: ≈.

arc
Part of the circumference of a circle.

area
The 2-D measure of the size of a surface. Measured in 'square' units: mm^2, cm^2, m^2, km^2.

array
An arrangement of numbers, shapes or objects in rows of equal size and columns of equal size, used to find out how many altogether.

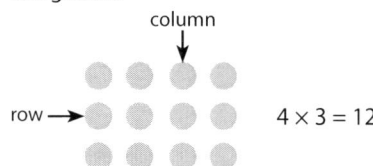

$4 \times 3 = 12$

ascending/descending order
Ascending order: rank values from smallest to largest.
Descending order: rank values from largest to smallest.

associative law
A mathematical law or rule where numbers can be grouped in different ways when adding or multiplying, without changing the total, e.g. $(a + b) + c = a + (b + c)$ and $(a \times b) \times c = a \times (b \times c)$.

augend
The number being added to in an addition calculation. See also *addend*.

average
The middle value of a set of numbers. It is found by adding all the numbers together and dividing by how many numbers there are. See also *mean*.

axis, axes
Scale lines, usually vertical and horizontal, used to define positions of points on a grid or graph.

axis of symmetry
An axis of symmetry divides the shape into two identical parts. Also called a mirror line.

B

balance
Things are balanced when both sides have equal value, e.g. $1000 g = 1 kg$, $3 + 6 = 10 – 1$.

bar chart
A statistical diagram using bars to show the frequency of outcomes.

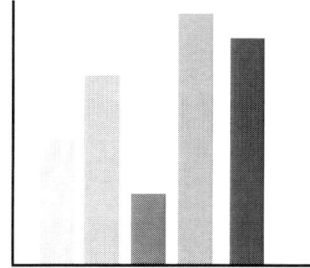

Glossary

bar line chart
A statistical diagram using lines to show the frequency of discrete outcomes.

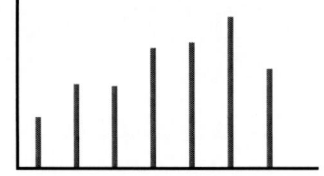

base, square-based
The flat surface underneath a 3-D shape. A square-based pyramid has one square base and four triangular faces.

Base 10 system
This is another name for the decimal number system. It increases and decreases by powers of 10. When we multiply a number by, e.g. 10, the digits move one place to the left because the number is made ten times bigger. When we divide by, e.g. 100, the number is 100 times smaller and the digits move two places to the right.

block diagram
A diagram showing statistical information. Each block stands for one object or event.

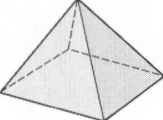

Dice throws

breadth
The same as width.

C

calendar
A list of the days of the year, arranged by month, week and day.

capacity
The amount a container can hold, e.g. the capacity of a 2 l bottle is 2 litres, the capacity of a football stadium is the amount of people it will hold. See also *volume*.

Carroll diagram
A Carroll diagram sorts objects according to a criteria and not that criteria. Can be several criteria but always the criteria and not the criteria, e.g. odd numbers/not odd numbers, multiples of 5/not multiples of 5, dogs/not dogs.

category
A group of elements or numbers all with the same property, e.g. dogs, cats, rats are all in the category 'animals'.

Celsius
A scale used to measure temperature. Sometimes called Centigrade. Units are °C.

centilitre
One hundredth of a litre. Symbol: cl. 100 cl = 1 l.

centimetre
A unit of length, $\frac{1}{100}$ of 1 metre. Symbol: cm.

centre
A point at the exact middle of a shape. The centre of a circle is the same distance from all points on its circumference.

century
100 years.

change
The money left over when buying something with a note or coin bigger than the amount needed. The change is given back to the buyer.

chart
A statistical diagram.

circle, circular
A set of points that are all a fixed distance (the radius) from a point (the centre). Like a circle.

circumference
The perimeter of a circle. The set of points a fixed distance from the centre of a circle. See also *arc*.

clock, clock face, hands
A clock is used to show and record time. It can have a circular face with revolving hands to mark hours and minutes, or it can have a digital display.

clockwise
A rotation or turn in the same direction as the movement of the hands on a clock. See also *anticlockwise*.

column
A vertical list of elements or numbers, usually in a table or an array.

combinations
Different combinations made from a selection, e.g. the various different outfits which can be made by choosing one hat and one coat to wear from three hats and four coats.

commutative
Addition and multiplication are commutative. It doesn't matter which way you add or mulitply in, the answer is always the same. Same answer, different calculation, e.g. $3 + 4 = 4 + 3$. But subtraction and division are not commutative, e.g. $7 - 2 \neq 2 - 7$.

compound number
A number that is not a prime number.

compound shape
A compound shape consists of two or more simple shapes such as a triangle placed on a square or oblong on top of a square. Also known as a composite shape.

concentric
Circles which share the same centre.

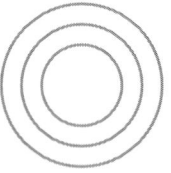

cone
A 3-D shape with a flat, circular face and a curved face. It has one apex directly above the circular base.

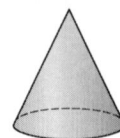

congruent
Shapes are congruent if they are exactly the same shape and size.

consecutive
Numbers that follow each other in a linear pattern, e.g. 3, 4, 5; 60, 70, 80; 17, 19, 21.

construct
To draw a shape accurately using a ruler, compasses and a protractor.

coordinate
An ordered pair of (x, y) values that define the position of a point on a Cartesian plane. In 3-D (x, y, z).

corner
A point on a 2-D shape where sides meet. Properly called a vertex (plural, vertices).

cube
A 3-D shape made from six identical squares which all meet at right angles, e.g. a cube of sugar.

cube number, cubed
Formed when a number is multiplied by itself and then by itself again. 2 cubed = $2 \times 2 \times 2 = 8$. The cube numbers are a sequence 1^3, 2^3, 3^3 and so on, which gives the numbers 1, 8, 27, 64, 125 and so on. See also *square number*.

cubic millimetres (mm³), cubic centimetres (cm³), cubic metres (m³), cubic kilometres (km³)
Metric measurements of liquid and solid volume. 1 mm³ is the volume enclosed in a cube of length 1 mm, etc.

cuboid
A 3-D shape made from six rectangles. Two or four of the rectangles could be squares, e.g. a cereal box. A cube is a special sort of cuboid.

currency
A money system. In the UK, the currency is pounds sterling (£). In the EU, the currency is the euro (€).

curved
A line that is not straight, e.g. a circle, or a surface that is not flat, e.g. an egg.

curved surface
A surface of a 3-D shape which is not flat, e.g. the surface of a sphere or cylinder.

cylinder, cylindrical
A 3-D object with circular ends and a uniform cross-section. The top is vertically above the base. Like a cylinder.

D

data
Numbers collected from a questionnaire or survey. Pieces of information usually represented in a special way, e.g. on bar charts and pie charts.

database
A method of storing data, often in large tables on a computer.

date
How we record the passing of time. Usually given as day of the month, month and then year, e.g. 3rd April 2015.

decimal, decimal fraction, decimal point, decimal place, decimal equivalent
Fractions as tenths, hundredths and so on represented as digits after a decimal point, e.g. 0.253 is equivalent to $\frac{2}{10} + \frac{5}{100} + \frac{3}{1000}$ or $\frac{253}{1000}$.

degree
Symbol: °. A unit used to measure the size of an angle. There are 360° in one complete turn. Also a unit of temperature.

denominator
The number underneath the vinculum in a fraction. Also called the divisor.

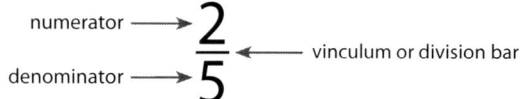

diagonal
A straight line inside a shape that goes from one corner to another (but not an edge).

diagram
A sketch or accurate drawing of a mathematical shape or problem.

diameter
A line passing across a circle, or a sphere, which passes through the centre. See also *radius*.

difference
The result of a subtraction. The difference between 12 and 5 is 7. See also *minuend, subtrahend*.

digit
A symbol from 0–9 in the decimal system. Used to show value. The value of each digit depends on its position, e.g. in 200, the digit 2 represents two hundreds.

digit total/sum
The sum of all the digits in a number, e.g. the digit sum of 435 is $4 + 3 + 5 = 12$. This carries on to $1 + 2 = 3$, so the digit total of 435 is 3.

digital clock, digital time
A system that shows the time as numbers. It can use the 12-hour or the 24-hour clock. 6 o'clock in the evening would show as 06.00 p.m. or 18:00.

discount
A reduction offered on the price of an item for sale.

distance apart … between … to … from
The length of the shortest line joining two points.

distribution
In statistics. The distribution of a set of values.

distributive law
When adding or multiplying, the numbers can be rearranged to support calculating, e.g. $2 \times 13 \times 5 = (2 \times 5) \times 13 = 10 \times 13 = 130$ and $a(b + c) = ab + ac$.

dividend
The number that is divided in a division calculation, e.g. in $12 \div 6 = 2$, 12 is the dividend. See also *denominator, division bracket, divisor, quotient*.

dividing
The process of division.

divisibility
Whether a number can be divided without remainder. All even numbers are divisible by 2.

division
A mathematical operation which groups a number into a given number of parts, e.g. $12 \div 4$ is 12 divided into four parts each of value 3. It is the inverse operation to multiplication.

division bracket
The half box around the dividend in a division. See also *dividend*.

division fact
A division statement likely to be frequently used, so worth memorising.

Glossary

division (on a scale)
The intervals on a scale, on a ruler or a graph axis.

divisor
The number that is used to divide in a division sum, e.g. in $12 \div 6 = 2$, 6 is the divisor. See also *denominator, dividend, quotient*.

dodecahedron
A 3-D polyhedron with 12 faces. A regular dodecahedron has pentagonal faces.

double
To multiply by 2.

E

edge
The line made where two faces of a 3-D shape meet. See also *face, vertex*.

eighths
The fraction of a whole obtained when it is shared into eight equal pieces.

equal sharing
To divide a number or set of items into equal parts.

equals
Symbol: =. Is the same as and equivalent to, e.g. $5 + 3 = 7 + 1$.

equation
A mathematical statement showing an equality, e.g. $10 \times 2 = 4 \times 5$ or $2x + 6 = 16$.

equilateral triangle
A triangle with three equal sides and three equal angles of 60°.

equivalent, equivalent to
Symbol: ≡. Two numbers or expressions that are equal, but which can be in a different form, e.g. £1 ≡ 100p.

equivalent fractions
Fractions with the same value, e.g. $\frac{1}{4} = \frac{2}{8} = \frac{3}{12}$. These are equivalent fractions.

estimate
An approximate answer, often used to check a complex calculation.

even
A whole number which is divisible by 2. It is a multiple of 2. See also *odd*.

F

face
A flat surface of a 3-D shape. See also *edge* and *vertex*.

factor
Numbers that divide exactly into a number are its factors, e.g. the factors of 12 are 1, 2, 3, 4, 6, 12.

factor pair
Two factors that multiply together to give the number. The factor pairs of 12 are 1×12, 2×6, 3×4.

factorise
To write a number or algebraic expression as a product of two or more factors.

flat
In 2-D and faces of 3-D shapes, not curved.

foot, feet
An imperial unit of length, approximately 30 cm. 12 inches = 1 foot and 3 feet = 1 yard.

formula, formulae
A mathematical sentence using letters or symbols (variables), e.g. area of a rectangle = length × width or $a = l \times w$.

fraction
Part of a whole, written as one number divided by another. In the fraction $\frac{3}{5}$, the numerator 3 is above the vinculum and the denominator 5 is below.

frequency table
A statistical table listing various outcomes and the frequency that they occur.

G

gallon
An imperial measure of capacity. 1 gallon is approximately 4.5 litres. See also *pint*.

gram
Symbol: g. A unit of mass. There are 1000 grams in a kilogram. See also *kilogram*.

graph
A diagram showing the relationship between two sets of numbers.

greater than
Also called more than. Symbol: >. Used when comparing the size of two quantities or measures. 10 is greater than 7, or 10 > 7. See also *less than*.

greater than or equal to
Symbol: ≥. An inequality showing the lowest value a number can take. $n \geq 7$ means n can have any value from 7 upwards. See also *less than or equal to*.

greatest value, least value
The highest or lowest value that can occur.

grouping
To divide, objects and numbers can be shared or grouped. Grouping is putting objects or numbers into groups of a particular size.

H

half
When a whole is divided into two equal parts.

half past
A measure of time. Half (an hour) past, so half past 5 is the same as 5:30 and 30 minutes past 5. See also *o'clock*.

halfway between
The midpoint between two values, e.g. 15 is halfway between 10 and 20.

heavier than, lighter than
Comparing two masses or weights, e.g. 4 kg is heavier than 3 kg, 3 kg is lighter than 4 kg.

heaviest, lightest
Comparing two or more masses or weights, e.g. of 5 kg, 6 kg and 10 kg, 5 kg is the lightest, 10 kg is the heaviest.

heavy, light
Words used to compare mass or weight.

hemisphere
Half of a sphere.

heptagon, heptagonal
A 2-D shape with seven straight sides.

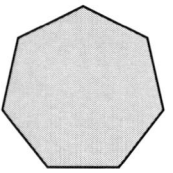 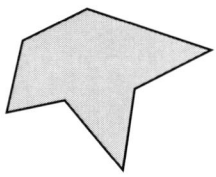

hexagon, hexagonal
A 2-D shape with six straight sides.

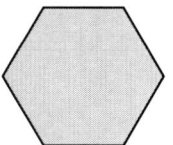 

hollow
Having an outline or surface that curves inwards, e.g. the inside of a hemisphere.

horizontal
Parallel to the horizon. See also *vertical*.

hour
Symbol: h. A measure of time. There are 24 hours in a day and 60 minutes in one hour. See also *minute*, *second*.

hour hand
The hand on a clock that measures the hours. One complete revolution takes 12 hours. See also *minute hand*.

hundred
One hundred, 100, is ten tens or one more than 99.

hundred thousand
100 000.

hundreds
The position in a number where the digit represents hundreds, e.g. in 278 there is a digit 2 in the hundreds place, so there are 2 hundreds.

hundreds boundary
When counting from tens to hundreds, the hundreds boundary is crossed.

hundredths
A fraction $\frac{1}{100}$ or 0.01.

I

imperial unit
A non-metric unit of measure, e.g. inches, yards, miles, pints. Many are still in common use.

in every, for every
A way of expressing proportion (in every) and ratio (for every), e.g. One in every ten pupils has a dog; For every teacher there are 15 students. See also *ratio*.

inch, inches
An imperial unit of length, approximately 2.5 cm. 12 inches = 1 foot.

integer, positive, negative
An integer is a whole number which can be positive or negative, e.g. −4, −2, 4, 100.

intersecting, intersection
Where two lines or curves cross.

inverse
Inverse operations leave the original value unchanged. The inverse of + 4 is − 4. The inverse of × 4 is ÷ 4 or × $\frac{1}{4}$. The inverse 'undoes' the action.

irregular
Not regular. A shape with sides and angles that are not equal.

isosceles triangle
A triangle with two equal sides and two equal base angles. A right-angled isosceles triangle has one right angle.

K

kilogram
Symbol: kg. A unit of mass. There are 1000 grams in a kilogram. See also *gram*.

kilometre
A metric measure of distance. 1 km = 1000 m.

kite
A quadrilateral with two pairs of equal adjacent sides.

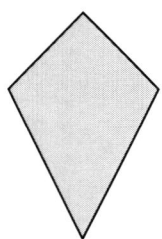

L

least popular, least common
In statistics. The value or outcome that happens least often. See also *most common*.

length, height, width, depth
Words used to describe lengths of lines and shapes, e.g. a cuboid has length 5 cm, width 3 cm and height 6 cm.

less than
Used when comparing the size of two quantities or measures, e.g. 7 is less than 10. See also *more than*.

less than or equal to
Symbol: ≤. An inequality showing the highest value a number can take. $n \leq 7$ means n can have any value up to and including 7. See also *greater than or equal to*.

line
A line is straight. It has no thickness and extends in both directions without ending.

line graph
A statistical graph with a continuous line showing the trend or variation in a value.

line segment
Part of a line that has a starting and ending point.

line symmetry
A 2-D object has line symmetry if it can be folded into two identical halves along a mirror line. Each half is a mirror image of the other.

line of symmetry

linear number sequence
A sequence of numbers that increases by a constant difference, e.g. 9, 13, 17, 21, 25, and so on.

Glossary

litre
Symbol: l. A measure of capacity. 1000 millilitres = 1 litre.

long, longer, longest
A comparison of lengths, e.g. a line is 3 cm, 3 cm is longer than 2 cm. Three lines are 4 cm, 6 cm and 8 cm. The longest length is 8 cm.

M

mass
A metric measure of the amount of matter in an object. Measured in grams (g), kilograms (kg) or tonnes (t). The mass of an object does not change, but its weight alters with any changes in the force of gravity.

maximum/minimum value
The largest/smallest value a number or variable can take.

mean
A measure of average. Mean = total of all data values ÷ number of data points. See also *median, range*.

measure, measurement
The size of a unit, e.g. we can measure area in square metres. Also means the act of measuring something.

measuring cylinder
A graduated cylinder for measuring volume and capacity accurately.

measuring scale
A way of measuring using a line or a dial with equal divisions, like on a ruler.

median
A measure of average. The middle number or value when all the elements of the data set are in ascending (or descending) order. If there is no middle value, then the mean of the two middle values. See also *mean, mode, range*.

mental calculation
Doing a calculation in your head, but perhaps with jottings.

metre
Symbol: m. A unit of length equal to 100 centimetres. 100 centimetres = 1 metre.

metric unit
Any unit used to measure on a metric scale, e.g. kilograms, centimetres, litres. All based on the decimal system.

mile
An imperial measure of distance. Used in the UK and US to measure distances between places. 5 miles is approximately equivalent to 8 kilometres.

millennium
A thousand years (10 centuries).

millilitre
Symbol: ml. A measure of capacity. 1000 millilitres = 1 litre.

millimetre
One thousandth of a metre. 1000 mm = 1 m.

million
1 000 000.

minuend
The starting number in a subtraction calculation, e.g. 10 (the minuend) – 3 (the subtrahend) = 7 (the difference). See also *subtrahend, difference*.

minus
Symbol. Another word for subtract.

minute
Symbol: min. A measure of time. See also *second, hour*.

minute hand
The hand on a clock face that measures the minutes. One complete revolution takes 60 minutes (one hour). See also *hour hand*.

mixed number
A number with both a whole number part and a fractional part, e.g. $3\frac{1}{2}$.

money
Coins and notes used to buy goods and services.

more than
Also called greater than. Symbol: >. Used when comparing the size of two quantities or measures. 10 is more than 7 or 10 > 7. See also *less than*.

more than or equal to
Symbol: ≥. An inequality showing the lowest value a number can take. $n \geq 7$ means n can have any value from 7 upwards. See also *less than or equal to*.

most common
In statistics. The most frequently occurring outcome. See also *least common*.

multiple, multiple of
A multiple is the product of two numbers, e.g. the multiples of 7 are 7, 14, 21, 28 and so on.

multiplicand
A number to be multiplied, e.g. in 6 × 3 = 18, 6 is the multiplicand. See also *multiplier*.

multiplication
A mathematical operation.

multiplication fact
A multiplication statement likely to be frequently used, so worth memorising, e.g. the multiplication table.

multiplication table
A list of multiplication facts for a given multiple, often learned by heart.

multiplier
The multiplying number, e.g. in 6 × 3 = 18, 3 is the multiplier. See also *multiplicand*.

multiply
Symbol: ×. A mathematical process equivalent to repeated addition, e.g. 2 × 4 = 2 + 2 + 2 + 2 = 8 or repeated grouping.

N

negative numbers
Numbers below zero on the number line. Read as negative 1, negative 2 and so on. See also *integer*.

net (open, closed)
The compound shape resulting from opening out a 3-D shape to show its 2-D faces and how they are connected. A one-piece set of connected 2-D shapes which can be folded to make a 3-D shape.

nth term
An algebraic expression that gives the value of any term in a sequence from its position in the sequence. An unknown value.

number
A label given to a quantity, using numerals. There are many different types of number, including counting numbers 0, 1, 2, 3 and so on; fractions; negative numbers; ordinal numbers.

number bonds/pairs
Pairs of numbers with a particular total, e.g. the number bonds for 10 are all pairs of whole numbers, like 2 and 8, which add up to 10.

number statement
A mathematical statement using numbers, also called a number sentence, e.g. 4 + 5 − 1 = 8.

numeral
A symbol used to represent a number. We use arabic numerals 0-9, but there are also Roman numerals and other systems.

numerator
The number above the vinculum in a fraction.

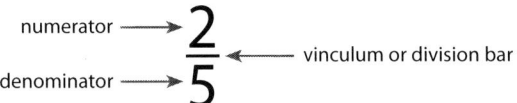

O

oblong
An irregular rectangle. A 2-D shape with two pairs of opposite sides that are equal and the angles are 90°. See also *square*.

obtuse angle
An angle between 90° and 180°. See also *acute, reflex angle*.

octagon, octagonal
A 2-D shape with eight straight sides.

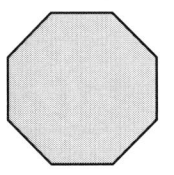 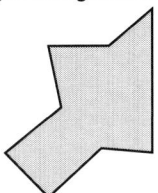

o'clock
A way of describing an exact hour time, e.g. 5 o'clock means the time is 5:00. See also *half past*.

octahedron, octahedral
A 3-D shape with eight triangular faces.

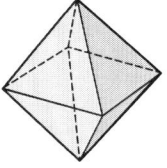 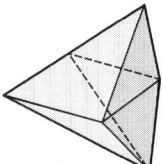

odd
A whole number which has a remainder of 1 when divided by 2. It is not a multiple of 2. See also *even*.

one hundred less/more
A number one hundred whole units more or less than another number. 900 is a hundred less than 1000 and 100 more than 800.

one less
The number one whole before that number on an number line, e.g. 9 is one less than 10.

one more
The number one whole after that number on a number line, e.g. 9 is one more than 8.

one third
A fraction obtained when a whole is divided into three equal parts.

ones
When counting individual items, the next counting number is allocated to the set each time one more is counted. 9 is the largest number of ones. See also *single-digit*.

ones boundary
When counting from a decimal to a whole number, the ones boundary is crossed. See also *tenths boundary*.

ordinal number
A number that tells the order of something, e.g. in a list 1st, 2nd, 3rd, and so on.

ounce
An imperial measure of mass. Symbol: oz. 1 ounce is approximately 28 g. 16 oz = 1 pound.

outcome
One of the possible results from a statistical experiment or trial, e.g. when tossing a coin there are two equally-likely outcomes: heads or tails.

P

p.m.
From Latin post-meridian, meaning after midday. 14:00 on the 24-hour clock is 2:00 p.m. See also *12-hour time*.

parallel
Lines that are the same distance apart and never meet.

parallelogram
A 2-D shape with two pairs of opposite sides that are equal and parallel. A rectangle is a special parallelogram, with all the angles 90°.

parts of a whole
A fraction of a whole number or object. If there are five equal parts of a whole then each part is $\frac{1}{5}$.

pattern
A regular arrangement of shapes or numbers that follows a rule.

pentagon, pentagonal
A 2-D shape with five straight sides.

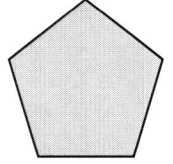 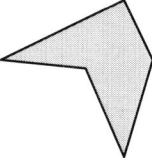

percentage, per cent, %
A fraction or mixed number expressed as hundredth parts, e.g. $\frac{1}{2} = \frac{50}{100} = 50\%$.

perimeter
The total distance measured around the outside of a 2-D shape or area. Calculated by adding the lengths of all the sides.

perpendicular
At right-angles to. Horizontal lines are always perpendicular to vertical lines.

pictogram
A picture to show statistical information. A picture is used to represent one or a number of elements.

pie chart
A statistical diagram that shows proportions of quantities as slices of a circle (a pie).

Glossary

pint
An imperial measure of capacity. There are 8 pints in 1 gallon.
1 litre is approximately 1.75 pints.

place, place value
Place value has several aspects to it. One is positional, which is
where the digit of a number is placed, e.g. in 345, the digit 3 is
positioned in the hundreds. Another is multiplicative, which is
when we multiply the digit by its position to get its true value.
So the 3 in 345 is multiplied by 100 to give 300. A third is additive.
This is when all the individual values of the digits are added
together to give the whole number, e.g. 300 + 40 + 5 = 345.

plane
A flat surface.

polygon
The general name for 2-D shapes with three or more straight
sides. Includes triangle (three sides), quadrilateral (four sides),
pentagon (five sides), and so on.

polyhedron
The general name for 3-D shapes with straight sides. Plural
polyhedra. Includes tetrahedron, prisms, pyramids.

pound
An imperial measure of mass. Symbol: lb. 2.2 lb is approximately
1 kg. See also *ounce*.

prime factor
A factor of a number that is also a prime number, e.g. the prime
factors of 12 are 2 and 3, since $12 = 2 \times 2 \times 3 = 2^2 \times 3$.

prime number
A number with only two factors, itself and 1. 1 is not a prime
number.

prism
A 3-D shape with two identical and parallel ends, joined by
rectangular faces. The cross-section of a prism is always the same
shape and size as the ends.

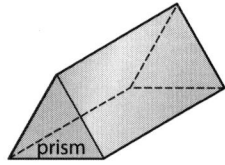
prism

product
The result of multiplying two numbers, e.g. the product of 4 and
3 is $4 \times 3 = 12$.

profit, loss
The money made or lost in a financial transaction. Can be
expressed as a money value or as a percentage.

proper/improper fraction
A proper fraction is a fraction that is less that 1, with the
numerator less than the denominator, e.g. $\frac{2}{5}$. In an improper
fraction, the numerator is larger than the denominator, e.g. $\frac{5}{2}$.

pyramid, square-based
A 3-D shape with a square base and four triangular faces.

Q

quadrant
One of the four regions formed by the x- and y-axes on a
Cartesian graph.

quadrilateral
A 2-D shape with four straight sides.

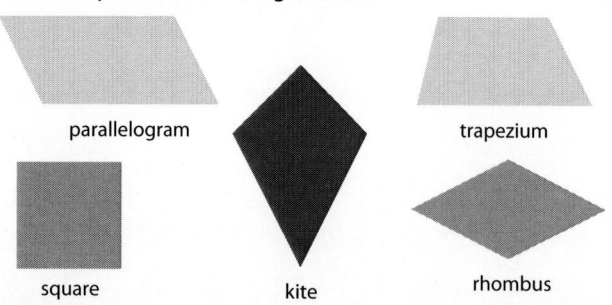
parallelogram   trapezium
square   kite   rhombus

quarter
When a whole is divided into four equal parts.

quarter past, quarter to
15 minutes past the hour or 15 minutes before the hour,
e.g. quarter to 12 is 11:45, quarter past 12 is 12:15.

questionnaire
A set of questions given to people to fill in, in order to collect
data for analysis. See also *survey, data*.

quotient
The answer to a division calculation, e.g. in $12 \div 6 = 2$, 2 is the
quotient. See also *denominator, dividend, divisor*.

R

radius
Any straight line segment from the centre of a circle to the edge
(circumference). The radius is half of the diameter. See also
diameter.

range
A measure of statistical spread. The difference between the
highest and lowest values in a set of data. See also *mean, median*.

ratio
A comparison of parts, usually expressed in its simplest form,
using a colon, e.g. 12 boys and 15 girls expressed as a ratio is
12:15 or 4:5.

rectangle, rectangular
A four-sided 2-D shape with four right angles and equal opposite
sides. A square is a regular rectangle with all four sides equal.
An oblong is an irregular rectangle.

rectilinear
A rectangular shape.

reduced to, simplify
To reduce or simplify a fraction or ratio, divide both numbers by
the highest common factor, e.g. $\frac{6}{9} = \frac{2}{3}$.

reflect, reflection
To transform an object by reflecting it in a mirror line. The image
is the same shape and size as the object.

reflective symmetry
A figure or object
has reflective
symmetry if there
is a line (2-D) or a
plane (3-D) which
divides the shape
into two identical
parts.

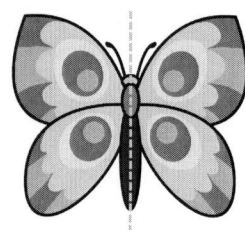
line of symmetry

Glossary

reflex angle
An angle greater than 180°. See also *acute, obtuse angle*.

regular
A 2-D shape with all the sides equal length and equal angles.

remainder
The number left over after a division sum, e.g. 13 ÷ 3 = 4 remainder 1.

rhombus
A 2-D shape with four equal sides and equal opposite angles.

right angle
A quarter of a full turn. 90°.

right-angled triangle
A triangle with one right angle. Can be isosceles or scalene.

Roman numerals
Numbers used by the Romans. Digits have no place value, e.g. II = 2 , VI = 6, LX = 60.

rotate, rotation
To transform an object by turning it a given direction and angle round a fixed point. The image is the same shape and size as the object.

round up, round down
A method of approximation. 37 rounds up to the nearest 10 so gives an approximation of 40, but 34 rounds down to the nearest 10 so gives an approximation of 30. Digits 4 or less round down and digits 5 or more round up, so 750 to the nearest 100 is 800.

row
A horizontal arrangement of, e.g. objects, shapes or numbers. See also *array*.

rule
An instruction for carrying out a mathematical operation or continuing a pattern. It can be written using symbols or words. See also *sequence*.

S

scalene triangle
A triangle with no equal sides or angles.

scales
A way of measuring using a line with equal divisions, like on a ruler. Also a device for measuring weight.

second
Symbol: s. A measure of time. There are 60 seconds in one minute. See also *minute*, *hour*.

semi-circle
Half of a circle, made from half of the curved circumference and a diameter.

sequence
A set of numbers made by following a given rule, e.g. the multiples of 3 are 3, 6, 9 and so on.

sevenths
The fraction of a whole obtained when it is cut into seven equal pieces.

shape
A 2-D or 3-D object.

sharing
A model for division, e.g. 10 ÷ 2 = 5 is 10 shared between 2, giving 5 each. Links closely with fractions, e.g. 10 shared between 2 is 5, so 5 is half of 10.

short, shorter, shortest
Words used when comparing lengths or height, e.g. a line is 3 cm, 2 cm is shorter than 3 cm, three lines are 4 cm, 6 cm and 8 cm. The shortest length is 4 cm.

side
A 2-D shape or figure has sides which are line segments. These line segments form the boundary of the shape. See also *corner*.

single-, 2-, 3-digit numbers
The number of digits in a number, e.g. 3 is a single-digit number, 13 is a 2-digit number and 213 is a 3-digit number.

sixths
The fraction of a whole obtained when it is cut into six equal pieces.

sorting
Classifying objects, shapes or numbers into groups according to their properties.

sphere, spherical
A 3-D shape where every point on the surface is the same distance from the centre, like a ball.

square
A regular quadrilateral where all the sides are equal.

square millimetre (mm²), square centimetre (cm²), square metre (m²)
Metric units of measure of area equivalent to a square 1 mm by 1 mm, a square 1 cm by 1 cm or a square 1 m by 1 m. Symbols: mm², cm² and m².

square number, squared
The square numbers are a sequence 1^2, 2^2, 3^2, formed by multiplying each number by itself. This gives the numbers 1, 4, 9, 16, 25 and so on. See also *cube number*.

statement
A number sentence, e.g. 2 + 4 = 6.

statistics
The branch of mathematics which studies the collection, representation and interpretation of data.

subtract
To do a subtraction calculation.

subtraction
A subtraction finds the difference between two numbers. Also called taking away, e.g. 10 (the minuend) – 3 (the subtrahend) = 7 (the difference). See also *minuend*.

subtraction fact
A subtraction statement likely to be frequently used, so worth memorising.

subtrahend
The number that is subtracted from the minuend.

sum
The answer to an addition calculation. The sum of 4 and 5 is 9. See also *total*.

surface
The face or faces of a 3-D shape. They can be flat like the face of a cube or curved like a sphere.

survey
A survey collects data for analysis. See also *questionnaire, data*.

Glossary

symmetry, symmetrical
A figure has line symmetry if it can be folded along a mirror line into two halves which are mirror images of each other. It has rotational symmetry if it can be rotated to give an identical shape.

line of symmetry

T

table
An arrangement of numbers or objects in rows and columns. See also *array*.

take away
Another name for subtraction. See also *subtraction*.

tall, taller, tallest
A comparison of two or more heights, e.g. Janet is 130 cm tall and John is 128 cm tall. Janet is taller than John, but Sam is the tallest.

tally
A set of marks used for quick and accurate counting. Usually counting in sets of 5 with four downward strokes and the 5th stroke is a diagonal line across the four downward strokes.

tally chart
A table used to collect information using tally counting.

temperature
A measure of hotness. Usually in degrees Celsius or degrees Fahrenheit. Symbol: °C or °F.

ten less
The number ten before that number on a number line, e.g. 40 is ten less than 50.

ten more
The number ten after that number on a number line, e.g. 50 is ten more than 40.

ten thousand
10 000.

tens boundary
When counting from ones to tens, the tens boundary is crossed.

tenths
The fraction of a whole obtained when it is cut into ten equal pieces. The basis for the decimal system of counting.

tenths boundary
When counting from a hundredth to a tenth, the tenths boundary is crossed. See also *ones boundary*.

tetrahedron
A 3-D shape with four triangular faces.

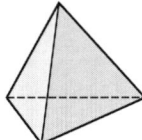

thousand less/more
The number one thousand whole units more or less than another number. 9000 is a thousand less than 10 000 and 11 000 is a thousand more than 10 000.

thousandths
$\frac{1}{1000}$ = 0.001.

three-quarters
A fraction of a whole. Three parts of a whole that has been divided into four equal parts.

 $\frac{3}{4}$

timetable
A table listing start and finish or arrival and departure times of activities or events, e.g. a school timetable or a public transport timetable.

title
A sentence to describe or explain a chart, graph or diagram.

tonne
A metric measure of mass. 100 kilograms = 1 tonne.

total
The answer to an addition calculation. The total of 4, 3 and 5 is 12. See also *sum*.

translate, translation
To transform an object by moving it a given distance and direction. The image is the same shape and size as the object and in the same orientation.

trapezium
A quadrilateral with one pair of parallel sides. It can also be isosceles.

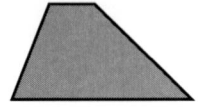 

triangle, triangular
A 2-D shape with three straight sides.

triangular prism
A 3-D shape with two identical and parallel triangular ends, joined by three rectangular faces.

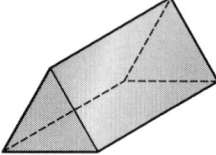

turn (whole turn, half turn, quarter turn, three-quarter turn)
A rotation about a point or line, like a hand around the clock face or a door about the join to the door frame. A whole turn is one complete revolution.

U

units
The standard measures, e.g. the units of length are metres, centimetres.

unknowns
Numbers to be found by solving equations and formulae. Represented by letters or shapes.

V

variable
A quantity that can take a range of different values. Represented by letters.

Venn diagram
A diagram of interlocking circles, used to sort numbers or objects by category.

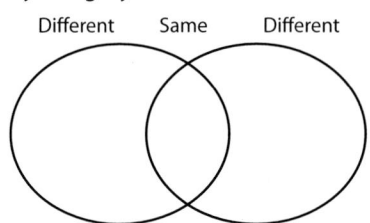